T0214475

Lecture Notes in Artificial Intelligence 11309

Subseries of Lecture Notes in Computer Science

LNAI Series Editors

Randy Goebel
  University of Alberta, Edmonton, Canada
Yuzuru Tanaka
  Hokkaido University, Sapporo, Japan
Wolfgang Wahlster
  DFKI and Saarland University, Saarbrücken, Germany

LNAI Founding Series Editor

Joerg Siekmann
  DFKI and Saarland University, Saarbrücken, Germany

More information about this series at http://www.springer.com/series/1244

Shouyi Wang · Vicky Yamamoto
Jianzhong Su · Yang Yang
Erick Jones · Leon Iasemidis
Tom Mitchell (Eds.)

Brain Informatics

International Conference, BI 2018
Arlington, TX, USA, December 7–9, 2018
Proceedings

 Springer

Editors
Shouyi Wang
University of Texas at Arlington
Arlington, TX, USA

Vicky Yamamoto
University of Southern California
West Hollywood, USA

Jianzhong Su
Department of Mathematics
University of Texas at Arlington
Arlington, TX, USA

Yang Yang
Maebashi Institute of Technology
Gunma, Japan

Erick Jones
The University of Texas at Arlington
Arlington, USA

Leon Iasemidis
Louisiana Tech University
Arlington, TX, USA

Tom Mitchell
Carnegie Mellon University
Pittsburgh, PA, USA

ISSN 0302-9743   ISSN 1611-3349   (electronic)
Lecture Notes in Artificial Intelligence
ISBN 978-3-030-05586-8   ISBN 978-3-030-05587-5   (eBook)
https://doi.org/10.1007/978-3-030-05587-5

Library of Congress Control Number: 2018963586

LNCS Sublibrary: SL7 – Artificial Intelligence

This Springer imprint is published by the registered company Springer Nature Switzerland AG
The registered company address is: Gewerbestrasse 11, 6330 Cham, Switzerland

Preface

Brain informatics (BI) is an emerging interdisciplinary research field with the vision of studying the brain from the informatics perspective. Firstly, brain informatics combines the efforts of cognitive science, cognitive psychology, neuroscience, etc. to study the brain as a general information processing system. Secondly, new informatics equipment, tools, and platforms pave the way for an imminent revolution in understanding the brain. Thirdly, starting from its proposal as a field, one of the goals of brain informatics is to build improved, inspiring, and transformative artificial intelligence. The BI conference is established as a unique interdisciplinary forum that attracts experts, researchers, practitioners, and industry representatives from neuroscience, psychology, cognitive science, machine learning, data science, artificial intelligence (AI), and information and communication technology (ICT) to facilitate fundamental research and innovative applications on brain informatics and brain-inspired technologies.

The series of Brain Informatics conferences started with the WICI International Workshop on Web Intelligence Meets Brain Informatics, held at Beijing, China in 2006. The second, third, fourth, and fifth BI conferences were held in Beijing, China (2009), Toronto, Canada (2010), Lanzhou, China (2011), and Macau, SAR China (2012), respectively. In 2013, the conference title was changed to Brain Informatics and Health (BIH) with an emphasis on real-world applications of brain research in human health and well-being. BIH 2013, BIH 2014 and BIH 2015, BIH 2016 were held at Maebashi, Japan, Warsaw, Poland, London, UK, and Omaha, USA, respectively. In 2017, the conference went back to its original design and vision to investigate the brain from an informatics perspective and to promote a brain-inspired information technology revolution. Thus, the conference name was changed back to Brain Informatics at Beijing, China, in 2017. In 2018, this grand event was held in Arlington, Texas, USA. The BI 2018 conference was hosted by The University of Texas at Arlington, Web Intelligence Consortium (WIC), IEEE Computational Intelligence Society, and the International Neural Network Society.

The 2018 International Conference on Brain Informatics (BI 2018) provided a premier international forum to bring together researchers and practitioners from diverse fields for the presentation of original research results on brain informatics, brain-inspired technologies, and brain and mental health applications. The BI 2018 conference solicited high-quality papers and talks with world-class keynote speeches, featured talks, panel discussions, and special topics workshops. Many world leaders in brain research and informatics gathered for this year's BI meeting, including Arthur Toga, Tom Mitchell, Leon Iasemidis, Chris Eliasmith, Andreas Tolias, Guoming Luan, and many other outstanding researchers.

The theme of BI 2018 was "Advancing Innovative Brain Informatics Technologies from Fundamental Research to Real-World Practice." This volume contains 46 high-quality papers accepted and presented at BI 2018, which was held in Arlington,

Texas, USA, during December 7–9, 2018. The authors and attendees came from all over the world. The BI 2018 proceedings papers address broad perspectives of brain informatics that bridges scales that span from atoms to thoughts and behavior. These papers provide a good sample of state-of-the-art research advances on brain informatics from methodologies, frameworks, techniques to applications and case studies. The selected papers cover five major tracks of brain informatics including: (1) Cognitive and Computational Foundations of Brain Science, (2) Human Information Processing Systems, (3) Brain Big Data Analytics, Curation, and Management, (4) Informatics Paradigms for Brain and Mental Health Research, (5) Brain–Machine Intelligence and Brain-Inspired Computing. The BI 2018 conference enhanced the efforts to promote the five tracks of brain informatics research and their important real-world applications.

The conference promoted transformative research to inspire novel conceptual paradigms and innovative technologies and designs that will benefit society. In particular, big data analytics, machine learning, and AI technologies are transforming brain informatics research and facilitating real-world BI applications. New data fusion and AI methodologies are developed to enhance human interpretive powers when dealing with large neuroimaging data sets, including fMRI, PET, MEG, EEG, and fNIRS, as well as data from other sources like eye-tracking and wearable, portable, micro, and nano devices. Brain informatics research creates and implements various tools to analyze all the data and establish a more comprehensive understanding of human thought, memory, learning, decision-making, emotion, consciousness, and social behaviors. These methods and related studies will also assist in building brain-inspired intelligence, brain-inspired computing, human-level wisdom-computing paradigms and technologies, improving the treatment efficacy of mental health and brain disorders.

We would like to express our gratitude to all BI 2018 conference committee members for their instrumental and unwavering support. BI 2018 had a very exciting program with a number of features, ranging from keynote talks to technical sessions, workshops/special sessions, and panel discussion. This would not have been possible without the generous dedication of the Program Committee members in reviewing the conference papers and abstracts, the BI 2018 workshop and special session chairs and organizers, and our keynote and feature speakers in giving outstanding talks at the conference. BI 2018 could not have taken place without the great team effort of the local Organizing Committee and generous support from sponsors. We would especially like to express our sincere appreciation to our kind sponsors, including The University of Texas at Arlington, the Center on Stochastic Modeling, Optimization, and Statistics (COSMOS), Center for Assistive Technologies to Enhance Human Performance (iPerform), Web Intelligence Consortium (http://wi-consortium.org), International Neural Network Society (https://www.inns.org), IEEE Computational Intelligence Society (http://cis.ieee.org), Springer-Nature, Springer LNCS/LNAI (http://www.springer.com/gp/computer-science/lncs), and International Neuroinformatics Coordinating Facility (INCF, https://www.incf.org).

Special thanks go to Juzhen Dong and Yang Yang for their great assistance and support with the CyberChair submission system. We also thank the Steering

Committee co-chairs, Ning Zhong and Hanchuan Peng, for their help in organizing and promoting BI 2018. We are grateful to Springer's *Lecture Notes in Computer Science* (LNCS/LNAI) for their sponsorship and support. We thank Springer for their help in coordinating the publication of this special volume in an emerging and interdisciplinary research field.

October 2018

Shouyi Wang
Vicky Yamamoto
Jianzhong Su
Yang Yang
Erick Jones
Leon Iasemidis
Tom Mitchell

Organization

General Chairs

Tom Mitchell   Carnegie Mellon University, USA
Leon Iasemidis   Louisiana Tech University, USA
Ning Zhong   Maebashi Institute of Technology, Japan

Program Committee Chairs

Jianzhong Su   The University of Texas at Arlington, USA
Vicky Yamamoto   University of Southern California, USA
Yu-Ping Wang   Tulane University, USA

Organizing Chairs

Shouyi Wang   The University of Texas at Arlington, USA
Erick Jones   The University of Texas at Arlington, USA

Workshop/Special Session Chairs

Felicia Jefferson   Fort Valley State University, USA
Chou, Chun-An   Northwestern University, USA
Fenghua Tian   The University of Texas at Arlington, USA
Jing Qin   Montana State University, USA

Tutorial Chairs

Yang Yang   Maebashi Institute of Technology, Japan
Vassiliy Tsytsarev   University of Maryland, USA

Publicity Chairs

Paul Wen   University of Southern Queensland, Australia
Huiguang He   Chinese Academy of Sciences, China
Mufti Mahmud   University of Padua, Italy

Steering Committee Chairs

Ning Zhong   Maebashi Institute of Technology, Japan
Hanchuan Peng   Allen Institute for Brain Science, USA

Program Committee

Agnar Aamodt	Norwegian University of Science and Technology, Norway
Jun Bai	Institute of Automation, Chinese Academy of Sciences, China
Quan Bai	Auckland University of Technology, New Zealand
Sylvain Baillet	McGill University, Canada
Katarzyna Blinowska	University of Warsaw, Poland
Kristofer Bouchard	Lawrence Berkeley National Laboratory, USA
Nizar Bouguila	Concordia University, Canada
Weidong Cai	The University of Sydney, Australia
Lihong Cao	Communication University of China, China
Zhigang Cao	Chinese Academy of Sciences, China
Mirko Cesarini	University of Milano-Bicocca, Italy
W. Chaovalitwongse	University of Arkansas, USA
Jianhui Chen	Beijing University of Technology, China
Kan Chen	The University of Texas at Arlington, USA
Kay Chen	The University of Texas at Arlington, USA
Joe Chou	Northeastern University, USA
Eva Dyer	Emory University and Georgia Institute of Technology, USA
Frank Emmert-Streib	Tampere University of Technology, Finland
Denggui Fan	University of Science and Technology Beijing, China
Yong Fan	University of Pennsylvania, USA
Philippe Fournier-Viger	Harbin Institute of Technology (Shenzhen), China
Richard Frackowiak	Ecole Polytechnique de Lausanne, Switzerland
Min Gan	Fuzhou University, China
Geoffrey Goodhill	University of Queensland, Australia
Jerzy Grzymala-Busse	University of Kansas, USA
Lei Guo	The University of Texas at Arlington, USA
Mohand-Said Hacid	Université Claude Bernard Lyon 1, France
Bin He	University of Minnesota, USA
Huiguang He	Chinese Academy of Sciences, China
Gahangir Hossain	Texas A&M University-Kingsville, USA
Frank Hsu	Fordham University, USA
Jiajin Huang	Beijing University of Technology, China
Zhisheng Huang	Vrije University of Amsterdam, The Netherlands
Felicia Jefferson	Fort Valley State University, USA
Tianzi Jiang	Chinese Academy of Sciences, China
Xingpeng Jiang	Central China Normal University, China
Hanmin Jung	Korea Institute of Science and Technology Information, South Korea
Jana Kainerstorfer	Carnegie Mellon University, USA
Yongjie Li	University of Electronic Science and Technology of China, China

Youjun Li	Beijing University of Technology, China
Peipeng Liang	Capital Normal University, China
Feng Liu	Harvard Medical School, USA
Lin Liu	Tsinghua University, China
Sidong Liu	University of Sydney, Australia
Tianming Liu	University of Georgia, USA
Weifeng Liu	China University of Petroleum, China
Yan Liu	The Hong Kong Polytechnic University, SAR China
Thomas loeger	Texas A&M University College Station, USA
Lucelene Lopes	Pontifical Catholic University of Rio Grande do Sul, Brazil
Roussanka Loukanova	Stockholm University, Sweden
Xiaoqiang Lu	Chinese Academy of Sciences, China
Anthony Maeder	Flinders University, Australia
Duoqian Miao	Tongji University, China
Mariofanna Milanova	University of Arkansas at Little Rock, USA
Randall O'Reilly	University of Colorado Boulder, USA
Hernando Ombao	King Abdullah University of Science and Technology, Saudi Arabia
Vasile Palade	Oxford University, UK
Valentina Poggioni	University of Perugia, Italy
Hosseini Rahilsadat	The University of Texas at Arlington, USA
Phill Kyu Rhee	Inha University, South Korea
Abdel-Badeeh Salem	Ain Shams University, Egypt
Alberto Sanna	The Scientific Institute San Raffaele, Italy
Divya Sardana	University of Cincinnati, USA
Christina Schweikert	St. John's University, USA
Andrzej Skowron	Warsaw University, Poland
Neil Smalheiser	University of Illinois, USA
Diego Sona	Istituto Italiano di Tecnologia, Italy
Piotr S. Szczepaniak	Technical University of Lodz, Poland
Ryszard Tadeusiewicz	AGH University of Science and Technology, Poland
Xiaohui Tao	University of Southern Queensland, Australia
Kuttiyannan Thangavel	Periyar University, India
Fenghua Tian	The University of Texas at Arlington, USA
Sunil Vadera	University of Salford, UK
Egon Van den Broek	Utrecht University, The Netherlands
Juan Velasquez	University of Chile, Chile
Frank van der Velde	Leiden University, The Netherlands
ZhiJiang Wan	Maebashi Institute of Technology, Japan
Changdong Wang	Sun Yat-sen University, China
Dongqing Wang	Qingdao University, China
Guoyin Wang	Chongqing University of Posts and Telecommunications, China
Lipo Wang	Nanyang Technology University, Singapore
Shouyi Wang	The University of Texas at Arlington, USA

Contents

Brain Big Data Analytics, Curation and Management

Brain-Machine Intelligence and Brain-Inspired Computing

Cognitive and Computational Foundations of Brain Science

Emotion Recognition Based on Gramian Encoding Visualization

Jie-Lin Qiu[1(✉)], Xin-Yi Qiu[2], and Kai Hu[1]

[1] Shanghai Jiao Tong University, Shanghai, China
Qiu-Jielin@sjtu.edu.cn
[2] Sun Yat-sen University, Guangzhou, China

Abstract. This paper addresses the problem that emotional computing is difficult to be put into real practical fields intuitively, such as medical disease diagnosis and so on, due to poor direct understanding of physiological signals. In view of the fact that people's ability to understand two-dimensional images is much higher than one-dimensional signals, we use Gramian Angular Fields to visualize time series signals. GAF images are represented as a Gramian matrix where each element is the trigonometric sum between different time intervals. Then we use Tiled Convolutional Neural Networks (tiled CNNs) on 3 real world datasets to learn high-level features from GAF images. The classification results of our method are better than the state-of-the-art approaches. This method makes visualization based emotion recognition become possible, which is beneficial in the real medical fields, such as making cognitive disease diagnosis more intuitively.

Keywords: Emotion recognition · EEG · Gramian Angular Fields
Tiled CNN · Medical diagnosis

1 Introduction

With the continuous development of computer vision technology, its application scope is much more extensive than before. Increasing number of industries begin to seek the use of visual technology to solve the problem in practice. At present, the importance of affective computing is getting more and more attention. However, the current calculation method based on EEG and other signal data is mainly time series signals [1,3], which is difficult to be put into real use due to its poor understandability. In view of the fact that people's ability to understand two-dimensional images is much larger than that of one-dimensional signals, we encode the time series data into images for visualization. After that we use Tiled convolutional neural networks [23] for emotion classification. Our method outperforms the state-of-the-art classification results and is more effective to be put into real medical fields.

© Springer Nature Switzerland AG 2018
S. Wang et al. (Eds.): BI 2018, LNAI 11309, pp. 3–12, 2018.
https://doi.org/10.1007/978-3-030-05587-5_1

2   Related Work

Emotion is a subjective, conscious experience when people facing internal or external stimuli, and it is crucial for communication, decision making and human-machine interface. Emotion recognition can be performed through facial movement, voice, speech, text, and physiological signals [8]. Among these approaches, emotion recognition from electroencephalography (EEG) has attracted increasing interest [2,7].

We want to solve the problem by encoding time series data as images to allow machines to recognize and classify the time series data like human vision. Time series recognition has been well studied in speech and audio area. Researchers have successfully used combinations of HMMs with acoustic models based on Gaussian Mixture models (GMMs) [9,10]. Deep neural network is a potential approach to produce the posterior probabilities over HMM states. Deep learning has become increasingly popular since the introduction of effective ways to train multiple hidden layers [11] and has already been proposed as a replacement for GMMs to model acoustic data in speech recognition tasks [12]. These Deep Neural Network - Hidden Markov Model hybrid systems (DNN-HMM) achieved brilliant performance in a variety of speech recognition tasks [13–15]. This success comes from learning distributed representation through a deep structure and unsupervised pre training for the Boltzmann machine (RBM) by stacking a single layer.

Convolutional neural networks (CNN) [16] is also widely used in computer vision. CNN exploits translational invariance within their structures by extracting features through receptive fields [17] and learn with weight sharing, becoming the state-of-the-art approach in various image recognition and computer vision tasks [18–20]. Since unsupervised pretraining has been shown to improve performance [21], sparse coding and Topographic Independent Component Analysis (TICA) are integrated as unsupervised pretraining approaches to learn more diverse features with complex invariances [22,23].

CNN is proposed for speech processing to maintain the invariance of time and frequency by LeCun and Bengio. Recently, CNN has shown the ability of further improving hybrid model performance by applying convolution and max-pooling in the frequency domain on the TIMIT phone recognition task [24]. A heterogeneous pooling approach proved to be beneficial for training acoustic invariance in [25]. An exploration of further finite weight allocation and weighted softmax aggregation layer has been proposed to optimize the CNN structure for speech recognition tasks [26]. In addition to audio and voice data, less work explores feature learning in the typical time series analysis tasks of the current depth learning architecture. Our direction is to encode EEG time series as images and to use deep learning architectures in computer vision to learn features and identify structure in time series.

In this paper, we encoded EEG time series data as images using Gramian Angular field (GAF). We selected 3 real time series dataset and applied deep Tiled Convolutional Neural Networks (Tiled CNN) with a pretraining stage that exploits local orthogonality by Topographic ICA [23] to represent the time series.

By comparing our results with the state-of-the-art representation and classification methods, we show that our approach achieves better performance than the state-of-the-art methods while exploring a relatively small parameter space.

3   Dataset

We evaluate the performance of the approaches on two real-world dataset, the SEED[1] dataset, the SEED IV dataset, and the DEAP[2] dataset.

- **SEED.** The SEED dataset contains EEG signals of three emotions (positive, neutral, and negative) from 15 subjects. All subjects were watching 15 four-minute-long emotional movie clips while their signals were collected. The EEG signals were recorded with ESI NeuroScan System at a sampling rate of 1000 Hz with a 62-channel electrode cap. To compare with previous work, we used the same data which contained 27 experiments from 9 subjects. Signals recorded while the subject watching the first 9 movie clips were used as training datasets for each experiment and the rest were used as test datasets.
- **SEED IV.** The SEED IV dataset contains EEG features in total of four emotions (happy, sad, fear, and neutral) [6]. There were 72 film clips in total for four emotions and forty five experiments were taken by participants to assess their emotions when watching the film clips with keywords of emotions and ratings out of ten points for two dimensions: valence and arousal.
- **DEAP.** The DEAP dataset contains EEG signals and peripheral physiological signals of 32 participants. Signals were collected while participants were watching one-minute-long emotional music videos. We chose 5 as the threshold to divide the trials into two classes according to the rated levels of arousal and valence. We used 5-fold cross validation to compare with Liu *et al.* [3] and Tang *et al.* [4].

4   Encoding Time Series Data into Images by Gramian Angular Field

Inspired by previous work on the duality between time series and complex networks [5,27,28], the type of image is a Gramian Angular field (GAF), in which we represent time series in a polar coordinate system instead of the typical Cartesian coordinates. In the Gramian matrix, each element is actually the cosine of the summation of angles.

Given a time series $X = \{x_1, x_2, ..., x_n\}$ of n real-valued observations, we rescale X so that all values fall in the interval $[-1, 1]$ or $[0, 1]$ by:

$$\tilde{x}^i_{-1} = \frac{(x_i - max(X) + (x_i - min(X))}{max(X) - min(X)} \qquad (1)$$

---

[1] http://bcmi.sjtu.edu.cn/~seed/.
[2] http://www.eecs.qmul.ac.uk/mmv/datasets/deap/.

$$or \quad \tilde{x}_0^i = \frac{x_i - min(X)}{max(X) - min(X)} \tag{2}$$

Thus we can represent the rescaled time series $\tilde{X}$ in polar coordinates by encoding the value as the angular cosine and the time stamp as the radius with the equation below:

$$\phi = arccos(\tilde{x}_i), -1 \le \tilde{x}_i \le 1, \tilde{x}_i \in \tilde{X}, r = t_i/N, t_i \in N \tag{3}$$

In the equation above, t_i is the time stamp and N is a constant factor to regularize the span of the polar coordinate system. This polar coordinate based representation is a novel way to understand time series. As time increases, corresponding values warp among different angular points on the spanning circles, like water rippling. The encoding map has two important properties. First, it is bijective as $cos(\phi)$ is monotonic when $\phi \in [0, \pi]$. Given a time series, the proposed map produces one and only one result in the polar coordinate system with a unique inverse map. Second, as opposed to Cartesian coordinates, polar coordinates preserve absolute temporal relations.

Rescaled data in different intervals have different angular bounds. [0,1] corresponds to the cosine function in $[0, \pi/2]$, while cosine values in the interval $[-1,1]$ fall into the angular bounds $[0, \pi]$. They can provide different information granularity in the Gramian Angular Field for classification tasks, and the Gramian Angular Difference Field (GADF) of [0,1] rescaled data has the accurate inverse map. This property actually lays the foundation for imputing missing value of time series by recovering the images.

After transforming the rescaled time series into the polar coordinate system, we can easily exploit the angular perspective by considering the trigonometric sum/difference between each point to identify the temporal correlation within different time intervals. The Gramian Summation Angular Field (GASF) and Gramian Difference Angular Field (GADF) are defined as follows:

$$GASF = [cos(\phi_i + \phi_j)] = \tilde{X}' \cdot \tilde{X} - \sqrt{I - \tilde{X}^2}' \cdot \sqrt{I - \tilde{X}^2} \tag{4}$$

$$GADF = [sin(\phi_i - \phi_j)] = \sqrt{I - \tilde{X}^2}' \cdot \tilde{X} - \tilde{X}' \cdot \sqrt{I - \tilde{X}^2} \tag{5}$$

I is the unit row vector $[1, 1, ..., 1]$. After transforming to the polar coordinate system, we take time series at each time step as a 1-D metric space. By defining the inner product:

$$< x, y >_1 = x \cdot y - \sqrt{1 - x^2} \cdot \sqrt{1 - y^2} \tag{6}$$

$$< x, y >_2 = \sqrt{1 - x^2} \cdot y - x \cdot \sqrt{1 - y^2} \tag{7}$$

Two types of Gramian Angular Fields (GAFs) are actually quasi-Gramian matrices $[< \tilde{x}_1, \tilde{x}_1 >]$.

The GAFs have several advantages. First, they provide a way to preserve temporal dependency, since time increases as the position moves from top-left to bottom-right. The GAFs contain temporal correlations because $G_{i,j||i-j|=k}$ represents the relative correlation by superposition/difference of directions with respect to time interval k. The main diagonal $G_{i,i}$ is the special case when $k = 0$, which contains the original value/angular information. From the main diagonal, we can reconstruct the time series from the high level features learned by the deep neural network (Fig. 1).

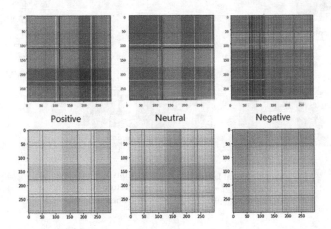

Fig. 1. GADF (first row) and GASF (second row) visualized images of SEED dataset with label Positive, Neutral and Negative.

5 Tiled Convolutional Neural Networks

Tiled Convolutional Neural Networks [23] are a variation of Convolutional Neural Networks that use tiles and multiple feature maps to learn invariant features. Tiles are parameterized by a tile size k to control the distance over which weights are shared. By generating multiple feature maps, Tiled CNN learns a complete representation through unsupervised terrain ICA (TICA) pre-training.

A typical TICA network is actually a double-stage optimization process with square and square root nonlinearities in each phase, respectively. In the first stage, the weight matrix W is learned while the matrix V is hard-coded to represent the topographic structure of units. More precisely, given a sequence of inputs x^h, the activation of each unit in the second stage is (Fig. 2):

$$f_i(x^h; W, V) = \sqrt{\sum_{k=1}^{p} V_{ik}(\sum_{j=1}^{q} W_{kj}x_j^h)^2} \qquad (8)$$

TICA learns the weight matrix W in the second stage by solving the following:

$$maximize: \sum_{h=1}^{n} \sum_{i=1}^{p} f_i(x^h; W, V) \quad subject\ to: WW^T = I \qquad (9)$$

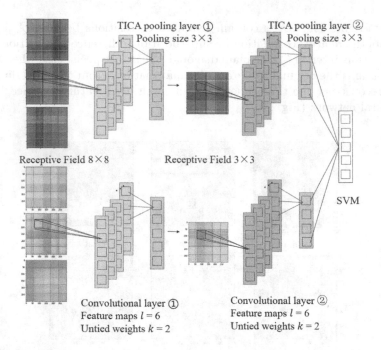

Fig. 2. The framework of Tiled CNN network used in our experiment.

Above, $W \in R^{p \times q}$ and $V \in R^{p \times p}$ where p is the number of hidden units in a layer and q is the size of the input. V is a logical matrix ($V_{i}j = 1$ or 0) that encodes the topographic structure of the hidden units by a contiguous 3×3 block. The orthogonality constraint $WW^T = I$ provides diversity among learned features.

GAF images are not natural images because they have no natural concepts such as edges and angles. Therefore, we propose to take advantages of unsupervised pre-training of TICA to learn many diversified features with local orthogonality. In addition, [23] empirically demonstrate that tiled CNNs perform well with limited labeled data because Partial weight binding requires fewer parameters and reduces the need for large amounts of labeled data. Our data from SEED and DEAP datasets tend to have few instances, which is suitable for using tiled CNNs. Typically, tiled CNNs are trained with two hyperparameters, the tiling size k and the number of feature maps l. In our experiment, we use grid search to adjust them.

6   Emotion Classification

We apply Tiled CNN to classify GAF images on 3 datasets. We trained two networks, each of which contained GASF and GADF visualized images respectively, and applied a linear SVM at the last layer as classifier. Our results are better than the state-of-the-art approach [4]. The datasets are pre-split into training and testing sets for experimental comparisons. For each dataset, the table gives

its name, the number of classes, the number of training and test instances, and
the length of the individual time series.

6.1   Experimental Setting

In our experiments, the size of the GAF image is regulated by the the number of PAA bins S_{GAF}. Given a time series X of size n, we divide the time
series into S_{GAF} adjacent, non-overlapping windows along the time axis and
extract the means of each bin. This enables us to construct the smaller GAF
matrix $G_{S_{GAF} \times S_{GAF}}$. The Tiled CNN is trained with image size $\{S_{GAF}\} \in$
$\{16, 24, 32, 40, 48\}$ and quantile size $Q \in \{8, 16, 32, 64\}$. At the last layer of the
Tiled CNN, we use a linear soft margin SVM and select C by 5-fold cross validation over $10^{-4}, 10^{-3}, ..., 10^4$ on the training set.

For each input of image size S_{GAF} and quantile size Q, we pretrain the Tiled
CNN with the full unlabeled dataset to learn the initial weights W through
TICA. Then we train the SVM at the last layer by selecting the penalty factor
C with cross validation. Finally, we classify the test set using the optimal hyperparameters $\{S, Q, C\}$ with the lowest error rate on the training set. If two or
more models tie, we prefer the larger S and Q because larger S helps preserve
more information through the PAA procedure and larger Q encodes the dynamic
transition statistics with more detail. Our model selection method provides ver-
satility and is not computationally expensive.

6.2   Results and Discussion

We use Tiled CNNs to classify GAF representations on the 3 datasets. The
classification accuracy is shown in Tables 1, 2 and 3.

Table 1. Average accuracies (%) of different approaches on SEED dataset

	Feature fusion	BDDAE	Liu et al. [3]	Tang et al. [4]	Our approach
Accuracy (%)	83.80	88.98	91.01	93.97	**94.33**
Std	16.38	12.51	8.23	7.03	**6.94**

Table 1 shows the comparison results of different approaches on SEED
dataset. BDDAE achieved higher classification accuracy and less std than SVM
based feature fusion. Liu et al. used RBM pre-training to build a multi-modal
autoencoder model performed better results of 91.01% [3]. Tang et al. used
Bimodal-LSTM to make fusion by considering timing and classification layer
parameters and achieved the state-of-the-art performance [4]. In our model, we
extracted high-level representations and achieved better results with classification accuracy of 94.33% and std of 6.94.

For SEED IV dataset, we regard Zheng et al.'s deep learning results as our
baseline [6]. We compare our DCCA model with different previous methods.

Table 2. Average accuracies (%) and standard deviation of different approaches for four emotions classification on SEED IV dataset

	CCA	SVM	BDAE [6]	Our approach
Accuracy (%)	49.56	75.88	85.11	**86.76**
Std	19.24	16.14	11.79	**10.45**

Table 2 presents that BDAE achieved better results than SVM based feature fusion. Compared with CCA based approach and other methods, we conclude that DCCA model which coordinated high-level features achieved better results.

Table 3. Average accuracies (%) of different approaches on DEAP dataset

	Feature fusion	AutoEncoder [2]	Liu *et al.* [3]	Tang *et al.* [4]	Ours
Valence (%)	65.29	74.49	85.20	83.82	**84.19**
Arousal (%)	65.43	75.69	80.50	83.23	**83.87**

Table 3 demonstrates comparison results of different methods on DEAP dataset for two dichotomous classification. Liu *et al.*'s multi-modal autoencoder model achieved higher accuracy than AutoEncoder [2]. Then Tang *et al.* used Bimodal-LSTM and achieved the state-of-the-art accuracy [4]. As for our method, we learned high-level features of GAF encoded images and achieved better results than the state-of-the-art method with mean accuracies of 84.19% and 83.87% for valence and arousal classification.

Furthermore, some people may think this visualizing time series data approach is no use to for there existing effective ways to analyze it, such as RNNs, LSTMs, and so on. But when coming to real world applicants, it is not the case. Most doctors and patients lack sensitivity to data analysis compared with researchers. For now, the situation in the diagnosis of cognitive diseases is mainly based on questionnaires, which is very subjective, because it is difficult to use physiological data as the main detection method for the complexity and non-intuitive nature of physiological signals. So after communicating with many hospitals, we proposed such a visualization method, hoping to provide a more objective analysis of relevant disease diagnosis.

7   Conclusions and Future Work

We put up a new direction for emotion classification by encoding time series data into novel representations GAF images, then extracted high-level features from these using Tiled CNN for emotion recognition. We show that our method can produce better results compared to the state-of-the-art methods on two real world datasets when searching a relatively small parameter space.

Important future work will apply more practical datasets to the current method to improve the algorithm and will consider other visualization methods. At present, only three and four emotion labels are used to discriminate. In the future, we will consider six types of emotion labels of signals to be encoded for visualization and classification and explore more efficient framework. We have cooperated with hospitals and hope to gradually discover new breakthroughs in visual applications during assisting cognitive disease diagnosis.

References

1. Tzirakis, P., Trigeorgis, G., Nicolaou, M.A., Schuller, B.W., Zafeiriou, S.: End-to-end multimodal emotion recognition using deep neural networks. IEEE J. Sel. Top. Signal Process. **11**, 1301–1309 (2017)
2. Lu, Y., Zheng, W.-L., Li, B., Lu, B.-L.: Combining eye movements and EEG to enhance emotion recognition. In: IJCAI (2015)
3. Liu, W., Zheng, W.-L., Lu, B.-L.: Multimodal emotion recognition using multimodal deep learning. CoRR, vol. abs/1602.08225 (2016)
4. Tang, H., Liu, W., Zheng, W.-L., Lu, B.-L.: Multimodal emotion recognition using deep neural networks. In: Liu, D., Xie, S., Li, Y., Zhao, D., El-Alfy, E.-S.M. (eds.) ICONIP 2017, Part IV. LNCS, vol. 10637, pp. 811–819. Springer, Cham (2017). https://doi.org/10.1007/978-3-319-70093-9_86
5. Zheng, W.-L., Zhu, J.-Y., Peng, Y., Lu, B.-L.: EEG-based emotion classification using deep belief networks. In: 2014 IEEE International Conference on Multimedia and Expo (ICME), pp. 1–6 (2014)
6. Zheng, W.-L., Liu, W., Lu, Y., Lu, B.-L., Cichocki, A.: Emotionmeter: a multimodal framework for recognizing human emotions. IEEE Trans. Cybern. **99**, 1–13 (2018)
7. Schuller, B.W., Rigoll, G., Lang, M.K.: Hidden Markov model-based speech emotion recognition. In: ICME (2003)
8. Kim, K.H., Bang, S.W., Kim, S.R.: Emotion recognition system using short-term monitoring of physiological signals. Med. Biol. Eng. Comput. **42**, 419–427 (2004)
9. Reynolds, D.A., Rose, R.C.: Robust text-independent speaker identification using Gaussian mixture speaker models. IEEE Trans. Speech Audio Process. **3**(1), 72–83 (1995)
10. Leggetter, C., Woodland, P.C.: Maximum likelihood linear regression for speaker adaptation of continuous density hidden Markov models. Comput. Speech Lang. **9**, 171–185 (1995)
11. Hinton, G.E., Osindero, S., Teh, Y.W.: A fast learning algorithm for deep belief nets. Neural Comput. **18**(7), 1527–1554 (2006)
12. Rahman Mohamed, A., Dahl, G.E., Hinton, G.E.: Acoustic modeling using deep belief networks. IEEE Trans. Audio Speech Lang. Process. **20**, 14–22 (2012)
13. Hinton, G.E., et al.: Deep neural networks for acoustic modeling in speech recognition: the shared views of four research groups. IEEE Signal Process. Mag. **29**, 82–97 (2012)
14. Deng, L., Hinton, G.E., Kingsbury, B.: New types of deep neural network learning for speech recognition and related applications: an overview. In: 2013 IEEE International Conference on Acoustics, Speech and Signal Processing, pp. 8599–8603 (2013)

15. Deng, L., et al.: Recent advances in deep learning for speech research at Microsoft. In: 2013 IEEE International Conference on Acoustics, Speech and Signal Processing, pp. 8604–8608 (2013)
16. LeCun, Y.: Gradient-based learning applied to document recognition (1998)
17. Hubel, D.H., Wiesel, T.N.: Receptive fields, binocular interaction and functional architecture in the cats visual cortex. J. Physiol. **160**, 106–154 (1962)
18. Lawrence, S., Giles, C.L., Tsoi, A.C., Back, A.D.: Face recognition: a convolutional neural-network approach. IEEE Trans. Neural Netw. **8**(1), 98–113 (1997)
19. Krizhevsky, A., Sutskever, I., Hinton, G.E.: Imagenet classification with deep convolutional neural networks. In: NIPS (2012)
20. LeCun, Y., Kavukcuoglu, K., Farabet, C.: Convolutional networks and applications in vision. In: Proceedings of 2010 IEEE International Symposium on Circuits and Systems, pp. 253–256 (2010)
21. Erhan, D., et al.: Why does unsupervised pre-training help deep learning? J. Mach. Learn. Res. **11**, 625–660 (2010)
22. Kavukcuoglu, K., et al.: Learning convolutional feature hierarchies for visual recognition. In: NIPS (2010)
23. Le, Q.V., Ngiam, J., Chen, Z., Hao Chia, D.J., Koh, P.W., Ng, A.Y.: Tiled convolutional neural networks. In: NIPS (2010)
24. Abdel-Hamid, O., Rahman Mohamed, A., Jiang, H., Penn, G.: Applying convolutional neural networks concepts to hybrid nn-hmm model for speech recognition. In: 2012 IEEE International Conference on Acoustics, Speech and Signal Processing (ICASSP), pp. 4277–4280 (2012)
25. Deng, L., Abdel-Hamid, O., Yu, D.: A deep convolutional neural network using heterogeneous pooling for trading acoustic invariance with phonetic confusion. In: IEEE International Conference on Acoustics, Speech and Signal Processing, pp. 6669–6673 (2013)
26. Abdel-Hamid, O., Deng, L., Yu, D.: Exploring convolutional neural network structures and optimization techniques for speech recognition. In: INTER-SPEECH (2013)
27. Campanharo, A.S.L.O., Sirer, M.I., Malmgren, R.D., Ramos, F.M., Amaral, L.A.N.: Duality between time series and networks. PloS One **6**, e23378 (2011)
28. Wang, Z., Oates, T.: Encoding time series as images for visual inspection and classification using tiled convolutional neural networks (2014)

EEG Based Brain Mapping by Using Frequency-Spatio-Temporal Constraints

Pablo Andrés Muñoz-Gutiérrez[1]([⊠]), Juan David Martinez-Vargas[2],
Sergio Garcia-Vega[4], Eduardo Giraldo[3], and German Castellanos-Dominguez[4]

[1] Universidad del Quindío, Armenia, Colombia
pamunoz@uniquindio.edu.co
[2] Instituto Tecnológico Metropolitano, Medellín, Colombia
[3] Universidad Tecnológica de Pereira, Pereira, Colombia
egiraldos@utp.edu.co
[4] Signal Processing and Recognition Group,
Universidad Nacional de Colombia, sede Manizales, Manizales, Colombia

Abstract. In this paper an improvement of the dynamic inverse problem solution is proposed by using constraints in the space-time-frequency domain. The method is based on multi-rate filter banks for frequency selection of the EEG signals and a cost function that includes spatial and temporal constraints. As a result, an iterative method which includes Frequency-Spatio-temporal constraints is proposed. The performance of the proposed method is evaluated by using simulated and real EEG signals. It can be concluded that the enhanced IRA-L1 method with the frequency-spatio-temporal stage improves the quality of the brain reconstruction performance in terms of the Wasserstein metric, in comparison with the other methods, for both simulated and real EEG signals.

Keywords: Dynamic inverse problem
Frequency-Spatio-temporal constraints

1 Introduction

Neural activity estimation is now considered as an important tool for assisted diagnosis of brain related diseases. The inherent dynamic of electroencephalographic (EEG) signals and its corresponding resolution in time is a key factor to analyze complex behaviours. In addition, when the estimation of neural activity is performed from EEG (known as dynamic inverse problem) an improvement of the resolution obtained by using functional Magnetic Resonance Imaging (fMRI) methods is achieved. However, in order to obtain a reliable neural activity reconstruction the inclusion of spatial and temporal constraints is mandatory in the solution of the dynamic inverse problem [1]. Moreover, frequency behaviour of EEG signals related to several pathological activity are also important for diagnosis support, which are usually analyzed by using non-stationary signal processing methods like

© Springer Nature Switzerland AG 2018
S. Wang et al. (Eds.): BI 2018, LNAI 11309, pp. 13–21, 2018.
https://doi.org/10.1007/978-3-030-05587-5_2

Wavelet Transform (WT) or Short-Time Fourier Transform [2–4]. In this way, several efforts have been made to include frequency constraints in the solution of the dynamic inverse problem [5,6].

A new WT has been proposed to investigate the functions and importance of transform sparseness in solving EEG/MEG inverse problems using L_1–norm regularizations, this wavelet is applied in irregular cortical surface [3]. Another work proposes a graph based framework for fMRI brain activation mapping which exploits the spectral graph wavelet transform (SGWT), the approach is based on spatial multi-scale transforms to exploit to take advantage of the geometrical structures of the gray matter [2].

The most of applications for WT and EEG have been addressed to pattern recognition, e.g., epileptic seizures detection using a hierarchical EEG classification system as shown in Ref. [7], this work used the entropy method with the best wavelet packet to detect epileptic seizures; in this way, another work used both discrete WT and Wavelet Packet (WP) decomposition together with statistical measures (to extract the relevant features) and machine learning algorithms, to detect and predict epileptic seizures [8].

Dynamic inverse solution with frequency-spatio-temporal constrains, that improves the brain activity reconstruction, is proposed in this work. First, the EEG signals is processed through a multi-rank filter for frequency selection and second, the processed signals are used within a cost function as spatial and temporal constrains. Finally, an iterative algorithm with frequency-spatio-temporal constrains is presented and its performance is evaluated by using simulated and real EEG signals. The proposed method Iterative Regularization Algorithm-L1 (IRA-L1), with the frequency-spatio-temporal stage, was compared with other approaches and can be concluded that IRA-L1 improves the quality of the brain reconstruction performance in terms of the Wasserstein metric, for both simulated and real EEG signals. This paper is structured as follows: In Sect. 2 a description of the methods proposed in this work are presented. In Sects. 3 and 4 a comparison analysis for simulated EEG and real EEG signals is presented. Finally, in Sect. 5 the conclusions and final remarks are presented.

2   Materials and Methods

The EEG computed from a known underlying neural activity for a time window can be described by the following output equation:

$$Y = MX + \Upsilon \tag{1}$$

where $Y \in \mathbb{R}^{d \times N}$ is a segment of EEG, being d the number of channels and $X \in \mathbb{R}^{n \times N}$ is a segment of neural activity being n the number of sources where the neural activity is known, and with N the total number of samples.

2.1   Multi-rate Filter Banks

In order to include frequency constraints in the estimation of neural activity, a decomposition of the EEG is performed. In this way, the EEG segment Y can be decomposed in several frequency bands by using multi-rate filter banks (MFB). That task can be performed by considering $V_{(j,i)}$ the subspace that represent a frequency band, and being $j = 0, \ldots, J$ the number of decomposition levels, and $i = 0, \ldots, 2^j - 1$ the number of frequency bands of each level, which satisfies that: $V_{(j,i)} = V_{(j+1,2^i)} \oplus V_{(j+1,2^i+1)}$. That can be achieved if the filters are selected with special properties like orthogonality or bi-orthogonality [9].

This decomposition in multiple frequency bands allows a detailed analysis of each band. However, a subset of frequency bands can be used for reconstruction of an approximated EEG by any cost function, for example an energy based cost function, where the approximated EEG can be obtained as

$$\hat{Y} = \sum_{j \in E} \tilde{Y}_j \tag{2}$$

being E the subset of frequency bands whose retained energy is over a threshold, and being $\tilde{Y}_j$ the $j-th$ frequency band. Therefore, by considering (2), the neural activity can be also decomposed in frequency bands according to (1) as follows:

$$Y_j = M X_j + \Upsilon_j \tag{3}$$

It can be seen that an approximated reconstruction can also be obtained by considering the selected frequency bands of the EEG as proposed in (2).

2.2 Inverse Problem with Frequency-Spatio-Temporal Constraints

By considering (1) and (2), an inverse problem based on a frequency selection EEG can be obtained as follows:

$$\underset{X_j}{\text{minimize}} \quad \|Y_j - M X_j\|_2^2 \tag{4a}$$

$$\text{subject to} \quad \|X_j\|_1^1 \tag{4b}$$

$$\|L X_j\|_2^2 \tag{4c}$$

where the solution is the reconstructed activity $\widehat{X}$ which includes frequency-spatio-temporal constraints. It can be seen that the optimization problem (4) is solved for each frequency bands (frequency constraint) by including sparsity constraint with an $l - 1$ norm (spatial constraint), and an $l - 2$ norm (temporal constraint). Being L an operator that compute the temporal evolution of estimated activity X (differences between consecutive columns).

3 Experimental Framework

Two methods for brain activity reconstruction are compared in this work, Multiple Sparse Priors (MSP) and IRA-L1, the performance is compared with MFB decomposition using the best tree and without MFB decomposition. The results are analyzed for both simulated and real EEG signals.

3.1   Simulated Active Sources

An analysis of the subspace mapping is performed with simulated EEG signals by considering the underlying neural activity known and by selecting, randomly, the location of the active sources in the brain. Two considerations for underlying activity dynamics as follows:

Database 1: According to [10], two sources in the range of 8 to 13 Hz were randomly located in the brain how alpha oscillations and with activity X sampled to 100 Hz. Besides, independent brain noise time series were generated and randomly located at 500 locations whose main feature was 1/f-shaped (pink noise) power and random phase spectra. These noise sources were distributed from the entire cortical surface and the EEG signals and the EEG signal y_k was generated by multiplying the neural activity x_k with the leadfield matrix M as described in Eq. (1). In this case was considered a SNR in the range of 0.1 to 0.9%.

Database 2: Three sources were activated according to the following expression: $x_i(t_k) = \exp\left(-\frac{1}{2}\left(\frac{t_k - c_i}{\sigma}\right)\right)^2 \sin\left(2\pi f_i t_k\right)$, being c_i the center of the windowed signal in seconds, and f_i the frequency of the signal, with $i = 1, \ldots, 3$. The c_i and f_i were selected in the following ranges $c_i : [0.5, 1.5]$ seconds and randomly in $f_i : [1, 20]$ Hz. In order to measure the performance of the method for several randomly selected source positions and robustness, 300 trials (60 for each SNR) with SNRs (0, 5, 10, 15 and 20 dB) [1]. As described in Eq. (1), the EEG was generated by multiplying X by the lead field matrix M.

The lead-field matrix used to generate the EEG signals for both databases is obtained from the so-called New York Head model as used in [10]. This head model combines a highly detailed magnetic resonance (MR) image of the average adult human head with state-of-the-art finite element electrical modeling. The model holds $n = 2004$ sources and $d = 108$ electrodes.

3.2   Real EEG Signals

The methods IRA-L1 and MSP with and without the MFB decompositions are evaluated using real EEG signals, where the ground truth is assumed relying upon multi-modal solutions. The paradigm has been set up by [11], where eighteen healthy young adults (eight female) were drawn from the MRC Cognition and Brain Sciences unit Volunteer Panel. In this paradigm were used 300 different faces (150 were from famous people and 150 were from unfamiliar (previously unseen) people) and 150 different scrambled faces. The faces or scramble faces were presented in a repeated way or after a lag of 5–15 intervening items. Finally, ERP of 15 subjects are selected for each one of the 3 stimulus and it is very important that each patient has his own forward model (lead-field matrix).

3.3   Performance Measure

To measure the performance of the proposed algorithms (IRA-L1 [1] and MSP [12]) is the Wasserstein metric, also termed the Earth Mover's Distance (EMD).

The EMD is a measurement of the amount of energy required to move the estimated brain mapping solution to the original simulated neural activity [1].

4   Results

The temporal (left) and frequency (right) dynamics of the simulated sources on the Database 1 are shown in Fig. 1. The source activity can be seen that it is mainly concentrated in the range of 8 to 13 Hz. It means that the relevant information should be able to localize the main EEG generators inside such frequency range.

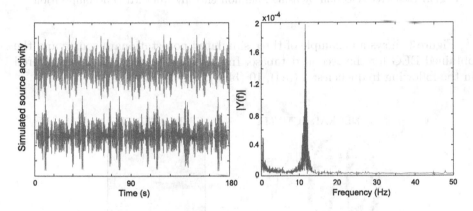

Fig. 1. Simulated EEG for two sources according to the Database 1

The MFB decomposition, for the database above mentioned, is shown in Fig. 2. It should be highlighted that almost the 90% of the EEG total energy is retained in subspaces $V_{(4,2)}$ and $V_{(4,3)}$, these subspaces (6.25 and 12.5 Hz) are within the frequency range of the activity simulated. Therefore, the EEG recording Y is projected into several sub-spaces $V(j,i)$, being $j = 0, \cdots, J$ the number of decomposition levels, and $i = 0, \cdots, 2^j - 1$ the number of sub-bands for each level. The best tree was automatically calculated in $J = 4$ using the Shannon entropy of each subspace as cost function and the retained energy criterion was set at each subspace such as it does not exceed the 50% of the total signal energy. As a result, we obtained that the EEG recording can be decomposed into the following subspaces: $V_{(0,0)} = V_{(1,1)} \oplus V_{(2,1)} \oplus V_{(3,0)} \oplus V_{(4,2)} \oplus V_{(4,3)}$.

It could be corroborated that the proposed MFB decomposition has an inherent property of automatic sub-bands selection. Therefore, according to the energy and entropy criteria, the brain activity can be reconstructed with the more relevant frequency bands. Once the best tree is estimated, the neural activity estimation is carried out employing solely the selected sub-spaces.

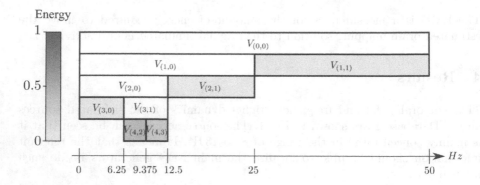

Fig. 2. Best tree selection by using Shannon entropy from MFB decomposition

Figure 3 shows an example of three simulated non-stationary source and the obtained EEG for the second database. In this case, the sources were centered in the following frequencies: 4 (red), 10 (blue), and 16 (orange).

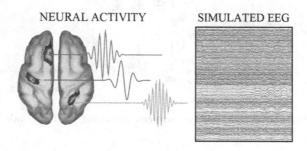

Fig. 3. EEG and three active sources randomly located with different frequencies. (Color figure online)

More than 90% of the total EEG energy was covered for the sub-spaces $V_{(4,1)}$, $V_{(4,2)}$, and $V_{(4,6)}$ with central frequencies of 6.25, 9.375, and 18.75 Hz (Fig. 4) after the signal was decomposed by using MFB. It must be remarked that the obtained results or each subspace directly correspond to each simulated active source. Therefore, the proposed method is able to optimally estimate the frequency bands of interest, under non-stationary conditions.

In Fig. 5 can be seen the EMD mean and standard deviation after 60 repetitions at each SNR level for the proposed algorithm with the database 2. The locations and the central frequency are randomly selected for each repetition. The best neural activity reconstruction were reached by applying the methods with the MFB decomposition step. It must be highlighted that the results with IRA-L1-MFB overcomes the remaining comparison methods (case with non-stationary sources). IRA-L1-MFB deals with the data non-stationarity in two

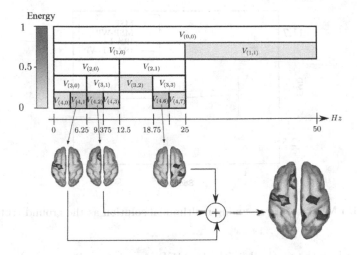

Fig. 4. MFB decomposition for three sources

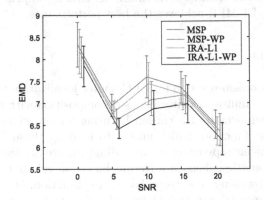

Fig. 5. Setup 2 EMD comparison for 60 repetitions of three randomly located sources at each SNR level

different ways: (i) by splitting the time-varying EEG spectrum into several subspaces using the MFB step, and (ii) by imposing smooth temporal transitions within the estimated sources, yielding an improved non-stationary source reconstruction.

For real EEG database, the ground truth used as estimated reference activity was EEG and MEG multimodal data. The neural activity was estimated for each of the three stimulus conditions, namely, faces, famous faces, and scrambled faces and for each methods to the averaged ERP time series of each subject. Therefore, with these estimations was possible to calculate the EMD between the ground truth and the active sources with each activity estimation algorithm. The last figure (Fig. 6) shows the EMD mean and standard deviation for the 15 subjects under each stimulus condition and, the best results (the lower EMD)

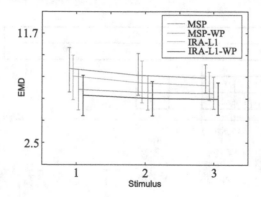

Fig. 6. EMD measure assuming multimodal solution as the ground truth.

were obtained by the methods with the MFB step, hence, it means closer reconstruction to the ground truth. Furthermore, as ERPs comprise non-stationary brain activity, IRA-L1-MFB achieves the best performance.

5   Conclusions

The novel inverse problem solution for EEG source localization is presented, this method is based on a multi-rate filter banks decomposition with frequency bands selection. Relevant information is chosen by using an automatic method based on the entropy cost function, which allows to identify those frequency bands on the threshold the entropy criteria. Accordingly, there are two inherent properties namely: automatic subspace selection based on relevant EEG frequency bands information by using an entropy based cost function, brain mapping with frequency-spatio-temporal constraints into the dynamic inverse problem solution. This method shown that can efficiently select the relevant frequency bands where the activity is spatially and temporal located, and hence, the brain activity reconstruction can be done for each frequency band. Besides, the MFB step can be used in applications to choose relevant information by applying the entropy based cost function, and then, this information can be used to rebuild the neural activity located in specific frequency bands.

Acknowledgments. This work was carried out under the funding of the Departamento Administrativo Nacional de Ciencia, Tecnología e Innovación (Colciencias). Research project: 111077757982 "Sistema de identificación de fuentes epileptogénicas basado en medidas de conectividad funcional usando registros electroencefalográficos e imágenes de resonancia magnética en pacientes con epilepsia refractaria: apoyo a la cirugía resectiva".

This work is also part of the research project "Solución del problema inverso dinámico considerando restricciones espacio-temporales no homogéneas aplicado a la reconstrucción de la actividad cerebral" funded by the Universidad Tecnológica de Pereira under the code E6-17-2.

References

1. Giraldo, E., Martinez-Vargas, J., Castellanos-Dominguez, G.: Reconstruction of neural activity from EEG data using dynamic spatio-temporal constraints. Int. J. Neural Syst. **26**(7), 16500261–165002615 (2016)
2. Behjat, H., Leonardi, N., Sörnmo, L., Ville, D.V.D.: Anatomically-adapted graph wavelets for improved group-level fMRI activation mapping. NeuroImage **123**(Supplement C), 185–199 (2015)
3. Liao, K., Zhu, M., Ding, L.: A new wavelet transform to sparsely represent cortical current densities for eeg/meg inverse problems. Comput. Methods Programs Biomed. **111**(2), 376–388 (2013)
4. Lina, J., Chowdhury, R., Lemay, E., Kobayashi, E., Grova, C.: Wavelet-based localization of oscillatory sources from magnetoencephalography data. IEEE Trans. Biomed. Eng. **61**(8), 2350–2364 (2014)
5. Gramfort, A., Strohmeier, D., Haueisen, J., Hämäläinen, M., Kowalski, M.: Time-frequency mixed-norm estimates: Sparse m/eeg imaging with non-stationary source activations. NeuroImage **70**, 410–422 (2013)
6. Castaño-Candamil, S., et al.: Solving the eeg inverse problem based on space-time-frequency structured sparsity constraints. NeuroImage **118**, 598–612 (2015)
7. Wang, D., Miao, D., Xie, C.: Best basis-based wavelet packet entropy feature extraction and hierarchical eeg classification for epileptic detection. Expert. Syst. Appl. **38**(11), 14314–14320 (2011)
8. Alickovic, E., Kevric, J., Subasi, A.: Performance evaluation of empirical mode decomposition, discrete wavelet transform, and wavelet packed decomposition for automated epileptic seizure detection and prediction. Biomed. Signal Process. Control **39**(Supplement C), 94–102 (2018)
9. Zhao, L., Jia, Y., Xie, Y.: Robust transcale decentralised estimation fusion for multisensor systems based on wavelet packet decomposition. IET Control Theory Appl. **8**(8), 585–597 (2014)
10. Haufe, S., Ewald, A.: A simulation framework for benchmarking EEG-based brain connectivity estimation methodologies. Brain Topography, 1–18 (2016)
11. Henson, R., Wakeman, D.G., Litvak, V., Friston, K.J.: A parametric empirical bayesian framework for the EEG/MEG inverse problem: generative models for multi-subject and multi-modal integration. Front. Human Neurosci. **5**(76), 1–16 (2011)
12. Friston, K., et al.: Multiple sparse priors for the M/EEG inverse problem. NeuroImage **39**(3), 1104–1120 (2008)

An EEG-Based Emotion Recognition Model with Rhythm and Time Characteristics

Jianzhuo Yan[1,2,3] and Sinuo Deng[1,2,3(✉)]

[1] Faculty of Information Technology,
Beijing University of Technology, Beijing 100124, China
yanjianzhuo@bjut.edu.cn, dsn0w@emails.bjut.edu.cn
[2] Beijing Advanced Innovation Center for Future Internet Technology,
Beijing University of Technology, Beijing 100124, China
[3] Engineering Research Center of Digital Community,
Beijing University of Technology, Beijing 100124, China

Abstract. As a senior function of human brain, emotion has a great influence on human study, work, and all aspects of life. Correctly recognizing human emotion can make artificial intelligence serve human being better. EEG-based emotion recognition (ER) has become more popular in these years, which is one of the utilizations of Brain Computer Interface (BCI). However, due to the ambiguity of human emotions and the complexity of EEG signals, the EEG-ER system which can recognize emotions with high accuracy is not easy to achieve. In this paper, based on the time scale, we choose recurrent neural network as the breakthrough point of the screening model. And according to the rhythmic characteristics and temporal memory characteristics of EEG, we propose a Rhythmic Time EEG Emotion Recognition Model (RT-ERM) based on the valance and arousal of LSTM. When using this model, the classification results of different rhythms and time scales are different. Through the results of the classification accuracy of different rhythms and different time scales, the optimal rhythm and time scale of the RT-ERM model are obtained, and the classification of emotional EEG is carried out by the best time scales corresponding to different rhythms, and we found some interesting phenomena. Finally, by comparing with other existing emotional EEG classification methods, it is found that the rhythm and time scale of the model can provide a good accuracy rate for RT-ERM.

Keywords: EEG · Emotion recognition · Rhythm and time characteristics
LSTM

1 Introduction

Analysis of EEG from the time domain mainly includes two perspectives: One is task-related EEG delay characteristics, which are mainly analyzed by event-related potentials; the other is memory-related EEG period characteristics, which are closely related to the memory attributes in cognitive theory. Previous studies have shown that emotions have a short-term memory attribute, that is, emotions will continue for some time until the next emotional stimulus, and this phenomenon can be measured using brain electricity [1]. Because short-term EEG signals are usually considered to be stable,

S. Wang et al. (Eds.): BI 2018, LNAI 11309, pp. 22–31, 2018.
https://doi.org/10.1007/978-3-030-05587-5_3

most studies use 1–4 s EEG signals to identify emotional states [2]. This article mainly focuses on emotion-related temporal memory attributes, and explores the association effects between different time scales and emotional states under different rhythms.

We add the concept of window function on the basis of the traditional full-response time-scale analysis, and determine the local brainwave component of the time-varying signal through the constant movement of the window function. The wavelet transform method is used to extract the EEG signals of different rhythms, and then the whole time domain process of the rhythmic brain wave is decomposed into countless equal-length sub-processes, each sub-process is approximately stable, and then the subsequent analysis and processing are performed. Due to the instability of physiological signals, the long-window physiological signal variability is large, and short-term windows do not provide sufficient information, so choosing a suitable length of time window is crucial for the accuracy and computational efficiency of emotion recognition [3]. The windowing method can be used to estimate the start and duration of different emotional states (such as high arousal). Especially when we use movie clips or music videos to induce emotions, different stimulus materials have different durations, and due to the different plots of the stimulus material, the induced emotions are fast and slow. Therefore, it is more practical and useful to estimate the start and duration of different emotional states through windowing.

Recurrent neural networks inspired and validated by cognitive models and supervised learning methods have been proven to be effective methods for simulating the input and output of sequence forms (especially data in temporal form). For example, in the fields of cognitive science and computational neuroscience, many physiological research results have laid the foundation for the study of circulatory neural net-works [4]. On the other hand, the idea of biological heuristics has also been validated by various experiments [5]. Based on the above theoretical support, we use the recur-rent neural network to simulate and identify the emotional EEG signals at multiple time scales.

In the next section, we will talk about the study about physiological characteristics (time characteristics) of emotional EEG first, and then tap, analyze and apply the binding relationship between emotion and rhythm and the relationship between emotion and time. The following sections will elaborate on the relevant technologies, principles, and methods involved in the model.

2   Method

2.1   Rhythm and Time Characteristics Analysis of EEG

A large number of studies of neurophysiological and cognitive science have shown that the brain has time consistency and delay in the process of emotional processing, memory attributes. This paper uses the LSTM neural network to explore the binding relationship between emotion and time scale under different shock rhythms, and then to serve for emotional recognition. The LSTM-based EEG "time" characteristic analysis mainly includes three parts: rhythm signal extraction, time scale division, and emotion recognition analysis. The following is a detailed explanation.

Rhythm Signal Extraction. We use the discrete wavelet transform to extract the rhythm of the full-band EEG signal. The formula is as follows:

$$W_f(j,k) = \int_R 2^{\frac{j}{2}} f(t)\overline{\psi(2^J t - k)}\,dt \tag{1}$$

Among them, $\psi_{j,k}(t) = |a|^{-\frac{1}{2}}\psi\left(\frac{t-b}{a}\right) = 2^{\frac{j}{2}}\psi(2^J t - k) j, k \in Z$, j and k are scale parameters. With the change of j, $\psi_{j,k}(t)$ is in different frequency bands in the frequency domain. With the change of k, $\psi_{j,k}(t)$ is in different time bands in the time domain.

Different from the analysis of wavelet parameters with different rhythms, we consider the time properties of different rhythms. Therefore, to reconstruct the wavelet coefficients, the time domain signals corresponding to different rhythms are obtained. The formula is as follows:

$$f(t) = C\sum_{j=-\infty}^{+\infty}\sum_{k=-\infty}^{\infty} W_f(j,k)\psi_{j,k}(t) \tag{2}$$

Division of Time Scales. According to different time scale analysis requirements, the rhythm signal is segmented using a rectangular window function. The time scales for the segmentation are: 0.25 s, 0.5 s, 0.75 s, 1 s, 2 s, 3 s, 4 s, 5 s and 6 s, as shown in Fig. 1.

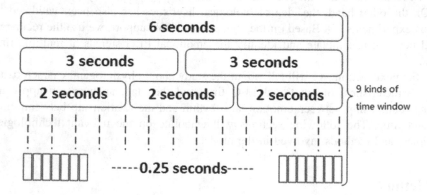

Fig. 1. Block diagram of window segmentation.

2.2   Long-Short Memory Neural Network

Recurrent Neural Network (RNN) is a very effective connection model. On the one hand, it can learn input data at different time scales in real time. On the other hand, it is also possible to capture the model state information of the past time through the loop of the unit in the model and have the function of the memory module. The RNN model was originally proposed by Jordan [6] and Elman [7], and subsequently de-rived many different variants, such as time delay neural network (TDNN) [8] and echo oscillating network (ESN) [9], etc. Due to the special design of recursion, RNN can theoretically learn history event information of any length. However, the length of the standard RNN model learning history information is limited in real application. The main problem is that the given input data will affect the status of the hidden layer unit, which will affect the output of the network. With the increase of the number of cycles, the output data of the network unit will be affected by exponential growth and decrease, which is defined as the gradient disappearance and gradient explosion problem [10]. A large number of research efforts have attempted to solve these problems, the most popular being the long short-term memory neural network structure proposed by Hochreiter and Schmidhuber in 1997 [11].

The LSTM network structure is similar to the standard RNN model except that its hidden layer's summation unit is replaced by a memory module. Each module contains one or more self-connected memory cells and three multiplication units (input gates, output gates, and oblivion gates). These multiplication units have writing, reading, and reset functions. Since these multiplication units allow the LSTM's memory unit to store and retrieve long-term information from the network, the gradient disappearance problem can be mitigated.

The learning process of LSTM is divided into two layers, forward propagation and back propagation. The back propagation process of LSTM calculates the loss function based on the output of the model training and the real tag, and then adjusts the weight of the model. Currently, two well-known algorithms have been used to calculate and adjust the weights in the back-propagation process: one is real-time recurrent learning (RTRL); the other is back propagation through time (BPTT). In this article, we use BPTT for training because it is better understood and has less computational complexity.

Since the LSTM model was proposed, it has been widely applied to a series of tasks that require long-term memory, such as learning context-confirmed statements [12] and requiring precise timing and counting [13]. In addition, the LSTM model is also widely used in real life, such as protein structure prediction [14], music generation [15], and speech recognition [16].

3 LSTM-Based EEG Emotion Recognition Model

Different from the analysis part, in this part, we directly use the optimal time and rhythm characteristics obtained from the analysis to construct an EEG emotion recognition method (RT-ERM) based on the "rhythm-time" characteristic inspiration, and then conduct emotion recognition. The analysis framework is shown in Fig. 2. The input is original Multi-channel EEG signal, and the output is the emotion classification which is based on the valence and arousal.

Step 1. The RT-ERM method receives the multi-channel original EEG signals:

$$X(t) = \left[x^{CH_1}(t), x^{CH_2}(t), \cdots, x^{CH_n}(t)\right] \in R^{n \times N} \tag{3}$$

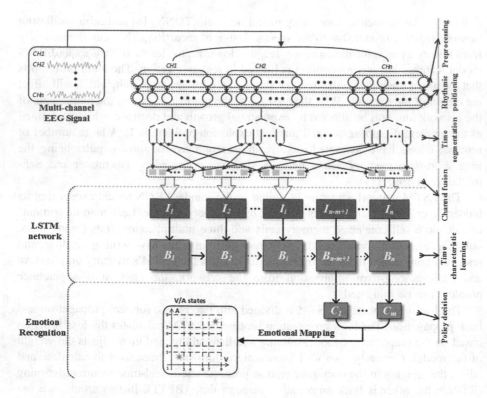

Fig. 2. An emotion recognition model inspired by "Rhythm-Time" characteristic

where n is the number of brain leads, N is the number of sample points, and $x^{CH_i}(t)$ is the brain electrical signal of the i-th channel.

Then we use the open source toolbox EEGLab to perform the technique of artifact removal and blind source separation based on independent component analysis for multi-channel EEG signals. The most representative signal in each brain power source as follow:

$$S(t) = \left[s^{CH_1}(t), s^{CH_2}(t), \cdots, s^{CH_n}(t)\right] \in R^{n \times N} \tag{4}$$

Step 2. Furthermore, the EEG signal is down-sampled to 256 Hz to obtain the preconditioned EEG signal, as follows:

$$F(t) = \left[f^{CH_1}(t), f^{CH_2}(t), \cdots, f^{CH_n}(t)\right] \in R^{n \times M} \tag{5}$$

where M is the number of channel sample points after downsampling. Rhythm extraction is performed on the preprocessed EEG signal to obtain a rhythm signal of interest:

$$F_\kappa(t) = \left[f_\kappa^{CH_1}(t), f_\kappa^{CH_2}(t), \cdots, f_\kappa^{CH_n}(t) \right] \in R^{n \times M} \tag{6}$$

where κ represents the emotion-related rhythm obtained from the analysis.

Step 3. Let tS be the time scale and sR be the sampling frequency, cut and merge the rhythm signals as follow:

$$I_\kappa(t) = \left[I_\kappa^1(t), I_\kappa^2(t), \cdots, I_\kappa^T(t) \right] \in R^{E \times T} \tag{7}$$

where $E = n * tS * sR$, T is obtained by dividing the total sample time by tS, and the EEG data vector of the i-th time node as follows:

$$I_\kappa^i(t) = \begin{bmatrix} f_\kappa^{CH_1}(ts * sR * (i-1), tS * sR * i), \ldots \\ \ldots, f_\kappa^{CH_n}(ts * sR * (i-1), tS * sR * i) \end{bmatrix} \tag{8}$$

Step 4. After being cut and merged, the signal $I_\kappa(t)$ is input into the LSTM model for recognition learning.

Step 5. Finally, the results of the emotion classification based on the valence and arousal of emotion is obtained by using the output of the LSTM network.

4   Results and Discussion

4.1   Data Description

EEG Data. The performance of the proposed emotional recognition model is investigated using DEAP Dataset. DEAP [17] is a multimodal dataset for analysis of human affective states. 32 Healthy participants (50% female), aged between 19 and 37 (mean age 26.9), participated in the experiment. 40 one-minute long excerpts of music videos were presented in 40 trials for each subject. There are 1280 (32 subjects × 40trials) emotional state samples. During the experiments, EEG signals were recorded with 512 Hz sampling frequency, which were downsampled to 256 Hz and filtered between 4.0 Hz and 45.0 Hz, and the EEG artifacts are removed.

Sample Distribution. Based on the above DEAP dataset, the proposed model is learned and tested for classifying the negative-positive states (ScoreV $\leq$ 3 or $\geq$ 7) and passive-active states (ScoreA $\leq$ 3 or $\geq$ 7), respectively. The sample size of negative state is 222; the sample size of positive state is 373; the sample size of passive state is 226; the sample size of active state is 297.

4.2 Assessment Method Overview

This section uses the Accuracy indicators to measure the final classification results. Their formula and definition are as follows:

Accuracy (ACC) measures the overall effectiveness of the classification model, which is the ratio of the correct sample size to the total sample size. The formula is:

$$Accuracy = \frac{TP + TN}{TP + TN + FP + FN} \times 100\% \qquad (9)$$

Among them, TP indicates that the sample belongs to the positive class and is also recognized as a positive class; FP indicates that the sample belongs to a negative class and is identified as a positive class; TN indicates that the sample is a negative class and is also identified as a negative class; FN indicates a positive class Cases identified as negative.

In this paper, positive classes correspond to high-price (HV) and high arousal (HA) states, while negative classes correspond to states of low valence (LV) and low arousal (LA). In addition, a 10-fold cross-validation method was used to verify the validity of the identification, and the average (Mean) and standard deviation (Std.) of the evaluation index were calculated.

4.3 Analysis of Binding Relationship Between Time and Rhythm

Based on the analysis method in Sect. 3, the "rhythm-time" characteristics of EEG under emotional valence and arousal were analyzed separately. The following are the results and discussion of analysis methods.

Table 1 is the recognition result obtained for different time scales for the EEG signals corresponding to the dimension of emotion valence under θ, α, β, and γ rhythms, respectively.

Table 1. The classification results of RT-ERM with different time scales for each rhythm under the dimension of emotion valence

Time Scale	ACC of Assessment Method (Mean ± Std.)			
(s)	θ/%	α/%	β/%	γ/%
0.25 s	56.35 ± 2.4113	60.27 ± 4.1427	60.29 ± 4.7628	58.17 ± 3.1975
0.5 s	59.50 ± 3.5681	58.17 ± 3.1975	57.91 ± 2.0398	58.18 ± 4.1395
0.75 s	58.97 ± 4.8805	59.76 ± 4.4014	62.12 ± 5.7946	58.69 ± 2.3590
1.0 s	58.44 ± 3.6729	58.43 ± 3.8471	59.47 ± 2.6751	59.23 ± 3.1682
2.0 s	61.59 ± 4.8816	60.53 ± 5.1299	60.02 ± 3.4931	60.54 ± 4.2358
3.0 s	59.49 ± 3.1551	58.97 ± 3.7542	58.18 ± 2.9866	59.48 ± 2.9294
4.0 s	59.49 ± 5.5365	58.17 ± 2.9786	61.07 ± 6.5296	59.48 ± 5.7782
5.0 s	58.70 ± 3.9015	59.22 ± 8.0870	59.48 ± 3.3671	60.52 ± 4.7069
6.0 s	58.70 ± 3.9015	61.06 ± 3.4886	57.79 ± 2.4043	58.96 ± 2.6829

As can be seen from the table, under θ rhythm, the time scale of 2 s corresponds to the best recognition effect, under α rhythm, the time scale of 0.25 s corresponds to the best recognition effect, under β rhythm, the time scale of 0.75 s corresponds to the best recognition effect, under γ rhythm, the time scales of 2 s and 5 s correspond to the best recognition effect.

Table 2 is the recognition result obtained for different time scales for the EEG signals corresponding to the dimension of emotion arousal under θ, α, β, and γ rhythms, respectively.

Table 2. The classification results of RT-ERM with different time scales for each rhythm under the dimension of emotion arousal

Time Scale (s)	ACC of Assessment Method (Mean ± Std.)			
	θ/%	α/%	β/%	γ/%
0.25 s	67.00 ± 7.3143	63.75 ± 3.4003	58.75 ± 3.5794	61.25 ± 3.9131
0.5 s	69.10 ± 4.2131	58.25 ± 6.8965	60.75 ± 4.8798	60.00 ± 5.1234
0.75 s	62.25 ± 2.8394	60.25 ± 4.8023	63.50 ± 3.0000	58.75 ± 2.7951
1.0 s	64.25 ± 3.7165	58.24 ± 4.8916	63.00 ± 4.8476	59.50 ± 1.8708
2.0 s	64.57 ± 1.9910	60.75 ± 2.5124	59.00 ± 3.3911	61.50 ± 5.0249
3.0 s	61.00 ± 5.3851	56.25 ± 2.3048	56.25 ± 5.6181	59.50 ± 1.5000
4.0 s	57.75 ± 4.9307	59.50 ± 2.4494	58.50 ± 5.0249	59.25 ± 5.2500
5.0 s	61.00 ± 2.7838	58.00 ± 4.4441	58.25 ± 3.3634	59.50 ± 4.4441
6.0 s	62.50 ± 4.8734	60.25 ± 4.5345	59.75 ± 3.4369	57.50 ± 2.9580

As can be seen from the table, under θ rhythm, the time scale of 0.5 s corresponds to the best recognition effect, under α rhythm, the time scale of 0.25 s corresponds to the best recognition effect, under β rhythm, the time scale of 0.5 s and 0.75 s correspond to the best recognition effect, under γ rhythm, the time scales of 0.25 s and 2 s correspond to the best recognition effect.

4.4 Emotion Recognition Results Comparison and Analysis

From Table 3, it can be seen that, currently, most of the emotion recognition studies using the DEAP database select a time window of 1 to 8 s, and the time window with the highest recognition accuracy rate is 1 to 2 s.

In the statistical results in Table 4–9, for valence, RT-ERM can obtain the highest average recognition accuracy (62.12%) at the time scale of 0.75 s and β rhythm, and the recognition accuracy rate reaches up to 76.3%; In terms of arousal, RT-ERM can obtain the highest average recognition accuracy (69.1%) at the time scale of 0.5 s and θ rhythm, and the recognition accuracy rate reaches 82.5%. Through the statistical results, we found that the LSTM-based deep learning network can effectively identify the emotional state and obtain a good recognition effect.

Table 3. Comparison of results that Use EEG Signals of DEAP Dataset for Emotion Recognition

Literature	Emotion category	Window's length	Classification	The highest classification accuracy (Acc/%)
Rozgić et al. [18]	Arousal/2	1 s/2 s/4 s/8 s (1 s step length)	SVM KNN	68.4/2
	Valence/2			76.9/2
Zhuang et al. [19]	Arousal/2	1 s (0.1 s step length)	SVR	68.4/2
	Valence/2			76.9/2
Yoon et al. [3]	Arousal/2	2 s (1 s step length)	Bayesian based on sensor convergence	70.1/2
	Valence/2			70.9/2
Sepideh et al. [20]	Arousal/2	1 s	KNN, QDA, LDA	74.2/2
	Valence/2			72.33/2
Our work	Arousal/2	<1 s	RT-REM	69.1 (82.5)/2
	Valence/2			62.12 (76.3)/2

5   Conclusions

This paper discusses the temporal memory characteristics of the brain in the process of emotional information processing, and then discusses the theoretical basis and advantages of the cyclic neural network when it is used in the mining analysis of temporal characteristics, and then constructs a model of sentiment analysis and recognition to achieve effective recognition and analysis of emotions. In this paper, we discussed the emotion mechanism under different time scales corresponding to different rhythms, using the rhythm oscillation mechanism as the default mode of the brain. We found that different rhythms and different emotional states correspond to similar and different time mechanisms through experimental results. For example, high rhythms (such as β and γ rhythm, etc.) have a high correlation with the expression of valence emotions, and low rhythms (such as θ rhythm) have a high correlation with the expression of arousal emotions. It is noteworthy that the smaller time scale shows better recognition performance no matter in the valence or arousal state. In summary, the "rhythm-time" characteristics obtained through RT-ERM affective model analysis not only have a greater significance for the in-depth understanding of the physiological properties of the brain in the process of emotional information processing, but also help guide the application of emotion recognition model based on physiological inspiration.

Acknowledgements. This work is supported by the CERNET Innovation Project (No. NGII20170719). We sincerely thank Hongzhi Kuai for the helpful discussion on the experiment design and the equipment support.

References

1. Khosrowabadi, R., Wahab, A., Ang, K.K., Baniasad, M.H.: Affective computation on EEG correlates of emotion from musical and vocal stimuli. In: Proceedings of the IJCNN, pp. 1168–1172. IEEE Press, Atlanta (2009)
2. Esslen, M., Pascual, M.R.D., Kochi, K., et al.: Brain areas and time course of emotional processing. Neuroimage 21(4), 1189–1203 (2014)
3. Yoon, H.J., Chung, S.Y.: EEG-based emotion estimation using Bayesian weighted-log-posterior function and perceptron convergence algorithm. Comput. Biol. Med. 43(12), 2230–2237 (2013)
4. Hopfield, J.J.: Neural networks and physical systems with emergent collective computational abilities. Proc. Natl. Acad. Sci. 79(8), 2554–2558 (1982)
5. Schuster, M., Paliwal, K.K.: Bidirectional recurrent neural networks. Signal Process. 45(11), 2673–2681 (1997)
6. Jordan, M.I.: Attractor Dynamics and Parallelism in a Connectionist Sequential Machine, pp. 112–127. IEEE Press, Amherst (1990)
7. Elman, J.L.: Finding structure in time. Cogn. Sci. 14(2), 179–211 (1990)
8. Lang, K.J., Waibel, A.H., Hinton, G.E.: A time-delay neural network architecture for isolated word recognition. Neural Netw. 3(1), 23–43 (1990)
9. Jaeger, H.: The "Echo State" Approach to Analysing and Training Recurrent Neural Networks. überwachtes lernen (2001)
10. Hochreiter, S.: Untersuchungen zu Dynamischen Neuronalen Netzen. PhD thesis, Institut für Informatik, Technische Universität München (1991)
11. Hochreiter, S., Schmidhuber, J.: Long Short-Term Memory. Neural Comput. 9(8), 1735–1780 (1997)
12. Gers, F.A., Schmidhuber, J.: LSTM Recurrent Networks Learn Simple Context Free and Context Sensitive Languages. IEEE Trans. Neural Netw. 12(6), 1333–1340 (2001)
13. Gers, F., Schraudolph, N., Schmidhuber, J.: Learning Precise Timing with LSTM Recurrent Networks. J. of Mach. Learn. Res. 3, 115–143 (2002)
14. Hochreiter, S., Heusel, M., Obermayer, K.: Fast model-based protein homology detection without alignment. Bioinformatics 23(14), 1728 (2007)
15. Eck, D., Schmidhuber, J.: Finding temporal structure in music: blues improvisation with LSTM Recurrent Networks. In: Proceedings of the 12th IEEE Workshop on Neural Networks for Signal Processing, pp. 747–756. IEEE, Martigny (2002)
16. Graves, A., Schmidhuber, J.: Framewise phoneme classification with bidirectional LSTM and other neural network architectures. Neural Netw. 18(5–6), 602–610 (2005b)
17. Koelstra, S., et al.: Deap: a database for emotion analysis using physiological signals. IEEE Trans. Affect. Comput. 3(1), 18–31 (2012)
18. Rozgić, V., Vitaladevuni, S.N., Prasad, R.: Robust EEG emotion classification using segment level decision fusion. In: IEEE International Conference on Acoustics, Speech and Signal Processing, pp. 1286–1290. IEEE, Vancouver (2013)
19. Zhuang, X., Rozgic, V., Crystal, M.: Compact unsupervised EEG response representation for emotion recognition. In: IEEE-EMBS International Conference on Biomedical and Health Informatics (BHI), pp. 736–739. IEEE, Valencia (2014)
20. Sepideh, H., Keivan, M., Motie, N.A.: The Emotion Recognition System Based on Autoregressive Model and Sequential Forward Feature Selection of Electroencephalogram Signals. J. Med. Signals Sens. 4(3), 194–201 (2014)

Influence of Realistic Head Modeling on EEG Forward Problem

Ernesto Cuartas Morales[1(✉)], Yohan Ricardo Céspedes Villar[2],
Héctor Fabio Torres Cardona[3], Carlos Daniel Acosta[1],
and German Castellanos Dominguez[1]

[1] Signal Processing and Recognition Group, Universidad Nacional de Colombia,
Km 9 Vía al Aeropuerto la Nubia, Manizales, Colombia, Manizales, Colombia
{ecuartasmo,cdacostam,cgcastellanosd}@unal.edu.co
[2] Centro de Bioinformática y Biología Computacional de Colombia - BIOS,
Bogota, Colombia
yohan.cespedes@bios.co
[3] Universidad de Caldas, Manizales, Colombia
hectorfabiotorres@gmail.com

Abstract. We study the influence of realistic head modeling on the
EEG forward problem. To this end, we define a high-resolution patient-
specific realistic head model from 3T-MRI and DWI data. Further, we
performed a nine tissues segmentation and a white matter anisotropy
estimation. Then we solve the forward problem using a state-of-the-art
FDM solution that allows volumetric voxelwise anisotropic definition in
a reciprocity sensors space. Finally, we compared the 9-tissues realistic
head model against the commonly used 5-tissues isotropic representation.
Our results show significant potential deviations due to the white matter
anisotropy, and radio to tangential patterns in the outer skull regions as
a direct effect of essential tissues like fat or muscle. Moreover, we analyze
the dipole estimation errors in a parametric inverse setup, finding DLE's
larger than 20 mm. Additionally, we study the influence of neglecting the
blood vessels, finding DLE's larger than 4 mm in deep brain areas.

Keywords: Forward modeling · Conductivity anisotropy
Finite differences

1 Introduction

To date, the influence of the forward modeling on EEG source localization tasks
(ESI) has been studied, revealing the necessity of more accurate and realistic
forward solutions. This aspect is crucial not only for investigative purposes, but
also for surgery planning and brain disorder treatments. To deal with the forward

This research was supported by the research project 36706 "BrainScore: Sistema compositivo, gráfico y sonoro creado a partir del comportamiento frecuencial de las señales
cerebrales", funded by Universidad de Caldas and Universidad Nacional de Colombia.

S. Wang et al. (Eds.): BI 2018, LNAI 11309, pp. 32–40, 2018.
https://doi.org/10.1007/978-3-030-05587-5_4

problem within EEG source analysis, however, the solution of Poisson's equation for a multilayer conductor volume must be performed, taking into account the boundary conditions correctly. Moreover, forward modeling of realistic free-form head volumes is only achievable using numerical approximations.

In this regard, a more realistic representation of head volumes may be of benefit. In practice, a realistic head volume can be obtained from neuroimages such as MRI or CT containing a large number of slices in a series of two-dimensional images. Every slice must be registered in the same coordinate system to obtain a coherent three-dimensional volume. After the registration stage, the volume contains the information of head tissues codified in intensity values, that can be segmented to generate a labeling map holding compartments for specific tissues. In particular, the scalp (where the EEG electrodes are placed), the skull, the cerebrum spinal fluid, the gray matter, and the white matter are the most commonly considered tissues in the forward modeling. Most of the solutions, nowadays, use five tissues segmentations, neglecting essential compartments like eyes, fat, muscle, or even blood vessels. Due to the direct impact of the forward modeling on EEG source localization, we build a patient-specific and realistic head model holding nine tissues, and anisotropic white matter modeling in a $1\,\text{mm}^3$ volumetric segmentation. Further, we use conductivity values from multiple works, including low-frequency conductivity values from IT'IS database.

In this work, we use state-of-the-art finite differences forward volumetric modeling (FDM) in a reciprocity setup to analyze the influence of realistic head data in the forward problem. Our results show that neglecting the important tissue compartments in the forward modeling can induce dipole localization errors larger than $20\,\text{mm}$, and significant potential deviations in the electric field propagation across the conductivity head volume.

2 Methods

2.1 EEG Forward Problem

The EEG forward problem involves the calculation of potentials $\phi(r)$ induced by a primary current density $J(r)$ in a head volume $\Omega \in \mathbb{R}^3$ with $\partial\Omega \in \mathbb{R}^2$ boundary, holding inhomogeneous and anisotropic conductivity $\Sigma(r) \in \mathbb{R}^{3\times3}$. The quasi-static approximation of Maxwell's equations can be formulated, leading to the Poisson's equation as follows [8]:

$$\nabla\cdot(\Sigma(r)\nabla\phi(r)) = -\nabla\cdot J(r), \ \forall r \in \Omega \tag{1}$$

$$\phi(r)|_{\Gamma_l}^+ = \phi(r)|_{\Gamma_l}^- \ \text{on} \ \Gamma_l, \ \forall l = 1,\ldots,N \tag{2}$$

$$(\Sigma(r)\nabla\phi(r))\cdot\hat{n}(r)|_{\Gamma_l}^+ = (\Sigma(r)\nabla\phi(r))\cdot\hat{n}(r)|_{\Gamma_l}^-, \ \text{on} \ \Gamma_l \tag{3}$$

$$(\Sigma(r)\nabla\phi(r))\cdot\hat{n}(r)|_{\partial\Omega} = 0, \ \text{on boundary} \ \partial\Omega \tag{4}$$

where r is a specific head volume position, N is the number of interfaces Γ_l (i.e., head layers), $\hat{n}(r) \in \mathbb{R}^3$ is a unit vector normal to Γ_l at r, and $g(r)|_{\Gamma_l}^{\pm}$

stands for the trace of function $g(\boldsymbol{r})$ from both sides of the l-th interface Γ_l. Furthermore, the solution of Eq. 1 requires establishing proper boundary conditions between adjacent compartments having different conductivities. Thus, Eqs. 2, and 3 stands for the Dirichlet and Neumann flux conditions respectively, while Eq. 4 (or non-flux homogeneous Neumann condition) implies that no current can flow out through the human head interface $\partial\Omega$ into the air [9].

2.2 Solving the Forward Problem with FDM

The solution of the Poisson Eq. 1 for realistic free-form head volumes is only possible using numerical approximations. In particular, individual magnetic resonance (MR) and/or computed tomography (CT) images can be segmented into different tissue types, such as white and grey matter (WM/GM), cerebrospinal fluid (CSF), skull, skin, among others. Recently, diffusion-weighted imaging (DWI) has also been used to determine the anisotropy profile of brain structures base on the movement of water molecules, being particularly important for modeling anisotropic properties in the WM. After segmentation labeling, and local anisotropic conductivity tensors estimation, we solve the EEG forward problem in a reciprocity setup for a given electrode configuration using the iLU-preconditioner FDM technique introduce by [1].

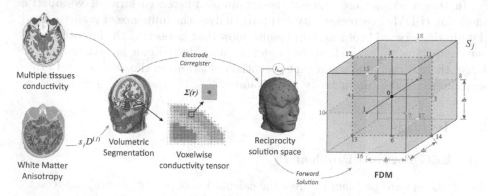

Fig. 1. Forward anisotropy modeling: The Figure illustrates from left to right multiple tissues conductivities and withe matter estimation that are included in the volumetric segmentation. The solution is carried out in a voxelwise conductivity framework for a *lead-field* reciprocity space of a corregistered electrode data set. Finally, forward calculations are carrier out using the FDM algorithm.

Figure 1 shows the realistic head modeling methodology pipeline, for which we define 9 different tissue conductivities for an MRI based tissue-labeling segmentation in a $1\,\mathrm{mm}^3$ space as in [10]. The segmentation allows a voxelwise conductivity distribution for the FDM that can be isotropic or anisotropic taking known conductivity parameters from the literature (Table 1). In addition, we estimate the WM anisotropy using DWI data. Further, we define a reciprocity solution for the EEG sensors space, that is solved using the FDM technique.

3   Experimental Setup

3.1   Realistic Patient-Specific Head Model (RHM)

We build a realistic, high-resolution, patient-specific volume conductor model from neuroimages, including anisotropic skull and white matter modeling. Further, we use T1, IDEAL T2 and diffusion-weighted imaging (DWI) MR scans acquired from a healthy 32-years-old male in the Rey Juan Carlos University, Medicine Faculty, Medical Image Analysis and Biometry Lab, Madrid, Spain.

Acquisition: MR images are acquired by $3.0T$ MR scanner (General Electric Signa HDxt), using the body coil for excitation and an 8-channel quadrature brain coil for reception. Imaging was performed using an isotropic $3DT1w$ SPGR sequence for the following parameters: TR= 8, 7 ms, TE= 3.2 ms, TI= 400 ms, NEX= 1, acquisition FOV= 260 mm, matrix= 320×160, resolution $1 \times 1 \times 1$ mm, flip angle 12; an IDEAL $T2$ sequence with TR= 3000 ms, TE= 81.9 ms, NEX= 6, FOV= 260 mm, acquisition matrix 320×160, flip angle 90; a Time of Flight (TOF) sequence consisting of 8 volumes with 6 slices overlap and TR= 20 ms, TE= 2.1 ms, NEX= 1, acquisition FOV= 224 mm, matrix 224×224, resolution $1 \times 1 \times 1$ mm, flip angle 15; and a DWI sequence with TR= 9200 ms, TE= 83.8 ms, TI= 0 ms, NEX= 1, acquisition FOV= 240 mm, matrix 100×100, flip angle 90, directions 45, thickness 2 mm.

Segmentation: Image preprocessing was performed using 3D Slicer built-in modules. The preprocessing steps included: MRI bias correction (N4 ITK MRI bias correction), and Registration (BRAINS) for movement correction. Cortical Segmentation, including brain white matter (WM) gray matter (GM), and cerebro-spinal fluid (CSF), was performed in the T1-weighted volume using *FreeSurfer*. The skull was estimated using a multi-atlas and label fusion-based approach. To this end, we applied to a CT database the Simultaneous Truth and Performance Level Estimation (STAPLE) algorithm. The remaining CSF was computed as the residual of the skull and the brain segmentation using a GNU Octave script. To segment the skin we use the background noise variance and thresholds of the anisotropically filtered volume as in [10]. Then, Gaussian smoothing was applied to reduce aliasing artefacts in the skin surface and to ensure a minimum of 2 voxels thickness for the skin volume. The eyeballs were segmented by applying a threshold and edge detection algorithm to the IDEAL in-phase head sequences. We also performed a smooth approximation of the main arteries by using an expectation-maximization algorithm to the median filtered TOF images. The remaining tissue was classified in muscle and fat/cartilage, using the expectation-maximization algorithm on the IDEAL fat and water images.

Finally, all available data (T1, T2, and DWI) was aligned with a voxel similarity-based affine registration procedure to correct subject orientation and geometrical distortions. Then, all registered DWI data were re-sampled to have

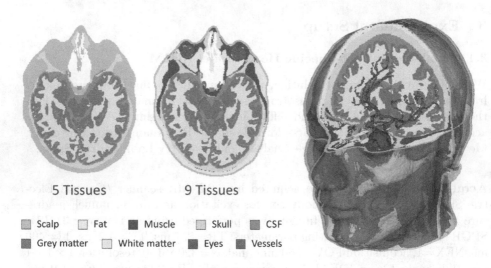

Fig. 2. RHM segmentation.

a unique size $1 \times 1 \times 1$mm by using the FSL toolbox [5]. The final head model is shown in Fig. 2 holding 9 different tissues namely: skin, skull, cerebro spinal fluid (CSF), grey matter (GM), white matter (WM), muscle, fat, eyeballs and vessels, including also a $1\,mm^3$ DWI. Furthermore, we refer to this dataset as realistic head model (RHM). Figure 2, shows a 5-layer, and a 9-layer segmentation for the RHM model.

Modeling White Matter Conductivity Anisotropy: We use diffusion tensor imaging (DTI) data to determine the conductivity tensors in the WM compartment. Therefore, we the DTI data from the 45 gradient directions of the DWI as in [12]. Then, we calculate the conductivity tensors $\boldsymbol{\Sigma}^{(j)}_{WM}$ from the DTI tensors $\boldsymbol{D}^{(j)} \in \mathbb{R}^{3\times3}$ using a local linear relationship $\boldsymbol{\Sigma}^{(j)}_{WM} = s_j \boldsymbol{D}^{(j)}$, as suggested in [11]. Furthermore, the scalar factor s_j can be obtained as follows:

$$s_j = \frac{\sigma^{iso}_{WM}}{(\lambda_1 \lambda_2 \lambda_3)^{1/3}}, \tag{5}$$

where $\sigma^{iso}_{WM} = 0.14$ S/m is the isotropic conductivity value for the white matter, and λ_1, λ_2, and λ_3 are the eigenvalues of the local tensor $\boldsymbol{D}^{(j)}$.

Head Tissue Conductivities: Table 1 show the considered isotropic conductivities for this work (last column), taking into account multiple previous ESI studies [6,11] and including also the IT'IS Foundation database holding a large list of low frequency tissue conductivities [2]. Magnitudes are given in Siemens per meter (S/m).

Table 1. Considered head tissue isotropic conductivities (S/m).

Compartment	Wolters 2006 [12]	Montes 2013 [6]	Vorwerk 2014 [11]	Gabriel 1993[2]	Selected
Skin	0.3300	0.3279	0.4300	-	0.4300
Skull	0.0042	0.0105	0.0100	-	0.0105
CSF	1.7900	1.7857	1.7900	1.7800	1.7900
GM	0.3300	0.3300	0.3300	0.2390	0.3300
WM	0.1400	0.1428	0.1400	0.1280	0.1400
Muscle	-	-	-	0.3550	0.3550
Fat	-	-	-	0.0573	0.0573
Eyes	-	-	-	1.5500	1.5500
Vessels	-	-	-	0.2800	0.2800

Electrodes: We performed fiducial-based similarity transformations to align the EEG electrodes to the head volume. Finally, we project each electrode position towards the center direction of the head volume to ensure that the electrode is surrounded by scalp voxels, guaranteeing that the electrode voxel is not surrounded by air as suggested in [3].

3.2 Parametric Inverse Solution

A parametric inverse solution can be estimated for a reference head model with electrode potentials V_R, compared against a tested head model with electrode potentials V_T, using the same electrode reciprocal space as follows:

$$RRE = \min_{(\tilde{r},\tilde{\mathbf{d}})} \left\{ \frac{\left\| V_R - V_T\left(\tilde{r},\tilde{\mathbf{d}}\right) \right\|_2^2}{\|V_R\|_2^2} \right\} \tag{6}$$

$$DLE = \|\hat{r} - r\|_2 \tag{7}$$

where $V_R \in \mathbb{R}^{N_E \times 1}$ are the electrode potentials of the reference model, usually the most realistic or complex head model. $V_T\left(\tilde{r},\tilde{\mathbf{d}}\right) \in \mathbb{R}^{N_E \times 1}$ are the electrode potential of a tested model, that must be iteratively recalculated to minimize the Eq. 6 as in [7]. Thus, solving the Eq. 6 for a single dipole from the reference model $(r, \mathbf{d})$, we obtain a single dipole from the test model $(\tilde{r}, \tilde{\mathbf{d}})$ that can be compared to obtain the dipole localization error (DLE) using positions r and $\tilde{r}$ (Eq. 7).

4 Results

4.1 Influence of Multiple Tissue Conductivity Modeling in the Potential Fields Propagation

We position a single dipole in the GM cortical-motor area (positive Z orthogonal axis). Then, we calculate reciprocity forward solutions using FDM and a

128 biosemi electrode distribution considering two head models, namely a fully isotropic 5-tissues medium and the 9-tissues with anisotropic WM medium. Further, we analyze the differences in the equipotential lines propagation to study the electric field differences for the considered head models.

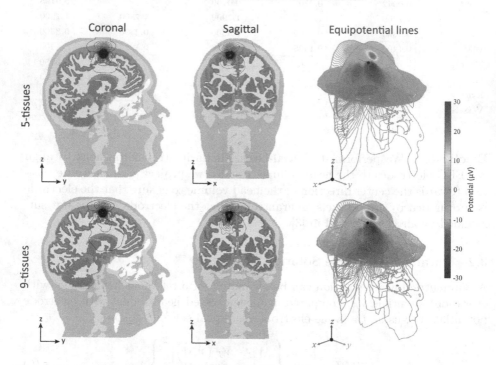

Fig. 3. Sagittal, coronal and tridimensional views of the equipotential lines propagation from a single dipole in the GM, for both, a full isotropic 5-tissues model (top) and the 9-tissues with anisotropic WM model (button).

We show a three-dimensional render of orthogonal planes containing the equipotential lines distribution for the dipole source represented in the Fig. 3 as a black dot, including also coronal and sagittal views for the two considered models. The results show essential differences in the equipotential lines between the different models. Further, for the 5-tissues case, the lines are smooth, and the electric fields easily reach the scalp surface. In comparison, for the 9-tissues medium, the equipotential lines tend to align with the local anisotropy eigenvectors, showing irregular patterns in the WM area, and tangential to radial restrictions in the compartments beneath the skin (fat and muscle areas).

4.2   Dipole Estimation Error in Realistic Head Modeling

We use the 9-layers RHM with WM anisotropy (Fig. 2) as the reference model. Additionally, we used the 5-tissues segmentation for the RHM model as the test model in a parametric inverse setup.

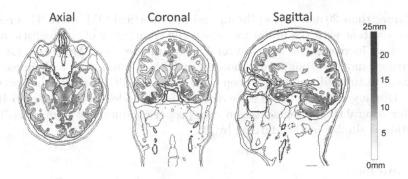

Fig. 4. Dipole localization errors for a 9-tissues segmentation against a simplify 5-tissues head model.

Figure 4 shows Axial, Coronal and Sagittal planes for the *DLE* comparing the 9-layer reference model against the simplistic 5-layer test model using the RHM data. Results show *DLE* larger than 20 mm in the deep brain and inter-cortical GM areas. We also analyze the influence of blood vessels modeling for 9-tissues reference model compared against an 8-tissues test model without blood vessels segmentation compartments. Remaining tissues where considered isotropic with conductivity values taken from Table 1.

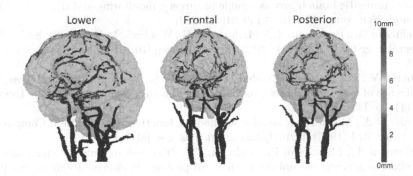

Fig. 5. Dipole localization errors due to neglecting the anisotropic blood vessels.

Figure 5 shows three different views (frontal, posterior and bottom), for a *DLE* 3D map, revealing that neglecting the blood vessels induce *DLE* larger than 10 mm in zones near to the Willis polygon (deep brain areas). Moreover, mean *DLE* was 4 mm for the GM area, and potentials propagation differences can be larger than 30μV in zones near the corpus callosum.

5   Concluding Remark

We analyze the influence of multiple tissues definition for the 9–layer and the commonly used 5–layer head data. Our parametric inverse solution results show

DLE larger than 20 mm in deep brain and inter-cortical GM areas. This result is also consistent with the literature, where the complexity of the realistic head model often increases the accuracy of ESI techniques [11]. Moreover, for the blood vessels modeling our results show mean *DLE* of 4 mm, with a big impact in zones near to the Willis polygon (deep brain areas) resulting in *DLE* larger than 10 mm. Our suggestion is to use more detailed head models in forward modeling, including several tissues segmentation with proper conductivity definitions. This suggestion is similar to the affirmed by [4].

References

1. Cuartas-Morales, E., Daniel-Acosta, C., Castellanos-Dominguez, G.: iLU preconditioning of the anisotropic-finite-difference based solution for the EEG forward problem. In: Ferrández Vicente, J.M., Álvarez-Sánchez, J.R., de la Paz López, F., Toledo-Moreo, F.J., Adeli, H. (eds.) IWINAC 2015. LNCS, vol. 9107, pp. 408–418. Springer, Cham (2015). https://doi.org/10.1007/978-3-319-18914-7_43
2. Gabriel, C.: Compilation of the dielectric properties of body tissues at RF and microwave frequencies. Environmental Health (1993)
3. Hallez, H., Staelens, S., Lemahieu, I.: Dipole estimation errors due to not incorporating anisotropic conductivities in realistic head models for EEG source analysis. Phys. Med. Biol. **54**(20), 6079 (2009)
4. Irimia, A., et al.: Electroencephalographic inverse localization of brain activity in acute traumatic brain injury as a guide to surgery, monitoring and treatment. Clin. Neurol. Neurosurg. **115**(10), 2159–2165 (2013)
5. Jenkinson, M., Beckmann, C.F., Behrens, T.E., Woolrich, M.W., Smith, S.M.: FSL. NeuroImage **62**(2), 782–790 (2012). https://doi.org/10.1016/j.neuroimage.2011.09.015
6. Montes, V., van Mierlo, P., Strobbe, G., Staelens, S., Vandenberghe, S., Hallez, H.: Influence of skull modeling approaches on EEG source localization. Brain Topogr. **27**(1), 95–111 (2013)
7. Nelder, J.A., Mead, R.: A simplex method for function minimization. Comput. J. **7**(4), 308–313 (1965). https://doi.org/10.1093/comjnl/7.4.308
8. Rahmouni, L., Mitharwal, R., Andriulli, F.P.: Two volume integral equations for the inhomogeneous and anisotropic forward problem in electroencephalography. J. Comput. Phys. **348**, 732–743 (2017)
9. Stenroos, M., Sarvas, J., et al.: Bioelectromagnetic forward problem: isolated source approach revis(it)ed. Phys. Med. Biol. **57**(11), 3517 (2012)
10. Torrado, C.A.H.T.J., et al.: High-Field MRI Planning Patient-Specific Tissue Model Segmentation in MRI. In: ISMRM 2014 (2014)
11. Vorwerk, J., Cho, J.H., Rampp, S., Hamer, H., Knösche, T.R., Wolters, C.H.: A guideline for head volume conductor modeling in EEG and MEG. NeuroImage **100**, 590–607 (2014)
12. Wolters, C.H., Anwander, A., Tricoche, X., Weinstein, D., Koch, M.A., Macleod, R.S.: Influence of tissue conductivity anisotropy on EEG/MEG field and return current computation in a realistic head model: a simulation and visualization study using high-resolution finite element modeling. NeuroImage **30**(3), 813–826 (2006)

Computational Model for Reward-Based Generation and Maintenance of Motivation

Fawad Taj[✉], Michel C. A. Klein, and Aart van Halteren

Behavioural Informatics Group, Department of Computer Science,
Vrije Universiteit Amsterdam, Amsterdam, The Netherlands
fawadtajl@gmail.com,
{michel.klein,a.t.van.halteren}@vu.nl

Abstract. In this paper, a computational model for the motivation process is presented that takes into account the reward pathway for motivation generation and associative learning for maintaining motivation through Hebbian learning approach. The reward prediction error is used to keep motivation maintained. These aspects are backed by recent neuroscientific models and literature. Simulation experiments have been performed by creating scenarios for student learning through rewards and controlling their motivation through regulation. Mathematical analysis is provided to verify the dynamic properties of the model.

Keywords: Motivation · Cognitive modelling · Reward-based learning

1 Introduction

Motivation is an important internal process for any human to achieve their targets and goals. Motivation is a complex topic which is usually mixed with desire, value and goal, that's why there is no consensus on whether the motivation is a state or a process. A number of psychological theories on motivation exists for example learning theory, attribution theory, self-determination theory etc. [1, 2]. A motivation may be intrinsic or extrinsic or other. A motivation that leads to perform any behavior or activity for self-enjoyment is known as intrinsic motivation, whereas the extrinsic motivation, on the other hand, is to act for external rewards. For example, research student has extrinsic motivation to write, if they do so in the hope of getting published or being famous.

A reward is an environmental stimulus that pulls people to act in a particular way. it is extremely useful and mostly used force in any learning environment. Neuroscientific examinations of motivation have set up the framework which provides a way to design different models or systems. From the neuroscience knowledge, two constructs are so relevant for consulting psychology. Firstly, how much motivation is linked to the past and how reinforcement learning is used to learn and storing it in the memory [3]. For good reason, we evolved to be highly sensitive to learn where we receive rewards and to work hard to recreate the situations that brought them about. This reinforcement leaning is implemented in our model through the body loop. Reinforcement of new behavior is extremely difficult because it means working against this powerful well

S. Wang et al. (Eds.): BI 2018, LNAI 11309, pp. 41–51, 2018.
https://doi.org/10.1007/978-3-030-05587-5_5

system. Thus usually, it is grounded in the neuroscience of motivation and reinforcement learning is to start behavior change with modest rewards [2].

Moreover, to maintain motivation continues learning and memory is required. Dopamine neuro transmitter plays an important role in learning, memory and habit formation [4]. According to reinforcement theory magnitude of leaning depends on the dopamine release. To release a proper amount of dopamine, the reward frequency and time should be maintained. Otherwise repeated use of reward increase expectation will decrease the learning rate or make it static at the end. In proposed model control state is used to check for continues use of reward for certain action, which gets activated if the reward is always repeated which cause the motivation down and the agent start moving to next action. To maintain motivation it is usually suggested to give a surprising reward with cognitive gap [1].

The paper is structured as follows. Section 2 consists of detail discussion about all the neurological background for reward pathway and reward prediction error. Section 3 presents the model and the temporal causal network modelling approach. In Sect. 4 the simulation of the scenario of the computational model is discussed. Section 5 consists of the mathematical analysis of some of the dynamic properties of the model. Finally, Sect. 6 contains the conclusion.

2 Background

2.1 Motivation Generation; Reward Pathway

The primary region of the brain that is associated with reward is the dopamine pathway and it is widely known as the reward pathway. Dopamine neuro transmitter is produced in a ventral tegmental area (VTA), passes through Globus Pallidus and releasees into the nucleus accumbens (NAcc) [5]. Dopamine pathway is divided into mesolimbic dopamine system and the mesocortical dopamine system. The mesolimbic is in charge of reward anticipation and learning. Whereas the mesocortical system includes, encoding the relative value of the reward and goal-directed behavior [1]. The main brain area that are involved in reward processing are VTA, NAcc, the amygdala, the hippocampus, ventromedial prefrontal cortex, adjacent medial orbitofrontal cortex (vmPFC/mOFC), lateral orbitofrontal cortex (lOFC), anterior cingulate cortex (ACC) and a lateral anterior prefrontal cortex (aPFC) [5]. All the species ae preprogrammed to approach primary rewards (food, sexual excitement etc.), but in case of secondary rewards like money, the OFC encodes and represents the associative value of reward and update the value for future decision making.

The reward system induce positive emotion that make the organism approach, or increase the frequency of target behavior. The choice of an action depends on reward mechanisms, as a form of valuing of the options [6]. Taking decision for action among the available options depend on the valuing process, every available reward option is coupled with an associated feeling related to valuation whether that option will provide satisfaction or not. For this mode among the available option one having strongest valuated feeling performs as a GO signal through the body loop and else are NO–GO options. The as-if body loop consists of [7]:

sensoryrepresentation → preparationforbodilychanges → feltemotionsensoryrepresentation → preparationforbodilychanges → feltemotion

2.2 Motivation Maintenance; Reward Prediction Error

As the stimulus-action-outcome is learned through the reinforcement and feeling, now the level of reward predication error (RPE) has to been balanced to maintain the motivation. From neuroscience prospective, dopamine plays a major role in motor performance conditioning learning and memory. Insufficient amount of dopamine causes stiffness and paralysis and excessive dopamine may result in behavioral disorders such as schizophrenia, impulse control disorder etc. [1]. The expectation about the reward makes an RPE unbalanced, positive RPE is generated when an outcome is better than expected reward or unexpected rewards are given, whereas negative RPE is generated when the outcome is worse than expected rewards or expected rewards are omitted [1]. The brain region involved in value signals are the amygdala, orbitofrontal cortex (OFC), ventromedial prefrontal cortex (vmPF), and ventral & dorsal striata and some others.

From Psychological prospect, repeated use of reward increase expectation which leads to reducing positive RPE, and reach to stable stage latter in time [1]. To maintain student motivation, a certain amount of dopamine should be release during the pursuit of target the behavior. The dopamine can be released by changing the type or frequency of reward.

A stimulus-action generates the associated feeling via recursive body and as-if body loops [7, 8], which can predict the consequences and satisfaction of particular option before taking action. This is done by evaluating the options using loops involving interaction between feeling and preparation. The connections from feeling to preparation can be either assumed static or adaptive. In this article we used adaptive connection strengths because here learning is involved which is usually a transfer from previous experiences [9].

3   Computational Model

In this section, the proposed computational model is discussed, based on the literature described in Sect. 2. The process starts with an external stimuli cause the agent to take some action to fulfil its goal. In relation to a goal (in our simulation it is learning Dutch language), particular actions are considered and the extent to which they will provide a feeling of satisfaction.

Furthermore, causal relationships in the model are based on the neurological literature presented in the Sect. 2; they do not take specific neurons into consideration but use more abstracted cognitive or mental states for the design of the model (through an interlevel relation between the neurological level and the cognitive/affective mental modelling level). An overview of the model is depicted in Fig. 1. The concepts used are explained in Table 1.

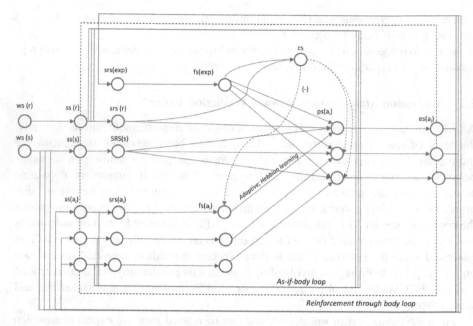

Fig. 1. Computational model for motivation through reward.

The temporal causal-network modelling approach [10, 11] has been used for modelling. The temporal dimension enables the modelling of cyclic causal relations with exact timing. In broader terms, there are some similarities between artificial neural networks and this approach, for example in the case of continuous time and recurrent, but there are important differences as well. For example, no hidden layer exists that do not represent any real-world phenomena; each state within this approach should be clearly defined with exact causal and temporal dimensions.

The models in temporal causal network modelling approach can be represented in two ways: conceptual representation and numerical representation. Both types of representation can be easily transformed into each other in a systematic manner.

Conceptual representation can be done through graphs or matrices. Whereas graphical representation involves states which represent some real world phenomena and the arrows show the causal relation between two states. Some additional information is given below:

- Value of connection (ωX, Y) representing strength of causality and it value ranges between [−1, 1].
- How fast a state Y can change upon casual impact. Speed factor is denoted by ηY, and value ranges between [0, 1].
- For multiple impacts on state Y, combination function cY(...) is used to combine the effect. There are a number of combination functions defined, varying from simple sum function to advance logistics function.

Table 1. The process and related states with description.

Process	Formal States name	Informal name	Description
Environment	ws(w)	World state	The world situation the person is facing, the stimulus, in the example w is a Dutch language book
	ss(w)	Stimulus State for World	The person senses the world through the sensor state
Motivation generation	srs(w)	Sensor representation state for World	Internal representation of sensory world information on w
	ss(r)	Sensory state of reward	Sensing reward through sensors
	srs(r)	Sensory representation of reward state.	Mental representation of reward
	ps(ai)	Preparation for i^{th} action	The human maintains an action/body representation srs(a) in the brain. Before performing an action, a feeling state FS(a) for action is generated by predictive as-if body loop
	fs(ai)	Feeling state of ith action	
	es(ai)	Execution state of ith action.	The execution of action change the situation and used to learn through body loop.
Maintenance of motivation	srs(exp)	Sensory representation state of expectation	The continues use of reward stop the learning process through the feeling sate FS(exp)
	fs(exp)	Feeling state of expectation	
	cs	Control state	Control state activated when expectation get higher using same reward

The conceptual representation of model can be translated into numerical representation as follow. For any state Y at any time point t, Y(t) denotes the activation value of Y. The causal impact of state X on Y at time point t, can be defined by:

$$\textbf{Impact}_{X,Y} = \omega_{X,Y}X(t). \tag{1}$$

Total aggregated impact of the multiple impact on state Y at time t combined by combination function cY(...) can be defined by

$$\begin{aligned}\textbf{aggimpact}_Y(\textbf{t}) &= c_Y(\text{impact}_{X1,Y}, \text{ impact}_{X2,Y}, \text{ impact}_{X3,Y}, \cdots) \\ &= c_Y(\omega_{X1,Y}X_1(t), \omega_{X2,Y}X_2(t), \omega_{X3,Y}X_3(t), \ldots)\end{aligned} \tag{2}$$

the aggimpact$_Y$(t) will have upward or downward effect at time point t, but how fast this change takes place depends on the speed factor η_Y,

$$Y(t+\Delta t) = Y(t) + \eta Y \ [\text{aggimpact}_Y(t) - Y(t)] \Delta t \qquad (3)$$

The following difference and differential equation can be obtained for state Y:

$$Y(t+\Delta t) = Y(t) + \eta Y \ [c_Y(\omega_{X1,Y}X_1(t), \omega_{X2,Y}X_2(t), \omega_{X3,Y}X_3(t), \ldots) - Y(t)]\Delta t \qquad (4)$$

$$dY(t)/dt = \eta Y \ [c_Y(\omega_{X1,Y}X_1(t), \omega_{X2,Y}X_2(t), \omega_{X3,Y}X_3(t), \ldots) - Y(t)] \qquad (5)$$

In the proposed model, the advanced logistic sum combination function alogistic$_{\sigma,\tau}$ (...) (Eq. 6) is used as the standard combination function for all state except ws(r) and ss(r) (Eq. 7), where simple identity function is used:

$$c_Y(V1, \ldots Vk) = \text{alogistic}\sigma, \tau V1, \ldots, Vk)$$
$$= (1/1 + e^{-\sigma(v_1 + \ldots + v_k - t)} - 1/1 + e^{\sigma,\tau}), t(1 + e^{-\sigma,\tau}) \qquad (6)$$

$$cY(V) = \text{id}(V) = V \qquad (7)$$

The feeling state act as a measuring and valuating state, the association between good feeling about certain action can be learnt over time based on past experiences. For this a Hebbian learning mechanism has been used by which such connections may automatically emerge or strengthen. The connections from feeling fs(a_i) to preparation ps(a_i) with weights ωfs(a_i), ps(a_i) have been made adaptive [12, 13]. The numerical representation of Hebbian learning is [10]:

$$\omega_{fs(ai),ps(ai)}(t+\Delta t) = \omega_{fs(ai),ps(ai)}(t) + [\eta \ \text{fs}_{ai}(t)\text{ps}_{ai}(t)(1 - \omega_{fs(ai),ps(ai)}(t)) - \zeta\omega_{fs(ai),ps(ai)}(t)] \Delta t \qquad (8)$$

4 Simulation

A number of simulations have been performed to test the model using MATLAB environment. One of the scenario discussed in this paper is as follow

Consider an academic situation where a student Marvik intended to learn the Dutch language. Mavrick has three options, firstly, start reading a book, secondly use internet and lastly attend the classes. The process is complimented by the teacher through verbal praise (reward-driven approach) for first of his action. This reward leads Marvik to work hard to get the reward and eventually ends in leaning language. By reinforcement rule, he associated the target behavior with reward. But always having the same reward he gets demotivated and starts losing that behavior.

The following is a brief summary of the agent's internal causality when given stimulus 's' and reward 'r' as inputs

I. External stimulus 's' and reward 'r' will occur and trigger preparation of action a_i.

II. Based on the preparation state for a_1, the sensory representation of the (positive) predicted effect of a_1 is generated.

III. The execution of a_1 increase the expectation for the reward 'r'.

IV. The control state gets activated after some threshold when expectation gets high with the same reward.

V. To take negative prediction error into account, the activation of control state slow down the learning or even stop it.

The combination function, initial value and speed factor for each state are given in Table 2, whereas Table 3, defines the connection weights between states.

Table 2. The parameters for combination function (alogistic) for given model.

States	Parameters (σ, τ)	States	Parameters (σ, τ)
ws(s)	$\sigma = 5, \tau = 0.5$	fs(exp)	$\sigma = 6, \tau = 0.7$
ss(s)	$\sigma = 5, \tau = 0.5$	ps(a1)	$\sigma = 6, \tau = 0.7$
ss(a1)	$\sigma = 5, \tau = 0.6$	ps(a2)	$\sigma = 6, \tau = 0.7$
ss(a2)	$\sigma = 5, \tau = 0.6$	Ps(a3)	$\sigma = 6, \tau = 0.7$
ss(a3)	$\sigma = 5, \tau = 0.6$	es(a1)	$\sigma = 9, \tau = 0.4$
srs(r)	$\sigma = 6, \tau = 0.5$	es(a2)	$\sigma = 9, \tau = 0.4$
srs(s)	$\sigma = 6, \tau = 0.5$	es(a3)	$\sigma = 9, \tau = 0.4$
srs(a1)	$\sigma = 6, \tau = 0.6$	fs(a1)	$\sigma = 3, \tau = 0.6$
srs(a2)	$\sigma = 6, \tau = 0.6$	fs(a2)	$\sigma = 3, \tau = 0.6$
srs(a3)	$\sigma = 6, \tau = 0.6$	fs(a3)	$\sigma = 3, \tau = 0.6$
srs(exp)	$\sigma = 6, \tau = 0.7$	cs	$\sigma = 4, \tau = 0.7$

Table 3. Connection weights.

Connection	Weight	Connection	Weight	Connection	Weight
$\omega_{ws(r),ss(r)}$	1	$\omega_{srs(a1),fs(a1)}$	1	$\omega_{es(a1),ss(s)}$	1
$\omega_{ws(s),ss(s)}$	1	$\omega_{srs(a2),fs(a2)}$	1	$\omega_{es(a2),ss(s)}$	1
$\omega_{ss(r),srs(r)}$	1	$\omega_{srs(a3),fs(a3)}$	1	$\omega_{es(a3),ss(s)}$	1
$\omega_{srs(r),ps(a1)}$	1	$\omega_{fs(a1),ps(a1)}$	1	$\omega_{es(a1),srs(a1)}$	1
$\omega_{srs(r),ps(a2)}$	1	$\omega_{fs(a2),ps(a2)}$	1	$\omega_{es(a2),srs(a2)}$	1
$\omega_{srs(r),ps(a3)}$	1	$\omega_{fs(a3),ps(a3)}$	1	$\omega_{es(a3),srs(a3)}$	1
$\omega_{srs(exp),fs(exp)}$	1	$\omega_{ps(a1),es(a1)}$	0.3	$\omega_{es(a1),srs(exp)}$	1
$\omega_{ps(a1),srs(a1)}$	1	$\omega_{ps(a2),es(a2)}$	0.3	$\omega_{es(a2),srs(exp)}$	1
$\omega_{ps(a2),srs(a2)}$	0.4	$\omega_{ps(a3),es(a3)}$	0.3	$\omega_{es(a3),srs(exp)}$	1
$\omega_{ps(a3),srs(a3)}$	0.4	$\omega_{fs(exp),ps(a1)}$	1	$\omega_{fs(exp),cs}$	1
$\omega_{ps(a1),srs(r)}$	1	$\omega_{fs(exp),ps(a2)}$	1	$\omega_{srs(r),cs}$	1
$\omega_{ps(a2),srs(r)}$	1	$\omega_{fs(exp),ps(a3)}$	1	$\omega_{cs,fs(a1)}$	-0.4
$\omega_{ps(a3),srs(r)}$	1	$\omega_{cs,ps(a3)}$	0.4	$\omega_{cs,ps(a2)}$	0.4

In the scenario, the strength of the connection weights ωfs(a$_i$), ps(a$_i$) from feeling to the considered preparation state, change over time through the hebbian learning mechanism. Initial values for all states have been chosen 0 except the world state ws (s) = 1 and ws(r) = 1, which depends on the scenario. The simulation is executed for some scenarios for 480 time points; the time step $\Delta t = 0.1$, learning rate $\eta = 0.2$ and extinction rate for all three states is $\zeta = 0.095$, when hebbian learning is used.

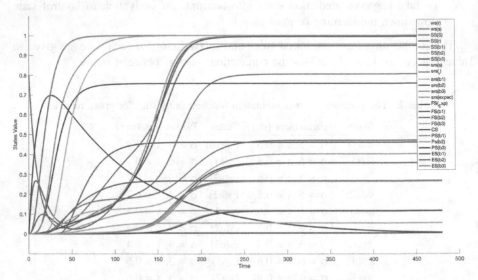

Fig. 2. The figure shows the overall execution of the model. Initially the **Preparation state** for action 1 is highly activated due to reward, then latter due to over expectation, control state gets activated and other action starts emerging.

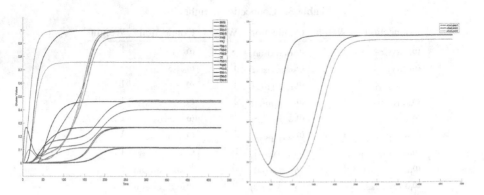

Fig. 3. The preparation and the feeling for action a$_1$ get higher.

Fig. 4. The first action is learned earlier than other two.

In Fig. 2, an agent takes an action among the available options after the onset of the stimulus. As soon as it gets the reward for the selected action, the pleasure feelings originated which force the agent to perform the action in a more rapid way. This behavior can be clearly seen in Fig. 2, the preparation of action get higher as soon as the reward has been anticipated.

Moreover, the Fig. 3, shows the learning for the connections between feeling and the preparation of action. It can be seen that first action has been learned quite earlier than the other two actions because the agent learning process has been ignited by the release of dopamine through reward (see Fig. 4). Lastly, the continuous use of the reward increase expectation and which lead to slow learning or even make learning to asymptote. This behavior is implemented through control state which gets activated when the value of rewards and the expectation gets higher, the red line from control to feeling state of action is suppressed and leaning gets stops.

5   Mathematical Analysis for Hebbian Learning

Mathematical analysis of certain properties (equilibria, monotonicity an limit cycle) of a model can help verifying the dynamics of a model. Equilibrium is the property where for some values for the state no change occurs and how this may depends on the values of the parameters of the model and/or the initial values of the states [14]. For Hebbian adaption it can also be analyzed from the difference or differential equation.

Here the focus is on ω from the Eq. 8 it can be analyzed when the following cases occurs:

$$\mathbf{d}\omega(t)/dt > 0 \Leftrightarrow \eta\ \mathrm{fs}_{ai}(t)\mathrm{ps}_{ai}(t)(1 - \omega_{\mathrm{fs}(ai),\mathrm{ps}(ai)}(t)) - \zeta\omega_{\mathrm{fs}(ai),\mathrm{ps}(ai)}(t)] > 0\ (\text{Increasing}) \quad (9)$$

$$\mathbf{d}\omega(t)/dt = 0 \Leftrightarrow \eta\ \mathrm{fs}_{ai}(t)\mathrm{ps}_{ai}(t)(1 - \omega_{\mathrm{fs}(ai),\mathrm{ps}(ai)}(t)) - \zeta\omega_{\mathrm{fs}(ai),\mathrm{ps}(ai)}(t)] = 0\ (\text{stationary}) \quad (10)$$

$$\mathbf{d}\omega(t)/dt < 0 \Leftrightarrow \eta\ \mathrm{fs}_{ai}(t)\mathrm{ps}_{ai}(t)(1 - \omega_{\mathrm{fs}(ai),\mathrm{ps}(ai)}(t)) - \zeta\omega_{\mathrm{fs}(ai),\mathrm{ps}(ai)}(t)] < 0\ (\text{Decreasing}) \quad (11)$$

As we are interested in stationary points the Eq. 10 can be further reduced and t is left out for convenience: $[\eta\ \mathrm{fs}_{ai},\mathrm{ps}_{ai}(1 - \omega_{\mathrm{fs}(ai),\mathrm{ps}(ai)}) - \zeta\omega_{\mathrm{fs}(ai),\mathrm{ps}(ai)}] = 0$

$$\Leftrightarrow \omega_{\mathrm{fs}(ai),\mathrm{ps}(ai)} = \eta\ \mathrm{fs}_{ai},\ \mathrm{ps}_{ai}/\zeta + \eta\ \mathrm{fs}_{ai},\mathrm{ps}_{ai}$$

$$\Leftrightarrow \omega_{\mathrm{fs}(ai),\mathrm{ps}(ai)} = 1/1 + \zeta/(\eta\ \mathrm{fs}_{ai},\mathrm{ps}_{ai})\ (\text{when both states value} > 0) \quad (12)$$

$$\Leftrightarrow \eta\ \mathrm{fs}_{ai},\ \mathrm{ps}_{ai}(1 - \omega_{\mathrm{fs}(ai),\mathrm{ps}(ai)}) - \zeta\omega_{\mathrm{fs}(ai),\mathrm{ps}(ai)}] = 0(\text{when both states value and}\ \zeta = 0) \quad (13)$$

The Table 4, shows the equilibrium values by Eq. 12, the deviation between the values on left and right side of equation are less than 0.03. It can be concluded that the analysis of equilibria gives an evidence that the model was correctly implemented.

Table 4. Equilibrium value confirmation.

Time step	Connection value $\omega_{fs(ai),ps(ai)}$	State Values	Speed factor η	Extinction ζ	Equilibrium by Eq. 12
3183	$\omega_{fs(a1),ps}$ $_{(a1)} = 0.8299$	0.4634, 0.9999	0.2	0.095	0.8196
3127	$\omega_{fs(a2),ps}$ $_{(a2)} = 0.8321$	0.4725, 0.9966	0.2	0.095	0.8201
3193	$\omega_{fs(a2),ps}$ $_{(a2)} = 0.8089$	0.4047, 0.9966	0.2	0.095	0.8301

6 Conclusion

The model presented in this paper is a neurologically inspired computational model for reward-based learning by involving a number of internal and external factors. The focus of this paper is to formalise the dynamics and interaction of internal states which are involved in decision making and associative learning. The model based on internal prediction in combination with associated feelings for valuation of the available actions.

The simulation results suggest that this model is capable of learning of making action choices on the one hand and through levels of expectation in relation to various types of actions on the other hand. The proposed computational model for making reward-based learning can be used to develop motivation monitoring intelligent systems that can help and support persons with motivation toward achieving his/her goals and targets. In future work, the model will be extended with motivation regulation strategies, and further focus will be on the social and environmental factors.

References

1. Kim, S.I.: Neuroscientific model of motivational process. Front. Psychol. **4**, 98 (2013)
2. Mowrer, O.: Learning theory and the Symbolic Processes. Wiley, New York (1960)
3. Berridge, K.C.: Motivation concepts in behavioral neuroscience. Physiol. Behav. **81**(2), 179–209 (2004)
4. Ashby, F.G., Turner, B.O., Horvitz, J.C.: Cortical and basal ganglia contributions to habit learning and automaticity. Trends Cogn. Sci. **14**(5), 208–215 (2010)
5. Rushworth, M.F., et al.: Frontal cortex and reward-guided learning and decision-making. Neuron **70**(6), 1054–1069 (2011)
6. Elliott, R., Friston, K.J., Dolan, R.J.: Dissociable neural responses in human reward systems. J. Neurosci. **20**(16), 6159–6165 (2000)
7. Damasio, A.R.: The feeling of what happens: body and emotion in the making of consciousness. N. Y. Times Book Rev. **104**, 8 (1999)
8. Fabrega Jr., H.: The feeling of what happens: body and emotion in the making of consciousness. Psychiatr. Serv. **51**(12), 1579 (2000)
9. Damasio, A.R.: The somatic marker hypothesis and the possible functions of the prefrontal cortex. Phil. Trans. R. Soc. Lond. B **351**(1346), 1413–1420 (1996)

10. Treur, J.: Dynamic modeling based on a temporal–causal network modeling approach. Biol. Inspired Cogn. Arch. **16**, 131–168 (2016)
11. Treur, J.: The ins and outs of network-oriented modeling: from biological networks and mental networks to social networks and beyond. In: Proceedings of the 10th International Conference on Computational Collective Intelligence, ICCCI, vol. 18 (2018)
12. Gerstner, W., Kistler, W.M.: Mathematical formulations of Hebbian learning. Biol. Cybern. **87**(5-6), 404–415 (2002)
13. Bi, G.-q., Poo, M.-m.: Synaptic modification by correlated activity: Hebb's postulate revisited. Annu. Rev. Neurosci. **24**(1), 139–166 (2001)
14. Treur, J.: Network-Oriented Modeling. Springer, Cham (2016). https://doi.org/10.1007/978-3-319-45213-5

Current Design with Minimum Error in Transcranial Direct Current Stimulation

Jing Qin[1]([✉])(iD), Yushan Wang[2], and Wentai Liu[2]

[1] Department of Mathematical Sciences, Montana State University,
Bozeman, MT, USA
jing.qin@montana.edu
[2] Department of Bioengineering, University of California, Los Angeles, CA, USA
{yushanwang,wentai}@ucla.edu

Abstract. As a non-invasive brain stimulation technology, transcanial direct current stimulation (tDCS) has been recently attracting more and more attention in research and clinic applications due to its convenient implementation and modulation of the brain functionality. In this paper, we propose a novel multi-electrode tDCS current configuration model that minimizes the total error under the safety constraints. After rewriting the model as a linearly constrained minimization problem, we develop an efficient numerical algorithm based on the alternating direction method of multipliers (ADMM). Numerical experiments have shown the great potential of the proposed method in terms of accuracy and focality.

Keywords: transcranial Direct Current Stimulation (tDCS)
Human head model · Multi-electrode stimulation · Safety constraints
Alternating Direction Method of Multipliers (ADMM)

1 Introduction

Transcranial direct current stimulation (tDCS) is an emerging non-invasive brain stimulation technology that applies a small amount of direct currents on the electrodes placed on a human scalp surface to elicit modulation of neural activities [14]. It serves as an important therapeutic tool in clinics to treat psychiatric conditions and neurological diseases, including depression [3], Parkinson's disease [6], and epilepsy [1]. The tDCS modulates brain functions mainly through two ways. Firstly, it affects the neuronal activities directly by inducing the cortical changes. Secondly, it affects the neuronal network dynamics by either enhancing or hindering the synaptic transmission ability.

Although tDCS has a lot of practical advantages such as the portability, flexibility and tolerable stimulation duration, it faces several challenges such as the limited stimulation intensity and focality of detecting the stimulating electric field (e-field). To address these issues, many optimization based methods have

© Springer Nature Switzerland AG 2018
S. Wang et al. (Eds.): BI 2018, LNAI 11309, pp. 52–62, 2018.
https://doi.org/10.1007/978-3-030-05587-5_6

been developed in the past. In particular, least squares methods are proposed to design the configuration of electrodes to minimize a second-order error [5]. In addition, several constraints are considered, including the maximum allowable value for the intensity for each electrode and the current sum due to the safety regulations, and the zero net current flow according to the reservation law. Similar to the beamforming problem, the linearly constrained minimum variance (LCMV) method is proposed in [5] to minimize the total power while utilizing the remaining degrees of freedom. However, LCMV suffers several drawbacks. Firstly, since minimization of the ℓ_2-norm leads to a result with uniformly distributed errors, there is no guarantee that the resulting electric field exhibits a maximum at the target. Then an undesired cortex region may be stimulated in the LCMV results. Lastly, it causes the high possibility to get an empty solution set. One can also see that if the current intensity is smaller in the target regions, then the reconstructed electrodes are more focalized. Recently, weighted least squares methods are proposed to improve the accuracy, such as Minimize the Error Relative to No Intervention (ERNI) [12]. To maximize the intensity along a desired direction at the target region, a linear objective function that describes the projected intensity is also used [9,13].

Besides, errors with unknown statistics occur inevitably due to the signal transmission in tDCS. In the signal/image processing community, it is well known that the ℓ_1-norm data fidelity is more robust to various noise/error types than its ℓ_2-norm counterpart [4,10]. Different from ℓ_2-norm minimization resulting in uniform error distribution, minimization of the ℓ_1-norm of the error vector leads to a sparse solution with nonuniform error distribution. In the pursuit of high electrode focality, we propose a ℓ_1-norm fidelity based model with the three commonly used constraints due to the safety regulation. By expressing the constraints using the indicator functions, we are able to convert the proposed nonlinear constrained minimization problem into a linear constrained one. Based on the alternating direction method of multipliers (ADMM), we derive an efficient numerical algorithm to solve the proposed model. In particular, each subproblem in the algorithm has a closed-form solution which brings computational convenience. Numerical experiments on multiple data sets have shown the proposed effectiveness and flexibility in achieving the ideal current configuration.

The rest of the paper is organized as follows. Section 2 describes the proposed mathematical model for the optimal configuration of tDCS electrode currents. To solve this minimization problem with linear constraints, we derive an efficient numerical algorithm base on ADMM. In Sect. 3, two sets of simulation experiments are conducted to verify the effectiveness of the proposed method. Finally, we draw conclusions and discuss future works in Sect. 4.

2   Methods

2.1   Simulation of a Realistic Head Model

The computational realistic head model utilized in our study is the anatomical template from Fieldtrip [11], which is derived from the Statistical Parametric

Mapping (SPM) Canonical Brain. The model contains essential parts in our study, including scalp, skull, cerebrospinal fluid (CSF), and the cortex. The boundaries of all the tissue layers of the model were first saved in stereolithography (STL) format, and then converted to the solid models using SolidWorks https://www.solidworks.com/. In addition, we also constructed 342-electrode system for the head model, the location of which is based on the international electroencephalography (EEG) system. The electrodes consist of the metal layer and the gel layer, where the gel layer lays between the metal and scalp as the real clinical application. Both of the layers have the same diameter of 6 mm and thickness of 1 mm. Figure 1 shows the head model and the distribution of electrodes.

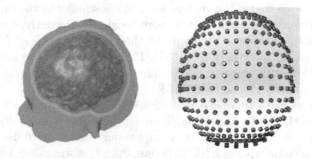

Fig. 1. Illustration of the head model and the electrode distribution.

Under the quasi-static condition, the injected current at each electrode has a linear relationship with the e-field value in each voxel, which is exactly the single element of the lead field matrix. Using FEM and solving Laplace equation in the realistic head model, we obtain one column by assigning a unit current (1mA) to that corresponding electrode and then complete the lead field matrix by repeating 342 times. All the simulation work is done by COMSOL Multiphysics 5.2 https://www.comsol.com/.

2.2   Proposed Mathematical Model

Let m be the number of voxels, n the number of electrodes, $\mathbf{s} \in \mathbb{R}^n$ the electrode current, $\mathbf{e}_d$ the desired e-field distribution of the cortex, $\mathbf{e}_0$ the desired electric field distribution of the target region, and $K \in \mathbb{R}^{m \times n}$ be the lead field matrix. In general, the desired electric field $\mathbf{e}_d$ and the electrode current $\mathbf{s}$ are linearly related through $K\mathbf{s} = \mathbf{e}_d + \varepsilon$ where $\varepsilon \in \mathbb{R}^m$ is an error term. Denote $I_{\max}$ the maximal direct current and I_{total} the total currents injected into the head. Due to the safety regulations, the magnitude of each electrode current can not exceed $I_{\max}$, and the sum of all currents in magnitude should be no more than $2I_{total}$. In addition, the conservation law of currents requires that the sum of all currents is zero. By taking all factors into consideration, we define the following feasible set

$$S = \{\mathbf{s} \in \mathbb{R}^n : |s_i| \leq I_{\max}, \sum_{i=1}^{n} |s_i| \leq 2I_{total}, \sum_{i=1}^{n} s_i = 0\}. \quad (1)$$

Next we introduce the ℓ_∞-norm and the ℓ_1-norm of a vector, i.e., $\|\mathbf{x}\|_\infty = \max_{1 \leq i \leq n} |x_i|$ and $\|\mathbf{x}\|_1 = \sum_{i=1}^{n} |x_i|$ for any $\mathbf{x} \in \mathbb{R}^n$. Using the vector norms, we can get an equivalent form of (1)

$$S = \{\mathbf{s} \in \mathbb{R}^n : \|\mathbf{s}\|_\infty \leq I_{\max}, \quad \|\mathbf{s}\|_1 \leq 2I_{total}, \quad \mathbf{s}^T \mathbf{1} = 0\}, \quad (2)$$

where $\mathbf{1} = (1, \ldots, 1)^T \in \mathbb{R}^n$. From the practical perspective, we wish that the generated electric field can reach the desired value at the target region while small errors are allowed at the other regions, which causes the error vector ε to be sparse. To enhance the sparsity of ε and allow a nonuniform distribution of errors, we propose the following model that minimizes the total error

$$\min_{\mathbf{s} \in S} \|K\mathbf{s} - \mathbf{e}_d\|_1. \quad (3)$$

Notice that the objective function in this problem is convex and non-differentiable but not strongly convex as the widely used total error power or its weighted variants [5], i.e., $\|W(K\mathbf{s} - \mathbf{e}_d)\|_2^2$ with the matrix of weights W. To handle this non-differentiability, we first convert (3) into a linearly constrained problem, and then resort to ADMM which can split multiple operators in the objective function and involve the fast proximal operator of the ℓ_1-norm.

2.3   Proposed Numerical Algorithm

In this section, we propose an efficient algorithm to solve (3). Recently, ADMM has become one of the most popular optimization methods with guaranteed convergence in a variety of application problems [2,7,8]. Given a convex linear constrained minimization problem whose objective function consists of multiple separable terms, ADMM aims to split the entire problem into several subproblems and alternate updating variables iteratively. At each iteration, each subproblem can either have a closed-form solution or be solved efficiently. However, ADMM introduces multiple auxiliary variables corresponding to the linear constraints. To reduce the number of auxiliary variables, we first express the solution variable using the linear constraint in S. It is worth noting that maintaining this linear constraint will induce one additional auxiliary variable and one more penalty in the augmented Lagrangian function which causes slightly slower convergence. Since $\mathbf{s}^T \mathbf{1} = 0$, i.e., $\mathbf{1}^T \mathbf{s} = 0$, we can deduce that $\mathbf{s}$ is in the nullspace of $\mathbf{1}^T$, denoted by $\mathcal{N}(\mathbf{1}^T)$. Let $B \in \mathbb{R}^{n \times (n-1)}$ be a *null-space basis matrix* of $\mathbf{1}^T$, i.e., the range of B satisfies $\mathcal{R}(B) = \mathcal{N}(\mathbf{1}^T)$. Then the rank-nullity theorem yields that there exists $\mathbf{x} \in \mathbb{R}^{n-1}$ such that $\mathbf{s} = B\mathbf{x}$. For example, we can choose

$$B = \begin{bmatrix} 1 & 1 & \cdots & 1 \\ -1 & 0 & \cdots & 0 \\ & & \cdots \cdots & \\ 0 & 0 & \cdots & -1 \end{bmatrix}_{n \times (n-1)}.$$

One can see that the columns of B form a basis of $\mathcal{N}(\mathbf{1}^T)$. By introducing the null-space basis matrix B of $\mathbf{1}^T$, the proposed model (3) turns into

$$\min_{\substack{\mathbf{s} \in C_1, \mathbf{z} \in C_2 \\ \mathbf{x}, \mathbf{y} \in \mathbb{R}^n}} \|\mathbf{y}\|_1, \quad \text{s.t.} \quad \mathbf{s} = B\mathbf{x}, \ \mathbf{y} = K\mathbf{s} - \mathbf{e}_d, \ \mathbf{z} = \mathbf{s}. \tag{4}$$

Here C_1 and C_2 are convex sets which are defined to be $C_1 = \{\mathbf{s} \in \mathbb{R}^n : \|\mathbf{s}\|_\infty \leq I_{\max}\}$ and $C_2 = \{\mathbf{z} \in \mathbb{R}^n : \|\mathbf{z}\|_1 \leq 2I_{total}\}$, respectively. Next we define an augmented Lagrangian function

$$\mathcal{L}(\mathbf{s}, \mathbf{x}, \mathbf{y}, \mathbf{z}, \widehat{\mathbf{x}}, \widehat{\mathbf{y}}, \widehat{\mathbf{z}}) = \|\mathbf{y}\|_1 + \frac{\rho_1}{2}\|\mathbf{s} - B\mathbf{x} + \widehat{\mathbf{x}}\|_2^2 + \frac{\rho_2}{2}\|\mathbf{y} - K\mathbf{s} + \mathbf{e}_d + \widehat{\mathbf{y}}\|_2^2$$
$$+ \frac{\rho_3}{2}\|\mathbf{z} - \mathbf{s} + \widehat{\mathbf{z}}\|_2^2 + \iota_{C_1}(\mathbf{s}) + \iota_{C_2}(\mathbf{z}).$$

Here ι_Ω is the indicator function defined by $\iota_\Omega(\mathbf{x}) = 0$ if $\mathbf{x} \in \Omega$ and ∞ otherwise. Note that $\mathbf{x} \in \mathbb{R}^{n-1}$, $\widehat{\mathbf{x}}, \mathbf{s}, \mathbf{z}, \widehat{\mathbf{z}} \in \mathbb{R}^n$, $\mathbf{y}, \widehat{\mathbf{y}}, \mathbf{e}_d \in \mathbb{R}^m$, $B \in \mathbb{R}^{n \times (n-1)}$ and $K \in \mathbb{R}^{m \times n}$.

We first group the two sets of variables $(\mathbf{x}, \mathbf{y}, \mathbf{z})$ and $\mathbf{s}$ and then apply ADMM. Since $\mathcal{L}$ is separable with respect to the respective variables $\mathbf{x}, \mathbf{y}, \mathbf{z}$, we can further obtain the following form with four subproblems

$$\begin{cases} \mathbf{s} \leftarrow \operatorname*{argmin}_{\mathbf{s}} \frac{\rho_1}{2}\|\mathbf{s} - B\mathbf{x} + \widehat{\mathbf{x}}\|_2^2 + \frac{\rho_2}{2}\|\mathbf{y} - K\mathbf{s} + \mathbf{e}_d + \widehat{\mathbf{y}}\|_2^2 + \frac{\rho_3}{2}\|\mathbf{z} - \mathbf{s} + \widehat{\mathbf{z}}\|_2^2 + \iota_{C_1}(\mathbf{s}) \\ \mathbf{x} \leftarrow \operatorname*{argmin}_{\mathbf{x}} \frac{\rho_1}{2}\|\mathbf{s} - B\mathbf{x} + \widehat{\mathbf{x}}\|_2^2 \\ \mathbf{y} \leftarrow \operatorname*{argmin}_{\mathbf{y}} \|\mathbf{y}\|_1 + \frac{\rho_2}{2}\|\mathbf{y} - K\mathbf{s} + \mathbf{e}_d + \widehat{\mathbf{y}}\|_2^2 \\ \mathbf{z} \leftarrow \operatorname*{argmin}_{\mathbf{z}} \frac{\rho_3}{2}\|\mathbf{z} - \mathbf{s} + \widehat{\mathbf{z}}\|_2^2 + \iota_{C_2}(\mathbf{z}) \\ \widehat{\mathbf{x}} \leftarrow \widehat{\mathbf{x}} + \mathbf{s} - B\mathbf{x} \\ \widehat{\mathbf{y}} \leftarrow \widehat{\mathbf{y}} + \mathbf{y} - K\mathbf{s} + \mathbf{e}_d \\ \widehat{\mathbf{z}} \leftarrow \widehat{\mathbf{z}} + \mathbf{z} - \mathbf{s} \end{cases}$$

The parameters ρ_1, ρ_2, ρ_3 are all positive real numbers. Note that the parameters ρ_1 and ρ_3 can be skipped in the respective $\mathbf{x}$-subproblem and $\mathbf{z}$-subproblem since scaling of the objective function in an optimization problem makes no impact on the solution. Firstly, the $\mathbf{s}$-subproblem has a least-squares solution restricted to the set C_1

$$\mathbf{s} \leftarrow \operatorname{proj}_{C_1} (\rho_1 I_n + \rho_2 K^T K + \rho_3 I_n)^{-1} (\rho_1 (B\mathbf{x} - \widehat{\mathbf{x}}) + \rho_2 K^T (\mathbf{y} + \mathbf{e}_d + \widehat{\mathbf{y}}) + \rho_3 (\mathbf{z} + \widehat{\mathbf{z}})). \tag{5}$$

Here the projection operator $\operatorname{proj}_{C_1}(\cdot)$ is essentially the projection onto the ℓ_∞-ball defined componentwise by $\left(\operatorname{proj}_{\|\cdot\|_\infty \leq c}(\mathbf{x})\right)_i = \min(c, \max(-c, x_i))$. In fact, the number of parameters in the $\mathbf{s}$-subproblem can be reduced to two after scaling. Similarly, the $\mathbf{x}$-subproblem has a least-squares solution

$$\mathbf{x} \leftarrow (B^T B)^{-1} B^T (\mathbf{s} + \widehat{\mathbf{x}}). \tag{6}$$

Next, the $\mathbf{y}$-subproblem has a closed-form solution

$$\mathbf{y} \leftarrow \operatorname{shrink}(K\mathbf{s} - \mathbf{e}_d - \widehat{\mathbf{y}}, 1/\rho_2). \tag{7}$$

Here the shrinkage operator (a.k.a. the proximal operator of ℓ_1-norm) shrink$(\cdot, \cdot)$ is defined componentwise by $\left(\text{shrink}(\mathbf{x}, \sigma)\right)_i = \text{sign}(x_i) \max(|x_i| - \sigma, 0)$. Lastly, similar to the s-subproblem, the z-subproblem has a least-squares solution restricted to the set C_2 and thus

$$\mathbf{z} \leftarrow \text{proj}_{C_2}(\mathbf{s} - \hat{\mathbf{z}}). \tag{8}$$

Similar to $\text{proj}_{C_1}(\cdot)$, the operator $\text{proj}_{C_2}(\cdot)$ is the projection onto the ℓ_1-ball defined by

$$\text{proj}_{\|\cdot\|_1 \leq c}(\mathbf{x}) = \begin{cases} \mathbf{x}, & \text{if } \|\mathbf{x}\|_1 \leq c, \\ \frac{c\mathbf{x}}{\|\mathbf{x}\|_1}, & \text{if } \|\mathbf{x}\|_1 > c. \end{cases}$$

Similar to [2], it can be shown that the proposed algorithm converges to the solution of (3) with convergence rate $O(1/k)$ where k is the iteration number.

3   Experimental Results

3.1   Experimental Design

The computational experiments are designed to compare the performance of several methods, including the conventional two pad electrodes, the constrained least squares (CLS) method, LCMV, maximum intensity (MI) method and the proposed one. In the experiments, we choose two different anatomical target types: single target and multiple targets. The single target contains only one active voxel in the motor cortex, shown in Fig. 2(a). The desired intensity is set to be 0.3 V/m [12]. This single target experiment aims to simulate the performance when algorithms are applied to the common clinical use. The test multiple targets are acquired from the results of the EEG source localization, shown in Fig. 3(a). The desired maximum intensity $\mathbf{e}_o$ restricted on those three target regions are 0.3727 V/m, 0.3522 V/m and 0.2841 V/m, respectively. The multiple-target experiment can help exam the performance of EEG-guided brain stimulation. In both experiments, we fix $I_{\max} = 2$ mA and $I_{total} = 4$ mA.

3.2   Comparison Metrics

To make comparison fair and comprehensive, we use three quantitative evaluation criteria, i.e., the stimulation precision, accuracy and intensity. Similar to the existing studies, we measure the stimulation precision (focality) by calculating the "half-max radius" [5] with a unit of millimeter (mm). By default, all length units are the millimeter. The difference is that we define $\mathbf{r}_{0.5} = \mathbf{r}\big|_{E(\mathbf{r})=0.5}$ to be the radius that contains half of the total energy. Here the portion of the energy contained within a circle of increasing radius around the mass center, denoted by $E(\mathbf{r})$, is defined by

$$E(\mathbf{r}) = \frac{\sum_{i \in \Gamma(\mathbf{r})} \|\mathbf{e}(\mathbf{r}_i)\|_2^2}{\sum_i \|\mathbf{e}(\mathbf{r}_i)\|_2^2},$$

where the $\Gamma(\mathbf{r})$ is the set containing all the voxels that lie within a distance of $\mathbf{r}$ from the center of the target region. Higher value of $\mathbf{r}_{0.5}$ indicates the more spread-out e-field distribution, while lower $\mathbf{r}_{0.5}$ suggests a better focality case that most of the energy are concentrated in a small region and it has better focusing capability. Target Error (TE) is the second criterion which is designed to evaluate the stimulation accuracy. The first and second metrics are the mass center of the target region and the activation region. Next, we define the third metric to assess the TE, which is the Euclidean distance between these two mass centers, i.e.,

$$ TE = \|MC_0 - MC\|_2, \quad MC_{j0} = \frac{\sum_i \mathbf{e}_0(\mathbf{r}_i)_j \cdot \mathbf{r}_{ij}}{\sum_i \mathbf{r}_{ij}}, \quad MC_j = \frac{\sum_i \mathbf{e}(\mathbf{r}_i)_j \cdot \mathbf{r}_{ij}}{\sum_i \mathbf{r}_{ij}}, $$

for $j \in \{x, y, z\}$. The last criterion is the intensity of the target region in V/m. If the target region contains more than one voxel, we will compare both the average intensity and the maximum intensity of the target region. According to the literature and clinical records, tDCS will be efficient enough when the produced intensity is about 0.2 V/m$\sim$ 0.3 V/m at the target region [12]. In addition, clinical application favors the result that is close to the desired e-field distribution in the target region. Note that we evaluate the performance of each target region separately if we stimulate the multiple targets at the same time.

3.3   Results

In the single target study, we first simulated the e-field distribution produced by the conventional electrode configuration (CEC). From the Fig. 2, one can see that this conventional montage will cause an effect on not only the motor cortex region, but also the other regions nearby, like the auditory cortex. Here we skip LCMV for comparison due to its failure to produce feasible results under the total current constraints. MI sacrifices even more focality to produce higher e-field intensity at the target area. On the contrary, CLS reduces the intensity to achieve better stimulation accuracy and precision. However, it is about two orders of magnitude less than the conventional system, which is not sufficient for the clinical treatment. The proposed result with $\rho_1 = 1$, $\rho_2 = 5$, and $\rho_3 = 4$ maintains a good balance among intensity, accuracy and precision, shown in Fig. 2. By enlarging the value of ρ_3, we can get a much more focal and accurate stimulation while maintaining the sufficient intensity with fewer iterations. Quantitative evaluation results are shown in the Table 1.

For the multiple targets study, conventional electrode is no longer applicable. Moreover, for this complicated stimulation pattern, LCMV has no feasible solution due to its strict constraints as we discussed in Sect. 1. Therefore, we can only compare the results of the constrained least squares, maximum intensity and proposed method with $\rho_1 = 10$, $\rho_2 = 10^{-2}$, and $\rho_3 = 10^{-1}$. The e-field distribution patterns are shown in the Fig. 3, and detailed quantitative evaluations are shown in the Table 2. The maximum intensity method, as expected, produces the highest intensity among the all methods being compared. However, it influences

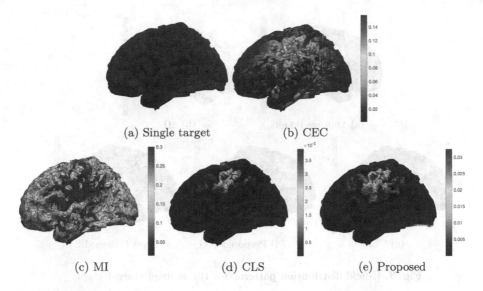

(a) Single target   (b) CEC

(c) MI   (d) CLS   (e) Proposed

Fig. 2. E-field distribution patterns for the single-target case.

Table 1. Quantitative evaluation comparison of various single-target results with the desired e-field distribution at the target $\|e_o\|_2 = 0.3$.

	Intensity	Focality	TE
CEC	0.1571	61.6189	13.8624
MI	1.4572	69.5048	27.1784
CLS	0.0039	17.5171	2.0436
Proposed	0.0325	18.5877	5.9834

the entire left side cortex and has the largest target errors in all three target regions. The constrained least squares method mimics the desired electric field distribution pattern, but the intensity is almost an order of magnitude less than the desired intensity, which is not sufficient for real applications. We also include the results obtained by applying the proposed method with two different sets of parameters ρ_1, ρ_2, ρ_3. The first result with $\rho_1 = 10, \rho_2 = 10^{-2}, \rho_3 = 10^{-1}$ (see Fig. 3(d)) is similar to the constrained least squares one that can successfully produce the desired pattern and has small target errors in all three target regions, but the intensity is not strong enough. The second result with $\rho_1 = 10, \rho_2 = \rho_3 = 10^6$ (see Fig. 3(e)), which is less focal compared to the first pattern, achieves the higher intensity that is more appropriate for clinical applications than the other results. In the meanwhile, it still has small target errors and the focality is much better than the maximum intensity method. Overall, the proposed method can achieve a well-balanced result with high intensity, accuracy, and focality.

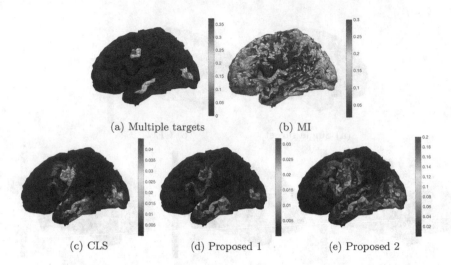

(a) Multiple targets   (b) MI

(c) CLS   (d) Proposed 1   (e) Proposed 2

Fig. 3. E-field distribution patterns for the multiple-target case.

Table 2. Quantitative evaluation comparison of various multiple-target results. The desired e-field distribution at the three targets are 0.3727 V/m, 0.3522 V/m, and 0.2841V/m, respectively.

	Intensity			Focality			TE		
MI	0.6032	0.3880	0.8406	57.0119	91.6543	46.8141	25.4935	27.2086	14.9702
CLS	0.0303	0.0297	0.0449	15.7622	14.8578	20.1903	10.7691	4.1970	4.7183
Proposed 1	0.0111	0.0125	0.0281	31.8789	13.1003	27.5492	11.6089	5.8121	3.3800
Proposed 2	0.0648	0.0876	0.1493	31.1384	23.7444	24.5476	12.7423	9.6420	6.2396

From the two experiments above, one can see several advantages of the proposed method over the state-of-the-art methods. First, the proposed method provides flexibility to achieve different desirable results by adjusting the values of ρ_1, ρ_2, ρ_3 within a limited number of iterations. The penalty parameters ρ_1, ρ_2, ρ_3 play an important role in balancing the trade-off between the intensity and the stimulation accuracy/precision at each iteration. As a matter of fact, another related method-weighted least squares (WLS)-has been proposed in [5]. However, WLS is complicated for implementation, since it requires the intervene of a clinician to specify the weight of the error term at each voxel. Moreover, the WLS results can not be directly predicted by the weighting parameters, which also makes it time consuming. By contrast, the proposed method can produce various favorable e-field distribution patterns easily. Second, the proposed method can produce effective stimulation pattern with reasonable stimulation accuracy and precision. Last but not least, the proposed method has empirically been shown to provide minimum error solutions with high accuracy and focality for clinical applications.

4 Conclusions

In this work, we propose a practically useful multi-electrode tDCS configuration model with the ℓ_1-norm fidelity and multiple constraints due to the safety consideration. To handle the non-differentiability of the objective function in the model, we rewrite the problem by the change of variables and then apply ADMM to derive an efficient numerical algorithm. Simulation experiments have demonstrated the flexibility of this method, i.e., yielding different desirable stimulation patterns by varying the parameters. By qualitatively and quantitatively comparing with other state-of-the-art methods, the proposed method has shown the great potential in providing optimal results with high accuracy and focality.

Acknowledgments. The research of Jing Qin is supported by the NSF grant DMS-1818374.

References

1. Auvichayapat, N., et al.: Transcranial direct current stimulation for treatment of refractory childhood focal epilepsy. Brain Stimul.: Basic Transl. Clin. Res. Neuromodul. **6**(4), 696–700 (2013)
2. Boyd, S., Parikh, N., Chu, E., Peleato, B., Eckstein, J.: Distributed optimization and statistical learning via the alternating direction method of multipliers. Found. Trends® Mach. Learn. **3**(1), 1–122 (2011)
3. Brunoni, A.R., et al.: The escitalopram versus electric current therapy for treating depression clinical study (ELECT-TDCS): rationale and study design of a non-inferiority, triple-arm, placebo-controlled clinical trial. São Paulo Med. J. **133**(3), 252–263 (2015)
4. Chan, T.F., Esedoglu, S.: Aspects of total variation regularized l_1 function approximation. SIAM J. Appl. Math. **65**(5), 1817–1837 (2005)
5. Dmochowski, J.P., Datta, A., Bikson, M., Su, Y., Parra, L.C.: Optimized multi-electrode stimulation increases focality and intensity at target. J. Neural Eng. **8**(4), 046011 (2011)
6. Fregni, F., et al.: Noninvasive cortical stimulation with transcranial direct current stimulation in parkinson's disease. Mov. Disord. **21**(10), 1693–1702 (2006)
7. Gabay, D., Mercier, B.: A dual algorithm for the solution of nonlinear variational problems via finite element approximations. Comput. Math. Appl. **2**, 17–40 (1976)
8. Glowinski, R., Marrocco, A.: Sur l'approximation, par elements finis d'ordre un, et la resolution, par, penalisation-dualité, d'une classe de problems de dirichlet non lineares. Revue Française d'Automatique, Informatique, et Recherche Opéationelle **9**, 41–76 (1975)
9. Guler, S.: Optimization of focality and direction in dense electrode array transcranial direct current stimulation (tDCS). J. Neural Eng. **13**(3), 036020 (2016)
10. Li, F., Osher, S., Qin, J., Yan, M.: A multiphase image segmentation based on fuzzy membership functions and L1-norm fidelity. J. Sci. Comput. **69**(1), 82–106 (2016)
11. Oostenveld, R., Fries, P., Maris, E., Schoffelen, J.M.: FieldTrip: open source software for advanced analysis of MEG, EEG, and invasive electrophysiological data. Comput. Intell. Neurosci. **2011**, 1 (2011)

12. Ruffini, G., Fox, M.D., Ripolles, O., Miranda, P.C., Pascual-Leone, A.: Optimization of multifocal transcranial current stimulation for weighted cortical pattern targeting from realistic modeling of electric fields. Neuroimage **89**, 216–225 (2014)
13. Sadleir, R., Vannorsdall, T.D., Schretlen, D.J., Gordon, B.: Target optimization in transcranial direct current stimulation. Front. Psychiatry **3**, 90 (2012)
14. Woods, A.J., et al.: A technical guide to tDCS, and related non-invasive brain stimulation tools. Clin. Neurophysiol. **127**(2), 1031–1048 (2016)

Assessment of Source Connectivity for Emotional States Discrimination

J. D. Martinez-Vargas[1], D. A. Nieto-Mora[1], P. A. Muñoz-Gutiérrez[2(✉)],
Y. R. Cespedes-Villar[3], E. Giraldo[4], and G. Castellanos-Dominguez[5]

[1] Instituto Tecnológico Metropolitano, Medellín, Colombia
[2] Universidad del Quindío, Armenia, Colombia
pamunoz@uniquindio.edu.co
[3] Centro de Bioinformatica y Biologia Computacional de Colombia - BIOS,
Manizales, Colombia
[4] Universidad Tecnológica de Pereira, Pereira, Colombia
egiraldos@utp.edu.co
[5] Signal Processing and Recognition Group, Universidad Nacional de Colombia,
Sede Manizales, Colombia

Abstract. In this paper a novel methodology for assessing source connectivity applied to emotional states discrimination is proposed. The method involves (i) designing the set of Regions-of-interest (ROIs) over the cortical surface, (ii) estimating the ROI time-courses using a dynamic inverse problem formulation, (iii) estimating the pairwise functional connectivity between ROIs, and (iv) feeding a Support Vector Machine Classifier with the estimated connectivity to discriminate between emotional states. The performance of the proposed methodology is evaluated over a real database where obtained results improve state-of-the-art methods that either compute connectivity between pairs of EEG channels or do not consider the non-stationary nature of the EEG data.

Keywords: EEG inverse problem · Connectivity
Emotional states discrimination · Regions of interest

1 Introduction

In the recent past, *electroencephalography* (EEG) has been increasingly employed as a non-invasive technique in understanding the brain functions and neural dynamics in humans, mainly, because of the following reasons: (*i*) The ease of manipulation at a low implementation cost, (*ii*) The ability to measure real-time responses directly from the neural activity without delays [1], (*iii*) The high temporal resolution that allows the research of many different kinds of dynamic brain activation during multiple cognitive tasks [2].

Particularly, EEG analysis is a valuable tool for studying the brain functionality and interaction patterns of neural activity across space, time, and frequency [3]. In this regard, neural synchronism has been explored as a feature to

© Springer Nature Switzerland AG 2018
S. Wang et al. (Eds.): BI 2018, LNAI 11309, pp. 63–73, 2018.
https://doi.org/10.1007/978-3-030-05587-5_7

determine normal and pathological behaviour of brain dynamics, as it is a direct measure of the connectivity among brain regions [4]. This normal or abnormal synchronization can be analyzed for the complete frequency spectrum of the EEG signals or for specific frequency bands [5].

Moreover, there are several methodologies for assessing connectivity from EEG recordings. For instance, connectivity metrics can be directly applied at the scalp level, i.e., computing the pairwise connectivity between EEG channels [6]. However, these metrics computed based on non-invasive recordings might be producing misleading interactions due to the volume conduction problem [7]. An alternative is to compute the connectivity metrics at the source level, applying as previous step a source reconstruction technique [8]. Those methods commonly include designing a set of Regions of interest (ROIs) and estimating their time-courses for applying the connectivity metrics. However, most source reconstruction techniques lack on considering the non-stationary nature of brain activity, which might hidden the actual brain interactions.

In this work a novel method for assessment of source connectivity applied to emotional states discrimination is proposed, where a dynamic inverse problem based on regions of interest (ROIs) is included. The performance of the method is evaluated for real EEG signals, where the proposed method outperforms the state-of the art-methods where the connectivity among EEG channels is usually considered. This paper is organized as follows: in Sect. 2 the mathematical background of the proposed method is presented, in Sects. 3 and 4 the experimental setup and the results are discussed, and in Sect. 5 the conclusions and final remarks are presented.

2   Materials and Methods

2.1   EEG Forward Problem Formulation Within Regions of Interest - ROIs

With the aim of representing the electromagnetic field magnitude measured by the scalp, we assume the following linear model [9]:

$$Y = LJ + \Xi, \tag{1}$$

where $Y \in \mathbb{R}^{C \times T}$ is the EEG data measured by $C \in \mathbb{N}$ sensors at $T \in \mathbb{N}$ time samples, $J \in \mathbb{R}^{D \times T}$ is the amplitude of $D \in \mathbb{N}$ current dipoles (or sources), which are distributed throughout the cortical surface with a fixed orientation perpendicular to it, and $L \in \mathbb{R}^{C \times D}$ is the gain matrix (termed *lead field matrix*), relating the source strengths to the measured EEG data. Also, the effect of noise on the brain activity measured by EEG recordings is modeled by the error matrix $\Xi \in \mathbb{R}^{C \times T}$, so that the uncorrelated noise is assumed to be a Gaussian-distributed random process with zero mean and covariance matrix $Q_\Xi \in \mathbb{R}^{C \times C}$.

The problem in (1) might be reformulated by including a spatial basis set, henceforth Regions of Interest - ROIs, which are both locally smooth and spatially confined. Consequently, the current density can be formulated by a linear combination of $S \in \mathbb{N}$ ROIs $\boldsymbol{\Phi} \in \mathbb{R}^{D \times S}$, as described below:

$$J = \boldsymbol{\Phi}H, \tag{2}$$

where $\boldsymbol{H} \in \mathbb{R}^{S \times T}$ are the weights introduced to reflect the desired ROI properties.

As no information about the cortical areas related to emotional processes is considered, ROIs are designed to be Gaussians centered at some dipole locations. As a results, the entire ROI set covers as much of the cortical surface as possible. Consequently, denoting the i-th dipole location by $\boldsymbol{x}_i$, the basis function centered at $\boldsymbol{x}_i \in \mathbb{R}^{1 \times 3}, \forall i \subset D$ and evaluated at $\boldsymbol{x}_j \in \mathbb{R}^{1 \times 3}, \forall j = 1, \ldots, D$, is given by [10,11]:

$$\boldsymbol{\Phi}(i,j) = exp(-d_g\{\boldsymbol{x}_i, \boldsymbol{x}_j\}/\sigma^2), \tag{3}$$

where $d_g\{\boldsymbol{x}_i, \boldsymbol{x}_j\}$ stands for the geodesic distance between the $i-$th and $j-$th dipoles.

2.2   EEG Inverse Problem for Estimating ROI Time-Courses

After defining the spatial properties of the ROI set, the next step is to estimate the parameters that rule its temporal activity. In turn, combining (1) and (2) generates that each row of $\boldsymbol{H}$ draws the brain activity evolution along time (time-courses) of each basis function or ROI. Thus, estimation of $\boldsymbol{H}$ is carried out by minimizing the fused Lasso (FL) cost function:

$$\widehat{\boldsymbol{H}} = \underset{H}{\mathrm{argmin}}\{\|\boldsymbol{Y} - \boldsymbol{L}\boldsymbol{\Phi}\boldsymbol{H}\|_F^2 + \lambda_s\|\boldsymbol{H}\|_1 + \lambda_t \sum_{t \in T-1} \|\boldsymbol{h}_{t+1} - \boldsymbol{h}_t\|_1\},$$

where $\boldsymbol{h}_\tau \in \mathbb{R}^{R \times 1}$ is the $\tau-$th column of $\boldsymbol{H}$, $\lambda_s \in \mathbb{R}^+$ and $\lambda_t \in \mathbb{R}^+$ are the spatial and temporal regularization parameters, respectively, and $\| \cdot \|$ stands for the L_p-norm

As demonstrated in [12], estimation of ROI time-courses using (4), encourages spareness and temporal homogeneity, benefiting a further source connectivity analysis. Optimization of (4) is carried out using FISTA algorithm detailed in [13]

2.3   Assessment of Pairwise Connectivity Between ROIs

Once we have estimated the ROI time-courses, we carry out a functional connectivity analysis, using the commonly used Magnitude Square Coherence (MSC) metric, to quantify linear synchrony in different frequency bands between pairs of ROIs. MSC has been commonly associated with information regarding emotions [14].

Thus, MSC evaluates large-scale neural interactions, where higher coherence values stand for greater interplay between the analyzed neural networks [4]. Consequently, the pair-wise MSC between two ROI time–courses r and r' can be computed as [15]:

$$\gamma_{r,r'}(f) = \frac{|S_{r,r'}(f)|^2}{|S_{r,r}(f)S_{r',r'}(f)|}, \quad \gamma_{r,r'} \in \mathbb{R}^+, \tag{4}$$

where $S_{r,r'}(f) \in \mathbb{R}^+$ is the cross-spectral density between ROI time-courses r and r' (columns r and r' of $\boldsymbol{H}$) at the frequency bin f. Moreover, $S_{r,r}(f) \in \mathbb{R}^+$ and $S_{r',r'}(f) \in \mathbb{R}^+$ are the auto-spectral densities of time–courses r and r', respectively.

3   Experimental Set–up

The proposed methodology for discriminating emotional states using source connectivity, involves the following stages: (i)Designing the ROI set $\boldsymbol{\Phi}$ as to cover the entire cortical surface; (ii)Estimating the ROI time-courses $\boldsymbol{H}$ by optimizing the FL cost function, (iii)Assessing the pairwise connectivity between ROIs, and (iv)Discriminating between emotional states using an SVM classifier.

3.1   EEG Data of Emotion Analysis

In this study, the EEG data used were obtained from the publicly available reservoir devoted to emotion analysis using physiological signals (DEAP) [16]. Thirty-two healthy participants (50% females and 50% males on average aging 26.9 years) were recruited and consented to participate in the study. Collecting EEG recordings by the BIOSEMI ActiveTwo system, data were acquired at a sampling rate 512 Hz, placing 32 electrodes on the surface scalp and according to the International 10–20 system. The applied pre-processing included the following steps: common referencing, down-sampling to 128 Hz, high-pass filtering from 4 Hz, and eye-blink artifact removal using independent component analysis.

Although the DEAP participants rated the felt emotion employing a discrete 9-point scale, the classification task had been relaxed by binarizing all subject's scores at the scale midpoint (i.e., at 5-point level), resulting in the basic setting of bi-class patterns (particularly, low versus high as pictured in Fig. 1). For each emotion classification task, therefore, we reflect the bi-class affective conditions: Valence (negative versus positive), Arousal (passive-active), Dominance (dominated-dominant), and Liking (dislike-like).

3.2   Benchmarking Connectivity Scenarios

Forward Model and ROI Definition: In order to provide the proposed source connectivity methodology with a suitable forward model, and in lack of individual Magnetic Resonance Images of each subject, we use the pre-computed lead

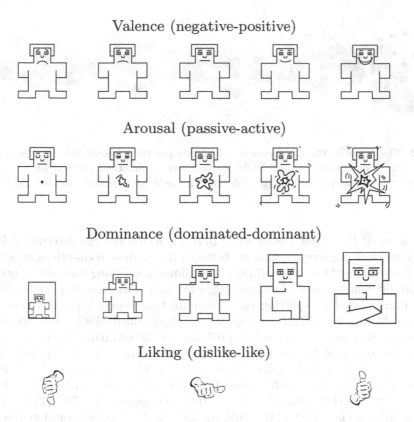

Valence (negative-positive)

Arousal (passive-active)

Dominance (dominated-dominant)

Liking (dislike-like)

Fig. 1. The Self-assessment manikins scales for valence, arousal, and dominance. The thumbs down/thumbs up symbols are for the liking scale.

fields provided by the so-called New York Model [17,18]. In this model, a Finite Element Model (FEM) is solved to generate the lead field, using a six tissue segmentation of the New York Head, including scalp, skull, CSF, gray matter, white matter, and air cavities. Summarizing, the model is reduced to the $C = 32$ electrodes available on the tested dataset, and for $N = 2000$ nodes (dipoles) of a cortical surface mesh.

Further, we select $R = 32$ dipoles (16 per hemisphere) distributed to cover the entire cortical surface as ROI centers. The spatial distribution of the source current amplitudes belonging to each ROI, namely, each column of Φ is modeled by a Gaussian function, as explained in Sect. 2.2. Moreover, the spatial standard deviation of the amplitude distribution is fixed to 10 mm. The amplitude of nodes outside the considered ROI is set to zero. Once the matrix Φ is created, each column is divided by its l_2 norm.

Figure 2 shows the electrode positions and some examples of ROIs plotted over the cortical surface.

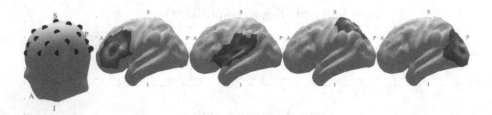

Fig. 2. The figure at the left shows the electrode positions, meanwhile the remaining ones show examples of the used ROIs plotted over a smoothed cortical surface. The markers correspond to Superior (S), Inferior (I), Posterior (P), and Anterior (A) brain axes.

Estimation of Pair-Wise Connectivity Between ROIs: For the determined ROI set, we measure the neural synchrony between the pairwise connections using the Magnitude Squared Coherence (MSC) that allows quantifying the linear synchronism in different frequency bands as suggested for emotion analysis in [5]. Thus, MSC is calculated by splitting each 1-minute time-course into thirty epochs, each one lasting $2\,s$ without overlap. Then, all obtained MSC values are averaged over the epochs to get a more reliable metric estimate. Moreover, MSC values are computed for ten EEG sub-bands: theta ($\theta = 4 - 8\,Hz$), low alpha ($l - \alpha = 8 - 10\,Hz$), high alpha ($h - \alpha = 10 - 12\,Hz$), alpha ($\alpha = 8 - 12\,Hz$), low beta ($l - \beta = 12 - 18\,Hz$), mid beta ($m - \beta = 18 - 24\,Hz$), high beta ($h - \beta = 24 - 30\,Hz$), beta ($\beta = 12 - 30\,Hz$), and gamma $\gamma = 30 - 45\,Hz$. Further, to get a holistic view of the MSC metric, the MSC is also computed in the range $4 - 45\,Hz$. At the end, for each frequency band, the pair-wise connectivity between ROIs are collected into a connectivity matrix $\boldsymbol{\Gamma} \in [0, 1]^{R \times R}$.

Further, due to the symmetric estimated connectivity matrices has all diagonal elements equal to one, only their upper diagonal entries are contemplated to create the feature representation matrix $\boldsymbol{\Upsilon} \in \mathbb{R}^{N_{tr} \times Q}$ (one per each considered frequency band), intending to have the minimum possible redundant information. Consequently, each row vector of $\boldsymbol{\Upsilon}$ comprises $Q = R'(R' - 1)/2$ features, encoding a single network frequency rhythm.

To compare the proposed methodology, we carry out the same experiment using as input to the connectivity analysis the pre-processed EEG data, i.e, we perform a sensor-level connectivity analysis, as the most common state-of-the-art method. Further, we also consider two state-of-the-art source estimation techniques, namely, S-FLEX [10] and Multiple Sparse Priors [19], which provide an excellent spatial localization of active sources, but does not consider the temporal brain activity dynamics.

Emotion Classification Accuracy: This measure is computed individually per subject, and each of the feature matrices $\boldsymbol{\Upsilon}$ estimated for each frequency band is individually used to feed a soft-margin support vector machine (SVM) classifier that is trained under the following leave-one-out cross-validation strategy: (*i*) From the $N_{tr} = 40$ trials per subject, 39 are used to train the SVM classifier, while the remaining trial set is devised for testing, (ii) we repeat the preceding stage over and over again until all samples have been used as the testing sample. The reason for using a leave-one-out cross-validation scheme is that the number of samples per subject is not enough for generating significant training and testing sets. Note that this strategy is the most used for emotion discrimination using the DEAP database [20].

Lastly, it is worth noting that the threshold of binarization applied to configure the high/low patterns makes the affective classes unbalanced for each subjective rate. To cope with this issue, we compute the F_1 score, as commonly used, to describe reliably the results of classifier performance.

4 Results

Figure 3 shows the F_1 score for all the considered subjects, and for each of the four considered classes, namely, Valence (V), Arousal (A), Dominance (D), and Liking (L). It must be noticed that for each class, we present the F_1 score associated with the frequency band reaching the highest performance. In turn, those frequency bands are gamma (V), theta (A), low-beta (D) and high-alpha (L), respectively.

It can be seen that for the total amount of trials the blue bars, which are related to the classification results using source level connectivity with dynamic estimation of the ROI time–courses as discriminant features, are higher than the remaining bars, which are related to the classification results by using either sensors level connectivity (red bars) or source level connectivity without considering the non-stationary nature of brain activity, i.e., MSP (orange bars) or S-FLEX (yellows bars) as source estimation methods.

Moreover, to confirm the insights provided by Fig. 3, we quantify the statistical difference regarding the F_1 score, validating whether the source connectivity performance over subjects is higher than the one obtained by the sensor level connectivity. To this end, a paired sample t–test is carried out in which the null hypothesis states that there are not significant differences between our proposal and the compared approaches in terms of the performed population mean values. Otherwise, the alternative hypothesis states that our population mean is greater than the ones of the comparison methods. The experiment is performed individually for each class, but also considering all the F_1 scores reached for all the tested classes in a single comparison scenario.

Table 1 summarizes the results of the t-test associated to the discrimination of emotional states. Comparing against the sensor level connectivity, it can be seen that in the Valence and Dominance emotions, where the proposed method outperform this state-of-the-art method, the null hypothesis of the test is rejected. Moreover, when considering the F_1 scores reached for all the tested classes, the test is also rejected, confirming our hypothesis that source level connectivity analysis is a suitable tool for discriminating between emotional states. Likewise, our methodology also overperforms the source connectivity approaches in most

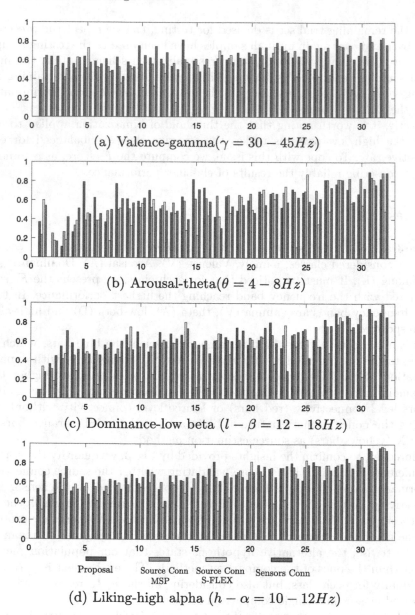

(a) Valence-gamma($\gamma = 30 - 45Hz$)

(b) Arousal-theta($\theta = 4 - 8Hz$)

(c) Dominance-low beta ($l - \beta = 12 - 18Hz$)

Proposal   Source Conn   Source Conn   Sensors Conn
              MSP   S-FLEX

(d) Liking-high alpha ($h - \alpha = 10 - 12Hz$)

Fig. 3. F_1 score of the classification results by using SVMs with leave-one-out validation.

cases, being the MSP based source estimation the most similar approach. As a result, we conclude that source connectivity estimation considering the non-stationary nature of brain activity is the most suitable approach for identifying connectivity patterns related to emotional processing.

Table 1. t−test associated to the discrimination of emotional states

		C1	C2	C3	C4	All
EEG	h	1	0	1	0	1
	t	1.8750	−0.0701	1.9576	1.0987	2.0275
	p	0.0351*	0.5277	0.0297*	0.1402	0.0223*
MSP	h	0	0	1	0	1
	t	0.9522	1.2588	2.0603	0.0644	2.2492
	p	0.1743	0.1087	0.0239*	0.4745	0.0131*
SFLEX	h	1	1	1	1	1
	t	0.0001**	0.0038**	0.0001*	0.0005**	$3.82e^{-12}$**
	p	0.0351*	0.5277	0.0297*	0.1402	0.0223*

5 Discussion and Conclusions

In this work we use source connectivity patterns for improving the discrimination of emotional states. Moreover, during training and validation of the proposed discrimination method, the following aspects need to be considered: The first aspect to reflect is the ROI selection. In this case, we use a set of ROIs in order to cover the entire cortical surface. However, the ROI selection could be performed according to the elicited brain activity [20], or according to the task in hand using Brodmann areas [21].

The next point to consider is the connectivity measure. Here, we use a commonly used functional connectivity metric, namely, the MSC, that quantifies linear synchrony in different frequency bands. Results clearly show that the frequency band at hand is an important factor to consider when analyzing different emotional states. However, some other aspects related to the nature of the brain activity synchronization, as its time evolution, should be considered in future works. Further, it must be noticed that we use, as discriminant features, the raw connectivity values to feed a SVM classifier trained under a leave-one-out cross-validation approach. Moreover, thought this training approach is valid for confirming that source-based connectivity features are more suitable that the sensor-level ones, a better feature extraction procedure, using graph metrics should also be considered.

Lastly, it is worth noting that we carry out a binary classification of emotions as previously reported in the literature, for instance, in [5]. However, other strategies of labeling should be considered to adequately describe the spatio-temporal patterns of emotion dimensions (like the use of regressions).

Acknowledgments. This work was carried out under the funding of COLCIENCIAS. Research project: 111077757982: "Sistema de identificación de fuentes epileptogénicas basado en medidas de conectividad funcional usando registros electroencefalográficos e imágenes de resonancia magnética en pacientes con epilepsia refractaria: apoyo a la cirugía resectiva".

References

1. Koppert, M., Kalitzin, S., Velis, D., da Silva, F.L., Viergever, M.: Dynamics of collective multi-stability in models of distributed neuronal systems. Int. J. Neural Syst. **24**(2), 1430004 (2014)
2. Lei, X., Wu, T., Valdes-Sosa, P.A.: Incorporating priors for EEG source imaging and connectivity analysis. Front. Neurosci. **9**, 284 (2015)
3. Schoffelen, J.M., Gross, J.: Source connectivity analysis with MEG and EEG. Hum. Brain Mapp. **30**(6), 1857–1865 (2009)
4. Hurtado-Rincón, J.V., Martínez-Vargas, J.D., Rojas-Jaramillo, S., Giraldo, E., Castellanos-Dominguez, G.: Identification of relevant inter-channel EEG connectivity patterns: a kernel-based supervised approach. In: Ascoli, G.A., Hawrylycz, M., Ali, H., Khazanchi, D., Shi, Y. (eds.) BIH 2016. LNCS (LNAI), vol. 9919, pp. 14–23. Springer, Cham (2016). https://doi.org/10.1007/978-3-319-47103-7_2
5. Gupta, R., Hur, Y.J., Lavie, N.: Distracted by pleasure: effects of positive versus negative valence on emotional capture under load. Emotion **16**(3), 328 (2016)
6. Chella, F., Pizzella, V., Zappasodi, F., Marzetti, L.: Impact of the reference choice on scalp eeg connectivity estimation. J. Neural Eng. **13**(3), 036016 (2016)
7. Lai, M., Demuru, M., Hillebrand, A., Fraschini, M.: A comparison between scalp- and source-reconstructed EEG networks. Sci. Rep. **8**(1), 12269 (2018)
8. Bastos, A.M., Schoffelen, J.M.: A tutorial review of functional connectivity analysis methods and their interpretational pitfalls. Front. Syst. Neurosci. **9**, 175 (2016)
9. Baillet, S., Mosher, J.C., Leahy, R.M.: Electromagnetic brain mapping. IEEE Signal Process. Mag. **18**, 14–30 (2001)
10. Haufe, S., et al.: Large-scale EEG/MEG source localization with spatial flexibility. NeuroImage **54**(2), 851–859 (2011)
11. Castaño-Candamil, S., Höhne, J., Martínez-Vargas, J.D., An, X.W., Castellanos-Domínguez, G., Haufe, S.: Solving the EEG inverse problem based on space-time-frequency structured sparsity constraints. NeuroImage **118**, 598–612 (2015)
12. Martinez-Vargas, J.D., Strobbe, G., Vonck, K., van Mierlo, P., Castellanos-Dominguez, G.: Improved localization of seizure onset zones using spatiotemporal constraints and time-varying source connectivity. Front. Neurosci. **11**, 156 (2017)
13. Chen, X., Lin, Q., Kim, S., Carbonell, J.G., Xing, E.P.: Smoothing proximal gradient method for general structured sparse regression. Ann. Appl. Stat. **6**(2), 719–752 (2012)
14. Gupta, R., Falk, T.H., et al.: Relevance vector classifier decision fusion and EEG graph-theoretic features for automatic affective state characterization. Neurocomputing **174**, 875–884 (2016)
15. Srinivasan, R., Winter, W.R., Ding, J., Nunez, P.L.: EEG and MEG coherence: measures of functional connectivity at distinct spatial scales of neocortical dynamics. J. Neurosci. Methods **166**(1), 41–52 (2007)
16. Koelstra, S., et al.: Deap: a database for emotion analysis; using physiological signals. IEEE Trans. Affect. Comput. **3**(1), 18–31 (2012)
17. Haufe, S., Ewald, A.: A simulation framework for benchmarking EEG-based brain connectivity estimation methodologies. Brain Topogr., 1–18 (2016). https://doi.org/10.1007/s10548-016-0498-y, ISSN 1573-6792
18. Huang, Y., Parra, L.C., et al.: The new york head- a precise standardized volume conductor model for EEG source localization and TES targeting. NeuroImage **140**, 150–162 (2016)

19. Friston, K., et al.: Multiple sparse priors for the M/EEG inverse problem. NeuroImage **39**(3), 1104–1120 (2008)
20. Padilla-Buritica, J.I., Martinez-Vargas, J.D., Castellanos-Dominguez, G.: Emotion discrimination using spatially compact regions of interest extracted from imaging EEG activity. Front. Comput. Neurosci. **10**, 55 (2016)
21. Hata, M., et al.: Functional connectivity assessed by resting state eeg correlates with cognitive decline of alzheimer's disease-an eloreta study. Clin. Neurophysiol. **127**(2), 1269–1278 (2016)

Rich Dynamics Induced by Synchronization Varieties in the Coupled Thalamocortical Circuitry Model

Denggui Fan[1(✉)], Jianzhong Su[2], and Ariel Bowman[2]

[1] School of Mathematics and Physics,
University of Science and Technology Beijing, Beijing 100083, China
worldfandenggui@163.com
[2] Department of Mathematics, University of Texas at Arlington,
Arlington, TX 76019, USA
su@uta.edu

Abstract. Epileptic disorders are typically characterized by the synchronous spike-wave discharges (SWD). However, the mechanism of SWD is not well-understood in terms of its synchronous spatio-temporal features. In this paper, based on the coupled thalamocortical (TC) neural field models we first investigate the SWD complete synchronization (CS), lag synchronization (LS) and anticipated synchronization (AS) mainly using the adaptive delayed feedback (ADF) and active control (AC). Then we explore the dynamics of 3-compartment coupled TC motifs with the interactive connectivity patterns of ADF and AC, as well as the various interactive weights. It is found that CS, LS and AS of motifs can coexist and transit between each other by changing the various interactive modes and weights. These results provide the complementary synchronization effects and conditions for the basic 3-node motifs. This may facilitate to construct the architecture based on patient EEG data and reveal the abnormal information expression of epileptic oscillatory network.

Keywords: Spike-wave discharges (SWD) · Synchronization control
Adaptive feedback control · Active control · Network motifs

1 Introduction

Many neurological diseases are caused by abnormal rhythms pertaining to synchronization behaviors of neuronal populations. Epileptic disorders, especially in children, are frequently characterized by spike-wave discharges (SWD), which

DF is supported by the National Natural Science Foundation of China (Grant No. 11702018) and the Project funded by China Postdoctoral Science Foundation (Grant Nos. 2016M600037 and 2018T110043).

S. Wang et al. (Eds.): BI 2018, LNAI 11309, pp. 74–84, 2018.
https://doi.org/10.1007/978-3-030-05587-5_8

are a striking nonlinear phenomenon observed in electroencephalogram (EEG) data. SWD is considered as a fundamental pathological behavior due to hyper-synchronised neural populations at the macroscopic level. However, SWD is not well-understood in terms of its synchronous spatio-temporal features, including synchronization mechanism, which may have potentially hampered the under-standing and diagnosis for epileptic seizures. Therefore, investigations for the synchronization conditions of SWD can yield meaningful insights into the under-lying dynamics of pathogenesis of this neurological disease, and provide predic-tions for further experiments.

Suffczynski et al. (2004) [1] developed a computational model of thalamo-cortical circuits based on relevant (patho) physiological data. It was revealed that the interruption of the normal activity may be due to bistable dynam-ics consisting of background state and seizure rhythm. Lytton et al. (1997) [2] mainly focused on the thalamic TC-RE circuit in a computer network model of spike-and-wave seizures and showed that dynamic interactions determine partial thalamic quiescence. Taylor et al. (2014) [3] developed a thalamocortical neu-ral field model, which can successfully simulate the SWD dynamics. Epilepsy regions are thought to be abnormally synchronized even between two remote seizure regions. However, these works mentioned above didn't model the dis-tant cortical regions. In particular, they didn't provided any insights into the synchronization dynamics of epileptic seizures. Therefore, in this paper, based on the coupled thalamocortical models we reviewed the common mechanisms for the (complete, lag and anticipated) synchronization control, which are then tested for the efficacy of these mechanisms on the SWD synchronization. In particular, we will investigate the motif synchronous dynamics of SWD. Such information can provide insight for understanding how epileptic patients' brain network structure forms when the brain develops highly synchronous SWD dur-ing seizure. Based on SWD patterns from patient EEG or fMRI data, one can select relevant synchronization mechanism and network structure to model these brain activities and their collective behavior.

The paper is organized as follows. Section 2 describes the single compart-ment thalamocortical model and the two coupled thalamocortical modules with a Drive-Response configuration (see Fig. 1). In Sect. 3, the complete, lag and anticipated synchronizations are investigated using the methods of sigmoidal activation coupling, delayed adaptive feedback and the active control, respec-tively. In Sect. 4, we will construct some typical motifs composed of 3 compart-ments thalamocortical columns to investigate the synchronization dynamics of 3-compartment motif. Section 5 presents a conclusion.

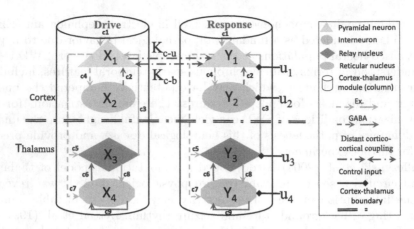

Fig. 1. Schematic of two-compartment coupled thalamocortical modules with a Drive-Response configuration. $X_1/Y_1, X_2/Y_2, X_3/Y_3$ and X_4/Y_4 represent the cortical pyramidal neuronal population, interneuronal population, thalamic relay nucleus and thalamic reticular nucleus, respectively. K_{c-u} and K_{c-b} represent the distant corticocortical uni-direction and bi-direction coupling functions which are time-dependent. Green arrows indicate the excitatory synaptic connectivity and red arrows indicate the inhibitory connectivity. $u_{1,2,3,4}$ represents the external control input into response module. (Color figure online)

2   Mathematical Models

The thalamocortical neural field model proposed by Taylor et al. [1] can be described as the following autonomous system,

$$\frac{dX_1}{dt} = \omega_1(h_1 - X_1 + c_1S[X_1] - c_2S[X_2] + c_3S[X_3]), \tag{1}$$

$$\frac{dX_2}{dt} = \omega_2(h_2 - X_2 + c_4S[X_1]), \tag{2}$$

$$\frac{dX_3}{dt} = \omega_3(h_3 - X_3 + c_5S[X_1] - c_6g[X_4]) \tag{3}$$

$$\frac{dX_4}{dt} = \omega_4(h_4 - X_4 + c_7S[X_1] + c_8g[X_3] - c_9g[X_4]) \tag{4}$$

where X_1, X_2, X_3 and X_4 are firing rates, i.e., the fractional firing activity in each neuronal populations. $h_{1,2,3,4}$ are additive input constants. $\omega_{1,2,3,4}$ are the timescale parameters. $c_{1,2,\dots,9}$ are the connectivity strengths within different neuronal populations whose linking rules essentially follow the experimentally known connection values. That is $c_1 = 1.8$, $c_2 = 1.5$, $c_3 = 1$, $c_4 = 4$, $c_5 = 3$, $c_6 = 0.5$, $c_7 = 3$, $c_8 = 10.5$, $c_9 = 0.2$, $h_1 = -0.35$, $h_2 = -3.4$, $h_3 = -2.0$, $h_4 = -5$, $w_1 = 26$, $w_2 = 32.5$, $w_3 = 2.6$, $w_4 = 2.6$. $S[x] = 1/(1 + \theta^{-x})$ and $g[y] = \alpha y + \beta$ are the activation functions of the cortical and thalamic modules, with $x = X_1, X_2, X_3, y = X_3, X_4$, respectively. Therein, $\alpha = 2.8, \beta = 0.5$, $\theta = 2.5 \times 10^5$. θ determines the steepness. It is noted that parametric values are set to make the cortical dynamics of the system show SWD discharges, as shown in Fig. 2.

The single thalamocortical model can be rewritten as follows:

$$X'(t) = \alpha + AX(t) + F(X(t)) \tag{5}$$

where

$$\alpha = \begin{pmatrix} \omega_1 h_1 \\ \omega_2 h_2 \\ \omega_3 h_3 \\ \omega_4 h_4 \end{pmatrix}, X(t) = \begin{pmatrix} X_1(t) \\ X_2(t) \\ X_3(t) \\ X_4(t) \end{pmatrix}, A = -\begin{pmatrix} \omega_1 & 0 & 0 & 0 \\ 0 & \omega_2 & 0 & 0 \\ 0 & 0 & \omega_3 & 0 \\ 0 & 0 & 0 & \omega_3 \end{pmatrix} F(X) = \begin{bmatrix} \omega_1(c_1 S[X_1] - c_2 S[X_2] + c_3 S[X_3]) \\ \omega_2 c_4 S[X_1] \\ \omega_3(c_5 S[X_1] - c_6 g[X_4]) \\ \omega_4(c_7 S[X_1] + c_8 g[X_3] - c_9 g[X_4]) \end{bmatrix}$$

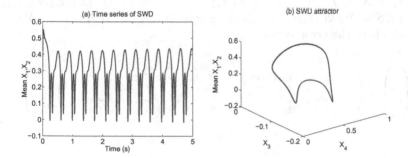

Fig. 2. Firing series and phase diagram of spike-wave discharges (SWD) in single-compartment thalamocortical module. (Color figure online)

3   Synchronization Dynamics of 2-Compartment Coupled Thalamocortical Models

The mechanism underlying the synchronization between distant cortical regions remains unclear. Coupling two thalamocortical modules may yield meaningful insights into this synchronous mechanism of epileptic seizures. In this section, we investigate the complete synchronization, lag synchronization and anticipated synchronization of the coupled thalamocortical modules with a Drive-Response configuration (Fig. 1), i.e., the coupled system has the stable solutions $y(t) = x(t)$, $y(t) = x(t - \tau)$ and $y(t) = x(t + \tau)$ ($\tau > 0$), respectively.

3.1   Complete Synchronization (CS) by Bidirectional Sigmoidal Coupling (SC)

It is believed that cortical excitatory pyramidal neurons in one region have sufficiently long axons which can produce significant propagation effect on neuronal populations within the other distantly located regions and also can be affected by these populations. This suggests the role for the cortical excitatory pyramidal neuron in modulating long distance cortical communication. Therefore, we coupled two thalamocortical modules using the pyramidal neuron populations. In particular, we model the coupling effect using a sigmoidal activation function, which is physiologically crucial and can transforms the average membrane potential of a population of neurons into an average pulse density of action potentials fired by the neurons. The equations can be written as follow,

$$\begin{cases} X'(t) = \alpha + AX(t) + F(X(t)) + K_1 S(Y_1(t)) \\ Y'(t) = \alpha + AY(t) + F(Y(t)) + K_1 S(X_1(t)) \end{cases} \tag{6}$$

Let the vector error state be $e(t) = Y - X$, $E(t) = S(Y) - S(X)$. Hence, $\dot{e}_i = \dot{Y}_i - \dot{X}_i$, $E_i = S(Y_i) - S(X_i)$ (i = 1, 2, 3, 4). $(E_1, E_2, E_3, E_4) = (S'(\xi_1)e_1, S'(\xi_2)e_2, S'(\xi_3)e_3, S'(\xi_4)e_4)$. where $S'(\xi_i) > 0, \xi_i \in (X, Y), (i = 1, 2, 3, 4)$ Then, the error system is:

$$\dot{e} = \begin{pmatrix} \dot{e}_1 \\ \dot{e}_2 \\ \dot{e}_3 \\ \dot{e}_4 \end{pmatrix} = \begin{pmatrix} -\omega_1 + (\omega_1 c_1 - K_1) S'(\xi_1) & -\omega_1 c_2 S'(\xi_2) & \omega_1 c_3 S'(\xi_3) & 0 \\ \omega_2 c_4 S'(\xi_1) & -\omega_2 & 0 & 0 \\ \omega_3 c_5 S'(\xi_1) & 0 & -\omega_3 & -\omega_3 \alpha c_6 \\ \omega_4 c_7 S'(\xi_1) & 0 & \omega_4 \alpha c_8 & -\omega_4(1 + \alpha c_9) \end{pmatrix} \begin{pmatrix} e_1 \\ e_2 \\ e_3 \\ e_4 \end{pmatrix} = \Delta e$$

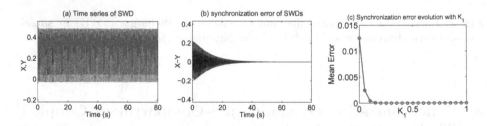

Fig. 3. (a) Time series and (b) complete synchronization error with $K_1 = 0.5$, as well as the (c) evolutions of synchronization error for the stable states with respect to the coupling function, K_1. (Color figure online)

Note that, it can be calculated from Δ that the appropriate large K_1 can make matrix Δ to have four eigenvalues with negative real parts. That means as K_1 increasing, the coupled system can reach to the complete synchronization. Figure 3 illustrates the effectiveness of this method.

3.2   Lag Synchronization (LS) Control Using Unidirectional Adaptive Delay Feedback (ADF)

Lag synchronization suggests that the dynamical variables of two coupled are synchronized with a time delay relative to each other [4,5]. Considering the following drive and response systems with adaptive delay feedback:

$$\begin{cases} X'(t) = \alpha + AX(t) + F(X(t)) \\ Y'(t) = \alpha + AY(t) + F(Y(t)) + K(X(t - \tau) - Y(t)) \end{cases} \tag{7}$$

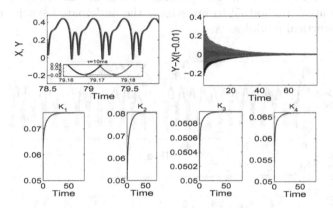

Fig. 4. Time series (upper-left panel), lag synchronization error with $\tau = 0.01s$ (upper-right panel) and the evolutions of adaptive coupling functions, K_1, K_2, K_3, K_4 (low panels). (Color figure online)

Let the vector error state be $e^\tau(t) = Y(t) - X(t-\tau)$, $E^\tau = S(Y(t)) - S(X(t-\tau))$, $\tau > 0$. Hence, $\dot{e}_i^\tau = \dot{Y}_i(t) - \dot{X}_i(t - \tau)$ ($i = 1, 2, 3, 4$). Then,

$$\begin{cases} \dot{e}_1^\tau = \omega_1(-e_1^\tau + c_1 E_1^\tau - c_2 E_2^\tau + c_3 E_3^\tau) - K_1 e_1^\tau \\ \dot{e}_2^\tau = \omega_2(-e_2^\tau + c_4 E_1^\tau) - K_2 e_2^\tau \\ \dot{e}_3^\tau = \omega_3(-e_3^\tau + c_5 E_1^\tau - c_6 \alpha e_4^\tau) - K_3 e_3^\tau \\ \dot{e}_4^\tau = \omega_4(-e_4^\tau + c_7 E_1^\tau + c_8 \alpha e_3^\tau - c_9 \alpha e_4^\tau) - K_4 e_4^\tau \end{cases} \tag{8}$$

where

$$\dot{K_1}(t) = \gamma_1(e_1^\tau)^2, \ \ \dot{K_2}(t) = \gamma_2(e_2^\tau)^2, \ \ \dot{K_3}(t) = \gamma_3(e_3^\tau)^2, \ \ \dot{K_4}(t) = \gamma_4(e_4^\tau)^2 \tag{9}$$

Hence, according to the LaSalle principal [6,7], we can obtained the following theorem.

Theorem 1. *All trajectories* $(X(t - \tau), Y(t)) \in R_X^4 \times R_Y^4$ *in (7) approach the manifold* $M = \{Y(t) = X(t - \tau) \in R^8, K = K_0 \in R^4\}$ *as time goes* *to infinity if $K_{1,2,3,4}$ satisfies the parameter update law (9), i.e.,* $\lim\limits_{t \to +\infty} e(t) =$ $\lim\limits_{t \to +\infty} Y(t) - X(t - \tau) = 0$ *and* $\lim\limits_{t \to +\infty} K(t) - K_0 = 0$. *That is also to say the response system asymptotically lag synchronise the drive system.*

Figure 4 illustrates the effectiveness of the proposed adaptive delay feedback method on SWD lag synchronization.

3.3 The Anticipated Synchronization (AS) by Unidirectional Active Control (AC)

Voss [8] discovered the anticipated synchronization. In the following, we will use the active control method [5] to investigate the anticipated synchronization of two thalamocortical modules.

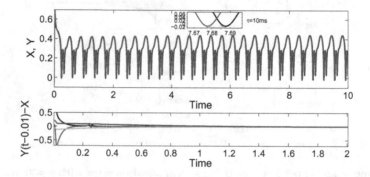

Fig. 5. Time series (upper panel) and anticipated synchronization error with $\tau = 0.01\,\mathrm{s}$ (low panel). (Color figure online)

Considering the following drive and response systems:

$$\begin{cases} X' = \alpha + AX + F(X) \\ Y' = \alpha + AY + F(Y) + U(X,Y) \end{cases} \tag{10}$$

where U(X,Y) is the nonlinear control function with respect to variables X and Y. Let the vector error state be $\bar{E}(t) = Y(t - \tau) - H(X(t)), \tau > 0$, where the smooth vector function $H(X(t)) = [H_1(X(t)), H_2(X(t)), H_3(X(t)), H_4(X(t))]^T$. The error dynamics of the drive-response system is:

$$\begin{aligned} \dot{\bar{E}}(t) &= \dot{Y}(t - \tau) - \dot{H}(X(t)) \\ &= AY(t - \tau) + F(Y(t - \tau)) \\ &\quad - DH(X(t))[AX(t) + F(X(t))] \\ &\quad + U(X(t), Y(t - \tau)) \end{aligned} \tag{11}$$

where $DH(X(t))$ is the Jacobian matrix of $H(X(t))$.

It is said that the drive system and response system are globally generalized anticipated synchronization, if there exist a smooth vector function $H(X(t))$ and controller $U(X(t), Y(t-\tau))$, such that all trajectories $(X(t), Y(t-\tau)) \in R_X^4 \times R_Y^4$ approach the manifold $\{Y(t-\tau) = H(X(t))\} \in R_X^4 \times R_Y^4$ as time goes to infinity, i.e., $\lim\limits_{t \to +\infty} \bar{E}(t) = \lim\limits_{t \to +\infty} Y(t-\tau) - H(X(t)) = 0$. This also implies that the error between the drive and response systems is globally asymptotically stable, i.e., all the eigenvalues of the error system have negative real parts. In particular, as for the anticipated synchronization, we have the following theorem.

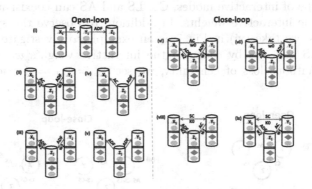

Fig. 6. Structures of nine 3-compartment thalamocortical motifs. SC, ADF and AC represent the 3 type of interactive approaches, i.e., sigmoidal coupling, adaptive delay feedback and active control, where K0, w0, w1 and w2 are the interactive weights, respectively. (Color figure online)

Theorem 2. *The anticipated synchronization of the drive-response system described in (10) can be achieved under the control law,*

$$U(X, Y(t-\tau)) = -AH(X(t)) - F(Y(t-\tau)) + DH(X(t))[AX(t) + F(X(t))] \quad (12)$$

where $H(X)=X$.

Figure 5 illustrates the effectiveness of the proposed active control method on SWD anticipated synchronization.

4   Synchronization Dynamics of 3-Compartment Thalamocortical Motifs

The conception of network motifs was first proposed by Milo et al. [9] to describe the interconnecting patterns occurring in complex networks at the microscale. In particular, 3-node motifs are mostly studied [10,11]. In addition, the spatial computational motifs across brain networks significantly affect neurological disorders such as epilepsy [12]. The epileptic oscillatory network includes various functional modules, e.g., network motifs, which work together to exhibit a highly efficient epileptic architecture. However, the synchronization dynamics of epileptic functional module network is still not well understood. In particular, the question how synchrony evolves in motifs is still unresolved. Therefore, investigations for the synchronization conditions of the neural modules can yield meaningful insights into the underlying dynamics of pathogenesis of neurological diseases and provide predictions for further experiments.

In this section, we propose 9 spatially extended 3-compartment coupled network motifs (Fig. 6), using the various SC, ADF and AC interactive modes with the different interactive weights, respectively. It can be seen from Fig. 7 that under the 3 type of interactive modes, CS, LS and AS can coexist in one motif by adjusting the interactive weights. In addition, to observe the synchronization evolutions, we take (vi) in Fig. 7 as an example to investigate the transitions of CS, LS and AS, by changing the interactive weights w_0, w_1 and w_2, respectively. Without loss of generality, we set $w_0 = w_1 = 1$ and gradually

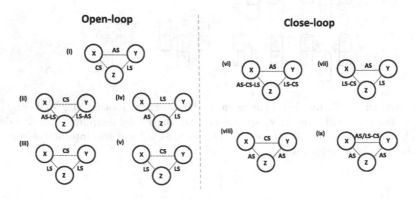

Fig. 7. The coexistence of complete synchronization (CS), lag synchronization (LS) and anticipated synchronization (AS), under the various interactive functions of 9 motifs corresponding to Fig. 6. (Color figure online)

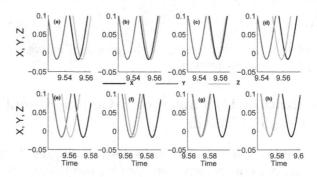

Fig. 8. Time series corresponding to the (vi) in Figs. 6 and 7. w0=w1=1, and w2=0(a), w2=0.1(b), w2=0.2822(c), w2=0.8(d), w2=2(e), w2=10(f), w2=60(g), w2=200(h), respectively. (Color figure online)

increase w_2. As shown in Fig. 8, X and Y always show anticipated synchronization. Y and Z firstly show the lag synchronization (LS) when weak weights $w_2 = 0, 0.1, 0.2822, 0.8, 2, 10$, corresponding to Figs. 8(a–f). However, the large weak weights $w_2 = 60, 200$ (Figs. 8(g–h)) can make Y and Z transit into the complete synchronization (CS). In particular, as for X and Z, it can be clearly seen that as w_2 increasing they transit from the anticipated synchronization (AS) (Figs. 8(a–b)), to CS (Fig. 8(c)) and LS (Figs. 8(d–h)), respectively.

In sum, the above results show that 3-compartment thalamocortical motifs can realized the coexistence and transition of CS, LS and AS, by changing the various interactive modes (SC, ADF and AC) and weights (w_0, w_1 and w_2).

5   Conclusion

In summary, based on the coupled thalamocortical neural field models we first investigated the complete, lag and anticipated synchronization (CS, LS and AS) of SWD, using the sigmoidal coupling (SC), adaptive delayed feedback (ADF) and active control (AC), respectively. We then proposed several typical motifs composed of 3 thalamocortical columns with the interactive connectivity mode of SC, ADF and AC, respectively. Simulation shows that various connectivity modes and interactive weights can make CS, LS and AS coexist and mutually transit in the motif. This finding complements and enriches the previous results regarding to the motif dynamics. The display of rich dynamics here provides a foundation for network modeling of patient EEG data, especially during the transition phase into highly synchronized states during the onset of brain diseases, such as Parkinsons disease or Epilepsy.

References

1. Suffczynski, P., Kalitzin, S., Da Silva, F.L.: Dynamics of non-convulsive epileptic phenomena modeled by a bistable neuronal network. Neuroscience **126**(2), 467–484 (2004)
2. Lytton, W.W., et al.: Dynamic interactions determine partial thalamic quiescence in a computer network model of spike-and-wave seizures. J. Neurophysiol. **77**(4), 1679–1696 (1997)
3. Taylor, P.N., et al.: A computational study of stimulus 1186 driven epileptic seizure abatement. PLoS One **9**(12), e114316 (2014)
4. Rosenblum, M.G., et al.: From phase to lag synchronization in coupled chaotic oscillators. Phys. Rev. Lett. **78**(22), 4193 (1997)
5. Yan, Z.: A new scheme to generalized (lag, anticipated, and complete) synchronization in chaotic and hyperchaotic systems. Chaos **15**(1), 13101 (2005)
6. LaSalle, J.: Some extensions of Liapunov's second method. IRE Trans. Circ. Theory **7**(4), 520–527 (1960)
7. Hale, J.K.: Dynamical systems and stability. J. Math. Anal. Appl. **26**(1), 39–59 (1969)
8. Voss, H.U.: Anticipating chaotic synchronization. Phys. Rev. E **61**(5), 5115 (2000)
9. Milo, R., et al.: Network motifs: simple building blocks of complex networks. Science **298**(5594), 824–827 (2002)

10. Sporns, O., Kotter, R.: Motifs in brain networks. PLoS Biol. **2**(11), e369 (2004)
11. Battiston, F., et al.: Multilayer motif analysis of brain networks. Chaos Interdiscip. J. Nonlinear Sci. **27**(4), Article no. 047404 (2017)
12. Gollo, L.L., Breakspear, M.: The frustrated brain: from dynamics on motifs to communities and networks. Phil. Trans. R. Soc. B **369**(1653), Article no. 20130532 (2014)

Human Information Processing Systems

Humans Have a Distributed, Molecular Long-Term Memory

John L. Pfaltz$^{(\boxtimes)}$

Department of Computer Science, University of Virginia, Charlottesville, USA
jlp@virginia.edu

Abstract. Most memory research has assumed that our long-term memories are somehow retained in our brain, usually by modified synaptic connections. This paper proposes a very different scenario, in which the basic substrate of these memories are molecules which flow within a newly discovered circulatory system similar to our lymph system. Moreover, the information bearing molecules are postulated to be cyclic protein polymers similar to the proteins found in all cell membranes.

Two network algorithms are presented which convert networks to, and from, such cyclic structures and seem to mimic the psychological processes of consolidation, recall, and reconsolidation.

1 Introduction

In 1968, Atkinson and Shiffrin [4] proposed a bipartite human memory consisting of short-term and long-term storage. This division has permeated current memory models because it is consistent with a considerable body of subsequent research. It is assumed that short-term memory is encoded by synaptic connections in the frontal lobe. But, the actual mechanism of long-term memory has never been very clear.

There is ample evidence that cognition and many memory processes occur within the neural network we call our "brain". The hippocampus seems to be particularly involved with memory encoding and recall [35]. So is it not surprising that it has been assumed that our long-term memories are stored within the brain itself. The plasticity of synaptic connections is often cited as the mechanism [32].

But does this make sense? Many unexpected long-term memories, such as "the color of our date's gown at the Junior prom" or "the nonsense words of the 'Jaberwocky' ", just seem to "flash back" unbidden. These are totally inconsequential (in a survival sense). Would an organism employ an expensive, high energy system such as our brain to actually store such data for many years? We think not.

In this paper we will propose a physically distributed, molecular long-term memory encoded as cyclic protein polymers. This is not an entirely new idea. Others have proposed molecular, non-neural, long-term memories *e.g.* [29], which are usually thought to be encoded by means of protein phosphorylation *e.g.* [13,14,27]. Similarly, the possibility that information might be distributed has

© Springer Nature Switzerland AG 2018
S. Wang et al. (Eds.): BI 2018, LNAI 11309, pp. 87–98, 2018.
https://doi.org/10.1007/978-3-030-05587-5_9

been observed, particularly in experiments with *Planaria* flatworms *e.g.* [19]. But, we are unaware of any proposal that these all together could constitute human long-term memory.

To do this we will make 6 key points.

- Storage of long-term data in a neural system is simply too expensive.
- Plants and other organisms without neural systems have mechanisms that react to environmental change.
- Eposidic human information is initially represented, in some form, by neural networks.
- There exist well-defined procedures that convert networks into "chordless cycle" structures and back again.
- Chordless cycle structures abound in every cell of our bodies and illustrate properties normally associated with vectors in a vector space.
- There have recently been found physical systems of unknown function that could circulate information throughout our bodies.

We have addressed the first bullet above. Each of the latter 5 bullets will be described in more detail in the remainder of this paper.

2   Primitive Memory

It is difficult to imagine any organism without a neural system having a "memory". But there is ample evidence that plants, even one celled bacteria have a rudimentary form.

Perhaps the most obvious, and first to be seriously studied, is *phototropism* in which plants grow towards a light source. It was known to Darwin that the *colepotile* (growing tip) is the sensor, and later the hormone *auxin* was identified as having a role in transmitting this information to elongate the proper cells in the stem [14]. One might not call this "memory"; but it clearly illustrates a non-neural sensing and transmission of information.

It can be argued that any reaction to a changing environment at least requires the ability to compare two time dependent states to determine a gradient. Baluška and Levin [5] cite many examples. Stock and Zhang [31] give a very detailed description of the biochemistry of "the so-called nanobrain, a sensory-motor regulatory organelle located at one or both poles of the [*E. coli*] cell that functions as a molecular brain to control motor function". This mechanism controls the movement of flagellar filaments so as to follow a nutrient gradient. Gagliano *et al.* [11] describe a fascinating experiment in which pea seedlings appear to "remember" an association between wind direction and a light source.

Even in multi-celled organisms with neural systems all information need not be concentrated in the brain. *Planaria* (flat worms) with a neural system and centralized brain have been widely studied. Like many primitive organisms, *planaria* can reproduce by lateral division, giving half their body, brain and neural system to each of the progeny. But, if cut transversely, the head will regenerate a new tail and the tail will regenerate a *new head*. This might be attributed to DNA; but McConnell *et al.* [15] demonstrated that the tail "remembered" episodic information with which it had been conditioned. This research has been critized for a small sample size and primitive methodology. But more recently, Neuhof, Levin and Rechavi [19] have reported similar results.

That shows that information can be represented and stored independent of a neural network.

Plants, one celled Ecoli bacteria and other primitive organisms are capable of storing information and reacting to change in their environment. But, these processes are limited and relatively slow. The evolution of neural cells and neural networks that appeared in the Cambrian era support a much more rapid response to environmental change, and a significant competitive advantage [27]. Yet, evolution often retains vestigal organs and procedures. Mechanisms found in plants and *planaria* may well have been retained in our evolution as long term storage.

3   Neural Systems

It is well established that the brain is the central organ by which we sense our environment, recognize change and, in general, "think". PET scans and other research has identified specific regions of the brain where various processes take place. For example, the prefrontal lobe of the hippocampus is associated with memory [6,35]; the visual cortex is known to be associated with that particular sense [28]. However, many finer details are still obscure. We do not know precisely how data is encoded; but it is assumed that its network structure is involved [9,30].

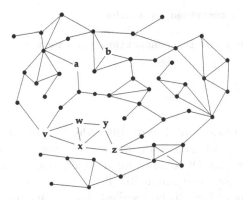

Fig. 1. A network graph $\mathcal{G}$ that might possibly model a neural configuration.

Graphs, such as Fig. 1, provide a reasonable model of network structure, in which nodes correspond to neurons and edges (links) denote connections between them. (Seven of the 53 nodes have been labeled for later reference.) In this network model, if x denotes a specific neuron, we let $x.\eta$ denote its "neighbors", that is all neurons to which it is connected. We assume η is *reflexive*, so $x \in x.\eta$. In Fig. 1, $x.\eta = \{v, w, x, y, z\}$ and $w.\eta = \{v, w, x, y\}$.

"Closure" is a mathematical concept that has proven useful in the analysis of a variety of network configurations [10]. We think closure is likely to be the basis of concept formation [22]. There are many different closure operators, which we generally denote by φ, but the one we use here is: "y is in the closure of x if all of y's neighbors are also neighbors of x". Or symbolically, $y \in x.\varphi$ if $y.\eta \subseteq x.\eta$.[1] In Fig. 1, w is in x-closure because $w.\eta \subseteq x.\eta$. This is a very simple closure process; but one which has been shown able to extract blobs within the visual pathway [26].

4   Consolidation and Recall

It is generally thought that long-term memories undergo a process that is commonly called "consolidation" [18]. Assuming that episodic events and other thoughts are somehow encoded in a neural configuration that can be modeled as a graph, we coded the procedure ω below to eliminate redundant elements and consolidate it into an irreducible form, $\mathcal{I}$.[2] A network is said to be irreducible if every node x is closed.

```
while there exist reducible nodes
   {
   for_each x in G
      {
      get x.nbhd
      for_each y in x.nbhd - x
         {
         if (y.nbhd contained_in x.nbhd
            {
            remove y and its connections from network
            }
         }
      }
   }
```

There is considerable indeterminism in this code; but we can prove that regardless of the order in which nodes are processed, every graph $\mathcal{G}$ has a unique irreducible form $\mathcal{I} = \mathcal{G}.\omega$. Of course, two distinct, but similar, network graphs $\mathcal{G}_1$ and $\mathcal{G}_2$ may have the same irreducible form, that is $\mathcal{G}_1.\omega = \mathcal{I} = \mathcal{G}_2.\omega$.

Long-term memories have to be recalled. Many have observed that "recall" involves a measure of active processing in our mind and that the recalled memory need not be a faithful copy of the stored episodic event [12,17]. Details are often changed.

---

[1] In mathematics, $\in$ and $\subseteq$ stand for "in" and "is a subset of" respectively.
[2] C++ source code for the following algorithms is available from the author.

The following simple procedure, ε, accepts an irreducible graph $\mathcal{I}$ and expands it. Given a node y, lines 6 and 7 choose a random subset of y, η to be the

```
for each y in I
    {
    while (|y.beta| > 1)
        {
        create new node z;
        S = choose_random_in (y.nbhd);
        z.nbhd = S;
        add {z} to N;
        }
    }
```

neighborhood of the new node z. (The operator $y.\beta$ in this code determines how many nodes should be expanded near y. Its specification is irrelevant to this paper.) Fig. 2(a) illustrates the irreducible graph $\mathcal{I}$ that results from applying the procedure ω to the graph of Fig. 1, together with (b) which is an expanded version of $\mathcal{I}$ which we might call $\mathcal{G}'$. $\mathcal{G}'$ is somewhat similar to $\mathcal{G}$, but not the same. Both networks of Fig. 2(a) and (b) were computer generated from that of Fig. 1. Networks of several thousands of nodes have been reduced and re-expanded using these codes.

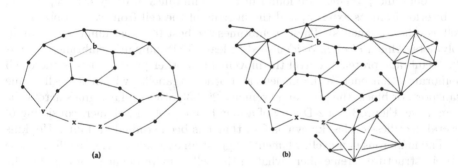

(a)   (b)

Fig. 2. (a) The irreducible consolidation, $\mathcal{I} = \mathcal{G}.\omega$ of Fig. 1, (b) An expansion (or recall) $\mathcal{G}'$, given $\mathcal{I}$.

If we consolidate the graph of Fig. 2(b) again, we will once again get the irreducible graph of Fig. 2(b). Many memory experts believe that "reconsolidation" is a fundamental aspect of memory maintenance [2]. We believe these two computer procedures constitute a reasonable, if abstract, model of the memory process.

5   Chordless Cycle Systems

The consolidation of the network of Fig. 1 which is shown in Fig. 2(a) consists of 6 cyclic structures, each a sequence of nodes, sometimes called a "path" which loops back to the starting node. This kind of cyclic structure, which we believe may be the basis of biological signaling and storage, needs more explanation.

A chord is a single edge, or link, that "short circuits" the cycle. If the dotted link between the nodes a and b were to exist, it would be a *chord*. The 6 cycles of Fig. 2(a) have no chords. It is a chordless cycle system. Chordal graphs, in which there are no chordless cycles, have been widely studied [16]; chordless cycle networks less so. It can be shown [23] that every node in an irreducible network, $\mathcal{I}$, must be a member of a chordless cycle of length ≥ 4.

Chordless cycle systems have the unique property that no cycle (regarded as a set of nodes) can be contained in another. This is sometimes called the Sperner property. Because of it, we can define a cycle composition operator which is analogous to vector composition in a vector space [24]. Indeed, each chordless cycle system can be shown to be a "matroid", or generalized vector space. The cycle system (or matroid) of Fig. 2(a) has rank 6 because it has 6 independent (basis) cycles and 20 distinct simple cycles, each behaving as an individual vector.

Vectors are often used to represent physical properties, and other forms of information. Cyclic structures can as well. Moreover, such molecular networks can be found throughout our bodies.

"Membrane proteins" are found in the membranes of every cell, separating its interior from its exterior, and the nucleus of the cell from its cytoplasm (as well as other organelles). These membranes are host to a vast number of protein polymers. Almén *et al.* have identified at least 6,718 human membrane proteins [3]. Membrane proteins control the movement of other proteins across these cell membranes that enclose the nucleus and other organelles within the cell. Some transport, or block, the protein movement [20,33], others relay signals across the membrane. Figure 3 is a 2-D view of a membrane protein polymer, consisting of several chordless cycles, known as Gr4 that has been studied at John's Hopkins [1]. The numerous non-cyclic filaments suggest an expanded form. In effect, these protein structures "remember" what in the cell's environment is "good" for the cell and what is not. It is not hard to visualize a similar mechanism operating on a multi-cellular level.

The "shape" of information can be important. The memory of our species, that is our DNA, is tightly bound in a double helix. It is virtually a ROM (read only memory) which must be essentially flawless. It is. But, our long-term memories must be loose enough to be "writable", and need not be perfect—just good enough. Systems of chordless cycles provide this kind of shape.

6   Mechanisms of Distributed Storage

Encoding information with an underlying cyclic structure seems plausible. The matroid properties ensure the expected mathematical richness; and the fact that

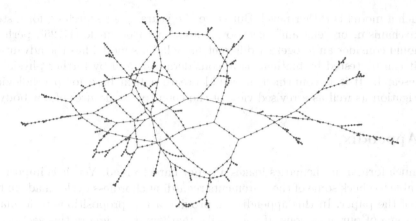

Fig. 3. A 2-dimensional rendition of the membrane protein polymer, Gr4.

biological versions exist in abundance provides further confirmation. It is the fact that the storage medium appears to be distributed (based on *planaria* and other studies) that has always seemed problematic.

That is why the recent paper by Benias, Wells, Carr-Locke, Theise, *et al.* [7] seems so important. The authors describe a new physiological system which is somewhat similar to our lymph system in that it is body-wide and flows by means of peristalsis. In their own words: "these anatomic structures may be important in cancer metastasis, edema, fibrosis and mechanical functioning of many or all tissues and organs. In sum, we describe the anatomy and histology of a previously unrecognized, though widespread, macroscopic, fluid-filled space within and between tissues, a novel expansion and specification of the concept of the human interstitium." Nowhere do the authors mention "memory"; but if their speculation regarding its possible role in cancer metastasis, then this unnamed structure is a conduit of protein information. It is reasonable to think that the hippocampus might be able to inject coded protein based information into this conduit, and later withdraw that information.

7   Discussion

While each of the 6 bullets presented in Sect. 1 can individually be well documented, the conclusion that taken all together they indicate a distributed circulatory long-term information store seems rather startling. Yet, it can make sense.

We envision processes in the hippocampus consolidating episodic experiences into cyclic polymer structures for storage, and expanding (recalling) them by means of phosphorylation to a more useful active form. The probability of recall would then be based on traditional diffusion properties. Of course, recall expansion must be a neural process based on a molecular stimulation.

Such a model is rather novel. But since the years spent searching for a storage mechanism, or "engram" have so far seemed to be futile [17, 25], perhaps we should consider an altogether different model. This model has the advantage that it can be tested by mathematical considerations and by further physiological research. If it is confirmed, it would create a firm base for psychological investigation as well as a revised view of the cognitive structures of our body.

8   Appendix

Too much formal mathematics makes a paper hard to read. Yet, it is important to be able to check some of the statements regarding chordless cycles made in the body of the paper. In this appendix we provide a few propositions to formally prove some of our assertions. If you dislike mathematics, ignore this section. It is not essential.

The order in which nodes, or more accurately the singleton subsets, of $\mathcal{N}$ are encountered can alter which points are subsumed and subsequently deleted. Nevertheless, we show below that the irreducible form $\mathcal{I} = \mathcal{N}.\omega$ will be unique, up to isomorphism.

Proposition 1. *Let $\mathcal{I} = \mathcal{N}.\omega$ and $\mathcal{I}' = \mathcal{N}.\omega'$ be irreducible subsets of a finite network $\mathcal{N}$, then $\mathcal{I} \cong \mathcal{I}'$.*

Proof. Let $y_0 \in \mathcal{I}$, $y_0 \notin \mathcal{I}'$. Then y_0 can be subsumed by some point y_1 in $\mathcal{I}'$ and $y_1 \notin \mathcal{I}$ else because $y_0.\eta \subseteq y_1.\eta$ implies $y_0 \in \{y_1\}.\varphi$ and $\mathcal{I}$ would not be irreducible.

Similarly, since $y_1 \in \mathcal{I}'$ and $y_1 \notin \mathcal{I}$, there exists $y_2 \in \mathcal{I}$ such that y_1 is subsumed by y_2. So, $y_1.\eta \subseteq y_2.\eta$.

Now we have two possible cases; either $y_2 = y_0$, or not.

Suppose $y_2 = y_0$ (which is often the case), then $y_0.\eta \subseteq y_1.\eta$ and $y_1.\eta \subseteq y_2.\eta$ or $y_0.\eta = y_1.\eta$. Hence $i(y_0) = y_1$ is part of the desired isometry, i.

Now suppose $y_2 \neq y_0$. There exists $y_3 \neq y_1 \in \mathcal{I}'$ such that $y_2.\eta \subseteq y_3.\eta$, and so forth. Since $\mathcal{I}$ is finite this construction must halt with some y_n. The points $\{y_0, y_1, y_2, \ldots y_n\}$ constitute a complete graph Y_n with $\{y_i\}.\eta = Y_n.\eta$, for $i \in [0, n]$. In any reduction all $y_i \in Y_n$ reduce to a single point. All possibilities lead to mutually isomorphic maps.   □

In addition to $\mathcal{N}.\omega$ being unique, we may observe that the transformation ω is functional because we can have $\{z\}.\omega = \emptyset$, thus "deleting" z, so ω maps every subset of N onto N_ω, Similarly, ε is a function because $\emptyset.\varepsilon = \{y\}$ provides for the inclusion of new elements. Both ω and ε are monotone, if we only modify its definition to be $X \subseteq Y$ implies $X.\varepsilon \subseteq Y.\varepsilon$, *provided $X \neq \emptyset$*.

The following proposition characterizes the structure of irreducible form.

Proposition 2. *Let $\mathcal{N}$ be a finite symmetric network with $\mathcal{I} = \mathcal{N}.\omega$ being its irreducible form. If $y \in \mathcal{I}$ is not an isolated point then either*

(1) there exists a chordless k-cycle C, $k \geq 4$ such that $y \in C$, or
(2) there exist chordless k-cycles C_1, C_2 each of length ≥ 4 with $x \in C_1$ $z \in C_2$
*   and y lies on a path from x to z.*

Proof. (1) Let $y \in \mathcal{I}$. Since y is not isolated, we let $y = y_0$ with $y_1 \in y_0.\eta$, so $(y_0, y_1) \in E$. Since y_1 is not subsumed by y_0, $\exists y_2 \in y_1.\eta$, $y_2 \notin y_0.\eta$, and since y_2 is not subsumed by y_1, $\exists y_3 \in y_2.\eta$, $y_3 \notin y_1.\eta$. Since $y_2 \notin y_0.\eta$, $y_3 \neq y_0$.

Suppose $y_3 \in y_0.\eta$, then $< y_0, y_1, y_2, y_3, y_0 >$ constitutes a k-cycle $k \geq 4$, and we are done.

Suppose $y_3 \notin y_0.\eta$. We repeat the same path extension. $y_3.\eta \not\subseteq y_2.\eta$ implies $\exists y_4 \in y_3.\eta$, $y_4 \notin y_2.\eta$. If $y_4 \in y_0.\eta$ or $y_4 \in y_1.\eta$, we have the desired cycle. If not $\exists y_5, \ldots$ and so forth. Because $\mathcal{N}$ is finite, this path extension must terminate with $y_k \in y_i.\eta$, where $0 \leq i \leq n - 3$, $n = |N|$. Let $x = y_0, z = y_k$.

(2) follows naturally.   □

Proposition 3. *Let $\rho(x, z)$ denote a shortest path between x and z in $\mathcal{N}$. Then for all $y \neq x, z, \in \rho(x, z)$, if y can be subsumed by y', then there exists a shortest path $\rho'(x, z)$ through y'.*

Proof. We may assume without loss of generality that y is adjacent to z in $\rho(x, z)$.

Let $< x, \ldots, x_n, y, z >$ constitute $\rho(x, z)$. If y is subsumed by y', then $y.\eta = \{x_n, y, z\} \subseteq y'.\eta$. So we have $\rho'(x, z) = < x. \ldots, x_n, y', z >$ of equal length. (Also proven in [21].)   □

In other words, y can be removed from $\mathcal{N}$ with the certainty that if there was a path from some node x to z through y, there will still exist a path of equal length from x to z after y's removal.

Figure 4 visually illustrates the situation described in Proposition 3, which we call a diamond. There may, or may not, be a connection between y and y' as indicated by the dashed line. If there is, as assumed in Proposition 3, then either y' subsumes y or *vice versa*, depending on the order in which y and y' are encountered by ω. This provides one example of the isomorphism described in Proposition 1. If there is no connection between y and y' then we have two distinct paths between x and z of the same length.

Fig. 4. A network diamond

In the following, we merely sketch the steps needed to show that any collection of chordless cycles can be regarded as a "matroid", or the analog of a vector space.

The cycles, C_i, C_k of an irreducible form $\mathcal{I}$ can be composed by retaining all links (edges) in either C_i or C_k but not both. It will be a new chordless cycle which we denote by $C_i \circ C_k$. Let Y be a collection $\{C_i, \ldots, C_k, \ldots, C_n\}$. By the span of Y, denoted $Y.\sigma$, we mean the collection of all possible cycles that can be generated by composition of some subset of the cycles in Y.

Lemma 1. *If $C_k = C_i \circ C_m$ then $C_i = C_k \circ C_m$.*

Proof. Let $C_k = C_i \circ C_m$, then $C_i = C_i \circ C_\emptyset = C_i \circ (C_m \circ C_m) = (C_i \circ C_m) \circ C_m = C_k \circ C_m$ $\square$

In Proposition 4, we show that the spanning operator is a closure operator. This is a rather different form of closure than that in Sect. 3 created by the neighborhood operator, η.

Proposition 4. *The spanning operator, σ is a closure operator over sets Y of cycles.*

Proof. To show that σ is a closure operator, we need show that for all sets X, Y (a) $Y \subseteq Y.\sigma$, (b) $X \subseteq Y$ implies $X.\sigma \subseteq Y.\sigma$, and (c) $Y.\sigma.\sigma = Y.\sigma$. It is evident that σ satisfies (a) and (b). Only (c) must be demonstrated.

Let Y be a set of cycles $\{C_i\}$. Suppose $C_m \in Y.\sigma.\sigma$ implying that there exists some sequence $1 \leq i \leq k$ such that $C_m = C_1 \circ \ldots \circ C_i \circ \ldots \circ C_k$, where $C_i \in Y.\sigma$, $1 \leq i \leq k$. Hence $C_i = C_{i_1} \circ \ldots \circ C_{i_n}$ where $C_{i_j} \in Y$. Thus, substituting for each i in the composition sequence for C_m above, we get $C_m = (C_{1_1} \circ \ldots \circ C_{1_n}) \circ (C_{2_1} \circ \ldots \circ C_{2_n}) \circ \ldots \circ (C_{k_1} \circ \ldots \circ C_{k_n})$ implying $C_m \in Y.\sigma$. $\square$

A closure system is said to be a matroid if it satisfies the Steinitz-MacLane exchange axiom [8,34], that is: if $x, y \notin Y.\sigma$ and $y \in (Y \cup x).\sigma$ then $x \in (Y \cup y).\sigma$.

Proposition 5. *Let $\mathcal{C}$ be a chordless cycle system and let σ be the spanning operator. The system $(\mathcal{C}, \sigma)$ satisfies the Steinitz-Maclane exchange axiom and is thus a matroid.*

Proof. By Proposition 4, σ is a closure operator. Let $C_i, C_k \nsubseteq Y.\sigma$ where $Y = \{\ldots, C_j, \ldots\}$. Suppose $C_k \in (Y \cup C_i).\sigma$ implying that $C_k = C_i \circ (\ldots C_j \ldots) = C_i \circ C_m$ where $C_m \in Y.\sigma$. Consequently, by Lemma 1 we have $C_i = C_k \circ C_m$ and $C_i \in (Y \cup C_k).\sigma$. $\square$

References

1. Afshar, A.A.S.: Systemic modeling of biomolecular interaction networks. Dissertation, Johns Hopkins University, October 2016
2. Alberini, C.M., LeDoux, J.E.: Memory reconsolidation. Curr. Biol. **23**(17), R746–R750 (2013)
3. Almén, M.S., Nordström, K.J.V., Fredriksson, R., Schiöth, H.B.: Mapping the human membrane proteome: a majority of the human membrane proteins can be classified according to function and evolutionary origin. BMC Biol., 1–14 (2009)

4. Atkinson, R.C., Shiffrin, R.M.: Human memory: A proposed system and its control processes. In: Spence, K.W., Spence, J.T. (eds.) The Psychology of Learning and Motivation: Advances in Research and Theory, vol. 2, pp. 89–195 (1968)
5. Baluška, F., Levin, M.: On having no head: cognition throughout biological systems. Front. Psychol. **7**(902), 1–19 (2016). https://doi.org/10.3389/fpsyg.2016.00902
6. Barker, G.R.I., Banks, P.J., Scott, H., Ralph, G.S., et al.: Separate elements of episodic memory subserved by distinct hippocampal-prefrontal connections. Nature Neurosci., 1–28 (2017). https://doi.org/10.1038/nn.4472
7. Benias, P.C., Wells, R.G., Carr-Locke, D.L., Theise, N.D., et al.: Structure and distribution of an unrecognized interstitium in human tissues. Sci. Rep. **8**(4947), 1–8 (2017). https://doi.org/10.1038/s41598-018-23062-6
8. Bonin, J.E., Oxley, J.G., Servatius, B. (eds.) Matroid theory. Contemporary Mathematics, #197. Amer. Math. Soc., Providence, RI (1995)
9. Bullmore, E.T., Bassett, D.S.: Brain graphs: graphical models of the human brain connectome. Annu. Rev. Clin. Psychol. **7**, 113–140 (2011)
10. Caspard, N., Monjardet, B.: The lattices of closure systems, closure operators and implicational systems on a finite set: a survey. Discret. Appl. Math. **127**(2), 241–269 (2003)
11. Gagliano, M., Vyazovstiy, V.V., Borbély, A.A., Grimonprez, M., Depczynski, M.: Learning by association in plants. Sci. Rep., 1–9, December 2016. https://doi.org/10.1038/srep38427
12. Gardiner, J.M.: Retrieval: on its essence and related concepts. In: Roediger III, H.L., Dudai, Y., Fitzpatrick, S.M. (eds.) Science of Memory: Concepts, pp. 221–224 (2007)
13. Glanzman, D.L.: PKM and the maintenance of memory. F1000 Biol. Rep. **5**(4), 1–9 (2013)
14. Liscom, E., Askinosie, S.K., Leuchtman, D.L., Morrow, J., Willenburg, K.T., Coats, D.R.: Growing towards an understanding of plant movement: emmanuel liscom. Plant Cell **26**, 38–55 (2014)
15. McConnell, J.V., Jacobson, A.L., Kimble, D.P.: The effects of regeneration upon retention of a conditioned response in the planarian. J. Comp. Physiol. Psychol. **52**(1), 1–5 (1959). https://doi.org/10.1037/h0048028
16. McKee, T.A.: How chordal graphs work. Bull. ICA **9**, 27–39 (1993)
17. Moscovitch, M.: Memory: why the engram is elusive. In: Roediger III, H.L., Dudai, Y., Fitzpatrick, S.M. (eds.) Science of Memory: Concepts, pp. 17–21 (2007)
18. Nadel, L.: Consolidation: the demise of the fixed trace. In: Roediger III, H.L., Dudai, Y., Fitzpatrick, S.M. (eds.) Science of Memory: Concepts, pp. 177–181 (2007)
19. Neuhof, M.: Levin, Michael, Rechavi, Oded: Vertically-and horizontally-transmitted - the fading boundaries between regeneration and inheritance in planaria. Biol. Open **5**, 1177–1188 (2016). https://doi.org/10.1242/bio.020149
20. Patel, S.S., Belmont, B.J., Sante, J.M., Rexach, M.F.: Natively unfolded nucleoporins gate protein diffusion across the nuclear pore complex. Cell **129**, 83–96 (2007)
21. Pfaltz, J.L.: Finding the mule in the network. In: Werner, R.A.B. (ed.) International Conference on Advances in Social Network Analysis and Mining, ASONAM 2012, Istanbul, Turkey, pp. 667–672, August 2012
22. Pfaltz, J.L.: Using closed sets to model cognitive behavior. In: Ray, T., Sarker, R., Li, X. (eds.) ACALCI 2016. LNCS (LNAI), vol. 9592, pp. 13–26. Springer, Cham (2016). https://doi.org/10.1007/978-3-319-28270-1_2

23. Pfaltz, J.L.: Computational processes that appear to model human memory. In: Figueiredo, D., Martín-Vide, C., Pratas, D., Vega-Rodríguez, M.A. (eds.) AlCoB 2017. LNCS, vol. 10252, pp. 85–99. Springer, Cham (2017). https://doi.org/10.1007/978-3-319-58163-7_6

24. Pfaltz, J.L.: Graph similarity defined by graph transformation. In: 2nd International Conference on Applied Math and Computational Science, p. 35 (abstract), Budapest, Hungary (2018)

25. Poo, M., Pignatelli, M., Ryan, T.J., Tonegawa, S., et al.: What is memory? The present state of the engram. BioMedCentral Biology, pp. 1–18, 2016. https://doi.org/10.1186/s12915-016-0261-6

26. Rosenfeld, A., Pfaltz, J.L.: Sequential operations in digital picture processing. J. ACM **13**(4), 471–494 (1966)

27. Sacktor, T.C.: Memory maintenance by PKMζ - an evolutionary perspective. Mol. Brain **5**(31), September 2012. https://doi.org/10.1186/1756-6606-5-31

28. Sarti, A., Citti, G., Petitot, J.: Functional geometry of the horizontal connectivity in the primary visual cortex. J. Physiol. Paris **103**(1–2), 37–45 (2009)

29. Sossin, W.S.: Molecular memory traces. Prog. Brain Res. **169**, 3–25 (2008)

30. Sporns, O., Honey, C.J., Kötter, R.: Identification and classification in brain networks. PLoS ONE **2**, e1049 (2007)

31. Stock, J.B., Zhang, S.: The biochemistry of memory. Curr. Biol. **23**(17), R741–R745 (2013)

32. Turner, P.R., O'Connor, K., Tate, W.P., Abraham, W.C.: Roles of amyloid precursor protein and its fragments in regulating neural activity, plasticity and memory. Prog. Neurobiol. **70**, 1–32 (2003)

33. Weis, K.: The nuclear pore complex: oily spaghetti or gummy bear? Cell **130**, 405–407 (2007)

34. Welsh, D.J.A.: Matroid Theory. Academic Press, London (1976)

35. Zeidman, P., Maguire, E.A.: Anterior hippocampus: the anatomy of perception, imagination and episodic memory. Nat. Rev. Neurosci. **17**, 1–26 (2016). https://doi.org/10.1038/nm.2015.24

Functional Connectivity Analysis Using the Oddball Auditory Paradigm for Attention Tasks

Juana Valeria Hurtado-Rincón[1(✉)], Francia Restrepo[2], Jorge Ivan Padilla[1,2,3], Hector Fabio Torres[3], and German Castellanos-Dominguez[1,2,3]

[1] Signal Processing and Recognition Group,
Universidad Nacional de Colombia, Bogotá, Colombia
jvhurtador@unal.edu.co
[2] Universidad Autónoma de Manizales, Manizales, Colombia
[3] Universidad de Caldas, Manizales, Colombia

Abstract. Nowadays, cognitive stimulus processing using Electroencephalographic (EEG) recordings is accomplished by analyzing individually the time-frequency information belonging to each EEG channel. Nevertheless, several studies have characterized cognitive functions as synchronized brain networks depending on the underlying neural interactions. As a result, connectivity analysis provides essential information for improving both the interpretation and interpretability of brain functionality under specific tasks. In this research, we perform functional connectivity analysis by measuring the stability of the phase difference between EEG channels, aiming to include synchronization patterns for studying the brain reaction to cognitive stimulus. Experiments are carried out in subjects responding to an oddball paradigm. Results show statistical differences between target and non-target labels, making the proposed methodology a suitable alternative to support cognitive neurophysiological applications.

Keywords: Brain connectivity · Phase synchronization
Electroencephalography · Oddball paradigm

1 Introduction

Studies of routine activities (like attention, perception, or decision-making) have been widely used in cognitive and clinical research of neurological diseases [12,19]. Because of the provided high temporal resolution and low implementation cost, electroencephalography (EEG) is a very suitable tool to investigate the brain activity patterns, mainly, in applications regarding the oddball paradigm experiments, in which two different testing sensory stimuli (i.e., *rare* and *frequent*) are randomly presented to a subject under examination. The rare stimuli, labeled as a target, are produced with a higher recurrence than the frequent stimuli, or non-target. In the oddball task, an evaluated subject must

© Springer Nature Switzerland AG 2018
S. Wang et al. (Eds.): BI 2018, LNAI 11309, pp. 99–108, 2018.
https://doi.org/10.1007/978-3-030-05587-5_10

distinguish either stimulus by pushing a button or mentally counting each target stimulus, while ignoring the non-targets occurrence.

In the stimulus processing, the event-related potentials (ERPs) are measured by averaging all EEG signals collected from a single subject, enabling to interpret the neural response and brain reaction to a given stimulus. A very studied component in ERPs is the P300 waveform, defined as an extended latency component appearing at 300–500 ms as a positive wave after each target stimulus is triggered. The detailed analysis of long latency components has been utilized in most cognitive and clinical neuroscience studies, widely performed by time-frequency methods, which are prone to be biased by the powerful individual channels [11,15]. In fact, the neuronal activity involved in cognitive functions is not evoked by the isolated brain regions, meaning that P300 waveforms are elicited by integrating structurally and functionally different brain areas [9,17].

Analysis of all neural interactions, termed brain connectivity, is assumed to provide additional valuable knowledge for better understanding of cognitive and clinical research [2]. In particular, EEG synchronization assessments are often used, which are intended to measure the phase synchronization intensity from neural models [3]. Since the volume conduction effect alters the electrical brain activity measured through scalp EEG, the synchronization values might not reflect brain activities accurately, producing spurious detection of connectivity and resulting in a high dimensional connectivity matrix containing real information and noise. In this regard, an analysis of significance based on inter-channel connections may elucidate the neural networks related with information processing [4,7].

In this work, we characterize the evoked responses through the functional connectivity quantified by the phase locking value (PLV), computing the pairwise relationships between all possible EEG channels. To investigate confidence of task-induced changes, the extracted PLV features are statistically tested to choose the most relevant ones, tending to identify the most significant EEG channel-to-channel connections; the statistical analysis is performed with the aim of identifying the channels and connections involved during attentional processes and memory work. The results performed on real-world EEG data, relying on the oddball experimental paradigm of cognitive evoked potentials, show that there are substantial differences in connectivity response to the discrimination of target and non-target.

2   Methods

Since the transient linking of different cognitive tasks is associated with the integration and interaction of different brain structures, long-range oscillatory phase synchronization is computed with the aim of searching spatially distributed patterns of coherent neural oscillations at specific frequencies, even if their amplitudes are uncorrelated [14]. To this end, the validation methodology appraises the following stages: (i) Computation of grand average ERP waveforms, (ii) Extraction of inter-channel connectivity features using PLV, and (iii) Estimation of a significant connectivity feature set.

2.1   Experimental Paradigm of Cognitive Evoked Potentials

ERP Data Description: The used EEG data were acquired from 25 children, aging from 5 to 16 years and having different education levels[1]. Children had been selected to fulfill the following exclusion criteria: intellectual disability, neurological antecedents, psychiatric hospitalization's history, autism, and related. The child's parents were also requested to sign written permission for authorizing their participation.

The experimental design is implemented using the oddball paradigm where, each subject listens to a series of tones, presented as auditive stimuli and labeled as target (rare) or non-target (frequent). Moreover, the subjects are instructed to pay attention to the targets and to count their incidence while ignoring the existence of non-targets tones. Each auditive stimulus (target or non-target) lasts 130 ms, holding a silent time between two consecutive stimuli of 1 s. The number of target-occurrence is fixed at 20% out of the total trials, while the non-target stimulus – the remaining 80%. The experiment contains approximately 200 trials. The oddball paradigm measures the perceptual discrimination between evoked event-related potential, in which the cognitive functions such as attention and work memory are necessary.

Grand Average Calculation: All employed EEG recordings were collected symmetrically using the International 10–20 system for 19-electrode placement. Further, the EEG data were sub-sampled at 250 Hz and segmented in N trials within the time interval, starting from -0.2 s to 1 s of the stimulus onset instant (0 s). Note that the interval measured between -0.2 s to 0 is termed baseline. For each child, representative ERP data are extracted by averaging across the segmented trial set, $\{Z_n \in \mathbb{R}^{C \times T} : n \in [1, N]\}$, where T is the number of time samples and $C = 19$ is the number of channels. Then, the grand average ERP waveform is estimated by averaging the data of the 25 subjects in this experiment, holding a sequence of positive and negative components. Additionally, with the aim of studying the active brain areas related to the stimuli processing, the spatial distributions of grand average energy are extracted from six-time intervals, starting from -0.2 to 1 s of the stimulus onset instant.

2.2   Extraction of Inter-channel Connectivity Features

Phase Locking Value (PLV): This synchrony measure represents the relations between phases at specific frequencies of coupled oscillating systems in which phases are adjusted as a function of their phase difference even if their amplitudes remain uncorrelated [14]. By using PLV, we quantify the instantaneous phase consistency between two brain activity signals recorded at different locations, relying on the response to a repeated stimulus. Specifically, PLV is

---

[1] Child population includes students of private and public schools of the city Manizales, Colombia.

employed, so that evaluates whether the phase difference of a couple of channels c and c' remains constant across the trial set, calculating the stable timing between scalp locations as [13]:

$$\gamma_{c,c'}(t)=\mathbb{E}\left\{|\exp\left(j(\Phi_n^{c'}(f,t)-\Phi_n^{c}(f,t))\right)|:n\in N, f\in F\right\},\in\mathbb{R}[0,1] \qquad (1)$$

where notation $\mathbb{E}\{\cdot\}$ stands for the common expectation operator, and $\Phi_n^{c}(f,t)$ is the instantaneous phase of n-trial, measured at c-electrode over $T\in N$ time samples and $F\in N$ frequency bins. Here, the instantaneous phase is computed using the continuous wavelet transform with a Morlet mother wavelet at frequency f as given in [1].

As suggested in [5], we remove the record of ongoing synchronization unrelated to task demands, applying baseline normalization of the computed PLV values by subtracting the mean (calculated for the baseline interval) from every data point. As a result, the lower the normalized PLV value $\overline{\gamma}_{c,c'}(t)$, the worse the synchronization between a tested couple of neural recordings at different scalp locations. That is, a zero value means a purely random rise and fall, while a unitary value means that one signal perfectly follows another.

In cognitive tasks, longer latency components, such as the P300, are related to the speed of stimulus evaluation since it appears when a cognitive function is performed during discrimination between the elicited stimuli. Nonetheless, the ERP waveform has low-frequency dynamics mostly under 30 Hz. Consequently, the connectivity analysis is conducted for the following four narrow-frequency bandwidths: $\delta \in [2,5]$ Hz, $\theta \in [5,8]$ Hz, $\alpha \in [8,12]$ Hz, and Low-$\beta \in [12,17]$ Hz.

At each frequency bandwidth, the functional connectivity feature set is pairwise computed over all available channels, yielding the channel-to-channel connection matrix for either testing condition: target $\Upsilon^{1}\in\mathbb{R}^{C\times C\times t}$ or non-target $\Upsilon^{0}\in\mathbb{R}^{C\times C\times t}$, each one holding elements $\overline{\gamma}_{c,c'}(t)$, respectively. Accordingly, 171 available connectivity features are estimated for each labeled stimulus and frequency bandwidth.

2.3   Estimation of Significant Connections

The extraction of all possible inter-channel interactions leads to connectivity matrices with a high amount of information, including redundant or worthless features for a specific task. Therefore, it becomes necessary to extract a set of connections to identify the discriminating properties of the estimated connectivity feature set [8]. Consequently, we conduct the statistical comparison of the obtained data for both stimuli. For each stimulus, a paired sample t-test is accomplished on the feature set split into six intervals of time: $-200 - 0, 0 - 200, \dots, 800 - 1000$ ms.

For assessing the connectivity difference with a confidence level across subjects, we use the null hypothesis to state that there are significant differences between the *target* and *Non-target* conditions, validating one by one each extracted feature. Otherwise, the alternative hypothesis asserts that the mean of one stimulus connection among subjects is higher than the another. Nonetheless, the amount of comparisons to be achieved is huge, diverging greatly from one trial to another. To deal with this issue, the set of most significant connectivity features is estimated by the Bonferroni correction, for which a connection becomes relevant if the null hypothesis is rejected with a corrected $p < 0.01$.

3   Results and Discussion

3.1   Visualization and Analysis of Connectivity

Figure 1 displays in the upper rows, the grand-average evolution over the time domain together with the topograms that are estimated for each considered time interval, revealing the spatially distributed patterns of neural activity. Thus, regardless the analyzed stimulus, each topogram points out on the almost non-response baseline interval. At the next time intervals, either response increases, resulting in a higher amplitude of target stimuli because of P300 component and making evident the brain regions that are mostly related to the P300 generation. As seen, the right frontal, temporal and parietal lobes are highly activated. In this regard, the parietal and temporal lobes handle all processing stimulus functions, which reach the central nervous system like the auditory stimulus processing and the discrimination between target and non-target stimuli. In turn, the frontal lobe activations (regarding the attention and working memory [18])

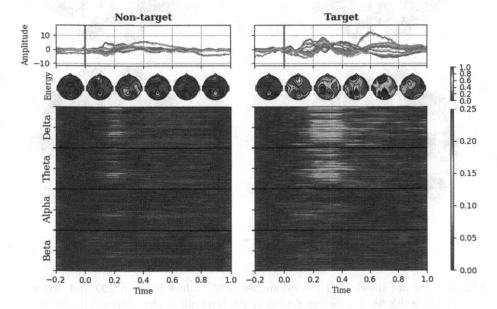

Fig. 1. Average of the estimated ERP waveforms for each one of tested children and PLV results. Top row, ERP Time evolution. Second row, Topograms of the energy spatial patterns. Bottom rows, Averaged PLV time evolution for the studied frequency bands.

can be detected starting at 200 ms after the target stimulus. This situation holds until the last split interval when neural activity patterns notoriously vanish. As a result, the presence of target ERP waveform can be correlated with the performing cognitive functions: attention and memory work.

As seen in the bottom rows of Fig. 1, the phase connectivity values rise as soon as the stimulus is triggered, making clear an important neural activity as a response to the elicitation. Note that the target responses prompt a higher amplitude in low-frequency bands, improving the discrimination between the target and non-target conditions. This behavior can be promoted by the low-frequency dynamics in ERP responses, reinforcing that cognitive brain processes are related to the low-frequency components of EEG activity [10]. On the opposite, PLV measurements do not seem discriminating between the labels in high-frequency bandwidths.

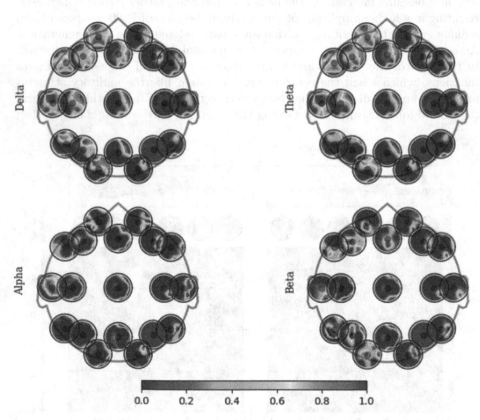

Fig. 2. Plots are showing all the normalized PLV values between 200 and 400 ms averaged by subjects. The figures represent the strength of the relationships between each channel (small circles) against the remaining channels, where the color represents the intensity of the connection between the specific channel and the scalp region (the red color states high intensity and the blue color states low activity), while the outside circle represents the whole scalp. (Color figure online)

As proposed in [16], the color graphs of Fig. 2 display the assessed phase interactions in target condition of each electrode with other brain areas in the interval between 200 and 400, ms when the P300 latency takes place. This time interval is selected because of the evident changes in the connectivity patterns seen in Fig. 1. So, the outside circle pictures the whole scalp, while the rings (at each electrode position) embrace the connectivity relationships between a specific electrode and remaining electrodes. As seen, the patterns of high connectivity of the target stimulus, involving the frontal brain areas, are distinguished in the analyzed interval. Moreover, Fig. 2 reveals that delta and theta bandwidths perform similar connectivity, showing high values at the frontal lobes, where the cognitive functions, as attention and memory, are generated to perform the discrimination process between conditions. Nevertheless, the previous behavior does not appear in the high-frequency bands. alpha and beta, where connectivity values are lower.

3.2 Significant Connections

Lastly, Fig. 3 displays the connections estimated as significant for the studied cognitive task. The blue lines represent the results of the t-test showing the statistical differences between the groups: target and non-target. The connections

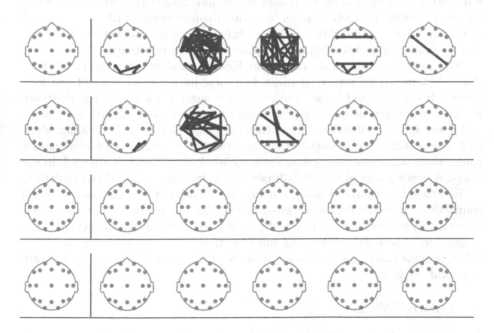

Fig. 3. Interchannel connections selected that are significantly different between the conditions target and non-target; these connections are presented as blue lines at each time interval and are the rejected PLVs in the performed t-test having higher p-value than the defined significant level (0.01). No significant connections are found in Alpha and Beta bands. (Color figure online)

were selected if rejected after the FDR correction ($p < 0.01$). The proposed analysis shows that the most informative neural, according to the connectivity patterns, are within 200 and 600 ms. Consequently, the connectivity patterns mostly appear within the time interval when it is expected that the subject is performing the attentional process and memory work. Moreover, the proposed analysis indicates that the main difference between target and non-target conditions concerning brain connectivity can be found in low-frequency bands, being associated with changes in theta and delta sub-frequency bands and involving connections between the frontal, temporal and parietal channels. These results are congruent with the findings in [6]. Finally, no statistically significant differences are found in the studied high-frequency bands.

4   Conclusions

In this work, we characterize the functional connectivity for the P300 component using the oddball paradigm. The synchronicity assessment is performed by the phase locking value, computing the pairwise relationships between the measured scalp EEG channels. Because there is a meager amount of significant differences in the phase-locking patterns between the triggered stimuli, we investigate the confidence of task-induced changes, relying on the p-value that is implemented as a statistical analysis. This methodology is used as a measure to identify and select the most significant EEG channel-to-channel connections. With the proposed framework we have studied the statistical differences in the connectivity patterns, and we have analyzed the behavior of phase networks in attention tasks.

The results performed on real-world EEG data show that the channel-to-channel connectivity present distinct temporal patterns for each of the four studied frequency bands. Also, the performed analysis indicates that there are substantial differences in connectivity response in the discrimination of target and non-target stimulus during the attention tasks. Moreover, the findings show that it is possible to differentiate the stimulus with a small set of low-frequency connections, and these connections are associated with the active channels in the time-frequency study of the oddball paradigm (frontal, temporal and parietal).

In general, with the proposed study, we found changes in the functional connectivity patterns that are related to the changes in the well studied ERP behavior. Therefore, we describe, in the sense of connectivity, the structure of the target and non-target auditory stimuli responses. From cognitive neuroscience, this technique contributes to the study of cognitive processes with very accurate temporal resolution.

5   Future Work

As a future work, the proposed methodology should be tested in the source space representation based on the EEG signals, facilitating the physiological interpretation of the active connections and regions during the task. Additionally, brain connectivity networks, using the selected connections should be created to implement graph theory measures, providing further features of brain organization.

Acknowledgements. This research is supported by the research project # 36706: "BrainScore: Sistema compositivo, gráfico y sonoro creado a partir del comportamiento frecuencial de las senãles cerebrales", funded by Universidad de Caldas and Universidad Nacional de Colombia.

References

1. Bob, P., Palus, M., Susta, M., Glaslova, K.: EEG phase synchronization in patients with paranoid schizophrenia. Neurosci. Lett. **447**(1), 73–77 (2008)
2. Brázdil, M., Mikl, M., Mareček, R., Krupa, P., Rektor, I.: Effective connectivity in target stimulus processing: a dynamic causal modeling study of visual oddball task. Neuroimage **35**(2), 827–835 (2007)
3. Doesburg, S.M., Emberson, L.L., Rahi, A., Cameron, D., Ward, L.M.: Asynchrony from synchrony: long-range gamma-band neural synchrony accompanies perception of audiovisual speech asynchrony. Exp. Brain Res. **185**(1), 11–20 (2008)
4. Fornito, A., Zalesky, A., Bullmore, E.: Fundamentals of Brain Network Analysis. Academic Press, Cambridge (2016)
5. Handy, T.C.: Brain Signal Analysis: Advances in Neuroelectric and Neuromagnetic Methods. MIT Press, Cambridge (2009)
6. Harper, J., Malone, S.M., Iacono, W.G.: Theta-and delta-band EEG network dynamics during a novelty oddball task. Psychophysiology **54**(11), 1590–1605 (2017)
7. van den Heuvel, M.P., de Lange, S.C., Zalesky, A., Seguin, C., Yeo, B.T., Schmidt, R.: Proportional thresholding in resting-state fMRI functional connectivity networks and consequences for patient-control connectome studies: Issues and recommendations. Neuroimage **152**, 437–449 (2017)
8. Hurtado-Rincón, J.V., Martínez-Vargas, J.D., Rojas-Jaramillo, S., Giraldo, E., Castellanos-Dominguez, G.: Identification of relevant inter-channel EEG connectivity patterns: a kernel-based supervised approach. In: Ascoli, G.A., Hawrylycz, M., Ali, H., Khazanchi, D., Shi, Y. (eds.) BIH 2016. LNCS (LNAI), vol. 9919, pp. 14–23. Springer, Cham (2016). https://doi.org/10.1007/978-3-319-47103-7_2
9. Ingber, L., Nunez, P.L.: Neocortical dynamics at multiple scales: EEG standing waves, statistical mechanics, and physical analogs. Math. Biosci. **229**(2), 160–173 (2011)
10. Inouye, T., Shinosaki, K., Iyama, A., Matsumoto, Y., Toi, S.: Moving potential field of frontal midline theta activity during a mental task. Cogn. Brain Res. **2**(2), 87–92 (1994)
11. Kiat, J.E., Long, D., Belli, R.F.: Attentional responses on an auditory oddball predict false memory susceptibility. Cogn. Affect. Behav. Neurosci., 1–15 (2018)
12. Kozlowska, K., Melkonian, D., Spooner, C.J., Scher, S., Meares, R.: Cortical arousal in children and adolescents with functional neurological symptoms during the auditory oddball task. NeuroImage Clin. **13**, 228–236 (2017)
13. Lachaux, J.P., Rodriguez, E., Martinerie, J., Varela, F.J., et al.: Measuring phase synchrony in brain signals. Hum. Brain Mapp. **8**(4), 194–208 (1999)
14. Lowet, E., Roberts, M.J., Bonizzi, P., Karel, J., De Weerd, P.: Quantifying neural oscillatory synchronization: a comparison between spectral coherence and phase-locking value approaches. PloS one **11**(1), 20 (2016)
15. Luck, S.J.: An Introduction to the Event-Related Potential Technique. MIT press, Cambridge (2014)

16. Nolte, G., Bai, O., Wheaton, L., Mari, Z., Vorbach, S., Hallett, M.: Identifying true brain interaction from EEG data using the imaginary part of coherency. Clin. Neurophysiol. **115**(10), 2292–2307 (2004)
17. Polich, J.: Updating P300: an integrative theory of P3a and P3b. Clin. Neurophysiol. **118**(10), 2128–2148 (2007)
18. Redolar Ripoll, D.: Cognitive Neuroscience. Editorial Panamericana, Madrid, p. 5 (2014)
19. Shim, M., Kim, D.W., Lee, S.H., Im, C.H.: Disruptions in small-world cortical functional connectivity network during an auditory oddball paradigm task in patients with schizophrenia. Schizophr. Res. **156**(2), 197–203 (2014)

Perspective Taking vs Mental Rotation: CSP-Based Single-Trial Analysis for Cognitive Process Disambiguation

Christoforos Christoforou[1,2]([⊠]), Adamantini Hatzipanayioti[3], and Marios Avraamides[4,5]

[1] Division of Computer Science, Mathematics and Science,
St. John's University, New York, NY, USA
christoc@stjohns.edu
[2] Division of Research and Development, R.K.I Leaders Ltd., Larnaca, Cyprus
[3] Max-Planck-Institute for Biological Cybernetics, Tuebingen, Germany
[4] Department of Psychology, University of Cyprus, Nicosia, Cyprus
[5] Research Centre on Interactive Media, Smart Systems,
and Emerging Technologies - RISE, Nicosia, Cyprus

Abstract. Mental Rotation (i.e. the ability to mentally rotate representations of 2D and 3D objects) and egocentric Perspective Taking (i.e. the ability to adopt an imagined spatial perspective) represent the two most well-known and used types of spatial transformation. Yet, these two spatial transformations are conceptually, visually, and mathematically equivalent. Thus, an active debate in the field is whether these two types of spatial transformations are cognitively and neurally distinct or whether they represent different manifestation of the same underlying core mental process. In this study, we utilize a machine learning approach to extract neural activity from electroencephalography (EEG) measures and identify neural differences between mental rotation and perspective taking tasks. Our results provide novel empirical evidence in support of the view that these two types of spatial transformation correspond to district cognitive processes at the neural level. Importantly, the proposed framework provides a novel approach that can facilitate the study of the neural correlates of spatial cognition.

Keywords: EEG · Single-trial · Machine learning · Spatial cognition

1   Introduction

The transformation of spatial relations is a fundamental skill that is inherent for many of the tasks we carry out in the course of our daily lives. Navigating in familiar and unfamiliar environments, avoiding obstacles during locomotion, providing navigation instructions to others, reasoning about how objects and scenes look from perspectives other than the one we occupy physically, all require transforming mentally a spatial memory we have previously stored about that

© Springer Nature Switzerland AG 2018
S. Wang et al. (Eds.): BI 2018, LNAI 11309, pp. 109–118, 2018.
https://doi.org/10.1007/978-3-030-05587-5_11

environment. Spatial transformations are also a core component of many aptitude tests as spatial skills in general are a good predictor for success in Science, Technology, Engineering, and Mathematics (STEM; [9]).

Two specific types of spatial transformation, whose behavioral effects have been thoroughly studied in Cognitive Science, are *Mental Rotation* and *Perspective taking*. In particular, mental rotation is believed to take place by rotating a reference frame that is intrinsic to an external object (i.e., object-centered reference frame) either to the upright or to the orientation of another object, in order to carry out a comparison. On the other hand, perspective taking entails mentally rotating an egocentric reference frame (i.e., a reference frame that is centered on the observer's body and oriented along with their facing direction) rather than an object-centered reference frame. Yet, both spatial transformations are conceptually, visually and mathematically equivalent, and exhibit equivalent behavior outcomes (i.e. their chronometric profiles are modulated by angular disparity [6]). Thus, an open question in the field of spatial cognition is to (i) determine whether these two spatial transformations constitute distinctive cognitive processes at the neural level and (ii) identify differential neural activity to characterize the neural underpinnings of behavioral effects observed under these spatial transformations (i.e. angular disparity effect).

A number of neuroimaging studies using functional magnetic resonance imaging (fMRI) suggest that despite some commonalities, mental rotation and perspective taking exhibit substantial differences in neural activation [5,10,11]. However, results from these studies rarely converge; that is, each study seems to paint a different picture (i.e., different brain areas are active and to a different extent). Thus, differences in neural measures found across the two transformations may still have been caused by methodological differences, e.g., different stimuli, different response requirements. Hence, one cannot conclude with certainty that the two types of spatial transformations are indeed distinct in terms of the underlying mental operations.

Multivariate single-trial analysis of neurophysiological measurements (such as EEG; Electroencephalography) provides a promising framework to isolate differential or congruent neural activity among cognitive processes and explore their links to behavioral observations. For example, a discriminant-based single-trial analysis was proposed in [8] to isolate neural measurements of perceptual decision making. A correlation-based single-trials analysis was proposed in [2] to detect neural activity associated with behavioral measurement of the stimulus-modality effect observed in cognitive treatment protocols for Traumatic-Brain Injury. Moreover, a multi-multivariate analysis on EEG measurement during video viewing was proposed to predict the preferential decision making of movie-goers to video [4]. In the context of brain-computer interfaces, multivariate single-trial analysis methods have been used extensively, for example, in detecting differential cognitive states of imagined limb movement [1], and in human-robot tele-operations [3]. However, to the best of our knowledge, such framework has not been explored in the context of spatial cognition.

To further examine the possibility of dissociation between mental rotation and perspective taking and to detect neural activity differential to the two conditions, in the current study we adopt a different approach from that of past studies. First, to avoid any confounds regarding the stimuli used or response execution, we have used identical displays for the two tasks and we avoid any type of response. Second, to compare neural activity across the two types of transformation we use a machine learning approach to extract neural activity from EEG measures. This novel approach identifies spatial projections that optimally isolate patterns of neural activity that differentiate the two conditions and could serve as indicators to subsequent studies to establish the neural correlates of behavioral findings in spatial cognition; such as, for example, the angular disparity effect.

2 Materials and Methods

2.1 Experiment Setup

We deployed our experimental paradigm as part of a broader study aiming to identify the neural correlates of the angular disparity effect observed in spatial perspective taking. For completeness, we provide a brief overview of the overall experiment setup and discuss in more detail the sections of the methods that relate to our current analysis.

The overall experiment involves two phases; a learning phase and a testing phase. During the learning phase, participants were immersed in a virtual environment depicting a square room with 8 objects placed at 45° intervals around the standpoint in the center of the room. The environment was created using Google Sketchup (Google Inc) and was displayed in VR using the Vizard VR Toolkit (Worldviz Inc). Participants viewed the array in a Virtual Reality Head-Mounted-Display and were asked to memorize the position of each object. Their memory was informally evaluated before the conclusion of learning phase by asking them to point with their arm to each object after all objects were hidden from view. Subsequently, in the testing phase participants were fitted with an active-electrode EEG cap and carried out three tasks: (i) an eye-calibration task, (ii) a short mental rotation and perspective taking task and, (iii) a longer perspective taking task that entailed localizing objects from imagined perspectives. In this study, we analyze the data from the mental rotation and perspective taking paradigm (ii above) and utilize data from the eye-calibration session (i above) to remove ocular artifacts. We describe these tasks in more detail below.

Participants. A total of 20 participants were recruited for the current study. Ages ranged from 19 to 24 years with the median age at 21 years. Participants received a small monetary compensation for their participation in the study. Informed consent was obtained from all participants in accordance with the international guidelines for research conduct and ethics.

Eye-Calibration Paradigm. Prior to the main experimental tasks, each participant performed a short eye-movement calibration task providing data for subsequent ocular artifact correction (see pre-processing section below). In this task, the participant was first asked to blink repeatedly for 10 s, and then, to make several horizontal and vertical saccades by following a fixation cross that moved on the screen from left to right for horizontal saccades and from top to bottom for vertical saccades. EEG data were recorded during the calibration session and accurate timings of these ocular tasks were included in the signal through the use of a trigger channel.

Mental Rotation vs Perspective Taking Session. During the "mental rotation vs perspective taking" session, participants were asked to imagine carrying out mental rotation and perspective taking tasks, over multiple trials. On each trial, participants were presented with a static image illustrating a 3D object and were instructed to either imagine the object rotating around its axis (i.e. to carry a mental rotation) or to imagine themselves walking around the object and inspecting it from every angle (i.e. to take an imagined perspective). Participants were instructed to maintain the imagined state for a period of 30 s, after which they were prompted to disengage from the activity, and the next trial begun. Each participant performed a total of 16 trials, 8 for each type of spatial transformation.

EEG Data Acquisition. EEG data were acquired continuously during the testing phase of the experiment using a Biosemi Active Two system (BioSemi, Amsterdam, Netherlands). Recordings were made with 64 active EEG electrodes positioned according the Biosemi's extended version of the 10/20 international system. In addition, Electrooculogram (EOG) signals were recorded from 8 external channels. Data were sampled at 512 Hz and the DC offset of all sensors was kept below 20 μV.

2.2   EEG Data Pre-processing

All pre-processing and data analysis were performed using custom MATLAB code (Mathworks Inc., Natick, MA, USA, MATLAB). A software-based 0.5 Hz high-pass filter was used to remove DC drifts, and a 50 Hz notch filter was used to minimize power-line interference. EEG and EOG data recorded during the calibration session were used to estimate spatial projections that captured the three types of ocular artifacts (eye-blinks, horizontal saccades, and vertical saccades). Subsequently, activity captured by these components was removed from the EEG recordings obtained during the "mental-rotation vs perspective taking" session using the method described in [7].

Dataset Definition. Two datasets were forked from the pre-processed EEG data by applying a band-pass filter on selected frequency bands. In particular, the first dataset was obtained by applying a band-pass filter in the alpha-band range (8 Hz–13 Hz) and the second by applying a band-pass filter in the lower beta-band range (13 Hz–20 Hz). Each dataset was then epoched into 16 segments (one for each imagined activity), ranging from 14 s prior to the end of the imagined activity to the end of that activity. Each segment was further split into fourteen non-overlapping, one-second windows. Each window was assigned a label indicating whether it corresponded to the "mental rotation" or the "imagined perspective taking" condition. The two resulting datasets are represented by the sets $\mathcal{D}^{(\alpha)}$ and $\mathcal{D}^{(\beta)}$ that are defined as follows:

$$\mathcal{D}^{(\alpha)} = \{\mathbf{X}_n^\alpha, y_n\}_{n=1}^N$$
$$\mathcal{D}^{(\beta)} = \{\mathbf{X}_n^\beta, y_n\}_{n=1}^N$$

where the superscript α and β indicate the alpha- and beta- band filtered data respectively, $\mathbf{X} \in \mathbb{R}^{D \times T}$ corresponds to a single EEG data trials of D channels and T temporal samples, N denotes the total number of trials, and $y \in \{-1, +1\}$ indicates the condition each trial is associated with (i.e. -1 corresponds to "Mental Rotation" and $+1$ denotes a "Perspective taking". In our specific dataset $D = 64, T = 512, N = 224$.

2.3 CSP-Based Single-Trial Analysis

Problem Setting. We consider a binary classification problem where each class corresponds to one of the two spatial transformations, mental rotation and perspective taking, and each observation correspond to a short time-window of EEG measurements. Let $y \in \{-1, +1\}$ be the class label and $\mathbf{X} \in \mathbb{R}^{D \times T}$ the band-pass processed EEG signal[1]. The classification problem can then be defined as follows: Given a set of training observation $\mathcal{D}^{(f)} = \{\mathbf{X}_n^f, y_n\}_{n=1}^N$, the task is to predict the class label y of an unobserved trial $\mathbf{X}$[2].

Common Spatial Pattern. In the context of brain-computer interfacing, Common Spatial Patterns (CSP) have been proven a powerful tool in classifying imaginary motor movements. In this study, we explore the use of CSP as a tool to extract discriminant features for the two cognitive processes under study. Intuitively, CSP learns the set of spatial projections of the EEG signal (i.e. weighted average across channels) that maximize the ratio of variance (i.e. power) in the spatially filtered signals of the two classes. This is achieved by the

---

[1] For clarity, here we assume that the signal X is already pre-processed and band-passed filter to either the alpha- or beta-band (as described in Sect. 2.2), and each trial is centered and scaled.

[2] Here $f \in \{\alpha, \beta\}$ indicates the band-pass filtered applied to the data during preprocessing.

simultaneous diagonalization of the covariance matrices corresponding to the two classes. Technically, let $\Sigma^{(+)}$ and $\Sigma^{(-)}$ be the covariance matrix of condition $y = +1$ and $y = -1$ respectively, defined as:

$$\Sigma^{(+)} = \frac{1}{|\mathcal{N}^{(+)}|} \sum_{i \in \mathcal{N}^{(+)}} \mathbf{X}_i^\top \mathbf{X}_i \qquad \Sigma^{(-)} = \frac{1}{|\mathcal{N}^{(-)}|} \sum_{i \in \mathcal{N}^{(-)}} \mathbf{X}_i^\top \mathbf{X}_i$$

where $\mathcal{N}^{(+)}$ and $\mathcal{N}^{(-)}$ are the set of trial indices that belong to class $y = +1$ and $y = -1$ respectively. The simultaneous diagononalization is then given by the solution of the generalized eigenvalue problem:

$$\Sigma^{(+)}\mathbf{w} = \lambda \Sigma^{(-)}\mathbf{w}$$

where λ and $\mathbf{w} \in \mathbb{R}^D$ are the eigenvalue and eigenvector of the order pair $(\Sigma^{(+)}, \Sigma^{(-)})$. We note that for any given eigenvector, eigenvalue pair $(\lambda_i, \mathbf{w}_i)$ the eigenvalue is given by $\lambda = \frac{\mathbf{w}^\top \Sigma^{(+)} \mathbf{w}_i}{\mathbf{w}^\top \Sigma^{(+)} \mathbf{w}_i}$. Thus, the eigenvalue captures the ratio between the variance of the two classes, once projected onto its corresponding eigenvector. For a more in depth treatment of CSP we refer the reader to the work of Blankertz et al. [1].

Features and Classification. In our study, we use the eigenvectors with the largest and smallest eigenvalue (denoted by $\mathbf{w}^{(max)}$ and $\mathbf{w}^{(min)}$, respectively), as spatial projections to transform each EEG trial. The former, defines the spatial filter that captures the maximum ratio of power under the first condition (i.e. $y = +1$), and the latter, the spatial projection with the maximal ratio of power under the second condition (i.e $y = -1$). Thus, given an EEG trail $\mathbf{X}_n$ the feature vector $\mathbf{x}_n$ is two dimensional vector given by:

$$\mathbf{x}_n = \mathbf{W}^\top \mathbf{X}_n \tag{1}$$

where $\mathbf{W} = [\mathbf{w}^{(max)}, \mathbf{w}^{(min)}]$. A logistic regression classifier is trained on the resulting feature vector.

2.4   Performance Metrics and Statistical Analysis

We report the five-fold cross-validation performance of the classifier in terms of the area under the *Receiver-operating characteristic* curve (AUC). Statistical significance of the AUC score for each dataset is obtained using permutation test (1000 permutations with randomized labels on each dataset). For group level comparisons, statistical significance is assessed using the Wilcoxon signed-rank test.

3   Results

The purpose of the study was to assess whether the single-trial analysis could isolate differential neural-activity between the two mental states ("mental rotation" and "imagined perspective taking"), and thus to provide evidence for their

Table 1. Classification performance across all participants and datasets.

Subjects	AUC score (alpha)	AUC score (beta)
1	0.64*	0.74*
2	0.83*	0.67*
3	0.66*	0.80*
4	0.68*	0.82*
5	0.65*	0.80*
6	0.78*	0.95*
7	0.56	0.51
8	0.71*	0.64*
9	0.75*	0.95*
10	0.53	0.55
11	0.70*	0.89*
12	0.75*	0.73*
13	0.54	0.79*
14	0.98*	0.97*
15	0.98*	1.00*
16	0.56	0.65*
17	0.64*	0.73*
18	0.56	0.76*
mean	0.7 ± 0.13	0.78 ± 0.14

dissociation in terms of the core mental processes involved. Here we summarize the results on the classification performance of single-trial analysis on data collected from all participants using the two band-pass datasets.

Table 1 summarizes the classification performance in terms of the area under ROC curve (AUC) for each participant and for each dataset. The p-values were calculated based on the distribution of AUC scores under the null hypothesis (i.e. the observation for the two condition come from are the same) using the permutation test. The mean AUC score across all participants was 0.70 ± 0.13 and 0.78 ± 0.14 for the alpha-band and beta-band dataset respectively.

Figure 2 shows the histogram of AUC scores of all participants relative to the distribution of AUC scores under the null hypothesis, for both datasets. The 99% significance AUC score level was estimated to 0.61 for both datasets. A Wilcoxon signed-rank test indicated that the median AUC scores on both the alpha- and beta- band dataset were statistically higher than the AUC 99% significant level threshold of the null hypothesis, $Z = 32, p < 0.02, Z = 8, p < 0.0001$, respectively.

The Receiver Operating Characteristic (ROC) curves that illustrate the performance classifier on the two datasets are shown in Fig. 1. Each ROC curve plots, for each subject, the true positive rate against the false positive rate of

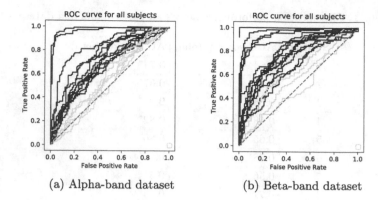

(a) Alpha-band dataset   (b) Beta-band dataset

Fig. 1. Receiver Operating Characteristic (ROC) curves that illustrates the performance of the classifier on the two datasets for each participant. Light-gray indicate ROC curves whose AUC score did not reach statistically significant level. The diagonal, dashed line shows ROC curve of a random classifer (i.e. guessing).

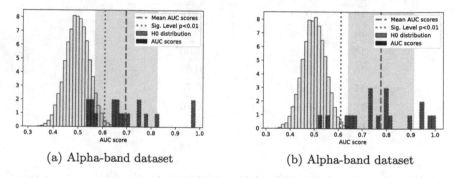

(a) Alpha-band dataset   (b) Alpha-band dataset

Fig. 2. The light-blue histogram shows the distribution of AUC scores, under the null hypothesis. The dark-bars show the histogram of AUC scores of all participants. The doted vertical line, marks the 0.99 significant level under the null hypothesis. The dashed vertical line denotes the mean AUC score across all participants. The shaded-band around the dashed line illustrates the region that is one standard deviation around the mean. The left figure, shows analysis results from the alpha-band datasets and the right figure shows results on the beta-band dataset (Color figure online)

the classifier at different threshold points. ROC curves whose AUC score is significantly higher than random performance (i.e. $p < 0.01$) are shown in dark black color while ROC curves whose AUC score is not significantly higher than random performance are drawn in light gray.

A second aim of this study was to explore the characteristics of neural-activity that differentiates among the two conditions. Figure 3 compares the classification performance of single-trial analysis, in terms of AUC scores, over the two datasets. A Wilcoxon signed-rank test indicated that median AUC scores on the

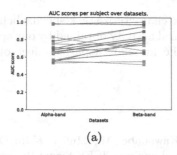 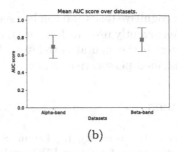

(a)   (b)

Fig. 3. Variation of AUC scores between the two datasets; per participant (left panel) and on average (eight figure). Error bars indicate mark one standard deviation around the mean.

beta-band dataset were statistically higher than the AUC scores of the alpha-band dataset, $Z = 28.00, p < 0.012$.

4   Discussion and Conclusion

In this paper, we propose a single-trial analysis approach to identify differential neural activity between two – conceptually equivalent- cognitive tasks, namely, mental rotation and perspective taking, in order to determine whether they can be considered distinct spatial transformations that rely on different core mental processes. In particular, we measured neural activity from participants while engaging in either mental rotation or perspective taking and learned spatial filters to isolated differential neural activity. We then used the overall power of the spatially projected signals to infer the underlying cognitive task using a logistic regression classifier. The degree to which the classifier correctly inferred the underling cognitive task served as an indicator of the level to which the two cognitive tasks engaged different neural processes.

A key finding of this study is novel empirical evidence in support of the hypothesis that Mental Rotation and Perspective Taking indeed arise from different neural processes. Our results show that the spatially filtered neural activity in the alpha- and beta-bands carry discriminant information about the activation of the two cognitive tasks. Indeed, classification accuracy on both alpha- and beta-band signals is significantly higher than random performance. Moreover, the classification performance on the beta-band signals ($AUC : 0.78$) is significantly higher than the classification performance on the alpha-band signals ($AUC : 0.70$). This finding suggests that beta-band likely carries additional discriminant information.

An important contribution of our study is that it provides a methodological approach to facilitate research on the neural underpinnings of spatial tasks. By isolating differential neural activity, our approach increases the overall signal-to-noise ratio allowing for the identification of more task-relevant metrics. Our approach can therefore be used as a pre-processing step to isolate differential activity in cognitive tasks and can be used to characterize task-specific behavioral effects. We currently use the differential neural activity obtained by our approach to characterize the neural correlates of the angular disparity effect observed during imagined perspective taking.

References

1. Blankertz, B., Tomioka, R., Lemm, S., Kawanabe, M., Muller, K.R.: Optimizing spatial filters for robust EEG single-trial analysis. IEEE Signal Process. Mag. **25**(1), 41–56 (2008)
2. Christoforou, C., Constantinidou, F., Shoshilou, P., Simos, P.: Single-trial linear correlation analysis: application to characterization of stimulus modality effects. Frontiers Comput. Neurosci. **7**, 15 (2013)
3. Christoforou, C., Mavridis, N., Machado, E.L., Spanoudis, G.: Android teleoperation through brain-computer interfacing: a real-world demo with non-expert users. In: IRIS2010, Nagoya, Japan, pp. 294–299 (2010)
4. Christoforou, C., Papadopoulos, T.C., Constantinidou, F., Theodorou, M.: Your brain on the movies: a computational approach for predicting box-office performance from viewer's brain responses to movie trailers. Frontiers Neuroinform. **11**, 72 (2017)
5. Keehner, M., Guerin, S.A., Miller, M.B., Turk, D.J., Hegarty, M.: Modulation of neural activity by angle rotation during imagined spatial transformations. Neuroimage. **33**, 391–398 (2006). https://doi.org/10.1016/j.neuroimage.2006.06.043
6. Kozhevnikov, M., Motes, M., Rasch, B., Blajenkova, O.: Perspective-taking vs. mental rotation transformations and how they predict spatial navigation performance. Appl. Cogn. Psychol. **20**, 397–417 (2006)
7. Parra, L., Spence, C., Gerson, A., Sajda, P.: Recipes for the linear analysis of EEG. Neuroimage **28**(2), 326–41 (2005). https://doi.org/10.1109/MSP.2008.4408441
8. Philiastides, M.G., Sajda, P.: Temporal characterization of the neural correlates of perceptual decision making in the human brain. Cereb. Cortex **16**, 509–518 (2005). https://doi.org/10.1093/cercor/bhi130
9. Wai, J., Lubinski, D., Benbow, C.: Spatial ability for stem domains: aligning over fifty years of cumulative psychological knowledge solidifies its importance. J. Educ. Psychol. **101**, 817–835 (2009)
10. Wraga, M., Shephard, J., Church, J., Inati, S., Kosslyn, S.: Imagined rotations of self versus objects: an fMRI study. Neuropsychologia **43**(5), 1351–61 (2005). https://doi.org/10.1016/j.neuropsychologia.2004.11.028
11. Zacks, J.M., Vettel, J.M., Michelon, P.: Imagined viewer and object rotations dissociated with event-related fMRI. J. Cognit. Neurosci. **15**, 1002–1018 (2003). https://doi.org/10.1162/089892903770007399

Using the Partial Directed Coherence to Understand Brain Functional Connectivity During Movement Imagery Tasks

Myriam Alanis-Espinosa(✉) and David Gutiérrez(✉)

Center for Research and Advanced Studies at Monterrey, 66600 Apodaca, Mexico
myriam.alanis@cinvestav.mx, dgtz@ieee.org
http://www.monterrey.cinvestav.mx/

Abstract. We propose to use the partial directed coherence (PDC) to analyze the coupling between pairs of electroencephalographic (EEG) measurements during movement imagery tasks, as well as the directionality of such coupling. For this, we consider the multivariate autoregressive model of the signals from a selection of eleven EEG channels that are assumed as a fully-connected measurement network. Then, we aim to find differences in connectivity patterns between motor imagery and resting state that arise in a brain-computer interface (BCI) system with visual feedback that controls the movement of a robot. Our preliminary results show that it is possible to relate the changes in the magnitude of the PDC to different connectivity patterns in the measurement network we have considered, and those changes are in agreement with brain functional connectivity that has been reported in other studies based mainly in magnetic resonance imaging.

Keywords: Brain-computer interfaces · Partial directed coherence
Functional connectivity

1 Introduction

A brain-computer interface (BCI) is a communication system that does not depend on peripheral nerves and muscles [13]. The primary goal of a BCI system is to enable basic communication to people that are unable to communicate due to amyotrophic lateral sclerosis (ALS), spine injury, cerebral palsy, among others that affect the path of the brain to control muscles. This can be achieved with non-invasive data-acquisition methods such as electroencephalography (EEG). One of the experimental paradigms used to control BCIs is motor imagery (MI), defined as a mental process by which a subject imagines a specific motor action.

Supported by the Mexican Council for Science and Technology (Conacyt) through Grant 220145.

S. Wang et al. (Eds.): BI 2018, LNAI 11309, pp. 119–128, 2018.
https://doi.org/10.1007/978-3-030-05587-5_12

Besides the control of a BCI, in neuroscience is of great interest the underlying interactions between different brain regions and whether they are causally connected.

Besides the main goal of using BCI in the context of control systems, great efforts are being made to explore the use of this tool in order to enhance our knowledge about brain function. Specifically, in regards to brain functional connectivity, different methods have been used together with BCI in order to relate the concept of *signal coupling* with the connectivity of different brain events. Such is the case of the coherence [12], or the partial directed coherence (PDC) [5] which allows us to analyze the influence or coupling exerted by a signal, in the frequency domain, on another one.

In this work, we are interested to gain further understanding about the functional connectivity that arises in the process of MI for BCI applications. Similar to the analysis proposed in [5], here we propose to use the PDC to analyze both the coupling between EEG measurements, as well as their directionality. Yet, in this paper we consider a fully-connected EEG sensor network comprised by the simultaneous measurements of eleven EEG channels, placed over the frontoparietal area which have already been considered as most relevant when studying motor tasks [6]. Then, we aim to compare the changes in connectivity of this complex network for the case of MI and resting states. Furthermore, we are interested to analyze different connectivity patterns that are related to different operational modes, specifically those related to the visual feedback provided to the users of a BCI system that controls the movement of a robot.

Based on these ideas, this paper is organized as follows: Sect. 2 presents the experimental design; Sect. 3 shows the comparison of the proposed PDC-based analysis during MI and resting state for real EEG data; in Sect. 4 results and future work are discussed.

2   Methods

The experimental design consists of two stages, in a similar fashion as in [8]. The first stage is the *traditional* BCI training (2D, monitor-based), where the subject performs imaginary movements according to the visual cues presented without feedback. The second stage is the BCI control task, which consist in providing visual feedback of the movements of the robot according to the cues presented.

2.1   Traditional BCI Training

In this stage, the subject begins with a BCI screening process from which user-specific parameters are extracted. The subject is required to perform either imaginary movements or to remain in resting state in response to the visual cue presented on a computer monitor while sitting on a chair. The cue is in the form of a red arrow pointing either left, right, upside and downside indicating whether the subject has to imagine closing and opening either the left hand, right hand, both hands or moving both feet, respectively. Each trial starts with a fixation cross for 3 s where the subject has to try to be with a neutral mind or rest followed by the visual cue presented during 4 s. Each trial has a random duration interval of 2.1 to 2.5 s between them to avoid adaptation [4]. During this interval the subject remains at rest. This sequence is shown in Fig. 1. Additionally, the subject has five minutes of rest between runs.

Forty EEG trials (ten for each class) are recorded in each of five runs. These EEG trials are used as *calibration* recordings to build a classifier for discriminating two different mental tasks. The task that shows highest separability versus resting state is used as the user-specific input for the BCI control task system in the online experiments.

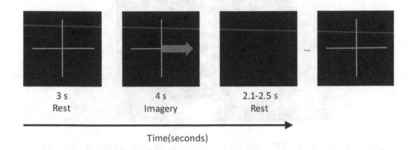

Fig. 1. Traditional BCI training sequence.

2.2   BCI Control Task

In this stage, we used the NAO humanoid robot as the device the BCI system is to control. The NAO robot is used mainly because of its capability of wireless communication and feasibility to communicate with the open source software platform OpenViBE, which is widely used for BCI development [11]. The NAO robot is placed in a hallway outside the experimental room. A Hero 4 camera streams video about the NAO robot and it is played on a tablet in front of the subject, as shown in Fig. 2. The main goal of the subject is to control the movement of the NAO robot with a personalized classifier. The subject receives visual feedback to help him/her in the modulation of the mental tasks in order to control the NAO robot.

The sequence of the experiment is shown in Fig. 3. At the beginning of the experiment, the subject remains in resting state for 15 s. Then, the following sequence is displayed in the screen: it starts with a green cross, followed by a black screen or a red arrow, and finally the letters FB (for *feedback*) appear. Each different screen appears for four seconds with a random time between each trial from 100 to 500 ms with a black screen. During the FB screen, the subject receives feedback looking at the screen of the tablet to see if the NAO robot moved or not according to the cue. When a MI task is detected, the robot walks a few steps forward, otherwise, the robot remains without change when resting state is detected. The subject is instructed to avoid blinking during the MI task to minimize noise in EEG data. Additionally, the subject has five minutes of rest between runs. The accuracy is recorded for each cue, which corresponds to the number of times that the subject correctly controlled the movement of the robot, as well as the number of times the robot halted during the subject's resting state.

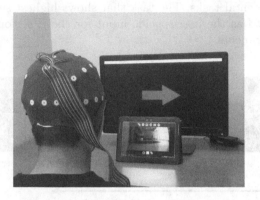

Fig. 2. Setup of the BCI control system at the experimental room.

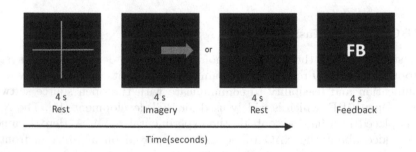

Fig. 3. BCI control task sequence.

2.3 EEG Data Acquisition and Preprocessing

The EEG signals are acquired with the TMSi MOBITA EEG amplifier over thirty-two electrodes uniformly distributed on scalp according to the international 10–20 system with ground on AFz. Impedance of all electrodes are kept below $5\,k\Omega$. Recordings are completed during daytime in a noise free and normally lighted room.

Signals are recorded at 1000 Hz, bandpass filtered with a zero-phase fourth-order Butterworth between 1 to 100 Hz band and a notch filter to remove artifact caused by electrical power lines in 60 Hz. Thereafter, EEG filtered signals are analyzed with BCI2000 offline tools to get a personalized feature for BCI control. This is done by the calculation of the r^2 values for all electrodes within 0–70 Hz for two cognitive states. In this way, the channels and frequencies with higher r^2 values are selected as features to train the classifier. More details on this process can be found at http://www.bci2000.org/mediawiki/index.php/User_Tutorial: Mu_Rhythm_BCI_Tutorial.

2.4   Feature Extraction and Classification

A Laplacian filter is implemented to each channel to increase the signal-to-noise ratio by enhancing the control signal and reducing noise [9]. This filter acts as a high-pass spatial filter that accentuates localized activity and reduces more diffuse activity. Thereafter the signals corresponding to MI and rest are extracted. The logarithmic band power is calculated over a one-second window with an overlap with the next one every 62.5 ms. The input of the classifier is a subset of these features.

A linear discriminant analysis (LDA) classifier is used to discriminate whether the class is a MI task or rest state. It receives the extracted features labeled by class from at least fifty trials each. LDA is a technique that finds the best combination of features that separate two or more types of classes [7]. The cross-validation of the classifier is made by a K-fold test of four partitions obtaining an accuracy of more than 70% for each class. Figure 4 shows an example of a classifier scenario trainer implemented in OpenViBE. This scenario produces a configuration file used for the BCI control task stage.

2.5   Partial Directed Coherence

The metric implemented to measure the connectivity between channels is the PDC [1], which is based on the Granger causality for the frequency domain which has been used to identify the direction of information flow and to quantify its strength. It consists in the implementation of a multivariate autoregressive model (MVAR) with a defined number of channels. In our case, bidirectional PDC is calculated between the EEG channels FP1, FP2, FC3, FCz, FC4, C3, Cz, C4, CP3, CPz, CP4, in a multivariate sense, which in total makes 110 directions. For each direction, the maximum PDC value is obtained for each trial over the α (8–12 Hz) and β (13–30 Hz) frequency bands. The time segment considered for PDC analysis is from 1 to 3 s after the cue is presented.

In each direction for a pair-of-channels (POCs), differences between resting state and MI are tested using the Wilcoxon rank-sum test. The null hypothesis is rejected with $p > 0.05$. If a channel pair direction showed differences, then it is considered to be significant. Once the significant channel pair directions are determined, the median over the trials for each of the frequency bands is calculated.

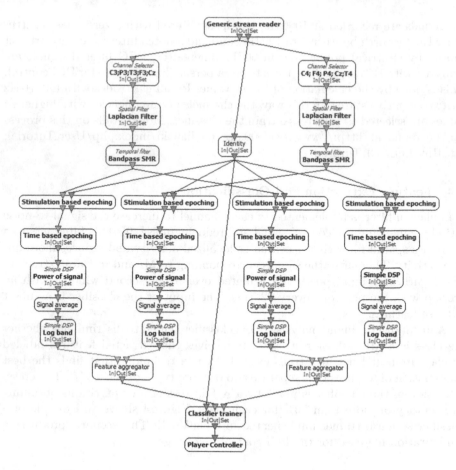

Fig. 4. Classifier scenario trainer implemented in OpenViBE.

The median value of the PDC is used to divide the POCs into three categories as in [10] but with different thresholds: POCs with *low* coupling have an indicator value below than 0.2, POCs with *medium* coupling have an indicator value between 0.2 and 0.6, and POCs with *high* coupling have an indicator value over 0.6.

3   Results

As proof-of-concept, we show the results for one of the subjects we have analyzed so far with the proposed methodology. The analysis was done only using the trials of resting state and MI that were correctly classified while controlling the BCI. First, we took the significant median PDC values that reached medium and high levels of coupling. Next, we considered only the 30% greatest values of the PDC in resting state and MI for each band. To illustrate this analysis,

Fig. 5 shows the PDC for each band, where the left colorbar represents the sum of all significant PDC values that were coupled to that channel, while the right colorbar corresponds to the value of the PDC for each coupling. The width of the arrow between electrodes represents the strength of the connection. Furthermore, Fig. 6 shows the connections that either increased or decreased from resting state to MI. Next, we discuss in further detail the results for each of the brain rhythms we analyzed.

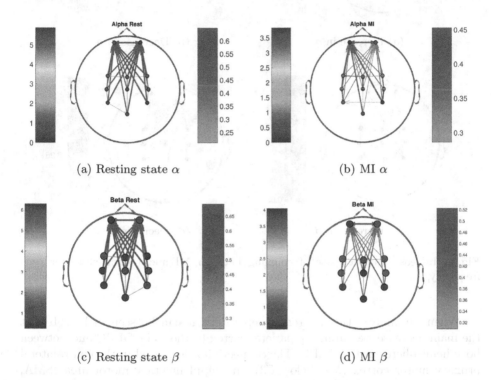

(a) Resting state α (b) MI α

(c) Resting state β (d) MI β

Fig. 5. Coupling between different channels for each frequency band during MI and resting state.

3.1 Alpha Band Analysis

For the resting state, the maximum PDC value is 0.6485 and it decreased to 0.4428 when the subject performed MI of the right hand (see Fig. 5a and b). We can identify that the information flow in resting state was mainly from the inferior parietal lobule (IPL, mainly covered by CP4 and CP3 channels) to the frontal lobe at the dorsolateral prefrontal cortex (DLPC) which is in agreement with the activation of the default mode network (DMN) [2]. From these signals, we may identify the right DLPC (below channel FP2) as an important sink. In the case of MI we can see that the most important sinks were in the DLPC (below FP1 and FP2), and the premotor dorsal area (PMd, below FC4) ipsilateral to MI.

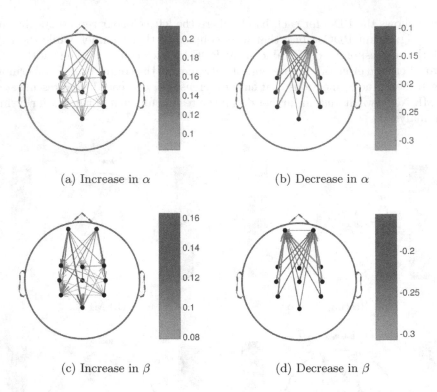

(a) Increase in α (b) Decrease in α

(c) Increase in β (d) Decrease in β

Fig. 6. Increase and decrease of coupling between MI and resting state for each frequency band.

When we analyze the differences separately, it can be seen in Fig. 6b that the main decrease was from the parietal cortex to the right DLPC and between both hemispheres at the DLPC. The connectivity decreased in the contralateral primary motor cortex (M1, below C3), the supplementary motor area (SMA, below FCz) with the DLPC. This suggests that the information flow change from the frontal area to parietal area, which may be a reflection of the frontoparietal attention network (FPAN). The main connectivity changes were in the M1 and SMA. The main increases were between the IPL to the M1 (with coupling CP4→C4 and CP3→C3). Interestingly, there was an increase from the SMA to bilateral PMd, and an increase from contralateral PMd to SMA as seen in [3].

3.2 Beta Band Analysis

For the resting state the maximum PDC value was 0.6911 and it decreased to 0.5222 when the subject performed MI of the right hand. Furthermore, the information flow went from the parietal lobe to the frontal lobe connecting them through the primary cortex (M1), which is in agreement with the DMN.

It can be seen that the most important sink was DLPF where the connectivity from the other regions was directed to this area. Finally, we noted an interesting interhemispheric bidirectional connectivity in DLPC (between channels FP1 and FP2).

In the case of MI, the contralateral sensorimotor area of MI (below C3) can be identified as an important source because there were notable flows outgoing to the frontal lobule (below FP1, FP2, CP3, C4 and FC4), and incoming flows from PM and IPL (below channels FC3 and CP3), contralateral to MI.

We can identify a notable decrease from the ingoing links of the frontal lobe of the right hemisphere(below FP2). We can observe an increase in connectivity from the frontal lobe all over to the parietal lobule. In bilateral M1 is where more changes happened between MI and resting state. The interhemispheric connectivity increased in both directions for the premotor cortex and IPL (FC3$\leftrightarrow$CP4 and FC4$\leftrightarrow$CP3). We have also noted an influence to SMA from the contralateral IPL and PMd, as reported in [3]. Finally, we can observe that the maximum value during MI task was in β rhythm. This was expected due to the fact that this is the frequency domain that corresponds to brain activities linked to movement imagination.

4 Conclusions

In this work we proposed a PDC-based analysis framework of the coupling between EEG measurements, as well as the directionality of such coupling, that has the potential to provide further understanding of the brain functional connectivity in BCI. We compared the changes in signal coupling of a fully-connected EEG sensor network between MI and resting state only for the cases where the subject could have the control of the robot through the BCI. Under these circumstances, different regions were found to have changes in coupling in α and β bands, mainly related to the DMN and FPAN in resting state and MI, respectively. Additionally, we found that the interhemispheric coupling between DLPC decreased from the resting state to MI, and the information flow increased from DLPC to the parietal cortex.

Here, as proof-of-concept, we presented the applicability of our method in real EEG measurements from a BCI system operated by one subject. Our preliminary results show great coincidence with other brain functional connectivity studies, mainly based in magnetic resonance imaging. Nevertheless, our future work will further analyze and validate our findings with data from more subjects. This will also allow to explore the possibility of finding connectivity patterns in the MI and resting state that are related to the visual feedback provided to the users of a BCI system.

References

1. Baccala, L., Sameshima, K.: Partial directed coherence: a new concept in neural structure determination. Biol. Cybern. **84**, 463–474 (2001)
2. Biazoli, C.E., et al.: Application of partial directed coherence to the analysis of resting-state EEG-fMRI data. Brain Connect. **3**(6), 563–568 (2013)
3. Chen, H., Yang, Q., Liao, W., Gong, Q., Shen, S.: Evaluation of the effective connectivity of supplementary motor areas during motor imagery using Granger causality mapping. NeuroImage **47**(4), 1844–1853 (2009)
4. Friedman, D., Leeb, R., Dikovsky, L., Reiner, M., Pfurtscheller, G., Slater, M.: Controlling a virtual body by thought in a highly-immersive virtual environment - a case study in using a brain-computer interface in a virtual-reality cave-like system (2007)
5. Gaxiola-Tirado, J.A., Salazar-Varas, R., Gutiérrez, D.: Using the partial directed coherence to assess functional connectivity in electroencephalography data for brain-computer interfaces. IEEE Trans. Cogn. Dev. Syst. **10**(3), 776–783 (2018)
6. Hanakawa, T., Dimyan, M.A., Hallet, M.: Motor planning, imagery, and execution in the distributed motor network: a time-course study with functional MRI. Cereb. Cortex (New York, NY) **18**(12), 2775–2788 (2008)
7. Kantardzic, M.: Data Mining: Concepts, Models, Methods and Algorithms. Wiley, New York (2002)
8. Leeb, R., Tonin, L., Rohm, M., Desideri, L., Carlson, T., Millan, J.D.R.: Towards independence: a BCI telepresence robot for people with severe motor disabilities. Proc. IEEE **103**(6), 969–982 (2015)
9. McFarland, D.J., McCane, L.M., David, S.V., Wolpaw, J.R.: Spatial filter selection for EEG-based communication. Electroencephalogr. Clin. Neurophysiol. **103**(3), 386–394 (1997)
10. Pasarica, A., Eva, O.D., Tarniceriu, D.: Analysis of EEG channel coupling for motor imagery applications. In: 2017 International Symposium on Signals, Circuits and Systems (ISSCS), pp. 1–4. IEEE (2017)
11. Renard, Y., et al.: Openvibe: an open-source software platform to design, test, and use brain-computer interfaces in real and virtual environments. Presence Teleoper. Virtual Environ. **19**(1), 35–53 (2010)
12. Salazar-Varas, R., Gutiérrez, D.: An optimized feature selection and classification method for using electroencephalographic coherence in brain-computer interfaces. Biomed. Signal Process. Control. **18**, 11–18 (2015)
13. Wolpaw, J.R., et al.: Brain-computer interface technology: a review of the first international meeting. IEEE Trans. Rehabil. Eng. **8**(2), 164–173 (2000)

Combining fMRI Data and Neural Networks to Quantify Contextual Effects in the Brain

Nora Aguirre-Celis[1,2(✉)] and Risto Miikkulainen[2]

[1] ITESM, E. Garza Sada 2501, Monterrey, NL 64840, Mexico
naguirre@cs.utexas.edu
[2] The University of Texas at Austin, 2317 Speedway, Austin, TX 78712, USA
{naguirre,risto}@cs.utexas.edu

Abstract. Does word meaning change according to the context? Although this hypothesis has existed for a long time, only recently it has become possible to test it based on neuroimaging. Embodiment theories of knowledge representation suggest that word meaning consist of a collection of attributes defined in terms of various neural systems. This approach represents an unlimited number of objects through weighted attributes and the weights may change in context. This paper aims at quantifying such dynamic meanings using computational modeling. A neural network is trained with backpropagation to map attribute-based representations to fMRI images of subjects reading everyday sentences. Backpropagation is then extended to the features, demonstrating how they change in different sentence contexts for the same word. Indeed, statistically significant changes occurred across similar contexts and across different subjects, quantifying for the first time how attribute weightings for the same word are modified by context. Such dynamic representations of meaning could be used in future natural language processing systems, allowing them to mirror human performance more accurately.

Keywords: Context effect · Concept representations · fMRI data analysis
Neural networks · Embodied cognition

1 Introduction

Embodiment theories of knowledge representation [1–3] propose that word meaning consist of a set of features, or attributes, that represent the basic elements of meaning. This approach provides an efficient method for representing an unlimited number of object types through weighted attributes. Recently it has become possible to ground this theory to brain imaging, mapping the semantic attributes to different brain systems. In particular, Binder et al. [4] identified a distributed large-scale brain network linked to the storage and retrieval of words. This brain network was used as the foundation for the Concept Attributes Representation (CAR) theory. CAR theory propose that words are represented as a set of properties that are basic components of meaning. Additionally, these properties are grounded in different neural systems such as sensory, motor, visual, spatial, temporal, affective, and others, based on the way concepts are experienced and acquired [4–7].

© Springer Nature Switzerland AG 2018
S. Wang et al. (Eds.): BI 2018, LNAI 11309, pp. 129–140, 2018.
https://doi.org/10.1007/978-3-030-05587-5_13

An intriguing challenge to such theories is that concepts are dynamic, i.e. word meanings are not fixed entries or lists of attributes, but dynamically processed each time a word is encountered [8]. For example, a pianist would invoke different aspects of the word piano depending on whether he will be playing in a concert or moving the piano. When thinking about a coming performance, the emphasis will be on the piano's function, including sound and fine hand movements. When moving the piano, the emphasis will be on shape, size, weight and other larger limb movements. It is possible to track the dynamic meanings of words by measuring how the attribute weighting changes across contexts.

The research stream of this paper aims to quantify this phenomenon through computational modeling. A neural network is trained to map brain-based semantic representations of words (CARs) into fMRI data of subjects reading everyday sentences. Backpropagation is then repeated separately for each sentence, reducing the remaining error by modifying only the CARs at the input of the network. As a result, the strengths of the attributes in the CARs change according to how important each attribute is for that sentence context.

Previous work with the available fMRI data set resulted in semantically meaningful changes. These changes were reported anecdotally in [9]. Word meaning was represented as a collection of attributes (CARs), grounded in observed brain networks. In two separate experiments, Multiple Linear Regression and a nonlinear Neural Network were used to map the CARs to the FMRI data in order to understand how the CARs could change to approximate the actual sentence representations seen in fMRI images. The results suggested that different features of word meaning were activated in different contexts. The linear mapping approach yielded disorganized results but the nonlinear mapping characterized the results in a meaningful manner.

In this paper, the CARs changes were analyzed more systematically. Interesting context effects were observed for different shades of meaning. Also, the changes in the CAR representations were averaged across subjects, and found to be statistically significant. In fact, the FGREP model captured the context of the sentence combining the meaning of the individual words. Based on this process, in the future it may be possible to create the word meaning dynamically in a natural language processing system, making it more sensitive to the semantic nuances that humans perceive and use.

The CARs theory is first reviewed, and the sentence collection, fMRI data, and word representation data described. The FGREP model is presented, followed by the experiments and how they were tested for statistical significance with the emphasis on aggregating context across subjects.

2   Concept Attribute Representation Theory

CARs represent the basic components of meaning defined in terms of observed neural processes and brain systems [4–7]. They are composed of a list of well-known modalities that correspond to specialized sensory, motor and affective brain processes, systems processing spatial, temporal, and casual information, and areas involved in social cognition. They capture aspects of experience central to the acquisition of event and object concepts (both abstract and concrete). For example, concept ratings on visual and sensory components include brightness, color, size, shape, temperature, weight, pain, etc. These aspects of mental experience model each word as a collection of a 66-dimensional feature vector that captures the strength of association between each neural attribute and the word meaning. Figure 1, shows the CAR for the concept *bicycle*.

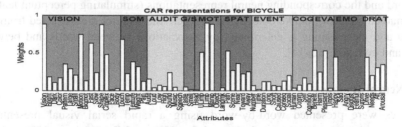

Fig. 1. Bar plot for the 66 semantic features in CAR theory. The ratings represent the basic features of *bicycle*. Given that is an object, it gets low weightings on human-related attributes: face, speech, head, and emotion and high weightings on visual, shape, touch, manipulation, and others.

The attributes were selected after an extensive body of physiological evidence based on two assumptions: (1) All aspects of mental experience can contribute to concept acquisition and consequently concept composition; (2) Experiential phenomena are grounded on neural processors representing a particular aspect of experience. For a more detailed account of the attribute selection and definition see [4–7]. Section 3.3 describes how the CAR ratings are acquired.

3 Data Collection and Processing

Three data sets were used for this study: the sentence collection prepared by Glasgow et al. [10], the Semantic Vectors (CAR ratings) for words obtained via Mechanical Turk [7, 11], and the fMRI images of the same sentence collection assembled by the Medical College of Wisconsin [11].

3.1 Sentence Collection and Semantic Word Vectors

The sentence set was prepared for use with neural data as part of the IARPA Knowledge Representation in Neural Systems (KRNS) Program [10]. The 240 sentences are composed by 2–5 content words from a set of 242 words (141 nouns, 39 adjectives and 62 verbs). The words were selected toward imaginable and concrete objects, actions, settings, roles, state and emotions, and events, (e.g. *couple, author, boy, theatre, hospital, desk, red, flood, damaged, drank, gave, happy, old, summer, chicken, dog*).

The 242 words (CAR) ratings were collected through Amazon Mechanical Turk [7, 11]. In a scale of 0–6, the participants were asked to assign the degree to which a given concept is associated to a specific type of neural component of experience (e.g. "To what degree do you think of a *bicycle* as having a fixed location, as on a map?"). Approximately 30 ratings were collected for each word. After averaging all ratings and removing outliers, the final attributes were transformed to unit length yielding a 66-dimensional feature vector (Fig. 1). Note that in this manner, the richness and complexity of representations is based on a direct mapping between the conceptual content of a word and the corresponding neural representations (stimulating perceptual features of the named concept), unlike other systems where the features are extracted from text corpora and the meaning is determined by associations between words and between words and contexts [12–14].

3.2 Neural Images

Sentences were presented word-by-word using a rapid serial visual presentation paradigm, with each content word exposed for 400 ms followed by a 200 ms inter-stimulus interval. Eleven subjects took part in this experiment producing 12 repetitions each. Participants viewed the sentences on a computer screen word by word while in the scanner. The data was acquired by the Center for Imagining Research of the Medical College of Wisconsin [11]. The fMRI voxels were preprocessed and transformed into a single sentence fMRI representation per participant (by averaging all the repetitions), with a final selection of 396 voxels per sentence on a scale from 0.2–0.8, for further use in the computational model.

3.3 Data Preparation

Because the neural data set did not include fMRI images for words in isolation, a technique developed by Anderson et al. [11] was adopted to approximate them. The voxel values for a word were obtained by averaging all fMRI images for the sentence where the word occurred. Thus, the vectors include a combination of examples of that word along with other words that appear in the same sentence. The final vector representations became the list of Synthetic Words (called SynthWord). Because of the limited number of combinations, some of these vectors became identical, and were excluded from the dataset.

Given the final selection of 237 sentences and 236 words (138 nouns, 38 adjectives and 60 verbs), the next step was to identify pairs of contrasting sentences with differences and similarities such as live mouse vs. dead mouse, family celebrated vs. happy family, and playing soccer vs. watching soccer. A collection of 77 such sentences, with different shades of meaning for verbs, nouns and adjectives, as well as different contexts for nouns and adjectives was assembled. This data set was used to prompt Words of Interest during the experimental process (Table 1).

Table 1. Sentences examples with differences and similarities in meaning. For instance, the role of the noun *soldier* is used in two different contexts, delivering medicine (good) vs. kicking the door (as an aggressive behavior).

SEMANTIC CONTRAST		SENTENCES
GOOD	94	*The soldier delivered the medicine.*
AGGRESSIVE	112	*The soldier kicked the door.*
ANIMAL	203	*The yellow bird flew over the field.*
	207	*The duck flew.*
OBJECT	210	*The red plane flew through the cloud.*
BAD PEOPLE	119	*The dangerous criminal stole the television.*
	152	*The mob was dangerous.*
NATURE	99	*The flood was dangerous.*

4   Computational Model

The technique for analyzing fMRI data is based on the FGREP neural network (Forming Global Representations with Extended BP, [15]). The neural network is trained to predict fMRI sentences (Fig. 2), by mapping CARWord (word attribute ratings) to SynthWord (fMRI synthetic words). SynthWords are combined, to form SyntSent for the predicted sentence, by averaging all words in the sentence. The SynthSent is then compared to the actual fMRISent (original fMRI data), to form a new error signal.

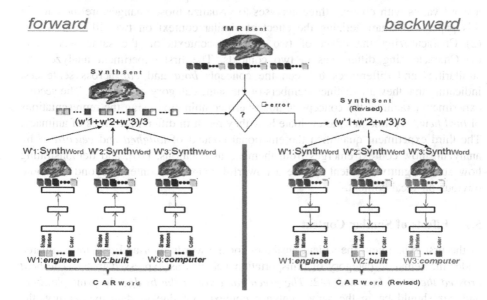

Fig. 2. The FGREP model to account for context effects. (1) Propagate CARWord to SynthWord. (2) Construct SynthSent by averaging the words into a prediction of the sentence. (3) Compare SynthSent against Observed fMRISent. (4) Backpropagate the error with FGREP for each sentence, freezing network weights and changing only CARWord. (5) Repeat until error reaches zero or CARs reach their upper or lower limits. The FGREP model captures context effects by mapping brain-based semantic representations to fMRI images.

The trained neural network is thus utilized to determine how the CARWords should change in the context of the sentence. That is, for each sentence, the CARWords are propagated and the error is formed as before, but during backpropagation, the network is no longer changed. Instead, the error is used to change the CARWords themselves (which is the FGREP method; [15]). This modification can be carried out until the error goes to zero, or no additional change is possible (because the CAR attributes are already at their max or min limits). Eventually, the revised CARWord represents the word meaning in the current sentence.

For the experiments, the FGREP model was trained 20 times with different random seeds for each of the eleven fMRI subjects. A total of 20 different sets of 786 context-based word representations were thus produced for each subject. In the experiments, the mean of the 20 representations was used for each word. Specific words to be analyzed (i.e. words of interest), were hand-picked from the list of contrasting sentences described in Sect. 3.3, to evaluate the performance of the model and the learned context-based representations. The changes for each attribute were evaluated with a paired t-test to determine which ones were statistically significant at the 95% level.

5 Results

The goal of the experiments was to characterize the changes that occur when a word is used in the context of a sentence. Since the importance given to individual attributes of a word varies with context, three analyses to visualize those changes are included in this paper: (1) Characterizing the effect of similar context on two different words, (2) Characterizing the effect of two different contexts on the same word, and (3) Characterizing differences in two contexts. The first experiment analyzed the similarities and differences between the concepts *boat* and *car* across sentences, indicating that they are distinct members of the same category of vehicles. The second experiment examined the conceptual noun-verb combination using the representations of *bird flew* vs. *plane flew*, to evaluate how they result in different degrees of animacy. The third experiment quantified the emotional context of *laughed* and *celebrated* by analyzing how context emerges from thematic associations, [16], and demonstrating how such cognitive content can be a powerful source of context beyond the more obvious physical context.

5.1 Effects of Similar Context

In the first experiment the salient attributes for the words *boat* and *car* are compared under the semantic category of transportation vehicles as expressed in 57: *The boat crossed the small lake* and 142: *The green car crossed the bridge*. In principle, *boat* and *car* should be in the same sentence context, but due to data availability, the experiment was designed with sentences that were similar and typical of those nouns. In CAR theory the activation of attribute representations is modulated continuously through attention and the interaction with context. Context draws attention to a subset of attributes, which are then enhanced, forming the basis for object categories. FGREP model quantified such enhanced representations for *boat* and *car*, revealing common underlying properties in the transportation vehicle category [7]. Due to space constrains, only two words are analyzed in this section, but different words were considered (*bicycle* vs. *plane; dog* vs. *mouse; horse* vs. *fish; tea* vs. *water*), with comparable results.

Figure 3 shows the results, averaged across subjects. For *boat* in sentence 57, there are changes on Vision, Large, Motion, Shape, Complexity, Weight, Sound, Manipulation, Path and Scene and event attribute Away, reflecting a large moving object. Evaluation and Emotion attributes of Benefit, Pleasant and Happy represent the experiential and personal nature of using a boat. Similarly, *car* in sentence 142 shows analogous activation for the same brain areas. Since both belong to the same semantic category, they share the similar context-related attribute enhancement. However, the distinctive weighting on these attributes sets them apart. The FGREP model was thus able to identify the effect of similar context on these two concepts across subjects.

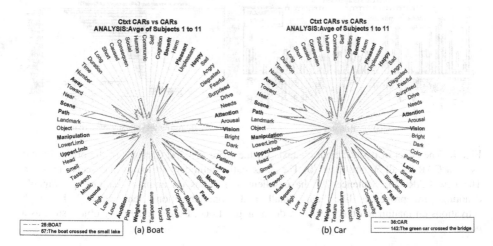

Fig. 3. The effect of similar context for the words *boat* and *car* averaged across subjects. Results are shown for the new CARs as an average of all subjects. The dotted lines indicate the original CARs and solid lines specify the context-based representations. Both plots display similar changes but the different weightings set them apart.

5.2   Effects of Different Contexts

In this experiment, the attributes of the noun-verb combination are analyzed for the word *flew*, as expressed in 200: *The yellow bird flew over the field*, and 207: *The red plane flew through the cloud*. According to CAR theory, noun-verb interactions arise within multiple brain networks, activating similar brain zones for both concepts. These interactions determine the meaning of the concept combination [7]. Since *bird* is a living thing, animate sensory, motor, affective, and cognitive experiences are activated, including attributes like Face and Speech. In contrast, *plane flew* has salient activations along animate dimensions such as Emotion, Cognition, and, Attention. Figure 4, shows the differences for *flew* in the two contexts. On the left side, all the 66 attributes are displayed and on the right side, only the statistically significant attributes. Due to space constrains, only Subject 9701 is presented, but the analysis was completed on all subjects and for diverse conceptual combinations (*small camera* vs. *small church*; *dangerous criminal* vs. *dangerous flood*; *injured horse* vs. *injured person*; *horse walked* vs. *person walked*), with similar effects.

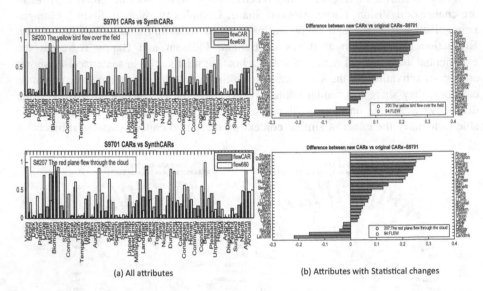

(a) All attributes   (b) Attributes with Statistical changes

Fig. 4. The effect of two different contexts for the word *flew*. (a) Changes of the original CAR vs. new CAR for all 66 attributes. (b) The statistically significant attributes in descending order. The new CARs for Sentence 200 have salient activations on animate features, presumably denoting *bird* properties like Pain, Small, and Communication. Sentence 207, has high activations on inanimate object features, describing a Loud, Large, and Heavy object such as a *plane*.

The results demonstrate context-dependent changes on Sentence 200 with salient activations on animate attributes like Face, Small, and Body, Pain, Audition, Music, Speech, Taste and Smell, as well as Communication and Cognition. In the other hand, Sentence 207 yields large changes on Vision, Color, Size, and Shape, Weight, Audition, Loud, Sound, Duration, Social, Benefit, Harm, and Attention. These results suggest that FGREP was able to determine the effect of two different contexts into the resulting CARs. As the context varies for each sentence representation, the overlap on neural representations create a mutual enhancement, producing a sharp difference between animate and inanimate contexts.

5.3 Characterizing Differences in Context

The third experiment examined the common emotional context in Sentences 4: *The wealthy family celebrated at the party*, and 14: *The couple laughed at dinner*, by how such cognitive content can be an instrumental source of context and demonstrating how context develops from external relations.

Many concepts such as *celebrated* and *laughed* refer to affective states and emotions, and other cognitive experiences. One advantage on using CARs is that such experiences count as much as sensory-motor experiences in grounding conceptual representations. When people "feel happy", they experience this phenomenon the same way as the sensory or motor events, except that the perception is internal. Similarly, to evaluate context in these sentences, CAR representations alone cannot capture the thematic associations between concepts (i.e., party, celebration, birthday cake, candles, laugh) unless additional sources provides it. Hence, the third experiment was designed to quantify that sort of context developed from external relations, i.e., spatial and temporal co-occurrence of events, captured by FGREP.

Figure 5 shows that these sentences resulted on very similar contexts, emphasizing Scenes, Events, and positive Emotions. Figure 5(a) shows the context CARs averaged for each sentence for all subjects. Both sentences are mostly similar on Spatial, Event, and Emotion attributes. Figure 5(b) aggregates these dimensions across the 12 corresponding brain areas according to the CAR theory. All subject brain signatures mainly differ in Gustatory, Motor, and Attention, possibly highlighting that laughing at dinner involves food and requires more head and upper body movements. In contrast, celebrating demands more Attention and Arousal. The results thus suggest that FGREP captures the thematic relations where the two contexts intersect semantically. They also validated that emotional content is a prominent and potentially powerful factor in sentence context, and there are subtle differences in it that can cause subtle differences in word meanings.

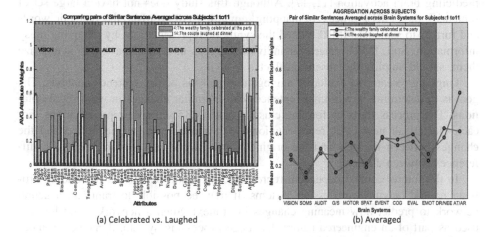

(a) Celebrated vs. Laughed   (b) Averaged

Fig. 5. Results featuring differences between two contexts averaged across subjects. (a) A comparison of the averaged attributes for each sentence representing *celebrated* and *laughed*. (b) Aggregation analysis across subjects for each brain zones. These context-based representations differ mostly in the Gustatory, Motor, and Attention zones, possibly emphasizing that laughing at dinner involves food and requires more movement than celebrating at the party, but the latter demands more Attention and Arousal.

Finding how sentence meaning is represented in the brain remains a major challenge [17]. The results in this experiment are significant because they indicate that FGREP captures the thematic knowledge of the sentences by mapping the heteromodal semantic representations (CAR) to fMRI data. By doing so, it is possible to look at the weightings of the brain systems for the entire sentence (as was done in Fig. 5b), although the thematic associations exposed by the model require further review.

6 Discussion and Further Work

The experiments in this paper suggest that different aspects of word meaning are weighted differently in distinct contexts, and it is possible to identify those changes for individual concepts, a combination of concepts, and for sentences by analyzing the corresponding fMRI images through the FGREP model. The changes in the CAR representations were averaged across subjects and found to be statistically significant. This result is remarkable considering that the dataset was not originally designed to answer the question of dynamic meaning. Limited by the data available, the experiments presented here address specific cases, however, by expanding the collection (e.g., identical contexts and contrasting contexts) the number of potential observations would increase, making it possible to test more systematically.

Synthetic words built by combining sentences where the word occurs is similar to many semantic models in Computational Linguistics [13, 14, 18]. Also, synthetic words formed by fMRI sentence representations has been successful in cases like predicting brain activation [11, 17]. Although this study does not have a large set of sentences, the FGREP process of mapping semantic CAR words to the synthetic words and further to sentences fMRI refined the synthetic representations by removing noisy information. Still, fMRI images for individual words instead of having to synthesize them, should amplify the observed effects.

Ongoing research is exploring aggregation analysis across sentence contexts. The goal is to determine how similar sentences cause similar changes in word representations. The process starts by forming clusters of the 237 sentence representations. For each cluster, all new CAR representations with similar roles are identified and the changes between the new and the original CARs averaged and correlated with differences between clusters.

In the future, context dependent representations could be utilized in building artificial natural language processing systems. It may be possible to train e.g. a neural network to predict how meaning changes in context. Such a network could be then used as part of an engineered natural language processing system, dynamically modifying the vector representations for the words to fit the context. Such a system should be more effective and more robust in its inference, and match human behavior better.

7 Conclusion

Concepts are dynamic; their meaning depends on context and recent experience. In this paper, word meaning was represented as a collection of attributes (CARs), grounded in observed brain systems. The FGREP Neural Network was trained to map CAR representations of words to fMRI images of subjects reading everyday sentences. Back-propagation was then extended to the CAR features, demonstrating how they change in different sentence contexts for the same word. The changes in the CAR representations were averaged across subjects and found to be statistically significant. In the future it may be possible to create such representations dynamically in a natural language processing system, making it more sensitive to the semantic nuances that humans perceive and use.

Acknowledgments. We would like to thank Jeffery Binder (Medical College of Wisconsin), Rajeev Raizada and Andrew Anderson (University of Rochester), Mario Aguilar and Patrick Connolly (Teledyne Scientific Company) for providing this data and insight for this research. This work was supported in part by IARPA-FA8650-14-C-7357 and by NIH 1U01DC014922 grants.

References

1. Regier, T.: The Human Semantic Potential. MIT Press, Cambridge (1996)
2. Landau, B., Smith, L., Jones, S.: Object perception and object naming in early development. Trends Cogn. Sci. **27**, 19–24 (1998)
3. Barsalou, L.W.: Grounded cognition. Annl. Rev. Psyc. **59**, 617–845 (2008)
4. Binder, J.R., Desai, R.H., Graves, W.W., Conant, L.L.: Where is the semantic system? A critical review of 120 neuroimaging studies. Cereb. Cortex **19**, 2767–2769 (2009)
5. Binder, J.R., Desai, R.H.: The neurobiology of semantic memory. Trends Cogn. Sci. **15**(11), 527–536 (2011)
6. Binder, J.R., et al.: Toward a brain-based Comp. Sem. Cogn. Neuropsychol. **33**(3–4), 130–174 (2016)
7. Binder, J.R.: In defense of abstract conceptual representations. Psychon. Bull. Rev. **23**, 1096–1108 (2016)
8. Pecher, D., Zeelenberg, R., Barsalou, L.W.: Sensorimotors simulations underlie conceptual representations: modality-specific effects of prior activation. Psychon. Bull. Rev. **11**, 164–167 (2004)
9. Aguirre-Celis, N., Miikkulainen R.: From words to sentences & back: characterizing context-dependent meaning rep in the brain. In: Proceedings of the 39th Annual Meeting of the Cognitive Science Society, London, UK, pp. 1513–1518 (2017)
10. Glasgow, K., Roos, M., Haufler, A. J., Chevillet, M., A., Wolmetz, M.: Evaluating semantic models with word-sentence relatedness. arXiv:1603.07253 (2016)
11. Anderson, A.J., et al.: Perdicting Neural activity patterns associated with sentences using neurobiologically motivated model of semantic representation. Cereb. Cortex 1–17 (2016). https://doi.org/10.1093/cercor/bhw240
12. Burgess, C.: From simple associations to the building blocks of language: modeling meaning with HAL. Behav. Res. Methods Inst. Com. **30**, 188–198 (1998)

13. Landauer, T.K., Dumais, S.T.: A solution to plato's problem: the latent semantic analysis theory. Psychol. Rev. **104**, 211–240 (1997)
14. Vinyals, O., Toshev, A., Bengio, S., Erham, D.: Show and tell: a new image caption generator. arXiv:1506.03134v2 (2015)
15. Miikkulainen, R., Dyer, M.G.: Natural language processing with modular PDP networks and distributed lexicon. Cogn. Sci. **15**, 343–399 (1991)
16. Estes, Z., Golonka, S., Jones, L.L.: Thematic thinking: the apprehension and consequences of thematic relations. Psychol. Learn. Motiv. **54**, 249–294 (2011)
17. Anderson, A.J., et al.: Multiple regions of a cortical network commonly encode the meaning of words in multiple grammatical positions of read sentences. Cereb. Cortex 1–16 (2018). https://doi.org/10.1093/cercor/bhy110
18. Mitchell, J., Lapata, M.: Composition in distributional models of semantics. Cogn. Sci. **38**(8), 1388–1439 (2010). https://doi.org/10.1111/j.1551-6709.2010.01106.x

Network Analysis of Brain Functional Connectivity in Mental Arithmetic Using Task-Evoked fMRI

Xiaofei Zhang[1,2,3,4,5](✉), Yang Yang[2,3,4,6], Ming-Hui Zhang[1,2,3,4],
and Ning Zhong[1,2,3,4,6]

[1] Faculty of Information Technology,
Beijing University of Technology, Beijing 100124, China
[2] Beijing Advanced Innovation Center for Future Internet Technology,
Beijing University of Technology, Beijing 100124, China
[3] Beijing International Collaboration Base on Brain Informatics and Wisdom
Services, Beijing 100124, China
[4] Beijing Key Laboratory of MRI and Brain Informatics, Beijing 100124, China
[5] School of Computer, Jiangsu University of Science and Technology,
Zhenjiang 212003, China
julychang@just.edu.cn
[6] Department of Life Science and Informatics, Maebashi Institute
of Technology, Maebashi, Gunma 371-0816, Japan

Abstract. Mental arithmetic is the complete use of brain functions to complete the basic arithmetic process without the aid of other tools and equipment. Neuroimaging studies of mental arithmetic have revealed some brain regions and networks associated with them. However, there are still many unsolved problems about the brain function network structure in mental arithmetic. We designed a mental arithmetic experiment consisting of four experimental conditions, and a group of 21 subjects were recruited in the experiment. The collected fMRI data was used to construct the brain functional connectivity network with atlas of Dosenbach-160. We used graph theoretic based network analysis method to calculate the small world attributes and network efficiencies of each subject's brain functional network, and tested the statistical differences between the experimental conditions. The results show that, when the human brain performs addition or subtraction, the functional connectivity network statistically shows a significant characteristic of small world from the resting state. And experiment condition of resting has a higher clustering coefficient over a continuous graph density than number matching, showing a more significant small world property. Results of network efficiency show that resting has slightly higher network-wide information exchange productivity than number matching. Furthermore, due to the limitations of the size of the recruited subjects, the report results can only be an exploratory attempt, which needs to be verified by a larger sample of data in the future.

Keywords: Mental arithmetic
functional Magnetic Resonance Imaging (fMRI) · Brain functional connectivity
Small world · Network efficiency

© Springer Nature Switzerland AG 2018
S. Wang et al. (Eds.): BI 2018, LNAI 11309, pp. 141–152, 2018.
https://doi.org/10.1007/978-3-030-05587-5_14

1 Introduction

Mental arithmetic is the complete use of brain functions to complete the basic arithmetic process without the aid of other tools and equipment. Some studies have shown that mental arithmetic significantly activate the anterior central gyrus and lobule of posterior parietal lobe, which are the centers of processing and working memory [1]. Even different subtypes in mental arithmetic differ in the extent to which brain regions are activated. Some evidence suggests that left inferior frontal gyrus, middle portion of dorsolateral prefrontal cortex, and supplementary motor area are more active in the process of subtraction than that of addition [2]. Other studies have found that mental arithmetic result in more intense activation of bilateral intraparietal sulci and inferior occipital gyrus, and a stronger connectivity between parietal and occipital than processing of arithmetic principles [3].

Neuroimaging techniques provide a very effective means for investigating the processes underlying the arithmetic calculation of human brain. The results of functional neuroimaging studies on humans, as well as neurophysiological records from single-cell of the monkey cortex, indicate that bilateral regions of the intraparietal sulcus is a key factor in the expression and processing of numerical values. And fMRI studies also show that intraparietal sulcus has similar activations in both numerical and non-numerical order judgements [4]. Numerous fMRI based studies on primates have found that numerical information is represented and processed in many areas of prefrontal and posterior parietal lobes, and intraparietal sulcus is a key node for the representation of numeric quantitative semantics [5]. Some fMRI study has even found that cognitive processes of mental subtraction and multiplication are dissociated [6].

Graph theoretic based complex network analyses used in relative researches have shown the potential different topological properties of brain networks, in which brain regions are represented as graph nodes, while anatomical and functional links between brain regions are represented as graph edges [7–9]. Many network analysis studies of the structural and functional connections of the brain shows that healthy human brains have distinct properties of small-world, including high clustering coefficient and low mean path length [10–14]. The magnitude of the clustering coefficient is directly proportional to the local efficiency and is used to measure the specialized processing (functional segregation) of the brain function in a specific sub-network. The mean path length is proportional to the global efficiency and is used to measure the distributed processing (functional integration) of the brain function among the various sub-networks [15]. Studies on these graph theoretic properties could elicit a good understanding of the organizing mechanism and dynamics of mental arithmetic in human brain.

In this paper, graph theoretic analysis is performed on task-state fMRI data to investigate the topological properties in whole-brain functional networks in 21 adults in a mental arithmetic experiment. The initial hypothesis is that the different conditions in the experiment have different network topologies and there are significant differences in global network metrics. In order to verify this hypothesis, we first construct a functional connectivity network for each experiment condition (number matching, resting, addition, subtraction), and then calculate the quantitative indicators of the network topology (small world properties and network efficiency), and statistically tested these indicators between experimental conditions. We calculated many global metrics, including clustering coefficient and network efficiency, for these functional connectivity networks. The comparisons between the experimental conditions are conducted with T-test. The whole framework of this study workflow is depicted in Fig. 1. Detailed experiment design and analysis procedures are described in Sect. 2.

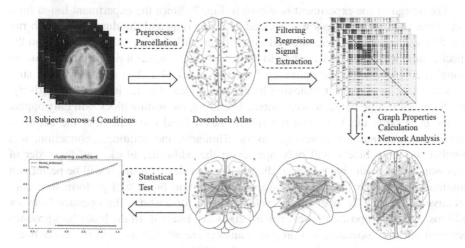

Fig. 1. Framework of the study design

2 Materials and Methods

2.1 Subjects

The mental arithmetic experiment was conducted in 21 Chinese university graduate students, including 12 males and 9 females, with an average age of 25.76 years and a standard deviation of 3.66. These subjects were right-handed, with an equal educational background, normal or corrected normal vision, and no neurological or psychiatric medical history. Before the experiment, each subject was given the possible natural reactions explanation, and also signed the informed consent form. This experiment was also approved by the Xuanwu Hospital Ethics Committee of Capital Medical University in Beijing.

2.2 Experiment Design

There were three kinds of trials in the experiment, which are addition, subtraction, and number matching of 2 digits. During the experiment, the subjects were subjected to these kinds of trials in the form of pictures. In order to focus on the neural mechanism of the simple addition, subtraction and number matching of the human brain, the trial excluded carrying and borrowing operation in the mental arithmetic problem. In each trial, there will be four pictures in sequence, of which the first and second are the two operands of these trials, the third is the operator, that is, plus or minus or hashtag, and the fourth is recommended answer. Subjects can select one of the two touch-touch buttons to click to determine whether the result in the fourth picture is correct. The hashtag is used for number matching and if the recommended answer is equal to one of the operands, then the subject should press the positive button. The subjects were asked to click as fast and accurate as possible, and the reaction time and accuracy of the results of the subjects were recorded.

The design of the experiment is shown in Fig. 2. Since the experiment lasted for a long time, the whole process was divided into two runs and the duration of each run was 552 s. The subjects were allowed to rest for a while between the two runs, and the specific time was adjusted according to the actual situation. Each run of the experiment contains 23 blocks, and the duration of each block is 24 s. The addition block, subtraction Block, and number matching block each appear 4 times in a run respectively, and there is a resting block between them. Therefore, the resting block will only appear on the even order block, so that the subject has a fixed rest time after the addition, subtraction, and number matching blocks. Similarly, the addition, subtraction, and number matching blocks will only appear on the odd-order block, and the order of appearance will ensure balance according to certain rules. Four trials will be performed continuously in each block. For example, the addition block will perform four consecutive additions. The operand in each trial lasts for 250 ms, the operator lasts for 500 ms, and the proposed answer lasts for 2000 ms. Intervals of the black backgrounds between operand, operator, and proposed answer are all 500 ms, and the black background after the proposed answer will last for 1500 ms.

2.3 fMRI Data Acquisition and Preprocessing

The data for this experiment was obtained by using a 3.0 Tesla MAGNETOM Trio Tim from Siemens Medical Systems in Erlanger, Germany, which has a 12-channel phased array head coil. We used foam fillings and headphones to limit the head movement of the subject and to reduce the noise generated during the scan. Anatomical image and functional images are acquired by using a T1 weighted 3D MPRAGE (magnetization prepared rapid gradient echo) sequence and EPI (echo-planar imaging) sequence respectively.

The preprocessing of the fMRI data consists of 4 steps. The first step is slice timing correction, where the middle slice is used as the reference slice. The second step is realignment, or motion correction, which solve the mismatch of the location of subsequent images in the time-series. The third step is spatial normalization, which helps inter-subject averaging and reporting of activations as co-ordinates within a known standard space. Here we used the MNI (Montreal Neurological Institute) space, and all volumes were re-sampled into $3 \times 3 \times 3$ mm3. The last step is smoothing, which helps the increasing SNR by removing high-frequency information, aligning all structures for inter-subject averaging, and increasing validity of statistics when using random of filed theory. We used 8-mm FWHM isotropic Gaussian kernel for convolution calculation in this step.

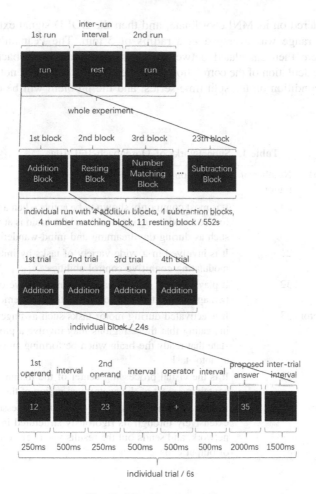

Fig. 2. Experiment paradigm

2.4   Construction of Functional Brain Networks

Since this study is a research on the neural mechanism of mental arithmetic with functional connectivity, it is necessary to consider not only the frequency band of BOLD signals, the selection of brain atlas, but also the re-ordering of fMRI images according to experiment trials when constructing the functional network of the subjects. In order to remove the linear drift in the BOLD signal, and the actual fMRI sampling rate is 2 s per scan, we did the filtering with range of 0.008–0.5 Hz. This was done by using REST [16], a software tool available at http://restfmri.net/forum/index.php (Table 1).

In order to extract signals from the corresponding voxels of the volume for correlation calculation, we used the Dosenbach-160 [17] atlas depicted in Fig. 3. Its 160 ROIs are obtained through meta-analysis, and each ROI is uniquely assigned to one of the six functional subnets of the Dosenbach-160 atlas. The extraction of each ROI time-series was centered on its MNI coordinate, and then the BOLD signal extracted by all voxels in this range was averaged at a radius of 5 mm. The Pearson's correlation coefficients were then calculated between time-series of all Dosenbach-160 ROIs. However, the calculation of the correlation coefficient matrix here does not consider the experimental condition on the split time-series, and the problem will be elaborated in the following.

Table 1. Subnetworks of Dosenbach-160 Atlas

No.	Subnetwork name	Number of regions	Description
1	Default	34	It is most commonly shown to be active when a person is not focused on the outside world and the brain is at wakeful rest, such as during daydreaming and mind-wandering
2	Fronto-Parietal	21	It is involved in a wide variety of tasks by initiating and modulating cognitive control abilities
3	Cingular-Opercular	32	It plays a more downstream role in cognitive control, perhaps associated with output gating of memory
4	Sensorimotor	33	It is activated during motor tasks such as finger tapping indicating that these regions may involve a pre-mediated state that ready the brain when performing and coordinating a motor task
5	Occipital	22	It is the visual processing center of the mammalian brain containing most of the anatomical region of the visual cortex
6	Cerebellum	18	It receives a modest number of inputs, processes them very extensively through its rigorously structured internal network, and sends out the results via a very limited number of output cells

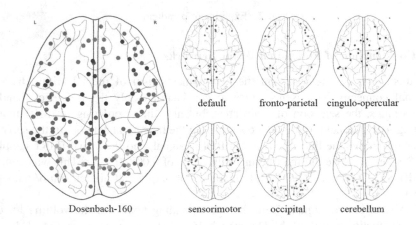

default   fronto-parietal   cingulo-opercular

Dosenbach-160   sensorimotor   occipital   cerebellum

Fig. 3. Atlas of Dosenbach-160 and its subnetworks

Due to the experimental design, blocks of the same condition type will be dispersed to different stages of the run. Therefore, when analyzing functional connectivity, it is necessary to consider how to deal with the discontinuous blocks of the same condition type. Two different data combination procedures, named block-wise connectivity and concatenated connectivity, were proposed [18]. The first way calculate time-series correlation within each block individually, and then average all blocks to result a single, average time-series correlation for each condition. The second way standardized each block to minimize the possibility of spurious correlations being induced due to changes in signal intensity or variability across blocks and then concatenated across blocks. Considering that the fMRI data have been normalized during preprocessing and filtering, and the effect of normalization again in each individual block is unknown, so we concatenated volumes across blocks and calculated the correlation for each condition.

After calculating the Pearson's correlation coefficient matrix under each condition of each subject, r-to-z conversion of the non-diagonal elements in the matrix can be performed to obtain a corresponding matrix of z-valued correlation coefficients. Figure 4 shows the matrix of z-valued correlation coefficients of subject 1 under four conditions. It can be seen visually that when subject 1 performs number matching and subtraction, there are more positive correlation edges in the whole brain network, which means more brain regions worked together. In the conditions of rest and addition, the positive correlation of the whole brain network is relatively small, indicating that there is no collaborative work in more brain regions. Of course, the more general conclusions need to be drawn based on the calculation of the network's indicators and statistical test of these indicators at group level.

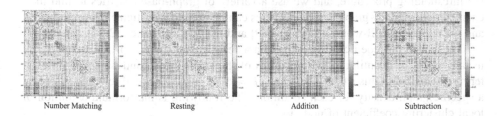

| Number Matching | Resting | Addition | Subtraction |

Fig. 4. Z-valued correlation coefficient matrices of subject 1

2.5 Thresholding of Graph Edges

To analyze the brain function network of mental arithmetic through the topological indicators in graph theory, it is necessary to convert the Z-valued correlation coefficient matrix into a binary matrix. Since there are a certain range of coefficients in the Z-valued correlation coefficient matrix, we used the thresholds to determine whether the edge corresponding to each unit in the matrix exists. The edge of the Z-valued correlation coefficient matrix greater than or equal to the current threshold is 1, otherwise it is 0, so that the binary matrix can be obtained to calculate the network topology indicators. In order to ensure that the comparison between the subjects can be mathematically compared, the thresholds of each subject is calculated according to the same graph density, which is the percentage of the maximum possible number of edges of the entire brain function network. We used the full range of graph density (1%–100%) and increment of 1% to examine the brain function network under different mental arithmetic conditions.

Figure 5 shows the connectome of the subject 1 under the condition of number matching, resting, addition, and subtraction when the graph density is 1%. Intuitively, it can be seen that the connectomes have different modes under different conditions, and the indicators of the graph need to be calculated to find out the patterns of mental arithmetic.

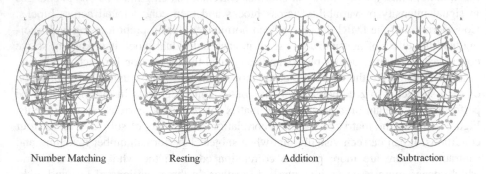

Number Matching   Resting   Addition   Subtraction

Fig. 5. Connectomes at graph density 1% of subject 1

2.6   Network Analysis Measures

A set of binary matrices was calculated from Z-valued correlation coefficient matrix with the thresholding procedure, and we use a variety of graph-based metrics to find their characteristics. Many graph theory measures can be used to investigate connectome [8], and we adopted small-world properties [19] and network efficiency [20] in this study.

The clustering coefficient and the characteristic path length of the network are usually used for quantifying the properties of the small-world, and we focus on clustering coefficient in this study. The graph $G = (V, E)$ was generated for each subject at a specific graph density for each condition. The following is the formula definition of local clustering coefficient of node v_i,

$$C_i = \frac{\left| e_{jk} : v_j, v_k \in N_i, e_{jk} \in E \right|}{k_i(k_i - 1)/2} \tag{1}$$

where N_i is all neighboring nodes of node v_i, e_{jk} is the existing edge between node v_j and node v_k which are two distinct neighboring nodes of node v_i. The numerator is the number of existing edges between neighboring nodes of node v_i. k_i is the number of neighboring nodes of node v_i. The denominator is the number of maximum possible edges between neighboring nodes of node v_i. The following is the formula definition of average clustering coefficient,

$$\bar{C} = \frac{1}{n}\sum_{i=1}^{n} C_i \tag{2}$$

where C_i is local clustering coefficient of node v_i, n is the number of nodes in the whole graph.

In this research, we focused on the global efficiency [20, 21] for the whole brain network which was constructed according to atlas of Dosenbach-160. The global efficiency, as a measure of information exchange productivity of the whole network, and the following is its formula definition in a graph G with N nodes,

$$E_{global} = \frac{1}{N(N-1)} \sum_{i \neq j \in G} \frac{1}{d_{i,j}} \tag{3}$$

where $d_{i,j}$ denotes the shortest path distance from node i to j.

2.7 Statistical Test

The graph theory indicators were calculated at each single graph density and form a functional curve, where the x-axis was represented as the graph density and the y-axis was represented as the graph theory indicator. To determine whether there exists significant difference between conditions in the graph theory indicators, we performed T-test on graph theory indicator at each graph density. Test results that show significant differences in continuous graph density were reported, and were used to analyze whether there are differences between different mental arithmetic conditions.

3 Results

When analyzing the indicators of the network in terms of sparsity, the graph density of 0.1 to 0.5 is recommended [19]. The results in Fig. 6(a) and (b) show that conditions of addition and subtraction have continuous graph densities in this region that are significantly higher than that of number matching. Explain that the human brain has smaller world properties compared to number matching when performing addition and subtraction. This indicates that during conditions of addition and subtraction, the functional network of the human brain is more segregated, and there are some subsystems that work relatively independently. Although the results do not show a significant difference in the whole or most of the range of graph density, it is necessary to consider the difference between actual Z-value ranges of the edges contained in different condition at same graph density.

Similarly, the results of Fig. 6(c) show that resting has a higher clustering coefficient over a continuous graph density than number matching, showing a more significant small world property. Explain that number matching is less obvious than resting, and there are no more obvious subsystems. Or, compared to resting, the brain function network corresponding to number matching has a global synergistic function.

The results of Fig. 6(d) show that resting has slightly higher network-wide information exchange productivity than number matching. Although the previous results show that resting is more of a small world than number matching, the actual global information exchange productivity also needs to comprehensively look at the information exchange anxiety in each subsystem and the information exchange productivity between subsystems. This requires a more detailed study of the network structure based on atlas of Dosenbach-160.

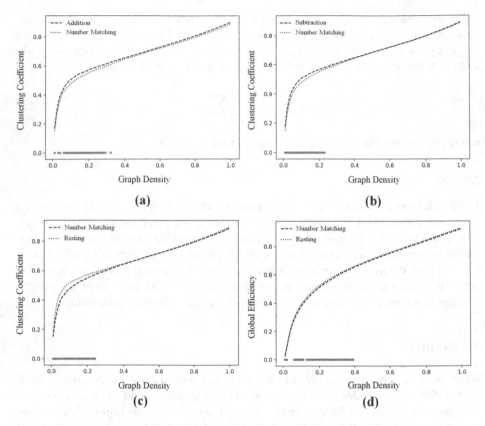

Fig. 6. Results with significant difference

4 Discussions

By using graph theory analysis and statistical test analysis, we studied the topological indicators of human brain function network under various mental arithmetic conditions in experimental design. As the hypothesis put forward at the beginning of the experiment, when the human brain performs addition or subtraction, the functional connectivity network statistically shows a significant difference from the resting state. That is, more subsystems are generated during addition or subtraction in human brain network. In some studies, it was found that there are differences in the degree of activation of a few brain regions when the human brain is undergoing addition and subtraction [2]. Therefore, the results of this study are not found to be significantly different between addition and subtraction on the global network, and the difference between them in network indicators requires specific functional subsystems and independent brain regions to be better studied.

The emergence of graph theory based on complex network analysis provides a new method for our studying of global and local brain function networks. Based on these methods, we have found that the addition and subtraction are with more characteristics of small world than that of the number matching. The analysis indicator used is the clustering coefficient. The higher the value of the clustering coefficient, the more cliques or subnets close to clique exist in the entire network. The distribution and structure of these cliques or subnets close to the clique also need to be studied at a more local level.

Finally, our research is only an attempt to study human brain and mental arithmetic through network analysis. More general findings need to replicate the current results by a larger number of samples. Once confirmed, these findings could form the basis for longitudinal studies testing important questions such as: (1) Which subsystems will be generated during the addition and subtraction process, which have an important impact on the small world attribute of the overall network; (2) Although addition and subtraction produce more subsystems, what is the difference between the number and type of these subsystems; (3) The whole network in the resting state will have a higher small world attribute than that of the number matching, and what is the difference compared to the network structure corresponding to addition and subtraction.

5   Conclusions

This paper studies the brain network topology and functional connectivity indicators during mental arithmetic by applying graph theory analysis and statistical tests. Based on the brain functional network constructed by atlas of Dosenbach-160, the experiment conditions of addition and subtraction show more significant small world attributes than number matching. At the same time, the experiment condition of number matching shows a more significant clustering coefficient and global efficiency than the resting. However, due to the limitations of the size of the recruited subjects, the report results can only be an exploratory attempt, which needs to be verified by a larger sample of data in the future. For the function network research of the human brain during mental arithmetic, the future direction needs to apply more atlases, and select the brain regions more relevant to the mental arithmetic for functional connectivity analysis. The design of the mental arithmetic experiment itself also needs to be more optimized, so as to better explore the structure and characteristics of the brain function network in each stage of mental arithmetic.

References

1. Wang, M., Wang, L.: Localization of the brain calculation function area with MRI. Chin. Sci. Bull. **46**(22), 1889–1892 (2001)
2. Yang, Y., et al.: The functional architectures of addition and subtraction: network discovery using fMRI and DCM. Hum. Brain Mapp. **38**(6), 3210 (2017)
3. Jie, L., et al.: The neural circuits for arithmetic principles. Neuroimage **147**, 432–446 (2016)
4. Ansari, D.: Effects of development and enculturation on number representation in the brain. Nat. Rev. Neurosci. **9**(4), 278–291 (2008)
5. Nieder, A., Dehaene, S.: Representation of number in the brain. Annu. Rev. Neurosci. **32**(1), 185–208 (2009)

6. Yi-Rong, N., et al.: Dissociated brain organization for two-digit addition and subtraction: an fMRI investigation. Brain Res. Bull. **86**(5–6), 395–402 (2011)
7. Bullmore, E., Sporns, O.: Complex brain networks: graph theoretical analysis of structural and functional systems. Nat. Rev. Neurosci. **10**(3), 186–198 (2009)
8. Rubinov, M., Sporns, O.: Complex network measures of brain connectivity: uses and interpretations. Neuroimage **52**(3), 1059–1069 (2010)
9. Stam, C.J.: Characterization of anatomical and functional connectivity in the brain: a complex networks perspective. Int. J. Psychophysiol. **77**(3), 186–194 (2010). Psychophysiology Official Journal of the International Organization of Psychophysiology
10. Strogatz, S.H.: Exploring complex networks. Nature **410**(6825), 268 (2001)
11. Stam, C.J.: Functional connectivity patterns of human magnetoencephalographic recordings: a 'small-world' network? Neurosci. Lett. **355**(1), 25–28 (2004)
12. Salvador, R., et al.: Neurophysiological architecture of functional magnetic resonance images of human brain. Cereb. Cortex **15**(9), 387–413 (2005)
13. Achard, S., et al.: A resilient, low-frequency, small-world human brain functional network with highly connected association cortical hubs. J. Neurosci. **26**(1), 63 (2006). The Official Journal of the Society for Neuroscience
14. He, Y., Chen, Z.J., Evans, A.C.: Small-world anatomical networks in the human brain revealed by cortical thickness from MRI. Cereb. Cortex **17**(10), 2407–2419 (2007)
15. Bassett, D.S., Bullmore, E.T.: Human brain networks in health and disease. Curr. Opin. Neurol. **22**(4), 340–347 (2009)
16. Song, X.W., et al.: REST: a toolkit for resting-state functional magnetic resonance imaging data processing. PLoS ONE **6**(9), e25031 (2011)
17. Dosenbach, N.U.F., et al.: Prediction of individual brain maturity using fMRI. Science **329**(5997), 1358–1361 (2010)
18. Cohen, J.R., D'Esposito, M.: The segregation and integration of distinct brain networks and their relationship to cognition. J. Neurosci. **36**(48), 12083 (2016). The Official Journal of the Society for Neuroscience
19. Watts, D.J., Strogatz, S.H.: Collective dynamics of 'small-world' networks. Nature **393**, 440–442 (1998)
20. Latora, V., Marchiori, M.: Efficient behavior of small-world networks. Phys. Rev. Lett. **87**(19), 198701 (2001)
21. Latora, V., Marchiori, M.: Economic small-world behavior in weighted networks. Eur. Phys. J. B-Condens. Matter Complex Syst. **32**(2), 249–263 (2003)

The Astrocytic Microdomain as a Generative Mechanism for Local Plasticity

Ioannis Polykretis, Vladimir Ivanov, and Konstantinos P. Michmizos$^{(\boxtimes)}$

Computational Brain Lab, Rutgers University, New Brunswick, NJ 08854, USA
konstantinos.michmizos@cs.rutgers.edu

Abstract. Mounting experimental evidence suggests that astrocytes have an active role in synaptic modification. A central premise is that they modify the structure and the function of the neuronal network but the underlying mechanisms for doing so remain elusive. Here, we developed a biophysically constrained 2D compartmental model of an astrocytic microdomain that suggests an explanation for the recently reported functional clustering of synapses. Our model followed the typical geometrical structure of astrocytes, comprising of functionally independent microdomains, and the spatial allocation of their sub-cellular organelles giving rise to (a) fast, process-specific and (b) delayed, microdomain-wide calcium waves. These waves encoded the neuronal activity into their spatial extent and interacted with each other to impose locally restricted synaptic weight modifications constrained in the microdomain. Our results give a possible explanation for the recently reported spatially clustered functional groups in dendritic spines, advocating the astrocytic microdomain as a fundamental learning unit in the brain.

Keywords: Astrocytes · Microdomain · Long term potentiation
Spatial clustering · Learning

1 Introduction

The involvement of astrocytes in information processing and learning has long been supported by experimental studies on their role in synaptic long term potentiation (LTP) [1–6] and depression (LTD) [7,8], and further spurred by recent findings that the astrocytic activity is not only necessary but also sufficient for memory formation and consolidation [9]. Astrocytes are found to modify synaptic strength by changing the neurotransmitters release probability of the presynaptic terminal [3,10], and increasing the number of receptors in the postsynaptic neuron [2,11]. However, the exact mechanisms that astrocytes use to mediate synaptic changes remain poorly understood.

Studies on neurons in the visual cortex have recently suggested a spatial clustering of functional synaptic groups. Specifically, dendritic spines, within less

© Springer Nature Switzerland AG 2018
S. Wang et al. (Eds.): BI 2018, LNAI 11309, pp. 153–162, 2018.
https://doi.org/10.1007/978-3-030-05587-5_15

than $\sim 10\,\mu m$ distance, tend to share receptive field properties, while more distant spines are functionally uncorrelated [12]. A possible explanation is that these clusters arise through spatially restricted mechanisms of plasticity [13,14], which are known to optimize long-term memory engram formation [15] and memory capacity [16]. Nonetheless, the underlying sub-cellular mechanisms generating the spatially localized plasticity are still elusive.

Interestingly enough, the dimensions of astrocytic microdomains (~ 10–$15\,\mu m^2$) [17–19] coincide with the reported maximum distance between functionally related spines [12]. The microdomains are ensembles of fine processes with highly-branching structure and close proximity to the synapses. They are found to function as independent cellular compartments [20]. Within them, distinct calcium waves [17,19,21] can be either localized in the vicinity of a synapse [22] or spread in the whole microdomain area [18,21]. The reported nonlinear interaction of these waves [21] further complicates the interpretation of their functional roles. Since calcium fluctuations within the microdomain can result into gliotransmitter release [1,2,8], it is reasonable to assume that the spatial extent of these waves might be constraining the reported astrocyte-induced synaptic modifications.

Current electrophysiological and calcium imaging techniques that map neural-glial networks at cellular resolution are challenged by the sheer size and volume of the vertebrate brain, the absence of a direct linkage between *in-vitro* cellular recordings and behavior, and the ineligibility of humans to become subjects in *in-vivo* optical cellular imaging techniques. A possible way to transcend these limitations is to develop biologically constrained models of astrocytic-neural networks. Here, we developed a 2D compartmental astrocytic model that suggests how the localized activity of the astrocytic microdomain can spatially restrict neuronal plasticity. Specifically, we show how astrocyte-induced slow inward currents (SICs) [23] affect the calcium concentration in the postsynaptic spines, resulting in potentiation [11] and functional correlation (Fig. 1.)

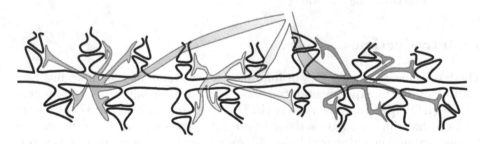

Fig. 1. Synaptic clustering through astrocytic-induced local plasticity, as suggested by our biophysically plausible computational model. Illustration of three distinct astrocytic microdomains ensheathing clustered fractions of a neural dendrite.

2 Methods

We designed a 2D astrocytic model, emulating the geometry as well as the main cellular compartments and their associated organelles. In this work, we focused on the astrocytic microdomain [17,19,22] (Fig. 2, inset). The intracellular mechanisms, which model the glutamate-induced production of the intermediate messenger molecule Inositol Triphosphate (IP_3) and the consequent generation of calcium oscillations, are described in our previous work [24].

We expanded our model [24] to include Voltage Gated Calcium Channels (VGCCs), a communication mechanism between the extracellular space and the astrocytic cytoplasm, as supported by experimental evidence [25,26]. As in neurons, these channels are activated by the cell's membrane depolarization. Interestingly, the astrocytic membrane potential is highly sensitive to the extracellular K^+ concentration; therefore, the release of K^+ from neuronal terminals during spiking activity increases the extracellular K^+ concentration, causing astrocytic depolarization [27,28]. This depolarization activates the VGCCs, inducing influx of calcium ions into the cell's cytoplasm. Since our initial model did not account for external calcium influx, we modified the calcium balancing mechanism parameters in the Perisynaptic Astrocytic Process (PAP) to $K_{bal} = 0.05\ \mu M$ and $v_{bal} = 0.9\ \mu M/s$, reported in [29]. To compute the intracellular calcium concentration (C), we started from the calcium current density (J) and transformed it to current (I), then to electric charge (Q), number of particles (N) and lastly moles (M), as follows:

$$J\left(\frac{\mu A}{cm^2}\right) \xrightarrow{\times S_\mu} I(\mu A) \xrightarrow[\mu A \times \Delta t]{\mu A = \mu C/s} Q(C) \xrightarrow[\div q_e]{\div \text{Ca valence}} N(\text{particles}) \xrightarrow{\div N_A} M(\text{mol}) \xrightarrow{\div V_\mu} C(M),$$

where S_μ is the average surface of a microdomain ($3 \times 10^{-6}\ cm^2$) [19], Δt is the simulation time step (1 ms), q_e is the electron charge, N_A is the Avogadro Number and V_μ is the average volume of a microdomain ($15\ \mu m^3$) [19]. This concentration was superimposed to the calcium concentration equation presented in our previous work [24]. Assuming that the extracellular K^+ does not spread beyond the microdomain, the depolarization and, hence, the calcium influx is localized to microdomains with active synapses.

We modeled only the low-threshold T-type VGCCs, which are the most responsive channels to the small astrocytic depolarizations caused by neuronal spiking activity. The contribution to the calcium influx by other subfamilies of VGCCs expressed in astrocytes [25,30] were considered negligible. The VGCCs were modeled using the Hodgkin-Huxley formulation [31], as shown below:

$$I_{Ca,T} = g_T m_T h_T (V - E_{Ca}), \quad m_T = \frac{1}{1 + e^{-\frac{V+63.5}{1.5}}}, \quad h_T = \frac{1}{1 + e^{\frac{V+76.2}{3}}}, \quad (1)$$

$$\tau_{m_T} = 65 e^{-(\frac{V+68}{6})^2}, \quad \tau_{h_T} = 50 e^{-(\frac{V+72}{10})^2} \quad (2)$$

Starting from a stimulation pattern [30 s–10 Hz] reported to induce membrane depolarization in astrocytes [32], we increased its duration to [45 s–10 Hz] to be able to observe the astrocytic repolarization, that took place after ~17 s [32].

The extended depolarization was used to calculate the current flowing through the VGCCs.

Astrocytes induced Slow Inward Currents (SICs) to the postsynaptic neurons. SICs were triggered when the microdomain calcium concentration surpassed a threshold value [23], as described below. The amplitude of SIC depended on the calcium level, as given by the experimentally fit function [23, 33]:

$$I_{astro} = 2.11 \frac{\mu A}{cm^2} ln(w)\Theta(lnw), where \quad w = [Ca^{2+}]/nM - 196.11 \tag{3}$$

and $\Theta(x)$ is the Heaviside function. The complete equation for SIC dynamics, activated at every calcium concentration peak, was:

$$I_{SIC}(t) = I_{astro}([Ca^{2+}_{peak}]) * n * \left(exp\left(\frac{t}{\tau^{SIC}_{decay}}\right) - exp\left(\frac{t}{\tau^{SIC}_{rise}}\right) \right) \tag{4}$$

where $\tau^{SIC}_{rise} = 50$ ms and $\tau^{SIC}_{decay} = 300$ ms are the time constants of the SIC and $n = \frac{6*6^{0.2}}{5}$ is a normalization constant [34] for exponential distributions, which assures that the biexponential distribution, before being multiplied by I_{astro}, is equal to one. Therefore, the resulting total current driving the postsynaptic neurons is modeled by $I_{total} = I_{basal} + I_{SIC}$, where I_{basal} is a basal presynaptic current.

This total postsynaptic current was mapped into calcium concentration in the postsynaptic dendritic spine, using a transformation similar to the one described above, but with four key differences: First, the SIC affected the postsynaptic neuron at multiple spines; experimental reports [35] suggest that an astrocytic microdomain contacts up to 36 spines of a neuronal dendrite with a particular distribution of extrasynaptic NMDA receptors (NMDARs) [36]. Second, the spine's small volume (0.01–0.1 μm^3) [37,38] and thin neck limited the diffusion from the spine to the dendrite. Hence, for modeling purposes, only NMDARs on the spines were considered. Third, only a fraction of the spinal extrasynaptic NMDARs, are affected by gliotransmission [39]. Therefore, only a fraction (10%) of the SICs was considered to alter the postsynaptic spine's calcium concentration. Fourth, the time that a calcium remains ion in the dendritic spines is ~15 ms [40].

Our model introduced plasticity in the postsynaptic neuron when the dendritic spine calcium concentration deviated from its steady-state (1 μM). Following the literature, the deviation was either a small (below threshold) but prolonged increase of calcium concentration, inducing LTD or a large (above threshold) and short increase inducing LTP [41–43]. To do this, we used the phenomenological model proposed by Abarbanel et al. [44] that accounts for the counterbalancing action of four calcium-dependent enzymes acting on the calcium-calmodulin kinase complex [41–43].

3 Results

Our model replicated the emergence of two types of experimentally reported calcium waves, whose complex interaction induces diverse synaptic plasticity throughout the astrocytic microdomain. Specifically, (T1) Voltage induced waves are produced upon activation of VGCCs, localized to the astrocytic microdomain filopodia, and (T2) agonist induced medium-scale waves are localized in the microdomain. Their interplay, leading to synaptic plasticity, is presented below.

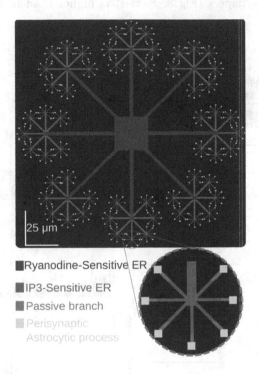

Fig. 2. Our proposed 2D model of an astrocyte controlling a spatial neural domain. The model preserves the basic compartments, their geometry and their main organelles.

Initial synaptic activity gave rise to (T1) calcium waves, which significantly delayed the onset of (T2) calcium waves. To show this, we stimulated 3 (active, Fig. 3, E, inset, point A) of the 7 synapses belonging to a single microdomain with a 10 Hz presynaptic firing activity for 45s (Fig. 3, A) to simulate the stimulation pattern used by Sibille *et al.* [32]. The 4 other synapses (inactive, Fig. 3, E, inset, point B) were driven with a 1 Hz firing rate to simulate idle activity. The initialization of the activity in the active synapses released K^+ to the extracellular space. This extracellular increase caused the depolarization of the whole astrocytic microdomain (Fig. 3, B), activating the VGCCs. The channels introduced calcium currents (Fig. 3, C, D) to the microdomain and increased the calcium concentration. These calcium concentration increases in the microdomain are interpreted as (T1) calcium waves (Fig. 3, F, left), limited to the thin processes. Due to the interaction between calcium and IP_3, this local wave suppresses IP_3 production (Fig. 3, E, left) and delays the (T2) calcium waves (Fig. 3, F, right) that can propagate through the entire microdomain.

The duration of synaptic stimulation defines the extent of plasticity. Short periods of activity induce plasticity only in the active synapses through (T1) waves. Persistent activity induces plasticity in all synapses of the microdomain, both active and inactive, through (T2) waves. The (T1) calcium concentration rise in the active synapses (Fig. 3, F, red) is higher than in the inactive ones

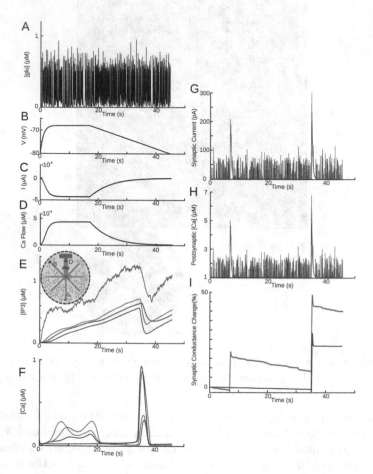

Fig. 3. Stochastic stimulation of synapses within the microdomain generates calcium waves and induces homo- and hetero-synaptic plasticity. Stochasticity is introduced into the model from the Poisson spike activity driving the Tsodyks-Markram model [51] of synaptic glutamate release, as in our previous work [24]. A. Glutamate release upon stimulating [10 Hz–45 s, as in [32]] 3 out of 7 synapses in the microdomain. B. Astrocytic membrane depolarization. C, D. Current flow through the VGCCs. E, F. Concentration of IP_3 and calcium, respectively, in the PAPs of active and inactive synapses. G. Synaptic current with the overlay of SICs in the active (red) and the inactive (blue) synapses H. SIC-induced calcium concentration in the postsynaptic spines. I. Homosynaptic (red) and heterosynaptic (blue) weight modifications in the postsynaptic spines (Color figure online)

(Fig. 3, F, blue). Contrary to the inactive synapses, the calcium concentration levels in the active synapses are sufficient [23,33] to induce a SIC. In the active synapses, the synaptic current is strengthened by the (T1)-induced SIC (Fig. 3, G, red), while there is no such SIC in the inactive synapses (Fig. 3, G, blue). Longer stimulation resulted in (T2) waves, which induced SICs in all the astrocytic microdomain synapses. (Fig. 3, G, red and blue). SICs increase the calcium concentration in the postsynaptic spines (Fig. 1, H), inducing increase of the synaptic conductance (Fig. 3, I). Hence, (T1) waves induce synaptic conductance increase only in the active synapses (Fig. 3, I, red, left), while (T2) waves induce synaptic conductance increase in all the microdomain synapses (Fig. 3, I, red, right).

The (T1) and (T2) waves induced different synchronization patterns in the postsynaptic neurons of the microdomain (Fig. 4). (T1) waves resulted in the synchronization of neurons with active presynaptic inputs, while (T2) waves resulted in the synchronization of all neurons controlled by the microdomain. Hence, neurons with active input experienced synchronization two separate times: at the

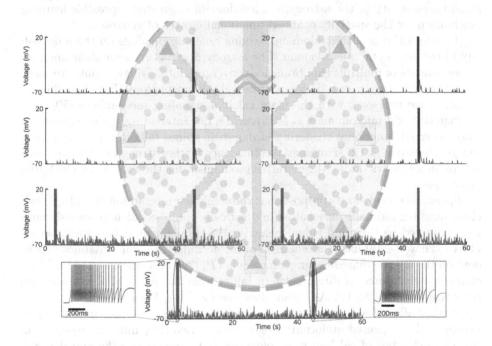

Fig. 4. Firing patterns of postsynaptic terminals (LIF, $R = 0.6 G\Omega$, $C = 100pF$) with active (red) and inactive (blue) presynaptic terminals. The active terminals are synchronized due to the SICs from the T1 and T2 waves, while the inactive ones are only synchronized due to the (T2)-induced SICs. The firing rate due to the weaker (T1)-induced SIC (left inset) is lower than the firing rate due to the (T2)-induced SIC (right inset). (Color figure online)

induction of SICs due to (T1) and (T2) waves. Furthermore, the higher amplitude (T2) waves caused faster postsynaptic firing rate than (T1) waves (insets).

4   Discussion

Our model suggests that the astrocytic microdomain, through complex calcium
wave interactions, imposes postsynaptic plasticity to cluster synapses, both spatially and functionally. Such clustering is known to improve the computational
power of neurons by increasing the flexibility of single dendrites [12,13]. It also
maximizes a dendrite's dynamic range and sensitivity by exploiting dendritic
non-linearities and passive integration [12,45,46]. The reported scale of synaptic
clustering aligns with the morphology and size of the microdomain [5,18,19,22].
Our model incorporated two generative mechanisms for calcium waves, at two
distinct spatial scales in the microdomain [17,22,47,48]. These seemingly simple
mechanisms exhibited complex wave interactions that drove synchronization [49]
and plasticity in postsynaptic sites. The modeling results of SIC-induced postsynaptic plasticity in the astrocytic microdomain suggested a possible learning
mechanism for the spatially confined functional cluster of synapses.

This hypothesis of microdomain learning crucially depends on the morphology of the astrocytic microdomain. The astrocytic structure near their fine processes consists of multiple thin branches converging into a single point. We modeled this key feature in our 2D compartmental cell morphology (Fig. 2), endowing
its miniscule processes with the main calcium signaling mechanisms [50]. The
average size of a microdomain is 5–15 μm [18,19]. Interestingly, the experimentally observed functional clustering of dendritic spines falls in a similar spatial
range of 5–10 μm [4,12]. This spatial coincidence further strengthens the hypothesis of an astrocytic-induced generative mechanism for the functional clustering
of synapses.

Specifically, our results propose that the combined interaction of multiple calcium signaling mechanisms resulted in drastically complex calcium wave dynamics, compared to their individual behavior. We implemented two such mechanisms: the well-established mechanism of intracellular calcium dynamics dependent on the intermediate messenger molecule IP_3 [29], and voltage-gated calcium
channels as a source of direct calcium influx from the extracellular space into
the cytoplasm [25,26,31]. As stand alone mechanisms, both generated calcium
waves that affect the microdomain in a uniform and predictable manner. Sur-
prisingly, this expected uniformity breaks down when they interact, resulting in
two distinct types of calcium wave patterns: fast, process-specific and delayed,
microdomain-wide waves. Process-specific waves arose from the uniform calcium
influx through VGCCs, modulated by local levels of IP_3 concentration as a
function of presynaptic activity. Therefore, process-specific (T1) calcium waves
were restricted only to processes with active presynaptic sites. Microdomain-
wide calcium waves emerged purely through intracellular calcium mobilization.
Importantly, we observed that process-specific waves significantly delayed their
onset, requiring longer presynaptic stimulation. Vast amounts of experimental

literature describe astrocytic calcium waves at different spatial and temporal scales [17,22,47,48], but their origin remains elusive. Our model paves the way for studying how the different reported calcium waves may interact in a functionally meaningful way.

Finally, our results propose that microdomains group spatially constrained clusters of synapses into single learning units via coordinated postsynaptic plasticity imposed by astrocytic calcium waves. Initially, calcium dynamics are limited to the faster, process-specific calcium waves resulting in selective potentiation of dendritic spines with active presynaptic sites. However, when the stimulation is significant enough in both strength and duration, this localized learning is further reinforced by a uniform postsynaptic potentiation imposed by the delayed microdomain-wide calcium wave. Therefore, dendritic spines with insignificant presynaptic activity still got potentiated as long as there was a subset of spines with significant, active presynaptic input. This modeling result aligns with the idea of homogeneous learning within a synaptic cluster. Accumulating experimental evidence shows that dendritic spines tend to group into learning [4] and functionally [12] similar clusters. To the best of our knowledge, our model is the first to propose an astrocytic-induced mechanism that leads to the functional clustering of dendritic spines. Overall, this work builds on the premise that glial cells are key cells in neural information processing [34,52] and aims to reveal their cellular mechanisms underlying normal behavior – and the pathophysiological deviations from it.

References

1. Gordon, G.R., Iremonger, K.J., Kantevari, S., Ellis-Davies, G.C., MacVicar, B.A., Bains, J.S.: Neuron **64**(3), 391–403 (2009)
2. Henneberger, C., Papouin, T., Oliet, S.H., Rusakov, D.A.: Nature **463**(7278), 232 (2010)
3. Perea, G., Araque, A.: Science **317**(5841), 1083–1086 (2007)
4. Harvey, C.D., Svoboda, K.: Nature **450**(7173), 1195 (2007)
5. Rusakov, D.A.: Nat. Rev. Neurosci. **16**(4), 226–33 (2015)
6. Yang, Y., et al.: Proc. Natl. Acad. Sci. **100**(25), 15194–15199 (2003)
7. Letellier, M., et al.: PNAS **113**(19), E2685–E2694 (2016)
8. Serrano, A., Haddjeri, N., Lacaille, J.-C., Robitaille, R.: J. Neurosci. **26**(20), 5370–5382 (2006)
9. Adamsky, A., et al.: Cell (2018)
10. Tewari, S., Majumdar, K.: J. Comput. Neurosci. **33**(2), 341–370 (2012)
11. Lisman, J., Yasuda, R., Raghavachari, S.: Nat. Rev. Neurosci. **13**(3), 169 (2012)
12. Scholl, B., Wilson, D.E., Fitzpatrick, D.: Neuron **96**(5), 1127–1138 (2017)
13. Larkum, M.E., Nevian, T.: Curr. Opin. Neurobiol. **18**(3), 321–331 (2008)
14. Winnubst, J., Lohmann, C.: Front. Mol. Neurosci. **5**, 70 (2012)
15. Govindarajan, A., Kelleher, R.J., Tonegawa, S.: Nat. Rev. Neurosci. **7**(7), 575 (2006)
16. Poirazi, P., Mel, B.W.: Neuron **29**(3), 779–796 (2001)
17. Di Castro, M.A., et al.: Nat. Neurosci. **14**(10), 1276–1284 (2011)
18. Grosche, J., Kettenmann, H., Reichenbach, A.: J. Neurosci. Res. **68**(2), 138–149 (2002)

19. Grosche, J., Matyash, V., Moller, T., Verkhratsky, A., Reichenbach, A., Kettenmann, H.: Nat. Neurosci. **2**(2), 139–43 (1999)
20. Araque, A., Martın, E.D., Perea, G., Arellano, J.I., Buño, W.: J. Neurosci. **22**(7), 2443–2450 (2002)
21. Perea, G., Araque, A.: J. Neurosci. **25**(9), 2192–2203 (2005)
22. Bindocci, E., Savtchouk, I., Liaudet, N., Becker, D., Carriero, G., Volterra, A.: Science **356**(6339), eaai8185 (2017)
23. Parpura, V., Haydon, P.G.: PNAS **97**(15), 8629–8634 (2000)
24. Polykretis, I., Ivanov, V., Michmizos, K.P.: International Conference on Neuromorphic Systems, ICONS 2018, 23–26 July 2018, Knoxville (2018)
25. Barres, B.A., Chun, L.L., Corey, D.P.: Glia **1**(1), 10–30 (1988)
26. Latour, I., Hamid, J., Beedle, A.M., Zamponi, G.W., Macvicar, B.A.: Glia **41**(4), 347–353 (2003)
27. Orkand, R., Nicholls, J., Kuffler, S.: J. Neurophys. **29**(4), 788–806 (1966)
28. Meeks, J.P., Mennerick, S.: Hippocampus **17**(11), 1100–1108 (2007)
29. De Pittà, M., Goldberg, M., Volman, V., Berry, H., Ben-Jacob, E.: J. Biol. Phys. **35**(4), 383–411 (2009)
30. Yan, E., Li, B., Gu, L., Hertz, L., Peng, L.: Cell Calcium **54**(5), 335–342 (2013)
31. Zeng, S., Li, B., Zeng, S., Chen, S.: Biophys. J. **97**(9), 2429–2437 (2009)
32. Sibille, J., Duc, K.D., Holcman, D., Rouach, N.: PLoS Comput. Biol. **11**(3), e1004137 (2015)
33. Nadkarni, S., Jung, P.: Phys. Biol. **1**(1), 35 (2004)
34. Kozachkov, L., Michmizos, K.P.: arXiv preprint arXiv:1702.03993 (2017)
35. Halassa, M.M., Fellin, T., Takano, H., Dong, J.-H., Haydon, P.G.: J. Neurosci. **27**(24), 6473–6477 (2007)
36. Petralia, R.S.: Sci. World J. **2012**, 10 (2012)
37. Harris, K.M., Jensen, F.E., Tsao, B.: J. Neurosci. **12**(7), 2685–2705 (1992)
38. Medvedev, N., Popov, V., Henneberger, C., Kraev, I., Rusakov, D.A., Stewart, M.G.: Philos. Trans. R. Soc. B **369**(1654), 20140047 (2014)
39. Papouin, T., Oliet, S.H.: Philos. Trans. R. Soc. B **369**(1654), 20130601 (2014)
40. Sabatini, B.L., Oertner, T.G., Svoboda, K.: Neuron **33**(3), 439–452 (2002)
41. Bear, M.F., Cooper, L.N., Ebner, F.F.: Science **237**(4810), 42–48 (1987)
42. Cormier, R., Greenwood, A., Connor, J.: J. Neurophy. **85**(1), 399–406 (2001)
43. Yang, S.-N., Tang, Y.-G., Zucker, R.S.: J. Neurophy. **81**(2), 781–787 (1999)
44. Abarbanel, H.D., Gibb, L., Huerta, R., Rabinovich, M.I.: Biol. Cybern. **89**(3), 214–226 (2003)
45. Polsky, A., Mel, B.W., Schiller, J.: Nat. Neurosci. **7**(6), 621 (2004)
46. Losonczy, A., Makara, J.K., Magee, J.C.: Nature **452**(7186), 436 (2008)
47. Kanemaru, K., et al.: Cell Rep. **8**(1), 311–318 (2014)
48. Rungta, R.L., et al.: Glia **64**(12), 2093–2103 (2016)
49. Fellin, T., Pascual, O., Gobbo, S., Pozzan, T., Haydon, P.G., Carmignoto, G.: Neuron **43**(5), 729–43 (2004)
50. Reyes, R.C., Parpura, V.: Neurochem. Int. **55**(1–3), 2–8 (2009)
51. Tsodyks, M.V., Markram, H.: Proc. Natl. Acad. Sci. U. S. A. **94**(2), 719–23 (1997)
52. Kozachkov, L., Michmizos, K.P.: arXiv preprint arXiv:1707.05649 (2017)

Determining the Optimal Number of MEG Trials: A Machine Learning and Speech Decoding Perspective

Debadatta Dash[1](✉) [iD], Paul Ferrari[2,3], Saleem Malik[4] [iD], Albert Montillo[5,6], Joseph A. Maldjian[5] [iD], and Jun Wang[1,7] [iD]

[1] Department of Bioengineering, University of Texas at Dallas, Richardson, USA
debadatta.dash@utdallas.edu
[2] Department of Psychology, University of Texas at Austin, Austin, USA
pferrari@utexas.edu
[3] MEG Laboratory, Dell Children's Medical Center, Austin, USA
[4] MEG Lab, Cook Children's Hospital, Fort Worth, TX, USA
saleem.malik@cookchildrens.org
[5] Department of Radiology, UT Southwestern Medical Center, Dallas, USA
Joseph.Maldjian@UTSouthwestern.edu
[6] Department of Bioinformatics, UT Southwestern Medical Center, Dallas, USA
Albert.Montillo@UTSouthwestern.edu
[7] Callier Center for Communication Disorders, University of Texas at Dallas, Richardson, USA
wangjun@utdallas.edu

Abstract. Advancing the knowledge about neural speech mechanisms is critical for developing next-generation, faster brain computer interface to assist in speech communication for the patients with severe neurological conditions (e.g., locked-in syndrome). Among current neuroimaging techniques, Magnetoencephalography (MEG) provides direct representation for the large-scale neural dynamics of underlying cognitive processes based on its optimal spatiotemporal resolution. However, the MEG measured neural signals are smaller in magnitude compared to the background noise and hence, MEG usually suffers from a low signal-to-noise ratio (SNR) at the single-trial level. To overcome this limitation, it is common to record many trials of the same event-task and use the time-locked average signal for analysis, which can be very time consuming. In this study, we investigated the effect of the number of MEG recording trials required for speech decoding using a machine learning algorithm. We used a wavelet filter for generating the denoised neural features to train an Artificial Neural Network (ANN) for speech decoding. We found that wavelet based denoising increased the SNR of the neural signal prior to analysis and facilitated accurate speech decoding performance using as few as 40 single-trials. This study may open up the possibility of limiting MEG trials for other task evoked studies as well.

Keywords: MEG · Speech · Wavelets · Artificial Neural Network

© Springer Nature Switzerland AG 2018
S. Wang et al. (Eds.): BI 2018, LNAI 11309, pp. 163–172, 2018.
https://doi.org/10.1007/978-3-030-05587-5_16

1   Introduction

Speech is an important inherent attribute of the humans for effective communication. Speech centers of the brain along with speech articulators function synergistically to produce speech. Epochs of air, originating from the lungs, with the help of pulmonary pressure are excited using the vocal cords at specifically designed frequencies, passed through the vocal tract to the oral cavity, modulated through various articulators such as the tongue, lips, and jaw and then are radiated as 'speech' from the mouth. Similarly, the speech centers of the brain include Wernicke's area: responsible for language recognition; Broca's area: responsible for constructing the sentence structure of speech; motor cortex: directs the motion of articulators; and auditory cortex: provides auditory feedback. With regard to the motor cortex, the left cerebral hemisphere of the brain consisting of bilateral supplementary motor area, the left posterior inferior frontal gyrus, the left insula, the left primary motor cortex, and temporal cortex is the major contributor towards the motor control of speech production [1]. Also, several sub-cortical areas of the brain such as basal ganglia help in voluntary motor control for language processing [2]; and cerebellum aids in the rhythmical organized sequencing of speech syllables [3]. While it is known that a myriad of brain regions participate in speech production, the true neural basis for speech production is still poorly understood.

A better understanding of the speech mechanism is critical to help the patients with severe neurological conditions (e.g., locked-in syndrome). Locked-in syndrome (patients are fully paralyzed but aware) usually occurs due to quadriplegia, severe brain damage, or neurodegenerative disease (e.g., amyotrophic lateral sclerosis, ALS) [4] and results in the inability to speak in otherwise cognitively intact individuals [5]. Neural signal based communication might be the only way to help these patients to resume a meaningful life with some level of verbal communication. Current Brain Computer Interfaces (BCIs) send directional commands to a computer based on the signal acquired from the brain without needing any acoustic sound production [6]. EEG is the present de-facto standard for BCIs owing to its characteristics of non-invasiveness, easy setup requirement and high-quality signal acquisition with high temporal resolution [7,8]. EEG-BCIs are believed to remain as the optimal choice for communication in paralyzed and completely locked-in patients with debilitating neurological diseases [9]. However, typical EEG-BCI experiments require the subjects to select letters from a screen with a visual/attention cue. This is time consuming with an average synthesis rate of 1 Word/Minute [10] and hence not suitable for spontaneous conversations in daily life. Recently, ECoG, which measures electric potentials directly from the brain surface [11], has also been used for decoding continuous spoken speech from the cortical surface [12]. However, it is invasive in nature and hence can not be used for data collection from healthy subjects. FMRI, on the other hand, estimates the neural activity from the voxels of the brain by measuring changes in blood oxygenation [13]. Although fMRI has a very high spatial precision [14] and has been used in related neuroscientific studies [15], its slow nature hinders in continuous speech recognition.

MEG measures the weak magnetic field induced synchronized neuronal ionic currents during synaptic transmission using very sensitive magnetometers positioned around the head [16]. The higher temporal resolution and quiet nature of MEG are advantageous over fMRI. It is also non-invasive and hence more practically suitable than ECoG. In contrast to EEG, the magnetic fields recorded by MEG are less distorted than the EEG recorded electric fields at skull and scalp. Also, it is reference-free and provides higher spatial resolution. Compared to other modalities MEG might be a better choice to analyze the neural dynamics during oromotor tasks of speech production. Moreover, prior studies on MEG for decoding speech [17–19] support its advantages over other approaches.

Despite the advantages, MEG signals are sensitive to background noise and motion artifacts. The motion of the facial muscles during speech utterance and eye blinks yield large artifacts in the MEG signals. The recorded magnetic field gradients are typically temporally averaged across trails to obtain an effective signal above background activity [20]. However, recording a large number of trials for the study of a particular stimulus evoked response can be very time consuming. The number of required trials for the study of a stimulus evoked response is a trade-off between the brain physiology (e.g., cell density, cell types, and location) and the maximum number of possible trials with similar performance level, maintaining a stable head position and avoiding eye blinks, etc. [21]. It has also been shown that ensembles containing too many trials can also be problematic [22]. With time, there is always a higher chance of motion artifact induction (due to head movement or eye blinks) which subsequently reduces the signal quality. Hence, the optimal number of trials of a MEG experiment is highly variable and is still debated. Very few studies have suggested a reasonable number of MEG trials as beyond either as many as possible [20] or typically between 100–300 [22]. However, no experimental evidence is given in these studies and the conclusions are made based on assumptions of good practice.

In this study, we aimed to determine the optimal number of MEG trials that are necessary and sufficient for effective speech decoding from the brain using a machine learning algorithm, which has rarely been studied, to our knowledge. We performed a speech decoding analysis based on a set of total trials from 5 to 70, respectively, where a high decoding accuracy indicates that more information is encoded in the signals. An optimal number of trials N will be determined if the decoding accuracy is decreased when the total number of trials is less than N and also if the accuracy is not significantly increased (remains at the similar level or even decreased) when the total number of trials is greater than N.

2   Data Collection

2.1   The MEG Unit

A 306 channel Elekta Triux MEG machine as shown in Fig. 1(a) was used in the experiment. The machine is equipped with 204 number of planar gradiometers and 102 number of magnetometers. The experiments were conducted at the MEG Center, Cook Children's Hospital, Forth Worth, Texas. The machine was housed within a two-layered magnetically shielded room, which reduced the interference of unwanted background magnetic fields. A 3 fiducial point based coordinate system was created for the subjects. Polhemus Fastrack digitalized 5 head-position-coils were used for the head positioning of the subjects inside the MEG scanner. Comfortable seating of the subjects inside the MEG unit was ensured with their arms resting on a table. A computer interfaced DLP projector was used to display the visual cue of the stimulus on a back-projection screen. The projector was situated at a distance of 90 cm from the MEG unit.

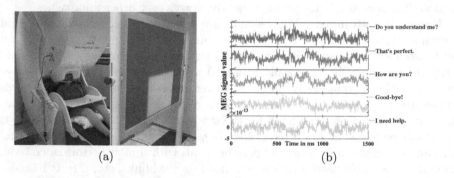

(a)   (b)

Fig. 1. (a) The MEG unit, (b) MEG signal for 5 spoken phrases with a sensor

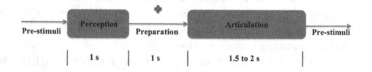

Fig. 2. Design of the experiment.

2.2   Participants and Protocol

Four young healthy, right-handed, English-speaking adults (2 males and 2 females) participated with their consent in the data collection. All the subjects had normal vision and had no speech, language, and/or cognitive disorders.

The experiment was designed as a delayed overt reading task. Subjects were asked to speak five short commonly used phrases: *Do you understand me*, *That's perfect*, *How are you*, *Good-bye*, and *I need help*. These sentences were chosen from Augmentative and Alternative Communication (AAC) data. The experiment was designed as 4 consecutive stages/segments: Pre-stimuli, Perception, Imagination (or preparation), and Articulation (Fig. 2). The pre-stimuli stage was a state of rest designed for 0.5 s. In the perception stage, a phrase stimulus was displayed on the screen for 1 s. During preparation, the subjects were asked to prepare the phrase displayed in the previous stage with a 1-s fixation cross displayed on the screen. In the final stage, the fixation was terminated by displaying a blank screen that signaled the subjects to speak the phrase (stimulus) at their natural speaking rate. The average time period of this articulation stage was 2 (up to 2.5) s. A total of 100 trials for each of the 5 stimuli were recorded after providing for roughly 1 s of non-movement baseline. To avoid the response suppression to repeated exposure the stimuli were presented in a pseudo-randomized order [23]. A prior training of subjects on sample stimuli was conducted to ensure subject compliance. The entire experiment lasted for an average of 45 min per subject. Sample MEG signals recorded through one of the sensors for the five phrases are displayed in Fig. 1(b).

2.3   Data Preprocessing

MEG signals were acquired with a 4 kHz sampling frequency. A band-pass filter of frequency range 0.1 Hz–1.3 kHz was applied to the MEG signals. Eye-blinking and cardiac signals were recorded using integrated bipolar EOG and EEG channels. Head motion of the subjects was tracked using a scanner based continuous head localization technique [24]. The articulated speech was recorded with a standard microphone attached to a transducer placed outside the magnetically shielded room. A custom air-pressure sensor was connected to an air-filled bladder attached below the jaw of the subjects. This recorded the jaw movements of the subjects during articulation by measuring the depression in the bladder. Both speech and jaw movement analog signals were fed into the MEG ADC channels and were digitized in real-time as separate channels. The data recorded through the MEG sensors were then epoched into trials from -0.5 to $+4.0$ s centered on stimulus onset. The trials that contained high motion artifacts were inspected visually and discarded [24]. Further, signals with erroneous movements due to incorrect articulation (started either before the cue to speak or existed within the baseline period for the next trial) were also removed. The remaining trials were then down sampled to 1 kHz. After preprocessing, a total of 1635 valid samples collected from the four subjects remained for analysis.

3   Methods

For unbiased data length among subjects, a maximum of 70 trials per phase per subject was considered for this study, as the minimum number of valid trials remained after processing for one subject was 73 for one phrase. In order to find the optimal number of trials, the data was partitioned into batches consisting $10n$ trials (for $n = 0.5, 1, 2, ...7$). Each batch was considered separately for analysis, denoised and then spatiotemporal wavelet features were extracted. An ANN model was trained with these features separately for each batch and the classification accuracies were compared. In our prior work [25], we had experimented with Gaussian Mixture Model (GMM) and Support Vector Machines (SVM), but these classifiers were not able to produce good decoding accuracy. We also tested Deep Neural Networks (DNN) for this purpose, but, as the data size was limited, it resulted in data generalization even with two hidden layers.

3.1 Wavelet Analysis

Before analysis, first the MEG acquired signals were denoised using a complex Morlet wavelet. These wavelets have a sinusoidal shape and are weighted by a Gaussian kernel. Morlet wavelets effectively capture the local harmonic components in the MEG time series and hence are popularly used in MEG data processing [26]. Complex Morlet Wavelet w in the time domain t at different frequencies f is given as:

$$w(t, f) = A \exp(-t^2/2\sigma_t^2) \exp(2i\pi ft) \tag{1}$$

where, $A = (\sigma_t\sqrt{pi})^{-1/2}$, t = time, σ_t = wavelet time period, and $i = \sqrt{-1}$. In our analysis $f_0/\sigma_f = 5$ was used, where σ_f is the shape of the Gaussian in the frequency domain and f_0 is the central frequency. The denoising was performed in the frequency range of 0.1–120 Hz to accommodate for neuromagnetic signals up to the high gamma frequency range with a central frequency at 1 Hz intervals.

Further, we decomposed the denoised signals into respective neural frequency bands by using a Discrete Wavelet Transform (DWT) approach to select the spatiotemporal features for further analysis. The underlying principle of wavelet analysis is to express a signal $\mathbf{X}$ as a linear combination of a particular set of functions, obtained by shifting and scaling a single function $\mathbf{\Psi}(t)$ as:

$$\mathbf{X}(a, b) = \frac{1}{\sqrt{a}} \int_{-\infty}^{\infty} \overline{\mathbf{\Psi}(\frac{t - b}{a})} \, \mathbf{x}(t)dt, \tag{2}$$

where, a and b are the scaling and shifting factors respectively. We have used Daubechies (db)-4 wavelet transform and performed a 5 level decomposition of the denoised MEG signal to find 5 different signals in the range of 0.1–4 Hz (delta), 4–8 Hz (theta), 8–15 Hz (alpha), 15–30 Hz (beta), 30–60 Hz (gamma), and 60–120 Hz (high gamma). Mathematically, the wavelet decomposition is represented as

$$s = a_5 + d_5 + d_4 + d_3 + d_2 + d_1 \tag{3}$$

where a_5 is the 5th level approximation of the signal representing the delta band frequency component whereas d_{1-5} are the respective layer detail components such that d_1 to d_5 represent high gamma, gamma, beta, alpha, and theta band frequency range respectively. Root Mean Square (RMS) values of the decomposed signals of all the trials were taken as the feature set to train the model.

3.2 Artificial Neural Network

A shallow ANN classifier was used in this study for its robust and effective non-linear computational modeling attributes of data classification. ANNs have been widely used in pattern classification problems to model the particular inputs leading to specific target outputs. The ANN model was designed to take the RMS values of the wavelet decomposed sensor signals in the input layer. A single hidden layer consisting of 256 nodes were used with random weights during initialization. The maximum number of epochs was set to 100 to properly train the model. A sigmoid activation function was used after the hidden layer which transformed the learned weights into a non-linear hyper-dimensional space. A 5 dimensional fully connected softmax layer was used as the final layer to represent the minimized cross-entropy of the 5 phrases. The weights (ω_{ij}) for nodes in the hidden layer of the ANN at iteration $(t + 1)$ are updated based on iteration (t) via back-propagation using a stochastic gradient descent as:

$$\omega_{ij}(t+1) = \omega_{ij}(t) + \eta \frac{\partial \mathbf{C}}{\partial \omega_{ij}}, \tag{4}$$

where $\mathbf{C}$ is the cost function, η is the learning rate set to 0.01, i and j are the input and hidden layer neuron labels respectively. The data was divided into three parts as training, testing and validation data. Training data consisted 70% of the whole data whereas the testing and validation data consisted 15% each of the whole data. The validation data was used to check for data over-fitting during training. Early stopping of the training resulted when the data starts to generalize with this approach. Further, we have experimented with various number of nodes to train the model to find that with a lower number of nodes the accuracy decreased whereas with higher node selection the performance of the model remained constant. Data over fitting resulted with more than 512 nodes in the hidden layer even after the 3rd epoch.

4   Results and Discussions

Figure 3 shows a comparison of the average speech decoding accuracies of the 4 subjects, obtained for each of the 4 stages of the speech production task at different trials. A peak at the 40th can be observed for the articulation, imagination and perception stages indicating the best performance with 40 number of trials. Although, as hypothesized, for the articulation and perception stage the speech decoding performance more or less saturated after 40 trials, the accuracy of imagination stage resulted in a continuous decrease. Although at present, there is no clear explanation for this behavior of the imagination stage, the absence of external stimuli or overt movement (For perception there were visual stimuli and during articulation, the produced overt speech sound was the feedback stimuli) might allow for more endogenous variability in the neural signal. After reaching optimal SNR, this variability may override any increased value of more trials.

To more accurately verify, if 40 is the optimal number, we performed the analysis with $32, 35, 37, 39, 41, 43, 45, 47$ and 49 trials. The pattern remained consistent with the best accuracy obtained with either 39 or with 40 number of trials. Further, for statistical validation, we implemented a 4-way ANOVA across trials with the four subjects as the 4 factors for each stage (pre-stimuli, perception,

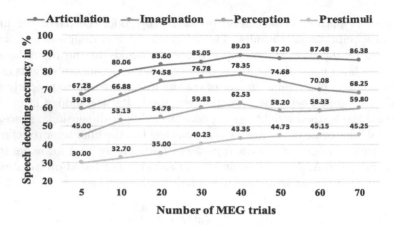

Fig. 3. Speech decoding accuracy at various total number of MEG trials

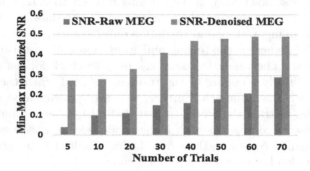

Fig. 4. Comparison of SNR for raw and denoised MEG signal at different trials

imagination, and articulation) respectively. Results indicated no statistically significant differences across subjects (p > .05) for each stage.

Figure 4 manifests the variation of the min-max normalized SNR of the raw MEG signal and wavelet decomposed MEG signal at different numbers of trials. It can be seen that, in case of the raw MEG signal, the SNR value was increased continuously with an increase in the number of trials. However, after denoising with wavelets, the SNR values were saturated after 40 trials. Hence, with proper denoising of the signal prior to analysis, 40 number of MEG trials could be sufficient for best speech decoding performance.

Among the 4 stages, during articulation, the highest model performance was obtained with an average accuracy of 89.03%. The average accuracy of 78.35% was maximum for classification of covert speech, i.e., during the stage of imagination. The additional involvement of the motor and auditory cortex regions of the brain to facilitate articulation and auditory feedback respectively could be the reason for the resulting higher accuracy in articulation. Perceived speech phrase classification was poorer. The pattern of increasing accuracy during the pre-stimuli stage can be clearly observed in the Fig. 3. Although, the subjects were at rest and the accuracy should be at the chance level for this stage, with an increase in the number of trials the speech decoding accuracy was increased. The most probable reason for this is that the subjects may have started to memorize the stimulus with time, as in total 5 number of stimuli were used.

Limitation. Although the results are promising, the dataset considered in this study is relatively small. A further analysis with a larger data set from more number of subjects is needed to validate these findings.

5   Conclusion

In this study, we investigated to determine the optimal number of MEG trials from a machine learning and speech decoding perspective. A total of 40 trials were found to be sufficient and necessary for the maximum speech decoding performance. Wavelet denoising resulted in a saturated SNR after 40 trials. Limiting the MEG trials will facilitate for huge improvement in experiment and computation time as well as cost reduction. We also demonstrated that speech decoding directly from the brain is possible with an accuracy of 89.03% during articulation whereas the imagined speech information can be extracted with an accuracy of 78.35%. Although 40 trials were obtained to be optimal for speech decoding task, it may not be optimal for other task-evoked MEG experiments.

Acknowledgment. This project was supported by the University of Texas System Brain Research grant and by the National Institutes of Health (NIH) under award number R03 DC013990. We thank Dr. Mark McManis, Dr. Ted Mau, Dr. Angel W. Hernandez-Mulero, Kanishk Goel and the volunteering participants.

References

1. Indefrey, P., Levelt, W.J.M.: The spatial and temporal signatures of word production components. Cognition **92**(1), 101–144 (2004)
2. Booth, J.R., Wood, L., Lu, D., Houk, J.C., Bitan, T.: The role of the basal ganglia and cerebellum in language processing. Brain Res. **1133**, 136–144 (2007)
3. Ackermann, H.: Cerebellar contributions to speech production and speech perception psycholinguistic and neurobiological perspectives. Trends Neurosci. **31**(6), 256–272 (2008)
4. Laureys, S.: The locked-in syndrome: what is it like to be conscious but paralyzed and voiceless? Progress Brain Res. **150**, 495–611 (2005). The Boundaries of Consciousness: Neurobiology and Neuropathology
5. Duffy, J.: Motor Speech Disorders Substrates, Differential Diagnosis, and Management, 3rd edn, p. 295. Elsevier, St. Louis (2012)
6. Herff, C., Schultz, T.: Automatic speech recognition from neural signals: a focused review. Front. Neurosci. **10**, 429 (2016)
7. Wolpaw, J.R., Mcfarland, D.: Control of a two-dimensional movement signal by a noninvasive brain-computer interface in humans. PNAS **51**, 49–54 (2004)
8. Yoshimura, N., et al.: Decoding of covert vowel articulation using electroencephalography cortical currents. Front. Neurosci. **10**, 175 (2016)

9. Birbaumer, N.: Brain computer-interface research: coming of age. Clin. Neurophysiol. **117**(3), 479–483 (2006)
10. Brumberg, J.S., et al.: Brain computer interfaces for speech communication. Speech Commun. **52**(4), 367–379 (2010)
11. Leuthardt, E.C., Cunningham, J., Barbour, D.: Brain-computer interface research. In: Guger, C., Allison, B., Edlinger, G. (eds.) Towards a Speech BCI Using ECoG. SpringerBriefs in Electrical and Computer Engineering, pp. 93–110. Springer, Heidelberg (2013). https://doi.org/10.1007/978-3-642-36083-1_10
12. Herff, C., et al.: Brain-to-text: decoding spoken phrases from phone representations in the brain. Front. Neurosci. **9**(217), 1–11 (2005)
13. Dash, D., Abrol, B., Sao, A., Biswal, B.: The model order limit: deep sparse factorization for resting brain. In: IEEE 15th International Symposium on Biomedical Imaging (ISBI), pp. 1244–1247 (2018)
14. Dash, D., Abrol, B., Sao, A., Biswal, B.: Spatial sparsification and low rank projection for fast analysis of multi-subject resting state fMRI data. In: IEEE 15th International Symposium on Biomedical Imaging (ISBI), pp. 1280–1283 (2018)
15. Formisano, E., De Martino, F., Bonte, M., Goebel, R.: Who is saying what? Brain-based decoding of human voice and speech. Science **322**, 970–973 (2008)
16. Cohen, D., Cuffin, B.N.: Demonstration of useful differences between magnetoencephalogram and electroencephalogram. Electroencephalogr. Clin. Neurophysiol. **56**(1), 38–51 (1983)
17. Chan, A.M., et al.: Decoding word and category-specific spatiotemporal representations from MEG and EEG. NeuroImage **54**(4), 3028–3039 (2011)
18. Wang, J., Kim, M., Hernandez-Mulero, A.H., Heitzman, D., Ferrari, P.: Towards decoding speech production from single-trial Magnetoencephalography (MEG) signals. In: IEEE International Conference on Acoustics, Speech and Signal Processing (ICASSP), pp. 3036–3040 (2017)
19. Dash, D., Ferrari, P., Malik, S., Wang, J.: Overt speech retrieval from neuromagnetic signals using wavelets and artificial neural networks. In: IEEE Global Conference on Signal and Information Processing (GlobalSIP) (2018)
20. Gross, J., Baillet, S., Barnes, G.R., Henson, R.N., Hillebrand, A., Jensen, O., Schoffelen, J.-M.: Good practice for conducting and reporting MEG research. Neuroimage **65**(100), 349–363 (2013)
21. Attal, Y., et al.: Modelling and detecting deep brain activity with MEG and EEG. IRBM - Biomed. Eng. Res. **30**, 133 (2009)
22. Burgess, R.C., Funke, M.E., Bowyer, S.M., Lewine, J.F., Kirsch, H.E., Bagi, A.I.: American clinical magnetoencephalography society clinical practice guideline 2: presurgical functional brain mapping using magnetic evoked fields. J. Clin. Neurophysiol. **28**, 355–361 (2011)
23. Grill-Spector, K., Henson, R., Martin, A.: Repetition and the brain: neural models of stimulus-specific effects. Trends Cogn. Sci. **10**(1), 14–23 (2006)
24. Cheyne, D., Ferrari, P.: MEG studies of motor cortex gamma oscillations: evidence for a gamma fingerprint in the brain? Front. Hum. Neurosci. **7**, 575 (2013)
25. Dash. D., Kim, M., Ferrari, P., Wang, J.: Brain activation pattern analysis for speech production decoding from MEG signals. In: 25th Annual meeting of Biomedical Engineering Society (BMES) (2018)
26. Tadel, F., Baillet, S., Mosher, J.C., Pantazis, D., Leahy, R.M.: Brainstorm: a user-friendly Application for MEG/EEG analysis. Comput. Intell. Neurosci. **8**, 8:1–8:13 (2011)

Brain Big Data Analytics, Curation and Management

Use of Temporal Attributes in Detection of Functional Areas in Basal Ganglia

Konrad A. Ciecierski(✉) (iD)

Research and Academic Computer Network, Warsaw, Poland
konrad.ciecierski@gmail.com

Abstract. Basal ganglia are a target for deep brain stimulation (DBS) in various neurological disorders like Parkinson's Disease (PD) or Dystonia. Due to the complex excitatory and inhibitory interactions between various components of basal ganglia, it is often as much important to stimulate certain regions as it is not to stimulate others. Such is the case in DBS surgery for PD where the goal is the stimulation of the Subthalamic Nucleus (STN) while the Substantia Nigra Pars reticulata (SNr) should not be stimulated. In this paper it is shown that use of temporal attributes extracted from microrecordings acquired during DBS procedure not only allows for better detection of the STN itself but also helps to prevent false positive identification of the SNr recordings as the STN ones.

Keywords: DBS (Deep Brain Stimulation)
STN (Subthalamic Nucleus) · SNr (Substantia Nigra Pars reticulata)
Teamporal fatures · Classification · Random Forest · SVM
Decision support system

1 Introduction

During the Deep Brain Stimulation (DBS) surgery for Parkinson's Disease (PD) the target for the stimulating electrode placement is Subthalamic Nucleus (STN) [1–3]. Surgery is a difficult one as the STN is small (9 by 4 by 7 mm) [2] and often poorly visible in Computer Tomography (CT) or Magnetic Resonance Imaging (MRI) results [1]. Misdetection of the STN and wrong placement of the stimulating electrode can cause very severe adverse effects as a result of the inhibition of the surrounding structures responsible for sensory, motor, autonomic and cognitive functions [4,5].

Very precise identification of the STN borders is therefore both difficult and extremely important [6]. To facilitate the localization of the STN, a two step procedure is applied. Firstly using fused CT with MRI scan, the expected localization of the STN is given. In the second phase, intra-surgically precise neurophysiological STN localization is obtained using analysis of the neurosurgical microrecordings [7].

© Springer Nature Switzerland AG 2018
S. Wang et al. (Eds.): BI 2018, LNAI 11309, pp. 175–185, 2018.
https://doi.org/10.1007/978-3-030-05587-5_17

During this phase an array of 3 to 5 parallel microelectrodes is inserted into the patient's brain using the stereotactic guidance system [1]. The electrodes are advanced towards the expected localization of the STN. From the depth that is roughly about 10 mm dorsal to the STN, electrodes are advanced in measured steps. At each step a multiunit simultaneous recording is obtained from all of the electrodes. After recording is done, the set of electrodes is advanced ventrally by 1 mm. Such steps are repeated for around 16 mm i.e. until the electrodes fully traverse the ventral border of the STN.

Developed computer based classifier determines then for each obtained recording if it has been recorded within STN or not. While this classifier obtains good results [7] it treats each recording separately. The knowledge about order in which recordings were obtained is not used. This is an important additional information as for example it is certain that if an increased activity is found below the STN ventral border it should not be classified as STN and is therefore a strong SNr indication [1,2]. This paper shows that use of such information improves classification results and also prevents miss-classification of the Substantia Nigra Pars reticulata (SNr) recordings as the STN ones.

2   DBS Data and Attributes

2.1   DBS Data

Data from DBS is recorded with great amplification, registered voltages are in ranges of microvolts and as such are very easily contaminated [1]. Because of that prior to calculation of any attributes the contaminating artifacts have to be removed [8].

2.2   Microrecording Based Primary Attributes

Attributes that are most discriminating when looking for the STN recordings are based on the signal's background [7]. For recorded signal, those attributes are: 80th percentile of absolute amplitude (**PRC80**), Root Mean Square (**RMS**), power calculated for frequencies below 500 Hz (**LFB**) and finally power calculated for frequencies between 500 Hz and 3 KHz (**HFB**). All those attributes are normalized according to the recording length and sensitivity of the given electrode [7]. In case of the Parkinson's Disease, some brain circuits in Basal Ganglia become aleterd in a pathological way [9]. This results in hyperactivity of the STN [1]. As the STN contains large amounts of small, densely packed neuron cells [2], when in hyperactive state it presents activity than can be detected by elevated values of primary attributes described above [7]. While the frequency range of the (**LFB**) attribute might seem to be broad, it is important to take into account that PD is highly heterogeneous. Various parts of the STN display different frequency characteristics but those characteristics are highly individual and cannot easily be generalized [10].

2.3   Temporal Attributes

Temporal attributes are calculated directly from four microrecording based primary attributes. For each primary attribute four temporal attributes are defined. Let's define set of primary attributes as

$$PAS = \{PRC80, RMS, LFB, HFB\} \tag{1}$$

Define also that for $a \in PAS$ the $a(e, d)$ denotes value of attribute a calculated for recording registered by electrode e at depth d.

Assuming that for given electrode e the recording started at depth d_B proceeded with step 1000 μm and ended at depth d_E such that $d_B < d_E$ one can for attribute $a \in PAS$ define a delta function at depth d [μm].

$$delta(a, e, d, s) = \begin{cases} 0 & iff \quad d - s < d_B \\ a(e, d) - a(e, d - s) & iff \quad d - s \geq d_B \end{cases} \tag{2}$$

Temporal attributes at depth d denote maximal positive and negative change in value of attribute a registered by given electrode e from the start of its recording pass.

This change is calculated between recordings separated by 1000 μm

$$DD1UP(a, e, d) = \max_{di \leq d} delta(a, e, di, 1000) \tag{3}$$

$$DD1DW(a, e, d) = \min_{di \leq d} delta(a, e, di, 1000) \tag{4}$$

or by 2000 μm

$$DD2UP(a, e, d) = \max_{di \leq d} delta(a, e, di, 2000) \tag{5}$$

$$DD2DW(a, e, d) = \min_{di \leq d} delta(a, e, di, 2000) \tag{6}$$

Knowing that all attributes are always calculated in context of given electrode e and depth d a simplified notation can be used:

$$DD1UP\_PRC80 = DD1UP(PRC80, e, d)$$
$$DD1DW\_PRC80 = DD1DW(PRC80, e, d)$$
$$DD2UP\_PRC80 = DD2UP(PRC80, e, d)$$
$$DD2DW\_PRC80 = DD2DW(PRC80, e, d)$$

In analogous way this notation can be extended to RMS, LFB and HFB attributes. Finally, define following sets of temporal attributes:

$$DD1UP = \{DD1UP\_PRC80, DD1UP\_RMS, DD1UP\_LFB, DD1UP\_HFB\}$$
$$DD1DW = \{DD1DW\_PRC80, DD1DW\_RMS, DD1DW\_LFB, DD1DW\_HFB\}$$
$$DD2UP = \{DD2UP\_PRC80, DD2UP\_RMS, DD2UP\_LFB, DD2UP\_HFB\}$$
$$DD2DW = \{DD2DW\_PRC80, DD2DW\_RMS, DD2DW\_LFB, DD2DW\_HFB\}$$

$$DD1 = DD1UP \cup DD1DW$$
$$DD2 = DD2UP \cup DD2DW$$
$$DD = DD1 \cup DD2$$

Examples showing values of primary attribute and based upon it temporal attributes can be seen of Figs. 1, 2 and 3. Figure 1 shows values of the RMS attribute calculated for pass of a single electrode.

As seen on Fig. 1 and confirmed also by the surgical protocol, the electrode passed through the STN at depths from -4000 μm to $+1000$ μm and then entered SNr at $+6000$ μm. As the SNr has been reached at $+6000$ μm, the electrode was not advanced any further.

From the Fig. 2 it is also evident that both $DD1UP\_RMS$ and $DD2UP\_RMS$ temporal attributes have distinct increase of their values at -4000 μm. It also noticeable at Fig. 3 that $DD2DW\_RMS$ show big decrease after exiting the STN at $+2000$ μm.

3   Evaluation and Interpretation

Quality of the attributes in classification has been tested on set of 18772 recordings registered during PD DBS surgeries. 14980 (79.80%) of them were assigned in surgical protocols as registered outside of the STN and here assigned to the $MISS$ class. 3792 (20.20%) of them were assigned in surgical protocols as registered within the STN and here assigned to the STN class. This means that classes are imbalanced and during classification it must be addressed.

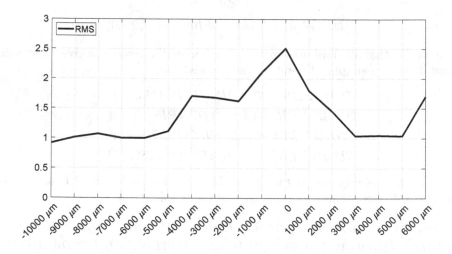

Fig. 1. Plot of the RMS attribute

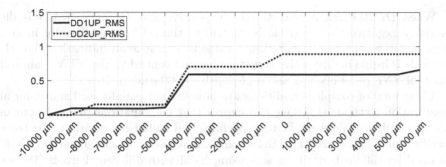

Fig. 2. Plot of the DD1UP_RMS and DD2UP_RMS attributes

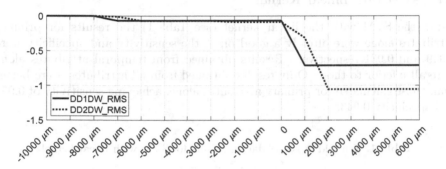

Fig. 3. Plot of the DD1DW_RMS and DD2DW_RMS attributes

Classifications have been made using two classifiers: Random Forest [11,12] and Support Vector Machine (SVM) [11]. In each case the classifier was used in a cost sensitive mode [13] to address the imbalance between classes.

As a measure of classification quality the sensitivity, specificity, accuracy and area under ROC (AUC) [14,15] have been calculated for each ten fold cross-validation.

Classifications were made using 5 different sets of attributes: primary attributes alone, $DD1$, $DD2$, $DD1 \cup DD2$ i.e. all temporal attributes and finally primary attributes together with temporal ones.

Looking at the Figs. 1, 2 and 3 one can notice a certain patterns that are especially evident with the $DD2UP\_RMS$ and $DD2DW\_RMS$ attributes.

When both $DD2UP\_RMS$ and $DD2DW\_RMS$ attributes are close to 0, the electrode is dorsal to the STN, it has not reached it yet.

When $DD2UP\_RMS$ is distinctively positive and $DD2DW\_RMS$ is close to 0, the electrode is inside the STN. It has already passed its dorsal border but has not yet passed the ventral border.

When $DD2UP\_RMS$ is distinctively positive and $DD2DW\_RMS$ is distinctively negative the electrode is ventral to the STN. Additionally in such situation, when the primary attribute value is high it is an indication that the electrode is inside highly active structure located ventral to the STN – an indication of SNr (see Figs. 1, 2 and 3 at depth +6000 μm) [1,2].

Those kind of complex conditions are however not equally well suited for all classification methods [16]. One can expect that combinations of conditions on various attribute values might be especially well suited for decision tree based classification approaches [17]. Below are comparisons of classification results obtained for different attribute sets using SVM with different kernels [18] and decision tree based Random Forest classifier.

3.1 SVM with Linear Kernel

Using the SVM with the linear kernel (see Table 1) the results for primary attributes alone were already a good ones, the sensitivity and specificity were 0.949 and 0.931 respectively. Results obtained from temporal attributes alone were all inferior to those. Only results obtained from all attributes, were better than those calculated for primary attributes alone, achieving sensitivity of 0.952 and specificity 0.943.

Table 1. Ten fold cross-validation results for SVM with linear kernel

Measure	Attribute set				
	Primary	$DD1$	$DD2$	DD	All
Sensitivity	0.949	0.832	0.882	0.884	**0.952**
Specificity	0.931	0.889	0.909	0.909	**0.943**
Accuracy	0.935	0.877	0.903	0.904	**0.945**
AUC	0.980	0.922	0.951	0.951	**0.984**

3.2 SVM with RBF Kernel

The SVM classifier with radial basis function (RBF) kernel (see Table 2) showed some improvement in relation to primary attributes only in the AUC parameter. Sensitivity, specificity and accuracy were in all cases inferior to those obtained from primary attributes alone. What is worth noticing is that even primary attributes taken together with temporal attributes were worse in majority of measures. It is clear that in case of this classifier addition of temporal attributes has worsened the overall results.

3.3   Random Forest

In case of this classifier the obtained results were much better than those achieved with the SVM classifier (see Table 3). Those good results are not unexpected as the Random Forest is a decision tree based classification method [17]. In case of $DD2$ set of attributes, all of the quality measures (Sensitivity, Specificity, Accuracy and AUC) were better than in case of primary attributes alone. Results obtained using DD set were even better and use of all attributes yielded best results.

Table 2. Ten fold cross-validation results for SVM with RBF kernel

Measure	Attribute set				
	Primary	$DD1$	$DD2$	DD	All
Sensitivity	0.957	0.895	0.914	0.920	0.954
Specificity	0.928	0.887	0.922	0.925	0.928
Accuracy	0.934	0.889	0.920	0.924	0.933
AUC	0.954	0.947	**0.959**	**0.965**	**0.977**

Table 3. Ten fold cross-validation results for Random Forest

Measure	Attribute set				
	Primary	$DD1$	$DD2$	DD	All
Sensitivity	0.920	0.911	**0.924**	**0.933**	**0.945**
Specificity	0.947	0.940	**0.957**	**0.961**	**0.969**
Accuracy	0.941	0.934	**0.951**	**0.955**	**0.964**
AUC	0.977	**0.979**	**0.985**	**0.988**	**0.991**

Having above findings, knowing than addition of temporal attributes can improve detection of the STN, one might wonder how inclusion of temporal attributes influence quality of classification of SNr data i.e. recordings registered and marked during surgeries as those from SNr.

For test purposes a modified version of cross-validation has been used. Data set of 18731 non SNr labeled recordings and a set of 41 SNr labeled recordings have been used. Each set has been partitioned 20 fold resulting in sets of recordings $\{recSTN_j\}_{j=1..20}$ and $\{recSNr_j\}_{j=1..20}$. In each batch, tests were run 20 times. On i^{th} run sets from following set

$$TRAIN_i = \{recSTN_j \cup recSNr_j \; : \; j \in \mathbb{N}, \; 1 \leq j \leq 20, \; j \neq i\} \qquad (7)$$

were used for training while the set of recordings

$$TEST_i = recSNr_i \qquad (8)$$

was used for testing – all tests were done using solely SNr recordings.

As a classifier the Random Forest with 100 trees was used. There were run total 100 batches i.e. 2000 Random Forest classifiers were constructed and evaluated. During the evaluation the score for the $MISS$ class was collected and number of false positive occurrences was counted.

As recordings coming from the SNr should all be of course classified as ones recorded outside of the STN, they all should be also assigned to the $MISS$ class. Therefore the score for the $MISS$ class should be close to 1.0.

On Fig. 4 there is a box-plot showing the score value distribution for the classification of the recording to the $MISS$ class. It is immediately evident that scores obtained when using all attributes are much higher which means that classifier based on all attributes is much less prone to produce false positives. False positive results might in turn lead to stimulation of the improper part of the brain and in effect lead to severe adverse effects [1].

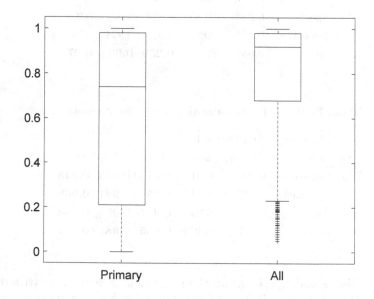

Fig. 4. Box plot of MISS class classification score

In 2000 of computed classifications, the classifiers based solely on primary attributes gave 38.51% of false positives while classifiers based on all attributes produced 17.46% of false positives. The number of false positives was by this reduced by more then 50%.

While the over 17% of false positives is not an excellent result, one must stress that for testing purposes only recordings from SNr were used and that while SNr distinct activity is spike related [19], the spiking activity was not taken into account during computation of any of primary attributes [7].

In Table 4 there are quartiles computed for the obtained score values.

Let's assume now the classification threshold to be at score value of 0.5.

Table 4. Quartiles for $MISS$ class score values

Attributes	Quartile		
	Q1	Q2	Q3
Primary	0.21	0.74	0.98
All	0.68	0.92	0.98

In case of primary attributes alone, some recordings between Q1 and Q2 have score values clearly less than 0.5 – they were thus wrongly classified to the STN class and were false positive cases.

In case of all attributes, the Q1 value is 0.68 (clearly above 0.5) and therefore all recordings falling between Q1 and Q3 were correctly classified to the $MISS$ class i.e. they all were true negatives.

4   Conclusions

In this paper it has been shown, that it is useful in classification of DBS recordings to take into account order in which they have been recorded by each of the electrodes. Knowing the standard approach [1] during DBS surgery for the Parkinson's Disease, this does provide an additional valuable information. It helps to prevent false positive detection of the highly active SNr [1,19] as the STN. It is especially important as in this type of surgery the STN not SNr should be the target of the stimulation [1].

Separate observation worth noticing is that temporal attributes that may inherit their values from dorsal depths are not universally well suited for all classification methods. In presented example, temporal attributes have improved results for Random Forest classifier to the point when the temporal attributes alone provided better results than primary attributes they were based upon (see Table 3). In case of Support Vector Machine classifier, there was some improvement only when using all attributes with linear kernel (see Table 1). In case of RBF kernel (see Table 2) only the AUC measure showed some improvement. With this kernel use of temporal attributes has in fact worsened all other tested classification measures i.e. sensitivity, specificity and accuracy. Other SVM kernels available in Matlab were also tested but obtained results were all uniformly much inferior to those obtained from primary attributes alone. Above findings are even more interesting knowing that SVM classifier is under typical circumstances particularly well suited for binary classification problems [18].

Described solution is presently in use during PD surgeries in Department of Neurosurgery, M. Sklodowska-Curie Memorial Oncology Center, Warsaw.

References

1. Israel, Z., Burchiel, K.J.: Microelectrode Recording in Movement Disorder Surgery. Thieme, New York (2011)
2. Nieuwenhuys, R., Voogd, J., Van Huijzen, C.: The Human Central Nervous System: A Synopsis and Atlas. Springer, Heidelberg (2007). https://doi.org/10.1007/978-3-540-34686-9
3. Pizzolato, G., Mandat, T.: Deep brain stimulation for movement disorders. Front. Integr. Neurosci. **6**, 2 (2012)
4. Anderson, P.B., Rogers, M.H.: Deep Brain Stimulation: Applications, Complications and Side Effects. Nova Biomedical Books, New York (2009)
5. Temel, Y., Blokland, A., Steinbusch, H.W.M., Visser-Vandewalle, V.: The functional role of the subthalamic nucleus in cognitive and limbic circuits. Progress Neurobiol. **76**(6), 393–413 (2005)
6. Priori, A., Egidi, M., Pesenti, A., Rohr, M., et al.: Do intraoperative microrecordings improve subthalamic nucleus targeting in stereotactic neurosurgery for Parkinson's disease? J. Neurosurg. Sci. **47**(1), 56 (2003)
7. Ciecierski, K., Raś, Z.W., Przybyszewski, A.W.: Foundations of recommender system for STN localization during DBS surgery in Parkinson's patients. In: Chen, L., Felfernig, A., Liu, J., Raś, Z.W. (eds.) ISMIS 2012. LNCS (LNAI), vol. 7661, pp. 234–243. Springer, Heidelberg (2012). https://doi.org/10.1007/978-3-642-34624-8_28
8. Ciecierski, K.A.: Methods of automatic artifact removal in neurobiological signals. In: Szewczyk, R., Zieliński, C., Kaliczyńska, M. (eds.) AUTOMATION 2018. AISC, vol. 743, pp. 72–81. Springer, Cham (2018). https://doi.org/10.1007/978-3-319-77179-3_7
9. Agid, Y.: Parkinson's disease: pathophysiology. Lancet **337**(8753), 1321–1324 (1991). https://www.thelancet.com/journals/lancet/article/PII0140-6736(91)92989-F/fulltext
10. Ciecierski, K.A., Raś, Z.W., Przybyszewski, A.W.: Frequency based mapping of the *STN* borders. In: Esposito, F., Pivert, O., Hacid, M.-S., Raś, Z.W., Ferilli, S. (eds.) ISMIS 2015. LNCS (LNAI), vol. 9384, pp. 386–395. Springer, Cham (2015). https://doi.org/10.1007/978-3-319-25252-0_42
11. Ciecierski, K.A., Raś, Z.W., Przybyszewski, A.W., Ciecierski, K.: Review of classification methods for intraoperative decision making for STN DBS in Parkinson disease
12. Qi, Y.: Random forest for bioinformatics. In: Zhang, C., Ma, Y. (eds.) Ensemble Machine Learning, pp. 307–323. Springer, Boston (2012). https://doi.org/10.1007/978-1-4419-9326-7_11
13. Sun, Y., Kamel, M.S., Wong, A.K.C., Wang, Y.: Cost-sensitive boosting for classification of imbalanced data. Pattern Recognit. **40**(12), 3358–3378 (2007)
14. Hajian-Tilaki, K.: Receiver operating characteristic (ROC) curve analysis for medical diagnostic test evaluation. Caspian J. Internal Med. **4**(2), 627 (2013)
15. Swets, J.A.: Measuring the accuracy of diagnostic systems. Science (1988). http://science.sciencemag.org/content/240/4857/1285.short
16. Statnikov, A., Wang, L., Aliferis, C.F.: A comprehensive comparison of random forests and support vector machines for microarray-based cancer classification. BMC Bioinform. **9**(1), 319 (2008). http://bmcbioinformatics.biomedcentral.com/articles/10.1186/1471-2105-9-319

17. Lior, R., et al.: Data Mining with Decision Trees: Theory and Applications, vol. 81. World Scientific (2014)
18. Williams, C.K.I.: Learning with kernels: support vector machines, regularization, optimization, and beyond. J. Am. Stat. Assoc. **98**(462), 489 (2003). https://dl.acm.org/citation.cfm?id=559923
19. Ciecierski, K.A., Mandat, T.: Detection of *SNr* recordings basing upon spike shape classes and signal's background. In: Ascoli, G.A., Hawrylycz, M., Ali, H., Khazanchi, D., Shi, Y. (eds.) BIH 2016. LNCS (LNAI), vol. 9919, pp. 336–345. Springer, Cham (2016). https://doi.org/10.1007/978-3-319-47103-7_33

Influence of Time-Series Extraction on Binge Drinking Interpretability Using Functional Connectivity Analysis

J. I. Padilla-Buriticá[1,3]([⊠]), H. F. Torres[2], E. Pereda[4], A. Correa[4],
and G. Castellanos-Domínguez[1]

[1] Signal Processing and Recognition Group,
Universidad Nacional de Colombia, Bogotá, Colombia
jipadilla@unal.edu.co
[2] Universidad de Caldas, Manizales, Colombia
[3] Diseño Electrónico y Técnicas de Tratamiento de Señal,
Universidad Politécnica de Cartagena, Cartagena, Spain
[4] Universidad de la Laguna, Santa Cruz de Tenerife, Spain

Abstract. Brain connectivity analysis has gained considerable importance in different cognitive tasks and the detection of pathological conditions. Despite recent advances in connectivity analysis, there are still problems to be solved, being a proper extraction of the time-series to characterize the regions of interest (ROI) one of the challenges. In this work, we examine the influence of the time-varying mean estimation on the brain connectivity analysis for control and binge drinkers subjects. The obtained results show that the performance of brain connectivity improves using the eigenvalue-based averaging since it may face better the nonstationarity behavior and inter-trial variability of MEG activity.

Keywords: Connectivity analysis · MEG inverse problem
Lagged phase synchronization

1 Introduction

The human brain is an organ with a set of complex networks, which can be affected by different factors, one of these factors is the consumption of harmful substances such as alcohol. In recent years, alcohol consumption has increased markedly, unfortunately, there are few works that have been carried out to analyze the toxic effect of alcohol on the brain, which is why it is considered a field of study to be developed. Some of the papers presented to study this effect are based on the analysis of cerebral connectivity, since the analysis of functional brain connectivity allows studying the interaction of different areas, as well as detecting abnormalities in the brain.

© Springer Nature Switzerland AG 2018
S. Wang et al. (Eds.): BI 2018, LNAI 11309, pp. 186–194, 2018.
https://doi.org/10.1007/978-3-030-05587-5_18

This analysis can be devised either in the MEG-channel or source space. In the first case, the MEG electrodes only detect summed activities of a large number of neurons, which are affected by the field spread effects, tend to bias the estimated neural activity and therefore the connectivity analysis [9]. Moreover, it is difficult to associate a physiological meaning with estimated connections since the measured signals are not located in the same spatial proximity to the underlying sources. In the second case, source reconstruction methods can take into account the cortical activity propagation across the scalp, increasing their performance in space and time domains. Besides, source solutions may support a better interpretation of the calculated interactions by their more direct association with the brain processes of integration and segregation [1], therefore, the functional connectivity analysis will be done on the source space.

To continue with the functional connectivity analysis on the sources, two aspects must be considered: the selection of the Regions of Interest (ROI) and the extraction of the time series belonging to the ROI. The selection of the ROI was made taking into account the Brodmann Regions that have been reported in other studies, such as areas affected by alcohol consumption. The second aspect will be the most important aspect of this work because it is a challenge to obtain an appropriate extraction of time series to characterize the ROI [11]. Mostly, the time-series extraction method focus on producing a single averaged time-course of MEG activity, relying on different estimates of time-varying means. However, each estimation is performed under diverse statistical assumptions, without taking into account the effects that can generate the method to obtain each time series [4].

In this work, we examine the influence of the time-varying mean estimation on the brain connectivity analysis for control and binge drinker subjects. The investigated averaging methods, which are commonly-used in literature, are the following: time-varying average and eigenvalue-based mean estimation. The comparison comprises three stages: (i) The activity in the source space is estimated through Empirical Bayesian Beamformer (BMF) [2]. (ii) Some regions of interest are selected, which in this case have been previously defined according to similar studies, taking into account the Brodmann's regions [3,12]. (iii) A connectivity brain measure is employed to quantify the changes in the information flow over the selected regions of interest. The obtained results show that the performance of brain connectivity improves using the eigenvalue-based averaging since it may face better the nonstationarity behavior and inter-trial variability of MEG activity.

2   Methods

2.1   Estimation of Brain Source Activity

With the aim of estimating a brain activity measured from M-EGG recordings, we will consider the distributed inverse solution $Y = LJ + \Xi$, where $Y \in \mathbb{R}^{C \times T}$ is the scalp M−EGG data measured by $C \in \mathbb{N}$ sensors at $T \in \mathbb{N}$ time samples, $J \in \mathbb{R}^{D \times T}$ is the amplitude of $D \in \mathbb{N}$ current dipoles, which are placed in each three-dimensional dimension and distributed through cortical surface. Also, the lead field matrix $L \in \mathbb{R}^{C \times D}$ holds the relationship between sources and M-MEG measurements, which can be assumed zero-mean Gaussian noise $\Xi \in \mathbb{R}^{C \times T}$, having matrix covariance $Q_\Xi = \sigma_\Xi^2 I_C$, where $I_C \in \mathbb{R}^{C \times C}$ is an identity matrix, and σ_Ξ^2 is the noise variance. Under these constraints, the measured brain source activity can be estimated as $\hat{J} = QL^\top(Q_\Xi + LQL^\top)^{-1}Y$, being $Q \in \mathbb{R}^{D \times D}$ the source covariance matrix.

As a rule, the source mapping approaches need spatial prior knowledge (priors) upon Q to include information derived from multiple modalities and/or subjects. In this regard, Empirical Bayesian Beamformer (BMF) relies on a prior that assumes a covariance matrix with elements q_{dd} in the main diagonal as follows [8]:

$$q_{dd} = (l_d^\top(YY^\top)l_d)^{-1}/\delta_d, \quad \forall d = 1, \ldots, D,$$

where $l_d \in \mathbb{R}^{C \times 1}$ is d−th column of L, and $\delta_d = 1/l_d^\top l_d$ is a normalization parameter.

2.2 Time-Series Extraction from Measured MEG Data

To perform the functional connectivity analysis, two tasks must be performed previously: selection of regions of interest (ROI), and extraction of time series from the selected ROI set [7]. In this study, we use l tags (with $l \in \mathbb{N}^{ROI}$) to designate the regions of interest associated with the Brodmann's areas Table 1; which have been chosen since they are affected by alcohol consumption [3]. We represent $\hat{J}_l$ as the set of time series estimated for the dipoles labeled l. Further, all time series extracted from the dipoles, belonging to each Brodmann's area, are encoded into matrix $\hat{J}_r = [\hat{J}_1, \hat{J}_2, \ldots \hat{J}_l]$. Nonetheless, we carry out the clustering of active brain sources, which are spatially adjacent and correlated to the studied phenomena, estimating the time-courses that properly describe the temporal patterns emerged in each region. Hence, an additional step must be accomplished to provide a single time series, aiming to characterize each ROI as a whole. To this end, a couple of reduction approaches are widely used:

- Time-varying mean value averaged across all dipoles at each ROI, that is, $x_r = \mathbb{E}\left\{\hat{J}_r : \forall i \in n\right\}$, being $\mathbb{E}\{\cdot\}$ notation for expectation operator.
- Time-curse of the eigenvectors associated with the maximal non-zero eigenvalues computed for the covariance matrix of $\hat{J}_r$ at each ROI as explained in [10].

2.3 Measure of Brain Connectivity

The lagged phase synchronization (LPS), noted as $\phi \in \mathbb{R}^+$, measures the relationship between a couple of time series, x and y, as follows:

$$\phi = \sqrt{1 - |S(\omega)|/|\Re(S(\omega))|} \tag{1}$$

whith $S \in \mathbb{C}$, the cross-spectral density matrix, defined as:

$$S(\omega) = \begin{bmatrix} S_{xx}(\omega) & S_{xy}(\omega) \\ S_{yx}(\omega) & S_{yy}(\omega) \end{bmatrix}$$

Where the diagonal elements of $S(\omega)$ reflect the power estimates of signals x and y, and the off-diagonal elements reflect the averaged crossspectral density terms. Notation $\Re$: stands for the real part of the matrix S.

3   Experimental Set-Up

Figure 1 shows the main schema for which we have studied the influence of the different forms of time series extraction, belonging to different ROI anatomically associated with the Brodmann's areas, using lagged phase synchronization (LPS) for connectivity analysis. We propose a methodology appraising the following stages: (i) MEG brain activity mapping, (ii) selection of regions of interest (ROI), (iii) Extraction of time series belonging to the ROI set and (iv) connectivity analysis.

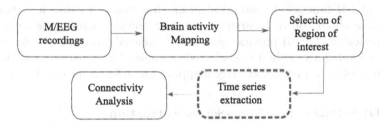

Fig. 1. Scheme of comparison between different methods for time series extraction in connectivity analysis. The block marked in dashed line is the subject of present study. The details of each step are described below.

3.1   MEG Database and Preprocessing

Four minutes of MEG signal were acquired (1000 Hz sampling rate and an online bandpass filter at 0.1−330 Hz) during eyes-closed resting state using a 306-channel (102 magnetometers and 204 gradiometers) system (Elekta©, VectorView). In this study, only magnetometers (102 channels) information was submitted to source and statistical analyses. The system was housed in a magnetically shielded room (VacuumSchmelze GmbH, Hanua, Germany). The head movement was monitored by means of four head-position indicator coils attached to the scalp. Ocular movements were tracked with two bipolar electrodes [5].

For the preprocessing, the raw recording data were at first submitted to Maxfilter software (v2.2, Elekta Neuromag) to remove external noise with the temporal extension of the signal space separation method with movement compensation. In this study, we used only magnetometers data in order to avoid mixing MEG sensors with different sensitivities or resorting to scaling. Accordingly, all of the magnetometer's resting state signals were automatically scanned for ocular, muscle and jump artifacts with Fieldtrip package (available online) and were visually confirmed by a MEG expert. The artifact-free data were segmented in continuous 4 seconds fragments (trials). At least 15 clean trials were obtained from all participants and preserved for further analyses. The number of surviving trials did not differ significantly between groups. To calculate the source reconstruction, the time series were filtered using a wavelet packet-based algorithm for the extraction of neural rhythms: $\theta : 4 - 7\,Hz$; $\beta : 14 - 30\,Hz$ and $\gamma : 30 - 50\,Hz$ [5].

3.2   Brain Activity Mapping

A source reconstruction was obtained using 8196 dipoles distributed through the brain for each of the subjects. Each dipole corresponds to a likely source location (based on single dipole models) and the separation between them is 5 mm. The leadfields are calculated using a single-sphere volume conductor model.

Concerning the choice of the prior set, Q in Sect. 2.1 is a diagonal matrix formed from a direct projection of the data into the source space. BMF uses a single, global functional-anatomical prior (functional because it is based on assumptions about source covariance and anatomical because it is constrained to the cortical manifold) provides just one estimated covariance component at the sensor level. This method was selected because of its satisfactory spatial and temporal resolution in brain activity mapping for different levels of SNR [2].

3.3   ROI Selection and Time-Series Extraction

Each source on the brain grid is anatomically associated with a Brodmann's area. Thus, 12 areas are selected previously, which are shown in Table 1, giving a total of 24 ROIs [7].

For the selected ROI, two forms of time series extraction are used, which are based on the mean and the decomposition in singular values. In different studies of functional connectivity, it is necessary for the choice of representative time series in the region of interest (ROI). The usual approach is to compute the mean value across the first eigenvector of ROI dipoles, which is further employed to calculate the measure of brain connectivity [6].

3.4   Connectivity Analysis

The significant differences between control subjects and binge subjects are shown in Figs. 2 and 3. We compared the results obtained with LPS (Eq. (1)), from the extracted time series with the average and the first eigenvector, in the complete set of regions of interest.

Table 1. Selected Brodmann's areas for connectivity analysis.

Anatomical regions	Brodmann area
middle temporal area (MT) ●	37
frontal eye fields (FEF) ●	6
superior parietal lobule (SPL) ●	7
anterior prefrontal cortex (aPFC) ●	10
Left dorsolateral prefrontal cortex (dlPFC) ●	9
Anterior cingulate cortex (aCC)	32
anterior inferior parietal lobule (aIPL) ●	40
anterior insula (aINS) ●	47
Posterior cingulate cortex (pCC) ●	23
posterior inferior parietal lobule (pIPL) ●	39
Visual fields (Vis) ●	18
auditory fields (Aud) ●	41

We obtain the connectivity results for the bands β and γ, afterwards we carried out a paired t-test, in which the null hypothesis is that there is greater connectivity in the control subjects than in the binge subjects ($\rho = 0.05$), and the results obtained are as follows:

In Figs. 2 and 3, the upper part shows the results obtained by means of the average and the lower part the results obtained with the first eigenvector. Also, the red color highlights the most representative connections for binge subjects that control subjects (with $\rho = 0.05$), the blue color shows the connections where the opposite happens.

There is a fronto-parietal coupling in the β rhythm as can be seen in Fig. 2, which is related to phase synchronizations during concentration and attention processes. It may also be noted that greater activity is maintained when the analysis is performed by the first eigenvector, and the connections on the brain decrease for the band β when the analysis is performed by the average. This aspect is very important, since we are analyzing the same frequency band and the representative connections in the brain cortex are different.

In Fig. 3 it can be seen that there is a less number of connections than for the band β, in both control subjects and binge subjects, on the other hand, the representative connections for the control largest eigenvalue). In addition, the connections over the parietal lobe decrease in the γ band. In general, for the rhythms β and γ it is possible to observe that the connections are different and change considerably depending on the method of time-series extraction, in spite of analyzing the same task.

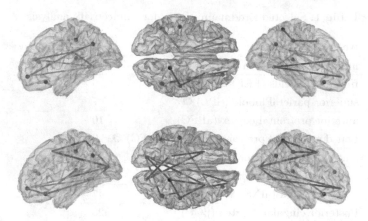

Fig. 2. Meaningful differences between binge (red line) and control(blue line) group in the connectivity analysis with the time series obtained with average (top) and the first eigenvalue (bottom) for β rhythm, with (LPS) and significant difference ($\rho = 0.05$) (Color figure online)

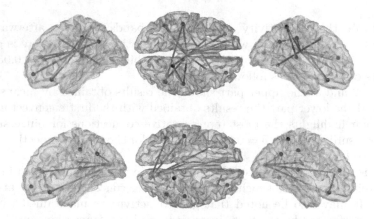

Fig. 3. Meaningful differences between binge (red line) and control(blue line) group in the conectivity analysis with the time series obtained with average (top) and the first eigenvalue (bottom) for γ rhythm, with (LPS) and significant difference ($\rho = 0.05$) (Color figure online)

4   Discussion and Concluding Remarks

We study the influence of the time series extraction method from different ROI on the brain connectivity analysis taking into account two methods for extracting the time series, based on the following steps:

1. Selection of brain mapping method, in this case we select BMF.
2. We apply two time series extraction from selected ROIs: we compute the average and the first eigenvector from predefined ROIs.

3. We estimate the connectivity measure using LPS between the extracted time-series.

The first task is related to the selected brain mapping method for imaging MEG activity. The tested method of brain mapping was BMF, the use of BMF improves identification of the source signals from MEG measurements [2], nevertheless, BMF tend to estimate several spurious activated areas, misleading the connectivity analysis. This effect appears to be directly related to the estimation complexity of the source covariance matrix [11].

Generally speaking, a challenging issue relating to brain connectivity analysis is how to extract the time series from the ROIs, since from these series, the analysis of functional connectivity is carried out, in which the different statistical relationships between the ROI are studied. Therefore, it is necessary to choose the method that best describes the dynamics of the time series, which are describing the behavior of all dipoles associated with an ROI. In the case of the average, there is a risk of eliminating components associated with phase change, while in the case of decomposition into eigenvectors, the assumptions are made about the probability distributions of the data, which leads to restrictions in the measure of connectivity.

Another aspect of consideration is the involved measure of connectivity analysis. Here, we have compared the changes of the LPS over the rhythms β and γ for the two methods for the time series extraction, it can be clearly noticed that the time series extraction method clearly influences the connectivity analysis. For instance, a poor time series extraction could lead to different physiological interpretations for the same task in the brain. As a result, the method for time series extraction must be chosen carefully in all studies conducted in brain connectivity. As future work, the authors plan to test the introduced approach over diverse paradigms, clustering, and connectivity measures. Furthermore, an online extension of the brain connectivity analysis can be proposed to include the temporal variations of the inter-channel relationships directly.

Acknowledgements. This research is supported by the research project *36706*: *BrainScore*: *"Sistema compositivo, gráfico y sonoro creado a partir del comportamiento frecuencial de las señales cerebrales"*, funded by Universidad de Caldas and Universidad Nacional de Colombia, JIPB is financed by Programa Nacional de Becas de Doctorado, convocatoria 647(2014).

References

1. Bastos, A.M., Schoffelen, J.M.: A tutorial review of functional connectivity analysis methods and their interpretational pitfalls. Front. Syst. Neurosci. **9**, 175 (2016)
2. Belardinelli, P., Ortiz, E., Barnes, G., Noppeney, U., Preissl, H.: Source reconstruction accuracy of MEG and EEG Bayesian inversion approaches. PloS one **7**(12), 51985 (2012)
3. Carbia, C., Cadaveira, F., Lopez-Caneda, E., Caamaño-Isorna, F., Holguín, S.R., Corral, M.: Working memory over a six-year period in young binge drinkers. Alcohol **61**, 17–23 (2017)

4. Cho, J.H., Vorwerk, J., Wolters, C.H., Knösche, T.R.: Influence of the head model on EEG and MEG source connectivity analyses. Neuroimage **110**, 60–77 (2015)
5. Correas, A., et al.: Functional and structural brain connectivity of young binge drinkers: a follow-up study. Sci. Rep. **6** (2016)
6. Gajdoš, M., Mračková, M., Elfmarková, N., Rektorová, I., Mikl, M.: 50. Comparison of canonical correlation analysis and pearson correlation in resting state fMRI in patients with parkinson's disease. Clin. Neurophysiol. **126**(3), 47–48 (2015)
7. Hata, M., et al.: Functional connectivity assessed by resting state EEG correlates with cognitive decline of Alzheimer's disease-An eLORETA study. Clin. Neurophysiol. **127**(2), 1269–1278 (2016)
8. Henson, R.N., Flandin, G., Friston, K.J., Mattout, J.: A parametric pmpirical bayesian framework for fMRI-constrained MEG/EEG source reconstruction. Hum. Brain Mapp. **31**(10), 1512–1531 (2010)
9. Mahjoory, K., Nikulin, V.V., Botrel, L., Linkenkaer-Hansen, K., Fato, M.M., Haufe, S.: Consistency of eeg source localization and connectivity estimates. Neuroimage **152**, 590–601 (2017)
10. Martinez-Vargas, J.D., Strobbe, G., Vonck, K., van Mierlo, P., Castellanos-Dominguez, G.: Improved localization of seizure onset zones using spatiotemporal constraints and time-varying source connectivity. Front. Neurosci. **11**, 156 (2017)
11. Padilla-Buritica, J.I., Martinez-Vargas, J.D., Castellanos-Dominguez, G.: Emotion discrimination using spatially compact regions of interest extracted from imaging EEG activity. Front. Comput. Neurosci. **10**, 55 (2016)
12. Spear, L.P.: Effects of adolescent alcohol consumption on the brain and behaviour. Nat. Rev. Neurosci. **19**(4), 197–214 (2018)

Regularized State Observers for Source Activity Estimation

Andrés Felipe Soler[1], Pablo Andrés Muñoz-Gutiérrez[2(✉)], and Eduardo Giraldo[1]

[1] Universidad Tecnológica de Pereira, Pereira, Colombia
{afsoler,egiraldos}@utp.edu.co
[2] Universidad del Quindío, Armenia, Colombia
pamunoz@uniquindio.edu.co

Abstract. The brain is a complex system and the activity inside can describe non-linear behaviors where the signals of the EEG which are taken from the scalp represent the mixture of the activity in each distributed source inside the brain. This activity can be represented by non-linear models and the inverse problem for source activity estimation can consider these models in the solutions. This paper presents the design of linear and nonlinear regularized observers for neural activity estimation, where the solutions involve a discrete physiologically-based non-linear model as spatio-temporal constraints. Furthermore, this document presents the estimation of the regularization hyper-parameters based on the application of a genetic algorithm over the Generalized Cross Validation cost function, which reduced the computational load. The aforementioned methods are compared with Multiple Sparse Priors (MSP) method of the state-of-the-art by using a simulated and real EEG signals.

Keywords: EEG inverse problem · Neuroimaging
Regularization parameters · Dynamic regularization

1 Introduction

The source activity estimation using EEG is an ill-conditioned and ill-posed inverse problem, with multiple solutions which are sensitive to noise in the measurement process, affecting the quality of the reconstruction. To overcome these difficulties the addition of spatial constrains in the solution process is used as in the methods Minimun Norm Estimates (MNE)[4], Weighted Minimun Norm Estimates (WMNE)[3] and Low Resolution Electrical Tomography (LORETA)[10]. Other method like Iterative Regularization Algorithm (IRA) [2] involves a temporal constraint based on one previous sample. In contrast to deterministic methods, Multiple Sparse Priors (MSP) [1] is based on a probabilistic framework and considers all the EEG data and assume that the sources are active in all the time window. However, the dynamical behavior is not considered in time [9]. In other hand, when the sources are active during all the

© Springer Nature Switzerland AG 2018
S. Wang et al. (Eds.): BI 2018, LNAI 11309, pp. 195–204, 2018.
https://doi.org/10.1007/978-3-030-05587-5_19

time in the EEG signals, the solutions show better reconstruction than MNE and LORETA in [6].

In this paper, the design of linear and nonlinear regularized observers for neural activity reconstruction is presented, where the solutions involve a discrete physiologically-based non-linear model as spatio-temporal constraints. In addition, the regularization hyper-parameters are selected by using a genetic algorithm. The paper is organized as follows: in Sect. 2 the proposed framework for source activity reconstruction and hyper-parameter estimation is presented. In Sect. 3 the results over real and simulated EEG signals are shown and finally in Sect. 5 the conclusions and final remarks are presented.

2   Materials and Methods

2.1   Forward and Inverse Problem Formulation

The EEG can be related to neural activity inside the brain through a forward problem described as a discrete state space model in the equation as follows

$$\boldsymbol{y}_k = \boldsymbol{M}\boldsymbol{x}_k + \varepsilon_k \tag{1}$$

EEG signals are represented by $\boldsymbol{y}_k \in \mathbb{R}^{d \times 1}$ where d is the number of electrodes on the scalp, the amplitude of n current dipoles $\boldsymbol{x}_k \in \mathbb{R}^{n \times 1}$ contains. $\boldsymbol{M} \in \mathbb{R}^{d \times n}$ is called the lead field matrix which relates the EEG with the neural activity at each source. The subscript k is the sample associated to the time instant $t_k = kh$ which represents the $k-$th sample of the EEG recording, where $k = 1, ..., N$, being N the total number of samples, and h the sample time. ε_k is an additive Gaussian noise with covariance a C_ε and zero mean. The inverse problem can be written like a minimization problem, like in [3] which involve a spatial constraint term with $l-2$ norm, the inverse problem can be formulated like:

$$\boldsymbol{J} = arg \min_{(\boldsymbol{x}_k, \rho)} \{||\boldsymbol{M}\boldsymbol{x}_k - \boldsymbol{y}_k||_2^2 + \rho^2 ||\boldsymbol{x}_k||_2^2\} \tag{2}$$

2.2   Discrete Physiologically Non-linear Model

In [8], a non-linear continuum model is presented, which consider a neural activity propagation, this model can be represented in space state model like below:

$$\frac{d\boldsymbol{v}}{dt} = \begin{bmatrix} 0 & 1 \\ \gamma^2 c_1 & -2\gamma \end{bmatrix} \boldsymbol{v}(t) + \begin{bmatrix} 0 & 0 \\ \gamma^2 c_2 & 0 \end{bmatrix} \boldsymbol{v}(t-t_0) + \begin{bmatrix} 0 & 0 \\ \gamma^2 c_3 & 0 \end{bmatrix} \boldsymbol{v}^2(t) + \begin{bmatrix} 0 & 0 \\ \gamma^2 c_4 & 0 \end{bmatrix} \boldsymbol{v}^3(t) + \begin{bmatrix} 0 \\ \gamma^2 \eta \end{bmatrix} \tag{3}$$

where the constant c_1 represents the instantaneous feedback due to nearby neurons, c_2 the delayed feedback via an extra-cortical loop with t_0 as the time delay of this feedback, γ is a characteristic decay rate of the field activity $\boldsymbol{x}(t)$ and η is a random white noise and it is considered as an external stimulus to perturb the brain states [7]. The variable $\boldsymbol{v}(t)$ is defined like:

$$\boldsymbol{v}(t) = \begin{bmatrix} \boldsymbol{x}(t) \\ \frac{d\boldsymbol{x}(t)}{dt} \end{bmatrix} \tag{4}$$

Applying the Taylor's approach forward differences for the derivative term in the Eq. (3), and following the procedure presented in [11] is possible to obtain the following model of the activity x_k in terms of the kth sample.

$$x_k = a_1 x_{k-1} + a_2 x_{k-2} + a_3 x_{k-\tau} + a_4 x_{k-2}^{\circ 2} + a_5 x_{k-2}^{\circ 3} \qquad (5)$$

being the terms $x_{k-2}^{\circ 2}$ and $x_{k-2}^{\circ 3}$ represent the corresponding Hadamard power of x_{k-2} the parameters of the model $a_1 \ldots a_5$ can be found through the equations presented in the discrete model in [11]. The variable τ represent the discrete version of the delayed feedback time t_0.

The activity in the distributed sources can be considered as a linear first order space state model like

$$x_k = f(x_{k-1}, \omega_k) + \eta_k \qquad (6)$$

with the dynamical output EEG equation are the same of Eq. (1). The first order observer consider f function as the evolution of the states as shown below

$$f(x_{k-1}, \omega_k) = a_1 x_{k-1} \qquad (7)$$

being the term ω a vector which contains the model parameters constants, in this case only the a_1 constant $\omega_k = a_1$. According to this information, the inverse problem can be performed involving an temporal term based on a l_2 norm to the inverse general problem presented in Eq. (2) as shown in the next expression

$$J = ||M x_k - y_k||_2^2 + \rho_k^2 ||x_k||_2^2 + \lambda_k^2 ||x_k - f(x_{k-1}, \omega_k)||_2^2 \qquad (8)$$

where ρ_k and λ_k are the regularization parameters of the spatial constraint and temporal constraint respectively. The estimation can be obtained finding the Jacobian with respect to x_k, equalling this to zero and solving for $\hat{x}_k$, the first order observer is represented by the follow equation

$$\hat{x}_k = (M^T M + \rho_k^2 I + \lambda_k^2 I)^{-1} (M^T y_k + a_1 \lambda_k^2 \hat{x}_{k-1}) \qquad (9)$$

In another case, the neural activity is considered as a linear second order space state model, involving the first delayed sample x_{k-1} and the linear terms of the second delayed sample x_{k-2} in a linear function f

$$x_k = f(x_{k-1}, x_{k-2}, \omega_k) + \eta_k \qquad (10)$$

where the function f consider the evolution of the states, like a linear combination of the two previously samples with the discrete constant models a_1 and a_2 like

$$f(x_{k-1}, x_{k-2}, \omega_k) = a_1 x_{k-1} + a_2 x_{k-2} \qquad (11)$$

the model parameters vector ω_k takes the structure $\omega_k = [a_1 \ a_2]^T$. Considering the second order term of the activity the new inverse problem can be represented by the next cost function

$$J = ||M x_k - y_k||_2^2 + \rho_k^2 ||x_k||_2^2 + \lambda_k^2 ||x_k - f(x_{k-1}, x_{k-2}, \omega_k)||_2^2 \qquad (12)$$

calculating the Jacobian with respect to $\boldsymbol{x}_k$, equalling to zero and solving for $\hat{\boldsymbol{x}}_k$, the second order observer can be represented by the follow expression

$$\hat{\boldsymbol{x}}_k = (\boldsymbol{M}^T \boldsymbol{M} + \rho_k^2 \boldsymbol{I} + \lambda_k^2 \boldsymbol{I})^{-1}(\boldsymbol{M}^T \boldsymbol{y}_k + \lambda_k^2(a_1 \hat{\boldsymbol{x}}_{k-1} + a_2 \hat{\boldsymbol{x}}_{k-2})) \tag{13}$$

For the non-linear estimation, all the terms of the non-linear model of the Eq. (5) are considered in the space state model involving the physiological model in to the observation process through the new function $\boldsymbol{f}$ like is shown below

$$\boldsymbol{x}_k = \boldsymbol{f}(\boldsymbol{x}_{k-1}, \boldsymbol{x}_{k-2}, \boldsymbol{x}_{k-\tau}, \boldsymbol{\omega}_k) + \eta_k \tag{14}$$

where $\boldsymbol{f}$ is now the non linear equation that considers the dynamical behavior of the system and takes the following structure

$$\boldsymbol{f}(\boldsymbol{x}_{k-1}, \boldsymbol{x}_{k-2}, \boldsymbol{x}_{k-\tau}, \boldsymbol{\omega}_k) = a_1 \boldsymbol{x}_{k-1} + a_2 \boldsymbol{x}_{k-2} + a_3 \boldsymbol{x}_{k-\tau} + a_4 \boldsymbol{x}_{k-2}^{\circ 2} + a_5 \boldsymbol{x}_{k-2}^{\circ 3} \tag{15}$$

where the model parameters vector $\boldsymbol{\omega}_k$ takes the structure $\boldsymbol{\omega}_k = [a_1 \ a_2 \ a_3 \ a_4 \ a_5]^T$. The states estimation can be performed by minimizing the new cost function J defined by

$$J = ||\boldsymbol{M}\boldsymbol{x}_k - \boldsymbol{y}_k||_2^2 + \rho_k^2 ||\boldsymbol{x}_k||_2^2 + \lambda_k^2 ||\boldsymbol{x}_k - \boldsymbol{f}(\boldsymbol{x}_{k-1}, \boldsymbol{x}_{k-2}, \boldsymbol{x}_{k-\tau}, \boldsymbol{\omega}_k)||_2^2 \tag{16}$$

where the estimation of the non-linear regularized observer can be represented by the follow expression

$$\hat{\boldsymbol{x}}_k = (\boldsymbol{M}^T \boldsymbol{M} + \rho_k^2 \boldsymbol{I} + \lambda_k^2 \boldsymbol{I})^{-1}(\boldsymbol{M}^T \boldsymbol{y}_k + \lambda_k^2(a_1 \hat{\boldsymbol{x}}_{k-1} + a_2 \hat{\boldsymbol{x}}_{k-2} + a_3 \hat{\boldsymbol{x}}_{k-\tau} + a_4 \hat{\boldsymbol{x}}_{k-2}^{\circ 2} + a_5 \hat{\boldsymbol{x}}_{k-2}^{\circ 3})) \tag{17}$$

2.3 Regularization Parameter Estimation

As a rule, the regularization observing process strongly depends of the regularization parameters, which directly can affect the quality of the neural activity reconstruction. In the presented methods two parameters have been considered, ρ_k associated to the spatial constraint and λ_k to the temporal constraint. Similar that in [2] a multiparameter generalized cross validation (GCV) can be performed for the regularized observers. The GCV method, considers the follow cost function defined as $\mathcal{G}(\lambda_k, \rho_k)$ for find this parameters

$$\mathcal{G}(\lambda_k, \rho_k) = \frac{||\boldsymbol{M}\boldsymbol{x}_k(\lambda_k, \rho_k) - \boldsymbol{y}_k||_2^2}{tr(\boldsymbol{I} - \boldsymbol{M}\boldsymbol{M}^\dagger(\lambda_k, \rho_k))^2} \tag{18}$$

being $\boldsymbol{M}^\dagger$ the regularized lead field matrix, this matrix is the same for the presented observers and can be computed using the next expression

$$\boldsymbol{M}^\dagger = (\boldsymbol{M}^T \boldsymbol{M} + \rho^2 \boldsymbol{I} + \lambda^2 \boldsymbol{I})^{-1} \boldsymbol{M}^T \tag{19}$$

A genetic algorithm (GA) to search optimal solution from a random population can be applied using the GCV cost function, where through of the following stages: compute and assign the fitness value, selection, crossover, mutation, elitism and new random member, is possible to find the regularization parameters.

The method consider an initial random population with two chromosomes $cr = 2$, corresponding to regularization parameters λ and ρ, the population only is created one time at the first sample and has n members. The random value range of the chromosomes is determined between zero and the maximum singular value of the matrix M. Then, the members are classified by a basic tournament, sorting the population according to the cost function $\mathcal{G}$ of each member, after, a set of parents is founded, this set called $P \in \mathbb{R}^{np \times cr}$ with np members are formed the union of two subsets $P = P_1 \cup P_2$, the subset $P_1 \in \mathbb{R}^{np_1 \times cr}$ contains the best np_1 members and the subset $P_2 \in \mathbb{R}^{np_2 \times cr}$ contains the worst np_2 members. The crossover process, where the children set are formed with chromosomes of different parents according to a randomly sort of the set P, and the number of children ns is defined by $ns = (2np) - 2$. After, the first nm members from the set P are chosen to be part of the mutated set $MU \in \mathbb{R}^{nm \times cr}$, where a random chromosome is replaced by a random number with the same criterion of the initial population, the chromosome to change is selected with equal probability between the two chromosomes. Then, the elitism set $E \in \mathbb{R}^{ne \times cr}$ are the best ne parents of the generation. In the last step, a set $N \in \mathbb{R}^{nw \times cr}$ where nw new members are created using the criterion of the initial population. Finally the set of the population for the next generation $NP \in \mathbb{R}^{n \times cr}$ formed by $NP = (E \cup S \cup MU \cup N)$.

3   Experimental Framework

3.1   Simulated EEG Data

The neuronal activity in the brain is simulated using a continuous space state model described in the Eq. (3), using the following values of the model parameters $c_1 = -3.2$, $c_2 = 2.8$, $c_3 = 0.05$, $c_4 = -0.1$ and $\gamma = 100$ taken from reference [8] where the constants correspond to a normal activity of one active source. The value of the activity is sampling at $F_s = 250\,\mathrm{Hz}$, the total time simulated is of $t = 1\,\mathrm{s}$ for sample quantity of $N = 250$ samples. The activity is located in a head model (lead field matrix M) which consider 8196 distributed sources in the brain and 128 sensor locations placed by the standard BIOSEMI-128 EEG on the scalp. Afterward, the EEG is calculated using the Eq. (1).

Two kind of simulation were made in this work, the first simulated data were used to compare the raw GCV with the improved GCV based on genetic algorithm to search optimal parameters of regularization:

Generalized Cross-Validation (GCV) and Genetic Algorithm GCV (GA-GCV) evaluation over simulated EEG dataset. To estimate the regularization parameters in each sample, two approach are considered, the standard GCV algorithm based on the *fminsearchbnd* Matlab^{TM} function and GCV based on genetic algorithm as a method of searching for minima. The parameters used in the GA-GCV are $cr = 2$, $np = 4$, $np_1 = 2$, $np_2 = 2$, $ns = 6$, $nm = 3$

and $nw = 2$. Where the relative error measurement is used to compare the performance of the methods, using the relative error as follow

$$RelE = \frac{||\hat{x}_k - x_k||_2^2}{||x_k||_2^2}. \qquad (20)$$

In order to analyze the computational time, five simulated EEG were generated with a different duration, $t = 1\,\mathrm{s}$, $t = 2\,\mathrm{s}$, $t = 3\,\mathrm{s}$, $t = 4\,\mathrm{s}$, $t = 5\,\mathrm{s}$ for $N = 250$, $N = 500$, $N = 750$, $N = 1000$ and $N = 1250$ samples respectively. Besides, the relative error was measured to both algorithms in terms of several signal noise ratio (SNR) conditions, 0dB, 5dB and 10dB and, in the same way, two cases were considered, three active sources and five active sources generated with the non-linear model Eq. (17). The tests were done in Matlab (2016b) and using a Processor Intel core i7-6700 with two cores on Windows 7 64-bits and RAM 8 GB.

Regularized Observers Evaluation Over Simulated EEG Dataset. The second test compare the performance in term of the relative error of the presented algorithms through this work, First order Observer with GA-GCV (FIO$_{GA}$), Second order Observer with GA-GCV (SEO$_{GA}$), Non-Linear Observer with GA-GCV (NLO$_{GA}$), Non-Linear Observer with standard GCV (NLO$_{GCV}$) and a method of the state-of-art MSP. The neural activity is placed in different locations into the brain, where the EEG is obtained by using the lead field matrix of 1, and the noise is added with a SNR value of 0dB, 5dB, 10dB and 15dB.

3.2   Regularized Observers Evaluation over Real EEG Database

This test was performed over real EEG signals. The neural activity is assumed relying upon multi-modal solutions. For this case, eighteen healthy young adults (eight female) were drawn from the MRC Cognition and Brain Sciences unit Volunteer Panel. There were 300 different faces and 150 different scrambled faces. Of the faces, 150 were from famous people and 150 were from unfamiliar (previously unseen) people. Each face or scrambled face was either repeated immediately or after a lag of 5–15 intervening items. From this data-set, Evoked Related Potentials of 15 subjects are selected for each one of the 3 stimulus [5]. It is noticeable that each patient has his own forward model and the lead field matrix M. The EEG was recorded from 70 Ag-AgCl electrodes in an elastic cap, according to the extended 10–10% system and using a nose electrode as the recording reference. The data were sampled with a frequency of $F_s = 1.1\,\mathrm{kHz}$.

In order to apply the proposed algorithms is necessary to adapt the discrete model of parameters of the activity involved in the vector ω_k to the sample frequency, the new value of the parameters used for the estimation with the real database are $a_1 = 1.818$, $a_2 = -0.8446$, $a_3 = 0.02314$, $a_4 = 0.0004132$ and $a_5 = -0.0008264$. The mean of the estimated activity in each one of the sources x_k is compared with a ground truth of each subject, and it was calculated with multi-modal technique which is given in the database [5].

4   Results and Discussion

The first results with simulated data were about the computational time in the estimation of the regularization parameters. In Table 1 the comparison between GCV and GA-GCV can be seen and is possible to observe that the GA-GCV method took much less time than the standard GCV, where this had a rate per second of 112.9 s against a 13.4 s of the GA-GCV.

Table 1. Comparative analysis of computational time of AG-GCV and standard GCV for several EEG duration.

EEG duration	AG-GCV	Standard GCV
1 s	13.4 s ± 0.5 s	112.9 s ± 1.1 s
2 s	26.1 s ± 0.6 s	231.4 s ± 1.9 s
3 s	37.6 s ± 0.7 s	336.1 s ± 2.7 s
4 s	49.9 s ± 0.8 s	450.2 s ± 3.7 s
5 s	61.6 s ± 1.2 s	560.1 s ± 4.6 s

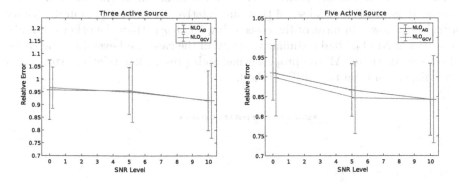

Fig. 1. Relative error for NLO_{AG} and NLO_{GCV}, with signal-noise ratio of 0dB, 5dB and 10dB for three and five active sources.

To analyze the two algorithms in terms of relative error were considered a simulations with three active sources and five active sources at several SNR conditions, 0dB, 5dB and 10dB, the results are showed in the Fig. 1. Where the relative error for the estimated neuronal activity was lower with standard GCV than AG-GCV for five active sources. Nevertheless, for three active sources the two solutions have similar values, even for SNR 0dB the AG-GCV present a low error value. The similar performance in the tuning of regularization parameters in terms of the relative error and the best performance in execution time, suggest that the AG-GCV can be used for a reliable regularization parameters estimation.

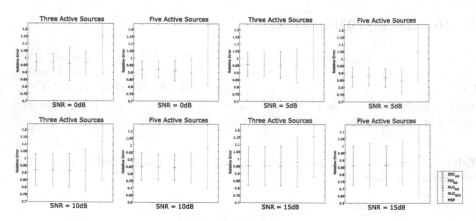

Fig. 2. Relative error for FIO_{AG}, SEO_{AG}, $NLAO_{AG}$, NLO_{AG}, NLO_{GCV} and MSP, with signal-noise ratio of 0dB, 5dB, 10dB and 15dB for three and five active sources.

Four simulated EEG dataset (with different SNR values 0dB, 5dB, 10dB and 15dB) were generated with three and five active sources to compare the observers (FIO_{AG}, NLO_{AG}, SEO_{AG}, NLO_{GCV} and MSP). In Fig. 2 the methods are compared in terms of the relative error over estimation of the location active sources. It is possible to observe that the relative error for the neural activity estimation is lower in most of the cases using NLO_{GCV} than the other methods, the values of NLO_{AG} had a similar value in all the cases and even in some cases, it had a lower value. All the proposed methods present low relative error and a lower dispersion than the MSP method.

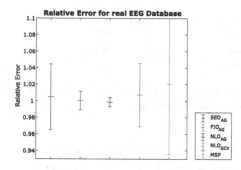

Fig. 3. Relative error for FIO_{AG}, SEO_{AG}, $NLAO_{AG}$, NLO_{AG}, NLO_{GCV} and MSP, with real EEG data.

The real EEG dataset was built with the signals taken to at least 15 subjects, the head model was provided for each of them and their ground truth too (calculated through multimodal technique) [5]. Source activity was estimated for each subject using the proposed methods, and its relative error was calculated using its respective ground truth. In Fig. 3 the relative error and standard deviation for each of the methods are shown. The outcomes suggest that the relative error is lower than the other methods in the NLO_{AG} and also is remarkable that the dispersion is lower. Regarding the result of MSP it has the same tendency that in the simulated data, because it has the higher dispersion and higher relative error than other methods.

5 Conclusions

The presented methods FIO, SEO and NLO are based on the dynamical characteristics of the activity and consider a physiologically meaningful model where the reconstruction of neural activity holds the spatio-temporal behaviour of the time series in terms of the temporal and spatial location of the sources. The usage of a linear and non-linear constraints for the temporal behaviour shows an improvement in terms of relative error when multiple sources are active simultaneously, guaranteeing the temporal smoothness of the solution, where the non-linear model of regularized observer NLO reached the best performance. In addition, the methods can be adapted to the characteristics of the EEG data.

For the regularization parameters the method GA-GCV reach a similar performance than the standard GCV in term of the results of the relative error, however the reduction of the computational load from approximately a rate of 112 s per 1 s of EEG to a 13 s per 1 s of EEG is an representative improvement.

The evaluation of the methods was performed over simulated and real EEG dataset, where the proposed methods overcome the different levels of signal noise ratio even when the noise added to the signals was the same amplitude than the EEG signals and considering that they were used the GA-GCV for the regularized parameters. The case of the methods whose consider linear spatio-temporal constraints of first order in FIO and second order in SEO kept a satisfactory performance. In addition, the method with the non-linear constraint with GA NLO_{AG} and with GCV NLO_{GCV} presented the better performance in terms of relative error.

Acknowledgment. This work was carried out under the funding of the Departamento Administrativo Nacional de Ciencia, Tecnología e Innovación (Colciencias). Research project: 111077757982 "Sistema de identificación de fuentes epileptogénicas basado en medidas de conectividad funcional usando registros electroencefalográficos e imágenes de resonancia magnética en pacientes con epilepsia refractaria: apoyo a la cirugía resectiva".

This work is also part of the research project "Solución del problema inverso dinámico considerando restricciones espacio-temporales no homogéneas aplicado a la reconstrucción de la actividad cerebral" funded by the Universidad Tecnológica de Pereira under the code E6-17-2.

Author Contributions. AFS and PAM conceived, designed and performed the experiments. EG analyzed the data. All the authors wrote and refined the article.

References

1. Friston, K., et al.: Multiple sparse priors for the M/EEG inverse problem. NeuroImage **39**(3), 1104–1120 (2008)
2. Giraldo-Suarez, E., Martinez-Vargas, J.D., Castellanos-Dominguez, G.: Reconstruction of neural activity from EEG data using dynamic spatiotemporal constraints. Int. J. Neural Syst. **26**(07), 1650026 (2016)
3. Grech, R., et al.: Review on solving the inverse problem in EEG source analysis. J. NeuroEng. Rehabil. **5**, 25 (2008)
4. Hauk, O.: Keep it simple: a case for using classical minimum norm estimation in the analysis of EEG and MEG data. NeuroImage **21**(4), 1612–1621 (2004)
5. Henson, R.N., Wakeman, D.G., Litvak, V., Friston, K.J.: A parametric empirical bayesian framework for the EEG/MEG inverse problem: generative models for multi-subject and multi-modal integration. Front. Hum. Neurosci. **5**, 1–16 (2011)
6. Hyder, R., Kamel, N., Tang, T.B., Bornot, J.: Brain source localization techniques: evaluation study using simulated EEG data. In: 2014 IEEE Conference on Biomedical Engineering and Sciences (IECBES), December, pp. 942–947 (2014)
7. Kim, J.W., Robinson, P.A.: Compact dynamical model of brain activity. Phys. Rev. E Stat. Nonlinear Soft Matter Phys. **75**(3), 1–10 (2007)
8. Kim, J.W., Shin, H.-B., Robinson, P.A.: Compact continuum brain model for human electroencephalogram. In: Proceedings of SPIE **6802**, 68020T–68020T-8 (2007)
9. López, J.D., Barnes, G.R.: Single: MEG/EEG source reconstruction with multiple sparse priors and variable patches. Dyna **79**(174), 136–144 (2012)
10. Pascual-Marqui, R.D., Michel, C.M., Lehmann, D.: Low resolution electromagnetic tomography: a new method for localizing electrical activity in the brain. Int. J. Psychophysiol. **18**(1), 49–65 (1994)
11. Soler, A.F.: Design of regularized state observer for estimation in large scale systems: source activity reconstruction from EEG signals. Master's thesis, Universidad Tecnológica de Pereira, Colombia (2018)

Distributional Representation for Resting-State Functional Brain Connectivity Analysis

Jiating Zhu$^{(\boxtimes)}$ and Jiannong Cao

The Hong Kong Polytechnic University, Hong Kong, China
sophie._z@163.com, csjcao@polyu.edu.hk

Abstract. Most analyses on functional brain connectivity across a group of brains are under the assumption that the positions of the voxels are aligned into a common space. However, the alignment errors are inevitable. To address such issue, a distributional representation for resting-state functional brain connectivity is proposed here. Unlike other relevant connectivity analyses that only consider connections with higher correlation values between voxels, the distributional approach takes the whole picture. The spatial structure of connectivity is captured by the distance between voxels so that the relative position information is preserved. The distributional representation can be visualized to find outliers in a large dataset. The centroid of a group of brains is discovered. The experimental results show that resting-state brains are distributed on the 'orbit' around their categorical centroid. In contrast to the mainstream representation such as selected network properties for disease classification, the proposed representation is task-free, which provides a promising foundation for further analysis on functional brain connectivity in various ends.

Keywords: Distributional representation
Functional brain connectivity · Categorical centroid
Outliers visualization

1 Introduction

A good low dimensional representation, which captures the important characteristics from the large information pool, is helpful in discovering new information across hundreds of brains. But due to the curse of dimensionality, it is not practicable to unfold raw functional magnetic resonance imaging (fMRI) data (4D tensor) directly into a vector to be trained via machine learning methods. The raw fMRI data is in large size (up to several gigabytes) and has inherent high levels of noise [1]. Studies using machine learning methods on low dimensional embedding of functional brain networks have been attempted. However, most of the recent researches on this topic are region-based [2–4], which consider

© Springer Nature Switzerland AG 2018
S. Wang et al. (Eds.): BI 2018, LNAI 11309, pp. 205–215, 2018.
https://doi.org/10.1007/978-3-030-05587-5_20

around a hundred regions. Nevertheless, region-based analysis limits the evaluation of inter-regional connectivities and restricts to certain anatomical areas. It has been discussed that voxel-based functional networks present features more prominently than region-based ones [5], such as small-world property.

Inspired from the text embedding method [6], which based on the distributed representation of words and documents, we propose a representation of the functional brain based on the connectivity distribution. The advantage of this novel representation is that it will not be affected by the errors from the alignment across brains.

The precise position and extent of the functional areas differ across individuals [7]. Even if 'perfect' anatomical alignment was possible, it would not align functional topography [8]. Currently, researchers use two approaches to compare a group of brains by either giving stimulus to the subjects or align different brains with anatomical masks. Both of the approaches will cause errors.

By investigating the proposed distributional representation, this paper aim to answer two questions:

(1) Is it possible to have a low dimensional representation for the whole functional brain connectivity in a voxel-level?
(2) How can we trust the prepossessed functional brain image data? Is it possible to find outliers only from the given data and eliminate them before further analysis?

2   Problem Definition

Definition 1. *A correlation matrix R captures the voxels' correlation information in a brain with N regions, where the entry r_{ij} is the Pearson's correlation coefficient value between regions i and j $(i, j = 1, ..., N)$. Here, a region refers to a three dimensional area in voxel-level (or higher region resolution).*

There will exist different correlation matrices for a specific brain with N regions due to different region partitions. Simply changing the numbering of the regions or assigning different anatomical positions for the regions will generate a different correlation matrix. Such a matrix has the ambiguity for representing the brain connectivity. Hence, we consider the distribution of correlation to avoid the ambiguity.

Definition 2. *A correlation distribution is a probability distribution that provides the probabilities of occurrence of different possible correlation values between voxels within a brain.*

In comparison with the correlation matrix, the correlation distribution loses the spatial information of the brain. Thus, we introduce a distance distribution to capture the information of the functional topology.

Definition 3. *A distance matrix D captures the voxels' relative position information in a brain with N regions, where the entry d_{ij} is the Euclidean distance between the centers of regions i and j $(i, j = 1, ..., N)$.*

Definition 4. *A distance distribution is a probability distribution that provides the probabilities of occurrence of different possible distance values between voxels within a brain. It depicts the spatial information of a brain by calculating the distribution of different possible values for the distance between a randomly selected pair of voxels.*

Definition 5. *A correlation-distance joint distribution is a probability distribution that provides the probabilities of co-occurrence of different possible correlation values and distance values between voxels within a brain.*

However, different distance values will give different contribution of spatial information to the joint probability distribution, because the distance distribution is a non-uniform distribution. To reduce this side effect, we consider a conditional distribution of correlation given distance.

Definition 6. *A correlation-distance conditional distribution is a probability distribution that provides the probabilities of occurrence of different possible correlation values between voxels when each of different possible values of the distance between voxels are given within a brain.*

Definition 7. *Distributional representation refers to an expression of functional brain connectivity by correlation distribution, correlation-distance joint distribution or correlation-distance conditional distribution.*

3 Distributional Representation Analysis

3.1 Data Description

The data we analyzed in this paper is from the ADHD-200 sample which collected resting-state fMRI scans from subjects with ADHD and typically developing controls in 8 international imaging sites. In this study, we only analyzed the preprocessed data from NYU with the largest number of subjects. The preprocessed data used NIAK pipeline and has extracted time courses from around 3000 regions of interests [9]. One or two resting-state fMRI scans were acquired for each subject in the NYU data. We picked the first scans (216 subjects) for analysis in this paper. The detailed information about the data can be found at http://preprocessed-connectomes-project.org/adhd200/.

3.2 Single Brain Analysis

We use a histogram to estimate the correlation distribution for a single subject. The data sample used for calculating the histogram is the upper triangle of the correlation matrix R, which is denoted by R_{tri}, where the entry in R_{tri} is $r_{ij}(i < j)$.

The histogram $R(r_k)$ for the correlation distribution is calculated by $R(r_k) = c_r(k)/(w_r n_r)$, where w_r is the bin width, n_r is the number of bins, $c_r(k)$ is the number of entries that fall into the kth bin. Thus, $r_k = (k - 1)w_r - 1$,

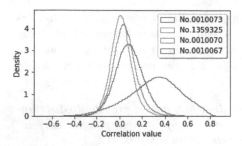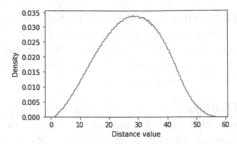

Fig. 1. Correlation distributions　　　　**Fig. 2.** The distance distribution

$k = 1, 2, ..., n_r$. Figure 1 shows the correlation distributions for 4 subjects by histograms, each with 200 bins over the range $[-1, +1]$. The correlation distributions in Fig. 1 look like Gaussian distributions.

Similarly, we use a histogram to estimate the distance distribution, taking the upper triangle D_{tri} of the distance matrix D as the data sample. The histogram $D(d_k)$ for the distance distribution is calculated by $D(d_k) = c_d(k)/(w_d n_d)$, where w_d is the bin width, n_d is the number of bins, $c_d(k)$ is the number of entries that fall into the kth bin. Thus, $d_k = (k-1)w_d, k = 1, 2, ..., n_d$.

Figure 2 shows the distance distribution by a histogram with 200 bins over the range $[0, 60]$. The distance distribution also looks like a Gaussian distribution. Theoretically, the spatial information (distance distribution) for every brain should be the same.

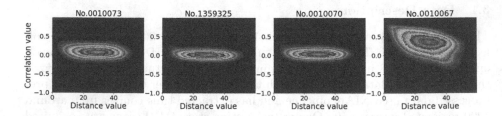

Fig. 3. Correlation-distance joint distributions

We use a two-dimensional histogram to estimate the correlation-distance joint distribution for a single subject. The two dimensional histogram is

$$h(r_i, d_j) = c_{rd}(i, j)/(w_r w_d n_r n_d), \tag{1}$$

where $c_{rd}(i, j)$ is the number of entries that fall into both the ith bin in $R(r_i)$ and the jth bin in $D(d_j)$. The two-dimensional histograms for the four subjects in Fig. 1 are shown in Fig. 3. We can see that the first three subjects from left to right look like two-dimensional Gaussian distributions. However, the last one (subject No. 0010067) has an obviously abnormal shape, whose alien features

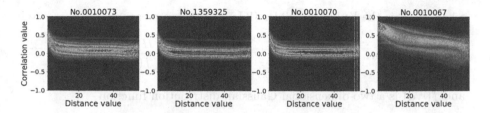

Fig. 4. Correlation-distance conditional distributions

can not be seen prominently in correlation distributions in Fig. 1. While the first three are marked 'pass', the subject No. 0010067 is marked 'questionable' in the quality control that come along with the preprocessed ADHD-200 NYU data. This means that our finding is consistent with the ground truth information.

In Fig. 3, the peaks (the smallest ovals) of the two-dimensional histograms all appear around the distance value 30. The reason is that the distance distribution, which also reaches its peak around 30 (see Fig. 2), affects the joint distribution. To eliminate such side effect, we introduce a conditional distribution to have a deeper investigation of the data. The two-dimensional histogram for estimating the correlation-distance conditional distribution for a single subject is

$$h(r_i|d_j) = h(r_i, d_j)/D(d_j). \tag{2}$$

Figure 4 shows the conditional distribution by a histogram with 200 bins in distance over the range $[1.55, 55]$ (the data around the two ends are removed due to the noise for visualization). As we can see from Fig. 4, correlation values tend to be higher around the shortest distance, which is consistent with our common knowledge that interactions are more active between neighboring voxels.

3.3 Group Analysis

To study the group characteristic in distributional representation, we first explore the centroid of the group and then focus on the divergence from the centroid in the group.

The following are four ways to represent the centroid.

- AJH: The accumulative two-dimensional joint histogram $H(r_i, d_j)$ as the centroid of a group with M subjects is calculated by

$$H(r_i, d_j) = \frac{1}{M} \sum_{b=1}^{M} h_b(r_i, d_j), \tag{3}$$

where $h_b(r_i, d_j)$ is the two-dimensional histogram for a subject numbered b in the group.
- EGD: The estimated two-dimensional Gaussian distribution $f_g(r, d)$ as the centroid is optimized by

$$f_g(r, d) = \arg \min_f D_{KL}(H(r, d) \| f(r, d)), \tag{4}$$

where D_{KL} is the Kullback-Leibler (KL) divergence measure,

$$D_{KL}(H(r,d)\|f(r,d)) = \sum_{i,j} H(r_i,d_j) \log \frac{H(r_i,d_j)}{f(r_i,d_j)}, \tag{5}$$

and $f(r,d)$ is a two-dimensional Gaussian distribution function

$$f(x,y) = A\exp(-a(x-x_0)^2 + 2b(x-x_0)(y-y_0) + c(y-y_0)^2). \tag{6}$$

– ACH: The accumulative two-dimensional conditional histogram $H(r_i|d_j)$ as the centroid is calculated by

$$H(r_i|d_j) = H(r_i,d_j)/D(d_j). \tag{7}$$

– ECD: The estimated two-dimensional conditional distribution $f_g(r|d)$ as the centroid is optimized by

$$f_g(r|d) = \arg\min_f D_{KL}(H(r|d)\|f(r|d)), \tag{8}$$

where $f(r|d) = f(r,d)/f(d)$, $f(d)$ is a one-dimensional Gaussian distribution function.

Figure 5 shows the centroid of a group in the four ways. The group contains 84 typically developing children in ADHD-200 NYU dataset. We kicked off the data that is marked as questionable in quality control, or the data that shows abnormal shape like the subject No. 0010067 in Fig. 3.

We calculate the KL divergence from the group centroid to each subject in the dataset. Furthermore, we fit two probability distribution functions to the KL divergence distribution. Figure 6 shows the KL divergence from the group centroid in four different aspects. The representation of each individual is the correlation-distance joint distribution if the centroid is represented by AJH or EGD, while the correlation-distance conditional distribution is applied when the centroid is represented by ACH or ECD. We can see that most of the KL

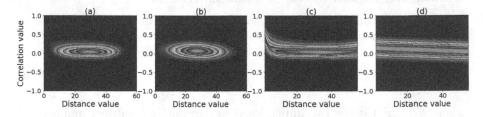

Fig. 5. Centroid for the group of typically developing children in ADHD-200 NYU dataset. (a) Accumulative two-dimensional joint histogram for the group centroid. (b) Estimated two-dimensional Gaussian distribution for the group centroid. (c) Accumulative two-dimensional conditional histogram for the group centroid. (d) Estimated two-dimensional conditional distribution for the group centroid.

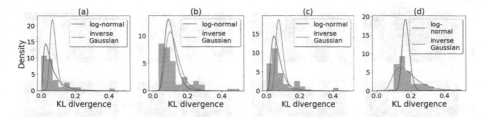

Fig. 6. Distributions of the KL divergence from the group centroid of typically developing children in ADHD-200 NYU dataset. The figure shows the histogram of the KL divergence values with 15 bins. (a) The divergence from the AJH centroid. (b) The divergence from the EGD centroid. (c) The divergence from the ACH centroid. (d) The divergence from the ECD centroid.

divergence values are below 0.2. This implied that most of the subjects cluster around the centroid. However, the shape of the probability distribution suggests that individuals in a group are gathered on an 'orbit' around the group centroid, not simply clustered closely around the group centroid. In Fig. 6(c), for instance, the probabilities for the individuals with very small KL values drop dramatically.

With a proper probability distribution function, the 'obrit' will be well depicted. It seems that the log-normal distribution is more suitable for estimating the KL divergence from the centroids of AJH and ACH, while the inverse Gaussian distribution is more suitable for the centroids of EGD and ECD.

A maximum likelihood estimation is used to estimate the parameters in the two probability distribution functions. Optimized parameters θ_g for a probability distribution function $f(kl_b|\theta)$ are calculated by

$$\theta_g = \arg\max_{\theta} \sum_{b=1}^{M} \log f(kl_b|\theta), \tag{9}$$

where $kl_b = D_{KL}(h_b||f_g)$ for the subject numbered b, $\theta = \mu$ if the probability distribution f is the single parameter inverse Gaussian distribution $f(x; \mu, \mu^2)$, or $\theta = (\mu, \sigma)$ if the probability distribution f is a log-normal distribution.

4   Results and Discussion

4.1   Outliers

We have a look at the correlation-distance joint distributions of total 216 subjects in preprocessed ADHD-200 NYU dataset. 15 obviously abnormal shapes are found (see Fig. 7), where 11 (73%) of them are marked as questionable in the quality control sheet.

The other four subjects are marked pass in the dataset. However, two of them (No. 3662296 and No. 6568351) have the same look (only a horizontal line appeared across the center) as the two questionable subjects (No. 0010015 and

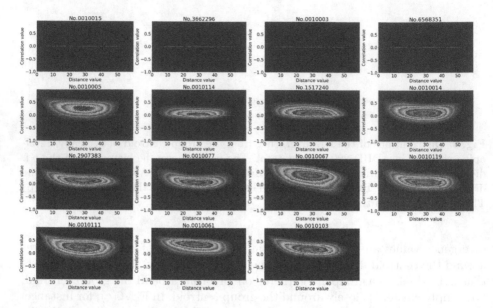

Fig. 7. Obviously abnormal shapes found manually.

No. 0010003) shown in the first row in Fig. 7. The third one (No. 0010114), on the second row at the second column, has the characteristic similar to the questionable subject No. 0010005 at the first column, where there suddenly appears a horizontal line across the center. The forth one (No. 1517240), next to the subject No. 0010114, also has the similar phenomenon, which seems to be collapsed to a horizontal line across the center, unlike other normal shapes that are symmetric-like. Thus, we believe that our distributional representation can provide useful information for finding alienated data.

4.2   Group Difference

We use two approaches to distinguish which group a subject belongs to. The typically developing children in ADHD-200 NYU dataset are regarded as a group named Typical, while subjects with ADHD-Combined, ADHD-Hyperactive /Impulsive or ADHD-Inattentive are regarded as a group named ADHD.

Simply comparing KL values $KL_{Typical}$ and KL_{ADHD} of an individual, we guess the individual falls into the group that has the smaller KL divergence to it. $KL_{Typical}$ is the KL divergence from the centroid of the group Typical to the individual distribution, while KL_{ADHD} is the KL divergence from the centroid of the group ADHD to the individual distribution. The number of individuals that are correctly found from each group is shown in the row labeled 'Compare KL' in Table 1.

The second way to guess the category of each individual is to estimate the probability of its KL value in each of the two groups Typical and ADHD, respectively, by an estimated probability distribution function $f(kl|\theta_g)$. We guess the individual falls into the group with the higher probability for its corresponding KL value. The results for the two probability distribution functions, namely log-normal and inverse Gaussian, are shown in the rows labeled 'Log-normal' and 'Inverse Gaussian', respectively, in Table 1.

Table 1. Different ways to recognize a group of subjects with four different centroid representations. The number of subjects in the group Typical is 84 and the number of subjects in the group ADHD is 89.

Centroid type		AJH	EGD	ACH	ECD
Compare KL	Typical	52 (62%)	55 (65%)	**72 (86%)**	51 (61%)
	ADHD	45 (50%)	38 (42%)	**64 (72%)**	54 (61%)
Inverse Gaussian	Typical	34 (40%)	52 (62%)	65 (77%)	26 (31%)
	ADHD	34 (40%)	24 (27%)	32 (34%)	58 (65%)
Log-normal	Typical	51 (61%)	37 (44%)	37 (44%)	17 (20%)
	ADHD	41 (46%)	49 (55%)	41 (46%)	69 (78%)
Centroid divergence		0.00103	0.00109	0.00217	0.00121

As shown in Table 1, the ACH approach has the best performance, where 86% of individuals in the group Typical are identified as Typical and 72% of individuals in the group ADHD are identified as ADHD. This performance is explainable. The divergence from the ACH centroid of the group ADHD to the ACH centroid of the group Typical is the biggest (see the bottom row). Hence, the two groups can be differentiated more easily. The ACH representation also has a significant improvement than the AJH representation, which justified that conditional distributions do eliminate the side effect of the unbalanced distance contributions to the joint distributional representations. Despite the fact that the two estimated probability distribution functions we attempted, namely Inverse Gaussian and Log-normal, do not show better performance, it is still possible to find appropriate estimation to improve the performance.

Because of the rough estimation, the estimated representations EGD and ECD do not have good performance on distinguishing groups (see columns labeled 'EGD' and 'ECD'). We can see from Fig. 5(c) and (d) that the estimated two-dimensional conditional distribution (ECD) loses some information at lower distance values in comparison with the accumulative two-dimensional conditional histogram (ACH). With a better estimation approach, we believe that the ECD representation will have a better performance.

5   Conclusion and Future Work

The greatest benefit of our distributional representation is that we can avoid the alignment errors when we compare a large group of brains. With our distributional representation, we can get a preview of the data and the data can be visualized to find outliers which might not be detected with a standard quality control procedure. The distributional representation persevered the majority connectivity information below the correlation value 0.7, which is around the commonly picked threshold for functional brain network analysis [5]. Although the dominant part of the representation stores the lower correlation values, it conveys the higher correlation information inside the distribution.

Instead of voxels' positions, the distance distribution between voxels is taken into consideration to preserve the spatial information in the functional brain, so that the position alignment can be avoided. The unbalanced contribution from the distance distribution is relived by a conditional distribution. Our quantitative results verified the effectiveness of the proposed conditional distribution (see Table 1).

An interesting thing is observed. The divergence distribution functions as an 'orbit', on which individuals are gathered around a group centroid. This phenomena, which needs further exploration, is beyond the conventional concept that similar subjects inhabit on the whole neighboring area around the centroid.

In the future, we will look for better distributional representation [10] and test our method on larger and various datasets to validate our findings. Novel analysis algorithms will be designed for various tasks, such as clustering and classification, on a basis of the distributional representation.

Moreover, it is possible to apply a distribution-based embedding method, such as the techniques in text embedding [6], to construct a task-free low dimensional representation for the whole functional brain connectivity in a voxel-level.

References

1. Norman, K.A., Polyn, S.M., Detre, G.J., Haxby, J.V.: Beyond mind-reading: multi-voxel pattern analysis of FMRI data. Trends Cogn. Sci. **10**(9), 424–430 (2006)
2. Cao, B., et al.: t-bne: Tensor-based brain network embedding. In: Proceedings of the 2017 SIAM International Conference on Data Mining SIAM, pp. 189–197 (2017)
3. Wang, S., He, L., Cao, B., Lu, C.T., Yu, P.S., Ragin, A.B.: Structural deep brain network mining. In: Proceedings of the 23rd ACM SIGKDD International Conference on Knowledge Discovery and Data Mining, pp. 475–484. ACM (2017)
4. Shen, H., Wang, L., Liu, Y., Hu, D.: Discriminative analysis of resting-state functional connectivity patterns of schizophrenia using low dimensional embedding of FMRI. Neuroimage **49**(4), 3110–3121 (2010)
5. Hayasaka, S., Laurienti, P.J.: Comparison of characteristics between region-and voxel-based network analyses in resting-state FMRI data. Neuroimage **50**(2), 499–508 (2010)
6. Tang, J., Qu, M., Mei, Q.: Pte: predictive text embedding through large-scale heterogeneous text networks. In: Proceedings of the 21th ACM SIGKDD International Conference on Knowledge Discovery and Data Mining, pp. 1165–1174. ACM (2015)
7. Nishimoto, S., Nishida, S.: Lining up brains via a common representational space. Trends Cogn. Sci. **20**(8), 565–567 (2016)
8. Chen, P.H.: Multi-view Representation Learning with Applications to Functional Neuroimaging Data. Ph.D. thesis, Princeton University (2017)

9. Bellec, P., Chu, C., Chouinard-Decorte, F., Benhajali, Y., Margulies, D.S., Craddock, R.C.: The neuro bureau adhd-200 preprocessed repository. Neuroimage **144**, 275–286 (2017)

10. Zhu, J., Cao, J.: Group analysis by visualized distributional representation for resting-state functional brain connectivity. In: Proceedings of the 14th International Conference on Semantics, Knowledge and Grids. IEEE (2018)

Deep Neural Networks for Automatic Classification of Anesthetic-Induced Unconsciousness

Konstantinos Patlatzoglou[1](✉) [ID], Srivas Chennu[1,2] [ID],
Mélanie Boly[3], Quentin Noirhomme[4], Vincent Bonhomme[5,6],
Jean-Francois Brichant[7], Olivia Gosseries[8], and Steven Laureys[8]

[1] University of Kent Chatham Maritime, Kent, UK
{kp356, sc785}@kent.ac.uk
[2] University of Cambridge, Cambridge, UK
[3] Department of Neurology and Department of Psychiatry,
University of Wisconsin, Madison, WI, USA
[4] Faculty of Psychology and Neuroscience,
Maastricht University, Maastricht, Netherlands
[5] GIGA - Consciousness, Anesthesia and Intensive Care Medicine Laboratory,
University and CHU University Hospital of Liege, Liege, Belgium
[6] Department of Anesthesia and Intensive Care Medicine, CHU University
Hospital of Liege, Liege, Belgium
[7] Department of Anesthesia, University of Liege, Liege, Belgium
[8] Coma Science Group, GIGA Consciousness, University and University
Hospital of Liège, Liège, Belgium

Abstract. Despite the common use of anesthetics to modulate consciousness in the clinic, brain-based monitoring of consciousness is uncommon. We combined electroencephalographic measurement of brain activity with deep neural networks to automatically discriminate anesthetic states induced by propofol. Our results with leave-one-participant-out-cross-validation show that convolutional neural networks significantly outperform multilayer perceptrons in discrimination accuracy when working with raw time series. Perceptrons achieved comparable accuracy when provided with power spectral densities. These findings highlight the potential of deep convolutional networks for completely automatic extraction of useful spatio-temporo-spectral features from human EEG.

Keywords: Consciousness · Anesthesia · EEG · Deep learning

1 Introduction

In the United States alone, 60,000 people receive general anesthesia (GA) every day for surgery [1]. Despite the obvious fact that GA fundamentally modulates brain activity, brain monitoring is not routine practice in the operating room, and is limited to proprietary systems which have produced mixed results, in part due to considerable interindividual variability [2]. Recent research into electroencephalographic (EEG) signatures of propofol-induced unconsciousness have highlighted the potential for improved brain monitoring [1, 3].

© Springer Nature Switzerland AG 2018
S. Wang et al. (Eds.): BI 2018, LNAI 11309, pp. 216–225, 2018.
https://doi.org/10.1007/978-3-030-05587-5_21

One of the challenges encountered in deploying novel EEG metrics of consciousness at the bedside is automation, in that they require expert analysis or interpretation of the data. To work towards addressing this challenge, we apply recent developments in artificial intelligence research, deep neural networks in particular, to the challenge of fully automated feature learning from EEG to detect states of unconsciousness due to propofol anesthesia. As there is no state-of-the-art deep learning model or reference dataset for EEG classification, we compare the performance of two widely used models, multilayer perceptrons (MLP) and convolutional neural networks (cNN), in their ability to discriminate states of unconsciousness from only 1 s of raw EEG data. With leave-one-participant-out-cross-validation, we show that cNNs achieve nearly 90% accuracy and significantly outperform MLPs, and generalize to data from participants unseen during network training.

2 Methods

2.1 Dataset Collection

The data used in this work were acquired from a propofol anesthesia study [4], in which the experimental design is described in detail. Briefly, the study was approved by the Ethics Committee of the Faculty of Medicine of the University of Liege, with participants giving written informed consent. Moreover, physical examination and medical history were obtained, in order to assure of any potential issues during anesthesia (e.g. pregnancy, trauma, surgery, mental illness, drug addiction, asthma, motion sickness).

Fifteen-minute spontaneous high-density electroencephalography (hd-EEG, 256 channel Hydrocel GSN) was recorded from 9 participants (mean age 22 ± 2 y, 4 males) during propofol anesthesia, at three different levels of consciousness, from fully awake, to mild sedation (slow response to command) and clinical unconsciousness (no response), as depicted in Fig. 1. Sedation procedure was monitored, while computer-controlled intravenous infusion was used to estimate effect-site concentrations of propofol. The level of behavioral consciousness was confirmed with the Ramsay scale, see [4] for details.

2.2 EEG Pre-processing

Minimal pre-processing steps were applied to the original data, in order to simulate a real-world scenario where deep learning could be applied to EEG data in real-time. Although raw EEG recordings tend to be noisy, the selection of the workflow was based on the notion of an automated feature extraction done by deep learning, along with a potential practical value of such implementation within a clinical context, where manual intervention and a priori knowledge of the signal would be infeasible.

Two different representations were extracted from the datasets, to compare the effects of using the raw time series versus a spectral representation. The latter has often been used in similar studies as a useful feature in EEG classification [5–8].

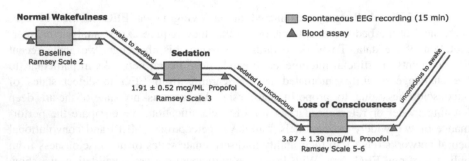

Fig. 1. Experimental design of the propofol anesthesia study. Participants underwent anesthetic induction into progressively deeper states of unconsciousness measured by behavior.

Raw Data Representation. For reducing the computational complexity of the deep learning pipeline, 20 electrodes of EEG data were examined, located as per the 10-20 system, namely: Fp1, Fp2, F7, F3, Fz, F4, F8, T3, C3, Cz, C4, T4, T5, P3, Pz, P4, T6, O1, Oz, and O2. Data were segmented into 1 s non-overlapping epochs and band-pass filtered between 0.5-40 Hz using a window FIR design (firwin, scipy). The vertex (Cz) electrode was the online reference, which was replaced by the average activity of all the 19 channels. Finally, the time series were down-sampled to 100 Hz, resulting in 100 samples per epoch. No manual artefact or bad channel rejection was performed other than the removal of the first 10 s of recording, which contained large unstable drifts. All pre-processing steps were implemented using the MNE-python library with default settings, unless specified otherwise.

Power Spectral Density Representation. To generate spectral representation of the EEG, raw data processed as above were submitted to the periodogram function (scipy) to obtain the power spectral density (PSD) of each channel and epoch. 201 points were used to compute the PSD, which resulted in 100 frequency bins (one-sided spectrum, dc coefficient removed). Importantly, this ensured that the dimensionality of the data was identical with both raw and PSD representations. The resulting dimension of each instance (epoch) was a 20 × 100 (channels x time samples/frequency bins) 2D-array for both representations.

Finally, the data were normalized by epoch using the scikit-learn library, before feeding them into the deep learning networks. This can be thought as normalizing the whole scalp activity for each epoch and participant independently. Although there are many ways to normalize the data (e.g. by time sample or by channel), this way was considered more appropriate in terms of its physical interpretation and practical application, as only data from the current epoch is required for applying the normalization.

2.3   Deep Learning Architectures

Two deep learning architectures were compared, as a way to investigate the suitability of such algorithms in classifying states of consciousness and extracting relevant features from the EEG. Convolutional neural networks (cNN) are a class of feed-forward networks that have become very interesting for end-to-end EEG research (both for analysis and interpretation of data) during the recent years. This architecture has shown to be very efficient in analyzing raw data (mostly from images), as it reveals spatial features across different levels of abstraction, using the convolution operation over local segments of the data [9]. In contrast, the Multilayer perceptron (MLP) network is a naïve implementation of a deep learning model, which can be used as a baseline for comparison (cNN can be thought as an MLP with a specialized structure).

Our aim here was not to optimize each network for the given task, but rather to compare them fairly, to reveal the computational advantages of each design. Hence the two models were compared with respect to their architectural sizes, which can be thought as the number of neurons/trainable parameters within each functional layer.

Convolutional Neural Network. The architecture of the cNN is a sequential model based on a simple design used in computer vision for hand-written digit classification (mnist example, Keras). The first functional layer (feature extraction) is a sequence of two convolutional layers, followed by a max-pooling and a dropout layer. The second functional layer (classification), consists of a fully connected layer, followed by a dropout layer and three softmax units (one for each conscious state). As a reference size, the original number of feature maps and hidden neurons were used, namely 32 for the 1st convolutional layer, 64 for the 2nd convolutional layer and 128 neurons for the 3rd dense layer. The patch window for max pooling was 2×2. Dropout rates were 0.25 and 0.5, respectively. Convolution windows were chosen with kernels 1×5 and 5×10 (1×1 strides), with the first layer only extracting temporal information (no padding used). Finally, all activation functions were relu units (except output layer). The model was trained using the categorical cross-entropy loss function and the Adadelta optimizer. Initialization of network weights was done with the Xavier uniform initializer. The cNN architecture is summarized in Fig. 2.

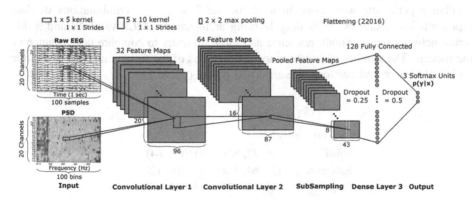

Fig. 2. Convolutional neural network architecture (reference size) for classifying the three conscious states: wakefulness, sedation, loss of consciousness. Raw EEG or PSD epochs were used as an input tensor.

Multilayer Perceptron. We employed a sequential MLP model designed to match the number of output neurons in each functional layer of the cNN (rather than equalising network layers). This ensured that the computational cost of each design was comparable in terms of training time. Both functional layers of the MLP consist of fully connected layers, followed by a dropout layer (2nd layer includes the three softmax units). The number of hidden units for the 1st layer was based on the number of neurons after the flattening in the cNN architecture (22016 for the reference size), while for the 2nd layer was kept the same. Activation functions, dropout rates and other model parameters during training were also kept the same with respect to the cNN. The MLP architecture is summarized in Fig. 3.

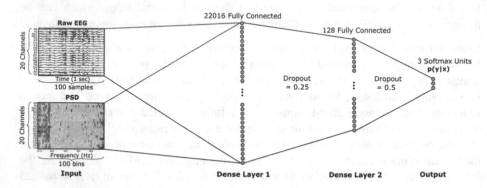

Fig. 3. Multilayer perceptron network architecture (reference size) for classifying the three conscious states. Raw EEG or PSD epochs were used as input tensors, after flattening the 2D-array into a 2000-dimensional vector.

2.4   Experiments

Twelve experiments were done in total for the $2 \times 2 \times 3$ combinations of data representations (Raw vs PSD), deep learning architectures (MLP vs cNN) and 3 different network sizes – small, reference and large, in order to compare performance of the models. The number of feature maps and neurons of the fully connected layers for each architecture and network size are listed below (Table 1).

Table 1. Network Sizes

Network size	cNN	MLP
Small	(16, 32, 64)	(11008, 64)
Reference	(32, 64, 128)	(22016, 128)
Large	(64, 128, 256)	(44032, 256)

To evaluate model performance, EEG data were divided into training and test sets. Previous studies have divided data from each participant proportionally into training and test sets [6, 10, 11]. However, an ideal but hard goal would be to generalize and predict states of consciousness in unseen participants. With this goal in mind, leave-one-participant-out cross validation (LOPOCV) was used for the training and testing of

the models, with each participant contributing 2700 instances on average (9 participants, 3 states, 15×60 1-s epochs ≈ 24300 total instances). Each instance was labeled
with one-hot encoding as the target vector, indicating one of the three sedation states.
Training was done with a batch size of 100 and for 10 runs (epochs). Models were
evaluated by their accuracy, computed as the percentage of epochs correctly predicted
in the left-out participant. All experiments were implemented in Python 3 using
Keras/Tensorflow on a CUDA NVIDIA GPU (Tesla P100).

3 Results

3.1 Architecture Comparison

The results from our 2×2 experimental design (Raw/PSD X cNN/MLP) were similar
for all three network sizes, and are summarized below. Reported figures and accuracies
are for the reference size networks depicted in Figs. 2 and 3.

Raw Data. With raw EEG input, the MLP achieved an average accuracy of 75.45%
across participants, with the cNN achieving 86.05% (Fig. 4). These accuracies are
significantly higher than the chance level accuracy of 33.33%. Cross-entropy loss on
the test set did not significantly decrease after the first epoch. Overall, the cNN was able
to achieve better accuracies for each state of consciousness and participant.

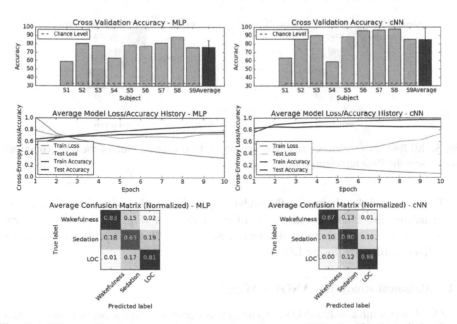

Fig. 4. MLP vs cNN (reference size) comparison for raw EEG classification of the three
conscious states. Cross validation accuracies, average model loss and confusion matrices are
shown for each architecture.

As seen in Fig. 4, the confusion matrices suggest that Wakefulness and LOC were not often confused. The intermediate state of Sedation was hardest to predict, due to individual variability in response to propofol. However, this would not present a problem in the clinical context, where anesthetic induction is much more rapid [10].

Power Spectral Density. With PSD input, the two architectures were equally capable in classifying states of consciousness (Fig. 5). In particular, the MLP performed better than when provided with raw time series as input, but the cNN did not (MLP: 83.4%, cNN: 87.35%). Importantly, cross-entropy loss revealed that the models converged faster using the PSD representation.

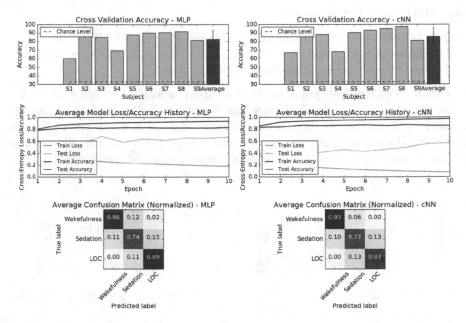

Fig. 5. MLP vs cNN (reference size) comparison for EEG classification of the three conscious states, using the PSD representation.

To understand the changes in the underlying EEG signal driving these accuracies, we visualized the PSDs in each state of consciousness (Fig. 6). As expected, we observed a decrease in alpha oscillations in Sedation, followed by the emergence of high-alpha oscillations during LOC.

3.2 Statistical Analysis – ANOVA Model

As a final step, a three-way ANOVA (type 2) was performed on the accuracies obtained in all twelve experiments across 2 architectures, 2 data representations and 3 model sizes, as summarized in Fig. 7 and detailed in Table 2.

The results of the ANOVA indicated that network architecture (cNN/MLP) was the strongest contributor to model performance (F = 10.6, p = 0.0015), while data

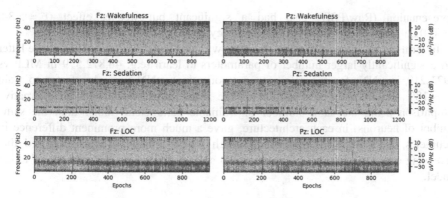

Fig. 6. Power spectral density (uV$^{2/}$Hz, dB) of the EEG epochs, divided by the sedation phases of the experiment. Representative frontal (Fz) and parietal (Pz) electrodes are shown.

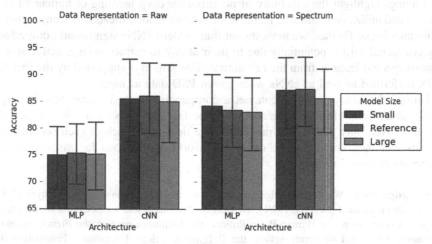

Fig. 7. Three-way ANOVA for the comparison of the data representations, architectures and network sizes. Error bars indicate 95% confidence interval.

Table 2. ANOVA Table

	Sum_sq	df	F	Pr(> F)
Architecture	1230.94	1	10.601	**0.0015**
Data Representation	620.06	1	5.340	**0.0229**
Model Size	14.34	2	0.061	0.9401
Architecture-Data Representation	351.13	1	3.024	0.0852
Architecture-Model Size	6.21	2	0.026	0.9735
Data Representation-Model Size	6.18	2	0.026	0.9737
Architecture-Data Representation-Model Size	0.85	2	0.003	0.9963
Residual	11146.71	96		

representation (Raw/PSD) also had a significant but weaker effect ($F = 5.34$, $p = 0.0229$), driven by the improved accuracy of MLPs with PSD data.

In terms of resource utilization, the cNN was also better than the MLP, as the latter had a significantly larger number of parameters to learn (e.g. 46,872,579 in MLP vs 2,921,219 in cNN, for the reference network size). cNN was also faster to train by $\sim 18\%$. Furthermore, a repetition of the above experiments with an alternative comparison using the same number of trainable parameters (rather than the same number of neurons) in each architecture, gave a much more prominent difference in accuracies, with the MLP performing much worse. Finally, we also verified that increasing epoch size from 1s through to 10 s did not improve performance of either model.

4   Discussion

Our findings highlight the capability of potential for deep learning of human EEG to discover and utilize generalizable features for automatic identification of consciousness during anesthesia. Further, we have shown that modern cNNs significantly outperform fully connected MLPs, potentially due to their ability to extract more effective spatio-temporo-spectral features from the raw signal. This notion is supported by the fact that MLPs performed as well as cNNs when given PSD data as input.

Though this study aimed to conduct a comparative analysis rather than hyperparameter optimization to maximize accuracy, the fact that cNNs were able to perform very well given only with 1 s of raw EEG data despite the lack of such optimization suggests that they could find utility in real-world applications for assessment and monitoring of consciousness.

Acknowledgements. We acknowledge funding from the UK Engineering and Physical Sciences Research Council [EP/P033199/1], the Belgian National Fund for Scientific Research, the European Commission, the Human Brain Project, the Luminous project, the French Speaking Community Concerted Research Action, the Belgian American Educational Foundation, the Wallonie-Bruxelles Federation, the European Space Agency, the University and University Hospital of Liège (Belgium). This research was undertaken with the support of the Alan Turing Institute (UK Engineering and Physical Sciences Research Council Grant EP/N510129/1).

References

1. Purdon, P.L., et al.: Electroencephalogram signatures of loss and recovery of consciousness from propofol. Proc. Natl. Acad. Sci. (2013). https://doi.org/10.1073/pnas.1221180110
2. Avidan, M.S., et al.: Prevention of intraoperative awareness in a high-risk surgical population. N. Engl. J. Med. (2011). https://doi.org/10.1056/NEJMoa1100403
3. Chennu, S., O'Connor, S., Adapa, R., Menon, D.K., Bekinschtein, T.A.: Brain connectivity dissociates responsiveness from drug exposure during propofol-induced transitions of consciousness. PLoS Comput. Biol. **12**, 1–17 (2016). https://doi.org/10.1371/journal.pcbi.1004669

4. Murphy, M., et al.: Propofol anesthesia and sleep: a high-density EEG study. Sleep **34**, 283–291 (2011). https://doi.org/10.1093/sleep/34.3.283
5. Schirrmeister, R.T., et al.: Deep learning with convolutional neural networks for EEG decoding and visualization. Hum. Brain Mapp. **38**, 5391–5420 (2017). https://doi.org/10.1002/hbm.23730
6. Stober, S., Cameron, D.J., Grahn, J.A.: Using convolutional neural networks to recognize rhythm stimuli from electroencephalography recordings. Neural Inf. Process. Syst. **2014**, 1–9 (2014)
7. Howbert, J.J., et al.: Forecasting seizures in dogs with naturally occurring epilepsy. PLoS ONE (2014). https://doi.org/10.1371/journal.pone.0081920
8. Park, Y., Luo, L., Parhi, K.K., Netoff, T.: Seizure prediction with spectral power of EEG using cost-sensitive support vector machines. Epilepsia (2011). https://doi.org/10.1111/j.1528-1167.2011.03138.x
9. Krizhevsky, A., Sutskever, I., Hinton, G.E.: ImageNet classification with deep convolutional neural networks. Adv. Neural Inf. Process. Syst., 1–9 (2012). http://dx.doi.org/10.1016/j.protcy.2014.09.007
10. Juel, B.E., Romundstad, L., Kolstad, F., Storm, J.F., Larsson, P.G.: Distinguishing anesthetized from awake state in patients: a new approach using one second segments of raw EEG. Front. Hum. Neurosci. (2018). https://doi.org/10.3389/fnhum.2018.00040
11. Korshunova, I., Kindermans, P.-J., Degrave, J., Verhoeven, T., Brinkmann, B.H., Dambre, J.: Towards improved design and evaluation of epileptic seizure predictors. IEEE Trans. Biomed. Eng. **65**, 502 (2017). https://doi.org/10.1109/TBME.2017.2700086

Efficient and Automatic Subspace Relevance Determination via Multiple Kernel Learning for High-Dimensional Neuroimaging Data

Murat Seçkin Ayhan[1](✉) and Vijay Raghavan[2]

[1] Institute for Ophthalmic Research, University of Tübingen,
72076 Tübingen, Germany
murat-seckin.ayhan@uni-tuebingen.de
[2] Center for Advanced Computer Studies, University of Louisiana,
Lafayette, LA 70503, USA
raghavan@louisiana.edu

Abstract. Alzheimer's disease is a major cause of dementia. Its pathology induces complex spatial patterns of brain atrophy that evolve as the disease progresses. The diagnosis requires accurate biomarkers that are sensitive to disease stages. Probabilistic biomarkers naturally support the interpretation of decisions and evaluation of uncertainty associated with them. We obtain probabilistic biomarkers via Gaussian Processes, which also offer flexible means to accomplish Multiple Kernel Learning. Exploiting this flexibility, we propose a novel solution, Multiple Kernel Learning for Automatic Subspace Relevance Determination, to tackle the challenges of working with high-dimensional neuroimaging data. The proposed Gaussian Process models are competitive with or better than the well-known Support Vector Machine in terms of classification performance even in the cases of single kernel learning. Also, our method improves the capability of the Gaussian Process models and their interpretability in terms of the known anatomical correlates of the disease.

Keywords: Gaussian processes · MRI · Alzheimer's Disease

1 Introduction

Alzheimer's disease (AD) is the 6th leading cause of death in the United States [2]. Its pathology induces complex spatial patterns of brain atrophy that evolve as the disease progresses [7]. The pathology mainly starts in and around the *hippocampus* and *entorhinal cortex*. However, by the time of a clinical diagnosis, the cerebral atrophy is widespread and it involves, to a large extent, temporal, parietal, and frontal lobes [7,24]. Also, the AD pathology does not necessarily conform to anatomical boundaries [7]. Thus, it is highly recommended that the entire brain, instead of predetermined *regions of interest (ROI)*, be examined for accurate diagnosis [7,24].

© Springer Nature Switzerland AG 2018
S. Wang et al. (Eds.): BI 2018, LNAI 11309, pp. 226–238, 2018.
https://doi.org/10.1007/978-3-030-05587-5_22

The most recent criteria and guidelines for AD diagnosis describe a *continuum* in which an individual experiences a smooth transition from functioning normally, despite the changes in the brain, to failing to compensate for the deterioration of cognitive abilities [2]. There are three stages of AD: (i) preclinical AD, (ii) Mild Cognitive Impairment (MCI) due to AD, and (iii) dementia due to AD. In the preclinical stage, measurable physiological changes may be observed; however, the symptoms are not developed [2]. MCI is a transitional state between normal aging and AD [17]. Individuals with MCI experience measurable changes in their cognitive abilities, which are also notable by family and friends, but the symptoms are not significant enough to affect the patient's daily life [2]. On the downside, MCI shares features with AD and it is likely to progress to AD at an accelerated rate [17].

Neuroimaging techniques like Positron Emission Tomography (PET) and Magnetic Resonance Imaging (MRI) are useful in identifying brain changes due to tumors and other damages that can explain a patient's symptoms. But, it is virtually impossible to visually detect a slight decrease in regional cerebral blood flow or glucose metabolism in cases of early AD [10]. On the other hand, voxel-based representations of neuroimagery can be used to perform both standardization and data-driven analysis of brain imagery [13,14]. [11] compared the accuracy of dementia diagnosis provided by radiologists to that of Support Vector Machines (SVMs) and argued that the accuracy of the computerized diagnosis of AD is equal to or better than that of radiologists. Overall, a general adoption of computerized methods for visual image interpretation for dementia diagnosis is strongly recommended [10,11,13,14]. In this respect, [11] stress the need for further research on probabilistic methods because medical experts could have more comfort from knowing the confidence levels associated with decisions and having better ability to interpret the models behind them.

In this study, we regard the induction of a probabilistic classifier as the creation of a *probabilistic biomarker* for *disease staging*. We propose to design probabilistic biomarkers via Gaussian Processes (GPs). GPs offer flexible means to carry out the Multiple Kernel Learning (MKL) and tackle the challenges of working with high-dimensional neurogimaging data. In this regard, we first investigate the conventional single kernel learning and postulate the advantages of using GP models rather than SVMs. Then, we extend the basic scheme towards MKL and propose a new variation of Automatic Relevance Determination (ARD). The proposed extension inherits the supervised feature selection characteristics of ARD and unites them with the automatic model selection capabilities of MKL.

2   Review

Kernel machines translate the data points into an Euclidean feature space and aim to solve the machine learning problems in the new space. In our review, we focus on supervised learning, for which the goal is to learn an appropriate function $y = f(\mathbf{x})$, where $\mathbf{x} = (x_1, x_2, ..., x_D)$ and D is the number of dimensions, that maps inputs to outputs, given a data set $\mathcal{D} = \{(\mathbf{x}_i, y_i)\}$ where $i = 1...N$.

In the context of kernel machines, it is assumed that there is a function $\phi(\mathbf{x})$ that translates inputs into a feature space and a kernel function $k(\mathbf{x}_i, \mathbf{x}_j) = \phi(\mathbf{x}_i)\phi(\mathbf{x}_j)^T$ implicitly achieves an embedding of observations into the feature space and yields the inner products. This is known as the *kernel trick* [20, 21].

2.1   Support Vector Machine

A typical SVM formulation in its dual form is

$$
\begin{aligned}
\min_{w,b,\varepsilon} \quad & \frac{1}{2}\boldsymbol{\alpha}^T Q \boldsymbol{\alpha} - \mathbf{e}^T \boldsymbol{\alpha} \\
s.t. \quad & \mathbf{y}^T \boldsymbol{\alpha} = 0, \\
& 0 \le \alpha_i \le C, \quad i \in \{1, \dots, N\},
\end{aligned}
\tag{1}
$$

where $\mathbf{e} = [1, \dots, 1]^T$, $C > 0$ is the regularization parameter, Q is an $N \times N$ positive semidefinite (PSD) matrix, $Q_{ij} = y_i y_j k(\mathbf{x}_i, \mathbf{x}_j)$ and $k(\mathbf{x}_i, \mathbf{x}_j)$ is a kernel function [6, 23]. A typical choice is a Radial Basis Function (RBF): $k_{RBF}(\mathbf{x}_i, \mathbf{x}_j) = \exp\left(-\gamma \|\mathbf{x}_i - \mathbf{x}_j\|^2\right)$. Once Eq. 1 is solved for $\boldsymbol{\alpha}$, the SVM decision function is

$$
f(\mathbf{x}_*) = \operatorname{sgn}\left(\sum_{i=1}^{N} y_i \alpha_i k(\mathbf{x}_i, \mathbf{x}_*) + b\right),
\tag{2}
$$

where b is the intercept term. For $\alpha_i \ne 0$, $\mathbf{x}_i$ is a *support vector*. Also, the output is a class label (-1 or $+1$) [6].

Training a typical SVM with an RBF kernel involves an exhaustive grid search for the values of hyperparameters C and γ [6]. For a large number of parameter configurations, the search becomes prohibitively expensive. In practice, it is conducted with respect to a finite set of *discrete* parameter configurations predefined by user. For each configuration, Eq. 1 must be solved for $\boldsymbol{\alpha}$ in order to obtain Eq. 2. Moreover, each decision function must be evaluated on a validation set in the search of the most plausible model.

Probabilistic Outputs. The SVM outputs can be calibrated to generate probabilistic information [18]. A sigmoid function, $\lambda(af(\mathbf{x}) + b)$, is fitted to the training set. Using class labels and decision values, a and b are estimated by maximizing the likelihood of training data [6, 27]. Since such a training may cause the model to overfit to the data, a *second-level* cross-validation (CV) is required in order to obtain acceptable decision values [6, 27]. Unfortunately, it causes a major overhead regarding the model selection due to nested validation procedures.

2.2   Gaussian Processes for Regression

A GP is specified by a mean function $m(\mathbf{x}_i)$ and a covariance function $k(\mathbf{x}_i, \mathbf{x}_j)$, which is analogous to a kernel. Given an observation $\mathbf{x}_i$ as input, the value of $f(\mathbf{x}_i)$

is a sample from the process [20]:

$$
\begin{aligned}
f(\mathbf{x}_i) &\sim \mathcal{GP}(m(\mathbf{x}_i), k(\mathbf{x}_i, \mathbf{x}_j)), \text{ where} \\
m(\mathbf{x}_i) &= \mathbb{E}[f(\mathbf{x}_i)] \\
k(\mathbf{x}_i, \mathbf{x}_j) &= \mathbb{E}[(f(\mathbf{x}_i) - m(\mathbf{x}_i))(f(\mathbf{x}_j) - m(\mathbf{x}_j))].
\end{aligned}
\tag{3}
$$

Equation 3 indicates that $f(\mathbf{x}_i)$ and $f(\mathbf{x}_j)$ are jointly Gaussian. For $j = 1...N$, $f(\mathbf{x}_i)$ depends on other observations, as well. Thus, covariance structure is crucial for GP learning. A simple covariance function that depends on an inner product of the input vectors is $k_{LIN}(\mathbf{x}_i, \mathbf{x}_j) = \sigma_f^2 (\mathbf{x}_i \cdot \mathbf{x}_j^T)$, where σ_f is the scale parameter. A more widely used one is the *squared-exponential (SE)* covariance function:

$$
k_{SE}(\mathbf{x}_i, \mathbf{x}_j) = \sigma_f^2 \exp\left(-\frac{\|\mathbf{x}_i - \mathbf{x}_j\|^2}{2\ell^2} \right),
\tag{4}
$$

where ℓ is the bandwidth parameter. Another example is the *neural network (NN)* covariance function:

$$
k_{NN}(\mathbf{x}_i, \mathbf{x}_j) = \sigma_f^2 \sin^{-1}\left(\frac{2\tilde{\mathbf{x}}_i^T \Sigma \tilde{\mathbf{x}}_j}{\sqrt{(1 + 2\tilde{\mathbf{x}}_i^T \Sigma \tilde{\mathbf{x}}_i)(1 + 2\tilde{\mathbf{x}}_j^T \Sigma \tilde{\mathbf{x}}_j)}} \right),
\tag{5}
$$

where $\tilde{\mathbf{x}} = (1, \mathbf{x})^T$ is an augmented input vector and Σ is a covariance matrix for *input-to-hidden* weights: $\mathbf{w} \sim \mathcal{N}(\mathbf{0}, \Sigma)$ [15,20,25].

Learning of Hyperparameters. A *GP-prior*, e.g., $\mathbf{f} \sim \mathcal{N}(\mathbf{0}, K)$, is a prior distribution over the latent variables. The covariance matrix K is dictated by the covariance function $k(\cdot, \cdot)$. Once combined with the likelihood associated with observed data, the GP-prior leads to a *GP-posterior* in a function space. This Bayesian treatment promotes the smoothness of predictive functions [25] and the prior has an effect analogous to the quadratic penalty term used in maximum-likelihood procedures [20].

Many covariance functions have adjustable parameters, such as ℓ and σ_f in Eq. 4. Learning in GPs is equivalent to finding suitable parameters for the covariance function. Given the target vector $\mathbf{y}$ and the matrix X that consists of training instances, this is accomplished by maximizing

$$
\log p(\mathbf{y}|X) = \underbrace{-\frac{1}{2}\mathbf{y}^T(K + \sigma_n^2 I)^{-1}\mathbf{y}}_{\text{data fit term}} \underbrace{-\frac{1}{2}\log |K + \sigma_n^2 I|}_{\text{complexity term}} \underbrace{-\frac{N}{2}\log 2\pi}_{\text{a constant}},
\tag{6}
$$

where σ_n is due to the Gaussian noise model, $y_i = f_i + \varepsilon$ and $\varepsilon \sim \mathcal{N}(0, \sigma_n^2)$. A large number of hyperparameters can be automatically tuned by maximizing Eq. 6 via *continuous* optimization. Equation 6 is solved once and no validation set is required, which is desirable when the sample size is small.

Predictions. GP regression yields a predictive Gaussian distribution (Eq. 7), from which a prediction $f_* = f(\mathbf{x}_*)$ is sampled, given the training instances X, target vector $\mathbf{y}$ and test input $\mathbf{x}_*$.

$$f_*|X, \mathbf{y}, \mathbf{x}_* \sim \mathcal{N}(\bar{f}_*, \mathbb{V}[f_*]), \text{ where} \tag{7}$$

$$\bar{f}_* = \mathbf{k}_*^T(K + \sigma_n^2 I)^{-1}\mathbf{y} \tag{8}$$

$$\mathbb{V}[f_*] = k(\mathbf{x}_*, \mathbf{x}_*) - \mathbf{k}_*^T(K + \sigma_n^2 I)^{-1}\mathbf{y} \tag{9}$$

and $\mathbf{k}_*$ is a vector of covariances between the test input $\mathbf{x}_*$ and the training instances. Equation 8 gives the mean prediction $\bar{f}_*$, which is the *empirical risk minimizer* for any symmetric loss function [20]. Equation 9 yields the predictive variance.

2.3 Gaussian Processes for Classification

Logistic regression (LR) is a well-known binary classifier, for which a sigmoid function assigns the class probabilities of a given input $\mathbf{x}_*$, i.e., $p(y_* = +1|\mathbf{x}_*) = \lambda(f_*) = \frac{1}{1+\exp(-f_*)}$. GP classification generalizes the idea and turns $\lambda(f_*)$ into a stochastic function, which implies a distribution over predictive probabilities. Once the *nuisance* parameters are integrated out, we obtain the *averaged predictive probability* via Eqs. 10 and 11 [20].

$$\bar{\lambda}(f_*) = \int \lambda(f_*)p(f_*|X, \mathbf{y}, \mathbf{x}_*)df_*, \text{ where} \tag{10}$$

$$p(f_*|X, \mathbf{y}, \mathbf{x}_*) = \int p(f_*|X, \mathbf{x}_*, \mathbf{f})p(\mathbf{f}|X, \mathbf{y})d\mathbf{f} \tag{11}$$

Due to discrete targets, the likelihood term is not Gaussian. Neither is the posterior distribution over the functions, $p(\mathbf{f}|X, \mathbf{y})$. Thus, the exact computation in Eq. 11 is intractable and we resort to approximation methods. A comprehensive overview of algorithms for approximate inference in GPs for probabilistic binary classification is provided [16]. We consider two of these solutions: Laplace Approximation (LA) and Expectation Propagation (EP). Basically, LA is simple and efficient, whereas EP is more sophisticated and accurate; however, the convergence of EP is not generally guaranteed [16].

2.4 Automatic Relevance Determination

A multipurpose covariance function can be written via a symmetric matrix M as in Eq. 12 [20].

$$k_{multi}(\mathbf{x}_i, \mathbf{x}_j) = \sigma_f^2 \exp\left(-\frac{(\mathbf{x}_i - \mathbf{x}_j)M(\mathbf{x}_i - \mathbf{x}_j)^T}{2}\right). \tag{12}$$

Possible choices for M are $M_1 = \ell^{-2}I$ and $M_2 = \text{diag}(\boldsymbol{\ell})^{-2}$ where $\boldsymbol{\ell} = [\ell_1, \ell_2, \cdots, \ell_D]$ is a vector of bandwidth parameters for each dimension. Depending on the choice of M_1 or M_2, Eq. 12 can perform as a standard Gaussian-shaped kernel or implement ARD [12, 15, 20], respectively. ARD effectively removes irrelevant features from inference by selecting large bandwidths for them. The process yields an explanatory and sparse subset of features [15, 20, 26]. But, its cost is $O(N^2)$ per hyperparameter [20], which makes it intractable for high-dimensional data.

3 Multiple Kernel Learning for Automatic Subspace Relevance Determination

MKL is a generalization of the single kernel learning, by which we can specify many kernels and simultaneously learn their properties. MKL delivers an optimal combination of kernels. Thus, it allows for *automatic model selection* and insights into the learning problem [5, 9].

ARD executed via M_2 in Eq. 12 is prohibitive for high-dimensional data. Given the flexibility of GPs and benefits of MKL, we investigate a new variation of ARD through multiple kernels. Our goal is to enable the expressiveness of ARD in high-dimensional settings. To this end, we propose an ARD procedure with respect to coarse groups, namely, *bags of features* rather than individual features. As the number of features bags will typically be significantly smaller than the number of features, we will dramatically reduce the number of hyperparameters, obtain a tractable ARD solution for high-dimensional data, and achieve sparsity at the level of feature bags. We call the new procedure Multiple Kernel Learning for Automatic Subspace Relevance Determination (MKL-AsRD).

It takes two basic steps to set up MKL-AsRD: (i) define the feature bags and (ii) assign the basis kernels accordingly. Then, each bag, which corresponds to a *subspace*, will be processed by a basis kernel and the information extracted from each will be weighted and combined into a final similarity measure. An MKLAsRD problem can be specified with $k(\mathbf{x}_i, \mathbf{x}_j) = \sum_{s=1}^{S} \beta_s k_s(\mathbf{x}_{is}, \mathbf{x}_{js})$, where $\mathbf{x}_i$ and $\mathbf{x}_j$ are the input vectors, s is the subspace indentifier, $k_s(\cdot, \cdot)$ is a *basis* kernel and β_s is the weight associated with the subspace. A subvector $\mathbf{x}_{is}$ denotes the part of the input $\mathbf{x}_i$ that lies in the subspace s, where $s \in \{1, 2, ..., S\}$. For $\beta_s \neq 0$, $\mathbf{x}_{is}$ and $\mathbf{x}_{js}$ are the relevant portions of inputs. Otherwise, $\mathbf{x}_{is}$ and $\mathbf{x}_{js}$ are effectively pruned away from the inference.

Adopting $k_{LIN}(\cdot, \cdot)$, $k_{SE}(\cdot, \cdot)$ and $k_{NN}(\cdot, \cdot)$ as *basis* kernels, we define three composite kernels: $k_{LINcomp}$, k_{SEcomp}, and k_{NNcomp}, where each subspace is assigned a local kernel. These kernel combinations indicate a conic sum where the mixing weights are restricted to be *non-negative*: $\beta_s = \sigma_{f_s}^2$. Due to the complexity term in Eq. 6, the parameters are driven towards zero, which leads to sparse combinations of kernel functions.

3.1 Domain-Knowledge for Feature Bags

Given a collection of 391 parametric images derived from PET scans and a taxonomy of 15,964 features that complies with the Talairach-Tournoux atlas, [3] hand-picked certain regions of the brain containing characteristic patterns of AD based on domain-knowledge and showed that the use of domain-knowledge improves the prior specification even in case of the single kernel learning. Then, [4] investigated more flexible and sensible prior specifications via k_{SEcomp}, and k_{NNcomp}. Given the taxonomy of 15 anatomical regions, they specified anatomically motivated kernels and integrated information from many regions, each of which exhibits certain characteristics regarding the progression of AD.

Neuroimaging procedures capture the snapshots of the metabolic demands or activities of neurons in the brain into 3D volumes, the structures of which are known beforehand. For instance, an MRI scan is acquired one *axial* slice at a time. These slices are combined into a big volume of brain imagery, following certain processing steps, i.e., slice timing corrections [1,22]. However, a taxonomy of voxels is not always available. In this regard, we consider the slices as feature bags, namely *pseudo* regions. In addition, we propose to use the spatial properties of voxels to come up with richer structural formations, e.g., cubes. One obvious advantage of using cubes is due to their ability to capture the 3D information about patterns in their proximity. A pattern of structural deformation that cuts across multiple slices may be captured by a single cube.

We explicitly use the domain-knowledge regarding the structural information of MRI scans in order to avoid expensive search procedures required to find plausible feature bags. We constrain the search to a particular setting defined with respect to slices and cubes. Our aim is to establish a proper trade-off for the supervised feature selection via MKL-AsRD and improve the classification performance and comprehensibility of the GP models.

4 Experiments

Table 1 describes the demographics of the patients in our MRI collection. There are three groups: Normal, MCI and AD (mild AD). The MCI group is the largest and the dataset is skewed. In order to obtain a balanced dataset, 755 scans were randomly sampled without replacement from each group. Statistical Parametric Mapping (SPM) [1] is also used to

Table 1. Demographics of MRI data.

	Number of subjects	Sex		Average age	Number of MRI scans
		M	F		
Normal	232	113	119	76.2	1278
MCI	411	267	114	75.5	2282
AD	200	103	97	76.0	
					755

normalize the image data into an International Consortium for Brain Mapping (ICBM) template [8,22]. Following the normalization, the dimensionality of neuroimages reduces from $170 \times 256 \times 256$ to $79 \times 95 \times 68$. Also note that no anatomical structure such as gray matter (GM), white matter (WM) or cerebrospinal fluid (CSF) is extracted. Instead, the whole brain data is deliberately preserved because brain atrophy can be measured both in GM and WM [7]. We simply let the machine learning software to figure out whatever is informative and determine the relevant portions of data.

We assume a typical SVM configuration as the baseline method and investigate the benefits of utilizing GPs for predictive modeling of AD. In this respect, our experimental setup is reminiscent of [4] which demonstrated the advantages of using GPs for the analysis of parametric images derived from PET scans. However, we use a larger collection of actual MRI scans, no taxonomy of voxels is present, and the dimensionality is much higher. Thus, we demonstrate the impact of MKL-AsRD under more complicated scenarios. Initially, we compare the performances of two kernel machines on the basis of single kernel learning. Then, we investigate the performance of MKL-AsRD. We do not consider SVM under MKL settings, mainly due to the computational costs involved in MKL. The single kernel learning results also support us in so doing. In addition to benchmarking, we identify the prominent portions of the brain through data analysis and interpret the results in a manner consistent with the AD pathology.

In order to estimate the generalization performances of the specified algorithms, we apply 10-fold CV and measure the *Area Under Curve (AUC)*. It is obtained via *Receiver Operating Characteristic (ROC)* analysis and summarizes the overall classification performance into one number. Based on the AUC scores, we compare the classification performances and test for significant differences.

For SVMs [6], we use a single linear kernel and the RBF kernel. A grid search is also performed using a fold of data. Thus, 80%, 10%, and 10% of data are used for training, validation, and testing, respectively. Also, we consider the generation of probabilistic outputs along with class labels for each SVM configuration tested. For GPs [19], we use $k_{LIN}(\cdot,\cdot)$, $k_{SE}(\cdot,\cdot)$, $k_{NN}(\cdot,\cdot)$, $k_{LINcomp}(\cdot,\cdot)$, $k_{SEcomp}(\cdot,\cdot)$, and $k_{NNcomp}(\cdot,\cdot)$. Since the GP models do not require validation sets, the training and test splits correspond to 90% and 10% of data. We fit a constant mean function to data and EP is used for inference, unless stated otherwise. The number of basis kernels, in the case of axial slices, is 68. For cube-shaped pseudo regions, we set the cube dimensions as $16 \times 16 \times 16$, which leads to 150 basis kernels, assuming that they are forbidden from overlapping. Despite the fixed number and layout of kernels, we learn the kernel properties automatically from data, which is central to MKL.

4.1   Results

From Fig. 1, we can tell that SVMs are fairly accurate. When we demand probabilistic outputs from SVMs, their performances are competitive with the basic configuration despite the use of smaller training sets. But, the generation of probabilities significantly complicates training. The differences between the performances of linear (LIN) and non-linear (RBF) SVMs indicate the non-linearity of the complex atrophy patterns.

GPs are usually preferable to SVMs. For Normal vs. AD and MCI vs. AD tasks, the GP models significantly outperform the baseline SVM. As for the Normal vs. MCI separation, the single kernel GPs are not significantly better than the baseline, due to marginal overlaps between the respective confidence intervals. Given that there is a large overlap between the spatial patterns of Normal and MCI classes, which has been reported by [7], the differences between SVMs and GPs may have been suppressed in this task. However, by the virtue of MKL-AsRD, GPs break the tie and outperform the baseline SVM, which is a linear one.

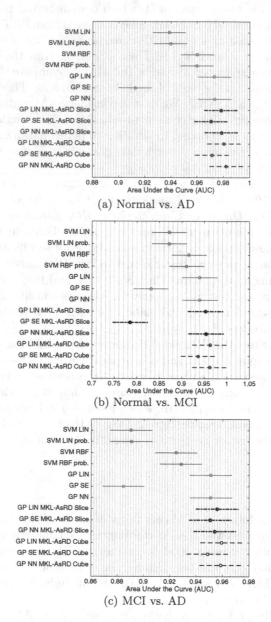

(a) Normal vs. AD

(b) Normal vs. MCI

(c) MCI vs. AD

Fig. 1. Average (mean) AUC results and comparison intervals for binary classification tasks. The confidence level is 95%. Two means are significantly different if their comparison intervals do not overlap. Also note that, due the convergence issues of EP during cross-validation, LA was used for inference for the following GP configurations: (a) GP SE MKL-AsRD Cube, (b) GP SE MKL-AsRD Slice and GP SE MKL-AsRD Cube, (c) GP SE MKL-AsRD Slice and GP SE MKL-AsRD Cube.

On top of that, GPs are preferable to non-linear SVMs, as well. Exceptions to these general takeaway messages are those with a single SE covariance function and two MKL-AsRD configurations in Fig. 1b: *GP SE MKL-AsRD Slice* and *GP SE MKL-AsRD Cube*. Due to the quadratic form in the exponent of Eq. 4, even the slightest change in a large number of input values easily causes the covariance between f_i and f_j to tend to zero. As a result, this function is not suitable for extracting a useful covariance structure from the high-dimensional neuroimaging data. The same phenomenon was reported based on the experiments with PET data [4]. In our defense, the poor performance of such GP models can be rectified by MKL-AsRD when the most relevant inputs are emphasized for the computation of covariance. In the exceptional case of GP SE MKL-AsRD Slice in Fig. 1b, the EP algorithm did not converge during a few iterations of the 10-fold CV, even

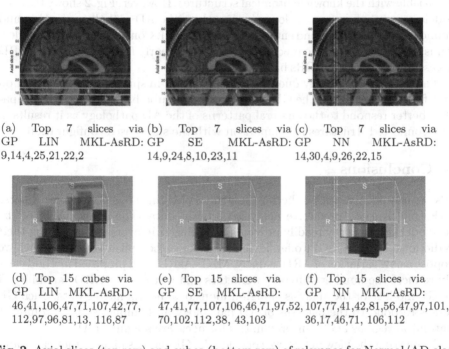

(a) Top 7 slices via GP LIN MKL-AsRD: 9,14,4,25,21,22,2

(b) Top 7 slices via GP SE MKL-AsRD: 14,9,24,8,10,23,11

(c) Top 7 slices via GP NN MKL-AsRD: 14,30,4,9,26,22,15

(d) Top 15 cubes via GP LIN MKL-AsRD: 46,41,106,47,71,107,42,77, 112,97,96,81,13, 116,87

(e) Top 15 slices via GP SE MKL-AsRD: 47,41,77,107,106,46,71,97,52, 70,102,112,38, 43,103

(f) Top 15 slices via GP NN MKL-AsRD: 107,77,41,42,81,56,47,97,101, 36,17,46,71, 106,112

Fig. 2. Axial slices (top row) and cubes (bottom row) of relevance for Normal/AD classification. Relevance scores are determined based on 10-fold CV. For each CV iteration, the mixing weights are normalized separately. Then, they are accumulated over iterations. Note that the normalized weights are always less than or equal to 1. Thus, the relevance scores are between 0 and 10. In this scheme, a relevance score towards the high end of the spectrum indicates that the associated slice or cube has been emphasized many times during our experiments. On the other hand, a score from the low end means that the slice/cube was pretty much ignored due to its low relevance to the classification task at hand. In the top row, the brighter (greener) a slice is, the more relevant it is. Similarly, in the bottom row, the brighter (grayer) a cube is, the more relevant it is. Invisible cubes are considered irrelevant due to their relevance scores and hence not shown in the figures. (Color figure online)

though the remaining iterations resulted in competitive performances. Due to the instability concerns, we resorted to LA throughout CV. Unfortunately, even the use of LA did not provide good estimates of mean and covariance. Nevertheless, the use of LA on other occasions, e.g., GP SE MKL-AsRD Cube in Fig. 1b, yielded competitive results.

Figure 1 also shows the competitiveness of the GP models equipped with linear covariance functions. Even a *single* function is quite satisfying in terms of classification performance. Considering the fewer hyperparameters and corresponding computational requirements, linear covariance function may be a natural choice for both single and multiple kernel learning scenarios.

Figure 2 shows the relevant portions of brain imagery determined via MKL-AsRD. We consider the relevant slices and cubes as the *regions of relevance (ROR)*. Since an anatomical taxonomy of them is not present, they are not exactly compatible with the known anatomical structures. However, Fig. 2 shows that the models generally focus on the lower brain, where the AD pathology starts in and around the hippocampus and entorhinal cortex [7, 24]. Considering that our collection is representative of the precursors of AD or its early forms only, MKL-AsRD successfully determines RORs based on the data.

The patterns of atrophy due to AD are bilateral in spite of greater impact on the left hemisphere [24]. The GP models with the cube-based MKL-AsRD capability better respond to the bilateral patterns of the AD pathology as it results in more connected structures in comparison with the slice-based configuration.

5   Conclusions

GPs are competitive with or better than the SVM which has been the workhorse of the multivariate predictive analysis of brain data. The added value of the GP models is that they readily provide probabilistic information regarding their predictions. Moreover, GPs offer flexible means to accomplish MKL, by which we propose a new variation of ARD, namely, MKL-AsRD. Our proposed method cleverly reduces the number of hyperparameters and restores the ARD capability of the GP models for the analysis of high-dimensional neuroimaging data. Such GP models respond to the patterns of AD pathology and emphasize the prominent anatomical regions and their proximities for accurate staging of AD.

Supporting the view of [11], we consider the GP models highly practical. Carefully trained and validated models can be deployed at neuroimaging centers in order to speed up the diagnostic processes with no compromise of accuracy and support accurate decision-making based on probabilistic reasoning in cases where there is a lack of access to an experienced physician.

Acknowledgements. Data used in this study are from the Alzheimer's Disease Neuroimaging Initiative (ADNI). For up-to-date information, see www.adni-info.org or adni.loni.usc.edu.

Majority of this work was completed at the Center for Advanced Computer Studies, University of Louisiana at Lafayette, where M.S.A completed his graduate studies under the supervision of V.R.

References

1. Ashburner, J., et al.: SPM8 Manual, July 2010
2. Association, A., et al.: 2018 Alzheimer's disease facts and figures. Alzheimers Dement. **14**(3), 367–429 (2018)
3. Ayhan, M.S., Benton, R.G., Choubey, S., Raghavan, V.V.: Utilization of domain-knowledge for simplicity and comprehensibility in predictive modeling of Alzheimer's disease. In: Proceedings of the 2012 IEEE International Conference on Bioinformatics and Biomedicine Workshops (BIBMW), BIBMW 2012, pp. 265–272 (2012)
4. Ayhan, M.S., Benton, R.G., Raghavan, V.V., Choubey, S.: Composite kernels for automatic relevance determination in computerized diagnosis of Alzheimer's disease. In: Imamura, K., Usui, S., Shirao, T., Kasamatsu, T., Schwabe, L., Zhong, N. (eds.) BHI 2013. LNCS (LNAI), vol. 8211, pp. 126–137. Springer, Cham (2013). https://doi.org/10.1007/978-3-319-02753-1_13
5. Bach, F.R., Lanckriet, G.R.G., Jordan, M.I.: Multiple kernel learning, conic duality, and the SMO algorithm. In: Proceedings of the Twenty-first International Conference on Machine Learning, ICML 2004, pp. 6–13 (2004)
6. Chang, C.C., Lin, C.J.: LIBSVM: a library for support vector machines. ACM Trans. Intell. Syst. Technol. **2**(3), 27:1–27:27 (2011)
7. Fan, Y., Batmanghelich, N., Clark, C.M., Davatzikos, C.: Spatial patterns of brain atrophy in MCI patients, identified via high-dimensional pattern classification, predict subsequent cognitive decline. NeuroImage **39**(4), 1731–1743 (2008). https://doi.org/10.1016/j.neuroimage.2007.10.031
8. Gupta, A., Ayhan, M.S., Maida, A.S.: Natural image bases to represent neuroimaging data. In: Proceedings of the 30th International Conference on Machine Learning (ICML-13), ICML 2013, June 2013
9. Hinrichs, C., Singh, V., Peng, J., Johnson, S.C.: Q-MKL:Matrix-induced regularization in multi-kernel learning withapplications to neuroimaging. In: NIPS, pp. 1430–1438 (2012)
10. Imabayashi, E., et al.: Superiority of 3-dimensional stereotactic surface projection analysis over visual inspection in discrimination of patients with very early Alzheimer's disease from controls using brain perfusion SPECT. J. Nucl. Med. **45**(9), 1450–1457 (2004)
11. Klöppel, S., Stonnington, C.M., Barnes, J., Chen, F., Chu, C., Good, C.D., Mader, I., Mitchell, L.A., Patel, A.C., Roberts, C.C., et al.: Accuracy of dementia diagnosis-a direct comparison between radiologists and a computerized method. Brain **131**(11), 2969–2974 (2008)
12. MacKay, D.J.C.: Bayesian methods for backpropagation networks. In: Domany, E., van Hemmen, J.L., Schulten, K. (eds.) Models of Neural Networks III. Physics of Neural Networks, pp. 211–254. Springer, New York (1996)
13. Matsuda, H.: Role of neuroimaging in Alzheimer's disease, with emphasis on brain perfusion spect. J. Nucl. Med. **48**(8), 1289–1300 (2007)
14. Minoshima, S., Frey, K.A., Koeppe, R.A., Foster, N.L., Kuhl, D.E.: A diagnostic approach in Alzheimer's disease using three-dimensional stereotactic surface projections of fluorine-18-FDG PET. J. Nucl. Med. **36**(7), 1238–1248 (1995)
15. Neal, R.M.: Bayesian Learning for Neural Networks. Springer, New York (1996). https://doi.org/10.1007/978-1-4612-0745-0
16. Nickisch, H., Rasmussen, C.E.: Approximations for binary Gaussian process classification. J. Mach. Learn. Res. **9**, 2035–2078 (2008)

17. Petersen, R.C.: Current concepts in mild cognitive impairment. Arch. Neurol. **58**(12), 1985 (2001)
18. Platt, J.C.: Probabilistic outputs for support vector machines and comparisons to regularized likelihood methods. Adv. Large Margin Classifiers **10**(3), 61–74 (1999)
19. Rasmussen, C.E., Nickisch, H.: Gaussian processes for machine learning (GPML) toolbox. J. Mach. Learn. Res. **9999**, 3011–3015 (2010)
20. Rasmussen, C.E., Williams, C.K.I.: Gaussian Processes for Machine Learning (Adaptive Computation and Machine Learning). The MIT Press, Cambridge (2005)
21. Schölkopf, B., Smola, A.J.: Learning with Kernels: Support Vector Machines, Regularization, Optimization, and Beyond. MIT Press, Cambridge (2001)
22. Thatcher, R.W.: Functional Neuroimaging: Technical Foundations. Academic Press, San Diego (1994)
23. Vapnik, V.N.: The Nature of Statistical Learning Theory. Springer, New York (1995). https://doi.org/10.1007/978-1-4757-3264-1
24. Whitwell, J.L., Przybelski, S.A., Weigand, S.D., Knopman, D.S., Boeve, B.F., Petersen, R.C., Jack, C.R.: 3D maps from multiple MRI illustrate changing atrophy patterns as subjects progress from mild cognitive impairment to Alzheimer's disease. Brain **130**(7), 1777–1786 (2007)
25. Williams, C.K.I., Barber, D.: Bayesian classification with Gaussian processes. IEEE Trans. Pattern Anal. Mach. Intell. **20**(12), 1342–1351 (1998)
26. Wipf, D.P., Nagarajan, S.S.: A new view of automatic relevance determination. In: Advances in Neural Information Processing Systems, pp. 1625–1632 (2007)
27. Wu, T.F., Lin, C.J., Weng, R.C.: Probability estimates for multi-class classification by pairwise coupling. J. Mach. Learn. Res. **5**, 975–1005 (2004)

Improving SNR and Reducing Training Time of Classifiers in Large Datasets via Kernel Averaging

Matthias S. Treder(✉)

School of Computer Science and Informatics, Cardiff University,
Cardiff CF24 3AA, UK
trederm@cardiff.ac.uk

Abstract. Kernel methods are of growing importance in neuroscience research. As an elegant extension of linear methods, they are able to model complex non-linear relationships. However, since the kernel matrix grows with data size, the training of classifiers is computationally demanding in large datasets. Here, a technique developed for linear classifiers is extended to kernel methods: In linearly separable data, replacing sets of instances by their averages improves signal-to-noise ratio (SNR) and reduces data size. In kernel methods, data is linearly non-separable in input space, but linearly separable in the high-dimensional feature space that kernel methods implicitly operate in. It is shown that a classifier can be efficiently trained on instances averaged in feature space by averaging entries in the kernel matrix. Using artificial and publicly available data, it is shown that kernel averaging improves classification performance substantially and reduces training time, even in non-linearly separable data.

Keywords: Kernel · Machine learning · Big data · SVM · FDA

1 Introduction

In neuroscience, machine learning has been applied as a statistical tool for investigating brain activity or structure, and as a computational model emulating brain activity [10]. In the first capacity, it has mostly been employed in the form of classifiers for applications such as multivariate analysis [7], classification of clinical data [13], and brain-computer interfaces [11]. Multivariate analysis of neuroimaging data poses several challenges, two of which are addressed here. Firstly, signal-to-noise ratio (SNR) in neuroimaging data is typically low [8]. Secondly, the increasing use of large-scale datasets [3] leads to unprecedented statistical power but also high computational demands for training a classifier.

Cichy and Pantazis [4] presented a simple technique that addresses both challenges at once. They had participants view images repeated 30 times each while MEEG was recorded. Trials from the same class were randomly partitioned

© Springer Nature Switzerland AG 2018
S. Wang et al. (Eds.): BI 2018, LNAI 11309, pp. 239–248, 2018.
https://doi.org/10.1007/978-3-030-05587-5_23

into groups of 5, averaged to $l = 30/5 = 6$ mean trials per class, and then used as input to a two-class linear Support Vector Machine (SVM). In [5] the authors averaged across groups of $l = 40$ trials. Obviously, averaging reduces the size of the data by a factor of l, avoiding a bottleneck in classifier training time. In addition, averaging improves SNR substantially as evidenced by the high classification performance reported by the authors [4,5].

As a linear operation, averaging only applies to linear classification tasks (see Fig. 1). Unfortunately, this precludes it from being used in kernel methods which can model more complex, non-linear relationships. Kernel methods are gaining popularity in social sciences [9] and in cognitive science [12], and they form the heart of the PRoNTo toolbox [15]. They are efficient when there is more variables than instances, such as in gene-expression data, since their complexity grows mainly with sample size [14,18]. More recently, multiple kernel learning has been explored for the classification of fMRI and EEG data [16,20].

The purpose of this paper is to extend the instance averaging approach of [4,5] to kernel methods. The basic idea is simple: kernel methods are non-linear in the original input space, but they act as linear models in a high-dimensional feature space. Therefore, instances can be averaged in feature space rather than in input space. It is shown that the necessary computations can be efficiently carried out in input space using the kernel trick. The benefits of kernel averaging are two-fold: a smaller kernel matrix allows for reduced classifier training times and less memory consumption. At the same time, the averaging increases the SNR of the data and hence classification performance.

The paper is structured as follows. At first, classification and averaging are formally introduced. The effect of data averaging is discussed for the input space and the feature space and an efficient computation using the kernel trick is presented. Subsequently, artificial data is used to illustrate that averaging instances in input space works for linearly separable data but not for linearly non-separable data, while kernel averaging works in both scenarios. Finally, four publicly available datasets are used to evaluate the effects of kernel averaging on classification performance and classifier training time.

2   Method

Let the i-th instance in a dataset be denoted as $\mathbf{x}_i \in \mathcal{X}$, where $\mathcal{X}$ is the *input space*. Each instance has a corresponding class label $y_i \in \mathcal{Y}$, where $\mathcal{Y}$ is the set of class labels. A classifier is a function $f : \mathcal{X} \mapsto \mathcal{Y}$ that maps an instance onto a predicted class label. For a binary classification task with class labels $+1$ and -1, any linear classifier can be written in the form

$$f(\mathbf{x}) = \mathrm{sgn}(\sum_i \alpha_i \, y_i \langle \mathbf{x}_i, \mathbf{x} \rangle) \tag{1}$$

where the $\mathbf{x}_i$'s are the training instances, $\mathbf{x}$ is a test instance, sgn is the signum function, and $\langle \cdot, \cdot \rangle$ is the standard dot product [14].

2.1   The Effect of Averaging

Let instances from a given class be drawn from a probability distribution $\mathcal{D}$ defined over $\mathcal{X}$, that is, $\forall i : \mathbf{x}_i \sim \mathcal{D}$. The average over l instances converges towards the expectation $\mathbb{E}[\mathbf{x}]$ in probability, that is, $\frac{1}{l}\sum_{i=1}^{l}\mathbf{x}_i \xrightarrow{P} \mathbb{E}[\mathbf{x}]$ as $l \to \infty$. Does a classifier applied to averages perform better than a classifier applied to the original instances? If the support of $\mathcal{D}$ is a convex set, averaging can likely improve class separation (Fig. 1a). However, if it is non-convex, averaging can be detrimental. In extreme cases, the expected value occupies a part of input space wherein instances from this class are never observed, i.e. $P(\mathbf{x} = \mathbb{E}[\mathbf{x}]) = 0$. For instance, in Fig. 1b the turquoise class inhabits a circular region of input space. The region is convex so that averages remain within the circular region. However, the region inhabited by the red class is not convex and averages can end up within the circle although red instances are never observed there.

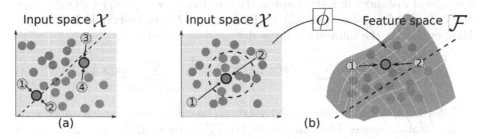

Fig. 1. Effect of averaging, illustrated for two classes (red and turquoise). (a) *Linear classifiers* use a linear decision boundary in input space (dashed line). When the red instances "1" and "2" are averaged (arrows), their average tends to be on the correct side of the hyperplane. The same applies to the turquoise instances "3" and "4". (b) *Kernel classifiers* use a non-linear decision boundary in input space (dashed circle). Averaging can pull the average onto the wrong side of the hyperplane even when the instances are on the correct side (see average of "1" and "2"). However, after projection into feature space using ϕ, data are linearly separable. (Color figure online)

2.2   Averaging Instances in Input Space

Cichy et al. [4,5] averaged sets of instances prior to linear classification. Linear classifiers partition input space into convex regions so that averaging improves performance if the data is linearly separable. This can easily be demonstrated for the special case of a multivariate Gaussian distribution, i.e. $\mathbf{x}_i \sim \mathcal{N}(\mathbf{m}, \boldsymbol{\Sigma})$ with mean $\mathbf{m}$ and covariance matrix $\boldsymbol{\Sigma}$. The distribution of the average across l instances is $\frac{1}{l}\sum_{i=1}^{l}\mathbf{x}_i \sim \mathcal{N}(\mathbf{m}, \boldsymbol{\Sigma}/l)$. In other words, the covariance matrix is scaled down by a factor of l. Since it is usually conceived of as the noise, averaged instances move closer to the class mean, increasing class separability. This approach is referred to as *instance averaging* in the rest of the paper.

2.3 Averaging Instances in Feature Space

Kernel classifiers partition input space into potentially non-convex regions. The data is implicitly projected to a high-dimensional *feature space* $\mathcal{F}$ by applying a function $\phi : \mathcal{X} \mapsto \mathcal{F}$. A linear classifier is then applied in $\mathcal{F}$. The formula in Eq. (1) applies when replacing $\mathbf{x}$ by $\phi(\mathbf{x})$:

$$f(\mathbf{x}) = \text{sgn}(\sum_i \alpha_i \, y_i \langle \phi(\mathbf{x}_i), \phi(\mathbf{x}) \rangle). \tag{2}$$

In other words, a kernel classifier acts as a linear classifier in feature space. Therefore, it is permissible to perform instance averaging *in feature space*. Next, an efficient way for averaging in feature space is developed.

If $\mathcal{F}$ is associated with a Reproducing Kernel Hilbert space, dot products in $\mathcal{F}$ can be represented by a kernel function $k : \mathcal{X} \times \mathcal{X} \mapsto \mathbb{R}$, $k(\mathbf{x}, \mathbf{x}') = \langle \phi(\mathbf{x}), \phi(\mathbf{x}') \rangle$. Crucially, this 'kernel trick' can also be used in order to train a classifier on averages of instances in feature space. To see this, let $\mathbf{z} = [\phi(\mathbf{x}_1) + \phi(\mathbf{x}_2) + ... + \phi(\mathbf{x}_l)]/l$ and $\mathbf{z}' = [\phi(\mathbf{x}'_1) + \phi(\mathbf{x}'_2) + ... + \phi(\mathbf{x}'_l)]/l$, $l \in \mathbb{N}$ be two such averages. Then exploiting the bilinearity of the dot product one obtains

$$\langle \mathbf{z}, \mathbf{z}' \rangle = \frac{1}{l^2} \sum_{i,j \in \{1,2,..,l\}} \langle \phi(\mathbf{x}_i), \phi(\mathbf{x}'_j) \rangle = \frac{1}{l^2} \sum_{i,j \in \{1,2,..,l\}} k(\mathbf{x}_i, \mathbf{x}'_j). \tag{3}$$

Inserting this result into Eq. (2) yields a classifier trained on instances averaged in feature space. The quantity in Eq. (3) corresponds to a single entry in the *averaged* kernel matrix. It is obtained by averaging several entries in the full kernel matrix. Therefore, this approach is referred to as *kernel averaging* in the rest of the paper.

2.4 Artificial Data

If the data is linearly separable, both instance averaging and kernel averaging should improve classification compared to no averaging. If the data is linearly non-separable, only kernel averaging should improve classification. To test this, three artificial datasets were generated and no averaging was compared to instance averaging and kernel averaging with groups of $l = 50$ instances. 'Linear' data was sampled from a multivariate Gaussian distribution in 10 dimensions. Four classes were created with different means but an equal covariance matrix sampled from a Wishart distribution. Two non-linearly separable datasets were generated in two-dimensional input space, a 'radial' (2 classes) and a 'checkerboard' (3 classes) dataset. For each dataset, 6000 data points were created and Gaussian noise was added to every point. The datasets are depicted in Fig. 2.

2.5 Real Data

To measure classification performance and computation time in real data, four publicly available datasets were analysed.

- *EEG* (http://bnci-horizon-2020.eu/database/data-sets). EEG from 11 participants performing an auditory oddball task [17]. Data were epoched in the interval [-0.2, 1] s and baseline corrected. Non-EEG channels were removed. To create a large dataset, trials from all participants were pooled, yielding 25,247 trials (instances), 63 variables (EEG electrodes), 241 time points, and 2 classes. Data was averaged in the typical interval for the P300 component (300–500 ms).
- *Gene expression* (http://archive.ics.uci.edu/ml/datasets/gene+expression+cancer+RNA-Seq). Part of the RNA-Seq (HiSeq) PANCAN dataset containing a random extraction of gene expressions of patients having different types of tumor [19]. It totals 801 instances, 20,531 variables, and 5 classes.
- *p53 mutants* (http://archive.ics.uci.edu/ml/datasets/p53+Mutants). The dataset models mutant p53 transcriptional activity (active vs inactive) based on data extracted from biophysical simulations [6]. It totals 16,772 instances, 5409 variables, and 2 classes.
- *Cardiotocography* (http://archive.ics.uci.edu/ml/datasets/Cardiotocography). Fetal cardiotocograms with classes corresponding to morphologic pattern [1]. It totals 2126 instances, 23 variables, and 10 classes.

2.6   Analysis

All analyses were conducted using MATLAB R2017a (Natick, USA) on an Intel Core i7-6700 CPU 3.40 GHz × 8 computer with 64 GB RAM running on Ubuntu 18.04. Kernel Fisher Discriminant Analysis (FDA) and SVM were considered as classifiers. For kernel FDA, an open-source implementation (https://github.com/treder/MVPA-Light/tree/devel) was used. For SVM, LIBSVM [2] was used. LIBSVM does not implement kernel averaging, but it allows for pre-computed kernels to be provided. For this reason, the kernel matrix was pre-computed for all analyses and manually averaged. The same kernel with the same hyperparameters was used for kernel FDA and SVM. For the simulations and the EEG and gene expression datasets, an RBF kernel was used. For the p53 mutants and the Cardiotocography datasets, a polynomial kernel was used. Hyperparameters were fixed to gamma=1/#variables, degree = 2, and coef0 = 0. All variables were z-scored.

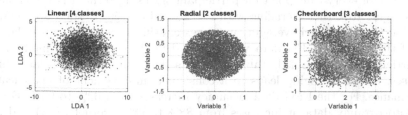

Fig. 2. Artificial datasets. The linear (Gaussian) dataset has been projected from 10 dimensions to the first 2 linear discriminant coordinates.

Five-fold cross-validation was used to estimate classification accuracy. The procedure was repeated 10 times. Training time corresponds to the time it takes to train a single classifier in one fold. Classification accuracy and training time were averaged across folds and repetitions. Its standard deviation was also calculated across folds and repetitions.

2.7 Complexity and Memory

Kernel averaging reduces the size of the kernel matrix by a factor of l. The complexity implications are discussed for kernel FDA and SVM. The most computationally demanding part of kernel FDA is an inversion and an eigenvalue decomposition of $n \times n$ matrices at a complexity of $\mathcal{O}(n^3)$. It is reduced to $\mathcal{O}(n^3/l^3)$ with kernel averaging. The complexity of the LIBSVM algorithm is reported as #iterations $\times$ $\mathcal{O}(n)$ if the $n \times n$ matrix can be cached [2]. Consequently, kernel FDA has a higher overall complexity than SVM and hence it should reap larger computational benefits from kernel averaging.

Memory consumption for storing the kernel matrix grows with n^2. For the largest dataset used in this paper (EEG data with 25,247 instances), the kernel matrix consumes about 2.3 GB RAM at single precision (4 bytes). The quadratic growth means that by just averaging 10 instances the memory required for the kernel matrix is reduced to about 23 MB, a factor of 100 smaller. The averaged kernel matrix can be built row-by-row or even entry-by-entry, so that the full kernel matrix is never actually required in memory.

3 Results

Figure 3 shows the results obtained on the artificial data. For linearly separable data, both instance averaging and kernel averaging improve classification performance from about 30% to about 80%. However, for the Radial and Checkerboard data, which are linearly non-separable, only kernel averaging leads to an improvement from about 60% to almost 100%. Instance averaging even has a slightly detrimental effect, leading to an accuracy $< 60\%$. Qualitatively, the same effects are observed for kernel FDA and SVM.

To illustrate the effect of kernel averaging on the EEG data, classification was performed for every time point for participant #1 using kernel FDA, comparing no averaging to kernel averaging with $l = 20$ and $l = 50$. Results are depicted in Fig. 4. Clearly, kernel averaging improves classification performance. For the rest of the analyses, EEG data was averaged in the 300–500 ms interval and all participants were pooled. Table. 1 depicts the results for the 4 datasets. In all cases, kernel averaging leads to a consistent improvement of classification performance. For the EEG data, accuracy increases from 62% to 99%. For the Cardiotocography data, it increases from 88% to 98% (kernel FDA) and 91% to 99% (SVM). Even for the gene expression and p53 mutants datasets, kernel averaging improves performance although the classification is almost at ceiling to start with. The results are consistent across classifiers and kernels.

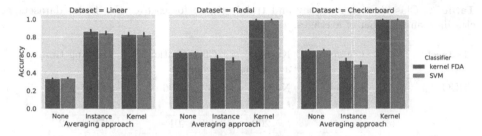

Fig. 3. Results on the artificial data. Similar results are obtained for kernel FDA (blue bars) and SVM (brown bars). When the data is linearly separable (Linear dataset), both instance averaging and kernel averaging improve classification performance. When the data is linearly non-separable (Radial and Checkerboard datasets), kernel averaging still improves classification performance but instance averaging does not. (Color figure online)

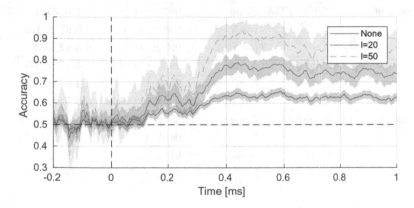

Fig. 4. Classification performance for participant #1 of the EEG dataset. Classification accuracy is plotted for every time point, comparing no averaging and kernel averaging with $l = 20$ and $l = 50$.

Kernel averaging also leads to a reduction of training time. This is especially evident for the two largest datasets, EEG and p53 mutants. In the EEG dataset, averaging $l = 200$ instances reduces training time from 248.07 s to 5.78 s for kernel FDA (40× faster), and from 15.67 s to 5.78 for SVM (3× faster). In the p53 mutants dataset, averaging $l = 10$ instances reduces training time from 151.25 s to 3.42 s for kernel FDA (40× faster), and from 4.17 s to 3.1 s for SVM (1.3× faster).

Table 1. Classification accuracy and training time for each of the 4 real datasets, classifier, and number of averages.

Dataset	Classifier	Kernel averaging	Classification accuracy	Training time [sec]
EEG	Kernel FDA	None	.62 ± .006	248.07 ± .49
		$l = 50$	.96 ± .02	7.06 ± .08
		$l = 200$	.99 ± .01	5.78 ± .12
	SVM	None	.62 ± .01	15.67 ± .26
		$l = 50$	.96 ± .02	7.06 ± .07
		$l = 200$	.99 ± .002	5.78 ± .16
Gene expression	Kernel FDA	None	.989 ± .007	.05 ± .04
		$l = 5$	1 ± 0	.01 ± .01
	SVM	None	.988 ± .007	.008 ± .003
		$l = 5$	1 ± 0	.006 ± .002
p53 mutant	Kernel FDA	None	.987 ± .002	151.25 ± 25.52
		$l = 5$	.993 ± .003	5.67 ± 1.2
		$l = 10$	.999 ± .002	3.42 ± .7
	SVM	None	.9933 ± .0013	4.17 ± .65
		$l = 5$	.9989 ± .0013	4.03 ± .67
		$l = 10$	.9998 ± .0004	3.1 ± .53
Cardiotocography	Kernel FDA	None	.88 ± .02	.635 ± .141
		$l = 5$	.98 ± .01	.075 ± .024
	SVM	None	.91 ± .01	.079 ± .019
		$l = 5$	.99 ± .01	.057 ± .011

4   Discussion

An approach for averaging data in high-dimensional feature space has been developed. The analysis of the artificial data shows that instance averaging (in input space) fails to improve classification performance when the data is linearly non-separable. In contrast, kernel averaging (in feature space) improves classification performance for both linearly separable and non-separable data. This illustrates that kernel averaging is a genuine generalisation of averaging to non-linear input spaces. In fact, instance averaging arises as a special case of kernel averaging when a linear kernel is used.

The analysis of 4 real datasets reveals a consistent improvement of classification performance by kernel averaging. Even classification on the gene expression and p53 mutants datasets improves significantly, despite the fact that performance is close to 100% to start with. Furthermore, there is a consistent reduction in training time. The benefit is most pronounced for kernel FDA with up to 40 times faster training on the EEG and p53 mutants datasets; smaller time benefits are obtained for SVM, in line with the complexity calculations.

Why not just subsample? For very large datasets, a simple alternative to kernel averaging is subsampling wherein just a subset of the data is selected. Because subsampling just discards large parts of the data, it does not offer the simultaneous improvement of SNR. However, if SNR is high to start with and performance is the only bottleneck, subsampling is a viable alternative.

How to interpret classification performance after averaging? If the classifier operates on averages rather than single instances, classification performance measures how well *groups of instances* can be classified. This nicely dovetails with many neuroscience applications. Often, a typical question is whether the classifier can differentiate between a patient group and a control group, or whether trials wherein participants viewed a face can be classified from trials wherein they viewed a scene. Whether or not a classifier trained using kernel averaging is also beneficial in the original, single-instance classification setting, is a separate question that will be addressed in future research.

How many instances should be averaged? The present results suggest that even for moderate values of l, such as 5 or 10, a significant improvement in class separability is achieved. For low SNR data such as EEG, larger values for l such as 20 or 50 can yield improvement without reaching ceiling performance. Conversely, l is bounded by data size. At least, l should be small enough such that a handful of averaged samples of each class occur in every training set.

Concluding, a novel kernel averaging approach has been developed that generalises the notion of instance averaging to kernel classifiers. It allows for a significant improvement of SNR in conjunction with computational benefits, particularly for large datasets.

References

1. Ayres-de Campos, D., Bernardes, J., Garrido, A., Marques-de Sá, J., Pereira-Leite, L.: Sisporto 2.0: a program for automated analysis of cardiotocograms. J. Matern. Fetal Med. **9**(5), 311–318 (2000). https://doi.org/10.1002/1520-6661(200009/10)9: 5⟨311::AID-MFM12⟩3.0.CO;2-9
2. Chang, C.C, Lin, C.J.: LIBSVM: A library for support vector machines. ACM Trans. Intell. Syst. Technol. **2**(3), 1–27 (2011)
3. Choudhury, S., Fishman, J.R., McGowan, M.L., Juengst, E.T.: Big data, open science and the brain: lessons learned from genomics. Front. Hum. Neurosci. **8**, 239 (2014). https://doi.org/10.3389/fnhum.2014.00239
4. Cichy, R.M., Pantazis, D.: Multivariate pattern analysis of MEG and EEG: a comparison of representational structure in time and space. NeuroImage **158**, 441–454 (2017). https://doi.org/10.1016/j.neuroimage.2017.07.023
5. Cichy, R.M., Ramirez, F.M., Pantazis, D.: Can visual information encoded in cortical columns be decoded from magnetoencephalography data in humans? NeuroImage **121**, 193–204 (2015). https://doi.org/10.1016/j.neuroimage.2015.07.011
6. Danziger, S.A., et al.: Predicting positive p53 cancer rescue regions using most informative positive (MIP) active learning. PLoS Comput. Biol. **5**(9), e1000498 (2009). https://doi.org/10.1371/journal.pcbi.1000498

7. Dima, D.C., Perry, G., Singh, K.D.: Spatial frequency supports the emergence of categorical representations in visual cortex during natural scene perception. NeuroImage **179**, 102–116 (2018). https://doi.org/10.1016/J.NEUROIMAGE.2018.06.033

8. Gonzalez-Moreno, A., et al.: Signal-to-noise ratio of the MEG signal after preprocessing. J. Neurosci. Methods **222**, 56–61 (2014). https://doi.org/10.1016/J.JNEUMETH.2013.10.019

9. Hainmueller, J., Hazlett, C., Alvarez, R.M.: Kernel regularized least squares: reducing misspecification bias with a flexible and interpretable machine learning approach. Polit. Anal. **22**(2), 143–168 (2014). https://doi.org/10.1093/pan/mpt019

10. Hinton, G.E.: Machine learning for neuroscience. Neural Syst. Circ. **1**(1), 12 (2011). https://doi.org/10.1186/2042-1001-1-12

11. Hwang, H.J., et al.: A gaze independent brain-computer interface based on visual stimulation through closed eyelids. Sci. Rep. **5**, 15890 (2015). https://doi.org/10.1038/srep15890

12. Jäkel, F., Schölkopf, B., Wichmann, F.A.: Does cognitive science need kernels? Trends Cogn. Sci. **13**, 381–388 (2009). https://www.sciencedirect.com/science/article/pii/S1364661309001430

13. Orrù, G., Pettersson-Yeo, W., Marquand, A.F., Sartori, G., Mechelli, A.: Using support vector machine to identify imaging biomarkers of neurological and psychiatric disease: a critical review. Neurosci. Biobehav. Rev. **36**(4), 1140–1152 (2012). https://doi.org/10.1016/j.neubiorev.2012.01.004

14. Schölkopf, B., Smola, A.J.: A short introduction to learning with kernels. In: Mendelson, S., Smola, A.J. (eds.) Advanced Lectures on Machine Learning. Lecture Notes in Computer Science, vol. 2600, pp. 41–64. Springer, Heidelberg (2003). https://doi.org/10.1007/3-540-36434-X_2

15. Schrouff, J., et al.: PRoNTo: pattern recognition for neuroimaging toolbox. Neuroinformatics **11**(3), 319–337 (2013). https://doi.org/10.1007/s12021-013-9178-1

16. Schrouff, J., Mourão-Miranda, J., Phillips, C., Parvizi, J.: Decoding intracranial EEG data with multiple kernel learning method. J. Neurosci. Methods **261**, 19–28 (2016). https://doi.org/10.1016/J.JNEUMETH.2015.11.028

17. Treder, M.S., Purwins, H., Miklody, D., Sturm, I., Blankertz, B.: Decoding auditory attention to instruments in polyphonic music using single-trial EEG classification. J. Neural Eng. **11**(2), 026009 (2014). https://doi.org/10.1088/1741-2560/11/2/026009

18. Wang, X., Xing, E.P., Schaid, D.J.: Kernel methods for large-scale genomic data analysis. Brief. Bioinf. **16**(2), 183–192 (2015). https://doi.org/10.1093/bib/bbu024

19. Weinstein, J.N., et al.: The cancer genome atlas pan-cancer analysis project. Nat. Genet. **45**(10), 1113–1120 (2013). https://doi.org/10.1038/ng.2764

20. Youssofzadeh, V., McGuinness, B., Maguire, L.P., Wong-Lin, K.: Multi-kernel learning with dartel improves combined MRI-PET classification of Alzheimer's disease in AIBL data: group and individual analyses. Front. Hum. Neurosci. **11**, 380 (2017). https://doi.org/10.3389/fnhum.2017.00380

Automatic Recognition of Resting State fMRI Networks with Dictionary Learning

Debadatta Dash[1]($\boxtimes$) (iD), Bharat Biswal[2], Anil Kumar Sao[3],
and Jun Wang[1,4] (iD)

[1] University of Texas at Dallas, Richardson, TX 75080, USA
{debadatta.dash,wangjun}@utdallas.edu
[2] New Jersey Institute of Technology, Newark, NJ 07102, USA
bharat.biswal@njit.edu
[3] Indian Institute of Technology, Mandi, HP 175005, India
anil@iitmandi.ac.in
[4] Callier Center for Communication Disorders, UT Dallas,
Richardson, TX 75080, USA

Abstract. Resting state functional magnetic resonance imaging (rs-fMRI) is a functional neuroimaging technique that investigates the spatially remote yet functionally linked neuronal coactivation patterns of the brain at rest. Non-invasiveness and task-free characteristics of rs-fMRI make it particularly suitable for aging, pediatric and clinical population. Researchers typically follow a source separation strategy to efficiently reconstruct the concurrent interacting resting state networks (RSN) from a myriad of whole brain fMRI signals. RSNs are currently identified by visual inspection with prior knowledge of spatial clustering of RSNs, as the variability and spatial overlapping nature of RSNs combined with presence of various sources of noise make automatic identification of RSNs a challenging task. In this study, we have developed an automated recognition algorithm to classify all the distinct RSNs. First, in contrast to traditional single level decomposition, a multi-level deep sparse matrix factorization-based dictionary leaning strategy was used to extract hierarchical features from the data at each level. Then we used maximum likelihood estimates of these spatial features using Kullback-Leibler divergence to perform the recognition of RSNs. Experimental results confirmed the effectiveness of our proposed approach in accurately classifying all the RSNs.

Keywords: Resting state networks · Dictionary learning · fMRI
KL divergence

1 Introduction

Functional connectivity is the statistical dependency of anatomically separated neuron populations interacting in a non-stationary way [1]. Investigation into functional connectivity provides important insights into human behavior and its alteration with neurogenerative diseases [2]. The paradigm of resting state functional magnetic resonance imaging has become a widely recognized neuroimaging modality to explore this functional connectivity in the resting brain. It is believed that cortical and sub-cortical

© Springer Nature Switzerland AG 2018
S. Wang et al. (Eds.): BI 2018, LNAI 11309, pp. 249–259, 2018.
https://doi.org/10.1007/978-3-030-05587-5_24

brain regions reflect a major pattern of ongoing connectome across the human brain at rest [1, 3, 4] indicating rs-fMRI as a robust measure of functional connectivity study. In rs-fMRI study, the subjects do not need to perform any explicit task in contrast to task-fMRI. This simplifies the experimental design by increasing subject compliance. Hence, rs-fMRI is more suitable to be applied to the pediatric and aging population as well as to neurologic patients.

The inter-synchronization of neuron clusters leading to functional connectivity is identified by spontaneous low frequency fluctuations in the Blood Oxygen Level Dependent (BOLD) signal [4] and those clusters are termed as Resting State Networks (RSN) [5] or Intrinsic Connectivity Networks (ICN) [6]. RSNs depict the spatial architecture of functional brain regions to study the temporal brain dynamics supporting the core cognitive and perceptual process of neural architecture [7]. The functional connectivity patterns of RSNs are found to be consistent within specific cerebellar and thalamic nuclei and provide reliable inferences about both cortico-cerebellar and cortico-subcortical connectivity estimates in a far better resolution compared with structural connectivity analysis.

Considering RSNs as different sources of functional connectome, based on the research question and framework design, the segregation of these functional networks can be approached either by a model-based clustering approach or by data driven analysis. Popular techniques of model driven methods are seed based cross-correlation (SCCA) [1, 8], multiple regression, generalized linear model (GLM) and recently popular graph theory analysis [9]. These methods use prior knowledge of the system under investigation to generate the RSNs and hence are subjected to experimental bias. On the other hand, data driven methods such as principal component analysis (PCA) [10], independent component analysis (ICA) [5], and sparse dictionary learning [11–13] etc. are bias free and compute the RSNs based on the statistical results obtained from data itself. ICA is the most popular approach among these data driven methods, but, recently, its inherent independence constraint criteria has been criticized [14].

Notably, DL has been increasingly used for rs-fMRI analysis as it decomposes these resting brain networks with ease by acting upon their sparsity attributes. Dictionary learning performs a source separation computation on the fMRI data to decompose into dictionary atoms (basis) and their corresponding representations by enforcing sparsity constraint onto the representations. After convergence, the representations denote the distinct RSNs. Mathematically, the data decomposition can be written as:

$$\mathbf{X} = \mathbf{DA} \tag{1}$$

Where, $\mathbf{X} \in R^{nmxv}$ is the multi-subject data matrix, $\mathbf{D} \in R^{nmxd}$ is the learned dictionary, $\mathbf{A} \in R^{dxv}$ is the learned representation matrix, n is the number of scans, m is the number of subjects under analysis, v is the number of voxels and d is the model order. Equation (1) can be solved by optimizing the following cost function:

$$argmin_{(\mathbf{D},\mathbf{A})} \left\| \mathbf{a}_{[i]} \right\|_1 \quad s.t. \quad \left\{ \left\| \mathbf{X} - \mathbf{D}\mathbf{A} \right\|_F \right\}^2 < \in \qquad (2)$$

Here, $\| \ \|_1$ is the sparsity promoting function l1-norm and $\| \ \|_F$ is the Frobenius norm. Rows $\mathbf{a}_{[i]}$ of the representation matrix $\mathbf{A}$ corresponds to d sparse RSNs. The convergence of the rows $\mathbf{a}_{[i]}$ to the distinct RSNs is automatically done by solving this cost function. However, Eq. (2) is jointly non-convex in $(\mathbf{D}, \mathbf{A})$ and hence becomes a non-deterministic polynomial-time (NP)-hard problem which can be typically solved using repeated alternative iterations of dictionary update (DU) and sparse coding (SC) steps [15, 16].

In this study, we have used the decomposition approach with dictionary learning, but instead of doing a single level decomposition, we adopted a multi-layer factorization strategy as proposed in our prior work [16] to extract multi-level hierarchical features. For recognition of RSNs, we estimated the probability score based on the maximum likelihood estimate computed through Kullback-Leibler (KL) divergence across RSNs. Based on this score, the RSNs are labeled and captioned. Although, the recognition of the RSNs has been studied previously with ICA [17] and Convolutional Neural Networks (CNN) [18] the recognition strategy implemented in these studies are computationally complex giving a lower performance. Our proposed approach has a simpler implementation but more effective in classifying the relevant RSNs.

2 Materials and Methods

2.1 Data

Three sets of data as detailed in [19–21] respectively are used for this experimentation. The first is Aging data, which contains 14 number of young and healthy adults (8 females and 6 males) of average 24 years of age. The subjects were recruited from the University of Texas at Dallas (UTD) and the University of Texas at Southwestern (UTSW). The data collection study was approved by institutional review boards (IRB) of both the institutions. Subject consent was taken prior to data collection. A Siemens Allegra three Tesla (3T) scanner was used to collect both task (finger tapping and digit symbol substitution) and resting state fMRI scans from the participants. Only the rest data is used for this study. 120 numbers of Echo Planar Images (EPI) were collected with a Field of View (FOV) of 220 mm and $64 \times 64 \times 32$ matrix dimension. The repetition time (TR) and the echo time (TE) was designed to be of 2 s and 30 ms respectively. A flip angle of 80 degrees was considered. The voxel resolution of the data was 3.4 mm $\times$ 3.4 mm $\times$ 4 mm.

A part of the Human Connectome Project (HCP) dataset (Beijing_Zang data) consisting of 48 young healthy subjects (28 females and 20 males) was also used as data for this study. The age of the subjects is in the range of 18-26 years. The matrix dimension of the data is $53 \times 63 \times 36$ whereas the voxel resolution is 3 mm $\times$ 3 mm $\times$ 3 mm. 119 number of EPI images were obtained from the fMRI scans of each subject. To check the reliability of the proposed algorithm for 'unhealthy' data, we chose the rs-fMRI scans of 40 adolescent subjects with ADHD disorder with their age varying from 7-21 years. The TR of the ADHD data is 2 s. The data was obtained from the preprocessed Neuroimage data from ADHD-200 consortium. Details of experimental parameters for the ADHD data acquisition is detailed in [21].

3 Data Preprocessing

Prior to analysis, the raw datasets were first preprocessed using the SPM-12 software [23] on a MATLAB 8.1 platform. The initial two scans of each subject were discarded from all the datasets to confirm the steady resting state of the brain. The rest of the valid images were then motion corrected with realignment function. Then, the images were co-registered to the anatomic brain images of the subjects. The deformation field maps from the subjects' structural scan images were used to normalize the functional images in the MNI space and then were resampled at a 3 mm^3 resolution. Default global signal regression and head motion correction were performed to realign the samples in the same space. Samples with large artifacts or erroneous behavior were discarded. Further, spatial smoothening of the functional images was done to reduce inter-subject variability by using a Gaussian Kernel with FWHM of 8 mm.

4 Proposed Approach

First, a multi-layer dictionary learning strategy is formulated with a model order of 20 for data decomposition. Considering $\mathbf{X}$ as the training fMRI data matrix, it is decomposed with 3 consecutive layers of factorizations as:

$$\mathbf{X} = \mathbf{D}_1\mathbf{A}_1 = \mathbf{D}_1\mathbf{D}_2\mathbf{A}_2 = \mathbf{D}_1\mathbf{D}_2\mathbf{D}_3\mathbf{A}_3 \tag{3}$$

$$\text{Where, } \mathbf{A}_1 = \mathbf{D}_2\mathbf{A}_2 \text{ and } \mathbf{A}_2 = \mathbf{D}_3\mathbf{A}_3 \tag{4}$$

In the first layer of decomposition, we projected the data into a lower temporal dimension utilizing the low-rank structure of fMRI signals. For this, we used the Fast Exemplar Selection (FES) algorithm [22, 24], which operates on the data such as:

$$\left\{ \left\| \mathbf{X} - \mathbf{D}_1\mathbf{D}_1^+\mathbf{X} \right\|_F \right\}^2 = 0, \text{s.t. } \mathbf{G} = \mathbf{D}_1^T\mathbf{D}_1 \text{ is invertible} \tag{5}$$

Where $\mathbf{D_1^+}$ represents the pseudo inverse of $\mathbf{D_1}$ and $\mathbf{G}$ is Gram matrix. Following this, $\mathbf{D_1^O}$ is obtained after orthogonalization via Gram-Schmidt process and then the low rank matrix $\mathbf{A_1}$ is computed as:

$$\mathbf{A_1} = \left(\mathbf{D_1^O}\right)^T\mathbf{X} \tag{6}$$

For the second and third layer, we implemented online dictionary learning (ODL) [15] which further decomposed the first layer representation matrix $\mathbf{A_1}$ simultaneously with each iteration t of first layer decomposition to find the representations as:

$$\mathbf{a_{2[i]}} = argmin_{(\mathbf{a2}\in R)}^v \left\{0.5 * \left(\left\|\mathbf{a_{1t}} - \mathbf{D_{1t-1}a_{2[i]}}\right\| + \lambda\|\mathbf{a_{2[i]}}\|_1\right)\right\} \tag{7}$$

where $\mathbf{a_2}$ is a row of $\mathbf{A_2}$ corresponding to the representations of $\mathbf{A_1}$ learned through dictionary $\mathbf{D_2}$. This second level dictionary $\mathbf{D_2}$ is iteratively updated as:

$$\mathbf{D_2} = argmin_{(\mathbf{D2})}\left[1/t\left\{\sum_{i=1}^{t}\left(0.5 * \left(\{\|\mathbf{a_i} - \mathbf{D_2a_{2i}}\|_2\}^2 + \lambda\|\mathbf{a_{2i}}\|_1\right)\right)\right]\right. \tag{8}$$

Here, λ is the regularization parameter. Similarly, $\mathbf{A_3}$ and $\mathbf{D_3}$ were also obtained with the same ODL approach. After 2nd level decomposition, the obtained representations contained the clusters of functionally similar networks. Then these clusters were refactorized to obtain the distinct RSNs in the third level. The axial maps obtained during the second- and third-layer decomposition is shown in Fig. 1. Once the dictionary was converged, the dictionary atoms responsible for corresponding networks were labeled as ground truth data label as shown in the following Table 1.

Table 1. Ground truth labels

i, j	j = 1	j = 2	j = 3	j = 4	j = 5
	Attention	Executive	Motor	Auditory	Visual
i = 1	aDMN	rFPE	SMN	Aud	VisP
i = 2	pDMN	lFPE	MN	Sal	VisM
i = 3	DAN	Pex	Cereb	VS	VisL
i = 4	PAN	CEN	–	–	VisO

Here j represents the 5 distinct clusters obtained at second level decomposition and i denotes the label of RSNs obtained while refactorizing the functionally similar clusters. It is important to note that, the j value can come anywhere between 1 to 20. But for simpler representation purpose we have devised the following table as the ground truth label matrix. During implementation, the true values of i and j were chosen for further computation.

The RSNs obtained in the final layer were indented and abbreviated as per the general convention [20] and as shown in Figs. 1 and 2: 1. anterior default mode (aDMN), 2. posterior default mode, 3. primary attention (PAN), 4. dorsal attention (DAN), 5. right fronto-parietal executive (rFPE), 6. left fronto-parietal executive (lFPE), 7. primary executive (Pex), 8. central executive (CEN), 9. sensory motor (SMN), 10. motor (MN), 11. cerebellum, 12. auditory (Aud), 13. salience (Sal), 14. ventral stream (VS), 15. primary visual (VisP), 16. medial visual (VisM), 17. lateral visual (VisL), and 18. occipital visual (VisO) network.

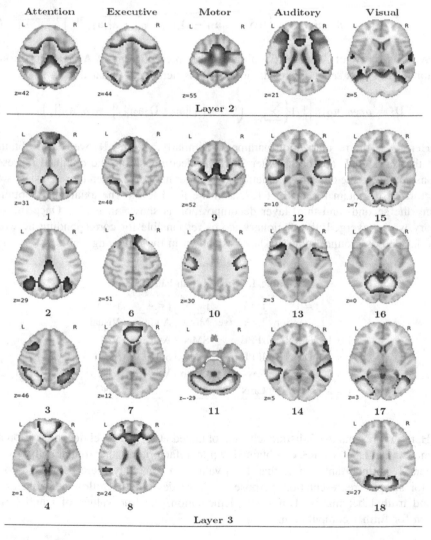

Fig. 1. Axial maps obtained at layer 2 and 3 from a training batch of rs-fMRI data.

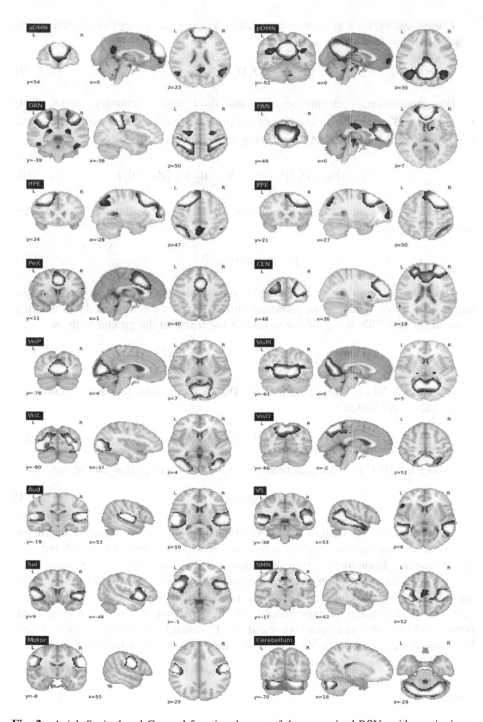

Fig. 2. Axial, Sagittal and Coronal functional maps of the recognized RSNs with captioning.

During testing, for a given new data matrix $\mathbf{Y}$, the same strategy of decomposition was followed to factorize Y as

$$\mathbf{Y} = \mathbf{D}_1' \mathbf{D}_2' \mathbf{D}_3' \mathbf{A}_3' \tag{9}$$

For recognition, only the second and third level dictionary atoms $\mathbf{d}_{2j}' \in \mathbf{D}_2'$ and $\mathbf{d}_{3j}' \in \mathbf{D}_3'$ were chosen to compute the probability score. First, we computed the maximum likelihood of the RSN belonging to a particular cluster as:

$$P_j = D_{2KLj}\left(\mathbf{D}_3' \| \mathbf{D}_2\right) = -\sum_{i,j} \mathbf{d}_{2j}' \log\left(\mathbf{d}_{3i} \big/ \mathbf{d}_{2j}'\right) \tag{10}$$

Where D_{2KL} is the KL-divergence from $\mathbf{D}_2$ to $\mathbf{D}_2'$. From this, the second level cluster can be identified by

$$j = \mathbf{argmax}_{\{j\}}\left(P_j\right) \tag{11}$$

Once the network cluster is identified, only those RSNs were chosen from the training set which lie under the particular cluster. Next, we computed the probability score of the test RSN being similar to one of the RSNs in the ground truth as:

$$P_i = D_{3KLi}\left(\mathbf{D}_3' \| \mathbf{D}_3\right) = -\sum_i \mathbf{d}_{3i}' \log\left(\mathbf{d}_{3i} \big/ \mathbf{d}_{3i}'\right) \tag{12}$$

D_{3KL} is the KL-divergence from $\mathbf{D}_3$ to $\mathbf{D}_3'$. Next, the total probability score of a given RSN is calculated as:

$$P = k\,P_{j+}\left(1-k\right)P_i \tag{13}$$

Where $k = (0,1)$ is a free parameter. Now the RSN recognition can be done as:

$$i = \mathbf{argmax}_{\{i\}}\left(P\right) \tag{14}$$

In other words, for each of the RSNs obtained from the test data, the maximum likelihood estimation was done by comparing it with the ground truth labeled data during training. In summary, given an unknown RSN, first, we found to which cluster (second level feature) it belongs and then which particular RSN was most similar to the test RSN in the given cluster. To deal with noise components, we chose a probability threshold of 0.5 (based on experimental observation) such that if $P < 0.5$, the component will be treated as a noise source and will be discarded from the recognition task. For most of the noise source-based networks, the P value was in the range of 0.1–0.3.

5 Results and Discussions

Figure 2. shows the recognized resting state fMRI networks based on the classification performance with the proposed approach. We have developed this recognition algorithm in such a way that the recognized network will be automatically captioned after decomposition. The labels can be seen on the top left corner of the functional maps. It is important to observe that all the RSNs obtained are spatially localized and free of pseudo activations. Due to multi-layer factorization, the noise suppression occurred twice and hence noise was reduced significantly. Also, during recognition, based on the experimental threshold, noise components are suitably discarded.

Moreover, this multi-layer decomposition is faster and more effective than a single layer decomposition approach as it operates with the lowest model order of 20, whereas for single level DL the model order varies between 40-50 or more based on the experimental design. We have used dictionary atoms instead of the representations as the features to compute the probability score. The choice of such a feature selection was inspired by the fact that the RSNs are spatially overlapped [18, 25, 26]. So, selecting the spatial features will decrease the recognition accuracy. Hence, for a better recognition performance, the basis (atoms) of the RSNs were chosen as the feature set instead of the representations.

Further, to validate our approach, we considered the rs-MRI data of different populations to classify the networks. For, instance we trained with HCP data to find the ground truth labels and then attempted to identify the RSNs of Aging data. We observed that within the same population all the networks are perfectly classified. However, when the training population data length was less than testing population data size, 2-3 networks were misclassified. In most of the cases, anterior and posterior default mode networks were misclassified indicating similar basis functions for these two networks. Similarly, when ADHD data was considered as the training dataset and when tested with the fMRI data of a healthy population (HCP or Aging), the recognition performance decreased. This result was expected as the attention networks of ADHD data is dissimilar to that of data obtained from healthy population. This theory was reflected in our experimental results as Primary and Dorsal attention networks were mostly misclassified. However, when trained with the healthy resting state fMRI data, all the resting state networks obtained from ADHD data were correctly classified including all the attention networks.

Although it is possible to find the sub-networks by simply putting a mask to the rs-fMRI data, automatic recognition is independent of such prior knowledge biased strategies. Moreover, the proposed approach is data driven and more robust to new data.

6 Conclusions

In this study, we have attempted for automatic recognition of resting state fMRI networks. We used a multi-layered dictionary learning to extract the hierarchical second and third level features and used KL divergence to recognize the distinct RSNs. Experimental results convey that the proposed approach is better compared to existing approaches in terms of network recognition as well as parcellation. The proposed approach is also computationally fast as it uses a very low model order for source separation and because of its hierarchical comparison approach. It was also observed that the recognition performance changes when different populations are chosen for training and testing. Also, a 100% accurate classification accuracy was obtained when the training data contained an equal or greater number of subjects than the testing data. In future, we will use Convolutional Neural Networks (CNN) in place of KL-divergence for a better and faster recognition performance.

Acknowledgment. This study was supported by the University of Texas System Brain Research grant and the National Institutes of Health (NIH) under award number R03 DC013990. We thank Kanish Goel and Beiming Cao for their valuable inputs. We also thank Dr. Bart Rypma and the volunteering participants for being of help in data collection.

References

1. Biswal, B., Yetkin, F.Z., Haughton, V.M., Hyde, J.S.: Functional connectivity in the motor cortex of resting human brain using echo-planar MRI. Magn. Reson. Med. **34**(4), 537–541 (1995)
2. Greicius, M.D., Supekar, K., Menon, V., Dougherty, R.F.: Resting-state functional connectivity reflects structural connectivity in the default mode network. Cereb. Cortex **19**(1), 72–78 (2009)
3. Buckner, R.L., et al.: Cortical hubs revealed by intrinsic functional connectivity: mapping, assessment of stability, and relation to Alzheimer's Disease. J. Neurosci. **29**(6), 1860–1873 (2009). The Official Journal of the Society for Neuroscience
4. Biswal, B., Kylen, J.V., Hyde, J.S.: Simultaneous assessment of flow and BOLD signals in resting-state functional connectivity maps. NMR Biomed. **10**, 165–170 (1997)
5. Beckmann, C.F., DeLuca, M., Devlin, J.T., Smith, S.M.: Investigations into resting-state connectivity using independent component analysis. Phil. Trans. R. Soc. London B Biol. Sci. **360**(1457), 1001–1013 (2005)
6. Seeley, W.W., et al.: Dissociable intrinsic connectivity networks for salience processing and executive control. J. Neurosci. **27**(9), 2349–2356 (2007)
7. Liu, X., et al.: Subcortical evidence for a contribution of arousal to fMRI studies of brain activity. Nat. Commun. **9**(1), 395 (2018)
8. Song, H., et al.: Love-related changes in the brain: a resting-state functional magnetic resonance imaging study. Front. Hum. Neurosci. **9**, 71 (2018)
9. Bullmore, E., Olaf, S.: Complex brain networks: graph theoretical analysis of structural and functional systems. Nat. Rev. Neurosci. **10**(3), 186–198 (2009)
10. Friston, K.J., Frith, C.D., Liddle, P.F., Frackowiak, R.S.J.: Functional connectivity: the principal-component analysis of large (PET) datasets. J. Cerebr. Blood F. Met. **3**, 5–14 (1993)
11. Li, H., Satterthwaite, T., Fan, Y.: Large-scale sparse functional networks from resting state fMRI. NeuroImage **156**, 1–13 (2017)
12. Eavani, H., et al.: Sparse dictionary learning of resting state fMRI networks. In: International Workshop on Pattern Recognition in NeuroImaging International Workshop on Pattern Recognition in Neuroimaging, pp. 73–76 (2012)
13. Dash, D., Sao, A. K., Wang, J., Biswal, B.: How many fMRI scans are necessary and sufficient for resting brain connectivity analysis? In: IEEE 6th Global Conference on Signal and Information Processing (GlobalSIP) (2018)

14. Lee, H.J., et al.: Activation of direct and indirect pathway medium spiny neurons drives distinct brain-wide responses. Neuron **9**, 412–424 (2016)
15. Mairal, J., Bach, F., Ponce, J., Sapiro, G.: Online dictionary learning for sparse coding. In: Proceedings of the 26th Annual International Conference on Machine Learning, ICML, pp. 689–696. ACM, New York (2009)
16. Dash, D., Abrol, V., Sao, A.K., Biswal, B.: The model order limit: deep sparse factorization for resting brain. In: IEEE 15th International Symposium on Biomedical Imaging (ISBI), pp. 1244–1247 (2018)
17. Lu, et al.: An automated method for identifying an independent component analysis-based language-related resting-state network in brain tumor subjects for surgical planning. Sci. Rep. **7**, 13769 (2017)
18. Zhao, Y., et al.: Automatic recognition of fMRI-derived functional networks using 3D convolutional neural networks. IEEE Trans. Biomed. Eng. **65**, 1975–1984 (2017)
19. Yuan, R., Di, X., Kim, E.H., Barik, S., Rypma, B., Biswal, B.: Regional homogeneity of resting state fMRI contributes to both neurovascular and task activation variations. Magn. Reson. Imaging **31**(9), 1492–1500 (2013)
20. Biswal, et al.: Toward discovery science of human brain function. Proc. Natl. Acad. Sci. **107**(10), 4734–4739 (2010)
21. The ADHD-200 Consortium. The ADHD-200 consortium: a model to advance the translational potential of neuroimaging in clinical neuroscience. Front. Syst. Neurosci. **6**, 62 (2018)
22. Dash, D., Abrol, V., Sao, A. K., Biswal, B.: Spatial sparsification and low rank projection for fast analysis of multi-subject resting state fMRI data. In: IEEE 15th International Symposium on Biomedical Imaging (ISBI), pp. 1280–1283 (2018)
23. SPM Homepage. https://www.fil.ion.ucl.ac.uk/spm. Accessed 29 June 2018
24. Abrol, V., Sharma, P., Sao, A.K.: Fast exemplar selection algorithm for matrix approximation and representation: a variant oasis algorithm. In: IEEE International Conference on Acoustics, Speech and Signal Processing (ICASSP), pp. 4436–4440 (2017)
25. Karahanoğlu, F.I., Van De Ville, D.: Transient brain activity disentangles fMRI resting-state dynamics in terms of spatially and temporally overlapping networks. Nat. Commun. **6**, 7751 (2015)
26. Zille, P., Calhoun, V.D., Stephen, J.M., Wilson, T.W., Wang, Y.: Fused estimation of sparse connectivity patterns from rest fMRI—application to comparison of children and adult brains. IEEE Trans. Med. Imaging **37**(10), 2165–2175 (2018)

Simultaneous EEG Analysis and Feature Extraction Selection Based on Unsupervised Learning

Badar Almarri[1,2]([✉]) and Chun-Hsi Huang[1]

[1] University of Connecticut, Storrs, CT 06268, USA
[2] King Faisal University, Al Hofuf 31982, Saudi Arabia
badar.almarri@uconn.edu

Abstract. Time-series EEG signals in a raw form are challenging to analyze, train, and compute. Several feature extraction methods, such as fast Fourier transform, wavelet transform, and time-frequency distributions, are commonly employed for this purpose. However, when applied to different datasets, the alignment between the method and machine learning algorithms varies significantly. Through an EEG experiment, we test a simultaneous analysis and unsupervised learning application that can effectively determine what feature extraction method will potentially lead to a higher prediction precision when the ground truth is provided by the participants at a later stage.

Keywords: EEG · Feature extraction · Clustering · Real time analysis

1 Introduction

The neural activities of the human brain have attracted the interest of scholars in a plethora of fields including psychology, medicine, and artificial intelligence, among many others. Methods by which it is possible to capture brain signals can take both invasive and non-invasive forms. Electroencephalography (EEG) and functional magnetic resonance imaging (fMRI) are non-invasive brain activity capturing and recording techniques that are popularly used in neuroscience studies. Non-invasive imaging or sensing outputs are inevitably prone to noise. Moreover, the massive feature space that each regional receptor (e.g., region-of-interest, ROI, in fMRI and electrodes in EEG) captures in a time-series manner creates a further level of complexity in dealing with neurological signals [17]. Hence, it is imperative that relevant features are extracted to optimize machine learning and develop a neurological understanding of their underlying relevance. [2,6,7].

In machine learning, the features extracted from the application-specific raw data contribute greatly to the reliability and accuracy of the learning algorithm outcomes. Those features reinforce the boundary decision to differentiate

© Springer Nature Switzerland AG 2018
S. Wang et al. (Eds.): BI 2018, LNAI 11309, pp. 260–269, 2018.
https://doi.org/10.1007/978-3-030-05587-5_25

between two different groups (e.g., high or low) in the case of a binary classification, for instance, [7].

Affective computing utilizes EEG to understand the underlying neurological interaction of subjects. Many researchers have investigated EEG signals in depth and applied different classification mechanisms to predict how humans will behave in reaction to different stimuli [5,9]. Aspects that are of interest can include human-computer interactions (HCIs), procedures like driving a car, or internal feelings and thoughts toward external stimuli. Emotion has been studied extensively in cases in which subjects are stimulated by multimedia. In most experiments, the signals that are recorded from subjects are classified based on some form of ground truth [12,23].

While subjects are undergoing an EEG experiment, it is often useful to provide a simultaneous analysis and understanding of the time-series signals [22]. The analytic feedback provides the experimenter with access to several advantages including early discovery of the validity and adjustment of the experiment. It can also be employed to verify subjects' feedback and real-time analysis and learning [10].

The rest of the paper is organized as follows: Sect. 2 presents an overview of subject-independent and unsupervised learning and provides details of the clustering methods employed in the current study. Section 3 describes the dataset. Section 4 outlines the methodology employed as we propose the epoched signal analysis and learning. Finally, the results and conclusion are presented in Sects. 5 and 6 respectively.

2   Background

2.1   Subject-Independent Learning

A subject-independent learning process is not determined by any particular subject. Rather, it represents a model for a stimulus in which different neurophysiological features from a variety of subjects contribute to the predictability task. In this approach, each stimulus takes the form of a unit model in which subjects are data points, each of whom has to provide feedback on their emotional states during the session stimulative environment.

The other form of learning in affective computing studies is subject dependent. However, subject-independent prediction offers several advantages over the subject-dependent approach. In subject-independent studies, we aim to verify the validity and effect of the event from different perspectives as opposed to being limited to the perspective of a single respondent. The vitality of subject-independent learning is clearly evident in brain-computer interaction (BCI) applications when the target is the stimulus (e.g., an event, a scene, etc.), and it is often seen in psychology and neuroscience studies. The opposite of that is when the target is a specific subject, and the goal is her or his neurological states toward different events.

2.2 Unsupervised Learning

The absence of ground truth is expected in many machine learning and data-driven applications. However, in some situations, ground truth may be unavailable. For example, if the nature of the data collection process does not call for labeling or feedback or the data exhibits noise, interruption, or loss. In these cases (and others), the cost of collecting the ground truth might be high (e.g., appointing doctors to label a lot of medical images).

Clustering [11] is the most popular algorithm in use for the purposes of unsupervised learning because it can discover separation and the level of density among data points. Other methods are principal component analysis (PCA), abnormality detection, and others.

In this study, we employed 3 well-known clustering algorithms, namely, k-mean clustering (using different distance metrics), spectral clustering, and genetic algorithms clustering to recognize the separability of features extracted from the recorded signals. k-mean is one intuitive clustering algorithm in which k points are selected randomly, and the data points are subsequently arranged according to their proximity to the selected points. A new mean is calculated, and the procedure is repeated until no data points move to the other cluster(s) [3]. Spectral clustering applies dimensionality reduction on the spectrum of the similarity matrix of the data points [14]. Genetic algorithms are utilized because of their ability to search for and identify clusters [13].

3 Dataset

Dataset: The dataset took the form of the DEAP (Dataset of Emotional Analysis using Physiological Signals [9]). It has the following specifications: 32 subjects, each has a multi-channel multidimensional array of size 40 * 40 * 8064, representing video * channel * data/signal). Of the 40 channels, 32 are EEG signals whereas the rest are other physiological measures. The ground truth data is also provided where subjects rated the stimuli based on how they felt when watching each stimulus (i.e. music video described in [9]). Four labels were provided - arousal, valence, dominance, and liking. In the current research, we were only concerned with EEG signals.

4 Methods

To deal with the EEG data in real time, it was vital to perform the heavy work as soon as an acceptable chunk of data was received. Each chunk of data, or epoch, was processed spontaneously. This included preprocessing, artifact removal, and feature extraction and selection, the latter of which is the most expensive part of the machine learning pipeline. In the proposed feature extraction method selection, we assumed the experimenter was going to apply stimuli in the same order for all subjects, and that each stimulus was applied simultaneously. On a practical level, the latter assumption is not easy to achieve; however, it can be accomplished by developing a synchronization procedure. A procedure of this nature was out of the scope of the current research; as such, we will validate this assumption.

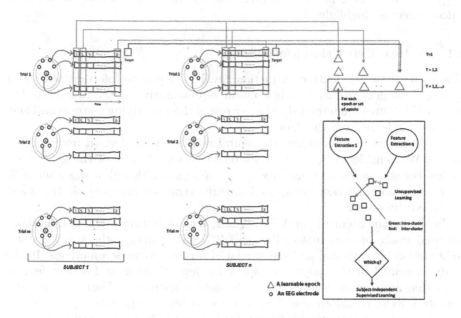

Fig. 1. An illustration of the proposed real time feature extraction.

Given n subjects and m stimuli in an EEG experiment, the objective of a subject-independent learning process is to build a learner, h; i.e.,

$$\mathbf{h} = X \to y \tag{1}$$

where X is a dataset that contains n subjects stimulated by jth stimulus (i.e. $j \in [1 - m]$). X needs to be transformed to $\hat{X}$ that suits the learner, h, better, and provides more insight about the neurosignals.

We defined an epoch size, referred to as w, and this represented the synchronization point that all subjects hypothetically needed to reach, see Fig. 1. Upcoming epochs go through the same process of feature extraction and feature extraction selection. Each w is considered to represent a learnable epoch; hence, in an unsupervised manner, we trained the current w of all subjects (subject 1, subject 2, ..., subject n). For each learnable epoch, we could then preprocess, transform, and extract features. Subsequent learnable epochs could be merged or may stand-alone, see comparison of one of the feature extraction method against the raw signal in Fig. 2. The merging of epochs represented the accumulative features extracted from the current and preceding epochs, which required a larger memory. On the other hand, individual epoch processing was lower cost and faster.

Subject-independent datasets (X) consist of m stimuli for each $i \in n$ subjects, and neural signals for ith subject using stimuli $j \in m$ is denoted as x_{ij}. Epochs, w, break down x_{ij} into x_{ijz} where z is the number of epochs, roughly of length $|x_{ij}|/w$. To be consistent with the literature notation, we will refer to x_{ijz} as x_i unless otherwise highlighted.

4.1   Feature Extraction Methods

Given raw data, x_i, feature extraction involves a process of transforming or mining x_i to generate $\hat{x}_i$ that is a useful representative of the raw data. The extracted features are intended to better reveal the underlying features and help the machine learn from the data.

As described in the dataset, the neural readings were derived from 32 electrodes. We considered $\hat{x}_i$ to be a stretched vector of each of the given electrodes. For simplicity, we considered x_i as one signal, although it was a set of 32 electrodes. In application, we applied feature extraction on every electrode and combined the results.

In the extant literature on EEG signals, tens of feature extraction methods are used solely or combinatorially. In [7,21] among many others, employed a combination of statistical and signal-related feature extraction methods. In the study described in this paper, we applied a few of the most frequent feature extraction approaches related to signals such as short-time Fourier transform, discrete wavelet transform and Teager-Kaiser energy coefficients separately and accompanied with statistical information such as the first 3 moments, standard deviation, and peak-to-peak, see details below:

Mean μ. In the time domain, the mean of a given epoch is formulated as follows:

$$\mu = 1/w \sum_{\tau=1}^{w} x_{i_\tau} \tag{2}$$

where τ is the discrete time of a signal where the given signal (i.e., epoch) is the sampling rate multiplied by the epoch size w.

Variance Var. Variance can be presented as the average power in a stochastic signal [21]:

$$Var = 1/w \sum_{\tau=1}^{w-1} x_{i_\tau}{}^2 \tag{3}$$

Standard Deviation σ [8]:

$$\sigma = \sqrt{1/w \sum_{\tau=1}^{w} (x_{i_\tau} - \mu)^2} \tag{4}$$

Skewness Skw [8]:

$$Skw = \sqrt{1/w \sum_{\tau=1}^{w} (x_{i_\tau} - \mu)^3 / \sigma^3} \tag{5}$$

Peak-to-peak PP [1]:

$$PP = x_{imax} - x_{imin} \tag{6}$$

Discrete Wavelet Transformation DWT. Wavelet transform decomposes a signal into a set of coefficients by scale, denoted as a, and transition, b, by the mother wavelet, Ψ. In this work, we employed Daubechies wavelet (DB4). Each level of scaling passed through a high- and low-pass filter. Then, a down-sampling (by 2) was processed. The main function is shown in 7:

$$DWT(a,b) = \int_{\tau=-\infty}^{\infty} x_i \Psi_{a,b}^*(\tau) \tag{7}$$

Short-Time Fourier Transform STFT. STFT works by sliding a window, w', throughout the given signal with some overlap. Since the proposed method is based on windowing in its core, we used $w = w^i$ if the size of w was small, and a smaller w^i size, otherwise. More details on STFT can be found in [16]:

$$STFT(m) = \sum_{\tau=-\infty}^{\infty} x_i w'(\tau - m) e^{-j\omega\tau} \tag{8}$$

Teager-Kaiser Energy Coefficients TKE. Although it was designed for speech analysis [19], TKE has also been applied in different signal applications, including EEG, to study the amplitude and frequency of the brain signals [15]. Kaiser's derivation of the discrete form is as follows [20]:

$$TKE = x_i(\tau)^2 - x_i(\tau - 1)x_i(\tau + 1) \tag{9}$$

4.2 Unsupervised Learning

Individual epochs captured from subjects are clustered to identify groups alike signals (i.e. subjects). We hypothesize that there should be an extent of separability, although it might be hard to identify. The goal here is to examine if there is some correlation between the clusters and the ground truth provided by members of the clusters.

Given $X_j w$ where j is in the range [1-m], we apply 5 clustering methods: (1) kMeans (distance: Manhattan), (2) kMeans (distance: Euclidean), (3) kMeans (distance: cosine), (4) genetic algorithm, and (5) spectral clustering.

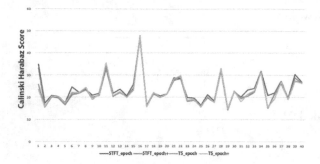

Fig. 2. Clustering performance evaluation of STFT against time-series in two different modes (epoch and epoch+). Epoch refers to individual epochs, and epoch+ refers to cumulative epochs.

To compare the clusters at an early stage at which ground truth labels are not yet provided, we used two different clustering evaluation metrics that do not compare with the ground truth: Calinski Harabaz Score and Silhouette Score.

Calinski-Harabaz Index [4] is a ratio of the between-clusters dispersion mean and the within-cluster dispersion. The higher the index, the better the clustering performance. Silhouette coefficient [18], on the other hand, is a real number in the range $[-1, +1]$, and is measured by two parameters for each data point: The mean distance between each point in a cluster and its pair, and the mean distance between each point and the point in the next nearest cluster.

4.3   Supervised Learning

We used five various classifiers: (1) linear support vector machine (Linear SVM), (2) radial base function (RBF) SVM, (3) decision tree (DT), (4) random forest (RF), and (5) AdaBoost. Those algorithms were selected because they have been employed intensively on problems of this nature with different feature extraction setups. We also expected this would facilitate a comparison with the separable clusters of subjects.

When this method is applied, the feature extraction method that performed better than the others is typically used to extract features that fit the subject-independent classifier. However, here, we fit all the classifiers to compare their results with clustering outcomes.

5   Results

In this work, we ran the proposed selection algorithm on six different feature extraction algorithms. The STFT, DWT, and Teager-Kaiser energy coefficients were run in isolation in one setup, while they were accompanied by statistical information, such as the first three moments, standard deviation, and peak-to-peak, in the second setup, Fig. 3.

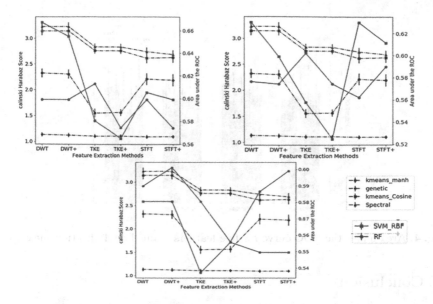

Fig. 3. Clustering performance evaluation for 6 feature extraction methods (note: + refers to the statistical features added to the extracted signal features). Two classifiers (SVM with RBF kernel and Random Forest) are plotted in blue. Upper-left: valence, Upper-right: Arousal, and Lower: Dominance

Due to imbalanced labeling, we used receiver operation characteristics (ROC). As opposed to relying on accuracy alone, the area under the curve was evaluated to measure performance. The former approach can be harmful in some situations. For example, if a class is major in training, and the model overfits it, the accuracy would be high, yet faulty.

As can be observed in Fig. 3, using DWT (with and without statistical information) outperforms the other feature extraction methods in this study. Both kmeans ($k = 2$), where the distance measure is cosine and spectral clustering exhibits a higher score than the other clustering algorithms. The K-means with the Manhattan measure of distance was consistent with the results presented in existing literature and our expectation that STFT and DWT would extract appropriate features for the learning process. Over the course of different runs, we observed how adding statistical features undermined the main feature extraction method.

In the current study, arousal and dominance predictability seemed to be higher than other affection measures (e.g., valence and dominance), see Fig. 4. RBF-kernelized SVM and AdaBoost exhibited a higher performance in terms of area under the ROC curve, reaching as high as 80%. Other learners did not perform consistently. We believe that the features that are extracted play a fundamental role in the fitting process, and that can be observed in the inconsistent feature-learner performance.

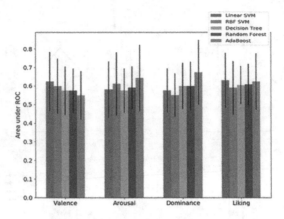

Fig. 4. Area under the ROC curve for five learners trained on 4 affection measures.

6 Conclusion

In the current study, we investigated different clustering methods to examine a range of the feature extraction methods that are frequently applied to EEG data. The findings revealed that DWT outperformed STFT and Teager-Kaiser energy. In terms of the classification aspect of the pipeline, SVM-RBF and AdaBoost outperformed other classifiers, especially in the arousal measure.

References

1. Abootalebi, V., Moradi, M.H., Khalilzadeh, M.A.: A new approach for EEG feature extraction in P300-based lie detection. Comput. Methods Programs Biomed. **94**(1), 48–57 (2009)
2. Amin, H.U., et al.: Feature extraction and classification for EEG signals using wavelet transform and machine learning techniques. Australas. Phys. Eng. Sci. Med. **38**(1), 139–149 (2015)
3. Arthur, D., Vassilvitskii, S.: k-means++: the advantages of careful seeding. In: Proceedings of the Eighteenth Annual ACM-SIAM Symposium on Discrete algorithms, pp. 1027–1035. Society for Industrial and Applied Mathematics (2007)
4. Caliński, T., Harabasz, J.: A dendrite method for cluster analysis. Commun. Stat. Theory Methods **3**(1), 1–27 (1974)
5. Frantzidis, C.A., et al.: Toward emotion aware computing: an integrated approach using multichannel neurophysiological recordings and affective visual stimuli. IEEE Trans. Inf. Technol. Biomed. **14**(3), 589–597 (2010)
6. Hong, K.S., Khan, M.J., Hong, M.J.: Feature extraction and classification methods for hybrid fNIRS-EEG brain-computer interfaces. Front. Hum. Neurosci. **12** (2018)
7. Jenke, R., Peer, A., Buss, M.: Feature extraction and selection for emotion recognition from EEG. IEEE T. Affect. Comput. **5**(3), 327–339 (2014)
8. Kevric, J., Subasi, A.: Comparison of signal decomposition methods in classification of EEG signals for motor-imagery BCI system. Biomed. Signal Process. Control **31**, 398–406 (2017)

9. Koelstra, S., et al.: Deap: a database for emotion analysis; using physiological signals. IEEE T. Affect. Comput. **3**(1), 18–31 (2012)
10. Lan, Z., Sourina, O., Wang, L., Liu, Y.: Real-time EEG-based emotion monitoring using stable features. Vis. Comput. **32**(3), 347–358 (2016)
11. Liu, C., Abu-Jamous, B., Brattico, E., Nandi, A.: Clustering consistency in neuroimaging data analysis. In: 2015 12th International Conference on Fuzzy Systems and Knowledge Discovery (FSKD), pp. 1118–1122. IEEE (2015)
12. Lotte, F., Congedo, M., Lécuyer, A., Lamarche, F., Arnaldi, B.: A review of classification algorithms for EEG-based brain-computer interfaces. J. Neural Eng. **4**(2), R1 (2007)
13. Maulik, U., Bandyopadhyay, S.: Genetic algorithm-based clustering technique. Pattern Recognit. **33**(9), 1455–1465 (2000)
14. Ng, A.Y., Jordan, M.I., Weiss, Y.: On spectral clustering: analysis and an algorithm. In: Advances in Neural Information Processing Systems, pp. 849–856 (2002)
15. O'Toole, J.M., Temko, A., Stevenson, N.: Assessing instantaneous energy in the EEG: a non-negative, frequency-weighted energy operator. In: 2014 36th Annual International Conference of the IEEE Engineering in Medicine and Biology Society, pp. 3288–3291. IEEE (2014)
16. Patkar, V.P., Das, L., Joshi, P.: Evaluation of PSE, STFT and probability coefficients for classifying two directions from EEG using radial basis function. In: 2015 IEEE International Conference on Computational Intelligence and Computing Research (ICCIC), pp. 1–4. IEEE (2015)
17. Rathore, S., Habes, M., Iftikhar, M.A., Shacklett, A., Davatzikos, C.: A review on neuroimaging-based classification studies and associated feature extraction methods for Alzheimer's disease and its prodromal stages. NeuroImage **155**, 530–548 (2017)
18. Rousseeuw, P.J.: Silhouettes: a graphical aid to the interpretation and validation of cluster analysis. J. Comput. Appl. Math. **20**, 53–65 (1987)
19. Vakman, D.: On the analytic signal, the Teager-Kaiser Energy algorithm, and other methods for defining amplitude and frequency. IEEE Trans. Signal Process. **44**(4), 791–797 (1996)
20. Wu, K., Zhang, D., Lu, G.: GMAT: Glottal closure instants detection based on the multiresolution absolute Teager-Kaiser energy operator. Digit. Signal Process. **69**, 286–299 (2017)
21. Xi, X., Tang, M., Miran, S.M., Luo, Z.: Evaluation of feature extraction and recognition for activity monitoring and fall detection based on wearable sEMG sensors. Sensors **17**(6), 1229 (2017)
22. Yap, H.-Y., Choo, Y.-H., Khoh, W.-H.: Overview of acquisition protocol in EEG based recognition system. In: Zeng, Y., He, Y., Kotaleski, J.H., Martone, M., Xu, B., Peng, H., Luo, Q. (eds.) BI 2017. LNCS (LNAI), vol. 10654, pp. 129–138. Springer, Cham (2017). https://doi.org/10.1007/978-3-319-70772-3_12
23. Zhong, M., Lotte, F., Girolami, M., Lécuyer, A.: Classifying EEG for brain computer interfaces using Gaussian processes. Pattern Recogn. Lett. **29**(3), 354–359 (2008)

Construction of Sparse Weighted Directed Network (SWDN) from the Multivariate Time-Series

Rahilsadat Hosseini$^{(\boxtimes)}$ ⓘ, Feng Liu, and Shouyi Wang

University of Texas at Arlington, Arlington, TX, USA
{rahilsadat.hosseini,feng.liu}@mavs.uta.edu, shouyiw@uta.edu

Abstract. There are many studies focusing on network detection in multivariate (MV) time-series data. A great deal of focus have been on estimation of brain networks using functional Magnetic Resonance Imaging (fMRI), functional Near-Infrared Spectroscopy (fNIRS) and electroencephalogram (EEG). We present a sparse weighted directed network (SWDN) estimation approach which can detect the underlying minimum spanning network with maximum likelihood and estimated weights based on linear Gaussian conditional relationship in the MV time-series. Considering the brain neuro-imaging signals as the multivariate data, we evaluated the performance of the proposed approach using the publicly available fMRI data-set and the results of the similar study which had evaluated popular network estimation approaches on the simulated fMRI data.

Keywords: Multivariate time-series
Sparse weighted directed network (SWDN) · fMRI

1 Introduction

MV time-series analysis is used to investigate the concept of connectivity in dynamic systems like physiological time series. Connectivity analysis can detect coupling which means the presence or absence of interactions between the processes and identify causality which means the presence of driver-response relationships. There are different approaches to transform MV time-series in to a network through mapping algorithms. A classic but popular approach is considering each one of time-series as a node, and the weight of the edge connecting nodes would be interdependency between pairwise data [1] like correlation matrices [2]. Another recent approach is mapping the time-series into abstract graphs [3] for example the visibility algorithms that is applied on uni-variate time-series [4]. Another way to perform connectivity assessment include linear MV autoregressive (MVAR) process, and deriving measurements like coherence, the partial coherence, the directed coherence and so on from the frequency domain. Dynamic dependence model (the extensions of multi-regression dynamic models (MDM)

© Springer Nature Switzerland AG 2018
S. Wang et al. (Eds.): BI 2018, LNAI 11309, pp. 270–281, 2018.
https://doi.org/10.1007/978-3-030-05587-5_26

[5]) is another available approach that map time-series to directed graphical models in which causality over time is decided based on the contemporaneous values of each one of the time-series as the predictor in a conditional relationship. Later, sparsity was induced to this network using sequential Bayesian mixture modeling [6].

There is a growing interest in brain network estimation. Brain connectivity/network reveals the linking patterns in the brain which happens in different layers from neurons to neural assemblies and brain structures. Brain connectivity involves 3 concepts: neuroanatomical or structural connectivity, functional connectivity and effective connectivity. Generally brain network estimation can be conducted in two main approaches, first, pairwise connectivity analysis like correlation, second, a convoluted approach to consider all the nodes globally like Bayes net modeling. Different methods can be applied on various brain imaging techniques. For example, MEG analysis of functional connectivity patterns based on the mutual information between wavelet time-series [7]. Another example is fNIRS (hemodynamic signals, such as HbO, HbR, and HbT responses) functional and effective connectivity analysis via Granger causality methods [8–10] and pair-wise temporal correlation [11]. The other significant group of studies focus on the analysis of fMRI network [12], using Granger causality [13] and dynamic causal modeling [14].

Smith et. al. [15] generated various fMRI simulations based on BOLD and evaluated the efficacy of different network construction methods. The 28 simulations varied based on simulation factors including number of nodes, session duration, TR/neural lag, noise, haemodynamic response function (HRF) standard deviation and other factors like shared inputs, global mean confound, bad ROI (mixed and new random), backward connections, cyclic connections, stronger connections, more connections, non-stationary & stationary connections and only-one-strong input. The tested network modeling techniques were correlation and partial correlation, regularized inverse covariance (ICOV), mutual information, Granger causality (conditional, pairwise, directed and causality difference) and related lag-based measures, PDC (partial directed coherence), DTF (directed transfer function), coherence, generalized synchronization (Gen Synch), Patel's conditional dependence measures, Byes Net and LiNGAM (Linear, Non-Gaussian, Acyclic causal Models). The four evaluation metrics were defined as follows: Z-score true positive (TP), Z-score false positive (FP), c-sensitivity i.e. the fraction of TPs that are estimated with higher connection non-normalized strengths than the 95th percentile of the raw non-normalized FPs and total number of true connections and lastly, d-accuracy i.e. mean fractional rate of detecting the correct directionality of true connections. Evaluation of the network methods are summarized as follow: first-rank performing methods with c-sensitivity about 90% were: Partial correlation, ICOV and the Bayes net. The second-rank with 70–80% were: full correlation and Patel's. The third rank with 50% were: MI, Coherence and Gen Synch. The forth rank with poor performance of under 20% were: the lag-based methods (Granger, PDC and DTF) and LiNGAM. Regarding the detection of the direction of the connection, none of the methods were accurate except Patel's with 65%. The effect of factors are summarized as follow: longer duration resulted in higher c-sensitivity and had strong dependency with detection of directionality. Duration was more effective than TR and TR was more effective than noise level. Bad RIO was significantly deteriorating. The number of nodes and the addition of a global mean confound had complex patterns of effect.

In this study, we aim to learn the structure of a multivariate time-series and construct a graphical data-driven model using minimum spanning tree, maximum likelihood and linear conditional Gaussian dependance. The biggest challenge in structure learning when having no prior knowledge about the structure, is finding the highest score structure which is NP-hard. A very complex yet powerful approach is Bayesian learning. However there are less computationally-complex approaches which are popular and commonly applied for example correlation, regularized inverse covariance and Granger causality. We apply the proposed network construction method to a variety of MV time-series in order to evaluate the efficacy of the method in comparison with other network estimation methods. As an example of the multivariate time-series, we applied the method to estimate functional connectivity in fMRI measurements which shows the temporal statistical correlation among neural assemblies. The fMRI data was publicly available from study [15]. We exploited the results from study [15] and compared the performance of SWDN using similar evaluation metrics including relative sensitivities to finding the presence of a direct network connection, ability to find the direction of the connection, and robustness against various network challenges.

2 Method

2.1 Data Description

As it has been explained in the previous section, we used the public fMRI data to evaluate the network detection. The BOLD timeseries fMRI data was generated based on dynamic causal modeling (DCM) in 28 sessions with 50 subjects, varying time-stamp points and simulated with different properties. The session properties are retrieved from the study [15] and is summarized in Table 1.

2.2 Maximum Spanning Tree (MST), Adjacency Matrix and Graph

Maximum spanning tree is the same as minimum spanning tree but with the selection of edges with maximum weigh at each iteration. Minimum spanning tree as a sub-network containing the strongest connections, has successfully been applied to detect the null model of connections that form the backbone structure of the brain to create an empirical reference [16], moreover to capture network alterations due to aging and disease in functional and structural imaging data [17–19]. We implemented the Prim's minimum spanning tree algorithm to find the underlying network. Prim's algorithm solves the problem

Table 1. Summary of the session properties of the simulated fMRI

Sim1, 5Nd, 200NTp	Baseline	Sim15, 5Nd, 200NTp	Stronger connection
Sim2, 10Nd, 200NTp	Baseline	Sim16, 5Nd, 200NTp	More connections
Sim3, 15Nd, 200NTp	Baseline	Sim17, 10Nd, 200NTp	Reduced noise
Sim4, 50Nd, 200NTp	Baseline	Sim18, 5Nd, 200NTp	Removed all HLV
Sim5, 5Nd, 1200NTp	1 h session	Sim19, 5Nd, 2400NTp	Increased neural lag
Sim6, 10Nd, 1200NTp	1 h session	Sim20, 5Nd, 2400NTp	Neural lag and removed HLV
Sim7, 5Nd, 5000NTp	4 h session	Sim21, 5Nd, 200NTp	2-group
Sim8, 5Nd, 200NTp	Shared input	Sim22, 5Nd, 200NTp	Nonstationary connection strength
Sim9, 5Nd, 5000NTp	Shared input	Sim23, 5Nd, 200NTp	Stationary connection strength
Sim10, 5Nd, 200NTp	Global mean confound	Sim24, 5Nd, 200NTp	Only one strong external input
Sim11, 10Nd, 200NTp	Bad ROI - mixed	Sim25, 5Nd, 100NTp	Reduced noise
Sim12, 10Nd, 200NTp	Bad ROI - mixed	Sim26, 5Nd, 50NTp	2.5 min session
Sim13, 5Nd, 200NTp	Backward connectionn	Sim27, 5Nd, 50NTp	Reduced noise
Sim14, 5Nd, 200NTp	Cyclic connection	Sim28, 5Nd, 100NTp	Reduced noise

Sim: simulation, Nd: number of Nodes, NTp: Number of time-points, HLV: haemodynamic lag variability

of finding acyclic set connecting all vertices in V with the minimal weight, $w(T) = \sum_{(u,v) \in T} w(u,v)$, for a given connected undirected graph $G = (V, E)$, where each edge (u, v) has a weight $w(u, v)$. Prim's algorithm starts with a spanning tree, containing arbitrary vertex and no edge, it repeatedly adds edges with minimum weight and grows the spanning with a vertex not in the tree in a greedy way. We defined a priority queue for the vertices not in the tree, using a pointer from adjacency matrix as the list of entry, in order to find the minimal edge connected to the tree. The key of the vertex is weight of the edge connecting it to the tree. This greedy algorithm works in $O((|V| + |E|) \log |V|) = O(|E| \log |V|)$ running time while loop runs $|V|$ times.

In maximum spanning tree, the set is found by vertices with maximum weight. Weight is calculated as the multivariate linear or nonlinear dependance matrix using pairwise mutual information (MI) and correlation. As described in the Algorithm 1, the tree starts with connecting all vertices ($v_{1...n} \in V$) to the root, then a queue is listed for entering the nodes (Q). The child (F) of the root, is decided by having the maximum weight ($keys(v)$) among all edges (E), if the weight of the new edge is greater than the current weight ($W(F, v) > keys(v)$). The selected (v) is then removed from the Q. This repeats till the queue become empty and predecessor (p) for all ($v \in Q$) is decided while root is the only vertex without parent. This procedure iterates for ($\forall root \in V$) and the best tree is selected based on the maximum likelihood of the ($data|G, model$).

The constructed tree is a compact joint representation over unstructured variable representation, much less smaller network. This tree network helps to speed up enumeration and eliminate variable and is the basis to construct the adjacency matrix. Adjacency matrix is a 0–1 matrix that takes a n-by-n weight matrix and returns a list of the maximum weight spanning tree. If there is a predecessor, then $pred(i) = 1$, otherwise it is zero. It can be either symmetric or non-symmetric. We converted the adjacency matrix to a graph by defining a matrix in size of adjacency matrix but with 2 columns. Column one defines

Algorithm 1. Maximum spanning tree (MST), an implementation of Prim's minimum spanning tree

---

$Q = V - \{root\}$
$p(v) = root \quad \forall v \in Q$
$keys(v) = W(root, v) \quad \forall v \in Q$
while $Q \neq \emptyset$ **do**
$\quad F = \underset{v \in Q}{\operatorname{argmax}}\, keys(v)$
$\quad Q = Q - \{F\}$
$\quad$ **for** $v \in Q$ **do**
$\quad\quad$ **if** $W(F, v) > keys(v)$ **then**
$\quad\quad\quad p(v) = F$
$\quad\quad\quad keys(v) = W(F, v)$

---

the existence of an edge (binary), column 2 defines the parent node, each row represents the child node. Adjacency matrix is used to calculate the linear parameters of the conditional Gaussian graphical model. There are two assumptions for simplicity and being allowed to use linear systems: all nodes follow Gaussian distribution [20] and child-parent (edge) have linear relationship [21].

Conditional Gaussian Distribution. We used the constructed graph to detect edges between children and parents, and to fit linear Gaussian between them. Next, we estimated parameters of the linear Gaussian model (β) using Eqs. (1, 2) where $C_{M \times 1}$ represents the child variable with M examples and $U_{M \times N}$ represents N parents ($U_1, \ldots, U_n$) each with M examples.

$$C|U \sim N(\beta(1) * U_1 + \beta(n) * U_n + \beta(n+1), \sigma^2) \tag{1}$$

$$\sigma = \sqrt{cov(C) - \sum(\sum(\beta * \beta'. * cov(U)))} \tag{2}$$

In Eq. (3), (A) represents the expectations matrix and is required to solve the linear system ($A \times \beta = B$) where (B) as the right hand side of the equation follows Eq. (4).

$$A = \begin{bmatrix} E[U_1] & E[U_2] & \ldots & E[U_n] & 1 \\ E[U_1 * U_1] & E[U_2 * U_1] & \ldots & E[U_n * U_1] & E[U_1] \\ \vdots & \vdots & \ldots & \vdots & \vdots \\ E[U_1 * U_n] & E[U_2 * U_n] & \ldots & E[U_n * U_n] & E[U_n] \end{bmatrix} \tag{3}$$

$$B = \begin{bmatrix} E[X] \\ E[X * U_1] \\ \vdots \\ E[X * U_n] \end{bmatrix} \tag{4}$$

We used log-likelihood to evaluate the data given the model and graph structure ($data|G, P$), where P is the structure array of estimated parameters (β) for the linear Gaussian. The selected model is the one with the maximum likelihood.

$$E(x) = \beta(0) + \beta(1) * U(1) + ... + \beta(n) * U(n) \tag{5}$$

$$p(v) = \sum(G == v)/|V| \tag{6}$$

$$\text{log-likelihood}(u|v) =$$

$$p(v) * \log(\sum(\exp((x - E(x))^2/2\sigma^2 - log(\sqrt{\pi}\sigma)))) \tag{7}$$

2.3   Network Evaluation Metrics

The four evaluation metrics were defined as follows: (1) normalized true positive (Z-score TP) i.e. normalized weight of the true connections (correctly detected edge when it existed in the ground-truth network), (2) normalized false positive (Z-score FP) i.e. normalized weights of the network for edges that are defined but should have been empty based on the ground-truth, (3) c-sensitivity i.e. the fraction of TPs that are estimated with higher connection non-normalized strengths than the 95th percentile of the raw non-normalized FPs and total number of true connections and (4) d-accuracy i.e. mean fractional rate of detecting the correct directionality of true connections which can be calculated as difference of normalized weights in $node_{ij}$ and $node_{ji}$.

3   Results

3.1   Comparing SWDN with Other Network Methods

In Fig. (1a, b, c and d) performance metrics Zscore TP, Zscore FP, c-sensitivity and d-accuracy are respectively calculated for SWDN. Based on the violin plots (vertical histograms that can depict multimodality), SWDN performs well in sessions 1, 5, 7, 15, 19 and 20, in which there is least overlap between distributions in Fig. (1a and b) meaning that the c-sensitivity distribution shown in Fig. (1c) has higher values with average mean and variance of 0.48 and 0.34 respectively. The sessions with very poor performance are 3, 4, 11, 12, 13, 16 and 24 in which c-sensitivity distribution has average mean and variance of 0.09 and 0.12 respectively.

The capability of the proposed method (SWDN) in detection of the ground-truth network is compared with other networks' capabilities which are retrieved from the study [15] and the results are summarized below. In each item, the italic font sentences summaries the results taken from the study [15] and the bold font sentences state the performance of SWDN.

In simulation 1, 2 and 3, Partial correlation, ICOV and the Bayes net performed about 90% of c-sensitivity, while lag-based methods (Granger, etc.) less than 20%. **The proposed method (SWDN) performed with average of 53% c-sensitivity with the standard deviation of .35 in sim1 and2 and outperformed lag-based methods including Granger but significantly reduced sensitivity to 17% in sim3.**

In simulation 4, full correlation, ICOV and Patel's all performed excellently. **In simulation 3 and 4 number of nodes increased to 15 and 50, SWDN's performance decreased, especially in sim4 to 10%**

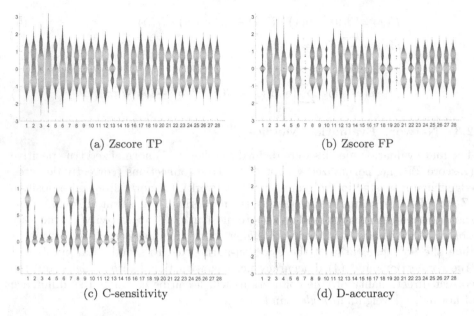

(a) Zscore TP   (b) Zscore FP

(c) C-sensitivity   (d) D-accuracy

Fig. 1. X-axis represents session IDs starting from 1 to 28, Y-axis represents the weights of all edges from all subjects.

In simulation 5 and 6, the duration was increased to 60 minutes, which caused the single lag-based method to reach higher sensitivity but poor d-accuracy suggested that it was not a trustworthy result. LINGAM was performing better in sim5 because of more time-points which improved better function for temporal ICA however, 10% reduced in sim6 because of more time-points. **SWDN performed 50% in sim5 but decreased in sensitivity in sim6 (24%) since there were more nodes.** *In Sim7 with 5 nodes and 250 min duration, LINGAM outperformed all other methods among all sessions (90%).* **SWDN increased sensitivity in sim7 to 55% because of the longer duration and less number of nodes comparing to sim5 and 6.**

In simulation 8 and 9, shared inputs deteriorated all estimation methods to 60% and below. **SWDN was not designed to capture shared inputs because it was based on minimum spanning tree (maximum of one parent for a child), therefore as expected the results was low and about 28–34% c-sensitivity.**

In simulation 10 with global mean confound, there was the same results as sim1. **SWDN achieved 48% c-sensitivity, outperforming lag-based methods but behind Bayes and Partial correlation.**

In simulation 11 and 12 with bad ROI (mixed or new random), the results were extremely bad, all the methods lower than 20% in sim11 but much better in sim12. **SWDN also performed poorly about 10% in both simulations.**

In simulation 13 with backward connections, all methods reduced sensitivity significantly with best method to be Bayes with 60% and Coherence, Gen Synch

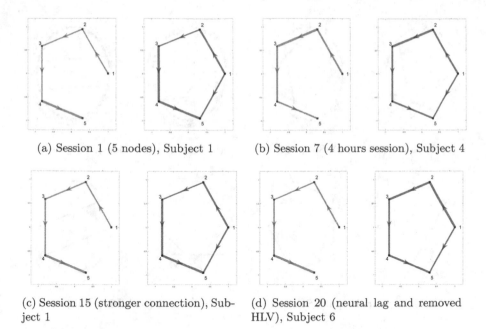

(a) Session 1 (5 nodes), Subject 1   (b) Session 7 (4 hours session), Subject 4

(c) Session 15 (stronger connection), Subject 1   (d) Session 20 (neural lag and removed HLV), Subject 6

Fig. 2. The best constructed network among subjects in a session by SWDN (in red, on the left) vs. the ground-truth network (in blue, on the right). These are the examples of excellent performance of SWDN under the promising circumstances like small network, longer duration, existence of strong connection and neural lag with removed HLV. Edge width is proportional to edge weight. (Color figure online)

and MI like the correlation measures, ICOV and Patel's, all being around 50%. **SWDN was not promising with 11%.**

In simulation 14, with cyclic connections, there were same results as sim1 but reduced d-accuracy. **SWDN was not designed to capture cyclic connections and achieved 30% c-sensitivity.**

In simulation 15, with stronger connection, Partial correlation, ICOV and the Bayes net methods achieved 90%. Full correlation and Patel's fell to around 60%. MI, Coherence and Gen Synch were unchanged, and, Partial MI increased to 85%. Lag-based methods were performing very poorly (less than 30%). **SWDN achieved 60% indicating that it outperformed lag-based methods in capturing stronger connections.**

In simulation 16, there were similar results as sim1 but lower sensitivity. **Expectedly, SWDN could not estimate network with many connections because it was designed to capture sparse network with the most significant edges, therefore performing poorly about 17%.**

In simulation 17, which could be compared with sim15, Partial correlation, ICOV and the Bayes net had excellent performance, while lag-based methods (Granger, etc.) less than 20%. MI and Coherence increased to 70s%. **SWDN with poor performance of 25% indicated that in comparison with**

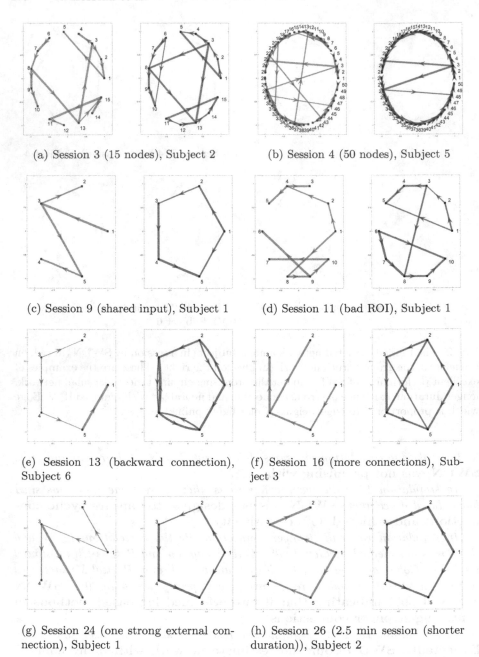

(a) Session 3 (15 nodes), Subject 2

(b) Session 4 (50 nodes), Subject 5

(c) Session 9 (shared input), Subject 1

(d) Session 11 (bad ROI), Subject 1

(e) Session 13 (backward connection), Subject 6

(f) Session 16 (more connections), Subject 3

(g) Session 24 (one strong external connection), Subject 1

(h) Session 26 (2.5 min session (shorter duration)), Subject 2

Fig. 3. The worst constructed network among subjects in a session by SWDN (in red, on the left) vs. the ground-truth network (in blue, on the right). These are the examples of poor performance of SWDN under the challenging circumstances like bigger networks, shared input, bad ROI (mixed nodes), existence of backward connection, many connections and one strong external connection in the ground-truth network and shorter duration. Edge width is proportional to edge weight. (Color figure online)

sim15 it performed equally or better than Granger methods. *Simulation 18 was similar to sim1 after removal of haemodynamic lag variability. The results were unchanged, all lag-based methods performed very poorly both with respect to c-sensitivity and d-accuracy.* **SWDN performed better than lag-based methods with 50% sensitivity indicating that existence of lag did not affect its performance.**

In simulations 19 and 20 with added neural lag, Partial correlation and ICOV achieved highest sensitivity 90s%, with some of the Granger approaches achieving 80s%. **SWDN achieved 53 to 60% sensitivity.**

Simulation 21 tested the sensitivity of the methods at detection of changes in connection strength among subjects. And introduced the most sensitive method as Patel's, with t = 7.4, Full correlation, Partial correlation, ICOV, Gen Synch and most of the Bayes net methods. **SWDN was not very sensitive with 27%.**

In simulation 22, there were non-stationary connection strengths. Bayes net methods, correlation and ICOV achieving the c-sensitivity (78% and 70% respectively). Coherence measures were expected to be promising but they were not. **SWDN was promising gaining 48% sensitivity.**

In simulation 23, there was stationary connection strength. Partial correlation and ICOV performed the best, but the Bayes net methods did not perform so well, falling to 60%. **SWDN performed poorly around 37%. The decrease in performance was similar to the Bayes Net methods comparing to sim22.**

In simulation 24 which was similar to sim15, but with only one strong external input, none of the methods had a c-sensitivity greater than 50%, and none had d-accuracy greater than 61%. Best performing methods Partial correlation and ICOV = 5 resulted in 40s% and the Bayes net models performed badly in 20s%. **SWDN performed similar to Bayes Net with 24% c-sensitivity.**

In simulations 25, 26 (shorter duration), 27 (shorter duration and reduced noise level) and 28 (reduced noise level), the three best-performing models resulted in 70s%, 50s%, 70s% and 80% sensitivity respectively. **SWDN achieved 36, 43, 43, and 38% c-sensitivity respectively.**

In Figs. 2 and 3 the excellent and poor performance of SWDN are respectively depicted via examples among subjects in each session. The examples are selected to visualize the strength and weakness of the method more clearly. SWDN is more efficient in estimation of the ground-truth network when it has less number of nodes and longer duration while it performs poorly with bigger networks and shorter duration. It was expected to have low sensitivity in estimation of specific networks (with complex simulation parameters) like backward, more connections, shared input and bad ROI because of the nature of spanning tree which is acyclic network with fixed number of edges in which each child node has maximum of one parent.

4   Conclusion

SWDN was capable of capturing the strongest sub-graph of the underlying network based on the MST algorithm. SWDN was more compatible with smaller networks meaning less number of nodes (refer to the good performance in sim1) and less number of edges (refer to poor performance in sim16) and longer duration of simulation (refer to the good performance in sim5, 7, 19 and 20). In 2 of the simulations (sim22 and 24) its performance was similar to Bayes Net, however it was much less complicated computationally and therefore less time-consuming. It outperformed lag-based methods like Granger (refer to sim1, 2, 14, 15, 17 and 18). With respect to the estimation of network connection directionality, SWDN was poor and was not able to detect higher than random accuracy. This conclusions is consistent with the results taken from study [15] which stated the d-accuracy of the methods to be at chance level (50%).

References

1. Lacasa, L., Nicosia, V., Latora, V.: Network structure of multivariate time series. Sci. Rep. **5**, Article no. 15508 (2015)
2. Hu, Y., Zhao, H., Ai, X.: Inferring weighted directed association network from multivariate time series with a synthetic method of partial symbolic transfer entropy spectrum and granger causality. PLOS ONE **11**(11), 1–25 (2016)
3. Zhang, J., Small, M.: Complex network from pseudoperiodic time series: topology versus dynamics. Phys. Rev. Lett. **96**, Article no. 238701 (2006)
4. Gutin, G., Mansour, T., Severini, S.: A characterization of horizontal visibility graphs and combinatorics on words. Phys. A Stat. Mech. Appl. **390**(12), 2421–2428 (2011)
5. Anacleto, O., Queen, C., Albers, C.J.: Multivariate forecasting of road traffic flows in the presence of heteroscedasticity and measurement errors. J. R. Stat. Society. Ser. C (Appl. Stat.) **62**(2), 251–270 (2013)
6. Zhao, Z.Y., Xie, M., West, M.: Dynamic dependence networks: financial time series forecasting and portfolio decisions. Appl. Stoch. Model. Bus. Ind. **32**(3), 311–332 (2016). asmb.2161
7. Siebenhhner, F., Weiss, S.A., Coppola, R., Weinberger, D.R., Bassett, D.S.: Intra- and inter-frequency brain network structure in health and schizophrenia. PLOS ONE **8**(8), 1–13 (2013)
8. White, B.R., et al.: Resting-state functional connectivity in the human brain revealed with diffuse optical tomography. NeuroImage **47**(1), 148–156 (2009)
9. Im, C.-H., Jung, Y.-J., Lee, S., Koh, D., Kim, D.-W., Kim, B.-M.: Estimation of directional coupling between cortical areas using near-infrared spectroscopy (NIRS). Opt. Express **18**(6), 5730–5739 (2010)
10. Yuan, Z.: Combining independent component analysis and granger causality to investigate brain network dynamics with fNIRS measurements. Biomed. Opt. Express **4**(11), 2629–2643 (2013)
11. Homae, F., et al.: Development of global cortical networks in early infancy. J. Neurosci. **30**(14), 4877–4882 (2010)
12. David, O.: fMRI connectivity, meaning and empiricism comments on: Roebroeck et al. The identification of interacting networks in the brain using fMRI: model selection, causality and deconvolution. NeuroImage **58**(2), 306–309 (2011)
13. Deshpande, G., Sathian, K., Hu, X.: Assessing and compensating for zero-lag correlation effects in time-lagged granger causality analysis of fMRI. IEEE Trans. Biomed. Eng. **57**(6), 1446–1456 (2010)

14. Friston, K.: Dynamic causal modeling and granger causality comments on: the identification of interacting networks in the brain using fMRI: model selection, causality and deconvolution. NeuroImage **58**(2), 303–305 (2011)
15. Smith, S.M., et al.: Network modelling methods for fMRI. NeuroImage **54**(2), 875–891 (2011)
16. van Dellen, E., et al.: Minimum spanning tree analysis of the human connectome. Hum. Brain Mapp. **39**(6), 2455–2471 (2018)
17. Stam, C.J., et al.: The relation between structural and functional connectivity patterns in complex brain networks. Int. J. Psychophysiol. **103**, 149–160 (2016). Research on Brain Oscillations and Connectivity in A New Take-Off State
18. Stam, C.J., Tewarie, P., Van Dellen, E., van Straaten, E.C.W., Hillebrand, A., Van Mieghem, P.: The trees and the forest: characterization of complex brain networks with minimum spanning trees. Int. J. Psychophysiol. **92**(3), 129–138 (2014)
19. Tewarie, P., van Dellen, E., Hillebrand, A., Stam, C.J.: The minimum spanning tree: an unbiased method for brain network analysis. NeuroImage **104**, 177–188 (2015)
20. Shmuel, A., Yacoub, E., Chaimow, D., Logothetis, N.K., Ugurbil, K.: Spatio-temporal point-spread function of fMRI signal in human gray matter at 7 tesla. NeuroImage **35**(2), 539–552 (2007)
21. Tak, S., Kempny, A.M., Friston, K.J., Leff, A.P., Penny, W.D.: Dynamic causal modelling for functional near-infrared spectroscopy. NeuroImage **111**(Supplement C), 338–349 (2015)

Preference Prediction Based on Eye Movement Using Multi-layer Combinatorial Fusion

Christina Schweikert[1(✉)], Louis Gobin[2], Shuxiao Xie[2],
Shinsuke Shimojo[3], and D. Frank Hsu[2]

[1] Division of Computer Science, Mathematics and Science,
St. John's University, Queens, NY 11439, USA
schweikc@stjohns.edu

[2] Laboratory of Informatics and Data Mining, Department of Computer
and Information Science, Fordham University, New York, NY 10023, USA

[3] Division of Biology and Biological Engineering/Computation and Neural
Systems, California Institute of Technology, Pasadena, CA 91125, USA

Abstract. Face image preference is influenced by many factors and can be detected by analyzing eye movement data. When comparing two face images, our gaze shifts within and between the faces. Eye tracking data can give us insights into the cognitive processes involved in forming a preference. In this paper, a gaze tracking dataset is analyzed using three machine learning algorithms (MLA): AdaBoost, Random Forest, and Mixed Group Ranks (MGR) as well as a newly developed machine learning framework called Multi-Layer Combinatorial Fusion (MCF) to predict a subject's face image preference. Attributes constructed from the dataset are treated as input scoring systems. MCF involves a series of layers that consist of expansion and reduction processes. The expansion process involves performing exhaustive score and rank combinations, while the reduction process uses performance and diversity to select a subset of systems that will be passed onto the next layer of analysis. Performance and cognitive diversity are used in weighted scoring system combinations and system selection. The results outperform the Mixed Group Ranks algorithm, as well as our previous work using pairwise scoring system combinations.

Keywords: Combinatorial Fusion Analysis (CFA)
Multi-layer Combinatorial Fusion (MCF) · Cognitive diversity
Machine learning · Preference detection

1 Introduction

Can we predict someone's preference between two face images based on his or her eye movements? There are many factors involved in forming our decision to find one image more appealing than another. Research by Frantz (1961) reveals that we tend to spend more time looking at objects that we prefer [3]. It has been shown that the type of images under consideration will determine whether novelty or past exposure will affect our preference [15]. When comparing faces, there are certain characteristics that are generally preferred such as symmetry and averageness; however, there are individual

S. Wang et al. (Eds.): BI 2018, LNAI 11309, pp. 282–293, 2018.
https://doi.org/10.1007/978-3-030-05587-5_27

and population variations [19]. Eye movements have been shown to expose information about our cognitive processes in a variety of scenarios [11, 26]. Gaze tracking data has been used in research on face image preference, as well as other areas including marketing [10] and text comprehension [21].

A study by Shimojo et al. [25] reveals a "gaze cascade effect" that develops in a two-alternative, forced choice (2AFC) preference task in which subjects are tasked with deciding which of two face images is more attractive. This research reveals the role of gaze in preference formation. An artificially-created bias of an observer's gaze can successfully bias the final preference decision, which indicated a causal role of such gaze bias as an implicit, somatic precursor of conscious preference decision. In the beginning of a trial, a subject's gaze time is evenly shared between the two images. However, as the exploration period progresses, the subject's gaze shifts toward the face he or she prefers, leading to an increasing probability that the subject is looking at the preferred face toward the end of the trial.

The eye movement dataset analyzed in this study has been designed and collected by Shimojo et al. [25] as part of their research work that characterizes preference formation with the gaze cascade effect. In a following work by Chuk et al. [2], Switching Hidden-Markov Models are used to identify two subgroups of subjects that exhibit different behavior in terms of gaze patterns and decision-making.

In our previous work on this dataset [22], we used the combinatorial fusion algorithm [7] to improve the prediction of face image preference. Scoring systems were created based on five attributes extracted from the data including: time spent on face in last 200 ms of trial, total time spent on face, gaze point count, interest sustainability, and region change frequency. The attributes relating to duration, point count, and interest sustainability were selected based on literature that relates more time spent looking at a face with preference, especially toward the end of the trial. [3, 25] The attribute that captures the number of edges between regions on a face was created to quantify the amount of exploration /movement within a face. It was demonstrated that combining multiple attributes can improve predictive performance; particularly, when the scoring systems are diverse. The concept of cognitive diversity, introduced by Hsu et al. [7, 8], is measured by comparing the rank-score characteristic functions of two scoring systems.

In this paper, we analyze the same data set using three machine learning algorithms (MLA): AdaBoost, Random Forest, and Mixed Group Ranks (MGR). In addition, a Multi-Layer Combinatorial Fusion (MCF) method is developed and applied to this eye movement dataset. Modeled after multi-layer feed-forward neural networks [5], MCF consists of an input layer, hidden layers, and an output layer. The scoring systems created from the gaze dataset are the input. Each internal layer consists of an "expansion" and "reduction" process (E/R). The "expansion" process involves performing a variety of score and rank combinations of given scoring systems. Performance and diversity are also used for weighted combinations. "Reduction" involves selecting a subset of resultant systems that will be passed to the next layer. Selection of these systems is done using performance and diversity as well. The E/R process continues until a stopping condition is met. At the last layer, the remaining systems are combined to obtain the final ranking. The MCF approach is also tested using cross-validation. MCF entails multiple layers of system combinations, as well as diversity and performance for subsystem selection at each layer; incorporating diversity and performance in selecting scoring systems for combination has been demonstrated to improve performance of the ensemble scoring system [8, 27].

The structure of the paper is as follows: Sect. 2 defines methods for combining multiple scoring systems including Combinatorial Fusion Analysis, machine learning algorithms, and MCF; Sect. 3 details the face preference classification experiment from dataset processing and attributes to the results for the previously mentioned methods; lastly, Sect. 4 concludes the paper with some observations and future work.

2 Methods for Combining Multiple Scoring Systems

2.1 Combinatorial Fusion Analysis

Applications that involve multiple features/indicators or multiple classifiers can be treated as multiple scoring system problems. The combinatorial fusion analysis methodology, as developed by Hsu et al. [7] defines a rank-score characteristic (RSC) function, combination methods, and a cognitive diversity measure to facilitate the comparison and fusion of multiple scoring systems. This combinatorial fusion approach has achieved successful results in areas ranging from virtual screening [27] and bioinformatics [16, 23] to information retrieval [9], text categorization [13], target tracking [18], and mobile network selection [12].

Consider a scoring system, A, on a set of trials, $D = \{d_1, d_2, ..., d_n\}$. This system consists of a score function from D to R (a set of real numbers), s_A, and a corresponding rank function from D to $N = \{1,2,...,n\}$ that is obtained by sorting the scores value in an ascending or descending order, r_A. The RSC function, f_A, is defined as:

$$f_A(i) = \left(s_A^o\ r_A^{-1}\right)(i),\ \text{for}\ 1 \leq i \leq n. \tag{1}$$

RSC functions characterize the scoring behavior of the system A. The Euclidean distance between the RSC functions of two systems is considered as the cognitive diversity between them [7, 8]. In this context, cognitive diversity between two systems, A and B, is computed as:

$$d(A, B) = d(fA, fB) = \sqrt{\sum_{i=1}^{n} \left((f_A(i) - f_B(i))\right)^2 / n}, \tag{2}$$

where n is the total number of trials used for training or testing. We then compute the cognitive diversity between each pair of scoring systems. Building on this is the concept of **diversity strength**, which captures how frequently a scoring system appears in the top 20% of system pairs, when ranked by cognitive diversity.

Score combination, SC, and rank combination, RC, functions are defined as the average score, or rank, of two or more scoring systems, respectively. Weights can also be incorporated into these functions to compute weighted score or rank combinations.

2.2   Machine Learning Algorithms (MLA)

AdaBoost and Random Forest are ensemble data mining methods that generally out-perform non-ensemble approaches. Boosting uses weights to combine classifier votes. In AdaBoost [4], training records are initially set with equal weights. After running each classification model, the weights of any records that are incorrectly classified are increased so that subsequent models will place more emphasis on these records. The weight of a classifier's final vote is a function of its error rate. Random forest [1] is an ensemble method that is comprised of randomly generated decision trees. Majority voting among all of the trees is used to determine the final class prediction.

Mixed Group Ranks (MGR) is a combination function proposed by Melnik et al. [20]. MGR is a rank-based combination method that balances confidence and prefer-ence. The MGR function is a weighted linear combination of the lowest ranks of all classifier subgroups.

The ensemble methods described in this section are commonly used and successful approaches. However, since they do not incorporate the concept of cognitive diversity among systems, there is an opportunity to address this in the MCF approach that is detailed in the following section.

2.3   Multi-layer Combinatorial Fusion (MCF)

A scoring system is created to represent each of the dataset attributes, more specifically, in our previous study [22] we have worked with five attributes: time spent on face in last 200 ms of trial (A), total time spent on face (B), gaze point count (C), interest sustainability (D), and region change frequency (E). (The attributes are described in Sect. 3.1 in detail.) The scoring systems consist of a score function and rank function on the set of trials $T = \{t_1, t_2, ..., t_{720}\}$. For each trial, the attributes have a value for the left face and a value for the right face. In order to have one score that represents an attribute at the trial level, we compute the score for a trial to be (attribute value for left face) – (attribute value for right face). Out of the 720 trials in the dataset, 357 subjects selected the left face and 363 selected the right face. Based on the way the scores are computed, the ideal rank function would rank all the left faces before the right faces. Therefore, we measure the performance of each scoring system by evaluating the percentage of top ranked faces that are left face (i.e. precision at top 50, 100, or 200).

The MCF method involves a series of layers that are generated through an iterative process of expansion (E) and reduction (R), which are explained in detail below. The expansion process includes the computation of a variety of system combinations including score and rank combinations, as well as weighted versions using diversity and performance. Reduction is a cut-off process that selects which scoring systems will be passed on to the subsequent layer. At each layer of analysis, we utilize two different reduction methods. Both approaches, sliding rule (SR) and half-half (HH) are based on performance and diversity.

Expansion Process. Using the combinatorial fusion method, we perform horizontal combinations of all subsets of scoring systems, including average and weighted average combinations at each level. Since there are 6 scoring systems at each layer (except the first), this includes 6-, 5-, 4-, 3-, and 2-combinations, giving us a total of 57 combinations. Since we perform both score and rank combinations, we have 57 * 2 combinations. As another case, we also compute weighted averages, with one version using performance as the weight and another using diversity. For the case including weighted averages, we have an additional 57 * 2 * 2 = 228 combinations, since the rank and score versions are also computed.

Reduction Process. The reduction process determines which scoring systems will be passed on to the next layer. We compute the performance and cognitive diversity strength for all scoring systems in a layer. Score functions for both performance and diversity strength are sorted in descending order, and a corresponding rank function is generated by assigning ranks in ascending order. Half-half (HH) and Sliding Rule (SR) methods are used to select the 6 "best" scoring systems at each layer.

1. **Half-half (HH)** selection: Evenly select the top 3 according to **diversity strength (DS)** and **performance (P)**, respectively. The performance selection is done first; if there are overlaps between the top 3 systems according to P and DS, we will select further down the DS list until 6 different scoring systems are selected.
2. **Sliding Ruler (SR)** selection: Given the ordered lists: DS and P, sorted from best to worst, we start at the beginning of the lists and then traverse both lists until we find 6 common systems. This ensures that we select the 6 systems that exhibit both high diversity strength and performance.

Stopping Condition. As two scoring systems become more similar, the cognitive diversity between them decreases. When cognitive diversity approaches zero, we may not see improved performance with more combinations /layers. When classifiers reach this critical point, we consider that they have converged.

Stopping conditions are set to prevent non-converging MCF schemes from running on forever, or even just for too long. Currently, we have two conditions that can stop the MCF algorithm from generating additional layers: The first condition is that the maximum number of layers allowed has been reached. That number is set by the user and should be decided on a case by case basis (size of the dataset, width of the layers, computing resources available and time available to run the algorithm). The second condition is if all scoring system pairs have a cognitive diversity of zero.

Since the maximum number of layers is set to 250 in this experiment, precision will be evaluated if the classifiers converge before it reaches 250 layers; otherwise, the process will be stopped at 250 considering the trade-off of between possible improvements in performance and computing time.

Precision Evaluation. We use precision to measure the classification performance of scoring systems and their combinations by comparing the predicted preferred face to the ground truth, which is the actual subject's preference. Performance evaluation is done in two steps:

1. The scores are sorted from highest to lowest. It is worth noting that the results may vary depending on which sorting algorithm is used, as various sorting algorithms may order identical scores differently. We are currently using the merge-sort sorting algorithm. It is a recursive algorithm that works by splitting a list until only lists containing one element remain; then, these lists are merged in an ordered manner to

obtain the final sorted list. Merge sort is considered a stable sort, since the original order of equal elements is maintained.
2. Compute the percentage of x highest scores that correctly predict the target class (such as top 50, 100, etc.).

We often have multiple objects with the same score; in this case, we take the middle rank and assign it as the rank for those objects with that same tied score

3 Classification Experiment

3.1 Eye Movement Dataset Description

Research by Shimojo et al. [24] has uncovered a connection between gaze saccade movements and preference decisions. As part of their work, they have designed and constructed a dataset for gaze analysis, which is the focus of this paper. The subjects in the study are presented with two computer-generated faces on a screen. The faces vary in terms of their features, symmetry, and have either a direct or averted gaze. In each trial, the subject is asked to select which face he/she finds more attractive. This preference decision, left or right face, is stored for each trial. During each trial, the eye movements of the subject are tracked. For each focus point, the x, y coordinates, as well as the duration time of focus on the point (in ms) are collected. The experiment involved 12 subjects, each of whom conducted 60 trials. Figure 1 shows one of the screens from a trial that includes the face images, along with the subject's gaze points. The face outlined in green indicates the subject's preference.

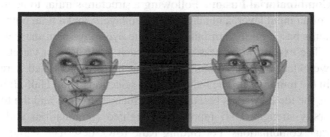

Fig. 1. An example trial image with eye movement plot.

Data Preprocessing. Since the images compared in this experiment are faces, it is natural to consider the significance of different regions of the face. Therefore, we map each of the raw x, y coordinates to one of the following facial regions: head, face, left eye, right eye, nose, and mouth. These regions are encoded in (ROI) mapping information, consisting of points that define polygons for each region: head (ellipse), face (pentagon), left eye (ellipse), right eye (ellipse), nose (triangle), and mouth (ellipse).

Within a trial, the subject's eye movement moves between the left and right side of the screen and within the left and right face images. For all of the points in a trial, we first test whether the x, y coordinate is on the left or right side of the screen. We can then use that particular face's ROI data to test whether the coordinate is located within one of the regions: face, left eye, right eye, nose, mouth, head, or none. For each face, we also compute the total time spent on each region.

Within a face, a subject's gaze can move from one region to another. For example, a subject may have a series of focus points in the head region and then shift focus to the mouth or nose. To represent this movement between regions, we generate an adjacency matrix to store the edges between regions for each face within a trial.

Eye Movement Attributes. After the preprocessing, we construct the following attributes: A: Time spend on face in the last 200 ms in a trial, B: Total duration of time spent on a face in a trial, C: Number of gaze points on a face, D: Sum of differences in time of consecutive gaze duration periods for a face, and E: Within a face, the number of shifts from one face region to another. More details on the attributes can be found in [22].

3.2   Implementation

Machine Learning Algorithms. AdaBoost (ADA), Mixed Group Ranks (MGR), and Random Forest (RF). The implementations of Random Forest and AdaBoost used are from the Scikit-learn library. The parameters set are: n_estimators = 1000 for Random Forest and 500 for AdaBoost. Both are set to use GridSearchCV. The other parameters have been set to their default values. Since no implementation of the Mixed Group Ranks algorithm was readily available, we chose to implement it in Python based on the description in [20]. We felt it was necessary to have a benchmark algorithm that had the same goals in design as MCF below.

Multi-layer Combinatorial Fusion. Following a structure similar to neural networks, MCF consists of an input layer, a number of hidden layers, and a final output layer. The 5 scoring systems based on the attributes from the eye movement dataset are input to the first layer. The expansion process occurs at each layer using a variety of both the average and weighted average combinations. The performance used here is the precision @200 in the training set. The reduction (R) selection, using Half-Half (HH), with width 6, selects the top 3 systems based on performance strength and the top 3 systems based on diversity strength. HH1 represents weighted combinations and HH2 represents the average combinations. For Sliding Rule (SR), described earlier, SR1 represents the weighted combinations and SR2 represents the average combinations. After one of the stopping conditions is met, the last layer uses rank average to combine the remaining scoring systems. Figure 2 illustrates the MCF architecture.

3.3   Results for Machine Learning and Multi-layer Combinatorial Fusion

Since the data contains a set of trials for each subject, the trials for each subject are kept together for testing and training. 3-fold cross-validation was used to run and evaluate Random Forest, AdaBoost, Mixed Group Ranks, and the MCF approach in order to compare the performances and to avoid overfitting. In the eye movement dataset, the 12 subjects were shuffled randomly. The 12 subjects are then divided into three groups. Since each group contains 4 subjects, there are 240 trials in each group. For each run, 1

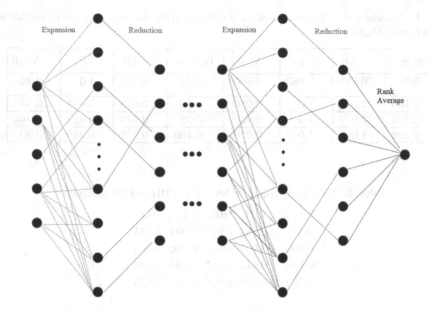

Fig. 2. Design of an MCF framework.

group out of 3 is set as the test data set and the remaining 2 groups are used as the training data set. Each possible configuration of the 3 groups is used. Therefore, the training datasets include a total of 480 trials and the testing datasets contain 240.

For each run, AdaBoost and Random Forest models were generated based on the training set and run on the test set. When running Mixed Group Ranks on the training datasets, we store which scoring system combination was selected within each subgroup, along with the weights. This information is then applied when using Mixed Group Ranks in the test dataset. For the MCF approach, the systems selected at each layer, along with the performance and diversity strength weights computed in training are used in the testing phase.

The training and testing results for AdaBoost, Random Forest, and Mixed Group Ranks are included in Table 1. Results for running the MCF method in the training and testing phases are included in Tables 2 and 3, respectively. Table 4 is a summary comparison of the algorithm results. For all training and testing results, the performance noted is the average performance of 3 runs.

3.4   Discussion

We observe in the results that the MCF algorithm, in any configuration, consistently outperforms MGR. Considering that we are working on a unique dataset with 720 trials, we will include MGR as a benchmark in future implementation of MCF on larger and more complex datasets so as to provide more insights into their relative strengths. MCF is more comparable to MGR, since they are both rank-based approaches. MCF demonstrates better precision than our previous study, which used pairwise scoring

Table 1. Training and testing precisions for AdaBoost (AB), Random Forest (RF) and Mixed Group Ranks (MGR).

Training	AB	RF	MGR	Testing	AB	RF	MGR
@50	0.988	0.980	0.900	@25	0.974	1.0	0.946
@100	1.0	1.0	0.950	@50	0.958	0.981	0.946
@150	1.0	1.0	0.940	@75	0.948	0.953	0.946
@200	1.0	1.0	0.910	@100	0.939	0.945	0.90

Table 2. Training precision for MCF using HH and SR reduction.

Training	HH1	HH2	SR1	SR2
@50	0.953	0.947	0.947	0.953
@100	0.967	0.963	0.960	0.963
@150	0.949	0.953	0.949	0.953
@200	0.923	0.918	0.917	0.920

Table 3. Testing precision for MCF using HH and SR reduction. *Note:* HH1 and SR1 use weighted combinations.

Testing	HH1	HH2	SR1	SR2
@25	0.960	0.947	0.960	0.960
@50	0.960	0.960	0.940	0.967
@75	0.947	0.951	0.947	0.947
@100	0.917	0.920	0.917	0.920

Table 4. Precision comparison among AdaBoost (AB), Random Forest (RF), Mixed Group Ranks (MGR), and MCF.

	AB	RF	MGR	MCF			
				HH1	HH2	SR1	SR2
Precision @200 *training*	1.0	1.0	0.910	0.923	0.918	0.917	0.920
Precision @100 *testing*	0.938	0.949	0.900	0.917	0.920	0.917	0.920

system combinations alone [22]. AdaBoost and Random Forest, as ensemble methods, perform very well, indicating the utility of these algorithms on this type of dataset.

When evaluating the results of different runs of cross-validation, we observe that class imbalance may affect performance. This underlines one of the main challenges when using ranking algorithms for classification. The exact proportion of the target class may not be known; however, it is an important consideration when setting the parameters of the algorithm to consider the variability in the target class distribution.

We can examine the performance of different gaze attribute combinations in MCF to gain insights into their role in preference detection. The best performing individual feature is A (duration in the last 200 ms of trial), which is consistent with existing research [25], demonstrating that subjects are more likely to be viewing the face they prefer toward the end of the trial. The feature combination with the best performance is when A is combined with D (interest sustainability), using score average. The second best combination involves the same features, but using score average weighted by performance. Though A is the best performing individual feature, it is interesting that performance increases when A is combined with D, which does not perform well on its own. This may indicate that, while we know subjects are more likely to be viewing their preferred face toward the end of the trial, the increase in the duration of sustained gaze intervals on a face also plays a role in decision formation. The third best feature combination is A, B (total duration), and D using performance-weighted score average.

The advantage of the MCF approach is that it performs layers of extensive combinations and selection until the generated combinations converge, meaning there is no longer any diversity among them. When all scoring system pairs have a diversity of zero, it indicates that their ranking behavior is the same. Then, based on the input features to the MCF framework, at this point we reach the theoretically-expected upper limit of performance, as further combinations would not yield any improvement. This is the rationale for using diversity as the stopping condition. The other possible stopping condition is a parameter for maximum number of layers, which depends on computing time and resources. The design of MCF is based on the idea that combining systems that exhibit relatively good performance and high diversity would lead to improved performance for the final combined system [8, 27].

4   Conclusion

This paper analyzes a dataset by combining multiple scoring systems using machine learning algorithms: AdaBoost, Random Forest and Mixed Group Ranks. In addition, the Multi-layer Combinatorial Fusion is introduced as a machine learning framework that incorporates concepts from combinatorial fusion analysis, such as scoring system combinations and cognitive diversity. Given a set of input scoring systems, the MCF model iterates through a series of layers that involve expansion (using a variety of system combinations) and reduction (selection of high performance and diversity scoring systems for the next layer). Finally, when a stopping condition is reached, the scoring systems at the last layer are combined using rank average, resulting in a ranked list. MCF has an advantage over other classifiers for applications that may require a relative ordering of records, as is the case with bioinformatics and information retrieval.

We build on previous analysis of an eye tracking dataset which aims to gain perspectives on how gaze tracking data can be used to predict face image preference. Random Forest, AdaBoost, Mixed Group Ranks, as well as MCF are applied to attributes extracted from an eye movement dataset to predict which face a subject will select as being more attractive. Based on the cross-validation performance, it has been demonstrated that MCF is a viable machine learning method.

Following are some items for further investigation:

- Test different parameters for the MCF model including the number of scoring systems selected in the reduction phase and the maximum number of layers. Enabling the algorithm to run more deeply has the potential for increased performance in cases where scoring systems take a longer time to converge.
- Use an ensemble approach by incorporating different algorithms as input to MCF and test the approach on larger-scale datasets.
- Explore additional features, such as a subject's previous exposure to an image and the gaze direction of the face images, which can be incorporated into MCF or other analysis.
- Use similarity mapping to perform cluster analysis to identify sub-groups of similar subjects and faces.
- Investigate how different subject subgroups form decisions differently by analyzing their exploration and decision phases. We can also compare various correlations between extracted features as to how they relate to different types of decision processes.
- Regarding gaze patterns for the face images, we can compare how different faces are viewed differently by subjects.
- Analyze the eye movement dataset from new perspectives and using different algorithms to contribute to the preference formation research related to eye tracking data.

References

1. Breiman, L.: Random forests. Mach. Learn. **45**, 5–32 (2001)
2. Chuk, T., Chan, A.B., Shimojo, S., Hsiao, J.H.: Mind reading: discovering individual preferences from eye movements using switching hidden Markov models. In: Papafragou, A., Grodner, D., Mirman, D., Trueswell, J.C. (eds.) Proceedings of the 38th Annual Conference of the Cognitive Science Society, p. 182. Cognitive Science Society, Austin (2016)
3. Fantz, R.L.: The origin of form perception. Sci. Am. **204**, 66–72 (1961)
4. Freund, Y., Schapire, R.E.: A decision-theoretic generalization of on-line learning and an application to boosting. J. Comput. Syst. Sci. **55**, 119–139 (1997)
5. Han, J., Kamber, M., Pei, J.: Data Mining: Concepts and Techniques, 3rd edn. Morgan Kaufmann, San Francisco (2012)
6. Ho, T.K., et al.: Decision combination in multiple classifier systems. IEEE Trans PAMI **16** (1), 66–75 (1994)
7. Hsu, D.F., Chung, Y.S., Kristal, B.S.: Combinatorial fusion analysis: methods and practice of combining multiple scoring systems. In: Hsu, H.H. (ed.) Advanced Data Mining Technologies in Bioinformatics, pp. 1157–1181. Idea Group Inc., Calgary (2006)
8. Hsu, D.F., Kristal, B.S., Schweikert, C.: Rank-score characteristics (RSC) function and cognitive diversity. In: Yao, Y., Sun, R., Poggio, T., Liu, J., Zhong, N., Huang, J. (eds.) BI 2010. LNCS (LNAI), vol. 6334, pp. 42–54. Springer, Heidelberg (2010). https://doi.org/10. 1007/978-3-642-15314-3_5
9. Hsu, D.F., Taksa, I.: Comparing rank and score combination methods for data fusion in information retrieval. Inf. Retr. **8**(3), 449–480 (2005)

10. Khushaba, R., et al.: Consumer neuroscience: assessing the brain response to marketing stimuli using electroencephalogram (EEG) and eye tracking. Expert Syst. Appl. **40**(9), 3803–3812 (2013)
11. König, P., et al.: Eye movements as a window to cognitive processes. J. Eye Mov. Res. **9**(5), 1–16 (2016)
12. Kustiawan, I., Liu, C.-Y., Hsu, D.F.: Vertical Handoff decision using fuzzification and combinatorial fusion. IEEE Commun. Lett. **21**, 2089–2092 (2017)
13. Li, Y., Hsu, D.F., Chung, S.M.: Combination of multiple feature selection methods for text categorization by using combinatorial fusion analysis and rank-score characteristic. Int. J. Artif. Intell. Tools **22**(2), 1350001 (2013)
14. Liao, H.I., Shimojo, S.: Dynamic preference formation via gaze and memory. In: Sharot, T., Dolan, R. (ed.) Neuroscience of Preference and Choice, pp. 277–292. Elsevier Inc. (2012)
15. Liao, H.I., Yeh, S.L., Shimojo, S.: Novelty vs. familiarity principles in preference decisions: task-context of past experience matters. Front. Psychol. **2**(43), 1–8 (2011)
16. Lin, K.L., et al.: Feature selection and combination criteria for improving accuracy in protein structure prediction. IEEE Trans. Nanobiosci. **6**(2), 186–196 (2007)
17. Little, A.C., Jones, B.C., DeBruine, L.M.: Facial attractiveness: evolutionary based research. Philos. Trans. R. Soc. B: Biol. Sci. **366**(1571), 1638–1659 (2011)
18. Lyons, D.M., Hsu, D.F.: Combining multiple scoring systems for target tracking using rank score characteristics. Inform. Fus. **10**(2), 124–136 (2009)
19. Mandler, G., Nakamura, Y., Van Zandt, B.J.: Exp. Psychol. Learn. Mem. Cogn. **13**, 646–648 (1987)
20. Melnik, O., Vardi, Y., Zhang, C.H.: Mixed group ranks: preference and confidence in classifier combination. IEEE Trans. Pattern Anal. Mach. Intell. **26**(8), 973–981 (2004)
21. Raney, G.E., Campbell, S.J., Bovee, J.C.: Using eye movements to evaluate the cognitive processes involved in text comprehension. J. Vis. Exp. JoVE **83**, 50780 (2014)
22. Schweikert, C., Shimojo, S., Hsu, D.F.: Detecting preferences based on eye movement using combinatorial fusion. In: Wang, Y., et al. (ed.) Proceedings of the 2016 IEEE 15th International Conference on Cognitive Informatics & Cognitive Computing (ICCI*CC 2016), pp. 336–343 (2016)
23. Schweikert, C., Brown, S., Tang, Z., Smith, P.R., Hsu, D.F.: Combining multiple ChIP-seq peak detection systems using combinatorial fusion. BMC Genom. **13**(Suppl 8), S12 (2012)
24. Shimojo, S., Simion, C., Changizi, M.: Gaze and preference – orienting behavior as a somatic precursor of preference decision. In: Adams, Jr., R.B., Ambady, N., Nakayama, K., Shimojo, S. (eds.) Social Vision, pp. 151–163. Oxford Univ. Press (2011)
25. Shimojo, S., Simion, C., Shimojo, E., Scheier, C.: Gaze bias both reflects and influences preference. Nat. Neurosci. **6**, 1317–1322 (2003)
26. Wang, Y., Wang, Y.: Cognitive informatics models of the brain. IEEE Trans. Syst. Man Cybern. Part C (Appl. Rev.) **36**(2), 203–207 (2006)
27. Yang, J.M., et al.: Consensus scoring for improving enrichment in virtual screening. J. Chem. Inform. Model. **45**, 1134–1146 (2005)

A Multilayer Network Approach
for Studying Creative Ideation from EEG

Rohit Bose[1], Kumar Ashutosh[2], Junhua Li[1], Andrei Dragomir[1],
Nitish Thakor[1], and Anastasios Bezerianos[1(✉)]

[1] Singapore Institute for Neurotechnology, National University of Singapore,
Singapore 117456, Singapore
eleba@nus.edu.sg
[2] Department of Electrical Engineering, Indian Institute of Technology,
Bombay 400076, India

Abstract. The neural mechanisms underlying creative ideation are not clearly understood owing to the widespread cognitive processes involved in the brain. Current research states alpha band's relation to creative ideation, as the most consistent finding. However, creative ideation appear at the signal level within multiple frequency bands and cross-frequency coupling phenomenon. To address this issue, we analyzed both within band and cross-frequency functional connectivity in a single framework using multilayer network. To further investigate the time evolution of creative thinking, we performed the analysis for three phases (early, middle and later). The experimental design used in this study consists of divergent thinking as an indicator of creativity where the subjects were instructed to give alternative uses of an object. As a control task, convergent thinking was used where the subjects were asked to list typical characteristics of an object. We evaluated global and nodal metrics (i.e., clustering coefficient, local efficiency, and nodal degree) for the three phases. Each metric was calculated separately for within band (intra layer) and cross-frequency (inter layer) connectivity. Paired t-test results showed significant difference in the later phase for both inter layer clustering coefficient and inter layer local efficiency. In nodal metrics, significant difference was observed in the later phase for intra layer degree and in all the phases for inter layer degree. The results from this study demonstrate that both the cross-frequency coupling and within-band connectivity can reveal more information regarding the neural processes related to creative ideation.

Keywords: Multilayer network · Supra-adjacency matrix
Creativity · Convergent and divergent thinking · EEG

This work is supported by the startup grant of Prof. N. Thakor.
R. Bose and K. Ashutosh—Equal contribution.

1   Introduction

Studying neural mechanisms associated with the creative process has been of high interest in the recent years. Creativity is difficult to define but can be generally described as the generation of ideas which are both novel and useful [4,11,30]. Several cognitive processes like episodic and semantic memory retrieval, working memory, attention, executive function, are associated with creative ideation [4,26].

Creativity analysis, so far, has been focused on individual frequency bands, mostly the alpha band power [15]. However, a lot of disagreement on the findings of creative analysis has been observed in the past literature [12]. Several studies have shown that high alpha power is associated with divergent thinking in the frontal region [3,16] whereas other studies have shown an increase in theta and beta power during creative thinking [8,28]. Additionally, gamma band has been found to increase 300 ms before the onset of "AHA moment" or subjective insight [18,31]. Therefore, all the frequency bands and their role in creative thinking should be considered for analysis. Cross-frequency coupling also plays a major role in many internal cognitive processes like decision making, memory etc. [6]. Recent findings show the role of theta and alpha coupling during various working memory task [1,14,19,21], which is associated with creative ideation [4,26]. However, the role of these processes in the time course of creative ideation has not been understood clearly. Therefore, to study the neural mechanisms during creative ideation, within band connectivity for all the frequency bands and cross-frequency coupling between them should be considered for analysis.

To account for the peculiarities of creativity related processes, we devised a framework based on multilayer networks. It is an effective tool that considers within band connectivity and cross-frequency coupling collectively in a single framework [9]. Multilayer network has found suitable application in dynamic connectivity analysis [2,25] and frequency based decomposition analysis of brain networks [10,35]. A simplified representation of the multilayer network is the supra-adjacency matrix, which consists of a block like structure. The diagonal blocks of the supra-adjacency matrix refer to as the within band connectivity and the off-diagonal blocks represents the between band connectivity [9,35].

In this paper, we aim to study the effects of within and cross frequency band connectivity during creative thinking using a multilayer network framework. We have performed the analysis separately for three different phases referring to the early, middle and later stage of the creative ideation. For each of these phases, we have evaluated global and nodal metrics to study the topological organizations of the brain regions separately for intra and inter layer connections.

2   Methodology

2.1   Participants

In this study, 16 subjects (7 females and 9 males; mean age: 23.44 and standard deviation: 2.39) were recruited from the National University of Singapore.

The subjects were right-handed and native speakers of English with normal or corrected-to-normal vision without having any prior history of CNS affecting drugs, mental or neurological diseases [26]. All the participants provided written consent prior to the experiment and monetary compensation was provided to each of them. The study was approved by the Institutional Review Boards of the National University of Singapore.

2.2   Experimental Protocol

Each of the divergent and convergent thinking tasks consisted of 15 trials. At the onset of each trial, a fixation cross was shown for 2–4 s followed by the name of the object. The length of each trial was 60 s where the subject were allowed to give as many responses within that duration. To perform a divergent thinking task, every subject were asked to think alternate use to daily objects like knife, paperclip etc. For a convergent thinking task, the subjects listed typical characteristics of the object. In rest of the paper, the divergent thinking task is referred to as Alternate Uses (AU) task and the convergent thinking task is referred to as Object Characteristics (OC) task. The object names used as stimuli were carefully selected so that they did not have multiple meanings and can be recognized by all subjects as everyday objects. The objects were selected randomly from a pool and then presented in a randomized order [26]. A short break was provided between two successive trials.

To maintain a good quality of the recordings and avoid muscle and other artifacts, the subjects were asked to press a key when they came up with an idea and wanted to vocalize it. After the subject finished speaking, the experimenter pressed another key to mark the end of the speaking period. These markers were used to extract the specific ideation interval corresponding to creative thinking and exclude the speaking durations from analysis.

2.3   EEG Data Acquisition

EEG data were collected using a WaveguardTM cap (CA-142; ANT Neuro, Netherlands) and a Refa TMSi amplifier (TMSI B.V., Netherlands). The EEG system comprised of 64 Ag/AgCl electrodes with 10k built-in resistor. The electrodes were placed in the 10–20 International system. Two of the auxiliary inputs to the amplifier were used for recording the vertical and the horizontal electrooculogram (EOG). The sampling rate was kept at 256 Hz and recorded using ASA-LabTM v4.7.12 (ANT Neuro, Netherlands), referenced using common average [26].

2.4   Data Preprocessing

The acquired EEG signal was initially bandpass filtered from 1 Hz to 40 Hz followed by a notch filter at 50 Hz. Independent Component Analysis (ICA) was applied using AMICA algorithm [27] to remove artifacts. The epochs associated with the AU and OC task were then extracted from the data. Further, every epoch was visually inspected and noisy epochs were rejected from the analysis. To study the time-course of creative thinking in the multilayer framework, the epochs were divided into three phases. These three phases correspond to first 1 s, middle 1 s and last 1 s of every epoch. Epochs having total duration below 3 s or above 15 s were rejected from the analysis.

2.5   Multilayer Network Construction

To construct the supra-adjacency matrix, we divided the EEG data into five frequency bands, namely θ, α_1, α_2, β and γ using Individual Alpha Frequency (IAF) [20]. For each frequency band, 62×62 adjacency matrix from within band connectivity was evaluated using Phase Lag Index (PLI) [24]. Similar adjacency matrix was evaluated from the cross-frequency coupling between each of the frequency band pair using Phase-to-Amplitude Coupling (PAC) [13]. The supra-adjacency matrix was then generated by combining all the adjacency matrices in a block structure such that the diagonal blocks/layers corresponds to the intra frequency connectivity and the off-diagonal blocks/layers corresponds to the inter frequency connectivity [5].

2.6   Global and Nodal Metrics

We investigated global network metrics to find out the topological organization of the brain connectivity during AU and OC. Clustering Coefficient (CC) [7, 29] is the measure of segregation in the network. It measures the fraction of neighbours which are neighbours themselves, forming a triangle [32]. Local efficiency (E_l) is a measure of the efficiency of information transmission within the local clusters in a graph [7, 29]. For every subject, these metrics were evaluated for all the layers. The mean of the metrics, across the layers was then evaluated separately for the inter and intra layers. Hence, CC_{intra} refers to the mean of the CC, averaged across the five intra layers and CC_{inter} refers to mean of the CC, averaged across the other off-diagonal inter layers. In a similar way, $E_{l_{intra}}$ and $E_{l_{inter}}$ were calculated.

The degree of a node refers to the number of edges linked with that node. High degree of a node corresponds to more information processing in that region and that node acts as a 'hub' in the network [29]. Similar to nodal metrics, degree of each node is averaged across the intra (Deg_{intra}) and the inter (Deg_{inter}) layers.

3   Results

The mean supra-adjacency matrix across all the subjects for later phase is shown in Fig. 1 for AU and OC. The five diagonal layers corresponds to the within band connectivity whereas the off-diagonal layers corresponds to the cross-frequency coupling. It can be observed that the alpha band has strong within band connectivity as well as strong cross frequency band connectivity with other frequency bands for both AU and OC task.

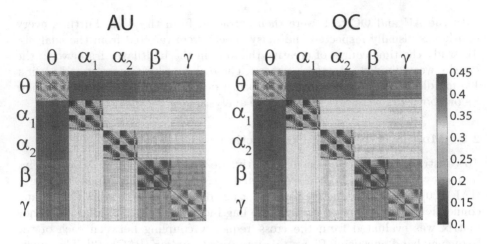

Fig. 1. Supra-adjacency plot across all the subjects for AU and OC task in later phase. The diagonal layers shows the within band connectivity matrix whereas the off-diagonal layers shows the cross-frequency connectivity matrix.

3.1 Global Network Characteristics

To observe the global topological organization of the brain network during AU and OC task, we evaluated the CC and E_l. Significant difference was only found in the later phase for the CC_{inter} (mean AU: 0.261 and mean OC:0.259, p-value < 0.01;paired t-test). For CC_{intra}, no significant difference was observed for all the three phases.

Similar results were observed also for E_l. Significant difference between AU and OC task was observed only in the later phase for $E_{l_{inter}}$ (mean value AU: 0.257 and mean OC: 0.255, p-value < 0.01;paired t-test). For $E_{l_{intra}}$, no significant difference was observed for all the three phases.

3.2 Nodal Network Characteristics

The intra and inter layer nodal degree calculated from the supra-adjacency matrix is shown in Fig. 2 and Fig. 3 with the significant nodes obtained from paired t-test. For Deg_{intra}, in early and middle phases, no significant difference was observed between AU and OC. The only significant difference observed is for later phase, in the right parieto-occipital regions. It should be noted that in the later phase for two electrodes, AF4 and C5, OC was significantly higher than AU. The degree was observed to be higher in the frontal regions in all the three phases for both AU and OC task.

For inter layer nodal degree, significant differences with AU > OC was observed for all the three phases. In early phase, the significant nodes are mostly clustered in the parietal and parieto-occipital region, mainly in the left hemisphere. In middle phase, the significant nodes are found to shift in the right hemisphere in the frontal, central, parietal and parieto-occipital regions. In later

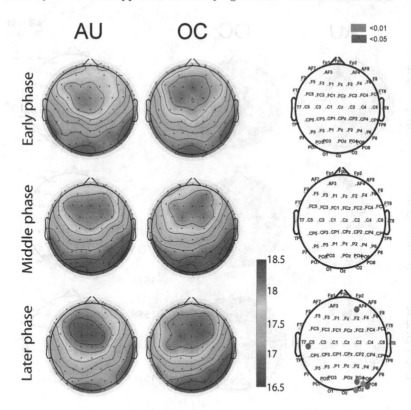

Fig. 2. Intra layer nodal degree for all the three phases. The first two columns shows the topographic maps of the nodal degree for AU and OC. The third column shows the significantly different nodes (AU > OC (except AF4 and C5 in the later phase where OC > AU)).

phase, the significant nodes were found in the left hemisphere in the frontal, central and temporal regions. Therefore, a hemispheric shift in significant degree of the nodes from early to middle phase and more clearly from middle to later phase was observed for inter layer degree. This observation was not found for Deg_{intra}.

4 Discussion

In this study, we studied the effect of all the frequency bands and the coupling between the bands in a multilayer framework for divergent and convergent thinking. Further, we also analyzed this effect in the early, middle and later phases of divergent thinking and compared with the convergent thinking.

From the supra adjacency matrix, α_1 and α_2 show high activity for both within band and cross-frequency couplings in all the phases (as shown in Fig. 1). This is in accordance to the most consistent finding in the creativity studies [15]. α_1 and α_2 are associated with different tasks and functions. For instance,

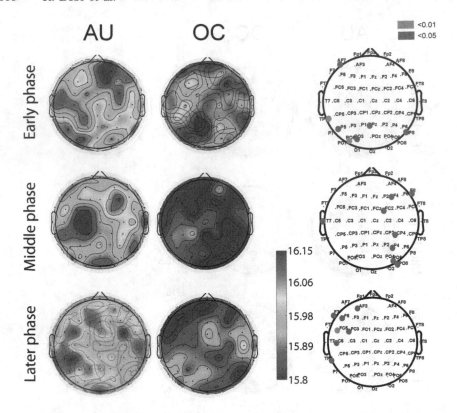

Fig. 3. Inter layer nodal degree for all the three phases. The first two columns shows the topographic maps of the nodal degree for AU and OC. The third column shows the significantly different nodes (AU > OC).

lower alpha is associated with alertness and vigilance whereas higher alpha is associated with more specific task demands like the semantic memory processing [12,22]. These cognitive functions are also associated with creative thinking in idea generation and evaluation phases [4]. In addition, we found that the cross-frequency coupling also plays a major role in divergent thinking which also supports the findings in [26]. Further, from Fig. 1, we observed that besides cross-frequency coupling of α band, other cross-frequency couplings like θ-β, θ-γ and β-γ also play an important role in creative thinking. To further investigate this aspect, we evaluated the global and nodal metrics separately for inter and intra layers to quantify our observation and find suitable biomarker for creative thinking.

In the global metrics, the topological alteration for AU and OC task was found similar for all the phases for CC_{intra} and El_{intra}. In contrast, CC_{inter} and El_{inter} show significant difference in the later phase. The later phase of the creative thinking has been associated with the subjective experience of insight or the "AHA moment" [18,23,31,34]. For both AU and OC task, a higher degree is observed in the frontal region. This region has also been found associated with divergent thinking [17]. In later phase, increase in alpha power in the right parietal region has been found in previous literature [18,23,31,34]. We found similar results for the Deg_{intra}. Deg_{inter} showed an interesting result for all the three phases. In the beginning of creative thinking (early phase), the significant nodes were found mostly in the left parietal and left parieto-occipital areas. In middle phase, the entire right hemisphere shows a higher degree for AU compared to OC with significant nodes located both in the right frontal, parietal and parieto-occipital regions. In later phase, lateralization of the brain is observed with a higher degree in the left hemisphere for AU compared to OC with significant nodes located in the left frontal, central and parietal regions. These results are in contrary to [33] where for alpha power, the right hemisphere has high alpha synchronization at the end of the ideation period. Moreover, for both nodal and global level, inter layer metrics show higher significance between AU and OC task. These findings suggest that cross-frequency coupling plays a major role in creative ideation and it is associated with important cognitive functions like working memory [1,14]. To illustrate the effectiveness of our approach, we compared the results obtained using only alpha band (both lower and upper) [15]. We observed that for global metrics, no significant difference was observed between AU and OC in both lower and upper alpha band for all the three phases. Hence, a single frequency band is not enough to explain the global characteristic of the brain network associated with creative ideation. Therefore, it can be concluded that the multilayer approach of combining multiple frequency bands is more effective compared to a single frequency band approach.

It should also be noted that the age group of the subjects has been restricted in this study(Min Age: 21 and Max age: 29). Hence, the observation made in this study are representative only for the young age group. In future studies we are planning to examine differences in creative ideation in young vs senior age groups.

5   Conclusion

In this study, we aimed to analyze the role of within frequency and cross-frequency interaction in different phases of creative ideation in a multilayer framework. Our findings suggest a major role of cross-frequency coupling for creative thinking in both global and nodal metrics. Among the three phases, significant change in the global organization (between AU and OC) was observed at the end of the creative thinking period. However, from the nodal aspect, difference between the AU and OC was observed in all the three phases. Overall, the results show the role of both inter and intra frequency connection as a potential biomarker for creative ideation. Further, the time-course analysis reveals that the brain connectivity for both inter and intra band connectivity, differs across different phases of creative ideation.

References

1. Axmacher, N., Henseler, M.M., Jensen, O., Weinreich, I., Elger, C.E., Fell, J.: Cross-frequency coupling supports multi-item working memory in the human hippocampus. Proc. Natl. Acad. Sci., p. 200911531 (2010)
2. Bassett, D.S., Wymbs, N.F., Porter, M.A., Mucha, P.J., Carlson, J.M., Grafton, S.T.: Dynamic reconfiguration of human brain networks during learning. Proceedings of the National Academy of Sciences (2011)
3. Bazanova, O., Aftanas, L.: Individual measures of electroencephalogram alpha activity and non-verbal creativity. Neurosci. Behav. Physiol. **38**(3), 227–235 (2008)
4. Beaty, R.E., Benedek, M., Silvia, P.J., Schacter, D.L.: Creative cognition and brain network dynamics. Trends Cogn. Sci. **20**(2), 87–95 (2016)
5. Brookes, M.J., et al.: A multi-layer network approach to MEG connectivity analysis. Neuroimage **132**, 425–438 (2016)
6. Canolty, R.T., Knight, R.T.: The functional role of cross-frequency coupling. Trends Cogn. Sci. **14**(11), 506–515 (2010)
7. Dai, Z., et al.: EEG cortical connectivity analysis of working memory reveals topological reorganization in theta and alpha bands. Front. Hum. Neurosci. **11**, 237 (2017)
8. Danko, S., Shemyakina, N., Nagornova, Z.V., Starchenko, M.: Comparison of the effects of the subjective complexity and verbal creativity on EEG spectral power parameters. Hum. Physiol. **35**(3), 381–383 (2009)
9. De Domenico, M.: Multilayer modeling and analysis of human brain networks. GigaScience **6**(5), 1–8 (2017)
10. De Domenico, M., Solé-Ribalta, A., Omodei, E., Gómez, S., Arenas, A.: Ranking in interconnected multilayer networks reveals versatile nodes. Nature Commun. **6**, 6868 (2015)
11. Diedrich, J., Benedek, M., Jauk, E., Neubauer, A.C.: Are creative ideas novel and useful? Psychol. Aesthetics Creativity Arts **9**(1), 35 (2015)
12. Dietrich, A., Kanso, R.: A review of EEG, ERP, and neuroimaging studies of creativity and insight. Psychol. Bull. **136**(5), 822 (2010)
13. Dimitriadis, S.I., Laskaris, N.A., Bitzidou, M.P., Tarnanas, I., Tsolaki, M.N.: A novel biomarker of amnestic MCI based on dynamic cross-frequency coupling patterns during cognitive brain responses. Front. Neurosci. **9**, 350 (2015)
14. Dimitriadis, S.I., Sun, Y., Thakor, N.V., Bezerianos, A.: Causal interactions between frontalθ-parieto-occipital$\alpha2$ predict performance on a mental arithmetic task. Front. Hum. Neurosci. **10**, 454 (2016)
15. Fink, A., Benedek, M.: Eeg alpha power and creative ideation. Neurosci. Biobehav. Rev. **44**, 111–123 (2014)
16. Fink, A., Neubauer, A.C.: EEG alpha oscillations during the performance of verbal creativity tasks: differential effects of sex and verbal intelligence. Int. J. Psychophysiol. **62**(1), 46–53 (2006)
17. Jauk, E., Benedek, M., Neubauer, A.C.: Tackling creativity at its roots: evidence for different patterns of EEG alpha activity related to convergent and divergent modes of task processing. Int. J. Psychophysiol. **84**(2), 219–225 (2012)
18. Jung-Beeman, M., et al.: Neural activity when people solve verbal problems with insight. PLoS Biol. **2**(4), e97 (2004)
19. Kawasaki, M., Kitajo, K., Yamaguchi, Y.: Dynamic links between theta executive functions and alpha storage buffers in auditory and visual working memory. Eur. J. Neurosci. **31**(9), 1683–1689 (2010)

20. Klimesch, W.: EEG alpha and theta oscillations reflect cognitive and memory performance: a review and analysis. Brain Res. Rev. **29**(2–3), 169–195 (1999)
21. Klimesch, W., Freunberger, R., Sauseng, P., Gruber, W.: A short review of slow phase synchronization and memory: evidence for control processes in different memory systems? Brain Res. **1235**, 31–44 (2008)
22. Klimesch, W., Sauseng, P., Hanslmayr, S.: EEG alpha oscillations: the inhibition-timing hypothesis. Brain Res. Rev. **53**(1), 63–88 (2007)
23. Kounios, J., et al.: The prepared mind: neural activity prior to problem presentation predicts subsequent solution by sudden insight. Psychol. Sci. **17**(10), 882–890 (2006)
24. Li, J.: Mid-task break improves global integration of functional connectivity in lower alpha band. Front. Hum. Neurosci. **10**, 304 (2016)
25. Mantzaris, A.V., et al.: Dynamic network centrality summarizes learning in the human brain. J. Complex Netw. **1**(1), 83–92 (2013)
26. Marmpena, M., Dimitriadis, S.I., Thakor, N., Bezerianos, A.: Phase to amplitude coupling as a potential biomarker for creative ideation: an EEG study. In: 2016 IEEE 38th Annual International Conference of the Engineering in Medicine and Biology Society (EMBC), pp. 383–386. IEEE (2016)
27. Palmer, J.A., Kreutz-Delgado, K., Makeig, S.: Amica: an adaptive mixture of independent component analyzers with shared components. Swartz Center for Computational Neuroscience, University of California San Diego, Technical report (2012)
28. Razumnikova, O.M.: Creativity related cortex activity in the remote associates task. Brain Res. Bull. **73**(1–3), 96–102 (2007)
29. Rubinov, M., Sporns, O.: Complex network measures of brain connectivity: uses and interpretations. Neuroimage **52**(3), 1059–1069 (2010)
30. Runco, M.A., Jaeger, G.J.: The standard definition of creativity. Creativity Res. J. **24**(1), 92–96 (2012)
31. Sandkühler, S., Bhattacharya, J.: Deconstructing insight: EEG correlates of insightful problem solving. PLoS one **3**(1), e1459 (2008)
32. Saramäki, J., Kivelä, M., Onnela, J.P., Kaski, K., Kertesz, J.: Generalizations of the clustering coefficient to weighted complex networks. Phys. Rev. E **75**(2), 027105 (2007)
33. Schwab, D., Benedek, M., Papousek, I., Weiss, E.M., Fink, A.: The time-course of EEG alpha power changes in creative ideation. Front. Hum. Neurosci. **8**, 310 (2014)
34. Sheth, B.R., Sandkühler, S., Bhattacharya, J.: Posterior beta and anterior gamma oscillations predict cognitive insight. J. Cogn. Neurosci. **21**(7), 1269–1279 (2009)
35. Tewarie, P., et al.: Integrating cross-frequency and within band functional networks in resting-state MEG: a multi-layer network approach. Neuroimage **142**, 324–336 (2016)

Estimating Latent Brain Sources with Low-Rank Representation and Graph Regularization

Feng Liu[1,2], Shouyi Wang[3(✉)], Jing Qin[4], Yifei Lou[5], and Jay Rosenberger[3]

[1] Massachusetts General Hospital, Harvard Medical School, Boston, MA, USA
[2] Picower Institue of Learning and Memory, MIT, Cambridge, MA, USA
liufengchaos@gmail.com
[3] Department of Industrial Engineering, University of Texas at Arlington,
Arlington, TX, USA
{shouyiw,jrosenbe}@uta.edu
[4] Department of Mathematical Sciences, Montana State University,
Bozeman, MT, USA
jing.qin@montana.edu
[5] Department of Mathematical Sciences, University of Texas at Dallas,
Richardson, TX, USA
yifei.lou@utdallas.edu

Abstract. To infer latent brain source activation patterns under different cognitive tasks is an integral step to understand how our brain works. Traditional electroencephalogram (EEG) Source Imaging (ESI) methods usually do not distinguish task-related and spurious non-task-related sources that jointly generate EEG signals, which inevitably yield misleading reconstructed activation patterns. In this research, we assume that the task-related source signal intrinsically has a low-rank property, which is exploited to infer the true task-related EEG sources location. Although the true task-related source signal is sparse and low-rank, the contribution of spurious sources scattering over the source space with intermittent activation patterns makes the actual source space lose the low-rank property. To reconstruct a low-rank true source, we propose a novel ESI model that involves a spatial low-rank representation and a temporal Laplacian graph regularization, the latter of which guarantees the temporal smoothness of the source signal and eliminate the spurious ones. To solve the proposed model, an augmented Lagrangian objective function is formulated and an algorithm in the framework of alternating direction method of multipliers (ADMM) is proposed. Numerical results illustrate the effectivenesks of the proposed method in terms of reconstruction accuracy with high efficiency.

Keywords: EEG Source Imaging
Low rank representation · Graph Regularization
Alternating direction method of multiplier (ADMM)

© Springer Nature Switzerland AG 2018
S. Wang et al. (Eds.): BI 2018, LNAI 11309, pp. 304–316, 2018.
https://doi.org/10.1007/978-3-030-05587-5_29

1 Introduction

As a direct measurement modality of neural electrical firing patterns, electroencephalogram (EEG) has a higher temporal resolution up to millisecond. EEG Source Imaging (ESI) aims to map from EEG recording on the scalp to the electrical potentials in the brain sources. ESI enables high temporal resolution noninvasive connectivity analysis in the source space, which is impossible using fMIR (low temporal resolution) or intracranial EEG (invasive) [1]. Since the number of electrodes usually is much smaller than that of brain sources, the ESI problem is highly ill-posed. A variety of methods have been proposed to address this challenging problem with different neurophysiological assumptions, formulated by various regularization techniques such as ℓ_1 or ℓ_2 norm, total variation norm [2] and others summarized in [3,4].

To encourage temporal smoothness, a number of regularization techniques based on spatiotemporal mixed norms have been developed, including Mixed Norm Estimates (MxNE) which uses $\ell_{1,2}$-norm regularization [5], time-frequency mixed-norm estimate (TF-MxNE) which uses structured sparse priors in time-frequency domain for better estimation of the non-stationary and transient source signal [6], and STOUT (spatio-temporal unifying tomography), which combines the advantage of Sparse Basis Field Expansions and TF-MxNE by imposing source current density into appropriate spatio-temporal basis functions.

One common limitation of the existing ESI algorithms is that they usually consider noises on the sensor level or the noise covariance in the source space. However, the spurious noise can be hard to estimate by a source covariance prior. If reconstructed, the estimated source is consisted of task-related source and spurious noise in the source space. The true task-related sources will be corrupted by spurious sources, which motivates us to develop new algorithms to find the true task-related source. There are two commonly accepted assumptions (1) spatially sparse (2) temporally continuous for the task-related source activation pattern, which inevitably leads to the low-rank property of the source space. To better discover the task-related source, we impose the low-rank penalty for source signal to estimate the latent sources with low-rank and sparse property, hoping to get rid of spurious source in the source space. Also, instead of imposing auto-regressive dynamical model, we use a nonparametric penalty term for temporal smoothness, which directly penalize dissimilarity of temporally neighboring samples. It is worth noting that we used the graph regularization term in our previous paper, however the graph is defined to be fully connected among all the points within one class [7–9], which inevitably drive all the activate patterns at different time points having the same magnitude, thus the dynamic behavior of the brain is oversimplified and its future application for realistic cases is limited.

In this paper, we propose a novel EEG source imaging model based on temporal graph regularized low-rank representation. The model is solved based on the alternating direction method of multipliers (ADMM) [10]. We conducted extensive numerical experiments to verify the effectiveness of discovering task related low-rank sources. The reconstructed solution is temporally smooth and spatially sparse. The contributions of our paper are summarized as follows:

1. A low-rank representation model (LRR) is proposed on EEG inverse problem from the low-rank property of true task-related source configurations.
2. We redefine the graph regularization to relieve the strong assumption in previous research and the newly defined graph regularization utilizes temporal vicinity information of samples to promote temporal smoothness.
3. A algorithm based on ADMM is given which is efficient extracting the low-rank task-related source patterns.

2   Inverse Problem and Temporal Graph Structures

2.1   The Inverse Problem

The cortex source electrical signal propagates to EEG sensors through a brain conductivity model which can be described as a linear mapping matrix called lead field matrix, given as follows,

$$X = LS + E \tag{1}$$

where $X \in \mathbb{R}^{N_c \times N_t}$ is the EEG data measured by N_c electrodes for N_t time points, $L \in \mathbb{R}^{N_c \times N_d}$ is the lead field matrix that maps the source signal to sensors on the scalp, each column of L represents the electrical field of one source at particular location to all the EEG electrodes, $S \in \mathbb{R}^{N_d \times N_t}$ represents the corresponding cortex potential in N_d sources locations for the N_t time instants. Since the number of sources is much larger than electrodes, solving S given EEG data X is ill-posed with infinite feasible solutions, which necessitates a regularization term to be imposed. Generally, an estimate of S can be done by minimizing a cost function, which is composed of a data fidelity term and a regularization term:

$$\arg \min_{S} \|E\|_F^2 + \gamma \Theta(S) \quad s.t. \quad X - LS = E, \tag{2}$$

where $\|\cdot\|_F$ is the Frobenius Norm. The penalty term $\Theta(S)$ is to encourage neurophysiologically plausible explanation and guarantees a unique solution.

2.2   Temporal Graph Embedding

A graph can be viewed as geometric neighborhood relationship between each vertex representing each data sample, the weight between vertex represents similarity between two points [11]. Inspired by the manifold theory [12], we use a regularization term to penalize the difference between two neighboring source signal. In our previous work, we use a graph regularization term to promote intra-class consistency [7], but the assumption is too strong by requiring all the reconstructed sources at different time points has the same location as well as signal magnitude as long as they belong to the same class. Now define a temporal graph regularization as

$$R_t(S) = \sum_{i,j=1}^{N} \|s_i - s_j\|_2^2 W_{ij}, \tag{3}$$

where s_i is the i-th column of the matrix S, and a binary matrix W is designed as follows,

$$W_{ij} = \begin{cases} 1, & \text{if } s_i \in N_k(s_j) \text{ or } s_j \in N_k(s_i) \\ 0, & \text{otherwise.} \end{cases}$$

The graph embedding matrix W contains temporal vicinity information. $N_k(s_i)$ is the set containing k temporally closest points to s_i. In this paper, we set $k = 1$. This formulation intends to force neighboring source signal having similar pattern. The benefits are twofold, one is for temporal smoothness of the task related activated source, another advantage is to make the spurious sources denoised since their intermittent pattern will otherwise increase the cost of objective function. By defining D as a diagonal matrix whose entries are row sums of the symmetric matrix W, i.e., $D_{ii} = \sum_j W_{ij}$, and denoting $G := D - W$, $R_t(S)$ can be rewritten as:

$$R_t(S) = \sum_{i,j=1}^{N} (s_i^T s_i + s_j^T s_j - 2s_i^T s_j) W_{ij} = \sum_{i}^{N} s_i^T s_i w_{ii} - \sum_{i,j=1}^{N} s_i^T s_j w_{ij}$$

$$= 2\operatorname{tr}(SDS^T) - 2\operatorname{tr}(SWS^T) = 2\operatorname{tr}(SGS^T), \tag{4}$$

where $\operatorname{tr}(\cdot)$ is the trace operator of a matrix, i.e., adding up all diagonal entries of a matrix.

3   Proposed EEG Source Imaging Model

3.1   Decomposition of True and Spurious Sources

In general, two types of noises should be considered, one originates from inaccurate measurement of the sensors modeled by Gaussian white noise, which is denoted as E in Eq.(1), the other type of noise is called biological noise that comes directly from the spontaneous activations in the source space, which are not task-related and termed as spurious source. The second types of noise (spurious sources) contributes to the EEG signal in the same way as the truth sources. This assumption make sense since it is commonly known that under resting states, our brain still generates EEG signal. A drawback of traditional models is that they did not separate the spurious sources from the true sources. The estimated source can be composed of both task-rated source and spurious sources. To address the above-mentioned problem, we propose to use a low rank constraint to extract the task related activation. The illustration for decomposition of source space as well as the whole procedure is given in Fig. 1, where S_1 has a low rank property and S_2 is sparse, and the sum of S_1 and S_2 is no longer low-rank, making X lose low-rank structure.

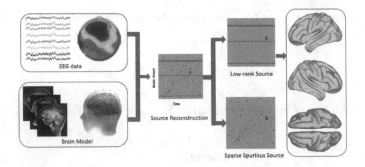

Fig. 1. Extraction of the low-rank true source from spurious source pipeline: After gathering the MRI scans of the head, tissue segmentation is conducted followed by mesh generation. By assigning conductivity values to different tissues and electrodes co-registered with the meshing model, boundary element method (BEM) was used to solve the forward model. Each triangle represents a brain source. The factual source signal S can be decomposed into two source matrix. The task related true sources S_1 have a low-rank property and the spurious sources S_2 are the sparse but not temporally consistent. The low-rank source solution is projected to cortex voxels to illustrate the activation pattern.

3.2   Low Rank Representation Model with Graph Regularization

We introduce our proposed model called Low-Rank Representation with Temporal Graph structures ESI (LRR-TG-ESI). The model is composed of data fitting term to explain the EEG data, temporal graph embedding regularization term that promotes temporal smooth, and a ℓ_1 norm for sparsity penalty and nuclear norm for the low-rank structure of the true source. The objective function is given below:

$$\min_{S,E} \|S\|_* + \lambda \|E\|_{1,1} + \beta \|S\|_{1,1} + \alpha \operatorname{tr}(SGS^T)$$
$$\text{s.t.} \quad X = LS + E, \tag{5}$$

where $\lambda, \beta, \alpha > 0$ are tuning parameters to balance the trade-off of different terms. Our proposed model is able to enforce row-sparse via low-rank and sparse regularization and temporal smoothness via temporal graph regularization while fitting the EEG data X. Although the graph regularization term has been discussed in our early paper [7], it is not defined on the temporal manifold, and the previous definition in [7] made a strong assumption to drive the magnitude of source signal to be similar intra-class. To promote the spatial smoothness, a total variation term can be imposed as another penalty term, such as first order total variation (TV) regularization in Ref. [2,13], fractional order TV in [8,14], and similar algorithm can be derived under the framework of ADMM, however further investigation of using spatial smoothing TV is our future work.

4   Optimization Algorithm

To solve (5), an algorithm in the framework of ADMM is developed. The augmented Lagrangian function of (5) is

$$L(S,M,E,T_1,T_2,\mu) = \|S\|_* + \lambda\|E\|_{1,1} + \beta\|M\|_{1,1} + \alpha\operatorname{tr}(SGS^T)$$
$$+ \langle T_1, X - LS - E\rangle + \langle T_2, M - S\rangle + \frac{\mu}{2} \times (\|X - LS - E\|_F^2 + \|M - S\|_F^2).$$
(6)

By some simple algebra, (6) can be reformulated as

$$L(S,M,E,T_1,T_2,\mu) = \|S\|_* + \lambda\|E\|_{1,1} + \beta\|M\|_{1,1} + \alpha\operatorname{tr}(SGS^T)$$
$$+ \frac{\mu}{2} \times (\|X - LS - E + \frac{T_1}{\mu}\|_F^2 + \|M - S + \frac{T_2}{\mu}\|_F^2) - \frac{1}{2}\mu(\|T_1\|_F^2 + \|T_2\|_F^2),$$
(7)

where T_1 and T_2 are Lagrangian multipliers and μ is a positive scalar which can be used as a step size. M is an auxiliary variable for S. The inner product of two arbitrary matrices A and B is denoted as $\langle A, B\rangle$, which is also equal to $\operatorname{tr}(A^T B)$. To minimize Eq. (7), the variables S, M, E, T_1 and T_2 can be updates alternately in a Gauss-Seidel manner by minimizing the augmented Lagrangian function with other variables fixed. For symbolic simplicity, we rewrite Eq.(7) as:

$$L(S,M,E,T_1,T_2,\mu) = \|S\|_* + \lambda\|E\|_{1,1} + \beta\|M\|_{1,1}$$
$$+ h(S,E,M,T_1,T_2,\mu) - \frac{1}{2}\mu(\|T_1\|_F^2 + \|T_2\|_F^2),$$
(8)

where

$$h(S,E,M,T_1,T_2,\mu) = \alpha\operatorname{tr}(SGS^T) + \frac{\mu}{2} \times (\|X - LS - E + \frac{T_1}{\mu}\|_F^2$$
$$+ \|M - S + \frac{T_2}{\mu}\|_F^2).$$
(9)

If the augmented Lagrangian function is difficult to minimize with respect to a variable, a linearized approximate surrogate function can used, hence the algorithm we used here bears the name Linearized Alternating Direction method [11,15]. Updating S by minimizing $h(S, E^k, M^k, T_1^k, T_2^k, \mu^k)$ (suppose we are at iteration k) is equivalent to minimize the following goal function with the other variables fixed:

$$L_S = \|S\|_* + h(S, E^k, M^k, T_1^k, T_2^k, \mu^k),$$
(10)

which is approximated by optimizing its linearizion at S^k plus a quadratic proximal term:

$$S = \operatorname*{argmin}_{S}\|S\|_* + \langle \nabla_S h(S^k), S - S^k\rangle + \frac{\eta}{2}\|S - S^k\|_F^2.$$
(11)

Here η is a constant satisfying

$$\eta > 2\alpha\|G\|_2 + \mu(1 + \|L\|_2^2), \tag{12}$$

where $\|\cdot\|_2$ is the spectral norm of a matrix, i.e, the largest singular value. As long as (12) is satisfied, (11) is a good approximate to (10). The solution to (11) has a closed form using a singular value thresholding operator (SVT) [16] given as:

$$S^{k+1} = \Theta_{\eta^{-1}}(S^k - \nabla_S h(S^k)/\eta), \tag{13}$$

where $\Theta_\varepsilon(A) = US_\varepsilon(\Sigma)V^T$ is the SVT operator, in which $U\Sigma V^T$ is the singular value decomposition of A and $S_\varepsilon(s)$ is defined as $\sin(x)\max(|x|-\varepsilon, 0)$. $\nabla_{S_1} h(S_1^k)$ is calculated as

$$\nabla_S h(S^k) = \alpha(S^k G + S^k G^T) + \mu L^T(LS - X + E - \frac{T_1}{\mu}) + \mu(S - M - \frac{T_2}{\mu})$$

To update M and E, it is equivalent to solve the following problem:

$$\underset{M}{\operatorname{argmin}} \frac{\mu}{2}\|M - S + \frac{T_2}{\mu}\|_F^2 + \beta\|M\|_{1,1} \tag{14}$$

$$\underset{E}{\operatorname{argmin}} \frac{\mu}{2}\|X - LS - E + \frac{T_1}{\mu}\|_F^2 + \lambda\|E\|_{1,1} \tag{15}$$

The general form of (14)–(15) is a ℓ_1 norm proximal operator defined as

$$\operatorname{prox}_\mu(V) = \arg\min_X \mu\|X\|_{1,1} + \frac{1}{2}\|X - V\|_F^2, \tag{16}$$

with $\mu > 0$. The above problem (16) has a closed form solution, called soft thresholding, defined by a shrinkage function,

$$\operatorname{shrink}(V, \mu) = (|V| - \mu)_+ \operatorname{sgn}(V),$$

where $(x)_+$ is x when $x > 0$, otherwise 0. The shrinkage function is defined as element-wise operator. Problem (14)–(15) has a close form solution described with the shrinkage function. After updating all the variables, these Lagrange multipliers are updated by

$$T_1 = T_1 + \mu(X - LS - E), \quad T_2 = T_2 + \mu(M - S). \tag{17}$$

The parameter μ is updated by $\mu = \min(\rho\mu, \mu_{max})$. A summarized algorithm is given as Algorithm 1. We initialize the S with the estimate S_0 from ℓ_1 solver.

It's worth noting that the data fitting term we use is $\ell_{1,1}$ norm of E in the model, and there are other options. Generally, if the Gaussian noise E is small, then the norm $\|E\|_F$, is an appropriate choice, but for random data corruption, $\ell_{1,1}$ should be used, and for sample specific data corruption, $\ell_{2,1}$ [17–19], should be used.

The above procedures are summarized in Algorithm 1. The convergence of Algorithm 1 can be easily derived from [15].

Algorithm 1. Source Imaging Based on Spatial and Temporal Graph Structures

> **INPUT:** Lead field matrix L, preprocessed EEG signal matrix X, graph matrix G,
> precalculated matrix D_α, parameters $\alpha, \zeta > 0$, and $\beta > 0$.
> **OUTPUT:** Source matrix S.
> **Initialize:** Set $S = S_0, J = 0, M = 0$.
> **while** not converged **do**
>   update S according to
> $S^{k+1} = \tilde{\Theta}_{\eta^{-1}}(S^k - \nabla_S h(S^k)/\eta)$,
>   update M according to Equation (14),
>   update E according to Equation (15),
>   update T_1, T_2 according to Equation (17),
>   update $\mu = \min(\rho\mu, \mu_{max})$,
> **end while**

---

5 Numerical Experiments

In this section, we conducted 2 experiments to illustrate the effectiveness of our proposed method. In the beginning, we tested different values for λ and β by setting $\alpha = 0$. Later, we illustrate the temporal smoothing functionality of the graph regularization term for corrupted source with abrupt signal jumps. In the second experiment, we give comprehensive numerical results by testing our algorithm against the benchmark algorithms to showcase the effectiveness of the proposed method in reconstructing task-related source, where we show that our algorithm can not only find the activated locations, but also reconstruct the time-course of source activation with high precision.

5.1 Experiments 1: Test LRR with Temporal Graph Prior

At each location, a time series with length of 500 were generated to represent the source activation time-course. At each time point, two randomly picked sources are activated to simulate the non-task related spurious noise with mean of 0 and variance to be 1. The task-related activate pattern has low-rank property, however, the noise corrupted source space is no longer low-rank. We repeated our experiment 50 times for all the combinations of λ and β, where $\lambda = \{0.01, 0.02, 0.03, 0.05, 0.1, 0.2, 0.5\}$ and $\beta = \{0.005, 0.01, 0.015, 0.02, 0.05, 0.1\}$. The reconstructed error (RE) metric used here is RE $= \|\hat{S} - S\|_2 / \|S\|_2$. The RE under different value of λ and β is given in Fig. 2. Next, we solve the LRR-TG-ESI problem (5) with graph regularization term to test its impact on the reconstructed signal. We assign different values $\{0.01, 0.02, 0.05, 0.1, 0.5\}$ for the graph regularization parameter α. The original source signal was smooth, then it was corrupted by random noise at some time points. There are also 2 randomly picked activated sources representing spurious sources with the mean of 0 and variance to be 1. The "temporal smoothing" impact of the graph regularization is shown in Fig. 3, where $\lambda = 0.02$ and $\beta = 0.01$. In Fig. 3, the original signal is corrupted and not smooth at some time points, we set the neighbor size to be

2 (the closest signal before and after the one to be estimated) when calculating the Laplacian matrix. It is evident from the formulation (3) that the graph regularization term will decrease the dissimilarity of the temporally neighbored reconstructed source. If α is set to be 0.5, the graph regularization term penalized heavily on the curvature of the reconstructed signal as is illustrated in Fig. 3. We can see that with the temporal graph prior, the reconstructed source is more smooth. It is worth noticing that the main purpose of temporal graph prior is not to smooth the time course for the activated locations, the main purpose is to filter out the spurious activations that are short transients with abrupt jumps. Combined with the low-rank prior, the temporal graph prior can filter the spurious activations and reconstruct the task related activated source. The randomly planted spurious sources are filtered out by penalizing the graph regularization and nuclear norm, and in most of the cases, the final rank is 2 can be achieved within a wide range of parameters.

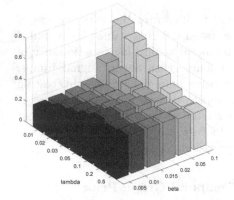 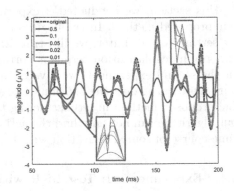

Fig. 2. Averaged reconstruction error and rank varying λ and β over 50 experiments. Average of reconstruction error for different λ and β

Fig. 3. Illustration of the smoothing effect of temporal graph regularization: reconstructed time courses from varied graph regularization parameters.

5.2 Experiments 2: Comprehensive Comparison with Benchmark Algorithms

The purpose of previous numerical experiments is to validate each term of the objective function and to understand their properties. The trade-off between low-rankness, data fidelity, sparsity, temporal smooth is fully discussed by varying different parameters. In this part, a comprehensive study is conducted to compare the proposed algorithm with the popular ESI algorithms such as MNE [20], sLORETA [21], and MCE with implementation of Homotopy and FISTA [7]. We generated independent sources in different ROIs for easy validation purpose, the number of independent sources of 2 and 3 corresponding to different rank of ground-truth source, and the spurious sources are generated by randomly activating the sources on the cortex with a random scalar whose mean value to be 0, and the variance is 1. Moreover, the noise on sensor level is also added to the EEG data. Two of the MCE algorithms are selected, which are Homotopy and FISTA [22].

To measure the performance, we introduced 5 metrics, including (1) CPU time in seconds, (2) rank of the calculated source, (3) Sparsity, measuring the number of nonzero elements in the source space at each time point, (4) Reconstruction Error (RE) defined in Sect. 5.1, (5) Localization Error (LE), which is calculated using the shortest path algorithm over the irregular meshes from the reconstructed source location to the ground truth location. The LE metric is the most important one since it measures the discrepancy in location, the other metrics give information of the property of the rendered solution. To calculate LE for each ROI with activated sources, we first locate the source with the largest activation magnitude in this ROI, and calculate the shortest path distance from the located source to the ground truth location. We conduct the same procedure for all the activated ROI, and calculate the average value of all the distances at each time point. The final LE is the averaged distance value for all the 500 time points for each experiment.

For our proposed algorithm, we set $\lambda = 0.01$ and $\beta = 0.01$, which were tested to have good performance for the same case when the rank is 2 and the number of the spurious activated source is 2 in previous experiment, and the graph parameter α is also set to be 0.01. 10 experiments were conducted under the same setting and the performance of all the algorithms are summarized in Tables 1 and 2 when true rank is 2 or 3. The SNR is calculated after the noise signal is generated and it was averaged from 10 experiments under the same experimental setting. As can be seen from the tables, our algorithm is the most accurate to locate the task related activated source. The CPU time of our algorithm is between Homotopy and FISTA algorithm.

Table 1. Source reconstruction performance comparison (Rank = 2)

Method	Rank = 2; SNR = −0.356 dB					Rank = 2; SNR = −1.12 dB					Rank = 2; SNR = −1.67 dB				
	Time	Rank	Sparsity	RE	LE	Time	Rank	Sparsity	RE	LE	Time	Rank	Sparsity	RE	LE
Homotopy	0.41	449	65	0.80	2.02	0.41	449.8	84.4	0.95	3.31	0.50	459.3	91.15	0.97	4.57
FISTA	2.76	500	1812.4	0.62	3.93	2.76	500	1920.4	0.89	9.39	2.73	500	1888.0	0.80	11.25
sLORETA	0.055	500	2004	1.18	33.5	0.05	500	2004	1.26	34.13	0.056	500	2004.0	1.32	38.31
WMN	8.4e-5	107	2004	0.99	22.6	8.4e-5	107	2004	0.99	31.47	8.4e-5	107	2004.0	0.99	28.46
Proposed	0.75	3.3	3.3	0.24	**0.145**	0.75	4.8	4.8	0.414	**1.94**	0.83	6.4	6.5	0.42	**2.27**

Table 2. Source reconstruction performance comparison (Rank = 3)

Method	Rank = 3; SNR = 0.938 dB					Rank = 3; SNR = −0.174 dB					Rank = 3; SNR = −0.784 dB				
	Time	Rank	Sparsity	RE	LE	Time	Rank	Sparsity	RE	LE	Time	Rank	Sparsity	RE	LE
Homotopy	0.36	445.4	77.6	0.64	5.18	0.48	464	87.2	0.68	6.1	0.46	474.1	92.5	0.84	5.88
FISTA	2.64	500	1812.5	0.69	9.33	2.56	500	1969.0	1.23	21.5	2.67	500	1939.2	0.94	17.44
sLORETA	0.057	500	2004	1.90	41.93	0.06	500	2004	1.81	43.9	0.05	500	2004.0	1.25	46.60
WMN	8.4e-5	107	2004	6.79	29.55	7.6e-5	107	2004	6.82	35.63	7.3e-5	107	2004.0	6.82	34.41
Proposed	0.72	5.2	5.2	0.43	**2.98**	0.80	6.1	6.1	0.488	**3.82**	0.75	7.3	7.3	0.45	**2.86**

6   Conclusion

In this paper, unlike the traditional model, we propose to estimate the latent source which is task-related but corrupted with spurious sources. To extract the discriminative task related source activation pattern, we come up with a new EEG source imaging model based on temporal graph structures and low-rank representation. The model is solved with an algorithm based on ADMM. Numerical experiments verified the effectiveness of the proposed work on discovering task related low-rank sources.

Acknowledgment. This work has been partially supported by the NSF funding under grant number CMMI-1537504 and DMS-1522786. The research of Jing Qin is supported by the NSF grant DMS-1818374.

References

1. Liu, F., Xiang, W., Wang, S., Lega, B.: Prediction of seizure spread network via sparse representations of overcomplete dictionaries. In: Ascoli, G.A., Hawrylycz, M., Ali, H., Khazanchi, D., Shi, Y. (eds.) BIH 2016. LNCS (LNAI), vol. 9919, pp. 262–273. Springer, Cham (2016). https://doi.org/10.1007/978-3-319-47103-7_26
2. Ding, L.: Reconstructing cortical current density by exploring sparseness in the transform domain. Phys. Med. Biol. **54**(9), 2683 (2009)
3. Grech, R., Cassar, T., Muscat, J., Camilleri, K.P., Fabri, S.G., Zervakis, M., Xanthopoulos, P., Sakkalis, V., Vanrumste, B.: Review on solving the inverse problem in EEG source analysis. J. Neuroeng. Rehabil. **5**(1), 1 (2008)
4. He, B., Sohrabpour, A., Brown, E., Liu, Z.: Electrophysiological source imaging: a noninvasive window to brain dynamics. Annu. Rev. Biomed. Eng. **20**, 171–196 (2018)
5. Gramfort, A., Kowalski, M., Hämäläinen, M.: Mixed-norm estimates for the M/EEG inverse problem using accelerated gradient methods. Phys. Med. Biol. **57**(7), 1937 (2012)
6. Gramfort, A., Strohmeier, D., Haueisen, J., Hämäläinen, M.S., Kowalski, M.: Time-frequency mixed-norm estimates: Sparse M/EEG imaging with non-stationary source activations. NeuroImage **70**, 410–422 (2013)
7. Liu, F., Rosenberger, J., Lou, Y., Hosseini, R., Su, J., Wang, S.: Graph regularized EEG source imaging with in-class consistency and out-class discrimination. IEEE Trans. Big Data **3**(4), 378–391 (2017)
8. Qin, J., Liu, F., Wang, S., Rosenberger, J.: EEG source imaging based on spatial and temporal graph structures. In: International Conference on Image Processing Theory, Tools and Applications (2017)
9. Liu, F., Hosseini, R., Rosenberger, J., Wang, S., Su, J.: Supervised discriminative EEG brain source imaging with graph regularization. In: Descoteaux, M., Maier-Hein, L., Franz, A., Jannin, P., Collins, D.L., Duchesne, S. (eds.) MICCAI 2017. LNCS, vol. 10433, pp. 495–504. Springer, Cham (2017). https://doi.org/10.1007/978-3-319-66182-7_57
10. Boyd, S., Parikh, N., Chu, E., Peleato, B., Eckstein, J.: Distributed optimization and statistical learning via the alternating direction method of multipliers. Found. Trends Mach. Learn. **3**(1), 1–122 (2011)

11. Yin, M., Gao, J., Lin, Z.: Laplacian regularized low-rank representation and its applications. IEEE Trans. Pattern Anal. Mach. Intell. **38**(3), 504–517 (2016)
12. Cai, D., He, X., Han, J., Huang, T.S.: Graph regularized nonnegative matrix factorization for data representation. IEEE Trans. Pattern Anal. Mach. Intell. **33**(8), 1548–1560 (2011)
13. Michel, V., Gramfort, A., Varoquaux, G., Eger, E., Thirion, B.: Total variation regularization for fMRI-based prediction of behavior. IEEE Trans. Med. Imaging **30**(7), 1328–1340 (2011)
14. Li, Y., Qin, J., Hsin, Y.L., Osher, S., Liu, W.: s-SMOOTH: sparsity and smoothness enhanced EEG brain tomography. Frontiers Neurosci. **10**, 543 (2016)
15. Lin, Z., Liu, R., Su, Z.: Linearized alternating direction method with adaptive penalty for low-rank representation. In: Advances in Neural Information Processing Systems, pp. 612–620 (2011)
16. Cai, J.F., Candès, E.J., Shen, Z.: A singular value thresholding algorithm for matrix completion. SIAM J. Optim. **20**(4), 1956–1982 (2010)
17. Nie, F., Huang, H., Cai, X., Ding, C.H.: Efficient and robust feature selection via joint $\ell_{2,1}$-norms minimization. In: Advances in Neural Information Processing Systems, pp. 1813–1821 (2010)
18. Du, S., Ma, Y., Ma, Y.: Graph regularized compact low rank representation for subspace clustering. Knowl.-Based Syst. **118**, 56–69 (2017)
19. Yin, M., Gao, J., Lin, Z., Shi, Q., Guo, Y.: Dual graph regularized latent low-rank representation for subspace clustering. IEEE Trans. Image Process. **24**(12), 4918–4933 (2015)
20. Hämäläinen, M.S., Ilmoniemi, R.J.: Interpreting magnetic fields of the brain: minimum norm estimates. Med. Biol. Eng. Comput. **32**(1), 35–42 (1994)
21. Pascual-Marqui, R.D., et al.: Standardized low-resolution brain electromagnetic tomography (sloreta): technical details. Methods Find. Exp. Clin. Pharmacol. **24**(Suppl D), 5–12 (2002)
22. Yang, A.Y., Sastry, S.S., Ganesh, A., Ma, Y.: Fast ℓ 1-minimization algorithms and an application in robust face recognition: a review. In: 2010 17th IEEE International Conference on Image Processing (ICIP), pp. 1849–1852. IEEE (2010)

Informatics Paradigms for Brain and Mental Health Research

Analysis of Epileptic Activity Based on Brain Mapping of EEG Adaptive Time-Frequency Decomposition

Maximiliano Bueno-López[1], Pablo A. Muñoz-Gutiérrez[2(✉)], Eduardo Giraldo[3], and Marta Molinas[4]

[1] Department of Electrical Engineering, Universidad de la Salle, Bogotá, Colombia
maxbueno@unisalle.edu.co
[2] Electronic Instrumentation Technology,
Universidad del Quindío, Armenia, Colombia
pamunoz@uniquindio.edu.co
[3] Department of Electrical Engineering,
Universidad Tecnológica de Pereira, Pereira, Colombia
egiraldos@utp.edu.co
[4] Department of Engineering Cybernetics,
Norwegian University of Science and Technology, Trondheim, Norway
marta.molinas@ntnu.no

Abstract. The applications of Empirical Mode Decomposition (EMD) in Biomedical Signal analysis have increased and is common now to find publications that use EMD to identify behaviors in the brain or heart. EMD has shown excellent results in the identification of behaviours from the use of electroencephalogram (EEG) signals. In addition, some advances in the computer area have made it possible to improve their performance. In this paper, we presented a method that, using an entropy analysis, can automatically choose the relevant Intrinsic Mode Functions (IMFs) from EEG signals. The idea is to choose the minimum number of IMFs to reconstruct the brain activity. The EEG signals were processed by EMD and the IMFs were ordered according to the entropy cost function. The IMFs with more relevant information are selected for the brain mapping. To validate the results, a relative error measure was used.

Keywords: Brain mapping · Empirical mode decomposition
Epilepsy · Signal analysis

1 Introduction

Richard Caton discovered electrical currents in the brain in 1875 and Hans Berger recorded these currents and published the first human Electroencephalogram (EEG) in 1924 [1]. The analysis of EEG signals has been very useful tool to support the medical diagnosis by extracting those meaningful features that can

© Springer Nature Switzerland AG 2018
S. Wang et al. (Eds.): BI 2018, LNAI 11309, pp. 319–328, 2018.
https://doi.org/10.1007/978-3-030-05587-5_30

allow to identify some diseases (for example, Alzheimer or epilepsy) or some disorders (for example, attention-deficit/hyperactivity disorder (ADHD) or autistic spectrum) or some changes in the signals in depth of anesthesia. Nevertheless, the EEG signals are very difficult to analyze in time and frequency due to their non-linear and non-stationary nature [2,3]. For this reason, EMD and Hilbert Huang Transform (HHT) have been used to analyze the EEG signals and they have allowed to obtain a better signal representation and to detect instantaneous frequencies (IF) that with other methods are difficult to observe [4]. By this way, the use of linear filters and pre-processing is not necessary. In [5], a method to quantify interaction between nonstationary cerebral blood velocity (BFV) and blood pressure (BP) is proposed for the assessment of dynamic cerebral autoregulation (CA) using HHT. In [6], the authors use Multivariate Empirical Mode Decomposition (MEMD), which allows to analyze multichannel signals directly; in that case, this method was used for a full data-driven analysis to decompose resting-state fMRI (functional Magnetic Resonance Imaging) data into different sub-bands looking for connectivity functions. Our paper has a similar purpose, but instead we use EEG signals and another brain reconstruction algorithm. The use of fMRI implies higher costs due to the equipment required for acquisition and processing of information. Different strategies have been used for the process of reconstruction of Neural Activity from EEG data, but to the best knowledge of the authors, EMD has been used for this purpose only recently. For neural activity reconstruction, an iterative regularized method that explicitly includes space (grounded in a physiological model) and time constraints within the dynamic solution of the EEG inverse problem, is presented in [7].

When medications for focal epilepsy are not effective, it is necessary to use invasive treatments how resective surgery where a part of the brain is removed. First, the sources or brain zones, where the epileptic seizures start, are located and second, the surgery is carefully performed. Sometimes, when the mapping is not the best, it is necessary an additional estimation of the zone that has to be removed. Therefore, intra-cranial electrodes are used and additional surgery is performed [8]. In this work, an improved technique to brain activity reconstruction is presented. This technique is based on data-driven and applies pre-processing stage of the EEG using empirical mode decomposition. The information is classified in frequency bands from IMFs and then a highly accurate brain mapping is performed to locate the active sources. To this end, an entropy cost function is proposed for the optimal selection of IMFs. The entropy is an indicator of the amount of information stored in a more general probability distribution and is a measure of the complexity of the time series [9]. Some previous works have considered the use of entropy to detection of epileptic seizure [10,11]. This paper is organized as follows: Sect. 2 gives an introduction to the essential concepts about EMD and EEG signals. The experimental setup is presented in Sect. 3 and the results obtained with the EEG signals are shown in Sect. 4. The discussion of the results is presented in Sect. 5. Finally, some conclusions are given in Sect. 6.

2   Methods

2.1   The Inverse Problem in EEG Signals

The following is the forward model of EEG generation:

$$y(t_k) = Mx(t_k) + \epsilon(t_k) \tag{1}$$

where $y(t_k) \in \mathbb{R}^d$ is the EEG and the neural activity is $x(t_k) \in \mathbb{R}^n$, with $t_k = kh$ the time at sample k being $k = 1, \ldots, T$ the number of samples, the sample time is h and the lead-field matrix $M \in \mathbb{R}^{d \times n}$, which relates the neural activity with the EEG. Different models can be used to simulated the evolution of $x(t_k)$ in time. It is possible to formulate an iterative inverse problem [7] based on regularized Tikhonov-Phillips functional, in order to estimate the neural activity $\hat{x}(t_k)$ for each measurement $y(t_k)$, as described in:

$$\hat{x}(t_k) = \arg\min_{x(t_k)} \|y(t_k) - Mx(t_k)\|_2^2 + \lambda_k \|x(t_k) - \hat{x}(t_{k-1})\|_2^2 \\ + \alpha_k \|x(t_k)\|_1 \tag{2}$$

where the regularization parameters λ_k and α_k are computed by generalized cross validation [7].

2.2   Empirical Mode Decomposition

The Empirical Mode Decomposition (EMD) is a data-driven time-frequency (T-F) method that allows to analyze multivariate signals in an adaptive way. A nonlinear and non-stationary signal $y(t_k)$ can be decompose into a sum of intrinsic mode functions (IMFs) using EMD and these IMFs satisfies two conditions [12]: first, *Zero mean defined by the symmetry between upper/lower envelopes* and second, *The amount of extrema and zero crossings must differ at most by one or be the same.*

$$y(t_k) = \sum_{i=1}^{N} \gamma_i(t_k) + r(t_k) \tag{3}$$

$\gamma_i(t_k)$ is obtained when EMD is applied over $y(t_k)$ and where i is the intrinsic mode function (IMF). The residual is $r(t_k)$ and N is the number of IMFs. The Hilbert transform can be applied to each IMFs and the instantaneous frequency is computed according to Eq. (4).

$$f_i(t) \triangleq \frac{1}{2\pi} \cdot \frac{d\theta_i(t)}{dt}, \tag{4}$$

being $\theta_i(t)$ the function phase of each IMF calculated from the analytical signal associated. Finally, the instantaneous frequency can be observed in the Hilbert Spectrum.

2.3 Entropy Function for Automatic IMF Selection

The proposed entropy function is the following:

$$e_i = -\sum_k \|\gamma_i(t_k)\|_2^2 \log(\|\gamma_i(t_k)\|_2^2) \tag{5}$$

It is applied over each IMF $\gamma_i(t_k)$ where e_i is the entropy of each IMF, and $e = [e_1 \ldots e_N]$. The estimated EEG signal $\tilde{y}(t_k)$ from IMFs with highest entropy (chosen automatically) is rebuilt according to the measured entropy e_i.

$$\tilde{y}(t_k) = \sum_{i \in O} \gamma_i(t_k) \tag{6}$$

being O the subset of of IMFs whose entropy e_i is over a threshold τ_e computed as follows

$$\tau_e = \frac{\max e - \min e}{2} + \min e \tag{7}$$

3   Experimental Setup

The performance of the aforementioned method is evaluated by using simulated and real EEG signals with epileptic activity. The experimental setup is divided in the following tasks:

1. EEG acquisition or simulation ($y(t_k)$) based on a nonlinear model.
2. Apply EMD on the EEG signal.
3. Optimal selection of IMFs using an entropy based cost function.
4. Reconstruction of a signal $\tilde{y}(t_k)$ based on the optimal selected IMFs according to (7).
5. Brain mapping of the neural activity based on the reconstructed signal.
6. Detection of focal origin of Epileptic seizures is performed by locating the source where the seizure is generated.

   Four methods are considered for brain mapping comparison to evaluate the performance of the proposed algorithm:

1. Brain mapping ($\hat{x}(t_k)$) using the EEG database $y(t_k)$ without EMD.
2. Brain mapping ($\hat{x}_{EMD}(t_k)$) using the reconstructed EEG $\tilde{y}(t_k)$ obtained from EMD standard decomposition and an entropy based IMF selection.
3. Brain mapping ($\hat{x}_W(t_k)$) using the reconstructed EEG $\tilde{y}_W(t_k)$ obtained from Wavelet Transform using Daubechies wavelet and three decompositions levels, where the level with highest energy is selected for reconstruction of the EEG.
4. Brain mapping ($\hat{x}_{WP}(t_k)$) using the reconstructed EEG $\tilde{y}_{WP}(t_k)$ obtained from Wavelet Packets decomposition using Daubechies wavelet and three decompositions levels, where the level with highest entropy is selected for reconstruction of the EEG.

A common procedure to evaluate the performance of brain mapping techniques is by using simulated EEG signals where the underlying brain activity is known. In this case, a measure of the brain mapping quality can be evaluated with the relative error measure [13] as follows:

$$e_s = \sum_k \frac{\|\widehat{x}(t_k) - x(t_k)\|_2^2}{\|x(t_k)\|_2^2} \tag{8}$$

$$e_{EMD} = \sum_k \frac{\|\tilde{x}_{EMD}(t_k) - x(t_k)\|_2^2}{\|x(t_k)\|_2^2} \tag{9}$$

$$e_W = \sum_k \frac{\|\tilde{x}_W(t_k) - x(t_k)\|_2^2}{\|x(t_k)\|_2^2} \tag{10}$$

$$e_{WP} = \sum_k \frac{\|\tilde{x}_{WP}(t_k) - x(t_k)\|_2^2}{\|x(t_k)\|_2^2} \tag{11}$$

being e_s the reconstruction error of the brain mapping estimation $\widehat{x}(t_k)$ resulting from $y(t_k)$, e_{EMD} the reconstruction error of the brain mapping estimation $\tilde{x}_{EMD}(t_k)$ resulting from $y(t_k)$, e_W the reconstruction error of the brain mapping estimation $\tilde{x}_W(t_k)$ resulting from $\tilde{y}_W(t_k)$ and e_{WP} the reconstruction error of the brain mapping estimation $\tilde{x}_{WP}(t_k)$ resulting from $\tilde{y}_{WP}(t_k)$.

3.1 Simulated EEG Signals

For the simulated database (SD-1) a complex nonlinear model of neural activity is used for EEG generation during an epileptic seizure based on [14] as follows

$$\begin{aligned} x(t_k) &= A_1 x(t_{k-1}) + A_2 x(t_{k-2}) \\ &+ A_3 x(t_{k-\tau}) + A_4 x(t_{k-1})^{\circ 2} + A_5 x(t_{k-1})^{\circ 3} + \eta(t_k) \end{aligned} \tag{12}$$

being $A_1 = a_1 I_n$, $A_2 = a_2 I_n$, $A_3 = a_3 I_n$, $A_4 = a_4 I_n$ and $A_5 = a_5 I_n$, where $I_n \in \mathbb{R}^{n \times n}$ is an identity matrix and $a_i \in \mathbb{R}$ are the model parameters which describe the dynamics of the brain activity, where $c_{k-1}^{\circ 2}$ denotes the Hadamard Power. The model parameter are set to $\tau = 20$, $a_1 = 1.0628$, $a_2 = -0.42857$, $a_3 = 0.008$, $a_4 = 0.000143$, $a_5 = -0.000286$, and $\|\eta(t_k)\| \leq 0.05$. The epileptic seizure is simulated at time $t_k = 0.5\,\mathrm{s}$ by modifying the values of a_1 from 1.0628 to 1.3, while a_2 from -0.428 to -1 over the entire diagonal. The simulated EEG $y(t_k)$ is obtained from $x(t_k)$ using (1) where $\epsilon(t_k)$ is set to achieve the Signal-to-Noise Ratios (SNRs) of 0, 5, 10, 15 and 20 dB, the sample rate is 250 Hz, and a number of $d = 128$ electrodes and $n = 8196$ sources are considered.

4 Results

After analyzing the database with the EMD, we obtained 6 IMFs per channel. In the IMF 2 in Fig. 1, it is possible to observe two areas in red that show how

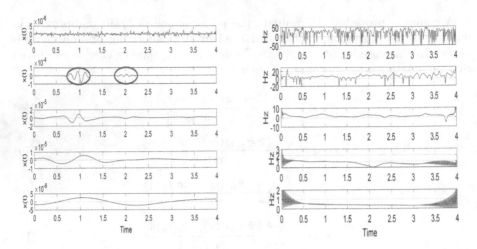

Fig. 1. IMF and IF of y_s for SD-1 using standard EMD

different frequencies (different oscillations) appear in the same IMF. In these IMFs the mode mixing problem is evident. An example of the retained energy and entropy for each IMF is presented in Fig. 2. In this example, the threshold is $\tau_e = 1930.9$ and then the EEG is reconstructed by using the IMF_1 and IMF_2. An example of the Hilbert spectrum is presented in Fig. 3, it is possible to see how the instantaneous frequency is changing with time. As expected, it is observed that the highest frequency is in IMF 1.

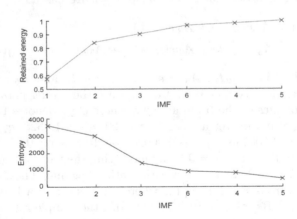

Fig. 2. Retained energy and entropy of $y(t_k)$ for SD-1 using standard EMD

A comparison of the original $y(t_k)$ and reconstructed $\tilde{y}(t_k)$ signals is presented in Fig. 4. The resulting brain mapping for each method is presented in Fig. 5.

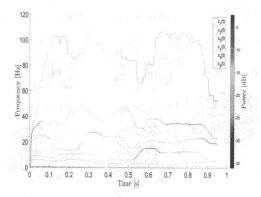

Fig. 3. Hilbert spectrum of $y(t_k)$ for SD-1 using standard EMD

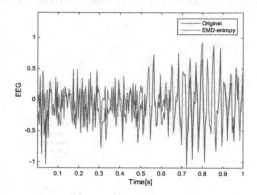

Fig. 4. Comparison of simulated $y(t_k)$ and optimally reconstructed $\tilde{y}(t_k)$ signals for SD-1 by using standard EMD for one channel

Relative error measure is used for evaluation and these results were obtained based on (8) $e_s = 1.3284$, $e_{EMD} = 1.2942$, $e_W = 1.3106$ and $e_{WP} = 1.2007$.

Showing that the best result is obtained for the brain mapping computed from the reconstructed neural activity using entropy-based selection of IMFs. An analysis based on 30 trials for each noise condition is shown in Fig. 6.

As shown in Fig. 6, the best results are achieved by the proposed method of EMD decomposition with automatic selection of relevant IMFs based on the entropy measure (EMD-entropy).

From the above, it can be seen an improvement of the source localization in terms of the relative error. That allows an improvement of epilepsy treatment when a smaller part of the brain needs to be removed.

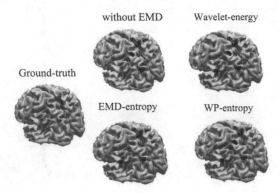

Fig. 5. Comparison of brain mapping obtained for simulated $x(t_k)$, estimated without EMD $\hat{x}(t_k)$ and optimally reconstructed $\tilde{x}(t_k)$ neural activity for SD-1

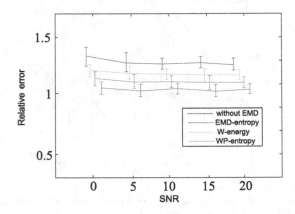

Fig. 6. Relative error comparison for SD-1 under several noise conditions

5   Discussion

First, it must be highlighted that this method allowed to reconstruct the brain activity from IMFs with relevant information for thi application. The problem of mode mixing was shown in [4] and therefore, the conclution was that the EMD does not have a good performance in decomposing and reconstructing the signals with low frequency. In Fig. 1 is possible to observe this phenomena. There are methodologies such as the masking signal [15] or Ensamble Empirical Mode Decomposition (EEMD) that can avoid this problem. However, the mode mixing does not disappear completely. When this technique is compared with strategies very common for this type of application such as Discrete Wavelet Transform (DWT), some factors can affect the performance in epileptic focus localization: the mother wavelet, the level of decomposition, frequency bands, and features. The validation allowed us to calculate the relative error and to affirm that the technique presented provides an accurate detection of sources associated to epileptic seizures.

In Fig. 5 is showed the brain activity reconstruction with raw data (without pre-processing) compared with reconstruction using EMD-entropy, wavelet-energy and WP-entropy. The reconstructions are not perfect, but they are very close to the ground-truth. The estimated relative errors allow to conclude that the estimated EEG from EMD-entropy was the lowest and the second lowest error was for WP-entropy (Fig. 6). The IMFs and levels for WP are selected automatically, and depending of the EEG the number of IMFs or levels for WP could change, but in either case the sources are located very close to ground-truth. The epileptic seizure was simulated at time $t_k = 0.5$ s and although time localization was not one of the purposes of this paper, in the Hilbert spectrum is possible to observe that the instantaneous frequencies associated with each IMF have a change in their behavior at exactly this time, therefore in order to automatically detect the beginning of an epileptic activity, an additional analysis of the instantaneous frequency could be performed.

6 Conclusions

An automatic detection of actives sources is presented. The method is based on EMD and entropy function for brain activity reconstruction. This strategy can be used to support medical diagnosis when is necessary the visual observations of EEG signals. The tests carried out with the simulated databases and the calculation of the relative error measure show an excellent performance of the proposed methodology.

Acknowledgment. This work was carried out during the tenure of an ERCIM 'Alain Bensoussan' Fellowship Programme, also under the funding of the Departamento Administrativo Nacional de Ciencia, Tecnología e Innovación (Colciencias). Research project: 111077757982 "Sistema de identificación de fuentes epileptogénicas basado en medidas de conectividad funcional usando registros electroencefalográficos e imágenes de resonancia magnética en pacientes con epilepsia refractaria: apoyo a la cirugía resectiva" and also this work is also part of the research project"Solución del problema inverso dinámico considerando restricciones espacio-temporales no homogéneas aplicado a la reconstrucción de la actividad cerebral" funded by la Universidad Tecnológica de Pereira under the code E6-17-2.

References

1. Im, C., Seo, J.M.: A review of electrodes for the electrical brain signal recording. Biomed. Eng. Lett. **6**(3), 104–112 (2016)
2. Subha, D.P., Joseph, P.K., Acharya, U.R., Lim, C.M.: EEG signal analysis: a survey. J. Med. Syst. **34**(2), 195–212 (2010)
3. Lin, K.Y., Chen, D.Y., Tsai, W.J.: Face-based heart rate signal decomposition and evaluation using multiple linear regression. IEEE Sens. J. **16**(5), 1351–1360 (2016)

4. Bueno-Lopez, M., Giraldo, E., Molinas, M.: Analysis of neural activity from EEG data based on EMD frequency bands. In: 24th IEEE International Conference on Electronics, Circuits and Systems (ICECS), Vol. 1, Batumi, Georgia, pp. 1–5. IEEE, December 2017
5. Men-Tzung, L., Kun, H., Yanhui, L., Peng, C., Vera, N.: Multimodal pressure-flow analysis: application of hilbert huang transform in cerebral blood flow regulation. EURASIP J. Adv. Signal Process. **2008**(1), 1–15 (2008)
6. Zhang, T., et al.: Multivariate empirical mode decomposition based sub-frequency bands analysis of the default mode network: a resting-state fmri data study. Appl. Inform. **2**(1), 2 (2015)
7. Giraldo-Suarez, E., Martinez-Vargas, J., Castellanos-Dominguez, G.: Reconstruction of neural activity from eeg data using dynamic spatiotemporal constraints. Int. J. Neural Syst. **26**(07), 1–15 (2016)
8. Plummer, C., Harvey, A.S., Cook, M.: EEG source localization in focal epilepsy: where are we now? Epilepsia **49**(2), 201–218 (2008)
9. Costa, M., Goldberger, A.L., Peng, C.K.: Multiscale entropy analysis of complex physiologic time series. Phys. Rev. Lett. **89**, 068102 (2002)
10. Xiang, J., et al.: The detection of epileptic seizure signals based on fuzzy entropy. J. Neurosci. Methods **243**(Suppl. C), 18–25 (2015)
11. Wang, L., et al.: Automatic epileptic seizure detection in EEG signals using multi-domain feature extraction and nonlinear analysis. Entropy **19**(6), 3–17 (2017)
12. Huang, N.E., et al.: The empirical mode decomposition and the Hilbert spectrum for nonlinear and non-stationary time series analysis. In: Proceedings of the Royal Society of London A: Mathematical, Physical and Engineering Sciences, vol. 454, no. 1971, pp. 903–995 (1998)
13. Grech, R., et al.: Review on solving the inverse problem in EEG source analysis. J. NeuroEngineering Rehabil. **5**(1), 25 (2008)
14. Munoz, P., Giraldo, E.: Time-course reconstruction of neural activity for multiples simultaneous source. In: IFMBE Proceedings CLAIB 2016, Vol. 60, Bucaramanga, Colombia, pp. iv/485–iv/488. Springer, October 2016
15. Deering, R., Kaiser, J.F.: The use of a masking signal to improve empirical mode decomposition. In: Proceedings of (ICASSP 2005) IEEE International Conference on Acoustics, Speech, and Signal Processing, 2005, vol. 4, pp. iv/485–iv/488, March 2005

Resting State EEG Based Depression Recognition Research Using Deep Learning Method

Wandeng Mao, Jing Zhu, Xiaowei Li$^{(\boxtimes)}$, Xin Zhang,
and Shuting Sun

School of Information Science and Engineering,
Lanzhou University, Lanzhou, China
{maowd16, zhujing, lixwei, zhangxin17,
sunsht17}@lzu.edu.cn

Abstract. Deep learning has obtained state-of-the-art performance in many fields with its powerful ability of representation learning. However, unlike other data, EEG signals have temporal, spatial and frequency characteristics. For the EEG based depression detection, how to preserve these features when EEG signals are fed into neural networks and select appropriate network structure to extract the corresponding inherent patterns is a problem that needs to be solved. Inspired by the application of deep learning in image processing, we used the distance-based projection method and the non-distance projection method to construct EEG signals as inputs of neural networks. Four different networks were used to extract inherent structure from constructed data. As a result, CNN outperformed other networks, with the highest classification accuracy of 77.20% using the non-distance projection method and 76.14% using the distance-based projection method. The results demonstrate that application of deep learning methods in the research of depression is feasible.

Keywords: Depression detection · EEG · Deep learning

1 Introduction

In the field of human brain research, it has been demonstrated by some studies that there is obvious difference in EEG signals between normal people and depression patients [1]. However, traditional machine learning methods widely used in EEG-based brain research mainly focus on various features extracted from EEG signals. This operation not only requires a large amount of prior knowledges and may leads to the loss of some potential information [2]. In contrast, deep learning can learn representations of data with multiple levels of abstraction and has dramatically improved the state-of-the-art in some domains such as speech recognition, visual object recognition, and object detection [3].

In order to achieve good performance, it is necessary to preserve these features of EEG signals as much as possible when the signals are fed into the deep learning models. In [4], series corresponding to different electrodes are arranged according to the number of electrodes and are constructed as two-dimensional frames containing

S. Wang et al. (Eds.): BI 2018, LNAI 11309, pp. 329–338, 2018.
https://doi.org/10.1007/978-3-030-05587-5_31

two dimensions of electrode number and time. In [5], the authors projected the electrodes from three-dimensional space to two-dimensional plane using polar projection. In [6], the authors arranged electrodes into a two-dimensional plane according to the relative position between the electrode pairs. Adjacent frames were arranged in chronological order into a sequence that represented the temporal features of EEG signals [5, 6].

It is also important to select appropriate deep learning models to extract inherent patterns from EEG signals. CNN (convolutional neural network) [7] was used in [4] and convolution operations across electrodes as well as that operations across time were introduced separately to extract corresponding spatial and temporal patterns. In [6], convolutional neural networks were used to extract inherent features from EEG data. In [5], the authors used methods of Maxpool, Temporal convolution, LSTM and Mixed LSTM/1DConv to process EEG data. In these studies, deep learning obtained better performance than traditional machine learning methods.

There are relatively few studies on the application of deep learning methods to the EEG signals based depression detection. In [8], the authors applied DBN to the detection of depression. However, the authors fed features extracted from EEG signals into DBN instead of other formats of EEG raw data. The operation of feeding features extracted from EEG signals into neural networks is not a reasonable choice because of some disadvantages. Therefore, in the task of depression diagnosis how to input the EEG signals in a reasonable form and use appropriate deep learning methods to process these data is the problem we try to solve in this paper.

In this paper, we collected resting state EEG signals from 34 subjects (17 normal subjects and 17 depressive subjects). Then, two methods described in [5, 6] were used to construct training samples, which were detailed described in Sect. 2.2. Finally, four deep learning models were applied to extract inherent patterns from data sequences and obtain the classification accuracy in task of depression detection, which were show in Sect. 2.3.

2 Subjects and Methods

2.1 Subjects and Experiment

17 depressive subjects and 17 normal subjects participated in the experiment. Before the collection, all participants completed the Mini and PHQ-9 [9] with the help of experienced psychiatrists. Psychiatrists determined whether subjects meet the enrollment conditions based on the interview and scales. We found there were not significant differences in age as well as gender while significant difference in PHQ-9 between the two groups (Table 1).

We collected five-minute resting-state EEG signal from each subject. Recruitment and data collection were completed in Lanzhou University Second Hospital.

Table 1. Basic information of depression group and control group

Variables (Mean ± S.D.)	Depression (n = 17)	Normal controls (n = 17)	$t/\chi2$	p
Gender (Males: Females)	11:6	13:4	$\chi2(1) = 0.452$	0.708
Age (Years)	33.35 ± 12.36	30.29 ± .9.68	t(32) = 0.803	0.428
PHQ-9	17.24 ± 5.21	3.47 ± 2.81	t(32) = − 9.582	0.000*

2.2 Frame Construction Method

Firstly, segments of 270 s in length from 15 s to 285 s was intercepted from five-minute EEG signal recordings. Then, selected signals was filtered to remove high-frequency noise, low-frequency drift and myoelectricity. After that, FastICA was used to remove the interference of the EOG on EEG signals [10]. Finally, Hanning filter was used to extract theta (4–8 Hz), alpha (8–13 Hz) and beta (13–30 Hz) bands, in which previous studies found that there were significant differences between depressed patients and normal people [11]. In order to meet the demand of deep learning for sample size, preprocessed signals were firstly cropped into 0.5-s segments with 0.1 s overlap between adjacent segments, which produced 674 segments per subject. For each segment, Auto-Regress model (AR model) was used to calculate the power spectral density for series of electrodes in each frequency band of theta, alpha and beta.

In order to ensure that inherent spatial and temporal patterns could be extracted from inputs by neural networks, characteristics of EEG signals should be preserved as much as possible when EEG signals were input to neural networks. In this paper, we used the power spectrum density of signals as the data to be processed and arranged adjacent frames into a sequence in chronological order to preserve temporal property. As for spatial information of EEG, we preserved this information by using two methods to project electrode position information from three-dimensional space to two-dimensional plane. One method is based on distance information between electrodes, which is called distance-based projection method, while another method uses relative position information between electrodes without considering distance information, which we refer to as non-distance mapping method.

2.2.1 Distance-Based Projection Method

The cap worn on the head could be viewed approximately as part of a sphere, and electrodes could be considered as points on the surface of the sphere. Based on the assumption, Azimuthal Equidistant Projection (AEP), also known as Polar Projection [12], could be used to project electrode coordinates from three-dimensional space to two-dimensional surface. Compared with using the x and y coordinates in original coordinates directly, this method preserves the topology of electrodes. AEP preserved the distance between electrodes to the central electrode but didn't preserve that information between any other electrode pairs (Fig. 1).

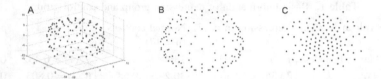

Fig. 1. Electrode locations projections. (A) Location of electrodes in the original 3-D space. (B) Location projections using the x and y coordinates of the original coordinates. (C) Location projections using AEP.

In order to generate data frames with size of 32 × 32, many points were introduced between and around the electrodes. Then, CloughTocher scheme [13] was used to estimate the numerical information of these points according to the information of electrodes around these points (Fig. 2).

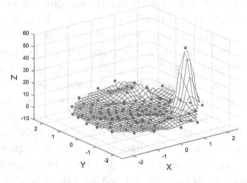

Fig. 2. Interpolation operation. X and Y denoted position information while Z for power spectral density. Red dots represented information of electrodes and the curved surface represented the frames generated by the interpolation operation.

2.2.2 Non-distance Projection Method

The device used in collection contained 128 electrodes, 64 out of which were selected according to the correspondence between the international 10–20 electrode positions with those sensors on the 128-channel HydroCel GSN [14]. Based on the relative position information between electrodes pairs, electrodes were arranged into a two-dimensional plane (Fig. 3). Then power spectrum was filled into the corresponding position to generate frames. This method preserved topological structure of sensors, but only considered relative positional relationship between electrode pairs regardless of corresponding distance information.

By performing the operations described above on different frequency band of subjects, we obtained three types of frames corresponding to theta, alpha and beta band respectively. Frames corresponding to different frequency bands were merged to form 3-channels frames similar to RGB images.

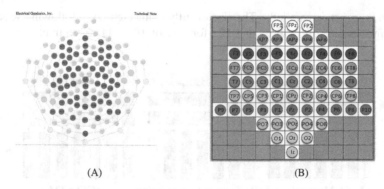

(A)   (B)

Fig. 3. (A) Distribution of electrodes. In this method, we used red painted electrodes to construct two-dimensional frames. (B) The arrangement of electrodes in the data frame. (Color figure online)

2.3 Architecture

The three-dimensional frames generated represent the distribution of EEG information over the scalp. Information changes between adjacent frames can reflect the activity of brain in the temporal dimension, and related temporal features could be used for depression recognition. In this paper, we used 7 temporally consecutive three-channel frames as a sequence to characterize temporal information of EEG signals. There was no overlap between adjacent sequences. In this paper, two different processing strategies were used to deal with temporal information of EEG: (1) We averaged seven frames in a sequence on each of the three channels and finally obtained a three-channel frame, which represented average state of EEG information over a period of time. Since these three-channel frames obtained by means of averaging contained temporal information, we only used ConvNets to extract spatial and frequency features from these frames in the following processing. (2) Sequences consisting of seven frames were fed into neural networks directly. In the following processing, CNN and RNN were used to extract temporal, spatial and frequency patterns from sequences.

For the first strategy, we used convolutional neural networks with relatively simple structure to learn spatial and frequency patterns of EEG. All convolutional layers used small receptive fields of size 3 × 3 and stride of 1 pixel with ReLU activation function. The inputs of convolution layer were padded with 1 pixel to preserve the spatial resolution after convolution. Max-pooling was performed over a 2 × 2 window with stride of 2 pixels [5]. Table 2 showed the ConvNet configuration we used. Besides, batch normalization [15] was added to the output of each convolutional layer. The size of fully connected layers was set to different number according to size of the two frames.

For the other approach, we used three different network architecture to process the frame sequence and evaluated their performance: (1) Max-pooling over time; (2) Temporal convolution; (3) LSTM [16] (Fig. 4). We first used 7 identical 4-layer ConvNets, which had the same configuration as that used previously, to process 7 frames in a sequence parallelly. The size of fully connected layer following was set to 256 for frames size of 32×32 and 128 for size of 10×11 respectively.

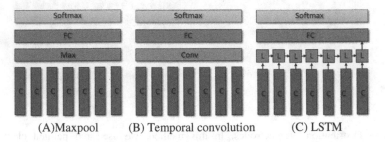

(A)Maxpool   (B) Temporal convolution   (C) LSTM

Fig. 4. Three different network architectures, the notation here is as follow. C: 4-layer ConvNet; Max: maxpool layer across time frame features; FC: fully-connected layer; Conv: 1-D convolution layer across time features; L: LSTM layer.

Table 2. ConvNets Configuration. The convolutional layer parameters were denoted as conv <receptive filed size>-<number of kernels>

A	B
Input (32×32 3-channel frame)	Input (10×11 3-channel frame)
Conv3-32	Conv3-32
Conv3-32	Conv3-32
maxpool	maxpool
Conv3-64	Conv3-64
maxpool	maxpool
Conv3-128	Conv3-128
FC-256	FC-64
softmax	softmax

Max-pooling: Max-pooling was performed over outputs of 7 parallel ConvNets which corresponded to features of different moments over time. Through this operation, the most obvious features of each dimension across time could be obtained.

Temporal Convolution: One-dimensional convolution operations were applied to outputs of previous parallel ConvNets. Using this approach, temporal features could be extracted from a set of feature maps corresponding to different moments. 64 1-D convolution kernels of size 3 and stride 3 were used in this method.

Long Short-Term Memory (LSTM): Long Short-Term Memory (LSTM) model [16] takes sequence as input and can extract inherent structures of inputs. Therefore, LSTM is a reasonable choice in capturing inherent temporal patterns of EEG signals. The architecture used in our research included one LSTM layer which contained 128 cells.

2.4   Training

We trained neural networks mentioned above by minimizing the cross-entropy loss function. As for the optimization algorithm, we selected Adam algorithm [17] with default parameters. The batch size used during training was set to 32. In addition, we used dropout [18] with keeping probability of 0.5 in fully-connected layers to mitigate overfitting. In this paper, we used 8-fold cross-validation, which had better classification performance than 5-fold and 10-fold cross-validation for our dataset, to evaluate the classification accuracy of different methods. The data sets were divided strictly according to the subjects, that is, the data corresponding to one subject didn't appear in the training set and the test set at the same time. Training interaction number was set to 15 epochs because models used could reach convergence before 15 epochs.

3   Results and Discussion

The three-channel frames obtained by two projection methods are shown in Fig. 5. Both methods reflect the distribution and transformation of EEG information over scalp. The distance-based projection method used more electrodes than the non-distance approach. From this point of view, the frames generated by distance-based method contained more information related to brain activity. However, the distance-based method didn't accurately preserve the relative distance between all electrode pairs in the coordinate transformation, which would affect the accuracy of subsequent interpolation operations. Besides, a large number of data points, most of which were obtained by the linear or non-linear combination of the information of surrounding electrodes, were introduced in interpolation operations. Compared with this situation, in the non-distance method value of each electrode was filled into the corresponding position in the frame, which might contribute to neural networks extracting inherent spatial patterns. Besides, there are not coordinate transformation and interpolation operations in non-distance projection method, and data frames generated by it has a smaller size. Therefore, it has lower time cost using data generated by non-distance method in deep learning models for the task of depression detection.

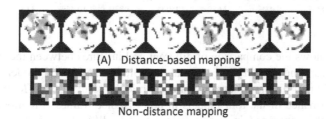

(A)   Distance-based mapping

Non-distance mapping

Fig. 5. An instance of the two projection methods in encoding EEG signals. Pictures shown in A and B are the projection results of the same data sequence by the two methods, respectively.

Table 3 shows the classification results of four network models on two different kinds of EEG frames. CNN architecture has the highest classification accuracy on both data frames, which are 76.14% and 77.20%, respectively. If the test set and training set are not divided strictly according to subjects, that is samples corresponding to one subject may appear in the training set and the test set at the same time, any combination of the four neural networks and the two frame construction methods described in this paper can obtain classification accuracy of more than 99%. Considering the practical application, it is necessary to strictly determine the division of the data set on the depression diagnosis. LSTM layers and convolution across time frames should be able to extract more temporal features which contribute to improving the classification performance than CNN mentioned above which simply averages the frame sequence. In [5], the classification accuracy of LSTM and Temporal convolution, which has the same structure as that used in our research, is higher than other models. This may mean that with the further optimization of parameter configuration, better result will be obtained in the task of depression detection. Besides, for non-distance frames, each of the four network architectures has a larger standard deviation in the classification accuracy, which means that the algorithm is more sensitive to the individual differences of subjects.

Table 3. Classification performance of different structures on distance-based and non-distance projection data. We use dis to represent distance-based data and non-dis to represent non-distance data.

Fold	CNN		Temporal conv		MAX		LSTM	
	Dis	Non-dis	Dis	Non-dis	Dis	Non-dis	Dis	Non-dis
1	74.74%	83.85%	74.33%	77.60%	75.00%	83.07%	74.22%	76.04%
2	85.16%	84.38%	75.78%	77.34%	73.18%	76.04%	85.94%	76.56%
3	72.92%	61.20%	67.45%	43.49%	58.59%	52.08%	71.88%	44.79%
4	85.51%	87.50%	77.08%	87.76%	75.52%	87.24%	74.48%	84.90%
5	78.91%	87.76%	64.32%	77.34%	63.28%	77.86%	69.27%	74.22%
6	66.41%	72.66%	62.50%	72.14%	64.58%	77.08%	72.40%	67.19%
7	78.65%	73.44%	52.34%	63.54%	66.41%	70.83%	57.03%	52.60%
8	66.84%	66.84%	68.40%	68.40%	64.06%	64.06%	62.33%	62.33%
Mean accuracy	76.14% ± 6.86%	77.20% ± 9.43%	67.78% ± 7.68%	70.95% ± 12.38%	67.58% ± 5.83%	73.53% ± 10.45%	70.94% ± 8.08%	67.33% ± 12.59%

Figure 6 shows the comparison of different architectures between the two mapping methods, we can find that CNN, Temporal convolution and MAX models have higher performance in non-distance mapping frames while the results of LSTM are lower. The average performance of the four models in non-distance frames is relatively better. In addition, for the caps used in our experiment, it is difficult to find an arrangement according to which all 128 electrodes are projected to 3-channel frames with preserving electrode topology. We tried to use 93 electrodes in the non-distance mapping method, but didn't achieve better results because of this issue. On the contrary, it is convenient to get the data frames through distance-based mapping as long as original coordinates of electrodes, which are easily acquired, are known.

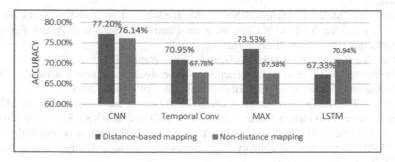

Fig. 6. Performance comparison of different architectures between the distance-based mapping method and the non-distance mapping.

4 Conclusion and Future Work

In this paper, two projection methods are applied to construct EEG signals as inputs of neural networks and four neural networks are used to complete the task of depression detection with constructed data. Combinations of these methods achieve acceptable results, which shows that projection methods can preserve features of EEG as much as possible when constructing inputs for neural networks and the four networks can effectively extract patterns related to depression from EEG. There are both advantages and disadvantages in each of projection methods. We compare these methods from their principle and actual performance, which could provide some suggestions for the use of the two methods.

However, the performance of methods described in this paper don't meet the requirements of clinical application due to some limitations. Besides, the number of available subjects is relatively small due to constraints such as cost and subject matching. In the future we will increase the sample size by collecting EEG signals from more subjects. We will also propose more appropriate deep learning models and parameter configurations to further improve the classification accuracy according to the development of deep learning and EEG research.

Acknowledgement. This work was supported by the National Basic Research Program of China (973 Program) [No. 2014CB744600]; the National Natural Science Foundation of China [Nos. 61632014, 61210010]; the International Cooperation Project of Ministry of Science and Technology [No. 2013DFA11140]; and the Program of Beijing Municipal Science & Technology Commission [No. Z171100000117005].

References

1. Debener, S., Beauducel, A., Nessler, D., Brocke, B., Heilemann, H., Kayser, J.: Is resting anterior EEG alpha asymmetry a trait marker for depression? Neuropsychobiology **41**, 31–37 (2000)
2. Ciregan, D., Meier, U., Schmidhuber, J.: Multi-column deep neural networks for image classification. In: 2012 IEEE Conference on Computer Vision and Pattern Recognition (CVPR), pp. 3642–3649. IEEE (2012)
3. LeCun, Y., Bengio, Y., Hinton, G.: Deep learning. Nature **521**, 436 (2015)
4. Schirrmeister, R.T., et al.: Deep learning with convolutional neural networks for EEG decoding and visualization. Hum. Brain Mapp. **38**, 5391–5420 (2017)
5. Bashivan, P., Rish, I., Yeasin, M., Codella, N.: Learning representations from EEG with deep recurrent-convolutional neural networks. arXiv preprint arXiv:1511.06448 (2015)
6. Carabez, E., Sugi, M., Nambu, I., Wada, Y.: Convolutional neural networks with 3D input for P300 identification in auditory brain-computer interfaces. Comput. Intell. Neurosci. **2017**, 9 (2017)
7. LeCun, Y., Bottou, L., Bengio, Y., Haffner, P.: Gradient-based learning applied to document recognition. Proc. IEEE **86**, 2278–2324 (1998)
8. Cai, H., Sha, X., Han, X., Wei, S., Hu, B.: Pervasive EEG diagnosis of depression using deep belief network with three-electrodes EEG collector. In: 2016 IEEE International Conference on Bioinformatics and Biomedicine (BIBM), pp. 1239–1246. IEEE (2016)
9. Kroenke, K., Spitzer, R.L.: The PHQ-9: a new depression diagnostic and severity measure. Psychiatr. Ann. **32**, 509–515 (2002)
10. Hu, B., et al.: EEG-based cognitive interfaces for ubiquitous applications: Developments and challenges. IEEE Intell. Syst. **26**, 46–53 (2011)
11. Omel'chenko, V., Zaika, V.: Changes in the EEG-rhythms in endogenous depressive disorders and the effect of pharmacotherapy. Hum. Physiol. **28**, 275–281 (2002)
12. Snyder, J.P.: Map Projections–A Working Manual. US Government Printing Office, Washington (1987). https://doi.org/10.3133/pp1395
13. Alfeld, P.: A trivariate clough—tocher scheme for tetrahedral data. Comput. Aided Geom. Des. **1**, 169–181 (1984)
14. Luu, P., Ferree, T.: Determination of the HydroCel Geodesic Sensor Nets' Average Electrode Positions and Their 10–10 International Equivalents. Inc, Technical Note (2005)
15. Ioffe, S., Szegedy, C.: Batch normalization: accelerating deep network training by reducing internal covariate shift. arXiv preprint arXiv:1502.03167 (2015)
16. Hochreiter, S., Schmidhuber, J.: Long short-term memory. Neural Comput. **9**, 1735–1780 (1997)
17. Kingma, D.P., Ba, J.: Adam: A method for stochastic optimization. arXiv preprint arXiv:1412.6980 (2014)
18. Hinton, G.E., Srivastava, N., Krizhevsky, A., Sutskever, I., Salakhutdinov, R.R.: Improving neural networks by preventing co-adaptation of feature detectors. arXiv preprint arXiv:1207.0580 (2012)

Tensor Decomposition for Neurodevelopmental Disorder Prediction

Shah Muhammad Hamdi[1](✉), Yubao Wu[1], Soukaina Filali Boubrahimi[1], Rafal Angryk[1], Lisa Crystal Krishnamurthy[2,3], and Robin Morris[3,4]

[1] Departement of Computer Science, Georgia State University, Atlanta, GA 30302, USA
{shamdi1,ywu28,sfilaliboubrahimi1,rangryk}@gsu.edu
[2] Center for Visual and Neurocognitive Rehabilitation, Decatur, GA 30030, USA
[3] Center for Advanced Brain Imaging, Georgia State University and Georgia Institute of Technology, Atlanta, GA 30302, USA
{lkrishnamurthy,robinmorris}@gsu.edu
[4] Department of Psychology, Georgia State University, Atlanta, GA 30302, USA

Abstract. Functional Magnetic Resonance Imaging (fMRI) has been successfully used by the neuroscientists for diagnosis and analysis of neurological and neurodevelopmental disorders. After transforming fMRI data into functional networks, graph classification algorithms have been applied for distinguishing healthy controls from impaired subjects. Recently, classification followed by tensor decomposition has been used as an alternative, since the sparsity of the functional networks is still an open question. In this work, we present five tensor models of fMRI data, considering the time series of the brain regions as the raw form. After decomposing the tensor using CANDECOMP/PARAFAC (CP) and Tucker decomposition, we compared nearest neighbor classification accuracy on the resulting subject factor matrix. We show experimental results using an fMRI dataset from adult subjects with neurodevelopmental reading disabilities and normal controls.

Keywords: fMRI · Tensor decomposition · Reading disabilities

1 Introduction

Brain Informatics, enriched by the advances of neuroimaging technologies such as Magnetic Resonance Imaging (MRI), Positron Emission Tomography (PET), and Electroencephalography (EEG), pose many challenges to data mining. These imaging modalities are noninvasive methods used to diagnose and investigate neurological and neurodevelopmental disorders. fMRI is a popular brain imaging technique, that records the change in Blood Oxygenation Level Dependent (BOLD) signals in different brain regions over time. Resting-state fMRI-based data analysis has facilitated diagnosis of several neurological and neurodevelopmental diseases such as Alzheimer's, Schizophrenia, Bipolar disorder, Attention-deficit/hyperactivity disorder (ADHD), Autism, and Dyslexia [1,2,5,15].

© Springer Nature Switzerland AG 2018
S. Wang et al. (Eds.): BI 2018, LNAI 11309, pp. 339–348, 2018.
https://doi.org/10.1007/978-3-030-05587-5_32

fMRI data can be represented in various forms, e.g., the sequence of 3D brain volumes over time, multivariate time series, and functional connectivity graphs. Given a training set of fMRI data representations of some human subjects and the associated labels of healthy/diseased, the task of binary classification aims to maximize classification accuracy on test data. Because of the advances in graph mining algorithms, most of the supervised learning studies on fMRI data take functional connectivity graphs (binarized by thresholding) as the inputs and transform the problem into graph classification [1–5]. Graph classification can be addressed by two approaches: structure-based approach and subgraph pattern-based approach. In structure-based approach, node-based features such as degree, PageRank score, and clustering coefficient [1,5] are calculated and each graph is transformed into a vector. In subgraph pattern-based approach [3], discriminative subgraphs are used as features.

When the fMRI data is represented by undirected and unweighted graphs, one big challenge is the correct representation of the graphs. Since the graphs are made by thresholding the functional connectivity matrices (each matrix element denotes the correlation of BOLD time series of two regions of interest or, ROIs), the sparsity of the generated graphs depends on the threshold value. Sparsity affects the performance of both graph classification approaches discussed above. Though most of the data mining papers disregard the edges with negative weights, it is still debated in the neuroscience community whether to keep or discard negative correlations [6].

To address this problem, some recent studies emerged with the idea of tensor-based modeling of fMRI data [7,8]. By stacking the functional connectivity matrices or the multivariate time series of the ROIs of all subjects, a third order tensor can be formed. By decomposing the tensor, we can identify the discriminative representations of subjects, so that subjects with neurological disease and normal controls can be easily separated.

In this work, we apply two well-known tensor decomposition methods, CP and Tucker decomposition, on five different tensor models of fMRI data, and compare the nearest neighbor classification performance on the resulting subject factor matrix. We evaluate the methods on a dataset containing fMRI data of normal adult controls and the subjects with reading disabilities, a neurodevelopmental disorder.

2   Related Work

fMRI data mining research can be divided into three categories: tensor imaging analysis, brain network analysis, and tensor decomposition-based analysis. Tensor imaging analysis deals with the raw fMRI images, i.e., the temporal sequence of brain volumes. Given a set of four-dimensional tensors and their corresponding case/control labels, the classification methods predict the labels of the unlabeled tensors. Vectorizing the tensors causes *curse of dimensionality*. Support Tensor Machine (STM) [9], which is a generalization of the Support Vector Machine (SVM) is proposed to address this issue.

Though the tensor imaging-based classification shows good classification accuracy, this approach could not identify the discriminating features required for interpretation. Wee et al. [1] used functional connectivity networks constructed from fMRI and DTI modalities to distinguish Mildly Cognitive Impaired (MCI) subjects from the healthy controls (MCI is the early stage of Alzheimer's disease). Their approach is an example of a structure-based graph classification approach. Given a functional network, weighted local clustering coefficient of each node is calculated, and the graph is represented by a vector consisting of these local connectivity measures. Then multi-kernel SVM is applied on this vector space. This model gives a ranking of the ROIs in terms of how well they are clustered with respect to other ROIs, which provides a good step towards the interpretability of the discriminating features. Jie et al. [5] presented another structure-based graph classification approach, where they use Weisfeiler-Lehman graph kernel [10] for computing the global connectivity features of each graph, which are used along with a local connectivity feature of weighted local clustering coefficient of each node. Considering the edge weights as the probabilities of the link between two nodes, Kong et al. [4] presented a discriminative subgraph feature selection method based on dynamic programming to compute the probability distribution of the discrimination scores for each subgraph pattern. In some cases of studies of neurological and neurodevelopmental disorders, along with the neuroimaging data, there are additional clinical, serologic and cognitive measures data from each subject that may be available. Cao et al. [3] presented a discriminative subgraph mining algorithm for brain networks which leverages such multiple side views-based data.

Recently, tensor decomposition is used to extract the latent discriminative features of each subject. In [7], tensors are formed by stacking the non-negative connectivity matrices of all subjects. The resulting tensor is decomposed with several constraints such as symmetry of the factor matrix representing the ROI space and orthogonality of the factor matrix representing the subject space in order to maximize the discrimination among the subjects of different classes. In [8], the time-sliced non-negative connectivity matrices are used to make the tensors in order to discover the latent factors of the time windows.

Tensor modeling, i.e., the proper construction of the tensor by stacking different types of data representations, is still a challenging problem. In this work, we present a comparative analysis of different tensor models and show the nearest neighbor classification performance after decomposing the tensors using CP and Tucker decompositions independently.

3   Tensor Decomposition

A multidimensional array is also known as a tensor. An N-th order tensor is the tensor product of N vector spaces, where each vector space has its own coordinate system. Decomposing higher order tensor into lower order tensors is a prominent research problem in mathematics. There are several tensor decomposition algorithms such as CP, Tucker, INDSCAL, PARAFAC2, CANDELINC,

DEDICOM, and PARATUCK2 [11]. In this paper, we consider third order tensors for fMRI data and consider CP and Tucker as the methods of tensor decomposition.

3.1 CP Decomposition

CP decomposition factorizes the tensor into a sum of rank one tensors. Given a third order tensor $\mathcal{X} \in \mathbb{R}^{I \times J \times K}$, where I, J and K denote the indices of tensor elements in three of its modes, CP decomposition factorizes the tensor in the following way.

$$\mathcal{X} \approx \sum_{r=1}^{R} \mathbf{a}_r \ \text{o} \ \mathbf{b}_r \ \text{o} \ \mathbf{c}_r = [\![\mathbf{A}, \mathbf{B}, \mathbf{C}]\!] \tag{1}$$

Here, o denotes the outer product of the vectors. R is a positive integer and also called the tensor rank. $\mathbf{a}_r, \mathbf{b}_r$, and $\mathbf{c}_r$ are vectors, where $\mathbf{a}_r \in \mathbb{R}^I$, $\mathbf{b}_r \in \mathbb{R}^J$, and $\mathbf{c}_r \in \mathbb{R}^K$ for $r = 1, 2, 3, \ldots R$. After stacking those vectors, we can get the factor matrices $\mathbf{A} = [\mathbf{a}_1, \mathbf{a}_2, \ldots \mathbf{a}_R]$, $\mathbf{B} = [\mathbf{b}_1, \mathbf{b}_2, \ldots \mathbf{b}_R]$, and $\mathbf{C} = [\mathbf{c}_1, \mathbf{c}_2, \ldots \mathbf{c}_R]$, where $\mathbf{A} \in \mathbb{R}^{I \times R}$, $\mathbf{B} \in \mathbb{R}^{J \times R}$, and $\mathbf{C} \in \mathbb{R}^{K \times R}$.

3.2 Tucker Decomposition

Tucker decomposition is a form of higher order Principal Component Analysis (PCA). A tensor is decomposed into a core tensor, which is multiplied by a matrix along its each mode. Tucker decomposition of a third order tensor $\mathcal{X} \in \mathbb{R}^{I \times J \times K}$ is given by,

$$\mathcal{X} \approx \mathcal{G} \times_1 \mathbf{A} \times_2 \mathbf{B} \times_3 \mathbf{C} = [\![\mathcal{G}; \mathbf{A}, \mathbf{B}, \mathbf{C}]\!] \tag{2}$$

Here, $\times_n$ denotes mode-n tensor product. $\mathbf{A} \in \mathbb{R}^{I \times P}$, $\mathbf{B} \in \mathbb{R}^{J \times Q}$, and $\mathbf{C} \in \mathbb{R}^{K \times R}$ are the factor matrices. These factor matrices can be thought as the principal components along each mode. The $\mathcal{G} \in \mathbb{R}^{P \times Q \times R}$ is the core tensor and its elements represent the interaction between those principal components.

Both CP and Tucker decomposition can be solved by Alternating Least Squares (ALS) optimization. After a random initialization of all factor matrices, ALS updates one factor matrix while keeping other two as fixed until convergence. The details of ALS optimization for CP and Tucker decomposition can be found in [11].

4   Modeling the fMRI Data in Tensors

In this section, we describe five tensorization schemata for the fMRI data. In Fig. 1, we visualize five models of the tensor. Among these five models, Tensor Model 3 was previously used in the literature [7], while we designed other four for the purpose of comparison. All the models of the tensors are third order. After tensorizing the data, we use CP and Tucker decomposition for computing the factor matrices. For the healthy/disabled prediction, we use only the factor matrix found in *subjects* mode. Factor matrices in other modes such as *ROIs* and *Timestamps* are out of the scope of this work.

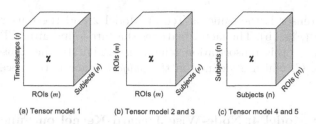

Fig. 1. Dimensions for fMRI data using third order tensor

4.1 Tensor Model 1: Stacked Multivariate Time Series

We have the dataset $D = \{A_1, A_2, \ldots, A_n\}$, where each matrix $A_i \in \mathbb{R}^{m \times t}$ is a multivariate time series, and their corresponding labels of healthy/disabled, which are given by $y_i = \{-1, +1\}$. Here, m denotes the number of ROIs, n denotes the number of subjects, and t denotes the number of time samples. In this tensorization scheme, we simply stack all A_i's together. Therefore, $\mathcal{X} = [A_1; A_2; \ldots, A_n]$ and $\mathcal{X} \in \mathbb{R}^{m \times t \times n}$ (Fig. 1a). After CP decomposition, we get three factor matrices $\mathbf{A}$, $\mathbf{B}$ and $\mathbf{C}$, where $\mathbf{A} \in \mathbb{R}^{m \times R}$, $\mathbf{B} \in \mathbb{R}^{t \times R}$ and $\mathbf{C} \in \mathbb{R}^{n \times R}$. After Tucker decomposition, we get three factor matrices of different number of columns, where $\mathbf{A} \in \mathbb{R}^{m \times P}$, $\mathbf{B} \in \mathbb{R}^{t \times Q}$ and $\mathbf{C} \in \mathbb{R}^{n \times R'}$. Therefore, $\mathbf{C}$ is the factor matrix in the *subject* space, where each row is a vector-based representation of each subject. Then, we split the rows (subjects) into train and test set, concatenate corresponding class label of each training subject, and train a classifier. Finally, we can evaluate the classification performance by predicting the class labels of the test subjects.

4.2 Tensor Model 2: Stacked Functional Connectivity Matrices

For each multivariate time series matrix A_i, we calculate Pearson correlation coefficient between each pair of time series. It gives us functional connectivity matrices $C_1, C_2, \ldots, C_n$, where $C_i \in \mathbb{R}^{m \times m}$. Each matrix C_i is symmetric and can be thought of as an adjacency matrix of an edge-weighted complete graph K_m. By stacking the C_i's one after another, we get a tensor $\mathcal{X} \in \mathbb{R}^{m \times m \times n}$ (Fig. 1b). After CP decomposition we get three factor matrices $\mathbf{A}$, $\mathbf{B}$ and $\mathbf{C}$, where $\mathbf{A} \in \mathbb{R}^{m \times R}$, $\mathbf{B} \in \mathbb{R}^{m \times R}$ and $\mathbf{C} \in \mathbb{R}^{n \times R}$. Since two modes are the same in the third order tensor, after CP decomposition we get two identical factor matrix, i.e., $\mathbf{A} = \mathbf{B}$. The similar case is also found in Tucker decomposition. In this tensor modeling scheme, $\mathbf{C}$ is the necessary subject factor matrix.

4.3 Tensor Model 3: Stacked Non-negative Functional Connectivity Matrices

Here, the matrices $C_1, C_2, \ldots C_n$ are thresholded by keeping only the non-negative matrix elements. Therefore, C_i's do not represent edge-weighted complete graphs, rather they denote weighted and undirected sparse graphs. The shape of the tensor is the same as Tensor Model 2 and the tensor is given by $\mathcal{X} \in \mathbb{R}^{m \times m \times n}$ (Fig. 1b). The factor matrices that are found after CP and Tucker decomposition in this tensorization scheme is similar to the Tensor Model 2. Factor matrix $\mathbf{C}$, which is defined in the *subject* space is the necessary factor matrix.

4.4 Tensor Model 4: Node-Wise Jaccard Kernel on Functional Connectivity Matrices

In this tensor model, we consider each C_i as an edge-weighted complete graph. For each pair of complete graphs, weighted Jaccard is calculated using the vectors represented by each node (vector of each node is found from the weights associated with the adjacent edges of that node). Given two vectors S and T, weighted Jaccard between them is [12]:

$$J(S,T) = \frac{\sum_k min(S_k, T_k)}{\sum_k max(S_k, T_k)} \qquad (3)$$

In Fig. 2, we show two example edge-weighted complete graphs. If g_i^j denotes the node j of graph g_i, then the calculation of node-wise Jaccard between these two edge-weighted complete graphs is as follows.

$$
\begin{aligned}
J(g_1, g_2) &= [J(g_1^A, g_2^A), J(g_1^B, g_2^B), J(g_1^C, g_2^C)] \\
&= [\frac{0.1 - 0.5}{0.2 + 0.3}, \frac{0.1 - 0.6}{0.2 - 0.4}, \frac{-0.5 - 0.6}{0.3 - 0.4}] \\
&= [-0.8, 2.5, 11]
\end{aligned}
$$

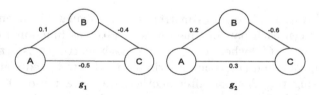

Fig. 2. Two edge-weighted complete graphs.

By calculating the node-wise Jaccard between each pair of complete graphs, we get a tensor $\mathcal{X} \in \mathbb{R}^{n \times n \times m}$ (Fig. 1c). After tensor decomposition, we get two identical factor matrices in the subjects space.

4.5 Tensor Model 5: Node-Wise Jaccard Kernel on Non-negative Functional Connectivity Matrices

In this model, we ignore the negative weighted edges in the complete graphs. Similar to the calculation of node-wise Jaccard described for Tensor Model 4, we get a tensor $\mathcal{X} \in \mathbb{R}^{n \times n \times m}$ (Fig. 1c). We similarly get two identical factor matrices in the subject space after tensor decomposition.

5   Experimental Evaluation

We used *Tensor Toolbox* [13] of MATLAB for computing CP and Tucker decomposition with ALS optimization. In this section, we show the performance of CP and Tucker decomposition on five tensor models.

5.1   Data Collection

In our dataset, the target neurodevelopmental disorder was reading disability. For the study, we used preprocessed resting-state fMRI scans of 27 adult subjects from the local community, 12 labeled as *struggling* readers (below-average reading test scores), and 15 labeled as *typical* (average on reading test).

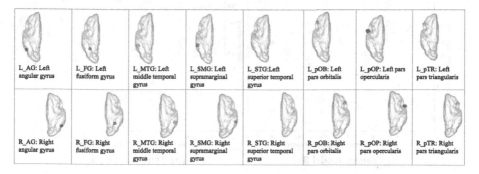

L_AG: Left angular gyrus	L_FG: Left fusiform gyrus	L_MTG: Left middle temporal gyrus	L_SMG: Left supramarginal gyrus	L_STG: Left superior temporal gyrus	L_pOB: Left pars orbitalis	L_pOP: Left pars opercularis	L_pTR: Left pars triangularis
R_AG: Right angular gyrus	R_FG: Right fusiform gyrus	R_MTG: Right middle temporal gyrus	R_SMG: Right supramarginal gyrus	R_STG: Right superior temporal gyrus	R_pOB: Right pars orbitalis	R_pOP: Right pars opercularis	R_pTR: Right pars triangularis

Fig. 3. Visualization of 16 ROIs in left and right hemisphere

The details of the preprocessing steps and experimental settings of this study can be found in [14]. We used 16 ROIs based on apriori reading research [15]. In Fig. 3, we show the visualization of these ROIs in left and right hemisphere of the brain. The preprocessing steps are done using AFNI, FSL, and FreeSurfer. After preprocessing, the number of voxels in one brain volume is $53 \times 63 \times 45$, while the repetition time (time between capturing two whole brain volume) is 2 s. Finally, using Conn [16] the multivariate time series and functional connectivity matrices of each subject are extracted. The length of each time series of each ROI is 125.

5.2   Evaluation Method

After obtaining the subject factor matrix by tensor decomposition, label information is concatenated and labeled representations of the subjects are fed into a classifier with a predefined train/test splitting strategy. In our experiments,

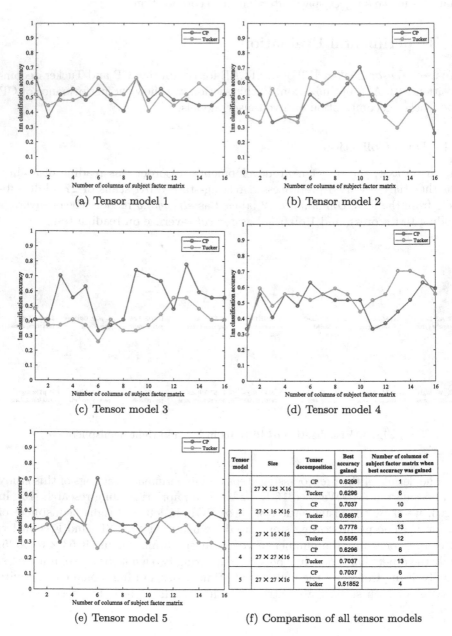

(a) Tensor model 1

(b) Tensor model 2

(c) Tensor model 3

(d) Tensor model 4

(e) Tensor model 5

(f) Comparison of all tensor models

Tensor model	Size	Tensor decomposition	Best accuracy gained	Number of columns of subject factor matrix when best accuracy was gained
1	27 × 125 × 16	CP	0.6296	1
		Tucker	0.6296	6
2	27 × 16 × 16	CP	0.7037	10
		Tucker	0.6667	8
3	27 × 16 × 16	CP	0.7778	13
		Tucker	0.5556	12
4	27 × 27 × 16	CP	0.6296	6
		Tucker	0.7037	13
5	27 × 27 × 16	CP	0.7037	6
		Tucker	0.51852	4

Fig. 4. Comparison of CP and Tucker decomposition on five tensor models on the basis of nearest neighbor classification on subject factor matrix

we chose nearest neighbor classifier (1nn) with Euclidean distance measure in order to evaluate discriminative subject representations in different subject factor matrices. As the train/test sampling method, we chose leave-one-out sampling because of the small number of samples. Leave-one-out is a special case of K-fold cross-validation while K is the number of samples. At i-th iteration of leave-one-out, all samples except the i-th one are used as training samples and the i-th sample is used as the test sample. Finally, the mean accuracy over all iterations is calculated.

5.3 Performances in Different Tensor Models

We varied the number of columns in the subject factor matrix from 1 to 16, since 16 is the minimum number of elements in three modes of the tensor (note that there are 16 ROIs, 27 subjects, and 125 timestamps). In Tucker decomposition, we fixed the number of columns in other factor matrices (ROIs and timestamps) same as their number of rows. Then, we evaluated the subject representations by feeding the subject factor matrix to the nearest neighbor classifier.

Figure 4a–e show the 1nn classification accuracy on the subject factor matrix found after CP and Tucker decomposition. Since ALS implementation of CP and Tucker decomposition is used, the resulting subject factor matrix depends on the initialization of other factor matrices representing ROIs and timestamps. Therefore, if we increase the number of columns of the subject factor matrix, which is equivalent to increasing the number of features in feature space, the classification accuracy may not increase linearly. The nonlinearity of accuracy with respect to the number of columns of the subject factor matrix is also supported by other studies [7,8]. In Fig. 4f, we summarized our findings by presenting the best accuracies along with the number of columns used in the subject factor matrix. Tensor Model 1 results in poor classification accuracy in both CP and Tucker decomposition, because it does not produce partially symmetric tensors like other models. CP decomposition performed better than Tucker decomposition in terms of best accuracy in all tensor models except Tensor Model 4. Tucker decomposition performed poor, especially when the non-negativity constraint is applied on the construction of the tensors (Tensor Models 3 and 5). Using CP decomposition on the tensor constructed from Tensor Model 3, we observed the best accuracy among all the experimental runs, which is 78%. Therefore, we validate the fact that for maximizing the classification accuracy, the combination of Tensor Model 3 and CP decomposition can be a good choice.

6 Conclusion

In this study, we have performed a comparative analysis of the tensor decomposition techniques for fMRI data. We evaluated five different tensor models, and showed the nearest neighbor classification accuracy on the subject factor matrix generated by CP and Tucker decomposition.

In the future, we aim to study the interpretability of the features (columns) of the factor matrices. Leveraging other factor matrices of ROIs and timestamps, and using them along with the subject factor matrix can result in more robust subject-based representations.

References

1. Wee, C.-Y., et al.: Identification of MCI individuals using structural and functional connectivity networks. Neuroimage **59**(3), 2045–2056 (2012)
2. Cao, B., et al.: Identification of discriminative subgraph patterns in fMRI brain networks in bipolar affective disorder. In: Guo, Y., Friston, K., Aldo, F., Hill, S., Peng, H. (eds.) BIH 2015. LNCS (LNAI), vol. 9250, pp. 105–114. Springer, Cham (2015). https://doi.org/10.1007/978-3-319-23344-4_11
3. Cao, B., Kong, X., Zhang, J., Philip, S.Y., Ragin, A.B.: Mining brain networks using multiple side views for neurological disorder identification. In: 2015 IEEE International Conference on Data Mining (ICDM), pp. 709–714. IEEE (2015)
4. Kong, X., Yu, P.S.: Semi-supervised feature selection for graph classification. In: Proceedings of the 16th ACM SIGKDD International Conference on Knowledge Discovery and Data Mining. pp. 793–802. ACM (2010)
5. Jie, B., Zhang, D., Gao, W., Wang, Q., Wee, C.-Y., Shen, D.: Integration of network topological and connectivity properties for neuroimaging classification. IEEE Trans. Biomed. Eng. **61**, 576–589 (2014)
6. Zhu, Y., Cribben, I.: Graphical models for functional connectivity networks: best methods and the autocorrelation issue. bioRxiv, p. 128488 (2017)
7. Cao, B., et al.: t-BNE: tensor-based brain network embedding. In: SIAM (2017)
8. Cao, B., Lu, C.-T., Wei, X., Yu, P.S., Leow, A.D.: Semi-supervised tensor factorization for brain network analysis. In: Frasconi, P., Landwehr, N., Manco, G., Vreeken, J. (eds.) ECML PKDD 2016, Part I. LNCS (LNAI), vol. 9851, pp. 17–32. Springer, Cham (2016). https://doi.org/10.1007/978-3-319-46128-1_2
9. Tao, D., Li, X., Hu, W., Maybank, S., Wu, X.: Supervised tensor learning. In: 5th IEEE International Conference on Data Mining. IEEE (2005)
10. Shervashidze, N., Schweitzer, P., Leeuwen, E.J.V., Mehlhorn, K., Borgwardt, K.M.: Weisfeiler-lehman graph kernels. J. Mach. Learn. Res. **12**, 2539–2561 (2011)
11. Kolda, T.G., Bader, B.W.: Tensor decompositions and applications. SIAM Rev. **51**(3), 455–500 (2009)
12. Huang, A.: Similarity measures for text document clustering. In: Proceedings of the 6th New Zealand Computer Science Research Student Conference (NZCSRSC 2008), Christchurch, New Zealand, p. 4956 (2008)
13. Bader, B.W., Kolda, T.G., et al.: Matlab tensor toolbox version 2.6, February 2015. http://www.sandia.gov/tgkolda/TensorToolbox/index-2.6.html
14. Krishnamurthy, V., et al.: Retrospective correction of physiological noise: impact on sensitivity, specificity, and reproducibility of resting-state functional connectivity in a reading network model. Brain Connect. **8**, 94–105 (2017)
15. Martin, A., Schurz, M., Kronbichler, M., Richlan, F.: Reading in the brain of children and adults: A meta-analysis of 40 functional magnetic resonance imaging studies. Hum. Brain Map. **36**(5), 1963–1981 (2015)
16. Whitfield-Gabrieli, S., Nieto-Castanon, A.: CONN: a functional connectivity toolbox for correlated and anticorrelated brain networks. Brain Connect. **2**(3), 125–141 (2012)

Feature Selection and Imbalanced Data Handling for Depression Detection

Marzieh Mousavian[1]([✉]), Jianhua Chen[1], and Steven Greening[2]

[1] Division of Computer Science and Engineering, School of EECS,
Louisiana State University, Baton Rouge, LA, USA
mmousa4@lsu.edu
[2] Psychology Department, Louisiana State University, Baton Rouge, LA, USA

Abstract. Major Depressive Disorder (MDD) is the most common disorder worldwide. Accurate detection of depression is a challenging problem. Machine learning-based automated depression detection provides useful assistance to the clinicians for effective depression diagnosis. One of the most fundamental steps in any automated detection is feature selection and investigation of the most relevant features. Studies show that regional volumes of the brain are affected in response to depression. Regional volumes are considered as features. The gray matter volumes' correlation with depression and the most effective gray volumes for depression detection is investigated in this study. Various feature selection techniques are studied, along with the investigation on the importance of resampling to handle imbalanced data, which is typically the case for depression detection, as the number of depressed instances is commonly a fraction of the entire data size. Experimental results using Random Forests (RF) and support vector machines (SVM) with a Gaussian kernel (RBF) as classifiers show that feature selection followed by data resampling gives superior performance measured by Area Under the ROC Curve (AUC) as well as prediction accuracy, and RF outperforms SVM for the depression detection task.

Keywords: Depression detection · Feature selection · Imbalanced data

1 Introduction

Depression or major depressive disorder is characterized by a persistent low mood [1]. Depression is the most common mental disorder worldwide [2] and its lifetime prevalence is 17% [3]. It significantly affects the quality of life and causes social and economic losses [1]. One of the main steps of depression detection is finding the most relevant features. Feature selection techniques are useful for accurate detection and prediction of depression at an individual patient.

Accurate detection and prediction of depression at an individual patient is a challenging problem. The diagnosis of MDD is mostly based on clinical signs and symptoms and there is a lack of neurobiological markers [4]. Neuro-biological markers would support diagnostic system and treatment decision. In practice, depression is mostly diagnosed by a clinical interview by considering some questions. The questions assess the typical symptoms of depression to measure the severity and depth of

© Springer Nature Switzerland AG 2018
S. Wang et al. (Eds.): BI 2018, LNAI 11309, pp. 349–358, 2018.
https://doi.org/10.1007/978-3-030-05587-5_33

depression symptoms [5]. Aaron Beck created the questions that are called Beck Depression Inventory (BDI) test. Using machine learning and automated method for depression detection is beneficial to help experts recognizing depression. Thus, an automatic medical diagnostic system would aid medical experts in their decision-making process [2]. One of the fundamental steps to detect depression accurately is choosing the most relevant features. Therefore, it is essential to use dimensionality reduction techniques and choose the best features.

Structural MRI (sMRI) is a non-invasive technique to study the brain structure. sMRI volume analysis of brain regions helps recognizing depressed versus non-depressed patients. Studies show that regional volumes of the brain are affected during the depression. According to Costafreda et al. [4] "In depression, volumetric and cellular deficits have most consistently been identified in the hippocampus, but as well in the anterior and posterior cingulate, orbitofrontal, lateral temporal and occipital cortices, and amygdala". Brain volume changes occur during the depression in the hippocampus, amygdala, anterior cingulate cortex, orbitofrontal cortex, dorsolateral prefrontal cortex, subgenual prefrontal cortex, putamen, caudate, and in the cerebrospinal fluid (CSF) [2]. Gray matter volume reductions have been found in anterior cingulate, orbitofrontal cortex, hippocampus and basal ganglia [6].

In this study, various dimensionality reduction techniques are applied to the data to find the best technique with the best classification result. Moreover, a support vector machine (SVM) is applied as a classifier for the selected features to investigate the prediction capability. The preprocessed neuroimaging scan's gray matter volumes for each region are referred to as features.

2 Related Works

Brain characteristics associated with depression are probed with different MRI modalities in machine learning literature. MRI modalities are generally categorized into structural and functional imaging methods [3]. Structural imaging is the most common modalities which are separated into T1-weighted and T2-weighted methods and Diffusion Tensor Imaging (DTI). Each method specialized for a different aspect of the brain [3].

In the literature of machine learning on sMRI for depressed patients, most studies had a limited small sample size, and features are extracted from T1-weighted images to model depression. In other words, features are chosen from anatomical changes as a biomarker for depression [3].

The available individual depression detection studies based on sMRI have utilized different features for detection. The features used were voxel-based morphometry, brain shape, and voxels intensity values [2]. Kipli and Kouzani [2] used brain sMRI volumetric features which refers to the feature measurement of the volume of selected brain regions and is carried out by summing all voxels within the traced regions of interest (ROIs). They used an ensemble of feature selection methods that combines wrapper and filter approaches to reduce features dimensionality based on feature degree of contribution [2].

2.1   Feature Selection

Feature selection is a fundamental step before applying a predictive model [7]. Feature selection methods identify the most relevant features and reduce the number of features while the most significant aspects of data are preserved [2, 3]. Brain regions identified during feature selection may offer an insight into effective brain regions in depression [7]. Various techniques are used for dimensionality reduction [8]. Feature selection techniques are consisting of either feature transformation into a lower dimensional space or selecting a subset of features without a transformation [9]. Unlike transforming features, choosing a subset of features does not change the representation of features [8].

Selecting a subset of features are widely separated into 'filter', 'wrapper' and 'embedded' methods on literature. These methods utilize feature ranking. Filter method provides a ranking of features, while wrapper and embedded methods give the best subset of features [2]. Filter techniques such as t-tests, F-statistic (ANOVA) and Pearson correlation coefficient use simple statistical measures (e.g. mean, variance, correlation coefficients) to rank features according to their relevance. Second, wrapper techniques use an objective function from a classification or regression machine learning model to rank features [7]. Lastly, embedded methods select relevant features as 'part' of the machine learning process by enforcing certain 'penalties' on a machine learning model [7]. Random forest (RF) and extra-trees (ET) are adopted as examples of embedded methods [10].

Transforming features methods contain principal component analysis (PCA) and autoencoders. PCA uses a linear combination of the data, however, autoencoder can use a non-linear combination [11]. The network structure can be designed that center of the network be smaller than the input [12].

2.2   Classifier

Most past studies on depression prediction have used support vector machine as a learning method for classification [3]. Support vector machine benefits from properties such as a reliable theoretical foundation and its insensitivity to high-dimensional data [3]. However, there are other methods that may perform equally well or better [3]. Therefore, other methods have been proposed in literature [6].

3   Our Method

The overall procedure for depression detection includes preprocessing and feature extraction, normalization, feature selection, balancing dataset, training the model, and classification. Figure 1 shows a schema of a classification task. In our study, we discuss 11 methods for feature subset selection and two methods for feature transformation. Then, we balance the dataset and apply the classification methods to classify depressed versus controls. Finally, we compare the results of classification using different feature selection methods.

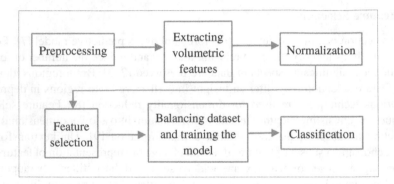

Fig. 1. Overall schema of classification of depressed versus non-depressed

3.1 Data

Data is provided from the NKI-Enhanced dataset (publicly available at http://fcon _1000.projects.nitrc.org/indi/pro/nki.html). A T1-weighted structural scan was acquired (MPRAGE: TR = 2500 ms; TE = 3.5 ms; flip angle 8°; FoV = 256 mm; voxel size 1 × 1 × 1 mm; full details at [5].

Preprocessing. Raw images are preprocessed using FreeSurfer software and volumetric attributes are extracted from sMRI data. White matter volume is discarded to focus on the gray matter in our study. In other words, redundant features are discarded and features that are related to gray matter regions are kept. Without discarding noisy feature, the classifier has a risk of overfitting, which means the machine learning model with poor generalization ability [7]. Table 1 shows datasets properties after preprocessing. 90 volumetric attributes are extracted from gray matter volume of the brain. Then data is normalized as describe under normalization section.

Table 1. Data structure contains 90 features initially and 420 records which includes 76 depressed patients and 344 control

Database	#Depressed	#Non-depressed	Total	Initial # of features
	76	344	420	90

Furthermore, the classification of depressed versus non-depressed is built out of BDI feature. The BDI threshold for classifying patients to depressed versus non-depressed is chosen 11 by the psychology expert on the authors' team. In other words, patients with BDI grater or equal to 11 are classified as depressed and others classified as non-depressed. Particularly, depressed would be the positive sample and is labeled by one while non-depressed is labeled as zero. The number of depressed versus non-depressed and initial number of features in our datasets is shown in Table 1.

Normalization. Due to the variability of head size between subjects that lead to the variability in total and regional brain volume, it is important to measure total intracranial volume (TIV equivalently intra-cranial volume: ICV). Studies show that adjustments for TIV increase the power of calculation for brain volumes [15]. To reduce the variability of head size between individuals, the gray matter volumes are divided by TIV in our study.

The next step is to normalize the data. In simple words, normalization adjusts different scales to a common scale. Feature scaling method is used for normalizing the features in the range [0, 1]. Formula 1 is used for rescaling the features.

$$(x - x_{min})/(x_{max} - x_{min}) \tag{1}$$

Next, feature selection techniques are used to get the most relevant features.

3.2 Feature Selection

Having irrelevant features reduce the accuracy of the model, therefore, it is essential to find the most important features. Feature selection techniques are used to find the most relevant features. It consists of selecting a subset of features and feature transformation. Selecting a subset of features involves feature ranking, and frequency calculation of features. Moreover, feature transformation method use a combination of features and create a new feature out of them to reduce the dimensionality.

We applied 13 feature selection methods in our study. These methods are commonly used in the literature. We applied ANOVA and Chi-square which is considered as Filter methods. Also recursive feature elimination (RFE) is utilized along with several estimators such as SVM, Random Forest Classifier, Random Forest regressor, Gradient Boosting Regressor, Linear regression and Logistic Regression as wrapper techniques. RFE is used along with 5-fold cross validation. Moreover, Extra Tree Classifier and Random Forest are selected as embedded techniques. Furthermore, PCA, and autoencoder are chosen to automatically transform data to a lower dimensional space. PCA learns the most important aspects of the whole dataset and autoencoder learns the low dimensional representation of data in each split on train data. In our method, we kept the ten best features of each of the 13 feature selection methods.

Our proposed method, based on voting, for selecting the top features proceeds as follows. Ten highest ranked features of each of the 11 methods are chosen, and the frequency of these features on the top 10 list are counted. Then, the top 10 most frequent features are chosen as our final features. The frequency of highest rank features is reported in Table 2. Furthermore, we compare the performance of our voting-based feature selection method with the 13 methods under result section.

After the feature selection step, the next step is imbalanced data handling which is done using oversampling or class weights. Then, data is classified using SVM and random forest classifier and the model is evaluated using 10-fold cross-validation. Evaluation metrics averaged over all 10 folds are reported.

3.3 Resampling

In most of the neurological studies, the number of positive samples is less than the number of negative samples. Therefore, the data is imbalanced. To deal with handling

Table 2. The most common features with their frequencies in 11 feature selection methods

Important features	Frequency
Left-Inf-Lat-Vent	6
Left-Accumbens-area	6
Left-Cerebellum-White-Matter	6
Right-Accumbens-area	5
Left-Cerebellum-Cortex	5
Brain-Stem	5
lh_inferiorparietal_volume	4
Left-Caudate	4
Left-Hippocampus	4
Left-Pallidum	4

imbalance data, there are two solutions. First, modifying training data using resampling methods or reweighting the samples. Second, changing the performance metrics. For imbalanced dataset, performance metrics F1-score (a weighted average over precision and recall) or area under Receiver Operating Characteristic (ROC) curve (AUC) could be a better measure for classifier quality [13]. Intuitively, AUC is the probability that a classifier will rank a randomly chosen positive example higher than a randomly chosen negative instance. In practice, the value of AUC varies between 0 and 1. Also, F1-score conveys the balance between precision and recall and reaches its best value at 1 and worst score at 0 [14]. We benefit from oversampling the minority class for classification in this study. Also, we report AUC as an evaluation metric.

3.4 Classification

For the classification performance evaluation, SVM with 'RBF' kernel and random forest (RF) are used as classifiers. We use stratified 10-fold cross validation which guarantee each fold preserves the percentage of samples for each class. Area under roc curve (AUC) and prediction accuracy are chosen for validation.

RBF is a Gaussian kernel with width parameter (gamma) and gamma shows the influence of each sample. The kernel comes in Formula 2. γ stands for gamma and must be greater than zero. In this study, we use default gamma which is 1/n features. Overestimating gamma leads to lose the non-linearity and behave linearly [16].

$$e^{-\gamma|x-x''|^2} \tag{2}$$

Random forest is an ensemble method which fits several decision trees to the data and average over trees. It uses a subset of data for each tree. In our study, subsamples are chosen without replacement. Random forest has the ability of overfitting. In our study, to avoid overfitting, minimum number of samples requires to be at each leaf is set to 10, and maximum depth of the tree is chosen 7.

4 Experimental Results and Discussion

An experiment is done using python 3.6. Python contains 'Skicit_learn 0.19.1' library which is used for feature selection and classification. Raw sMRI images are preprocessed using FreeSurfer software and volumetric features are extracted from different regions of interests (ROIs). Next, data is normalized due to the variety of head size. Different feature selection methods are utilized and features that are important in classification are identified. We suggest capturing features with the most repetitions among all methods. Table 2 shows the list of the most common features with their frequencies in the mentioned feature selection methods.

The ten most frequent features are as follows. Temporal horn of left lateral ventricle (Left-Inf-Lat-Vent), left nucleus accumbens (Left-Accumbens-area), and white matter of left hemisphere of cerebellum (Left-Cerebellum-White-Matter) are the most repetitive ones. Right nucleus accumbens (Right-Accumbens-area), left cerebellar cortex (Left-Cerebellum-Cortex), and Brain-Stem are ranked as the second frequent features. Moreover, left inferior parietal lobule (lh_inferiorparietal_volume), left caudate nucleus (Left-Caudate), left hippocampus proper (Left-Hippocampus), and left globus pallidus (Left-Pallidum) are stayed in the third place.

Having important features, our dataset needs to be balanced by using oversampling and adjusting class weight for depressed patients. Therefore, the new database is balanced and does not suffer from imbalanced problem. It is important to adjust the number of samples in each class, after applying feature selection. Otherwise, feature selection's assumption would be violated. In other words, feature selection methods assume that data is identically independent, however, applying oversampling leads to dependency of data. Tables 3 and 4 represents various feature selection methods along with our proposed method. Based on the voting method, ten features with the highest frequencies are chosen as important features. We apply random forest and SVM-RFE classifier on the balanced dataset. Also, area under roc curve and accuracy rate are reported as the evaluation metrics. Table 3 is the result of random oversampling, and Table 4 shows applying weights to the minority class.

It is important to note that due to the data imbalance issue, it may not be a good idea to focus on the accuracy as the major metrics for performance. Here the dataset has about 80% class zero objects. A base classifier declaring every record to be the majority class would have an accuracy of about 0.82. But such a classifier is hardly useful at all. In contrast, AUC, in this case, is a better criterion.

Results are the average over 10-fold cross-validation and are rounded to two decimal digits. Results illustrate that random forest classifier works well on our data. Also, voting method evaluation shows that its values are among the top three performances, although it is not the best feature selection method. Table points that RFE with linear SVM kernel and RFE along with random forest classifier as a kernel, works better than our voting method. However, proposed method performs better than most of the discussed feature selection methods.

Table 4 displays the performance of classifiers on the data which is balanced using class weights. Weight is chosen as 4.52 for depressed patients. The reason is 4.52 is the ratio of the number of samples from control class to number of samples from depressed

Table 3. Different feature selection methods with area under ROC curve and accuracy as evaluation metrics using random oversampling to adjust number of samples

Random oversampling	Random forest classifier		SVM (RBF)	
Feature selection	AUC	Accuracy	AUC	Accuracy
ANOVA	0.88	0.8	0.36	0.35
Chi-squared	0.89	0.8	0.3	0.32
RFE-SVM (C = 1)	0.86	0.78	0.3	0.32
RFE-SVM (C = 100)	**0.91**	**0.83**	0.28	0.33
RFE- Gradient boosting regressor	0.92	0.82	0.28	0.32
RFE- Random forest regressor	**0.91**	**0.83**	0.31	0.39
RFE-Random forest classifier	0.89	0.8	0.28	0.32
RFE- Linear regression	0.9	0.81	0.34	0.31
RFE- Logistic regression	0.89	0.8	0.28	0.32
Extra tree classifier	0.9	0.81	0.34	0.35
Random forest classifier	0.9	0.81	0.3	0.33
PCA	0.86	0.78	0.27	0.32
Autoencoder	0.47	0.59	0.47	0.48
Proposed voting method	**0.9**	**0.82**	**0.31**	**0.32**

Table 4. Different feature selection methods with area under ROC curve and accuracy as evaluation metrics using class weight to ensure the balanced dataset

Class-weight	Random forest classifier		SVM(RBF)	
Feature selection	AUC	Accuracy	AUC	Accuracy
ANOVA	0.54	0.68	0.52	0.56
Chi-squared	0.5	0.65	0.47	0.56
RFE-SVM (C = 1)	0.51	0.6	0.48	0.56
RFE-SVM (C = 100)	0.55	0.67	0.5	0.56
RFE- Gradient boosting regressor	0.52	0.67	0.38	0.56
RFE- Random forest regressor	0.5	0.66	0.38	0.56
RFE-Random forest classifier	0.56	0.68	0.39	0.56
RFE- Linear regression	**0.65**	**0.7**	0.52	0.56
RFE- Logistic regression	0.44	0.64	0.39	0.56
Extra tree classifier	0.5	0.64	**0.48**	**0.56**
Random forest classifier	0.46	0.65	**0.48**	**0.56**
PCA	0.52	0.68	0.38	0.56
Autoencoder	0.5	0.56	0.47	0.56
Proposed voting method	**0.56**	**0.69**	**0.5**	**0.56**

class. Results indicate that random forest is a better classifier than SVM. Also, comparing Tables 3 and 4 demonstrates that balancing data using random oversampling leads to better result than using class weights.

Table 5 displays baseline classifiers. First baseline classifier always classifies records to majority class. However, second baseline classifier directly applies to the imbalanced data with initial number of features. Comparing baseline with oversampling and adjusting weight results indicate that using random oversampling along with random forest as the classifier performs better than baselines.

Table 5. Baseline classifiers. Baseline 1 is a classifier that always predict the majority class (non-depressed), and baseline2 shows RF and SVM classifiers that apply to the raw data

	Classifier	AUC	Accuracy
Baseline 1	Dummy classifier that predicts everyone as 0	0.5	0.82
Baseline 2	Random forest classifier	0.48	0.82
	SVM classifier	0.45	0.82

5   Conclusions and Future Work

Depression is a mood disorder and is among highly prevalence disorders. Detecting the disorder in early stages can improve treatment process. Detecting depression, it is essential to find the most relevant feature. These features are the result of feature selection methods. Handling imbalanced data is applied using random oversampling and by adjusting class weights. SVM classifier with RBF kernel and random forest classifiers are performed. Classification performance is reported using the average of 10-fold cross-validation.

As a future work, we will apply different classification techniques to improve the classification accuracy and area under ROC curve. Also, we will apply deep learning methods and improve the depression detection.

References

1. Gong, Q., et al.: Prognostic prediction of therapeutic response in depression using high-field MR imaging. NeuroImage **55**, 1497–1503 (2011)
2. Kipli, K., Kouzani, A.: Degree of contribution (DoC) feature selection algorithm for structural brain MRI volumetric features in depression detection. Int. J. Comput. Assist. Radiol. Surg. **10**, 1003–1016 (2014)
3. Patel, M., Khalaf, A., Aizenstein, H.: Studying depression using imaging and machine learning methods. NeuroImage: Clin. **10**, 115–123 (2016)
4. Costafreda, S., Chu, C., Ashburner, J., Fu, C.: Prognostic and diagnostic potential of the structural neuroanatomy of depression. PLoS ONE **4**, e6353 (2009)
5. Fcon_1000.projects.nitrc.org. Accessed 28 Mar 2018
6. Mwangi, B., Matthews, K., Steele, J.: Prediction of illness severity in patients with major depression using structural MR brain scans. J. Magn. Reson. Imaging **35**, 64–71 (2011)

7. Mwangi, B., Tian, T., Soares, J.: A review of feature reduction techniques in neuroimaging. Neuroinformatics **12**, 229–244 (2013)
8. Hira, Z., Gillies, D.: A review of feature selection and feature extraction methods applied on microarray data. Adv. Bioinf. **2015**, 1–13 (2015)
9. Feature Selection/Extraction Dimensionality Reduction. http://vision.psych.umn.edu/users/schrater/schrater_lab/courses/PattRecog09/Lec17PattRec09.pdf. Accessed 28 Mar 2018
10. Hemphill, E., Lindsay, J., Lee, C., Măndoiu, I., Nelson, C.: Feature selection and classifier performance on diverse bio- logical datasets. BMC Bioinf. **15**, S4 (2014)
11. Geng, X., Xu, J.: Application of autoencoder in depression diagnosis. In: 3rd International Conference on Computer Science and Mechanical Automation, CSMA (2017)
12. Bosch, N., Paquette, L.: Unsupervised Deep Autoencoders for Feature Extraction with Educational Data (2018)
13. Unbalanced data and cross-validation|Kaggle. https://www.kaggle.com/questions-and-answers/27589. Accessed 28 Mar 2018
14. Scikit-learn-contrib/imbalanced-learn. https://github.com/scikit-learn-contrib/imbalanced-learn. Accessed 28 Mar 2018
15. Malone, I., et al.: Accurate automatic estimation of total intracranial volume: a nuisance variable with less nuisance. NeuroImaging **104**, 366–372 (2015)
16. Amami, R., Ayed, D.B., Ellouze, N.: Practical selection of SVM supervised parameters with different feature representations for vowel recognition. arXiv preprint arXiv:1507.06020 (2015)

Deep Convolutional Neural Networks for Automated Diagnosis of Alzheimer's Disease and Mild Cognitive Impairment Using 3D Brain MRI

Jyoti Islam[✉] and Yanqing Zhang

for the Alzheimer's Disease Neuroimaging Initiative*

Georgia State University, Atlanta, GA 30302, USA

jislam2@student.gsu.edu

Abstract. We consider the automated diagnosis of Alzheimer's Disease (AD) and Mild Cognitive Impairment (MCI) in 3D structural MRI brain scans. We develop an efficient deep convolutional neural network (CNN) based classifier by analyzing 3D brain MRI. The proposed model extracts features from the MRI scans and learns significant information related to Alzheimer's Disease (AD) and Mild Cognitive Impairment (MCI). We perform motion correction, non-uniform intensity normalization, Talairach transform, intensity normalization, and skull-stripping in the raw MRI scans. After that several 2D slices are generated, and center patch is cropped from the slices before passing them to the CNN classifier. Besides, we demonstrate ways to improve the performance of a CNN classifier for AD and MCI diagnosis. We conduct experiments using Alzheimer's Disease Neuroimaging Initiative (ADNI) dataset for classification of the AD, MCI and CN (normal/healthy controls) to evaluate the proposed model. The proposed model achieves 94.97% accuracy for AD/CN classification and 91.98% accuracy for AD/MCI classification outperforming baseline models and several competing methods from other studies.

Keywords: Deep learning · Convolutional neural network Alzheimer's Disease · MRI · Brain imaging

1 Introduction

Alzheimer's Disease (AD) is a progressive neurodegenerative disease that causes people to lose their memory, mental functions and ability to continue daily activities. AD is the most prevailing type of dementia, and Mild Cognitive Impairment

*Data used in preparation of this article were obtained from the Alzheimer's Disease Neuroimaging Initiative (ADNI) database (adni.loni.usc.edu). As such, the investigators within the ADNI contributed to the design and implementation of ADNI and/or provided data but did not participate in analysis or writing of this report. A complete listing of ADNI investigators can be found at: http://adni.loni.usc.edu/wp-content/uploads/how_to_apply/ADNI_Acknowledgement_List.pdf.

S. Wang et al. (Eds.): BI 2018, LNAI 11309, pp. 359–369, 2018.
https://doi.org/10.1007/978-3-030-05587-5_34

(MCI) is considered as the earlier stage of AD [1]. It is crucial to detect patient at MCI stage before the disease progress further as there is no cure for AD. Earlier diagnosis can help for proper treatment and prevent brain tissue damage. Magnetic Resonance Imaging (MRI) is a technique that creates a 3D representation of brain using magnetic fields and radio waves. Nowadays it is a standard practice to use MRI to detect changes in the brain caused by AD. Figure 1 shows some brain MRI images with different AD stages. The Hippocampus and cerebral cortex of the brain are shrunk, and ventricles are enlarged in the brain of AD patient. Hippocampus reduction causes cell loss and damages the synapses and neuron ends [21]. Structural MRI (sMRI) is helpful for measuring these progressive changes in the brain due to the AD. Deep learning technologies have achieved significant success in medical image analysis. We develop a deep convolutional neural network that learns essential features directly from the input MRI data to distinguish between CN, MCI and AD patients. We focus on the preprocessing steps and show that proper preprocessing of the data plays a vital role in accurate diagnosis. Hence, our primary contributions are two-fold: (a) We develop a deep convolutional neural network that can diagnosis MCI and AD patients from 3D MRI brain scans. (b) We devise an efficient approach to improve classification performance of an automated CNN classifier for Alzheimer's Disease diagnosis.

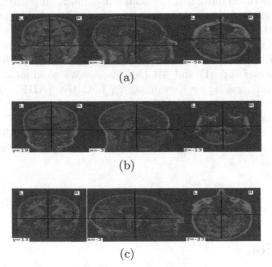

(a)

(b)

(c)

Fig. 1. Sample brain MRI images from ADNI database presenting different stages of Alzheimer's Disease. (a) normal/healthy controls (CN); (b) Mild Cognitive Impairment (MCI); (c) Alzheimer's Disease (AD).

2   Related Work

Researchers have been using machine learning techniques to build classifiers using imaging data and clinical measures for AD diagnosis. These studies have identified the significant structural differences in the regions such as the hippocampus and entorhinal cortex between the healthy brain and brain with AD. Different imaging modalities, such as structural and functional Magnetic Resonance Imaging (sMRI, fMRI), Position Emission Tomography (PET), Single Photon Emission Computed Tomography (SPECT), and Diffusion Tensor Imaging (DTI) scans can notice the changes causing AD due to the degeneration of brain cells. Several research works have been done using these neuroimaging techniques for AD Diagnosis. Moreover, information from multiple modalities have been combined to improve the diagnosis performance. In recent years, deep learning models specially Convolutional Neural Networks have demonstrated outstanding performance for medical image analysis. For neuroimaging data, deep learning techniques can discover the hidden representation and efficiently capture the disease-related pathologies. Gupta et al. [5] have developed a sparse autoencoder model for AD, Mild Cognitive Impairment (MCI) and healthy control (HC) classification. Payan et al. [19] trained sparse autoencoders and 3D CNN model for AD diagnosis. Brosch et al. [3] developed a deep belief network model and used manifold learning for AD detection from MRI images. Hosseini-As et al. [6] adapted a 3D CNN model for AD diagnostics. Liu et al. [16] developed a deep learning model using both unsupervised and supervised techniques and classified AD and MCI patients. Sarraf et al. [22] used fMRI data and deep LeNet model for AD detection. Suk et al. [25,26] developed an autoencoder network-based model for AD diagnosis and used several complex SVM kernels for classification. They have extracted low to mid level features from magnetic current imaging (MCI), MCI-converter structural MRI, PET data and performed classification using multi-kernel SVM. Cárdenas-Peña et al. [4] have developed a deep learning model using central kernel alignment and compared the supervised pre–training approach to two unsupervised initialization methods, autoencoders and Principal Component Analysis (PCA). Earlier we have developed several deep convolutional networks [8,10–12] to classify different stages of Alzheimer's Disease using OASIS dataset [18]. For our current work, we develop an efficient deep convolutional neural network based classifier and demonstrate better performance on the ADNI dataset [13].

3   Methods

3.1   Formalization

Let $x = \{x_i, i = 1, ..., N\}$, a set of MRI data with $x_i \in [0, 1, 2, ..., L-1]^{h*w*l}$, a three Dimensional (3D) image with L gray scale values, $h*w*l$ voxels and $y \in \{0, 1, 2\}$, one of the stages of AD where 0, 1, 2 refers to normal/healthy control (CN), Mild Cognitive Impairment (MCI), and Alzheimer's Disease (AD) respectively. We will construct a classifier,

$$f : X \to Y; x \mapsto y \tag{1}$$

that predicts a label y in response to an input image x with minimum error rate. The training process of the classifier would be an iterative process to find the set of parameters w, that minimizes the classifier's loss

$$L(w, X) = \frac{1}{n} \sum_{i=1}^{n} l(f(x_i, w), \widehat{c_i}) \tag{2}$$

where x_i is i^{th} image of X, $f(x_i, w)$ is the classifier function that predicts the class c_i of x_i given w, $\widehat{c_i}$ is the ground-truth class for i^{th} image x_i and $l(c_i, \widehat{c_i})$ is the penalty function for predicting c_i instead of $\widehat{c_i}$. We set l to the loss of cross–entropy,

$$l = - \sum_i \widehat{c_i} \, log \, c_i \tag{3}$$

3.2 Data Selection

For our proposed model, we have used 1726 MRI scans (347 AD, 537 CN, 806 MCI) of 479 patients from the Alzheimer's Disease Neuroimaging Initiative (ADNI) database (adni.loni.usc.edu). Specifically We used ADNI1:Annual 2 Yr 1.5T dataset for our model. The subjects were in the age range 55–92. The ADNI was launched in 2003 as a public-private partnership, led by Principal Investigator Michael W. Weiner, MD. The primary goal of ADNI has been to test whether serial magnetic resonance imaging (MRI), positron emission tomography (PET), other biological markers, and clinical and neuropsychological assessment can be combined to measure the progression of mild cognitive impairment (MCI) and early Alzheimer's disease (AD). Up-to-date information related ADNI database can be found at www.adni-info.org.

3.3 Data Preprocessing

We downloaded the raw Neuroimaging Informatics Technology Initiative (NiFTI) file format MRI scans from the ADNI website (http://adni.loni.usc.edu/). The structural MRI scans were acquired from 1.5T scanners. These MRI scans were already reviewed for quality and Gradient inhomogeneity correction (gradwarp), B1 non-uniformity correction, and N3 processing (to reduce residual intensity non-uniformity) were applied. Since the raw scans are not skull-stripped and have unnecessary information, we perform cortical reconstruction with Freesurfer image analysis suite (http://surfer.nmr.mgh.harvard.edu/). We use the function recon-all -autorecon1 which performs 5 out of 31 transformation processes done by Freesurfer. The five transformation processes are - Motion Correction and Conform, NonUniform intensity normalization (NU), Talairach transform computation, Intensity Normalization 1 and Skull Stripping. After these preprocessing steps we get a skull-stripped MRI scan with dimension

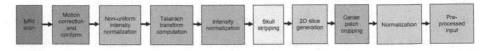

Fig. 2. 3D Brain MRI Preprocessing module.

$256 * 256 * 256$. Some slices from sample skull-stripped MRI scan of CN, MCI, and AD patients are shown in Fig. 3. We discard several slices at the beginning and at the end as they do not have any useful information. After that, we crop a $224 * 224$ center patch from each slice to reduce the background image region outside the brain tissue and perform image normalization.

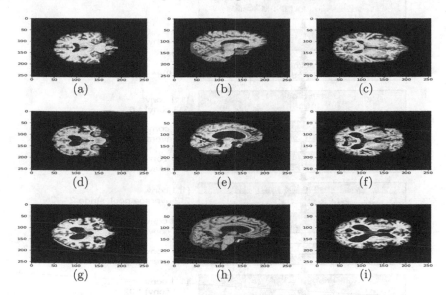

Fig. 3. Skull-stripped MRI slices presenting different AD stages. (a)–(c) CN; (d)–(f) MCI; (g)–(i) AD.

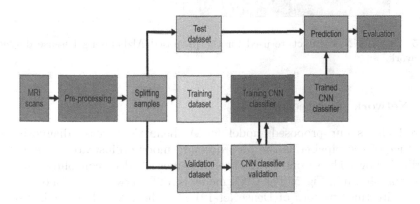

Fig. 4. Block diagram of the proposed Alzheimer's Disease diagnosis framework.

3.4 Data Augmentation

Data augmentation helps to increase the size of the dataset. For our work, we developed an augmentation scheme involving generating multiple slices from each

MRI scan. Slices are taken from different image plane: Axial or horizontal plane, Coronal or frontal plane, and Sagittal or median plane. Moreover, we applied Horizontal Flipping to increase the amount of training samples.

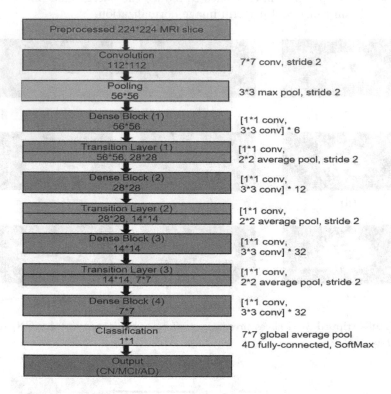

Fig. 5. Deep CNN architecture used for the proposed Alzheimer's Disease diagnosis framework.

3.5 Network Architecture

Figure 4 shows our proposed model for Alzheimer's Disease diagnosis. The first stage of the pipeline is the preprocessing module illustrated in Fig. 2 and described above. The second stage of the classifier is a deep convolutional neural network as shown in Fig. 5. The CNN model is a 2D network and follows a modified architectural pattern of DenseNet-121 [7]. The CNN classifier has several layers performing the convolution, batch normalization, rectified linear unit, and pooling operation. The layers follow a particular connection pattern known as dense connectivity [7]. We keep these layers very narrow (e.g., 12 filters per layer) and connect each layer to every other layer. Similar to [7], we will refer to the layers as dense layer and combination of the layers as dense block. Since all the dense layers are connected to each other, the ith layer receives the feature-maps $(h_0, h_1, h_2, ..., h_{i-1})$, from all previous layers $(0, 1, 2, ..., i-1)$. The network has a global feature map set, where each layer adds a small set of feature-maps. Each layer can access the gradients from the loss function and the original input in training time. As a result, the flow of information improves, and gradient flow becomes stronger in the network. Final classification is performed by the soft-max layer with three different output classes: CN, MCI, and AD. We optimized the CNN classifier using the Adam algorithm [14].

4   Experiments and Results

For our work, we used 80% data from the ADNI1 dataset as training set, and 20% as test dataset. From the training dataset, a random selection of 10% images is used as validation dataset. The experiments were performed using PyTorch framework. Transfer learning [9] was applied to pre-train the CNN classifier using Imagenet database [20]. The parameters used for training process are: learning rate: 0.0001, weight decay: 0.1 after every 7 epochs, and batch size: 16.

To improve the performance of CNN for AD diagnosis from 3D brain MRI, we studied the impact of several factors such as - network pre-training, image pre-processing, choosing random slice from the MRI as network input, and choosing specific slice from three different image plane (axial, sagittal, and coronal). Initially, we trained the network with raw MRI scans. For this approach, training

Table 1. Impact of different factors on proposed CNN

Methods	AD vs CN		
	Accuracy	Sensitivity	Specificity
Without Pre-training	75.98	78.45	71.43
Random slice	75.98	79.51	68.42
Axial slice	87.15	86.44	88.52
Sagittal slice	89.94	87.10	96.36
Coronal slice	94.97	94.33	95.89

Table 2. Impact of different CNN architecture on proposed diagnosis framework

Methods	AD vs CN		
	Accuracy	Sensitivity	Specificity
ResNet-18	86.03	85.12	87.93
ResNet-50	82.68	85.09	78.46
ResNet-101	83.79	88.18	76.81
ResNet-152	82.68	79.67	89.28
DenseNet-169	83.24	84.35	81.25
DenseNet-201	83.80	88.03	75.81
Proposed method	94.97	94.33	95.89

Table 3. Comparison with the State-of-the-Art. '–' indicates that result was not reported by the authors.

Methods	AD vs CN			AD vs MCI			MCI vs CN		
	Accuracy	Sensitivity	Specificity	Accuracy	Sensitivity	Specificity	Accuracy	Sensitivity	Specificity
Sergey et al. [15]	80.00	–	–	–	–	–	–	–	–
Beheshti et al. [2]	93.01	89.13	96.80	–	–	–	–	–	–
JLLR+DeepESRNET [24]	91.02	92.72	89.94	–	–	–	73.02	77.60	68.22
MOLR+DeepESRNET [24]	90.28	92.65	89.05	–	–	–	74.20	78.74	66.30
B. Shi et al. [23]	91.95	89.49	93.82	–	–	–	83.72	84.74	82.72
Liu et al. [17]	92.0	90.9	93.0	–	–	–	85.3	82.3	88.2
Aderghal et al. [1]	91.41	89.06	93.75	69.53	67.19	71.88	65.62	66.25	65.00
Proposed method	94.97	94.33	95.89	91.98	90.47	95.38	74.70	70.96	78.20

accuracy was more than 95%, but validation accuracy was around 68% which indicates the network lacks generalization. Pre-processed MRI data helped to solve this issue and improved performance of the CNN. Table 1 demonstrates the results of other experiments. From the results, we can see that choosing random slice from the MRI hampers the performance of the CNN classifier even with pre-trained network and pre-processed data. Moreover, the experimental results demonstrate that choosing slices from coronal view have a huge positive impact on the CNN classifier for AD diagnosis. Table 2 shows the effect of different CNN architecture on the performance of the proposed AD diagnosis framework. Here, it is evident that the proposed CNN classifier, shown in Fig. 5 outperforms the other baseline models. Our model is pre-trained with the Imagenet database [20] and we perform the training with the pre-processed coronal slices. These results also demonstrate that the performance of a CNN classifier vastly depends on the architecture and depth of the network. To validate the effectiveness of our model, we compare it with several state-of-the-art methods. The comparison result is shown in Table 3. Following previous approaches, we use accuracy, sensitivity and specificity for performance comparison. The result shows that our model outperforms other competing methods for AD/CN classification, AD/MCI classification and demonstrates comparable performance for MCI/CN classification. The proposed model follows a modified architectural pattern of DenseNet-121 and it outperforms DenseNet-169 and DenseNet-201. The later two models are much deeper and complex than DenseNet-121 and need lot more data for preventing over-fitting and better classification performance.

5 Conclusion

In this paper, we proposed a novel automated Alzheimer's Disease diagnosis framework and demonstrated ways to improve the performance of a CNN classifier. The experimental result shows that a pre-trained network with preprocessed slices from coronal view is a reliable technique for MCI and AD diagnosis. The performance of the proposed model shows that it can compete with other state-of-the-art methods for AD diagnosis using 3D brain MRI data. In future, we plan to extend our work to computer-aided diagnosis in other biomedical fields.

Acknowledgement. This study was supported by Brains and Behavior (B&B) Fellowship program from Neuroscience Institute of Georgia State University.

Data collection and sharing for this project was funded by the Alzheimer's Disease Neuroimaging Initiative (ADNI) (National Institutes of Health Grant U01 AG024904) and DOD ADNI (Department of Defense award number W81XWH–12–2–0012). ADNI is funded by the National Institute on Aging, the National Institute of Biomedical Imaging and Bioengineering, and through generous contributions from the following: AbbVie, Alzheimer's Association; Alzheimer's Drug Discovery Foundation; Araclon Biotech; BioClinica, Inc.; Biogen; Bristol-Myers Squibb Company; CereSpir, Inc.; Cogstate; Eisai Inc.; Elan Pharmaceuticals, Inc.; Eli Lilly and Company; EuroImmun; F. Hoffmann-La Roche Ltd and its affiliated company Genentech, Inc.; Fujirebio; GE Healthcare; IXICO Ltd.; Janssen Alzheimer Immunotherapy Research & Development, LLC.; Johnson & Johnson Pharmaceutical Research & Development LLC.; Lumosity; Lundbeck; Merck & Co., Inc.; Meso Scale Diagnostics, LLC.; NeuroRx Research; Neurotrack Technologies; Novartis Pharmaceuticals Corporation; Pfizer Inc.; Piramal Imaging; Servier; Takeda Pharmaceutical Company; and Transition Therapeutics. The Canadian Institutes of Health Research is providing funds to support ADNI clinical sites in Canada. Private sector contributions are facilitated by the Foundation for the National Institutes of Health (www.fnih.org). The grantee organization is the Northern California Institute for Research and Education, and the study is coordinated by the Alzheimer's Therapeutic Research Institute at the University of Southern California. ADNI data are disseminated by the Laboratory for Neuro Imaging at the University of Southern California.

References

1. Aderghal, K., Benois-Pineau, J., Afdel, K.: Classification of SMRI for Alzheimer's disease diagnosis with CNN: single Siamese networks with 2d+? approach and fusion on ADNI. In: Proceedings of the 2017 ACM on International Conference on Multimedia Retrieval, pp. 494–498. ACM (2017)
2. Beheshti, I., Demirel, H., Matsuda, H., Initiative, A.D.N., et al.: Classification of Alzheimer's disease and prediction of mild cognitive impairment-to-Alzheimer's conversion from structural magnetic resource imaging using feature ranking and a genetic algorithm. Comput. Biol. Med. **83**, 109–119 (2017)
3. Brosch, T., Tam, R., For the Alzheimer's Disease Neuroimaging Initiative: Manifold learning of brain MRIs by deep learning. In: Mori, K., Sakuma, I., Sato, Y., Barillot, C., Navab, N. (eds.) MICCAI 2013. LNCS, vol. 8150, pp. 633–640. Springer, Heidelberg (2013). https://doi.org/10.1007/978-3-642-40763-5_78
4. Cárdenas-Peña, D., Collazos-Huertas, D., Castellanos-Dominguez, G.: Centered kernel alignment enhancing neural network pretraining for MRI-based dementia diagnosis. Comput. Math. Methods Med. **2016**, 10 pages (2016)
5. Gupta, A., Ayhan, M., Maida, A.: Natural image bases to represent neuroimaging data. In: International Conference on Machine Learning, pp. 987–994 (2013)
6. Hosseini-Asl, E., Keynton, R., El-Baz, A.: Alzheimer's disease diagnostics by adaptation of 3d convolutional network. In: 2016 IEEE International Conference on Image Processing (ICIP), pp. 126–130. IEEE (2016)

7. Huang, G., Liu, Z., van der Maaten, L., Weinberger, K.Q.: Densely connected convolutional networks. In: Proceedings of the IEEE Conference on Computer Vision and Pattern Recognition (2017)

8. Islam, J., Zhang, Y.: Brain MRI analysis for Alzheimer's disease diagnosis using an ensemble system of deep convolutional neural networks. Brain Inform. **5**(2), 2 (2018)

9. Islam, J., Zhang, Y.: Visual sentiment analysis for social images using transfer learning approach. In: 2016 IEEE International Conferences on Big Data and Cloud Computing (BDCloud), Social Computing and Networking (SocialCom), Sustainable Computing and Communications (SustainCom) (BDCloud-SocialCom-SustainCom), pp. 124–130. IEEE (2016)

10. Islam, J., Zhang, Y.: An ensemble of deep convolutional neural networks for Alzheimer's disease detection and classification. arXiv preprint arXiv:1712.01675 (2017)

11. Islam, J., Zhang, Y.: A novel deep learning based multi-class classification method for Alzheimer's Disease detection using brain MRI data. In: Zeng, Y., et al. (eds.) BI 2017. LNCS, vol. 10654, pp. 213–222. Springer, Cham (2017). https://doi.org/10.1007/978-3-319-70772-3_20

12. Islam, J., Zhang, Y.: Early diagnosis of Alzheimer's disease: a neuroimaging study with deep learning architectures. In: Proceedings of the IEEE Conference on Computer Vision and Pattern Recognition Workshops, pp. 1881–1883 (2018)

13. Jack, C.R., et al.: The Alzheimer's disease neuroimaging initiative (ADNI): MRI methods. J. Magn. Reson. Imaging **27**(4), 685–691 (2008)

14. Kingma, D.P., Ba, J.: Adam: a method for stochastic optimization. arXiv preprint arXiv:1412.6980 (2014)

15. Korolev, S., Safiullin, A., Belyaev, M., Dodonova, Y.: Residual and plain convolutional neural networks for 3d brain MRI classification. In: 2017 IEEE 14th International Symposium on Biomedical Imaging (ISBI 2017), pp. 835–838. IEEE (2017)

16. Liu, F., Shen, C.: Learning deep convolutional features for MRI based Alzheimer's disease classification. arXiv preprint arXiv:1404.3366 (2014)

17. Liu, M., Zhang, D., Shen, D., Alzheimer's Disease Neuroimaging Initiative: Hierarchical fusion of features and classifier decisions for Alzheimer's disease diagnosis. Hum. Brain Mapp. **35**(4), 1305–1319 (2014)

18. Marcus, D.S., Wang, T.H., Parker, J., Csernansky, J.G., Morris, J.C., Buckner, R.L.: Open access series of imaging studies (OASIS): cross-sectional MRI data in young, middle aged, nondemented, and demented older adults. J. Cogn. Neurosci. **19**(9), 1498–1507 (2007)

19. Payan, A., Montana, G.: Predicting Alzheimer's disease: a neuroimaging study with 3d convolutional neural networks. arXiv preprint arXiv:1502.02506 (2015)

20. Russakovsky, O., et al.: ImageNet large scale visual recognition challenge. Int. J. Comput. Vis. (IJCV) **115**(3), 211–252 (2015)

21. Sarraf, S., Anderson, J., Tofighi, G.: DeepAD: Alzheimer's disease classification via deep convolutional neural networks using MRI and fMRI. bioRxiv, p. 070441 (2016)

22. Sarraf, S., Tofighi, G.: Classification of Alzheimer's disease using fMRI data and deep learning convolutional neural networks. arXiv preprint arXiv:1603.08631 (2016)

23. Shi, B., et al.: Nonlinear feature transformation and deep fusion for Alzheimer's disease staging analysis. Pattern Recognit. **63**, 487–498 (2017)

24. Suk, H.I., Lee, S.W., Shen, D.: Deep ensemble learning of sparse regression models for brain disease diagnosis. Med. Image Anal. **37**, 101–113 (2017)
25. Suk, H.I., Lee, S.W., Shen, D., Alzheimer's Disease Neuroimaging Initiative: Hierarchical feature representation and multimodal fusion with deep learning for ad/MCI diagnosis. NeuroImage **101**, 569–582 (2014)
26. Suk, H.-I., Shen, D., Alzheimer's Disease Neuroimaging Initiative: Deep learning in diagnosis of brain disorders. In: Lee, S.-W., Bülthoff, H.H., Müller, K.-R. (eds.) Recent Progress in Brain and Cognitive Engineering. TAHP, vol. 5, pp. 203–213. Springer, Dordrecht (2015). https://doi.org/10.1007/978-94-017-7239-6_14

Evaluating Mental Health Encounters in mTBI: Identifying Patient Subgroups and Recommending Personalized Treatments

Filip Dabek$^{(\boxtimes)}$, Peter Hoover$^{(\boxtimes)}$, and Jesus Caban$^{(\boxtimes)}$

National Intrepid Center of Excellence, Walter Reed National Military
Medical Center, Bethesda, MD, USA
{filip.j.dabek.ctr,peter.j.hoover2.ctr,jesus.j.caban.civ}@mail.mil

Abstract. Mild Traumatic Brain Injuries (mTBIs) are "poorly understood" [6] and often associated with psychiatric conditions [21]. While machine learning techniques have explored these comorbidities, the utilization of psychiatric Electronic Health Records (EHRs) poses unique challenges, but provides great promise in the understanding of the brain and the effect of an mTBI [3,14]. Therefore, in an effort to assist clinical practice in the field of mTBI, we present our work on utilizing EHR in which we apply machine learning models to identify and compare patient subgroups and explore algorithms to recommend patient catered treatment plans. Through this work, we aim to highlight effective techniques for handling the complexities of EHR and psychiatric-specific data.

Keywords: Traumatic brain injury · Machine learning
Mental health · Psychiatry · Healthcare application

1 Introduction

Mild Traumatic Brain Injuries (mTBIs), often referred to as concussions, are caused by "a severe external force or blow to the head or body that causes an alteration in neurologic functioning, with impairment in concentration, working memory, and executive functioning" [7]. While mTBIs continue to be a "poorly understood" injury [6], active research has identified a strong association between mTBIs and psychiatric conditions, such as Post Traumatic Stress Disorder (PTSD), depression, and anxiety [21]. These conditions can be better understood through the utilization of Electronic Health Records (EHRs) [13]. With the amount of patient information available within EHRs growing at a rapid pace [3] new techniques have been developed to more easily extract relevant patient information. This in turn, aids in the development of algorithms and models used in the assessment of treatment responses, intervention effectiveness, and patient-driven therapy [14].

F. Dabek and P. Hoover— Equal Contribution.

© Springer Nature Switzerland AG 2018
S. Wang et al. (Eds.): BI 2018, LNAI 11309, pp. 370–380, 2018.
https://doi.org/10.1007/978-3-030-05587-5_35

However, utilizing EHRs as a data source poses similar challenges as using data from any other domain [27]. Data is often presented with sparsity, incompleteness, and a significant amount of noise and bias. It is often difficult to provide a meaningful interpretation of the data given its high dimensionality [25]. When exploring EHRs specific to mental health, additional challenges must also be considered. These records contain information not easily measured, much of which require clinical interpretation. Due to the lack of concrete metrics available within these clinical records, there is a high reliance upon self-report questionnaires, which themselves present their own limitations. It often becomes difficult to effectively analyze and draw conclusions when there is a reliance on subjective reporting and interpretation.

Therefore, we present our work on effectively using this complex and difficult data on a sample population of service members diagnosed with a mTBI. These patients were admitted to an interdisciplinary 4-week intervention program for the evaluation and treatment of traumatic brain injury and subsequent comorbidities. Data collected prior to their admittance and throughout the program was used to build a more robust understanding of a patient makeup - determining pertinent features for our patient representation. This will assist clinicians in answering clinically relevant questions and provide personalized recommendations for treatment options.

To accomplish these objectives, our approach consists of three parts: (1) identify the different subgroups that exist within the population using clustering algorithms, (2) summarize the similarities and differences between the subgroups using statistical methods, and finally, (3) adapt and apply recommendation algorithms to provide a personalized and effective treatment plan for each patient.

2   Related Work

Previous research has explored the application of machine learning techniques within the healthcare sector. These studies have focused on the classification and predictability of models in an effort to provide improved and more accurate healthcare to patients. Newcomer et al. utilized a hierarchical clustering method to classify clinically relevant patients based on comorbidities [16]. Within a military population, Bailie et al. utilized the Neurobehavioral Symptom Inventory (NSI) to classify subgroups of patients based upon similar post-TBI symptoms [2]. Similarly, Chekround et al. explored a symptom clustering technique to better predict individual responses to certain antidepressants, reducing the potential for adverse drug responses [4]. Miotto et al. included medications, diagnostic codes, and free-text clinical notes within their deep neural network approach to predict outcomes and future diagnostics [14].

While previous research has focused on the utilization of EHR from multiple domains to improve patient outcomes, the various interventions patients receive are often disregarded. Therefore, we will specifically take advantage of the rich information embedded within psychiatric data by incorporating it into our patient representation.

3   Dataset

We compiled a population consisting of 518 service members who were admitted to an Intensive Outpatient Program (IOP), a four-week clinical intervention program catered towards service members suffering from traumatic brain injury (TBI) and/or psychological health (PH) issues. Electronic healthcare records (EHR) were obtained from patients both 365 days prior to their intake and during their attendance. Additionally, medications, diagnostic codes, and psychiatric clinical notes were gathered. Utilizing psychiatric initial evaluation clinical notes, an overall sentiment index was created per patient [17, 18, 22] to provide a clinical interpretation of a patients' overall well-being during their evaluation.

To assess subjective patient symptomatology and make use of the rich embedded knowledge contained within psychiatric data, self-reported surveys that are completed by patients during their attendance were gathered; namely: the Neurobehavioral Symptom Inventory (NSI), PTSD Checklist - military (PCL-m), and the Generalized Anxiety Disorder 7-item (GAD-7). These provide insight into a patient's self-report mental health condition. Admission survey scores were utilized in the clustering model while discharge scores were assessed in the evaluation of our model. Figure 1 displays the patient representative of this data.

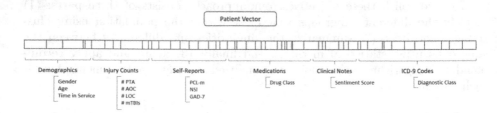

Fig. 1. An overview of the wide range of data utilized to build an overall representation of each patient.

4   Identifying Subgroups

With our dataset defined, we sought to identify subgroups of patients that underwent the 4-week Intensive Outpatient Program (IOP). By identifying these groups it is possible to gain a more in depth understanding of the types of patients that are admitted to this program as well as provide more personalized care that is catered for the specific type of patient.

To arrive at these subsets, we utilized clustering algorithms which allow for the processing of large amounts of sparse data and identified particular groupings. First we will describe the feature vectors utilized, followed by the exploration of said vectors, and finally we will outline the process for determining our final subgroups. Figure 2 provides a visual representation of this process.

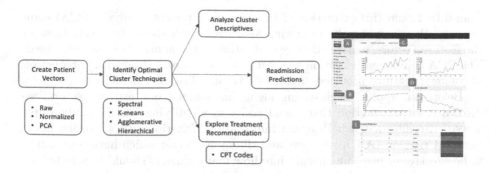

Fig. 2. Cluster exploration and assessment process.

Fig. 3. Our in-house exploration interface for evaluating our feature vectors and the results of various clustering algorithms.

4.1 Feature Vectors

The patient vector was formed to create an overall representation of the patient and encompassed the following elements:

- **Demographics:** Age, gender, & years of active duty military service.
- **Survey scores:** We chose to utilize Neurobehavioral Symptom Inventory (NSI), PTSD-Checklist-military (PCL-m), and the Generalized Anxiety Disorder (GAD-7) due to their particular insight into the behavioral health status of patients.
- **Diagnosis Codes:** The International Classification of Disease (ICD-10) diagnostic codes were grouped based upon their broad diagnostic categories. 'F' codes (mental and behavioral health conditions) were grouped individually to provide more detailed descriptions of patient's mental health status.
- **Injury Information:** Total counts of loss of consciousness (LOC), alternations of consciousness (AOC), and post-traumatic amnesia (PTA) were appended to our vector, due to their relevance to mTBI patients [26].
- **Medications:** Total medication prescriptions, grouped by class.
- **Psych Evaluation:** Utilizing a modified Finn Årup Nielsen (AFINN) lexicon on psychiatry evaluation notes, we obtained an overall sentiment score per patient. The AFINN classifies and provides weight on specific words and phrases held within text [18]. Modifications were made to include and reclassify clinically specific words and phrases.

4.2 Cluster Exploration

While the feature vectors that we created can effectively represent a patient's EHR and psychiatric specific data, we utilize the vectors in three different methods based on previous work [2]: (i) raw feature vectors, (ii) normalized vectors from 0 to 1, and (iii) extraction of Principal Component Analysis (PCA) components. By providing the clustering algorithm with these three variations of the feature vectors, a more effective evaluation of the analysis can be performed. The PCA component variation was utilized to determine if dimension reduction of collinear features provided any benefit to our clustering model.

Before we applied a clustering algorithm against our feature vectors, we defined a set of criterion that would assist in identifying our final subgroups. These criterion included: Bayesian Information Criterion (BIC), Akaike Information Criterion (AIC), variance, and silhouette score; which have been found to be effective at providing insight into how many clusters should be selected for a given model [1,12,20]. For each of these metrics, a common technique consists of plotting a graph of the number of clusters, k, against the metric and identifying the point at which increasing k provides a marginal increase in the metric: widely known as the elbow method [11,23,24].

To explore both the metrics and results of the clustering algorithms, we created an interface that utilized multiple methods of visual analytics to provide insights into the various results of the algorithms. Figure 3 provides an example of the interface which is described within the following sections:

(A) Contains controls for altering the type of feature vector to input into the algorithm (raw, normalized, or PCA components) as well as the features to utilize in the construction of the feature vector
(B) A toggle for switching the clustering algorithm and the number of clusters
(C) Three different tabs provide complex visualizations of the feature vectors
(D) Graphs for each of the four metrics for all values of k for the given algorithm
(E) A table providing a distribution breakdown of the clusters

4.3 Decision Process

The first algorithm that we tried was the k-means algorithm due to it being a standard algorithm that universally provides effective results [10]. However, upon loading our interface we quickly were able to see that the k-means algorithm performed poorly with our dataset. Moving away from the k-means algorithm, we explored two other algorithms - spectral clustering and agglomerative hierarchical clustering. For the spectral clustering algorithm we saw similar, ineffective results as the k-means algorithm. However, when examining the agglomerative hierarchical clustering algorithm we quickly were able to see that the distributions among the clusters throughout the scatter plots were separable.

Thus, we chose the agglomerative clusting algorithm and arrived at $k = 6$ for the number of clusters by using the previously defined metrics.

5   Subgroup Analysis

5.1   Overall Descriptions

The demographic means for each cluster are displayed within Table 1. While age and time in service among the groups appear to be well distributed, notable differences are shown between Cluster0 and Cluster1 when compared to the other groups. These clusters appear to represent our younger patients with fewer years of service.

Examining patient injuries among the clusters, the number of alterations of consciousness and total injuries were the statistically different injury counts. The average number of counts are displayed within Table 2. We can see that Cluster3 often exhibited the most injury counts overall, particularly within the total number of alterations and loss of consciousness.

Table 1. Demographics

Cluster	0	1	2	3	4	5
Age	34.4	32.7	39.4	38.67	39.1	37.8
TIS	12.4	11.5	18.6	17.4	16.8	15.4

TIS, Time in Service

Table 2. Average injury counts

Cluster	LOC	AOC	PTA	Total[a]
0	1.00	1.09	0.31	2.80
1	1.00	1.16	0.27	2.84
2	1.27	1.94	0.35	3.99
3	1.40	2.25	0.34	4.09
4	0.89	1.94	0.33	3.53
5	1.23	1.08	0.15	3.23

LOC, Loss of Consciousness; AOC, Alteration of Consciousness; PTA, Post-Traumatic Amnesia
[a] Kurskal-Wallis Analysis of Variance Significance at $\alpha = 0.05$

5.2   Cluster Utilization

Further exploring differences between the clusters, we evaluated the patients' healthcare utilization by examining medication prescriptions and clinical note sentiment analysis.

Because the clinic, at which patients are seen, treats and addresses issues of mental and behavioral health, we assessed the presence of 'F' diagnostic codes. These are codes associated with mental and behavioral health disorders. The average number of 'F' codes per cluster is displayed within Fig. 4. The most prominent of these codes are 'F43' and 'F07' which entail "Reaction to severe stress, and adjustment disorders" and "Personality and behavioral disorders", respectively. Again we notice the high utilization of these codes associated with Cluster0. We should also note the low average of "Reaction to severe stress, and adjustment disorders" within Cluster3 when compared to the other clusters.

Beyond diagnostic codes, we explored medication prescriptions among the clusters. As evident by Fig. 5 one particular group stood out. Cluster0 exhibited

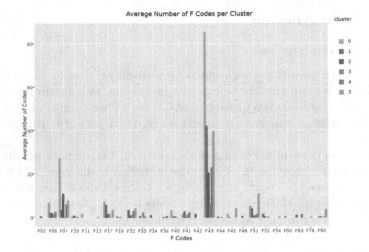

Fig. 4. Average number of F ICD-10 codes per cluster.

the most medication prescriptions. These medication classes included Narcotics, Anti-convulsants, SSRI's, and Barbiturates. Cluster0 medication prescriptions were statistically greater than any other group, as supported by a Kruskal-Wallis analysis test. The medications which did not statistically differ were antimalarials, glucocorticoids, and vitamins/minerals.

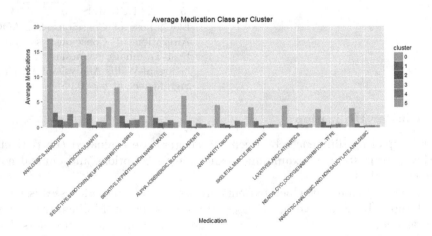

Fig. 5. Average medication class per cluster.

Through Natural Language Processing, the overall sentiment of patient Behavioral Health notes were assessed. While the majority of the clusters appear to have an overall positive clinical note sentiment, Cluster4 shows a substantially negative value. Table 4 shows the average sentiment per cluster. Conversely, Cluster3 shows the highest average sentiment.

Table 3. Cluster descriptions

Cluster	Description
0	High Medication Utilizers and F code diagnostics
1	Youngest sample with moderate medication use
2	Lowest Self-report scores - Low Symptomatology
3	High Injury Counts
4	Low clinical note sentiment and medication utilizers
5	High muscularskeletal diagnostic codes

Table 4. Sentiment

Cluster	Average sentiment
0	0.1033
1	0.2073
2	0.4163
3	0.6798
4	−1.2574
5	0.2188

5.3 Cluster Descriptions

After reviewing and assessing the similarities and differences, we constructed a brief description of each cluster which can be seen in Table 3. In this table it is possible to see the various subgroups of patients within our mTBI population. For example, we can see that Cluster0 consisted of patients that utilized the most amount of medications and were diagnosed with a large amount of "F" codes. Using this knowledge, a clinician can be better prepared when conducting an evaluation of their patient. These insights ultimately assist clinicians in developing a better understanding of their patient population.

6 Recommending Treatments

With an in-depth knowledge of the different types of patients that attend IOP programs, we have implemented and applied machine learning models for the recommendation of treatments to new patients that arrive at the clinic as well as patients that may readmit to the program.

Because we aim to provide personalized treatment plans for patients we utilize patient outcomes, which are encompassed by the three surveys that patients complete upon admission and discharge from the clinic: NSI, PCLM, and GAD7; as described in Sect. 3. However, as we are specifically interested in the mental health of the patient, we focus on the NSI survey as it directly pertains to the patients' symptomatology and general mental health.

We define the outcome of the patient as the change in the scores between admission and discharge where $\Delta NSI = NSI_{Dis} - NSI_{Admn}$, such that a negative value of ΔNSI indicates a reduction of symptoms and thus a desired outcome.

6.1 Admission

Finding Like Patients. We can leverage the existing feature vectors that we built and apply the k-nearest neighbors algorithm (kNN) [8] to identify similar patients and recommend treatments that were previously utilized, allowing for clinicians to follow similar care processes as previous cases.

Identifying Effective Treatments. While finding treatments that were given to similar patients can be effective at creating a consistent healthcare process, this process lacks the ability to identify treatments that result in positive patient outcomes. Therefore, we utilize gradient boosted trees in the XGBoost library [5] to build a classifier that predicts a patient's outcome, ΔNSI, based on the counts of different mental health treatments given to the patient in the past. Then using the feature importance functionality of the XGBoost library it is possible to identify the most effective treatments for each subgroup of patients.

Additionally, while running the classifier with an 80% training/20% testing split we found that providing the cluster index identified in Sect. 4 to the classifier caused for the mean accuracy to increase as well as for it to create a higher and tighter bound on the accuracy. Thus we can conclude that these clusters can be utilized across a wide range of tasks to quickly improve performance, due to the ability to partition the patients into similar groups.

6.2   Readmission

While it is hoped that patients will benefit from therapy, through a reduction in symptoms, there exists instances in which a patient may need to be readmitted for further treatment. In these cases, it is important to evaluate the treatments that a patient already received and identify alternative methods that may be more effective. Furthermore, at the point of readmission, there exists additional information pertaining to the patient outcomes that was not previously known. Therefore, we implemented a system akin to the recommendation systems that have been developed throughout different machine learning tasks.

A typical machine learning recommendation task consists of aggregating user movie ratings and then suggesting new movies based on the user's interests in relation to the general population. This task can be directly translated by relating the users to patients, the movies to treatments, and the ratings to the effect (outcome) that a treatment had on the patient. To accomplish this, we utilize a Python recommendation library, Surprise [9], and implement a content-based recommender [15,19].

7   Conclusion

Within this paper, we outlined our process and methodologies for the discovery of patient subgroups and personalized treatment plans for patients suffering from mTBI and subsequent comorbidities. While it is already assumed that treatments are catered to each individual patient, their responses to these treatments are not always straightforward. It can be difficult to gauge a patients' response to a particular therapy. Utilizing our proposed methodology allows for a more evidence-based intervention plan, relying upon previous success rates of treatments with patients of similar history and symptomatology.

Wile the main focus of this research dealt with mental health and responses to treatment, for the future we look forward to incorporating the vast array of therapies (CPTs) that patients undergo across other disciplines during their time at an IOP. To accomplish this task, we plan to explore machine learning models that are able to better handle such high dimensions and features, such as neural networks.

References

1. Almeida, H., Guedes, D., Meira, W., Zaki, M.J.: Is there a best quality metric for graph clusters? In: Gunopulos, D., Hofmann, T., Malerba, D., Vazirgiannis, M. (eds.) ECML PKDD 2011. LNCS (LNAI), vol. 6911, pp. 44–59. Springer, Heidelberg (2011). https://doi.org/10.1007/978-3-642-23780-5_13
2. Bailie, J.M., et al.: Profile analysis of the neurobehavioral and psychiatric symptoms following combat-related mild traumatic brain injury: identification of subtypes. J. Head Trauma Rehabil. 31(1), 2–12 (2016)
3. Blavin, F.E., Buntin, M.B.: Forecasting the use of electronic health records: an expert opinion approach. Medicare MedicaidRes. Rev.3(2) (2013)
4. Chekroud, A.M., Gueorguieva, R., Krumholz, H.M., Trivedi, M.H., Krystal, J.H., McCarthy, G.: Reevaluating the efficacy and predictability of antidepressant treatments: a symptom clustering approach. JAMA Psychiatry 74(4), 370–378 (2017)
5. Chen, T., Guestrin, C.: Xgboost: a scalable tree boosting system, pp. 785–794. ACM (2016)
6. Cifu, D.X., Caruso, D.: Traumatic Brain Injury. Demos Medical Publishing, New York (2010)
7. Conder, R.L., Conder, A.A.: Sports-related concussions. North Carolina Med. J. 76(2), 89–95 (2015)
8. Cover, T., Hart, P.: Nearest neighbor pattern classification. IEEE Trans. Inf. Theory 13(1), 21–27 (1967)
9. Hug, N.: Surprise, a Python library for recommender systems (2017). http://surpriselib.com
10. Jain, A.K.: Data clustering: 50 years beyond k-means. Pattern Recogn. Lett. 31(8), 651–666 (2010)
11. Kodinariya, T.M., Makwana, P.R.: Review on determining number of cluster in k-means clustering. Int. J. 1(6), 90–95 (2013)
12. Lletı, R., Ortiz, M.C., Sarabia, L.A., Sánchez, M.S.: Selecting variables for k-means cluster analysis by using a genetic algorithm that optimises the silhouettes. Anal. Chim. Acta 515(1), 87–100 (2004)
13. Meystre, S.M., Savova, G.K., Kipper-Schuler, K.C., Hurdle, J.F., et al.: Extracting information from textual documents in the electronic health record: a review of recent research. Yearb Med Inform 35(128), 44 (2008)
14. Miotto, R., Li, L., Kidd, B.A., Dudley, J.T.: Deep patient: an unsupervised representation to predict the future of patients from the electronic health records. Sci. Rep. 6, 26094 (2016)
15. Mooney, R.J., Roy, L.: Content-based book recommending using learning for text categorization, pp. 195–204. ACM (2000)
16. Newcomer, S.R., Steiner, J.F., Bayliss, E.A.: Identifying subgroups of complex patients with cluster analysis. Am. J. Managed Care 17(8), e324-32 (2011)
17. Ngoc, P.T., Yoo, M.: The lexicon-based sentiment analysis for fan page ranking in facebook. In: 2014 International Conference on Information Networking (ICOIN), pp. 444–448. IEEE (2014)

18. Nielsen, F.Å.: Afinn, March 2011. http://www2.imm.dtu.dk/pubdb/p.php?6010
19. Pazzani, M.J., Billsus, D.: Content-based recommendation systems. In: Brusilovsky, P., Kobsa, A., Nejdl, W. (eds.) The Adaptive Web. LNCS, vol. 4321, pp. 325–341. Springer, Heidelberg (2007). https://doi.org/10.1007/978-3-540-72079-9_10
20. Pelleg, D., Moore, A.W., et al.: X-means: extending k-means with efficient estimation of the number of clusters. ICML **1**, 727–734 (2000)
21. Schwarzbold, M., et al.: Psychiatric disorders and traumatic brain injury. Neuropsychiatric Dis. Treat. **4**(4), 797 (2008)
22. Silge, J., Robinson, D.: Text Mining with R: A Tidy Approach. O'Reilly Media Inc., Sebastopol (2017)
23. Thorndike, R.L.: Who belongs in the family? Psychometrika **18**(4), 267–276 (1953)
24. Tibshirani, R., Walther, G., Hastie, T.: Estimating the number of clusters in a data set via the gap statistic. J. Roy. Stat. Soc. Ser. B (Stat. Methodol.) **63**(2), 411–423 (2001)
25. Weiskopf, N.G., Hripcsak, G., Swaminathan, S., Weng, C.: Defining and measuring completeness of electronic health records for secondary use. J. Biomed. Inf. **46**(5), 830–836 (2013)
26. Wilk, J.E., Herrell, R.K., Wynn, G.H., Riviere, L.A., Hoge, C.W.: Mild traumatic brain injury (concussion), posttraumatic stress disorder, and depression in us soldiers involved in combat deployments: association with postdeployment symptoms. Psychosom. Med. **74**(3), 249–257 (2012)
27. Wu, J., Roy, J., Stewart, W.F.: Prediction modeling using EHR data: challenges, strategies, and a comparison of machine learning approaches. Med. Care **48**(6), S106–S113 (2010)

DeepDx: A Deep Learning Approach for Predicting the Likelihood and Severity of Symptoms Post Concussion

Filip Dabek[(⊠)], Peter Hoover[(⊠)], and Jesus Caban[(⊠)]

National Intrepid Center of Excellence, Walter Reed National Military
Medical Center, Bethesda, MD, USA
{filip.j.dabek.ctr,peter.j.hoover2.ctr,jesus.j.caban.civ}@mail.mil

Abstract. In the United States alone, an estimated 1.7 million traumatic brain injuries (TBIs) occur each year, leading to more than 1.3
million TBI-related emergency room visits and hospitalizations, as well
as thousands of deaths [9]. Following a mild TBI (mTBI) or concussion,
patients may experience physical, psychological, and cognitive deficits
lasting a period of hours, days, or for an extended period of time.
Although most people recover within days to weeks of injury, some report
persistent symptoms. Early detection, prognosis, and forecast of symptoms have the ability to improve the overall outcome of a patient, reduce
the cost associated with treatment, and provide important insights into
poorly understood brain injuries. This paper presents a deep learning
approach for predicting the onset of a new diagnosis and its severity
up to a year post concussion. Through the evaluation of our model we
show that with thirty TBI-related symptoms, we are able to correctly
predict the onset of a new symptom 93.49(±6.92)% of the time, and
when predicting the entire 12-months trajectory of a patient's symptoms we are able to exceed the expected 13.27% by more than doubling
it to 33.53%. In addition, we introduce the concept of a deep recurrent
neural network generating sample patients which can be used to derive
the different types of patients that exist within the population.

Keywords: Machine learning · Mild traumatic brain injury
Deep learning · Prediction · Symptoms

1 Introduction

A concussion is a poorly understood mild traumatic brain injury (mTBI) that
can alter the way the brain functions. In the United States alone, an estimated
1.7 million TBIs occur each year, leading to more than 1.3 million emergency
room visits, a quarter million hospitalizations, and 52 thousand deaths [9]. Due
to the poor understanding of mTBIs, it is difficult for a clinician and patient to
identify the symptoms that a patient will experience in both the short- and long-
term. Early detection and accurate forecasts of the onset of new symptoms have

© Springer Nature Switzerland AG 2018
S. Wang et al. (Eds.): BI 2018, LNAI 11309, pp. 381–391, 2018.
https://doi.org/10.1007/978-3-030-05587-5_36

the ability to improve the overall outcome of a patient, reduce the cost associated with treatment, and provide insights into this poorly understood brain injury.

Advances in big data and scalable analytical techniques open new opportunities by creating tools that use the patient's pre-existing conditions and longitudinal clinical trajectories to determine the likelihood of a patient developing psychological conditions. Along with these advances in techniques, during the last decade a significant amount of attention has been given to the acquisition of clinical data from patients suffering mTBI and psychological health (PH) problems after a concussion. The increased awareness has been in part driven by the Department of Defense (DoD) and many other government and private organizations that have been leading different efforts to raise awareness about the short- and long-term effects of concussions.

This paper presents a deep learning approach for predicting symptoms and their severity after a first diagnosis of a mTBI. We utilize a deep recurrent neural network (RNN) along with support vector machines (SVMs) to predict the likelihood of a symptom occurring in the future and a logistic regression model to approximate the severity of that symptom. In our results we found that our model was able to predict symptoms for a patient over a year after their concussion. Our paper is organized as follows: Sect. 2 describes some of the previous work involving mTBI. Section 3 describes our comprehensive dataset that was used to train and test different predictive models. Section 4 describes the data processing steps taken to format the data for an RNN. Section 5 describes the model that we have built using a deep RNN. Section 6 evaluates our model on both the raw accuracy and the approximation to the mean, while Sect. 7 presents four different sample generated patients; and finally Sect. 8 concludes the paper and describes some of the future work.

2   Background

Existing clinical literature has shown that a strong association exists between mTBI and various psychological conditions and symptoms [3]. Bryant et al. argued that the stress reaction caused by a concussion is a key factor in developing PTSD [1,2]. Another study found that soldiers that lose consciousness and subsequently were diagnosed with mTBI while deployed in Iraq were strongly associated with developing PTSD three to four months after returning home from combat [11]. In addition, research has found that patients with a concussion are susceptible to developing anxiety, depression, and other neuropsychological conditions [12,16]. In our own previous work we have utilized support vector machines (SVMs) and grammar-based approaches to model patients' clinical trajectories [4–6].

As of recent, much success has been shown with RNNs and long short-term memory (LSTM) [10,13,14] on sequential tasks. For instance, predicting the next character has made leaps in performance due to RNN's [17]. Therefore, we aim to utilize and apply the power of these RNNs to better model and understand a patient's trajectory.

3 Dataset

This study leverages electronic health records (EHRs) data retrospectively extracted from the DoD Health Services Data Warehouse (HSDW) under an approved IRB protocol. The HSDW contains longitudinal health record information for millions of active duty SMs as well as dependent beneficiaries, including direct care provided by the MHS as well as healthcare purchased through civilian health networks.

The data used for this project only included active duty mTBI patients with no history of a moderate or severe TBI and had at least a year worth of data before and after their first mTBI diagnosis. The metadata associated with each clinical encounter was extracted: date of encounter, appointment type, diagnosis codes, procedural codes were among this information. The resulting dataset consisted of 124,000 patients and 8.7 million TBI-related clinical encounters.

To build our model the dataset was defined to be $D = \{P_0, P_1, ..., P_n\}$ where each patient $P_i = <E_1, E_2, ...E_m>$ contains a timestamped series of encounters E_i arranged in a specific order with respect to the timestamps. The arrangement of the encounters can be used to derive temporal relationships within the data such as $E_i \prec E_{i+1}$ describing that E_i happened before E_{i+1}. Each encounter, E_i, contains a set of diagnoses such that $E_i = <d_1, d_2, ..., d_p>$ and $d_i \in \delta$ where $\delta = \{d_1, d_2, ..., d_n\}$ is a dictionary of event types. The set of possible diagnoses consisted included diagnosis-related group (DRG) for *Alzheimer's, Anxiety, Audiology, Behavioral, Cognitive deficits, Depression, Endocine dysfunction, Headache, Neurology, PTSD, Parkinson's, Seizure, Sleep, Speech, Stress, Vision.*

4 Feature Extraction

Because we seek to model the temporal relationships between encounters using recurrent nodes in a neural network, each patient was input over multiple time steps. This allows the network to learn the patient's history over time and predict over multiple timeframes into the future. However, utilizing the raw encounter data poses a problem for the network to learn patterns and trends; thus we needed to identify the features that would be utilized in our deep learning approach.

A simple approach to utilizing the raw patient encounters with an RNN would be to input the diagnoses at each encounter into the network such that the number of time steps for a patient corresponded to the number of encounters, $|P_i|$, that they underwent. However, this approach does not overcome the challenging aspect of the temporal data: that patient has a varying number of encounters and that the interval between encounters varies. These variations cause the network to have a difficult time to understand the patterns of a patient as it is unable to know whether they were close together or spread far apart. Due to little research being conducted into utilizing varying time intervals in RNN's, we chose to build on the rich existing literature on consistent and evenly spaced feature vectors.

To build an evenly spaced feature vector for each patient, we first identified a common reference point amongst all patients: the date of their first diagnosis of mTBI. Even though each patient experienced their first mTBI on a different date, this injury could serve as a reference point to align all of the patients. For example, the date of the first mTBI is represented as t_0, where the encounters that occur prior to the injury correspond to $E_i \forall t < 0$, and the encounters that occur after the concussion correspond to $E_t \forall t > 0$.

Using this reference point, we split the data before and after into one month intervals. This unit of time was chosen as we have found this to be the most effective for EHR data in the past [6]. Therefore, encounters in the month prior to the concussion corresponded to $E_t \forall - 30 \leq t < 0$, encounters in the month after the concussion corresponded to $E_t \forall 0 < t \leq 30$, etc. (where t is in days). For the purpose of this paper we only consider the encounters up to 365 days before and up to 365 days after the first mTBI, such that $-365 \leq t \leq 365$, which results in 24 total intervals (12 before the mTBI and 12 after). We define each of these month intervals as m spanning from -12 to 12.

With these intervals defined, we aggregated the number of occurrences of each diagnosis δ such that a vector of size $|\delta|$ is created for each interval corresponding to the number of times that the patient experienced that diagnosis in the time span. We defined each of these diagnosis counts as a patient's symptom for the month, such that $S_{dm} = |d|_m \ \forall d \in \delta$ would correspond to the feature vector for each corresponding month interval m. These vectors, S_{dm}, correspond to the symptoms that the patient experienced in each month before and after their concussion and are utilized in our deep learning model for prediction of future symptoms.

4.1   Symptom Severity

As the constructed feature vectors for each patient contain the raw number of encounters that a patient had for a specific diagnosis, we can assume that the count corresponds to the severity of their symptoms, such that more encounters indicate more severe symptoms and fewer encounters indicate less severe symptoms. Using this notion of severity the feature vector can be analyzed in two different ways: with and without severity.

To analyze the symptoms without severity we simply converted each feature vector to be binary, such that any values above 0 will be converted to 1: $S_{dm} = (bool)S_{dm} > 0 \ \forall d, m \in \delta, m$. This transformation causes each feature vector to represent whether or not a patient had an occurrence of a diagnosis in the indicated month interval, m. In addition, this transformation could be applied to only the targets of a network while leaving the inputs to be their raw values.

To analyze the symptoms with severity, the feature vector could be left with the raw values of encounters. However, as neural networks struggle with a wider range of values we normalize the values of the symptoms. Rather than normalizing all values to be between 0 and 1, we instead normalized the values such that all counts of zero remain 0 and that all counts above 0 are normalized between 0.5 and 1. The reason for this decision was to provide a clear linear boundary for a support vector machine (SVM) that will be utilized later in our deep learning approach. With this normalization technique, the boundary between symptoms that exist and those that do not is clearly defined as $[0, 0.5)$.

5 Deep Learning Model

We introduce our deep learning approach for modeling the patient's trajectory that consists of two parts: a deep recurrent neural network and a logistic regression model. The reasoning behind this decision was that it is difficult for a neural network to predict a wide range of values, 0 to 50, but it excels in binary decisions: 0 to 1. Therefore due to this limitation we utilize a neural network to predict the presence of a symptom and the logistic regression model to approximate the severity of the symptom.

5.1 Network

We begin by defining the input and output features that are utilized in our deep RNN. We utilize the feature vectors defined in Sect. 4 such that the input to the network is each month interval and the target of the network is each subsequent month interval normalized to not factor in the severity of the symptom, as defined in Sect. 4.1. The reason behind normalizing the targets to not include severity was due to the fact that neural networks excel at binary decisions of 0 to 1 more so than they do with a wide range of values, such as 0 to 50. By providing as input the severity of the symptom, the network is still able to make assumptions on the data and better predict the presence of a symptom in the future, but it is not required to identify the exact number of severity as that is assigned to the later logistic regression model.

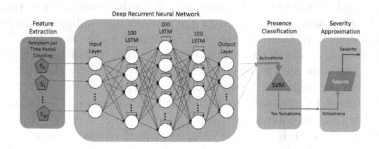

Fig. 1. An overview of our deep learning model.

Using the input and targets that we obtained, we constructed a three layer RNN using Theano [18] and Lasagne [8]. Each layer of the network consisted of LSTM nodes with a sigmoid activation function and varying number of hidden nodes: 100, 200, and 100. This varying configuration of nodes allows for the network to learn an abstract representation of the data before arriving at the final output. Also, to prevent the network from over-fitting, we placed a dropout layer before the first hidden layer, such that during training 20% of the inputs are randomly removed and not processed by the network [7,15,19]. The final architecture of our network can be seen in Fig. 1.

Next, as we are interested in the symptoms of the patient post concussion, only the targets after the first mTBI for each patient are evaluated. Figure 2 shows an example of this where the network is not expected to produce output for the 12 months prior to a concussion, but only when the patient experiences a concussion are the targets utilized.

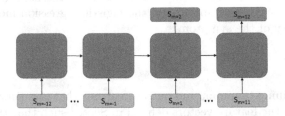

Fig. 2. An example of the network not being expected to produce targets for the first 12 time steps (a year before concussion), but once the concussion has occurred then the targets are produced (for the 12 months post concussion).

A common task for an output layer is to perform single label classification. This is typically achieved by applying a softmax activation on the output layer and then finding the node with the highest activation. However as there are many symptoms to predict we preformed multi-label classification on our network, where each output node utilized the sigmoid activation function and all of the symptoms will be predicted at the same time. With this configuration, we needed to identify the boundary in each node's activation that indicates the presence of a symptom or not. Therefore, we place a support vector machine (SVM) on each output node to classify the activation produced, as can be seen in Fig. 1. In addition, we were able to use the feature of SVMs where they provide the likelihood that the predicted classification for a sample is correct. This likelihood could be utilized by clinicians to better utilize, understand, and trust these predictions within the clinical setting.

Combining the deep RNN and SVMs, we trained our network by applying a train/validation/test split methodology and for each epoch: (i) pass the training data through the network, (ii) update the network parameters until satisfied using validation data, (iii) get the activation values for the training data, (iv) create an SVM and fit it with the activation values from the previous step and the training data targets, and (v) get the training and SVM losses. Thus, when the validation or test steps are taken, the latest SVM that was created in the last epoch is utilized.

5.2 Severity Approximation

As we obtained the classification of whether or not a patient will encounter a symptom in the future using the deep RNN and SVMs from the previous section, we needed to be able to approximate the severity of the symptom that the patient will experience. To provide this approximation, we utilized a logistic regression model for each symptom such that it takes in the activation of its corresponding output node and outputs the approximate number of times that the patient will experience that symptom in that month. This implementation allows for the logistic regression model to utilize the information that the network had learned throughout the patient's history.

6 Evaluation

To evaluate our architecture, consisting of an RNN, SVMs, and logistic regression models, on the dataset of patients that we defined previously, we analyze the accuracy of predicting the next month interval in various forms: individual symptoms, entire patient, and each individual month interval. Our evaluations were run with a train/validation/test split methodology where the 60% of the data was used for training, 20% was used for validation, and 20% was used for testing. The network was trained on 20 epochs with a batch size of 5,000, a loss function of binary cross entropy, and an update function of rmsprop with a learning rate of 0.3.

6.1 Without Severity

First, we analyze the model's ability to predict without taking severity into account, thus the model is simply predicting the presence of a symptom. Over all 30 symptoms that we evaluated, our model was able to correctly predict a symptom $93.49(\pm6.92)\%$ of the time and it was able to predict 35.33% of the feature vectors with complete accuracy. While 35.33% may appear to be low for predicting an entire feature vector, this is very promising as with 30 symptoms there exists a lot of noise and randomness with having perfect accuracy for a vector. Essentially, to be able to obtain a completely accurate feature vector we would expect to have an accuracy of about 0.9349^{30}, or 13.27%, which 35.33% is much larger than and thus the 35.33% statistic is a very positive one.

Table 1 shows a subset of symptoms as well as the 12 month intervals and their corresponding percentages for how often the symptoms or feature vector was correct within that window. In this data we can see that overall we were able to achieve high accuracy for the symptoms with a couple outliers. When looking at the month intervals we see that our network had a more difficult time predicting in the months closest to the concussion, but as time went on the accuracy increased. This initial accuracy in the first couple of months can be attributed to there being a lot of variability and unknown information in the dataset, but as time progresses then patients' symptoms begin to level out and become relatively controlled.

Table 1. Mean accuracy for without diagnosis severity

Symptom	Accuracy	Month	Accuracy
DirectCare	77.98%	1	89.08%
OutPatient	78.03%	2	91.50%
InPatient	98.82%	3	92.30%
MentalHealth	86.59%	4	92.86%
Ortho	89.40%	5	93.39%
Optom	95.10%	6	93.82%
PrimCase	95.35%	7	94.10%
ImSub	99.17%	8	94.42%
Ent	98.81%	9	94.80%
PTSD	73.96%	10	95.10%
Depression	89.11%	11	95.28%
DrugAbuse	98.72%	12	95.25%

6.2 With Severity

Second, we turn on the logistic regression piece of our model, as shown in Fig. 1, to analyze our model's effectiveness in predicting the severity of symptoms. Table 2 once again displays a subset of symptoms as well as the 12 month intervals. However, unlike Table 1, this table provides the mean differences between the actual and predicted symptom severity; thus these correspond to the overall symptom count rather than the accuracy of predicting each symptom. Similar to Sect. 6.1, we can see that the difference between the predicted and expected

Table 2. Mean differences (Predicted - Actual) for diagnosis severity

Symptom	Mean	Month	Mean
DirectCare	2.78 (±6.45)	1	0.69 (±3.43)
OutPatient	2.64 (±6.15)	2	0.45 (±2.45)
InPatient	0.02 (±0.3)	3	0.41 (±2.26)
MentalHealth	0.74 (±2.93)	4	0.37 (±2.06)
Ortho	0.57 (±2.16)	5	0.33 (±1.89)
Optom	0.06 (±0.28)	6	0.3 (±1.76)
PrimCase	0.7 (±1.38)	7	0.28 (±1.71)
ImSub	0.27 (±1.54)	8	0.26 (±1.66)
Ent	0.02 (±0.17)	9	0.23 (±1.54)
PTSD	0.32 (±1.8)	10	0.21 (±1.48)
Depression	0.44 (±1.85)	11	0.2 (±1.41)
DrugAbuse	0.09 (±0.66)	12	0.22 (±1.58)

values decrease as the patient is further from a concussion. However, there exists a large variety in the symptoms difference due to some symptoms having a large range of severity values while others have small ranges.

7 Patient Generation

A common task applied to RNN's is text generation where the network is trained on a corpus of text and then fed a begin token followed by each output character that is generated. This task highlights the network's ability to output a piece of text based on the style of writing that was learned from the training corpus. With the success produced by this task [17], we employ the same methodology to our deep learning model by providing an initial input history and allowing the model to generate the future diagnoses and their severity of the patient. Using this methodology we are able to identify a patient that the network sees as being the "common" patient followed within our dataset.

As our task requires 12 feature vectors corresponding to the 12 months prior to an mTBI, we created four fictitious patients that had just experienced a concussion and allowed the network to generate their future outlook. The four generated patients correspond to different types of patients: (A) a patient with zero history of symptoms prior to their first concussion, (B) a patient with no symptoms until 2 months before their concussion, (C) a patient with a lot of symptoms early in the year but none in the last 10 months before the concussion, and (D) a patient that experienced a multitude of symptoms the entire year before their concussion.

Upon generating the data for the four patients after their concussion, we analyzed the top five symptoms experienced by the patients. Table 3 contains the top five symptoms and displays the number of times that each patient would experience them in total over the year after their mTBI. In this table we can see that "OutPatient" and "DirectCare" encounters dominated amongst the patients, but that depression, drug abuse, and mental health were close behind. The results obtained from these four fictitious patients shows how our network can identify the makeup of our population as well predict the future of a newly given patient. In addition, by "peeking" into the SVM in our model utilized for presence classification, as shown in Fig. 1, we can provide a clinician and patient the probability of them having each symptom for each month interval.

Table 3. Top five symptoms predicted for patients A through D.

Symptom	Count	Per Patient
OutPatient	1344	336
DirectCare	1296	324
Depression	198	49.5
DrugAbuse	198	49.5
MentalHealth	125	31.25

8 Conclusion

In this paper we presented our deep learning approach for predicting the likelihood and severity of symptoms post concussion. For our approach we extracted feature vectors for each month interval before and after a concussion, containing a severity metric for each symptom that a patient may experience. Then we utilized these feature vectors in a deep RNN and an SVM for classification of whether or not the symptom will be experienced and a logistic regression model to predict the severity of each symptom. In our results we found that with thirty symptoms to predict, our model was able to correctly predict all of a patient's symptoms for a future month with 35.33% accuracy, which is promising given the expected 13.27% (as shown in Sect. 6.1) as well as the noise and variability that exists in patient data.

References

1. Bryant, R.A., Marosszeky, J.E., Crooks, J., Gurka, J.A.: Posttraumatic stress disorder after severe traumatic brain injury. Am. J. Psychiatry **157**(4), 629–631 (2000)
2. Bryant, R.A., et al.: Trajectory of post-traumatic stress following traumatic injury: 6-year follow-up. Br. J. Psychiatry **206**(5), 417–423 (2015)
3. Caban, J., Riedy, G., Oakes, T., Grammer, G., DeGraba, T.: Understanding the effects of concussion using big data. In: 2014 IEEE International Conference on Big Data (Big Data), pp. 18–23, October 2014. https://doi.org/10.1109/BigData.2014.7004387
4. Dabek, F., Caban, J.J.: A grammar-based approach to model the patient's clinical trajectory after a mild traumatic brain injury. In: 2015 IEEE International Conference on Bioinformatics and Biomedicine (BIBM), pp. 723–730, November 2015. https://doi.org/10.1109/BIBM.2015.7359775
5. Dabek, F., Caban, J.J.: Leveraging big data to model the likelihood of developing psychological conditions after a concussion. Procedia Comput. Sci. **53**, 265–273 (2015)
6. Dabek, F., Caban, J.J.: A neural network based model for predicting psychological conditions. In: Guo, Y., Friston, K., Aldo, F., Hill, S., Peng, H. (eds.) BIH 2015. LNCS (LNAI), vol. 9250, pp. 252–261. Springer, Cham (2015). https://doi.org/10.1007/978-3-319-23344-4_25
7. Dai, A.M., Le, Q.V.: Semi-supervised sequence learning. In: Advances in Neural Information Processing Systems, pp. 3061–3069 (2015)
8. Dieleman, S., et al.: Lasagne: first release, August 2015. https://doi.org/10.5281/zenodo.27878
9. Faul, M., Xu, L., Wald, M., Coronado, V.: CDC - TBI in the US Report - Traumatic Brain Injury - Injury Center. Centers for Disease Control and Prevention (2010)
10. Hochreiter, S., Schmidhuber, J.: Long short-term memory. Neural Comput. **9**(8), 1735–1780 (1997)
11. Hoge, C.W., Auchterlonie, J.L., Milliken, C.S.: Mental health problems, use of mental health services, and attrition from military service after returning from deployment to Iraq or Afghanistan. JAMA **295**(9), 1023–1032 (2006)
12. Kay, T.: Neuropsychological treatment of mild traumatic brain injury. J. Head Trauma Rehabil. **8**(3), 74–85 (1993). https://doi.org/10.1097/00001199-199309000-00009

13. Lipton, Z.C., Kale, D.C., Elkan, C., Wetzell, R.: Learning to diagnose with LSTM recurrent neural networks. arXiv preprint arXiv:1511.03677 (2015)
14. Miotto, R., Li, L., Kidd, B.A., Dudley, J.T.: Deep patient: an unsupervised representation to predict the future of patients from the electronic health records. Sci. Rep. **6**, 26094 (2016)
15. Pham, V., Bluche, T., Kermorvant, C., Louradour, J.: Dropout improves recurrent neural networks for handwriting recognition. In: 2014 14th International Conference on Frontiers in Handwriting Recognition, pp. 285–290, September 2014. https://doi.org/10.1109/ICFHR.2014.55
16. Schoenhuber, R., Gentilini, M.: Anxiety and depression after mild head injury: a case control study. J. Neurol Neurosurg. Psychiatry **51**(5), 722–724 (1988). https://doi.org/10.1136/jnnp.51.5.722
17. Sutskever, I., Martens, J., Hinton, G.E.: Generating text with recurrent neural networks. In: Proceedings of the 28th International Conference on Machine Learning (ICML-11), pp. 1017–1024 (2011)
18. Team, T.T.D., et al.: Theano: a python framework for fast computation of mathematical expressions. arXiv preprint arXiv:1605.02688 (2016)
19. Zaremba, W., Sutskever, I., Vinyals, O.: Recurrent neural network regularization. arXiv preprint arXiv:1409.2329 (2014)

Automatic Detection of Epileptic Spike in EEGs of Children Using Matched Filter

Maritza Mera[1]($\boxtimes$) (iD), Diego M. López[1] (iD), Rubiel Vargas[2] (iD),
and María Miño[3] (iD)

[1] Telematics Department, University of Cauca, Popayán, Colombia
{maritzag, dmlopez}@unicauca.edu.co
[2] Physics Department, University of Cauca, Popayán, Colombia
rubiel@unicauca.edu.co
[3] Pediatrics Department, University of Cauca, Popayán, Colombia
memino@unicauca.edu.co

Abstract. The Electroencephalogram (EEG) is one of the most used tools for diagnosing Epilepsy. Analyzing EEG, neurologists can identify alterations in brain activity associated with Epilepsy. However, this task is not always easy to perform, because of the duration of the EEGs or the subjectivity of the specialist in detecting alterations. **Aim**: To present an epileptic spike detector based on matched filter for supporting diagnosis of Epilepsy through a tool able to automatically detect spikes in EEG of children. **Results**: The results of the evaluation showed that the developed detector achieved a sensitivity of 89.28% which is within the range of what has been reported in the literature (82.68% and 94.4%), and a specificity of 99.96%, the later improving the specificity of the best reviewed work. **Conclusions**: Considering the results obtained in the evaluation, the solution becomes an alternative to support the automatic identification of epileptic spikes by neurologists.

Keywords: Matched filter · Spike detection · Epilepsy · Seizure

1 Introduction

Reading EEGs by specialists is a task which consumes a lot of effort and time due to the duration of EEG signal recordings. In general, EEG records have durations between 20 and 30 min and in some cases the records are even longer (48 or 72 h), representing one of the main causes of the high cost of diagnosing neurological diseases such as epilepsy [1]. In the same manner, the difficulty of diagnosing this kind of disease increases in developing countries, due to the lack of medical personnel; in countries like Colombia, for example, there is a rate of one neurologist per 200,000 inhabitants [2], as a result, it is difficult to guarantee diagnosis and timely attention to patients. The situation is more worrisome in the case of patients residing in rural areas because the specialists are located in the clinical centers of main cities.

S. Wang et al. (Eds.): BI 2018, LNAI 11309, pp. 392–402, 2018.
https://doi.org/10.1007/978-3-030-05587-5_37

Considering the above mentioned, automatic detection of different abnormal events present in EEG signals arises as an alternative to reduce the reading times of an EEG signal and increase the opportunity of EEG reading services, because once the abnormalities on the signal are identified, the specialist would only have to confirm or denied them.

The automatic reading of EEGs is a field of research in which different approaches have been developed in order to offer tools that facilitate the reading of EEG records, especially for those which are of long duration. In [3], the authors proposed to classify epileptiform events using time-frequency analysis and a random forest-based classifier, achieving an accuracy of 83%. Likewise, in [4] features extracted from wavelet coefficients are used to classify the EEG segments with a 93% sensitivity and specificity. In [5], a tool based on neural networks for the detection of epileptic seizures was developed, accomplishing an accuracy, specificity and sensitivity of 88.67%, 90% and 95% respectively.

Considering the above, the main challenge of the works that have been developed so far is to improve the percentages of effectiveness and reliability of the detection or classification of epileptic seizures. Due to epileptic discharges do not occur under the same pattern, thus, characterize and classify them under the same model can reduce the effectiveness of detection or classification. Consequently, some investigations have been developed for the identification of specific patterns in order to increase the reliability of the reading.

The objective of this research is to propose an epileptic spike detector based on matched filter for supporting diagnosis of Epilepsy through a tool able to automatically detect spikes in EEG of children. The automatic detection of spikes from an EEG waveform implies the identification of an epileptic spike template.

This paper has been organized as follows: Sect. 2 describes the dataset used to support the development and evaluation of the proposal, theorical description of the Matched Filter and the development of the detector to automatically identify epileptic spikes. In Sect. 3, the experimental evaluation of the sensitivity and specificity of the epileptic spike detector is presented. In Sect. 4 the discussion of the results and contributions are described. Finally, Sect. 5 describes the conclusions of the work.

2 Materials and Methods

This section presents a description of the main materials, methods and concepts considered for the implementation of the automatic detection of epileptic spikes in an EEG signal.

2.1 Database

For this research, 100 electroencephalograms from children with suspected epilepsy were collected. This collection was made as part of the Neuromotic project whose general objective is the development of a TeleEEG system to support the diagnosis of epilepsy in rural areas in Colombia [6]. As part of this project, the development of a component to support the reading of EEG by a neurology professional is sought.

In the construction of the dataset and in accordance with bioethics standards, an informed consent was obtained for each EEG record, the aforementioned consent was approved by the Ethics Committee of the Universidad of Cauca, Colombia. Each EEG record was acquired using the BWII EEG device and the BW Analysis software, both developed by Neurovirtual. The device has FDA certification.

Each EEG record was acquired under the electrode positioning system 10-20 [7], considering a sampling rate of 200 samples per second, and an approximate duration of 30 min. Some EEG records were taken in patients in the waking state (46 records) and others in sleep (54 records).

Once the records were digitized, they were evaluated by a neuropaediatrician who established the diagnosis. The EEGs diagnosed as abnormal went through an annotation process, in which segments with epileptic alterations were documented describing in detail the beginning and end of an epileptic abnormality.

2.2   Matched Filter

Matched filters are basic signal analysis tools used to extract known waveforms from a

Fig. 1. Detection scheme, after [8].

signal that has been contaminated with noise [8]. The model used for the extraction or detection of the wave can be seen in Fig. 1.

The scheme defined in Fig. 1 describes the implementation of a filter $h(t)$ to extract the signal $s(t)$ contaminated with noise $n(t)$, as a result of applying $h(t)$ it is obtained the hypothesis H_x. In this scheme, the null (H_0) and alternative (H_1) hypotheses are considered in Eqs. (1) and (2). If the waveform that is sought is present in the signal, hypothesis H_1 is confirmed, otherwise H_0 hypothesis is confirmed. In the context of the detection of epileptic spikes, $x(t)$ is a function describing the EEG measured brain activity, the noise $n(t)$ represents a normal brain activity of a patient (EEG base rhythm), the signal $s(t)$ the epileptic spike to be found, H_0 normal activity of the patient and H_1 the presence of the epileptic spike.

$$H_0 : x(t) = n(t) \tag{1}$$

$$H_1 : x(t) = s(t) + n(t) \tag{2}$$

This mechanism works very well in practice when a known pattern or waveform is sought, because the filter allows to maximize the SNR (signal noise ratio) of the filtered signal and reduce the effect of noise on the original signal [9]. However, when waveforms are not known, the method does not work efficiently.

In this work, the development of a tool that supports the diagnosis of epilepsy through the identification of epileptiform events is sought. For this purpose, a review has been made in the literature on characteristic patterns that describe the presence of an epileptic discharge. In this sense, it could be observed that epileptic seizures generate electric shocks on some areas of the brain generating unexpected changes in the waveform of EEGs. In some cases, the appearance of waveforms is identified periodically or semiperiodically or simply the disorganization of the electrical activity of the patient. Some of the most wanted patterns by neurologists during the inspection of EEGs correspond to peaks (narrow and broad). Considering the above, a tool that allows the automatic detection of spikes from an EEG waveform that works as a template is proposed. This template was constructed by averaging 25 segments diagnosed as spikes by a neuropediatric expert in reading EEGs. Figure 2(a) shows an example of the appearance of epileptic spikes in the base rhythm of the EEG wave on channels 17, 18, 22 and 23 of the EEG.

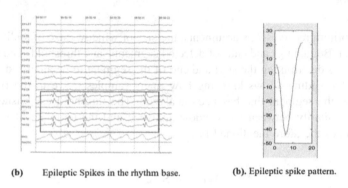

(b)   Epileptic Spikes in the rhythm base.   **(b).** Epileptic spike pattern.

Fig. 2. Epileptic Spikes in the rhythm base.

From the epileptic spikes detected, the epileptic spike pattern of Fig. 2(b) was constructed. Considering the visual analysis performed by the neurologist, it was defined that the size of the segments of epileptic spikes extracted should contain data of 15 samples, 13.33 ms, in order to capture the data from the beginning of the spike until the end of it.

2.3   Epileptic Spike Detector

Considering the wave pattern which describes an epileptic spike, a spike detector algorithm was constructed using matched filter and sliding windows over an EEG channel. The algorithm is defined below:

```
Algorithm 1. Spikes detector.
Void SpikesDetector (windowSize, slidingSize, pattern, EEGChannel, spikesBeginnings, spikesEnds, thresh)
    startIndex = 0
    maxIndex = Lenght (EEGChannel)
    b_matchedFilter = createMatchedFilter(pattern)
    while (startIndex< maxIndex) do
        segment = EEGChannel(:, startIndex: maxIndex + windowSize)
        matches = matchedFilter(segment, template, thresh, b_matchedFilter)
        if (isNotEmpty(matches)) do
            spikesBegginings.Add (startIndex)
            spikesEnds.Add (startIndex+windowSize)
            startIndex = startIndex + slidingSize
        else
            startIndex = startIndex + windowSize
        end if
```

The algorithm receives 7 as arguments, the size of window, size of sliding, pattern, EEG channel, Beginnings and ends of detected segments, and threshold. The size of the window allows determining the start and end of the segment to be analyzed, as well as the size of the sliding allows knowing how many samples move to the right of the beginning of the segment that has been analyzed. The threshold establishes the percentage of similarity between the window analyzed and the template of spikes. Figure 3 illustrates the afore mentioned process.

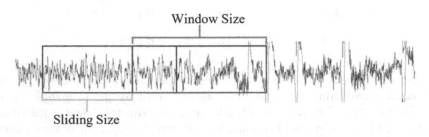

Fig. 3. Analysis scheme by window.

The *pattern* corresponds to the template constructed from the epileptic spikes, *EEGChannel* corresponds to a channel extracted from the EEG in which the pattern will be searched. *spikesBeginnings* and *spikesEnds* correspond to the arrangements where the beginnings and ends of the segments that have presence of the pattern of epileptic spikes are stored, and the function *createMatchedFilter* creates a matched filter based on the template. The algorithm analyzes the entire EEG channel while segments can be extracted through the sliding window, and for each window extracted a review is made with the Matched Filter to determine if this window has the presence of the epileptic spike pattern.

The algorithm that describes the Matched Filter is described below:

Algorithm 2. Matched Filter.
Var matches **MatchedFilter** (segment, template, thresh, b_matchedFilter)
    y = FilterSignal(b_matchedFilter, segment)
    u = template.'*template
    matches = ReviewThreshold (y,thresh,u)
    return matches
End MatchedFilter

Where *segment* describes segment to evaluate, *template* represents the epileptic spike pattern, *thresh* sets a detection threshold, which was established empirically in 0.9 by testing values between 0.6 and 1, *b_matchedFilter* contains the matched filter based on template, *y* contains the segment filtered with the matched filter, *u* stores the autocorrelation matrix of the template and function *ReviewThreshold* establishes if *y* exceeds the threshold. The autocorrelation matrix is used for detecting the appearance of patterns in a signal, in this case, the autocorrelation matrix was used for detecting the pattern of spikes in the brain activity.

3   Results

For the evaluation of the epileptic spike detector, 8 segments of EEG records extracted from the dataset of 100 patients were used. The final test used 60 min of recording of brain activity, these records were divided into 100 segments with 10 s of recording, 8 segments of these contained spikes. Considering the annotations made on the dataset, beginnings and ends of 56 segments in which epileptic discharges occur in the form of a spike are known. In this sense, the spike detector was used for each EEG segment and the correctly identified, badly identified and unidentified segments were counted to determine the sensitivity and specificity of the detection. Figure 4 describes examples of spikes (epilepsy episodes) contained in extracted segment with abnormalities.

Each segment described in Fig. 4 was reviewed by the detector of spikes. The results can be seen in Table 1.

In the results obtained, it can be seen that the number of spikes detected in each segment is greater than the actual number of spikes. With this in mind, each spike identified by the detector was reviewed to analyze the reason for the error. It was possible to identify that in some cases, a real spike was being identified twice or three times by the detector, due to the reduced size of the sliding window and in other cases, the abrupt fall of the slow waves that occur just after the spike occurrence is also considered by the detector. It is also important to mention that slow waves are also considered an abnormality by the neurologists annotating the EEG. Thus, the spikes detected with close beginnings (difference between beginnings less than 20 samples) were considered as a single one.

Considering the above, Table 2 presents the results of the evaluation eliminating repeated spikes, the detection of slow waves and the number of spikes not detected.

Segment 1: 7 spikes

Segment 2: 7 spikes

Segment 3: 6 spikes

Segment 4: 8 spikes

Segment 5: 6 spikes

Segment 6: 7 spikes

Segment 7: 6 spikes

Segment 8: 8 spikes

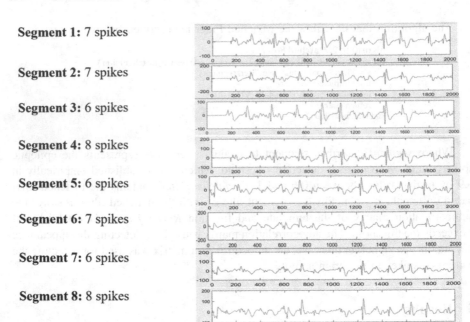

Fig. 4. Description of each segment.

Table 1. Results of the evaluation.

Segment	Real spikes	Spikes detected
S1	7	9
S2	7	29
S3	6	10
S4	8	16
S5	6	6
S6	7	19
S7	6	7
S8	8	14

Considering the results obtained in Table 2, it can be concluded that the built-in epileptic spike detector achieved a sensitivity of 89.28%. To calculate the sensitivity, the size of the segments (2000 samples) and the number of windows that were generated through the sliding window implemented in the detector were considered, which generated for each segment analyzed a total of 369 windows that had to be evaluated. Considering that there were 8 segments analyzed, 2,952 windows were revised, which allows obtaining a specificity of 99.96%

Table 2. Results of the evaluation.

Segment	Real spikes	Detected Spikes	Slow waves	Spikes not detected	Wrong detected spikes
S1	7	7	1	0	0
S2	7	7	12	0	1
S3	6	5	6	1	0
S4	8	7	6	1	0
S5	6	5	1	2	0
S6	7	7	9	0	0
S7	6	4	2	2	0
S8	8	8	5	0	0
TOTAL	**56**	**50**	**42**	**6**	**1**

4   Discussion

In this paper, the development of a new mechanism for the automatic detection of epileptic spikes based on the implementation of a matched filter and a template representing the waveform of an epileptic spike is presented. The tool developed reached a sensitivity of 89.28% and specificity of 99.96% in the identification of epileptic spikes on a dataset with EEG records of children.

The construction of the dataset arose as a need to have a set of training data which describes in detail the beginning and end of an epileptic abnormality, due to in the literature there are different datasets that only describe periods of time in which the appearance of an abnormality can be observed and then disorganization or new appearances of the abnormality. One example is the Physionet EEG database [10], which is one of the most widely used pediatric EEG databases. This database does not describe the exact segments of the start and end of specific abnormalities.

The main contribution of this work for the field of neurology is the implementation of a method that automatically detects epileptic spikes with high reliability with respect to the values found in the literature. This could decrease the reading time of EEGs and facilitate the diagnosis of Epilepsy by neurologists. Additionally, the proposed method was tested using real data from a Dataset built by the authors and annotated with the help of a neuropediatrician to document the exact segments where the epileptic abnormalities occur in electroencephalograms.

In previous investigations, many tools have been designed to detect points in EEG signals. The main objective of these in the majority is to reduce the reading time of the specialists, since normally they face large volumes of data [11]. In [12] the authors describe the development of a tool for the detection of epileptic spikes using neural networks, in which a PPV (positive prediction value) of 72.67% and a sensitivity of 82.68% were obtained. In [13], an approach is proposed to analyze the EEG record following a Markov paradigm in order to increase the sensitivity of the detection, however, the result becomes a solution with high computational complexity. In [14] a spike detector developed using analysis of energy and frequency changes is described, for this a SNEO (smoothed nonlinear energy operator) is used for testing different window functions, however, the results were performed using a dataset with animal records and the objective of the tool is to support real-time evaluation of EEGs. In [15] a detector of single spikes and spikes with slow waves is proposed. The results of the evaluation show that the built model improves the accuracy of the classification when the single spikes and spikes with slow waves are considered as different classes, however, the detection is performed in two stages, the first to detect a possible spike and the second one to extract features of the window and classify it as a spike, a spike with a slow wave or not spike, this could imply a greater computational load. In this study, the authors performed several configurations, obtaining a sensitivity between 87.9% and 94.4%, as well as a specificity between 86.7% and 92.3%.

Considering the works reviewed, the solution developed in this study obtained a sensitivity (89.28%) within the range of what has been reported in the literature (82.68% and 94.4%) and improving with 99.96% the specificity of 93% of the best reviewed work. This as consequence of the good template built for spikes in brain activity of the children and the threshold used for comparing the autocorrelation matrix of the window with the template, which was obtained empirically. Furthermore, it is expected that this proposal reduces the computational load due to it perform fewer stages compared with other approaches.

As future work the characterization of the greatest number of abnormalities associated with epilepsy in order to develop an epileptic event detector that includes abnormalities other than epileptic spikes is proposed. Considering that not all the abnormalities associated with epilepsy can be easily represented in a wave pattern, it is also recommended to include a classification process based on a process of feature extraction through signal processing to support the classification of the segments that cannot be represented through a wave pattern. Finally, the spike detector implemented in this project was tested using EEG records of children, however, this mechanism could be used to detect epileptic spikes in adult patients, since the waveform does not change.

5 Conclusion

This paper described the implementation of an epileptic spike detector through the development of a sliding windowing mechanism that allows to screen an EEG signal window by window and determine whether these correspond to epileptic spikes by comparing a template with each window using a matched filter. The template was constructed from the calculation of the average of 25 segments corresponding to 25 epileptic spikes and the Matched Filter method implemented achieved a sensitivity of 89.28% and a specificity of 99.96%. The main contribution of this work for the field of neurology is the implementation of a method that automatically detects epileptic spikes with high reliability with respect to the values found in the literature. This could potentially decrease the reading time of EEGs and facilitate the diagnosis of Epilepsy by neurologists.

Acknowledgements. The work is funded by a grant from the Colombian Agency for Science, Technology, and Innovation Colciencias – under Calls 715-2015, project: "NeuroMoTIC: Sistema móvil para el Apoyo Diagnóstico de la Epilepsia", Contract number FP44842-154-2016, and Call 647- 2015.

References

1. Garcés, A., Orosco, L., Diez, P., Laciar, E.: Automatic detection of epileptic seizures in long-term EEG records. Comput. Biol. Med. **57**, 66–73 (2015)
2. Liliana, J., Lara, A., Alexandra, M., Gómez, M., Gómez, F. R.: Informe Final Proyecto Estdio de disponibilidad y distribución de la oferta de médicos especialistas, en servicios de alta y mediana complejidad en Colombia. https://www.minsalud.gov.co/salud/Documents/Observatorio%20Talento%20Humano%20en%20Salud/DisponibilidadDistribuciónMdEspecialistasCendex.pdf. Accessed 06 Oct 2018
3. Fraiwan, L., Lweesy, K., Khasawneh, N., Wenz, H.: Automated sleep stage identification system based on time – frequency analysis of a single EEG channel and random forest classifier. Comput. Methods Programs Biomed. **108**(1), 10–19 (2011)
4. Tsalikakis, D.G., Tsipouras, M.G.: Epileptic seizures classification based on long-term EEG signal wavelet analysis. In International Conference on Biomedical and Health Informatics on proceedings Precision Medicine Powered by pHealth and Connected Health, Thessaloniki, Greece, pp. 165–169 (2017)
5. Acharya, U.R., Oh, S.L., Hagiwara, Y., Tan, J.H., Adeli, H.: Deep convolutional neural network for the automated detection and diagnosis of seizure using EEG signals. Comput. Biol. Med. **100**(1), 270–278 (2018)
6. Molina, E., Salazar-Cabrera, R., López, Diego M.: NeuroEHR: open source telehealth system for the management of clinical data, EEG and remote diagnosis of epilepsy. In: Figueroa-García, J.C., López-Santana, E.R., Rodriguez-Molano, J.I. (eds.) WEA 2018. CCIS, vol. 915, pp. 418–430. Springer, Cham (2018). https://doi.org/10.1007/978-3-030-00350-0_35
7. Quigg, M.: EEG Pearls: Acquisition of the Electroencephalogram 2, 1st edn. Elsevier, Charlottesville (2006)
8. Bancroft, J. C.: Introduction to Matched Filters. https://crewes.org/ForOurSponsors/ResearchReports/2002/2002-46.pdf. Accessed 06 Oct 2018
9. Hermand, J., Roderick, W.I.: Acoustic model-based matched filter processing for fading time-dispersive ocean channels: theory and experiment. IEEE J. Ocean. Eng. **18**(4), 447–465 (1993)
10. Goldberger, A.L., et al.: PhysioBank, PhysioToolkit, and PhysioNet components of a new research resource for complex physiologic signals. Compon. New Res. Resour. Complex Physiol. Signals **101**(23), 215–220 (2000)
11. Gaspard, N., Alkawadri, R., Farooque, P., Goncharova, I.I., Zaveri, H.P.: Clinical Neurophysiology Automatic detection of prominent interictal spikes in intracranial EEG: validation of an algorithm and relationsip to the seizure onset zone. Clin. Neurophysiol. **125**(6), 1095–1103 (2014)
12. Carey, H.J., Manic, M., Arsenovic, P.: Epileptic Spike Detection with EEG using Artificial Neural Networks. In: 2016 9th International Conference on Human System Interactions (HSI), pp. 89–95 (2016)

13. Kumar, H., Amit, G., Kohli, K.: EEG spike detection technique using output correlation method: a Kalman filtering approach. circuits. Syst. Signal Process **34**(8), 2643–2665 (2015)
14. Garg, H.K., Kohli, A.K.: Nonstationary-epileptic-spike detection algorithm in EEG signal using SNEO. Biomed. Eng. Lett. **3**(2), 80–86 (2013)
15. Liu, Y., Chou-Ching, L., Tsai, J.-J., Sun, Y.-N.: Model-based spike detection of epileptic EEG data. Sensors **13**, 12536–12547 (2013)

ƒASSERT: A Fuzzy Assistive System for Children with Autism Using Internet of Things

Anjum Ismail Sumi[1], Most. Fatematuz Zohora[1], Maliha Mahjabeen[1],
Tasnova Jahan Faria[1], Mufti Mahmud[2(✉)], and M. Shamim Kaiser[1(✉)]

[1] Institute of Information Technology, Jahangirnagar University,
Savar, Dhaka 1342, Bangladesh
mskaiser@juniv.edu
[2] Computing and Technology, School of Science and Technology,
Nottingham Trent University, Clifton Campus, Nottingham NG11 8NS, UK
mufti.mahmud@ntu.ac.uk, mufti.mahmud@gmail.com

Abstract. This work presents an assistive system for child with autism spectrum disorder (C-ASD). The main objective of this system is to reduce dependency on the caregiver and parent and thereby assisting them to make independent. Fuzzy logic based expert system is designed for the assisting system which will help in intervention strategies. The system collects data from four different sensors, such as GPS, heart beat, accelerometer and sound, and generates required notification for the parent, caregiver and C-ASD. The wearables-specifically smart watches- can be used to implement such system. A case study shows the proposed expert system is able to help the C-ASD to restore dysfunction.

Keywords: Fuzzy set · Knowledge base · Wearable devices
Caregiver · Brain disorder

1 Introduction

Autism Spectrum Disorder (ASD) or simply Autism refers to a complex neurological and developmental disability with a range of conditions characterized by difficulties with social and interpersonal skills, speech and nonverbal communication and by restricted and repetitive behavior. It appears early in childhood and lasts throughout a person's life. The learning, thinking, and problem-solving and other capabilities of people with ASD can range from gifted to severely challenged. Some children with ASD need a lot of help in their daily lives; others need less. In the care centers it is a hectic job for the caregivers to monitor and supervise each child with their discrete needs.

Computational intelligence has been widely used in responding to problems related to healthcare and rehabilitation. The examples range from using fuzzy based systems for rehabilitation [4] to advanced machine learning techniques to

© Springer Nature Switzerland AG 2018
S. Wang et al. (Eds.): BI 2018, LNAI 11309, pp. 403–412, 2018.
https://doi.org/10.1007/978-3-030-05587-5_38

find patterns in biological data [5]. A fuzzy rule-based strategy can be implemented in a domain specific expert system that constructs rules using fuzzy sets and fuzzy logic and uses those rules to make decisions or choices.

The emerging Internet of Things (IoT) – creates human-machine or machine-to-machine communications – can collect data from children with ASD using various sensors and forward these sensor data to expert systems which emulates the decision-making ability of a human expert. Overcoming many security concerns, IoT has been adopted to improve healthcare [6].

Sula and Spaho proposed a system for improving the communication and language skills of children with autism using a smart assistive environment in autism care centers which uses JXTA-Overlay platform and SmartBox device to monitor the children and creates P2P communication between children, caregivers and therapists [10].

Alwakeel et al. presented a machine learning based electronic system for autism activity recognition using wireless sensor network [2]. This system has three main components; wearable sensor device, parent application and machine learning algorithm to accurately detect the gesture and motion of autistic child.

Min introduced a wearable system which is based on accelerometer as wearable sensor, microphone and camera as static sensors to detect behavioral patterns of child with ASD within a room using time Frequency method to extract features and Hidden Markov Model to analyze accelerometer signal [7].

Goel and Kumar proposed a wearable smart locator band that helps keeping track of kids using GPS technology and can notify parents in case of any emergency using GSM technology [3].

Ahmed et al. presented a solar powered smart wearable health monitoring and tracking device which uses temperature sensor, pulse sensor and GPS and GSM technology to monitor the location and health condition of the children with ASD [1].

Min and Tewfik introduced an algorithm to detect repetitive patterns of child with ASD using wearable wireless accelerometer sensor system [8]. They used Linear Predictive Coding method and the roots of the polynomials for classification of normal and self-injurious behaviors.

In the care centers or special schools, it is not possible to provide one to one services, that is, one caregiver for one student with ASD. In addition, their need and may be situation dependent. Some of them may be sensitive to load noises, bright/dark lights, ochlophobic etc. Because of their neurological and physical disability of various types, they cannot express their feelings properly to their guardians regarding their needs. For this deficiency in communication an autistic child in care centers may wander around or exposed to risks when the caregivers are not around. In these cases it would be very helpful for the parents and caregivers if they can be notified about the child's whereabouts in a specific perimeter and can monitor and assist the child as well through an expert system.

In this paper we propose a fuzzy based expert system using IoT by which parents and caregivers can monitor the child's movement, health condition, responsiveness and probable interaction of the child with others from a remote place using an application in their smart devices and can be notified if there is any kind of danger to the child or the child goes outside of the area range. The children can also be notified about their scheduled routine from their wearable device if they cannot maintain their class or therapy schedule on their own. Sound sensor of the system can issue an alert to the parents and caregivers if the child is making any abnormal sounds or making sounds higher than normal amplitude level. Movement sensor of the system can detect repetitive patterns which may result in any kinds of aggressiveness in behavior of the child and can therefore issue an alert. GPS technology is used to track the location of the child and wireless networks to establish communication between the expert system and parents, caregivers and care center through an application. Our proposed system doesn't intend to eliminate face to face communication, but rather tries to increase child's independence in the care center or school premises with maintaining sufficient security measures. This smart and assistive environment can increase attention, self-reliance and decrease aggressive and anxiety related behaviors of the children with ASD.

The rest of the paper is organized as follows: In Sects. 2 and 3, we provide details of our proposed system and data acquisition strategy. In Sect. 4, we present and discuss experimental results obtained from autistic subjects. Then, in Sect. 5, we present conclusions and future work.

2 Proposed System Model

The proposed system comprised of three individual units titled sensing unit, data processing unit and application unit which is illustrated below with a block diagram in Fig. 1.

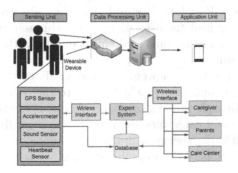

Fig. 1. Block diagram of proposed system

2.1 Sensing Unit

The sensing unit will consist of GPS sensor, accelerometer as in motion sensor, sound sensor and heartbeat sensor. A wearable device will be enabled by these sensors and it will operate as the sensing unit of this system. The wearable device includes the following sensing elements:

GPS Sensor. GPS sensor incessantly determines the child physical location using latitude, longitude and altitude, the time when the reading is taken, the current direction or heading of the child and their speed. Using this sensor we can monitor if the child is within the safe boundaries as they should be. If the current location detected by the GPS sensor does not match with the scheduled location of the child then the system generates an alarm.

Accelerometer. Accelerometer as in motion sensor, measures proper acceleration in 3d space such as left/right, up/down and forward/backward. Autistic child may often repeat some form of movements which are self-injurious behaviors and can lead them to danger. When such a repetitive movement is detected, the caregiver and parents will be notified immediately and the child will be taken care of.

Sound Sensor. Sometimes an autistic child may make various sounds for expressing happiness or anger or danger. The amplitude and the frequency of the sound are different for different behavioural situation. In addition, these amplitude and frequency pair is a subjective feature for each patient. The sound sensor can feed the sound signal to the data processing unit to detect any abnormal sounds.

Heartbeat Sensor. Heartbeat sensor detects any atypical heart activity such as missing pulse or rhythmic deficit. When engaging in sports or physical activities, some autistic children do not understand that they are getting too tired and further doing this may lead them to danger. So, this sensor detects the heart rate and issues an alert to the connected smart devices if the current heart rate crosses the normal limit.

The data of the positions, movements and vitals of the child will be collected from the sensors and then it will be sent to the data processing unit for further processing through wireless interface. And if it fulfills the conditions of notifying the parents and caregivers about any issue regarding the child's physical and mental health, the system will deliver the necessary information to the application unit as well as to the wearable device.

2.2 Data Processing Unit

Data processing unit consists of a fuzzy based expert system and an external database. Expert system will process the data coming from the sensing unit via wireless interface with the support of a properly enhanced knowledge base and inference engine. On the other hand, the external database will store necessary data from all of the units of the system and feed it back into the expert system. The collected data of child's physical location, repetition of movements of various kind, vitals and other corresponding data from the sensing unit will be inputted for the data processing unit to process the received data for determining a particular solution for each session with the intelligent expert system. After analyzing each session, a decision will be generated with additional command and information and it will be sent to the application unit via wireless interface as an alarm or a notification in the associated application as per their given instruction. Every decision along with its related information and commands respect to that decision will be sent to the external database as well to be stored for gaining new data set for the knowledge base of the expert system. The proposed expert system will be thoroughly discussed in the next section.

2.3 Application Unit

The monitoring and management application is installed on the smart devices for the parents, caregivers and the care center. It will work like the output section of the system because every processed data in each session will generate a result to decide what to do in the current situation along with the related information about the child and the system will always send these alerts or notices to the application unit for the parents and caregivers to be notified about any occurrence at any time. In this way, the transparency for children security and well-being in this system can be maintained radically.

3   Expert System for Assisting Child with ASD

The functional diagram of the proposed expert system is given below in Fig. 2.

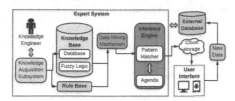

Fig. 2. Functional diagram of proposed expert system

The components of the expert system are a knowledge base; inference engine and user interface. The knowledge base contains specific and high-quality knowledge. Data, information, and past experience combined together are termed as knowledge. Explicit knowledge is required to exhibit higher intelligence. The knowledge base will be formed by readings from various experts, scholars, and the Knowledge Engineers. The knowledge engineer will categorize and organize the information in a meaningful way, in the form of IF-THEN-ELSE rules, to be used by interference machine.

3.1 Data Extraction and Fuzzy Set Generation

The data from the various sensors are collected and these raw data are transformed into a specific format by either moving average with amplitude method or the fast Fourier transform method [9]. Finally trapezoidal membership function is used to generate the fuzzy sets.

3.2 Fuzzy Rule Base

Fuzzy rule-based strategy is basically based on verbally constructed rules. Fuzzy rules are linguistic IF-THEN-ELSE formulations, used to conclude an output based on input variables by specifying fuzzy sets, each of which can be referred to as any form of linguistic values. Several rules constitute a fuzzy rule base. Therefore, here in this fuzzy rule base LOW, MEDIUM and HIGH are linguistic values of the linguistic variables such as Accelerometer, Sound sensor and Heartbeat sensor which work as premises and Hyperactivity as the consequence, after initiating the implication of the premises (Fig. 3).

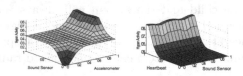

Fig. 3. Hyperactivity detection using FIS

Table 1. Determining mechanism for required attention and alert

GPS	Hyperactivity	Att. Required	Alert sent
IL	L	No	No
IL	M	Medium	Caregiver and parents
IL	H	High	Caregiver
OL	L	High	Caregiver
OL	M	High	Caregiver
OL	H	High	Caregiver

For the system to detect when to give attention to the child and to what extent, can be formulated using the same fuzzy rule-base approach in a different context where GPS locations (linguistic values- In Location (IL) and Out of location (OL)) and Hyperactivity values work as premises and required attention level as consequence of processing the input variables as shown in Table 1.

4   A Case Study

The functioning procedure for monitoring child's social interaction is shown in the flow chart in Fig. 4. First of all, the wearable device with GPS sensor, 3D-accelerometer, sound sensor and heartbeat sensor will have to be fully functional to carry out further procedures of the system. The GPS data will include child's physical location, current time, current direction the child is heading towards and their movement speed, which will be loaded instantly in the database. 3D-accelerometer will measure proper acceleration and detect movements which are self-injurious. Sound sensor will search for any abnormal sounds, atypical breathing pattern and change in amplitude level of the voice. Finally, the heartbeat sensor will check whether the heart rate crosses the normal limit or not. If any movement that is injurious to their health is observed, the caregiver and parents will be notified immediately and in the meantime the child's device will play some soothing audio records to attract their attention and calm them until the child is taken care of. In case of no destructive repetitive movements, the system will search for child's location within a specific range. If more than one child is found in the appropriate location, the distance among the GPS location of all the children in that area range will be compared. By comparing the distances, we can somewhat estimate the possibility of interaction among the children. If the system finds any child who is more than 5 m away from other children within a specific range, those children will be marked as deserted children and the system will alert the parents and caregiver to keep an eye on them for improving their social communication with others. Otherwise it will be considered that the children are having gentle interactions with the children nearby if no deserted children are found within the area range.

In addition to the functional procedures, this system will enable the child to perform their assigned daily activities on their own without any supplementary help. Figure 5 shows the schedule understanding flowchart for the child with ASD in the care center.

In autism care centers or schools, it is predetermined that the child is supposed to do some specific tasks in certain time periods as well as in some exact locations. We can get child's current location continuously from the GPS sensor attached with the wearable device. This information will be compared with the predefined scheduled location in the database if any task schedule of the child pops up. If both the location data matches it will be considered that the child is capable of maintaining the routine work independently. But in case of a total different situation, the system will generate an alarm to the connected devices and play an audio command in the child's device.

Let us present the result of our case study, for which we have experimented 12 subjects from Ananda Shala School. Ananda Shala is a special need-based education center of the Jahangirnagar University of Bangladesh and it is solemnly working for the autistic children and raising awareness among the people since its establishment. We have over 72 h of annotated data from these 12 children with autism. From the close observation period we have found that these children have the likelihood to take off the wearable device. The observation time

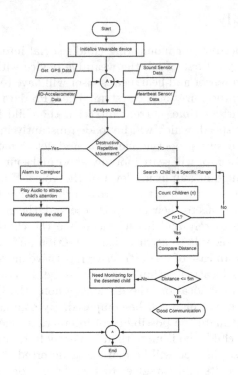

Fig. 4. Procedural flow chart for monitoring child's social interaction

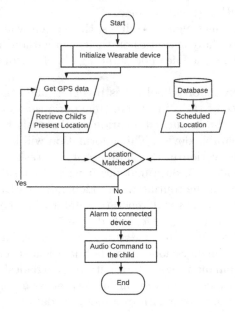

Fig. 5. Functional flow chart of schedule understanding mechanism

Table 2. Accuracy of fuzzy based assisting system

Proposed	Accuracy
Fuzzy logic	89%

for exhibiting this particular behavior in each subject was set to 30 min and for how long each of them carried the wearable device in that lapse of 30 min, is shown in the graph in Fig. 6a. Thus, from our survey, only 3 subjects carried the wearable device for the whole observation time and therefore, the average device wear-ability duration becomes 15.96 min for a observation period of 30 min.

Figure 6b shows number of times each object responded to the input to the wearable. It has been seen that each object's response frequency is proportional to wear-ability duration.

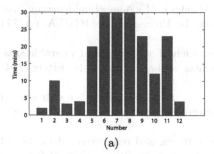
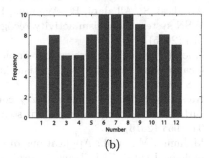

(a)   (b)

Fig. 6. (a) Distinction observed by device wear-ability duration. (b) Number of times objects are responded to the input.

From the analysis of acquired and annotated data with our predefined fuzzy sets and fuzzy logic, we were able to detect the accuracy of this fuzzy based expert system which is shown in Table 2. Heartbeat sensor, sound sensor and accelerometer, these three parameters were under consideration during the measurement of the system accuracy.

5   Conclusion

The paper describes a proposed assistive environment in autism care centers to make the children independent by reducing their dependency on caregivers and to ensure the parents about their child's safety. The assisting system uses a fuzzy logic based expert system which will be a necessary tool for guiding the child in the school premises by intervening different strategies. Thus, from our observations and data analysis, on the average, we are able to maintain 89% of total system accuracy of our proposed system. The successful implementation of the system requires various physical sensors enabled wearable device for the

C-ASD. The system is designed in a way that it can collect data from four different sensors (GPS, heartbeat, accelerometer and sound) and at the same time, it can generate and pass the obtained result as an alert or notification to the caregivers, parents and if necessary to the children through their wearable device. The case study shown in the previous section is a proof that the proposed system can be of greater assistance to deal with the dysfunctional characteristics of autistic children in the care center premises. In the future, we are planning to study a large number of children with various ages with detailed study on the performance evaluation of the defined fuzzy sets and fuzzy logic.

References

1. Ahmed, I.U., Hassan, N., Rashid, H.: Solar powered smart wearable health monitoring and tracking device based on GPS and GSM technology for children with autism. In: Proceedings of ICAEE, pp. 111–116 (2017)
2. Alwakeel, S., Alhalabi, B., Aggoune, H., Alwakeel, M.: A machine learning based WSN system for autism activity recognition. In: Proceedings of ICMLA, pp. 771–776 (2015)
3. Goel, I., Kumar, D.: Design and implementation of android based wearable smart locator band for people with autism, dementia, and alzheimer. Adv. Electr. **2015**, 1–8 (2015)
4. Kaiser, M.S., et al.: A neuro-fuzzy control system based on feature extraction of surface electromyogram signal for solar-powered wheelchair. Cogn. Comput. **8**(5), 946–954 (2016)
5. Mahmud, M., et al.: Applications of deep learning and reinforcement learning to biological data. IEEE Trans. Neural Netw. Learn. Syst. **29**(6), 2063–2079 (2018)
6. Mahmud, M., et al.: A brain-inspired trust management model to assure security in a cloud based IoT framework for neuroscience applications. https://doi.org/10.1007/s12559-018-9543-3. [ePub ahead of print]
7. Min, C.: Automatic detection and labeling of self-stimulatory behavioral patterns in children with autism. In: Proceedings of IEEE-EMBC, pp. 279–282 (2017)
8. Min, C.H., Tewfik, A.: Automatic characterization and detection of behavioral patterns using linear predictive coding of accelerometer sensor data. In: Proceedings of IEEE-EMBC, pp. 220–2233 (2010)
9. Santos, B.R., et al.: A method for automatic fuzzy set generation using sensor data. Intell. Autom. Soft Comput. **14**(3), 279–294 (2008)
10. Sula, A., Spaho, E.: Using assistive technologies in autism care centers to support children develop communication and language skills. A case study: Albania. Acad. J. Interdiscip. Stud. **3**(1), 203–212 (2014)

ADEPTNESS: Alzheimer's Disease Patient Management System Using Pervasive Sensors - Early Prototype and Preliminary Results

Tajim Md. Niamat Ullah Akhund[1], Md. Julkar Nayeen Mahi[1],
A. N. M. Hasnat Tanvir[1], Mufti Mahmud[2(✉)], and M. Shamim Kaiser[1(✉)]

[1] Institute of Information Technology, Jahangirnagar University,
Savar, Dhaka 1342, Bangladesh
mskaiser@juniv.edu
[2] Computing and Technology, School of Science and Technology,
Nottingham Trent University, Clifton Campus, Nottingham NG11 8NS, UK
mufti.mahmud@ntu.ac.uk, mufti.mahmud@gmail.com

Abstract. Alzheimer's is a catastrophic neuro-degenerative state in the elderly which reduces thinking skills and thereby hamper daily activity. Thus the management may be helpful for people with such condition. This work presents sensor based management system for Alzheimer's patient. The main objective of this work is to report an early prototype of an eventual wearable system that can assist in managing the health of such patients and notify the caregivers in case of necessity. A brief case study is presented which showed that the proposed prototype can detect agitated and clam states of patients. As the ultimately developed assistive system will be packaged as a wearable device, the case study also investigated the usability of wearable devices on different age groups of Alzheimer's patients. In addition, electro dermal activity for 4 patient of age group 55–60 and 60-7s years were also explored to assess the health condition of the patients.

Keywords: Sensor · Machine learning
Neurodegeneration · Wearable devices · Healthcare

1 Introduction

Alzheimer's is a disease that mostly relies on the behavior (e.g: memory counter parts, brain function involving) of the elderly age people. Increasing growth of population is a good factor for upholding the percentage of Alzheimer's in large quantities, especially in developing countries. It has been estimated that Alzheimer's will increase in a large quantity within the next 20 years among elderly people [13] and more or less, 115.4 million human will suffer in the long term factors, nearly in about 2050 [19]. In between the year 2000 to 2010 the

© Springer Nature Switzerland AG 2018
S. Wang et al. (Eds.): BI 2018, LNAI 11309, pp. 413–422, 2018.
https://doi.org/10.1007/978-3-030-05587-5_39

death penalty among elderly people have reached around 68% in comparing to the full population estimate [2]. There is hardly any better solution or cure for Alzheimer's in this modern era neither an accurate or reliable diagnosis; only some symptom based techniques are available for sub groups of patients. The expectation of life cycle after Alzheimer's diagnosis can lead to seven years in maximum [9] even though, Alzheimer's depends on environmental behaviors, genetic causes and lifestyle factors. These factors are merely effective approach to control Alzheimer's in the early detection with a good management strategy through a cognitive fashion. Moreover, in late 2010's there emerges some good strategic approaches through sensor based managements for the early detection of Alzheimer's [14].

Sensors or custom based electronic devices can act as a first party authority and detect symptoms of disease (e.g; behavior, walk pattern) in a low cost measurements which is a key point for early diagnosis of Alzheimer's in the developing countries. However; Internet-of-Things (IoT), Internet-of-Things driven cloud computing (IoTDC) are some of the sensor based approaches that can be carried on for the early diagnosis of Alzheimer's with better results. Dynamic time wrapping (DTW), machine learning based Kernel Null Foley-Sammon trans- form (KNFST), stochastic neighbor embedding (SNE) are some of the sensor based reliable approach that can attain 80% accuracy in early Alzheimer's diagnosis. The activity and behavioral complexities in terms of accuracy are the major lags for the disease diagnosis [3, 22]. On the contrary, sensor based machine learning (ML) training approach can work to record and estimate the behavioral patterns for the use of future classification, which is definitely a good form of Alzheimer's diagnosis with utmost accuracy [25].

In this paper work, the authors have discussed a wide range benefits of using sensors under different approaches of Alzheimer's disease detection with bare accuracy measures. The author's main target in this paper is to review their research work to show the possible usage of sensor based application models in disease inspection of Alzheimer's for a feasible reliable approach.

2   Literature Review

Alzheimer's is a disease that can be categorized as a memory loss in human brain for the elderly. It is a disorder of neurological functions in the brain whose attacking rate grows exponentially with age. [21] describes that the phases of Alzheimer's can be modeled into three stages. There are several promising methods for Alzheimer's disease detection in humans. [1] describes that there are statistically 67 percent chances in elderly people to have Alzheimer's.

Meanwhile, neurological examination of the brain, neuro-imaging and neurophysiological evaluation have shown a successful diagnosis of suspicious suffering with Alzheimer's at an accuracy of 90 percent. But these evaluation process takes a long time and also needs hospital facilities with very costly work progressions. However, early detection on Alzheimer's symptomatology is a new process that can overcome the time and cost process of disease evaluation. This process deals mainly with behavioral analyzing shifting techniques through automated computer aided diagnosis (ACAD). For every detection process accuracy is a dire need parameter for disease evaluation.

Non-invasive innovative diagnostic (NIID) is an another wide process terminology that can help early detection of Alzheimer's in some main modalities like psychological, cognitive and behavioral impairments. In case of rehabilitation perspectives, gait analysis enabled wireless sensors have shown greater performances. Gyroscope, accelerometer, magnatoresistive sensors, flexible goniometer, electromagnetic tracking system, sensing fabrics, piezocapasitive, piezoelectric sensors, EMG process and Xsens (custom made sensor, Netherlands) are some of the better options to work on.

However, [23] have described the analytical usefulness of body pattern based gait kinematic sensors in the interpretation of social applications and clinical diagnosis. They have also stated some better algorithmic reviews in their paper which can be carried through the sensor based development modules to gain better signals in case of performance efficiencies. In gait kinetics; ground reaction force (GRF) measurement is a good approach but not for stationery systems. Moreover, the authors have concluded that gait analysis using body orientation through wireless sensors can carry remarkable benefits for the early detection in Alzheimer's.

The dynamic time wrapping algorithm (DTW) uses various movement pattern of foot which is collected from wearable IoT devices. [24] have narrated a novel algorithm for the early detection of disease (e.g: Alzheimer's). The normal and disease affected people is identified using cross identification function. The main benefit of this algorithm is that it significantly compares the distances between segments then compute them through wrapping them in a time alignment fashion.

The built - in smart phone sensors can make a good help in managing the detection of Alzheimer's disease. [11] describes a self-learning scheme enabled algorithm for medical monitoring of human disease (e.g: Alzheimer's). The empirical study of the paper is to establish a self-learning classifier that works with maximum recognition ability of detecting human disease in the out most cases. In other words, electronic devices merging with actuators through the use of machine learning approaches have a great impact on early based Alzheimer's disease detection managements which is also a pattern of lower cost estimation disease evaluation method [15].

Mobile sensor based system with an artificial integrity based approach can made a good help in terms of Alzheimer's disease detection at an early stage. [20] have discussed about the cognitive impairment detection through behavior anomalies through smart-faber an android based system with artificial intelligence integrity that can detect behaviors of the elderly age citizen informing by their body functional abilities. In this case, 'smart-faber' is the pervasive controller for subject targeting.

3 System Model

The Micro-controller unit MCU will be connected with the wearable sensors and GPS. Wearable sensor includes pulse sensor, flex sensor, accelerometer, gyroscope, magnetometer, temperature sensor and force sensitive resistor. MCU will collect the sensor data with location and save them into the SD card and send them to cloud database via Internet connection. Then the collected data will be analyzed. Then machine learning will be applied on the processed data after processing analysis. Then system will take decision about the patient is attacked or not based on the machine learning result. If the patient is attacked then the alert service will notify the care giver with patient's current location (see Fig. 1). In the first part of our work we have worked with the EDA sensor and take data. The procedure of EDA sensor is defined in a diagram. We have made an early system prototype (see Fig. 2). The EDA sensor module collects the electro dermal changes from human screen and amplifies it. The amplified data goes to MCU with its analog read pin. Then the SD card module connected with the MCU saves the data in an micro SD card for further processing. Another feature of our project is the system can send a fast notification through SMS via the GSM module.

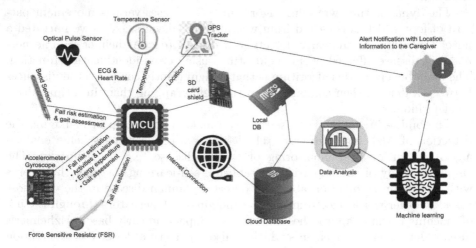

Fig. 1. System model.

3.1 Data Collection Using Pervasive System

We can collect Alzheimer's patient physical data with various sensor. The sensors send analog value to the MCU. We use some calculation to get the sensor value. Some sensor requires some library functions. We have applied optical pulse sensor to calculate pulse and ECG here. Flex sensor, FSR and gyroscope gives

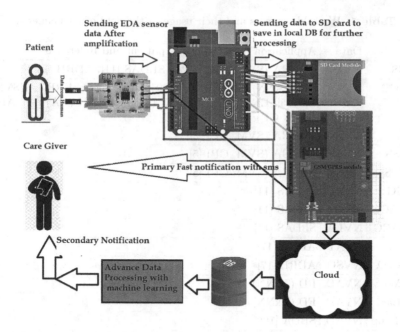

Fig. 2. EDA sensor working diagram.

the movement data in three axes. Then we can apply machine learning on the received data to realize patient condition. We have studied on the sensor used in the field of Alzheimer's and form a table containing wearable sensor, their data and suitable machine learning algorithm, see Table 1.

3.2   Management of Alzheimer's Patients

In our first prototype device we have added an EDA sensor with micro-controller. The micro-controller reads the analogue data from the sensor. In our future work the MCU is connected with the other above mentioned sensors. MCU saves the sensor data along with the location and time in an micro SD card through the SD card module. The data will be sent to an server in future. Our first prototype device have collected the EDA sensor data only. We applied machine learning algorithms on the data after processing. The machine learning algorithms compares the collected sensor data along with the previous Alzheimer's data set. Then the algorithm detects the patient is attacked or not on those particular time. If the patient is attacked by Alzheimer's according to the algorithm then the system will send an notification to the care giver of the patient through Internet or GSM after advanced processing of the sensor data. Then the care giver can take steps to help the patient. The system can send a fast primary notification through SMS via the GSM module to the care giver.

Table 1. Wearable sensors and their usage in the field of Alzheimer's.

Sensor	Data	Application for Alzheimer's patient and Reference
1. GS	NVAV	FREGA (SVM, GP) [5,24], SLDAS [11], ADRB [18]
2. ACC	NVAA	FD (TkNN) [6], SLDASguo2016smartphone, FREGA (SVM, GP) [5], ENEX (RM) [8], SC (CA) [12], HK (CA) [10], ADL (k-NN GP) [4], LC(SVM) [7]
3. FS	NVR	FREGA (SVM, GP) [5]
4. FSR	NVAD	FREGA (SVM, GP) [5]
5. EFS	NVAD	FREGA (SVM, GP) [5]
6. MG	NVAD	SLDAS [11]
7. GACC	NVGA	SLDAS [11]
8. LACC	NVLA	SLDAS [11]
9. PlS	NVAT	ADRB [17]
10. EDA	NVSC	ADRB [17]
11. Mic	NVAD	FD (TkNN) [6]
12. Bar	NVAD	FD (TkNN) [6]
13. Temp	NVAD	SBDA [18]
14. RFID	NVRF	FPF (TA) [16], LC (SVM) [7], SC (CA) [12], HK (CA) [10]

Legends: Fall risk estimation and gait assessment – FREGA; Self-learning data analysis scheme for patient's activity recognition - SLDAS; Detection of Alzheimer's Disease-Related Behaviors – ADRB; Numeric value of Angular velocity around the three axes – NVAV; Numeric value of Acceleration along the three axes of (x,y,z) – NVAA; Fall detection – FD; Fall risk estimation and gait assessment – FREGA; Self-care – SC; Housekeeping – HK; Activities of daily living – ADL; Leisure and communication – LC; Energy expenditure – ENEX; Self learning data analysis scheme for patients activity recognition – SLDAS; Numeric value of Resistance – NVR; Fall risk estimation and gait assessment – FREGA; Numeric value from analog data – NVAD; Numeric value of Gravitational acceleration along the three axes of (x,y,z) – NVGA; Numeric value of Linear acceleration without gravity along the three axis of (x,y,z) – NVLA; Numeric value against time – NVAT; Detection of Alzheimer's Disease Related Behaviors – ADRB; Continuous numeric value with time to plot graph – NVTP; Numeric value from changes in skin conductance resulting from the sympathetic nervous system activity – NVSC; Sensor-Based Detection Of Alzheimer's Disease – SBDA; Numeric value from digital radio frequency tag – NVRF; Food preparation and feeding – FPF; Force Sensitive Resistor – FSR; Electric Field Sensor – EFS; Electro Dermal Activity – EDA; Gaussian process – GP; Threshold based kNN Algorithm – TkNN; Threshold based Algorithm – TA; Regression Model – RM; Custom Algorithm – CA; Gyroscope – GS; Accelerometer – ACC; Flex Sensor – FS; Magnetometer – MG; Gravity Accelerator – GACC; Linear Accelerator – LACC; Pulse Sensor – PlS; Microphone – Mic; Barometer – Bar; Temperature – Temp

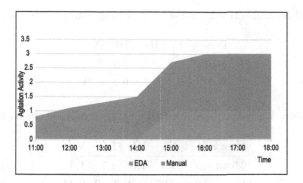

Fig. 3. Clam (0) and agitation (1) activities of an Alzheimer's patient recorded by a nurse. The similar activity is also recorded at different time by a automated sensor.

4   A Case Study

This section discusses a case study which involves nine Alzheimer's patients. The experimentation was conducted at the Institute of Mental Health, Dhaka by obeying the privacy rule of clinical research approved by the institute. The two states: *Clam* and *Agitated* were observed using manual and sensor based system. The manual data were collected by the nurse whereas the data for sensor based system were collected using wearable devices.

The observation of the nurse(s) and sensor data are found to be similar as shown in Fig. 3. The agitation and clam activity recorded by the sensor are recorded. The Clam state (denoted by 0) and Agitation state (denoted by 1) of an Alzheimer's patient.

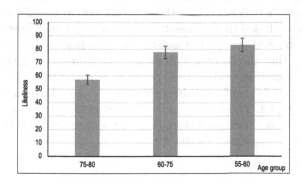

Fig. 4. Effect of various age group on the usage of smart watch. More age group Alzheimer's patents are reluctant to use the smart watch which can monitor the various activities

Figure 4 shows the effect of various age group on the usage of smart watch. The Alzheimer's patents belonging to the high age group were reluctant to use

Table 2. Electro dermal activity for age group 55–60 years

Person	I	II	III	IV
Mean	2.2	2.1	1.9	2
Std	0.2	0.22	0.2	0.31

Table 3. Electro dermal activity for age group 60–65 years

Person	I	II	III	IV	V
Mean	2	1.8	1.9	1.7	1.8
Std	0.3	0.27	0.26	0.29	0.28

the smart watch which can monitor the various physiological parameters or activities.

Electro Dermal activity (EDA) of a patient detects the state (calm/agitated condition) from the recorded sensor raw data. Tables 2 and 3 show EDA for various persons of age group 55–60 and 60-7s years. The data has been collected 10 times from each subject, then the mean and standard deviation are calculated. For these two age group the EDA based smartwatch can distinguish calm/distress condition with 83% accuracy. From these result, it has been found that the EDA reduces with the increase of age.

5   Conclusion

In this work, sensors-based management system for Alzheimer's patient is proposed. There are various sensors discussed which can be employed to tract and assist an Alzheimer's patient. A case study is conducted to find out the effectiveness of such sensor based management. It is found that such system can detect agitation and clam activity. As the assisting system may be incorporated in the portable devices, thus the effect of various age group on the usage of smart watch has been investigated. In addition electro dermal activity for 4 persons of age group 55–60 and 60-7s years were also explored. It is found that a generic system may not be developed. The system has to be customized based on the condition of a person. In future, machine learning based management will be employed to design a generic management system for the Alzheimer's patients.

References

1. Ahmed, O.B., et al.: Classification of Alzheimer's disease subjects from MRI using hippocampal visual features. Multimed. Tools Appl. **74**(4), 1249–1266 (2015)
2. Association, A., et al.: 2016 Alzheimer's disease facts and figures. Alzheimer's Dement. **12**(4), 459–509 (2016)
3. Aramendi, A.A., Aztiria, A., Basarab, A.: On the early diagnosis of Alzheimer's Disease from multimodal signals: a survey. Artif. Intell. Med. **71**, 1–29 (2016)

4. Atallah, L., Lo, B., King, R., Yang, G.Z.: Sensor placement for activity detection using wearable accelerometers. In: Proceedings of BSN, pp. 24–29 (2010)
5. Bamberg, S.J.M., et al.: Gait analysis using a shoe-integrated wireless sensor system. IEEE Trans. Inf. Technol. Biomed. **12**(4), 413–423 (2008)
6. Bianchi, F., Redmond, S.J., Narayanan, M.R., Cerutti, S., Lovell, N.H.: Barometric pressure and triaxial accelerometry-based falls event detection. IEEE Trans. Neural Syst. Rehabil. Eng. **18**(6), 619–627 (2010)
7. Bulling, A., Ward, J.A., Gellersen, H., Troster, G.: Eye movement analysis for activity recognition using electrooculography. IEEE Trans. Patt. Anal. Mach. Intell. **33**(4), 741–753 (2011)
8. Crouter, S.E., Clowers, K.G., Bassett Jr., D.R.: A novel method for using accelerometer data to predict energy expenditure. J. Appl. Physiol. **100**(4), 1324–1331 (2006)
9. Dauwels, J., et al.: Slowing and loss of complexity in Alzheimer's EEG: two sides of the same coin? Int. J. Alzheimer's Dis. (4), 10 (2011)
10. Farringdon, J., Moore, A.J., Tilbury, N., Church, J., Biemond, P.D.: Wearable sensor badge and sensor jacket for context awareness. In: Proceedings of ISWC, pp. 107–113 (1999)
11. Guo, J., Zhou, X., Sun, Y., Ping, G., Zhao, G., Li, Z.: Smartphone-based patients' activity recognition by using a self-learning scheme for medical monitoring. J. Med. Syst. **40**(6), 140 (2016)
12. Im, S., Kim, I.J., Ahn, S.C., Kim, H.G.: Automatic ADL classification using 3-axial accelerometers and RFID sensor. In: Proceedings of MFI, pp. 697–702 (2008)
13. Labate, D., Foresta, F.L., Morabito, G., Palamara, I., Morabito, F.C.: Entropic measures of EEG complexity in Alzheimer's disease through a multivariate multiscale approach. IEEE Sens. J. **13**(9), 3284–3292 (2013)
14. Lopez, D., Sekaran, G.: Climate change and disease dynamics - a big data perspective. Int. J. Infect. Dis. **45**, 23–24 (2016)
15. Mahmud, M., et al.: Applications of deep learning and reinforcement learning to biological data. IEEE Trans. Neural Netw. Learn. Syst. **29**(6), 2063–2079 (2018)
16. Patterson, D.J., Fox, D., Kautz, H., Philipose, M.: Fine-grained activity recognition by aggregating abstract object usage. In: Proceedings of ISWC, pp. 44–51 (2005)
17. Pedro, S.: Sensor-Based Detection of Alzheimer's Disease-Related Behaviours. University of Coimbra, Coimbra (2013)
18. Pedro, S., Quintas, J., Menezes, P.: Sensor-based detection of Alzheimer'S disease-related behaviors. In: Zhang, Y.-T. (ed.) The International Conference on Health Informatics. IP, vol. 42, pp. 276–279. Springer, Cham (2014). https://doi.org/10.1007/978-3-319-03005-0_70
19. Prince, M., Ali, G., Guerchet, M., Prina, M., Albanese, E., Wu, Y.T.: Recent global trends in the prevalence and incidence of dementia, and survival with dementia. Alzheimers Res. Ther. **8**, 23 (2016)
20. Riboni, D., et al.: SmartFABER: recognizing fine-grained abnormal behaviors for early detection of mild cognitive impairment. Artif. Intell. Med. **67**, 57–74 (2016)
21. Rosén, C., Hansson, O., Blennow, K., Zetterberg, H.: Fluid biomarkers in Alzheimer's disease-current concepts. Mol. Neurodegener. **8**(1), 20 (2013)
22. Tao, W., Liu, T.Z.R.F.H.: Gait analysis using wearable sensors. Sensor **12**(2), 2255–2283 (2012)
23. Tao, W., Liu, T., Zheng, R., Feng, H.: Gait analysis using wearable sensors. Sensors **12**(2), 2255–2283 (2012)

24. Varatharajan, R., Manogaran, G., Priyan, M., Sundarasekar, R.: Wearable sensor devices for early detection of Alzheimer disease using dynamic time warping algorithm. Clust. Comput. 1–10 (2017)
25. Zhou, X., Xu, J.: Identification of Alzheimer's disease-associated long noncoding RNAs. Neurobiol. Aging **36**(11), 2925–2931 (2015)

Uncovering Dynamic Functional Connectivity of Parkinson's Disease Using Topological Features and Sparse Group Lasso

Kin Ming Puk[1], Wei Xiang[2], Shouyi Wang[1(✉)], Cao (Danica) Xiao[3],
W. A. Chaovalitwongse[4], Tara Madhyastha[5], and Thomas Grabowski[6]

[1] Department of Industrial, Manufacturing and Systems Engineering,
University of Texas at Arlington, Arlington, USA
shouyiw@uta.edu
[2] Department of Computer Science and Engineering,
University of Texas at Arlington, Arlington, USA
[3] AI for Healthcare, IBM Research, Yorktown Heights, USA
[4] Industrial Engineering, University of Arkansas, Fayetteville, USA
[5] Integrated Brain Imaging Center, University of Washington, Seattle, USA
[6] Departments of Radiology and Neurology, University of Washington, Seattle, USA

Abstract. Neuro-degenerative diseases such as Parkinson's Disease (PD) are clinically found to cause alternations and failures in brain connectivity. In this work, a new classification framework using dynamic functional connectivity and topological features is proposed, and it is shown that such framework can give better insights over discriminative difference of the disease itself. After utilizing sparse group lasso with anatomically labeled resting-state fMRI signal, both discriminating brain regions and voxels within can be identified easily. To give an overview of the effectiveness of such framework, the classification performance with the network features extracted on dynamic functional network is quantitatively evaluated. Experimental results show that either single feature of clustering coefficient or combined feature group of characteristic path length, diameter, eccentricity and radius perform well in classifying PD, and as a result the identified feature can lead to better interpretation for clinical purposes.

Keywords: Parkinson's disease
Functional Magnetic Resonance Imaging (fMRI)
Dynamic functional connectivity · Sparse group lasso · Classification

1 Introduction

Functional connectivity refers to arbitrary relationships that might exist between the activations of distinct and often well separated neuronal populations, without any reference to physical connections or an underlying causal model [9].

© Springer Nature Switzerland AG 2018
S. Wang et al. (Eds.): BI 2018, LNAI 11309, pp. 423–434, 2018.
https://doi.org/10.1007/978-3-030-05587-5_40

In order to establish such connectivity, typical mathematical approaches including Pearson's correlation [13,23], covariance [28] and mutual information [5,29] are often used. Correlation is by far the most popular method in this regard.

Often, in calculating the connectivity strength between two voxels, entire segment of time-series is used, which is better known as static functional connectivity. On the contrary, dynamic functional connectivity (DFC) applies a moving/sliding window so that only part of time-series segment is used time for computing the connectivity measure [4,8,9]. It has been shown in previous studies and in this work that DFC is a better and more robust way of quantifying functional connectivity in human brain. Essential to the employment of DFC are the tuning of two parameters - length and speed of the moving window. If length is too long, almost the entire segment of time-series is used; on the contrary, if the length is too short, then the calculated connectivity is not able to capture the relationship between two voxels. On the other hand, if speed is too slow, overlapping of time-series signal may occur and temporal change of each subject's connectivity network is not obvious enough for meaningful comparison; alternatively, if speed is too fast, then change in connectivity network may be too abrupt. In this work, classifications using both static and dynamic functional connectivity are conducted to illustrate the robustness of the proposed framework.

Comparing networks is an enormously difficult task, especially when the size of networks is different and networks to be compared have different nodes. The most primitive approach which still enjoys wide popularity in recent decade would be to compare voxel-wise connectivity in a functionally connected network, better known as multi-voxel pattern analysis [16]. Indeed such a network can be obtained from employing a distance metric between time-series signal of any two voxels. The most popular metric is Pearson's correlation because of its computational efficiency as opposed to metrics such as mutual information and lagged correlation. However, this approach cannot compare two networks in general and cannot explain causation. Another approach is to extract topological features based on complex network theory [7,20,25,27]. A complex network can be loosely defined as one with non-trivial topological features [2] such that it cannot be easily characterized with the typical features such as degree and cycle. In light of these facts, this work aims at extracting topological features from functional connectivity network and conducting classification with them. If classification accuracy is high, it means that topological features used for classification are discriminative or "different" enough for further investigation on the disease itself. Therefore, instead of computing a wide range of topological features between the disease and control groups with a hope that significant difference can be found, classification can be conducted to seek promising discriminating features for further interpretation.

2 Material and Method

2.1 Participants

Experiment subjects include 24 patients with Parkinson's Disease and 21 healthy controls as recruited by Integrated Brain Imaging Center at the University of Washington. Their demographics are summarized in Table 1. Patients with PD were diagnosed by an experienced neurologist according to their medical history, neurological examination and exclusion of other neuropsychiatric diseases. Before conducting fMRI scanning, the Hoehn and Yahr Scale (H&Y) were assessed for subjects with PD. Majority of PD patients were at the early stage of the disease (H&Y I-II). Please note that subjects do not differ significantly in education or age. This research study was approved by the University of Washington Institutional Review Board. All participants provided written informed consent.

Table 1. This study includes 25 subjects with PD and 21 controls. Potential participants were excluded if they had a history of any primary neuro-degenerative disease other than idiopathic PD. PD patients did not differ significantly from controls on age, education, or Montreal Cognitive Assessment score.

Demographics	PD patient	Control	Total
No. of subjects	24	21	45
Age at scan	66.08 (10.27)	61.90 (10.00)	64.13 (10.25)
Male subjects	17 (71%)	9 (43%)	26 (58%)
Years of education	16.17 (2.12)	15.90 (2.39)	16.05 (2.23)
Hoehn and Yahr scale	2.04 (1−2.5)	N/A	N/A
Right-Handed subjects	20	19	39

2.2 Functional MRI Data Acquisition

The dataset used in this work is part of a larger study which consists of both task-based and resting-state runs [15]. The fMRI data were acquired using a Philips 3T Achieva MR System (software version 3.2.2; Philips Medical Systems, The Netherlands) with a 32-channel SENSE head coil. During each session, whole-brain axial echo-planar images (43 sequential ascending slices, 3mL isotropic voxels, field of view = 240 × 240 × 129, repetition time, TR = 2400 ms, echo time = 25 ms, flip angle = 79°, and SENSE acceleration factor = 2) were collected parallel to the anterior-commissure– posterior commissure (AC-PC) line for all functional runs. The first five dummy volumes in our fMRI acquisition are automatically discarded to achieve steady-state imaging. Run duration was 300 volumes (12 min) for the resting-state run and 149 volumes (5.96 min) for each task run. A sagittal T1-weighted 3D MPRAGE (176 slices, matrix size = 256. 256, inversion time = 1100 ms, turbo-field echo factor = 225, repetition time = 7.46 ms, echo time = 3.49 ms, flip angle = 7°, and shot interval = 2530 ms) with 1 mm isotropic voxels was also acquired for registration. Please note that this study only utilizes data from resting-state runs.

2.3   Classification Framework

The classification framework consists of preprocessing, selection of brain regions, dynamic functional connectivity at each selected brain region, extraction of topological features and ensemble learning.

Data Preprocessing. Functional images were processed identically using a pipeline developed using software from FSL, FreeSurfer, and AFNI. Data were corrected for motion using FSL MCFLIRT. The pipeline removed spikes using AFNI, performed slice timing correction using FSL, and regressed out time series motion parameters and the mean signal for eroded (1mm in 3D) masks of the lateral ventricles and white matter (derived from running FreeSurfer on the T1-weighted image). Three dimensional spatial smoothing was performed using a Gaussian kernel with a full width at half maximum (FWHM) of sigma = 3 mm. Co-registration to the T1 image was performed using boundary-based registration based on a white matter segmentation of the T1 image (epi_reg in FSL). A Temporally Concatenated Probabilistic Group Independent Components Analysis (TC-GICA) was implemented using Multivariate Exploratory Linear Decomposition into Independent Components (MELODIC) Version 3.12 to generate large-scale components across all restingstate scans for all participants. In this data set, a probabilistic Principal Component Analysis using the Laplace approximation to the Bayesian evidence of the model order estimated a 22-dimensional subspace into which data were projected. The whitened observations were decomposed into sets of vectors that described the signal variation across the concatenated time courses and across the spatial maps by optimizing for non-Gaussian spatial source distributions using a fixed-point iteration technique. A dual-regression approach implemented in FSL was used to identify session-specific time courses for each subject corresponding to the spatial maps identified in the ICA, then to identify session-specific spatial maps for each subject corresponding to these time courses. An average spatial map for each subject was created for each component of interest by averaging the Session 1 and Session 2 maps. A group-level analysis comparing PD patients with controls was performed by nonparametric testing (5000 permutations) on the single-subject spatial maps for the group-level components of interest. Maps were thresholded at a Bonferroni-corrected probability of 0.05 with threshold-free cluster enhancement.

MNI coordinates that have been identified as nodes in the default mode network (DMN) and republished by [22] were then selected. The detail of the 264 selected voxels (Power-264 Atlas) can be found in appendix. For each coordinate, a 10 mm diameter mask in standard space were created and transformed to subjects' native space to calculate mean subject-specific time courses for each region of interest. Readers are referred to [15] for the preprocessing detail of this retrospective study.

Dynamic Connectivity Analysis. Indeed, DFC works by selecting a time window of fixed length, and data points within which are used to calculate the

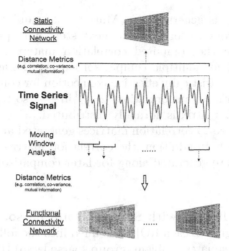

Fig. 1. An Illustration of Establishing Functional Network Using Dynamic Connectivity of fMRI Time-Series Signal: Static functional connectivity uses the entire segment of time-series signal in establishing connectivity, whereas dynamic functional connectivity uses part of the time-series signal at a time.

FC metric of interest. The window is then shifted in time by a fixed number of data points (ranging from a single data point to the length of a window) that defines the amount of overlap, if any, between successive windows [4,8]. Thus two parameters are required to compute the correlation matrix for DFC: length and speed of moving window. In this work, length (w) and speed (v) are chosen to be 24 TR (around 24 * 2.4 = 57.6 seconds) and 12 TR per each moving (around 28.8 s per each moving) based on the recommendation from [8] and the empirical result in this work. It follows that the number of moving window is $\lceil \frac{T-w}{v} \rceil = \frac{300-24}{12} = 23$.

A distinction between static and functional connectivity has to be made before proceeding (Fig. 1): for static functional connectivity, the value of T in Eq. 1 would be the full length of the time series signal (i.e. 300 TR in this study), whereas for dynamic functional connectivity, the value of T would be the length of moving window ($w = 24$).

Denote DFC network matrix at moving window w (where $w = 1, \ldots, 23$) as M_w, which is calculated with Pearson Correlation as follows [13]:

$$M_w(i,j) = \frac{\sum_{k=1}^{T}(x_k^i - \overline{x}^i)(x_k^j - \overline{x}^j)}{\sqrt{\sum_{k=1}^{T}(x_k^i - \overline{x}^i)^2}\sqrt{\sum_{k=1}^{T}(x_k^j - \overline{x}^j)^2}}. \tag{1}$$

In Eq. (1), denote the time-series vector at voxel i as $\boldsymbol{x}^i = [x_1^i, x_2^i, \ldots, x_T^i]$, where T is the length of the time-series signal. $\overline{x}^i$ and $\overline{x}^j$ are the mean of vectors $\boldsymbol{x}^i$ and $\boldsymbol{x}^j$. As a result, the correlation matrix is square and symmetric since $M(i,j) = M(j,i)$.

Each DFC matrix is generated via Matlab command "corr". To facilitate computation of network features in the next step, only positive part of correlation coefficient in the computed correlation matrix is used. Correlation matrix was corrected for multiple comparisons using Bonferroni correction at $p = 0.05$ to seek only statistically effective connection for consideration, and was z-transformed (Fisher's z-transformation, $z = \frac{1}{2}\ln\frac{1+r}{1-r}$) so that each correlation coefficient in the DFC matrix is normally distributed.

In the end, there are 23 correlation matrices generated at each selected brain region for each subject. In addition, the correlation matrices using static functional connectivity were generated along for later comparison between dynamic and static FC.

Selection of Brain Region with Sparse Group Lasso. The mean subject-specific time-series signal at each ROI is then fed into the following group sparse Lasso penalized least squares problem (group sparse lasso) [12] in order to select the relevant voxels which can most discriminate subjects with PD from those without it:

$$\min_{\mathbf{x}} \quad \frac{1}{2}||A\mathbf{x} - \mathbf{y}||_2^2 + \lambda_1||\mathbf{x}||_1 + \lambda_2 \sum_{i=1}^{g} w_i^g ||\mathbf{x}_{G_i}||_2 \qquad (2)$$

In the above, A is the matrix containing time-series signal (number of rows is 13,500 (300 TR[1] for each of the 45 subjects) and number of column is 264 (voxels)), $\mathbf{y}$ is the labeling of the subjects (1 is PD, -1 is control), $\mathbf{x}_G$ is the group labeling information (to be explained later in this section as in Table 2), and $\mathbf{x}$ is the solution of model (a vector of length 264, with each element corresponding to a voxel). After solving model (2), voxel i is chosen if $\mathbf{x}_i$ is not zero. As a property of group sparse Lasso, the ideal number of voxels and the groups chosen are as minimal as possible.

Benefits of employing group sparse lasso in an early stage of this framework include (1) alleviating subsequent computational burden of computing correlation matrix for quantifying the DFC and (2) discovery of network clusters with regard to group labeling of any designation. In this work, lobe-level anatomical labeling is used as obtained through Talairach Client 2.4.3 [10,11].

With parameter tuning, voxels from three regions - (3) right cerebrum-frontal lobe, (7) left cerebrum-parietal lobe and (8) left cerebrum-frontal lobe were selected.

Extraction of Topological Features. Using the result from last step, time series matrix for each subject can be substantially reduced because not all 264 voxels will be used in forming the functional connectivity network at each brain region. In other words, the time series matrix for each subject is reduced from number of time points (300 TR) by number of voxels (264) to number of time points by number of selected voxels at each brain region.

---

[1] 1 TR represents the time between two successive data points in the time-series signal.

Table 2. A List of Brain Regions Defined for Lobe-Level Anatomical Labeling by Talairach Client 2.4.3. 255 out of 264 voxels are anatomically labeled and thus be selected by sparse group lasso.

No	Region name	No of voxels	No	Region name	No of voxels
1	Left Cerebrum-Occipital Lobe	16	10	Right Cerebrum-Parietal Lobe	24
2	Right Cerebrum-Occipital Lobe	17	11	Right Cerebrum-Sub-lobar	15
3	Right Cerebrum-Frontal Lobe	43	12	Left Cerebrum-Sub-lobar	8
4	Left Cerebrum-Temporal Lobe	19	13	Right Cerebellum-Posterior Lobe	4
5	Left Cerebrum-Limbic Lobe	17	14	Right Cerebellum-Anterior Lobe	1
6	Right Cerebrum-Temporal Lobe	18	15	Left Cerebellum-Posterior Lobe	3
7	Left Cerebrum-Parietal Lobe	18	16	Inter-Hemispheric-*	1
8	Left Cerebrum-Frontal Lobe	39	17	Left Brainstem-Midbrain	1
9	Right Cerebrum-Limbic Lobe	10	18	Left Cerebellum-Anterior Lobe	1

As this work aims at investigating the discriminating features of PD, and it is essential to extract topological features from the reduced time-series data in order to classify between subjects with and without PD, and to characterize the disease itself. Features extracted from each DFC matrix M_w at moving window w are:

- Clustering Coefficient (CC): In layman's term, clustering coefficient is a measure of the extent to which one's friends are also friends of each other [26]. As a measure of functional segregation, it is equivalent to the fraction of the node's neighbors that are also neighbors of each other [30].
  There are different versions of clustering coefficient. Global clustering coefficient assess the overall level of clustering in a network [18] and is defined in [14,24] as

$$C = \frac{1}{|N|} \sum_{i \in N} C_i = \frac{1}{|N|} \sum_{i \in N} \frac{3 * \text{no. of triangles at node } i}{\text{no. of triples at node } i} = \frac{1}{|N|} \sum_{i \in N} \frac{2 * \text{tri}_i}{k_i(k_i - 1)} \tag{3}$$

where C_i is the global clustering coefficient of node i, N is the set of nodes/voxels in the network, tri_i[2] is the number of triangles around a node i, and k_i[3] is the degree of a node i.
It is further generalized to its weighted, undirected version in [17] as

$$C^w = \frac{1}{|N|} \sum_{i \in N} C_i^w = \frac{1}{|N|} \sum_{i \in N} \frac{2 * \text{tri}_i^w}{k_i(k_i - 1)} \tag{4}$$

where C_i^w is the global weighted clustering coefficient of node i and tri_i^w[4] the weighted geometric mean of triangles around node i. This is the version

---

[2] Mathematically, $t_i = \frac{1}{2} \sum_{j,h \in N} a_{ij} a_{ih} a_{jh}$, where a_{ij} is the connection status between i and j: $a_{ij} = 1$ when link (i, j) exists (when i and j are neighbors); $a_{ij} = 0$ otherwise ($a_{ii} = 0$ for all i).

[3] From the formula, C is only defined when k_i is larger than 1.

[4] Mathematically, $t_i^w = \frac{1}{2} \sum_{j,h \in N} (w_{ij} w_{ih} w_{jh})^{1/3}$, where w_{ij} is the connection weight between nodes i and j.

this work uses for classification. It is generated via the command "cluster-ing_coef_wu" of Brain Connectivity Toolbox [24].

Please note that this classification framework does not use the average of global weighted clustering coefficient at each node (C_i) as a single feature. Instead, the value of CC at each node is concatenated as a feature vector (i.e. $[C_1, C_2, \ldots, C_n]$, where n is the number of nodes/voxels in the DFC network). Doing so ensures robustness of classification and allows later investigation of the extent to which each node in a DFC network is clustered.

The value of CC (unweighted or weighted) is defined to be between 0 and 1. Obviously, a high value of this feature indicates that the presence of clustered connectivity at individual nodes of the DFC network, as its name implies.

Last but not least, local clustering coefficient assesses the clustering in a single node's immediate network. Since this work does not use this feature, it is not further explained. Readers are referred to [18, 19] for details.

- Characteristic Path Length (CPL): As a measure of functional integration, characteristic path length (also known as average shortest path length) shows us the general distance between two nodes in a network. It is simply the average shortest path length in the network [30] and is mathematically defined as

$$L = \frac{1}{|N|} \sum_{i \in N} L_i = \frac{1}{|N|} \sum_{i \in N} \frac{\sum_{j \in N, j \neq i} d_{ij}}{|N| - 1} = \frac{\sum_{i \in N} \sum_{j \in N, j \neq i} d_{ij}}{|N|(|N| - 1)} \quad (5)$$

where L_i is the average distance between node i and all other nodes, d_{ij} is shortest path length between nodes i and j and N is the set of nodes in the network. If the network is symmetric, it can be defined as [3]:

$$L_{\text{symmetric}} = \frac{2 \sum_{i \in N} \sum_{j > i} d_{ij}}{|N|(|N| - 1)} \quad (6)$$

The value of CPL is defined to be between 0 and 1. A low value of this feature indicates that the network is in very compact form as the distance between any two nodes in the network is relatively short; on the contrary, a high value indicates the network is in the form of a line [1].

- Eccentricity, Graph Radius, Graph Diameter: In the terminology of graph theory, eccentricity of a node i is the greatest graph distance between node i and any other nodes in the network. Graph radius is the minimum of eccentricity among all nodes in a network, whereas graph diameter is the maximum of eccentricity among all nodes in a network.

Diameter characterizes the distance between the two most distant node pairs in a network.

The value of these three features is defined to be 0 and $+\infty$ (when the network has disconnected components). They are generated via the command "charpath" of Brain Connectivity Toolbox [24].

In this work, these three features are not used directly as a single feature. Rather, the ratio of the feature over the number of nodes in the identified brain region is used. Classification with this feature in the same brain region is the same for either using the original value or the ratio of this feature. However, when this feature from different brain regions is used for classification, the ratio version of this feature would be more meaningful.

Classification with Ensemble Learning. As there will be more features than observations because of dynamic connectivity analysis, and an effective method of feature selection is desired. In this regard, minimum Redundancy Maximum Relevance (mRMR) feature selection [21] is used. mRMR aims at selecting a subset of feature set based on the statistical property of a target classification variable, subject to the constraint that the features are mutually dissimilar to each other but at the same time marginally similar to the target classification variable. Because of its first-order incremental nature, mRMR selects features very quickly without sacrificing classification performance. The number of features used in this work is 50.

After feature selection, classification consists of two parts as in:

- Single-Region Classification: At each brain region, a five-fold cross validation is conducted on the chosen features using support vector machine (SVM) with linear kernel [6].
- Ensemble learning with majority voting: The predicted labels from each brain region were combined together and a new label was "predicted" via majority voting. For example, if the predicted labels for regions 1, 2 and 3 are 1, -1 and -1, then the new predicted label is -1 under majority voting. In case of even number of brain region (e.g. gyrus-level anatomical labeling), the one with lowest accuracy was dropped so that no ties would occur.

3 Result

Tables 3 summarizes accuracy of the classification using different features. In addition to the classification performance from the single brain region, classification using features extracted from voxels of and classification with ensemble learning from all the identified brain regions are included for a fair and comprehensive review.

To begin with, feature "clustering coefficient" performed particularly well across three kinds of anatomical/functional labeling. On the contrary, "characteristic path length", "diameter", "eccentricity" and "radius" are not good for discrimination unless combined together for classification. Recall in the Sect. 2.3

Table 3. Classification accuracy using topological features extracted from the chosen three regions (1) right cerebrum-frontal lobe, (2) left cerebrum-parietal lobe and (3) left cerebrum-frontal lobe of lobe-level anatomical labeling.

Feat	Connectivity	Right cerebrum-frontal lobe	Left cerebrum-parietal lobe	Left cerebrum-frontal lobe	All nodes from 3 regions	Ensemble learning
1. CC	Static	62.22%	53.33%	51.11%	64.44%	71.11%
	Dynamic	82.22%	84.44%	95.56%	100.00%	97.78%
2. CPL	Static	51.11%	53.33%	53.33%	51.11%	51.11%
	Dynamic	37.78%	46.67%	46.67%	35.56%	37.78%
3. Diameter	Static	53.33%	55.56%	48.89%	53.33%	53.33%
	Dynamic	68.89%	46.67%	40.00%	44.44%	51.11%
4. ECC	Static	60.00%	62.22%	42.22%	60.00%	57.78%
	Dynamic	51.11%	51.11%	44.44%	68.89%	53.33%
5. Radius	Static	44.44%	53.33%	68.89%	62.22%	53.33%
	Dynamic	53.33%	55.56%	53.33%	53.33%	53.33%
6. CPL + ECC + Radius + Diameter	Static	57.78%	62.22%	42.22%	57.78%	51.11%
	Dynamic	91.11%	80.00%	95.56%	97.78%	100.00%
7. All features	Static	64.44%	53.33%	55.56%	51.11%	55.56%
	Dynamic	100.00%	91.11%	95.56%	95.56%	100.00%

that if difference of accuracy between single-region and multi-region classifications is too much or if the accuracy of multi-region (ensemble learning) classification is less than that of single-region classification, it is very likely that the feature is not a useful one. The accuracy with ensemble learning for these four features is generally lower than that with single-region classification. Besides, their accuracy with dynamic connectivity analysis is generally lower than that of the static one.

Nonetheless, features sets "CPL + ECC + Radius + Diameter" and "All Features" perform very well across three kinds of group labeling.

Last but not least, dynamic connectivity analysis is once again proofed to be more robust than that of the static one in this work, as illustrated by the difference between dynamic and static ones from the feature sets "clustering coefficient", "CPL + ECC + Radius + Diameter" and "all features".

4   Concluding Remark

This work proposes a new framework of diagnosing PD and seeking discriminating features of the disease itself using sparse group lasso, dynamic functional connectivity and topological features. It is relative easier to diagnose PD if different groups of topological features are combined together for classification, provided the right method of feature selection is used. However, it would be more difficult to do so with just a single group of features while maintaining high accuracy. Clustering coefficient, in this regard, is proofed to be a useful feature and as a result of this and the whole framework, discriminating voxels of PD in the identified brain region under default model network can be found. In addition to this contribution, the relative discriminative power of brain regions with three kinds of anatomical/functional labeling for PD is concluded. This work also attempts to answer one of the research questions in the fMRI research community - instead of finding discriminating voxels spread over different brain regions as in multi voxel pattern analysis [16], can we find discriminating brain regions instead? The answer is through the use of sparse group lasso. Researchers can later use other different kinds of labeling and evaluate the selection result accordingly. Last but not least, dynamic functional connectivity is once again proofed to be more robust than that of the static one.

References

1. Aftabuddin, M., Kundu, S.: AMINONET-a tool to construct and visualize amino acid networks, and to calculate topological parameters. J. Appl. Crystallogr. **43**(2), 367–369 (2010)
2. Arenas, A., Díaz-Guilera, A., Kurths, J., Moreno, Y., Zhou, C.: Synchronization in complex networks. Phys. Rep. **469**(3), 93–153 (2008)
3. Börner, K., Sanyal, S., Vespignani, A.: Network science. Ann. Rev. Inf. Sci. Technol. **41**(1), 537–607 (2007)
4. Byun, H.Y., Lu, J.J., Mayberg, H.S., Günay, C.: Classification of resting state fMRI datasets using dynamic network clusters. In: Workshops at the Twenty-Eighth AAAI Conference on Artificial Intelligence (2014)
5. Chai, B., Walther, D., Beck, D., Fei-Fei, L.: Exploring functional connectivities of the human brain using multivariate information analysis. In: Advances in Neural Information Processing Systems, pp. 270–278 (2009)
6. Cortes, C., Vapnik, V.: Support-vector networks. Mach. Learn. **20**(3), 273–297 (1995)
7. Estrada, E.: The Structure of Complex Networks: Theory and Applications. Oxford University Press, New York (2012)
8. Matthew Hutchison, R., et al.: Dynamic functional connectivity: promise, issues, and interpretations. Neuroimage **80**, 360–378 (2013)
9. Ioannides, A.A.: Dynamic functional connectivity. Curr. Opin. Neurobiol. **17**(2), 161–170 (2007)
10. Lancaster, J.L., et al.: Automated talairach atlas labels for functional brain mapping. Hum. Brain Mapp. **10**(3), 120–131 (2000)
11. Lancaster, J.L., et al.: Automated labeling of the human brain: a preliminary report on the development and evaluation of a forward-transform method. Hum. Brain Mapp. **5**(4), 238 (1997)
12. Liu, J., Ji, S., Ye, J., et al.: SLEP: sparse learning with efficient projections. Arizona State Univ. **6**, 491 (2009)
13. Loewe, K., Grueschow, M., Stoppel, C.M., Kruse, R., Borgelt, C.: Fast construction of voxel-level functional connectivity graphs. BMC Neurosci. **15**(1), 1 (2014)
14. Duncan Luce, R., Perry, A.D.: A method of matrix analysis of group structure. Psychometrika **14**(2), 95–116 (1949)
15. Madhyastha, T.M., Askren, M.K., Boord, P., Grabowski, T.J.: Dynamic connectivity at rest predicts attention task performance. Brain Connectivity **5**(1), 45–59 (2015)

16. Norman, K.A., Polyn, S.M., Detre, G.J., Haxby, J.V.: Beyond mind-reading: multi-voxel pattern analysis of fMRI data. Trends Cogn. Sci. **10**(9), 424–430 (2006)
17. Onnela, J.-P., Saramäki, J., Kertész, J., Kaski, K.: Intensity and coherence of motifs in weighted complex networks. Phys. Rev. E **71**(6), 065103 (2005)
18. Opsahl, T.: Triadic closure in two-mode networks: redefining the global and local clustering coefficients. Soc. Netw. **35**(2), 159–167 (2013)
19. Opsahl, T., Panzarasa, P.: Clustering in weighted networks. Soc. Netw. **31**(2), 155–163 (2009)
20. Papo, D., Buldú, J.M., Boccaletti, S., Bullmore, E.T.: Complex network theory and the brain. Phil. Trans. R. Soc. B **369**(1653), 20130520 (2014)
21. Peng, H., Long, F., Ding, C.: Feature selection based on mutual information criteria of max-dependency, max-relevance, and min-redundancy. IEEE Trans. Patt. Anal. Mach. Intell. **27**(8), 1226–1238 (2005)
22. Power, J.D., et al.: Functional network organization of the human brain. Neuron **72**(4), 665–678 (2011)
23. Richiardi, J., Eryilmaz, H., Schwartz, S., Vuilleumier, P., Van De Ville, D.: Decoding brain states from fmri connectivity graphs. Neuroimage **56**(2), 616–626 (2011)
24. Rubinov, M., Sporns, O.: Complex network measures of brain connectivity: uses and interpretations. Neuroimage **52**(3), 1059–1069 (2010)
25. Strogatz, S.H.: Exploring complex networks. Nature **410**(6825), 268–276 (2001)
26. Telesford, Q.K., Joyce, K.E., Hayasaka, S., Burdette, J.H., Laurienti, P.J.: The ubiquity of small-world networks. Brain Connectivity **1**(5), 367–375 (2011)
27. Van Wijk, B.C.M., Stam, C.J., Daffertshofer, A.: Comparing brain networks of different size and connectivity density using graph theory. PloS ONE **5**(10), e13701 (2010)
28. Varoquaux, G., Gramfort, A., Poline, J.-B., Thirion, B.: Brain covariance selection: better individual functional connectivity models using population prior. In: Advances in Neural Information Processing Systems, pp. 2334–2342 (2010)
29. Wang, Z., Alahmadi, A., Zhu, D., Li, T.: Brain functional connectivity analysis using mutual information. In: 2015 IEEE Global Conference on Signal and Information Processing (GlobalSIP), pp. 542–546. IEEE (2015)
30. Watts, D.J., Strogatz, S.H.: Collective dynamics of śmall-worldńetworks. Nature **393**(6684), 440–442 (1998)

Brain-Machine Intelligence and Brain-Inspired Computing

The Effect of Culture and Social Orientation on Player's Performances in Tacit Coordination Games

Dor Mizrahi[1], Ilan Laufer[1], Inon Zuckerman[1(✉)], and Tielin Zhang[2]

[1] Department of Industrial Engineering and Management,
Ariel University, Ariel, Israel
inonzu@ariel.ac.il
[2] Institute of Automation, Chinese Academy of Sciences, Beijing, China

Abstract. Social Value Orientation (SVO) is one of the main factors affecting strategic decision making. This study explores the effects of different cultural background on players' SVO as well as on their ability to coordinate in tacit coordination games. Tacit coordination games are coordination games in which communication between the players is not allowed or not possible. Our results showed that the two cultural backgrounds (Israelis and Chinese players) differ in the distribution of the SVO angle (a measure of the social orientation of the player), which is useful for predicting the cultural background of the player. Next, we explored the effects of the SVO value on players' strategies in tacit coordination games and demonstrated that players with different cultural backgrounds are endowed with different coordination abilities (as measured by a coordination index).

Keywords: Tacit coordination games · Social Value Orientation Support Vector Machine

1 Introduction

There is a substantial set of evidence from the social and behavioral sciences literature showing that individuals explicitly take into account the outcome of others when considering their course of action [1]. Moreover, the choices people make depend, among other things, on stable personality traits that affect the way they approach interdependent others. This theory was later denoted as the Social Value Orientation (SVO) theory, which has been since developed into a class of theorems [2]. The social orientation of a player is not an absolute value; it describes a spectrum of possible behaviors, in which one end of the spectrum denotes proself behavior, and the other end denotes prosocial behavior. The first aim of the current study (Aim #1) was to explore whether there are differences in the distribution of the SVO between two groups belonging to different cultural backgrounds (CBs), namely, Israeli (ICB) and Chinese (CCB), that were otherwise identical in terms of other demographic data. Based on the results of Aim #1, the second aim (Aim #2) was to predict the cultural

© Springer Nature Switzerland AG 2018
S. Wang et al. (Eds.): BI 2018, LNAI 11309, pp. 437–447, 2018.
https://doi.org/10.1007/978-3-030-05587-5_41

background (CB) as a function of the SVO values. Our third aim (Aim #3) was to examine the effect of the CB on the performance level in tacit coordination games.

2   The Influence of Cultural Background on the SVO Index

2.1   The SVO Measure

The SVO theory describes the preferences or motivations of Decision Makers (DMs) when allocating joint resources between the self and another person [1, 2]. The model represents four main categories that describe those preferences: Individualistic orientation – a DM who is only concerned with their own outcomes, Competitive orientation – a DM who aspires to maximize their own outcome, but in addition also minimizes the outcome of others, Cooperative orientation – a DM who tends to maximize the joint outcome, and Altruistic orientation – a DM who is motivated to help others at the expense of their own utility.

There are three main methods that were suggested over the years to measure the SVO in humans. The first is called the Ring method [3], which consists of 24 social dilemma games in which the subject must choose between two alternatives that represent different combinations of outcomes for themselves as well as for another person. Another measure is the Triple-Dominance measure [4] which consists of nine items while in each of them the subject needs to select one out of three possible own-other outcomes. The third and most recent measuring method is the Slider method [5], which is also considered to be the most accurate one.

In the slider method, the participant must answer only 6 questions. These questions contain a continuous scale; each point on the scale produces a different allocation of resources between him or herself and an unknown other. This method of measurement has two main advantages. First, instead of assigning the participant to one of four possible categories, the slider method produces a number called the SVO angle (see Eq. (1)). Second, this method provides a way to discern the attitude of the subject towards two relatively selected categories (Each cross-section of different categories is applied in each one of the six different questions – as presented in Fig. 1). The six questions were designed to explore all the possible relationships between the four main categories mentioned in the Ring method.

The SVO angle in the Slider method is calculated as the arctangent of the ratio between the average payments of the unknown player and the average payments of the decision maker. Both average payments are centered on the ring by subtracting the fixed value of 50, as can be seen in the following Eq. (1):

$$SVO^o = \arctan\left(\frac{\overline{A_o} - 50}{\overline{A_s} - 50}\right) \tag{1}$$

Figure 1 displays the Ring structure, along with the various categories and their relative position on it. The green lines are the continuous scales, which represent the different range of options for resource allocation that are associated with a single participant, in each one of the six questions in the Slider method. The answers of a

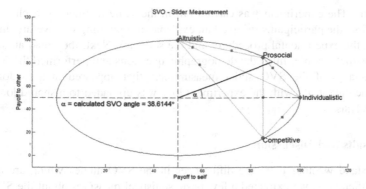

Fig. 1. SVO slider measurement method by using a graphical analysis (Color figure online)

randomly selected participant are displayed on the green scales along with the weighted SVO angle, calculated using Eq. (1), which represents subject's predicted behavior.

2.2   Experimental Setup

Experimental Goals. The main goal of the first experiment was to explore whether there are differences in the distribution of the SVO angles between two groups with identical demographic data, except for the CB of the group, that is, ICB versus CCB (Aim #1). We constructed a software that allowed us to calculate the SVO index of participants using the Slider method (Fig. 2).

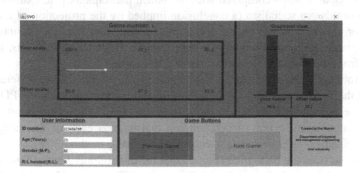

Fig. 2. SVO slider application window

Participants. The participants were composed of two different groups. The first contained 93 students from Ariel University that were enrolled in one of the courses on campus (49 of whom were female, 83 were right hand dominant, mean age $= \sim 23$, SD $= 1.97$). The second group contained 95 students at the University of Chinese Academy of Sciences (UCAS) that were enrolled in one of the courses on campus (36 of whom were female, 88 were right hand dominant, mean age $= \sim 23$, SD $= 1.89$).

Procedure. The experiment was carried out in the same manner for each of the two groups. First, the participants received an explanation regarding the overarching aim of the study, the experimental procedure, and the software. Next, they read an additional written instructions file, filled the demographic questions and performed the 6 resource allocation tasks of the SVO slider measurement that appeared in a random order. Finally, the output file with the experiment logs was uploaded to a shared location for offline analysis.

2.3   Results and Discussion

To understand whether there are differences in the SVO angles which are rooted in cultural differences, we extracted a few basic statistical measures about the SVO angle (Table 1):

Table 1. SVO angles statistics – CB compression

	Mean SVO angle	SVO angle – S.D.	Median SVO angle
Ariel university	31.3530	11.8833	35.9384
UCAS	21.6493	15.3722	23.0868

From the data presented in Table 1, it is possible to extract two main conclusions. First, by observing the average and median angle values, it is evident that the Chinese participants have a significantly smaller angle than their Israeli counterparts. This indicates a greater tendency for competitiveness and individualism on the part of Chinese participants when compared with the Israeli participants who exhibit a greater tendency towards pro socialism (a conclusion implied by the projection of the α angle obtained for each CB group on the SVO ring presented in Fig. 1). Second, we can observe a greater variability among Chinese relative to Israeli participants, as can be discerned from the standard deviation of the SVO angle.

To corroborate these conclusions, we produced a histogram of the different angles in each of the two groups, from which the probability density function (PDF) of the angle can be estimated (Fig. 3). On the histogram, "hard" decision boundaries were marked by pinpointing a line of demarcation that bounds each of the categories by which participants would be labeled with using the Ring methodology.

It is evident from the histogram (Fig. 3) that the distribution density function of the SVO angle is different between the CCB and the ICB groups (Aim #1). After performing two-sided two sample t-test, a significant difference between the groups was revealed (t (186) = 4.85; p < 0.001).

To strengthen our findings, we explored another feature associated with each of the six questions that were used in the Slider method. An answer to the Slider measurement questions produces two parameters: the amount of resources that participants assign to themselves and to the unknown other. In order to diminish the number of features, we devised a composite feature that combines the two pair of answers in a single-value manner as follows:

$$feature_i = \frac{(self\ payment)_i}{(other\ payment)_i} \qquad (2)$$

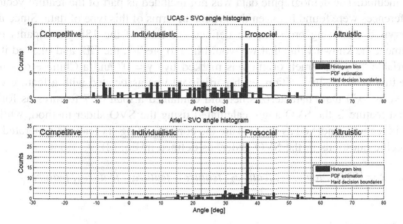

Fig. 3. SVO angle histogram and estimated PDF compression

Lower values of the composite feature for each question reflect a more pro-social tendencies, while higher values reflect a more individualistic or competitive tendencies. The median and mean values of the six features of each group are presented in Table 2. All six median values of the Chinese group are greater or equal than the corresponding values of the Israeli group (by 21.28% on average). These findings corroborate the results based on the SVO angle data presented before.

Table 2. SVO features statistics compression by cultural background

Feature index	Min value	Max value	UCAS mean	UCAS median	UCAS std	Ariel mean	Ariel median	Ariel std
1	1	5.666	1.973	1.388	1.507	1.391	1	1.029
2	2	5.666	2.549	2.368	0.859	2.442	2	0.927
3	0.5	1	0.916	1	0.131	0.946	1	0.123
4	0.5	5.666	2.012	1.328	1.575	1.346	1.006	1.150
5	0.5	2	1.217	1.169	0.407	1.064	1	0.286
6	1	2	1.318	1.216	1.336	1.135	1	0.240

3 Predicting Cultural Background Based on SVO Data

3.1 Problem Framework and Definitions

In the previous section we have seen that there are differences in the SVO distribution between the two culturally different groups. Our second aim was to predict CB as a function of the Slider model parameters values (Aim #2).

To do so we defined a vector of features that uses all the available data from the Slider method. The demographic data was not included as part of the feature vector, as no differences were found between the groups in terms of this type of data. Since this is a supervised clustering problem, we defined for each of the 188 participants in the experiment the known value that we would like to predict, the CB, and marked it with the variable "y". An Israeli origin was marked by "y = 0" and a Chinese origin was denoted by "y = 1". In addition, each participant was associated with a feature vector (marked by "x") that characterizes her and contained a total of 7 features as follows. The first feature is the SVO angle calculated using the SVO slider method, while the other six features (indexed as x_2 to x_7) are the corresponding six features generated from the specific questions in the SVO slider, as defined in Eq. (2).

$$x = [SVO^o, feature_1, feature_2, feature_3, feature_4, feature_5, feature_6] \tag{3}$$

3.2 Data Analysis

Dimensionality Reduction. To perform dimensionality reduction (e.g. [6]) we used the Principal Component Analysis (PCA) algorithm [7] to describe the data with only few important features. Table 3 displays the retained variance from the dimension reduction process as a function of the number of principal components.

Table 3. Retained variance as function of the number of principal components

Number of principal components	1	2	3	4	5	6	7
Retained variance [%]	48.01	65.81	78.02	85.53	92.84	98.90	100

The calculation of the retained variance was accomplished by comparing the original data with the reconstructed data, using the following formula:

$$retained\ variance = 1 - \frac{\frac{1}{m}\sum_{i=1}^{m}||x^{(i)} - x_{approx}^{(i)}||^2}{\frac{1}{m}\sum_{i=1}^{m}||x^{(i)}||^2} \tag{4}$$

As shown in Table 3, the various parameters are highly correlated, so most of the variance can be explained by only few important features. Specifically, 78% of the original variance can be accounted for by using only 3 features, and 95% of the original variance could be explained by using only 5 features. The model optimization process, described in the following chapters, revealed that the best results were achieved when we used only three PCA principals' components.

Model Selection. In order to predict the CB, we have to choose a prediction model. A significant consideration in choosing the model is the size of the data set (n = 188) and the number of features (k = 7) [8]. In our case, the amount of data is relatively small compared to the amount of data often used in common learning problems. Therefore we have chosen a model that is suitable to tackle such problems, namely, Support Vector Machine (SVM) [9]. SVM is suitable to handle small data sets since only selected samples, called support vectors, are used to create the separating hyperplane (the classifier decision boundary). SVM is the most known prediction model from a group of algorithms in machine learning which is referred to as "kernel methods". Kernel functions enable the model to predict high-order dimensions, without calculating the data coordinates in space, but rather by computing the inner products between all the pair samples in the data set [10].

$$\text{Polynomial Kernel: } K(x,y) = \left(x^T y + c\right)^d \tag{5}$$

$$\text{Radial basis function kernel: } K(x,y) = \exp(-\frac{||x - y||^2}{2\sigma^2}) \tag{6}$$

Model Optimization. In order to obtain the highest percentage of correct predictions we were required to optimize the SVM model. In the optimization process we used two different kernels, polynomial and radial basis functions. Here, we will present the optimization results of the polynomial kernel alone, which were slightly better, although the trends in the two cases were similar. The two main parameters we could control in the optimization process were the number of features (after dimensionality reduction using PCA algorithm), and the polynomial kernel order (d).

To determine the best model configuration, for each coupling (number of features and the kernel order), fifty independent cross-validation tests were performed. As is customary in the ML world, the percentage of disclosure relates only to the test group. It should be noted that at each run of the algorithm, the training group and the testing group were re-randomized. The sizes of the training group and the testing group were 70% and 30%, respectively. In addition to ensuring the convergence of the SVM price function in model training, which is done in an iterative way and may take a long time when it comes to a high-order kernel, we defined an upper limit of up to 750,000 optimization iterations. The average detection percentage for each pair of parameters examined in the model optimization process is displayed in the following heat map shown in Fig. 4.

Looking at the heat map, that represents the optimization process of the prediction model, it could be observed that there are three main areas: (1) The "Green" area: where the model produces low predictive values due to a definite bias, i.e. an over-fitting problem. That is, the combination of the simple hypothesis structure together

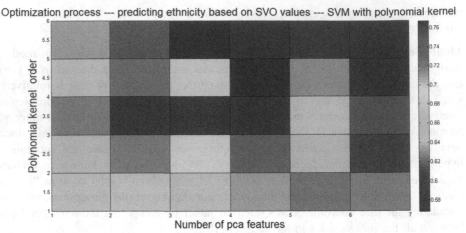

Fig. 4. SVM with polynomial kernel optimization process heat map (Color figure online)

with the quantity of features is insufficient to produce an optimal model. (2) The "Red" area: in which the configuration of the model produces optimum performance, both in terms of the hypothesis structure and number of features. Thus, this configuration of the model is optimal for the current data set. (3) The "Blue" area: in which the model produces low prediction percentages due to high variance, i.e. this area represents a state of overfitting. This phenomenon is caused by a large number of features that have a large mutual effect and the hypothesis that has a higher order complexity than the information.

After analyzing the heat map shown in Fig. 4, we determined the optimal configuration of the prediction model. With this configuration, we succeeded in producing the best model for the presented problem, with which we reached a correct detection ratio of 85.33% (the train-test ratio in this case was [0.6, 0.4]). Our model failed to classify only 6 Israelis (out of 36) and 5 Chinese students (out of 37).

4 Application - The Impact of Cultural Background Prediction on Tacit Coordination Problems

One of the significant skills required to facilitate Human-Robot Interaction (HRI) is coordination, i.e., the act of operating together harmoniously [11]. Effective coordination often requires building and maintaining appropriate common knowledge, beliefs, and assumptions that the involved parties share (e.g. [12, 13]). In this part of the study we would like to demonstrate whether CB affects the beliefs and basic knowledge used to coordinate human-machine operations (Aim #3).

Tacit coordination games are games in which two individuals are rewarded for making the same choice from the same set of alternatives, when communication between the two players is not possible. To determine whether the CB has an impact on the coordination process, the subjects were presented with the tacit coordination games immediately after filling the SVO questionnaire. In these games we asked the subjects to connect circles to squares (appearing on a screen) as they see fit, while trying to coordinate their answers with an unknown partner [14]. The coordination performance of the various players, and the perceived difficulty level of the game by the players was measured by the *Coordination index* (CI) measure that has been proposed by Mehta et al. [14]. The index is a statistical measure that quantifies the ability of subjects to coordinate in a specific game, and it measures the probability that two distinct individuals, chosen at random without replacement from the set of N individuals, choose the same label. The index value allows determining how difficult it is to coordinate in a specific game. Given a coordination game with the label set $\{l_1, ..l_n\}$ and any set of N individual players, when each of them plays the game only once with an unknown anonymous partner. For each label l_j let m_j be the number of individuals who choose it, then the coordination index c is given by:

$$c = \frac{\sum_j m_j (m_j - 1)}{N(N - 1)} \tag{7}$$

The CI index takes the value 1 (maximal value) if all individuals chose the same label and 0 (minimal value) if everyone chose a different label. If labels are chosen at random, the expected value of the index is $\frac{1}{N}$. The higher the CI, the easier it is to coordinate between two random players and vice versa, the lower the CI is, the easier it is to coordinate and the game is perceived as easier by the players. Analysis of the results of the tacit coordination games, and the calculation of the CI index for each CB in each game, shows that there was a difference in the perception of the games between the ICB and CCB groups. Games that were perceived as easy to coordinate in one group appeared to be complicated by the other group and vice versa. To illustrate this, we will focus on a specific game instance (#7; The full list of games and their corresponding number can be found in [14]). In this game, a single circle splits in half the distance between two squares into two equal sides, as shown in Fig. 5:

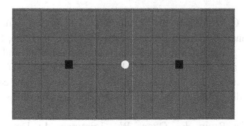

Fig. 5. "Assign Circles" – Game #7

While the CI value for the ICB group was 0.78, the value of the CCB group was about 0.5, which amounts to a random uniform selection. That is, while the Israeli players were able to coordinate in this game by identifying and implicitly agreeing that the square on the right side constitutes a focal point [15], the Chinese players failed to achieve such a coordination: the CCB group was unable to coordinate at all and the CI value approximated to the minimum possible value, which is obtained by random selection.

5 Conclusions and Future Work

This study has three major outcomes. First, it was demonstrated, for the first time, that the distribution of SVO values significantly varies between groups belonging to different CBs that share similar demographic characteristics (Aim #1). Second, it was shown that social measures, such as the SVO index, can be used to predict the CB of the player, ICB or CCB (Aim #2). Third, it was demonstrated that players from different CB groups differed in their approach to tacit coordination problems (Aim #3). These results open a variety of new research directions. First, it will be interesting to examine the distribution and quantity of the players' strategic profiles and discern the set of strategies and decision rules used by the players in each CB group. Second, we have seen that there was a significant difference in the SVO data between the two CB groups. Whereas the Israeli population has leaned towards a pro-social trend the Chinese population has leaned more towards competitiveness and individuality. However, these findings were obtained while the incentive for each player has not been contingent upon the answer they give. Thus, in future studies it will be worth examining the effect of the SVO index in games involving diverge interests. Although in this type of games players are also expected to coordinate their answers, different game outcomes are associated with different utilities for each of the players. Finally, it might also be interesting to explore whether the differences in perception of the difficulty level of coordination among subgroups of different CBs are accompanied by parallel changes in electrophysiological markers, signifying potential differences in the functionality of the underlying brain networks.

References

1. Balliet, D., Parks, C., Joireman, J.: Social value orientation and cooperation in social dilemmas: a meta-analysis. Group Process. Intergroup Relat. **12**(4), 533–547 (2009)
2. Bogaert, S., Boone, C., Declerck, C.: Social value orientation and cooperation in social dilemmas: a review and conceptual model. Br. J. Soc. Psychol. **47**(3), 453–480 (2008)
3. Liebrand, W., McClintock, C.: The ring measure of social values: a computerized procedure for assessing individual differences in information processing and social value orientation. Eur. J. Pers. **2**(3), 217–230 (1988)
4. Van Lange, P., De Bruin, E., Otten, W., Joireman, J.: Development of prosocial, individualistic, and competitive orientations: theory and preliminary evidence. J. Pers. Soc. Psychol. **73**(4), 733–746 (1997)
5. Murphy, R.O., Ackermann, K.A., Handgraaf, M.J.J.: Measuring social value orientation. Judgm. Decis. Mak. **6**(8), 771–781 (2011)
6. Yan, S., Xu, D., Zhang, B., Zhang, H., Yang, Q., Lin, S.: Graph embedding and extensions: a general framework for dimensionality reduction. IEEE Trans. Pattern Anal. Mach. Intell. **29**(1), 40–51 (2007)

7. Svante, W., Esbensen, K., Geladi, P.: Principal component analysis. Chemometr. Intell. Lab. Syst. **2**(1–3), 37–52 (1987)
8. Batista, G., Prati, R., Monard, M.: A study of the behavior of several methods for balancing machine learning training data. ACM SIGKDD Explor. Newsl. **6**(1), 20 (2004)
9. Mitchell, T.: Machine Learning. McGraw-Hill, New York (1997)
10. Shawe-Taylor, J., Cristianini, N.: Kernel Methods for Pattern Analysis. Cambridge University Press, New York (2004)
11. Malone, T., Crowston, K.: What is coordination theory and how can it help design cooperative work systems? In: Proceedings of the 1990 ACM Conference on Computer-supported Cooperative Work, New York (1990)
12. Klein, G., Woods, D., Bradshaw, J., Hoffman, R., Feltovich, P.: Ten challenges for making automation a "team player" in joint human-agent activity. IEEE Intell. Syst. **19**(06), 91–95 (2004)
13. Bradshaw, J., Dignum, V., Jonker, C., Sierhuis, M.: Human-agent-robot teamwork. IEEE Intell. Syst. **27**(2), 8–13 (2012)
14. Mehta, J., Starmer, C., Sugden, R.: The nature of salience: an experimental investigation of pure coordination games. Am. Econ. Rev. **84**(3), 658–673 (1994)
15. Steiner, P., Schelling, T.: The strategy of conflict. Economica **28**(109), 96 (1961)

Self-programming Robots Boosted
by Neural Agents

Oscar Chang$^{(\boxtimes)}$ iD

Yachay Tech University, Urcuqui 100650, Ecuador
ochang@yachaytech.edu.ec, ogchang@gmail.com

Abstract. This paper deals with Brain-Inspired robot controllers, based on a special kind of artificial neural structures that burn "dark" energy to promote the self-motivated initiation of behaviors. We exploit this ambient to train a virtual multi-joint robot, with many moving parts, muscles and sensors distributed through the robot body, interacting with elements that satisfy Newtonian laws. The robot faces a logical-mechanical challenge where a heavy, slippery ball, pressed against a wall has to be pushed up by means of coordinate muscles activation, where energy, timing and balancing conditions add noticeable technical complications. As in living brains our robots contains self-motivating neural agents that consumes energy and function by themselves even without external stimulus. Networks that handle sensory and timing information are combined with agents to construct our controller. We prove that by using appropriate learning algorithms, the self-motivating capacity of agents provides the robot with powerful self-programming aptitudes, capable of solving the ball lifting problem in a quick, efficient way.

Keywords: Neural agents · Self-programming robots · Artificial intelligence

1 Introduction

Deep Learning has made possible massively trained ANN capable of recognizing a specific human face in a blink [1, 2]. However, these powerful neural processors lack key a component of life: self-motivation. What internal force inspires a fruit fly? Comprehensive research [3, 4] has found that in ultimate navigating lifesaving situations, decisions in the drosophila fly's brain, with about 250.000 neurons, are taken by a reduced set of neurons that consume energy and originates inner noisy in the form of a few chaotic neurons outputs, initiating a major change in behavior (modification in flying direction, for instance).

So, at this scale the fly incorporates in its brain structure a compact number of neurons that are assigned *self-motivated behavior initiation attribute*s. As a magnificent consequence, this internal capacity converts the fly into a free running autonomous living creature, which can actuate even if no external stimulus is received.

At the bigger human brain scale the functioning of autonomous behaviors initiator is a much more elaborated matter, well documented by Raichel and his research team, by using modern functional magnetic resonance imaging (fMRI) [5, 6]. From these studies one noticeable finding is that the human brain never really rests but stays

© Springer Nature Switzerland AG 2018
S. Wang et al. (Eds.): BI 2018, LNAI 11309, pp. 448–457, 2018.
https://doi.org/10.1007/978-3-030-05587-5_42

always in constant, seemingly chaotic activity, burning a substantial amount of energy that seems to go nowhere. Raichel called this phenomenon "the brain dark energy" and his discovery change previous concept about brain functioning. This energy-burning attitude seems to be the common way of living brains and signs of it has been suggested in bees [7] and sub millimeter worms [8].

1.1 Processing Blocks and Sparseness

Brains are quite demarked conglomerates communicating though sparse coding. As example in the insects' brain the olfactory system two highly specialized and separate clusters of neurons (neuropils) handle smelling functions [9]. The first cluster called the antennal lobe (AL) captures information from olfactory receptor and send sparse information to another cluster: the Mushroom Body (MB). After unknown methods the MB acts as efficient classifier that learns from the environment with the sparse information coming from the AL. From the genetic point of view both AL and MB comes pre-packed, ready to go once assembled.

From our short journey through biological brains, we extract the following guidance for the design of self-learning robots:

- In behavior initiation a small set of neurons could assume big responsibilities.
- Whenever possible use preassembled robust, independent operative blocks.
- Whenever possible communicate through sparse code.
- Burn energy.
- Promote self-motivation.

1.2 Related Works

The utilization of artificial neural networks in robot control has had a vigorous recent history. In [10] a review of NN based robot control algorithms, including NN based manipulator control is presented. In [11] the authors describes a Convolutional Neural Network-Based Robot where classification is implemented by an end-to-end Convolutional Neural Network. In [12] the proof-of-principle of a system with dozens of neutrally-controlled joints is established. In [13] the authors solve partially observed domains using recurrent neural networks to solve the Morris water maze task.

In previous works [14] we proposed methods where robotic controlling was tied up with the inspiring concept of Programming with Neurons [15]. More recently we studied the applicability of internal neural behavior initiators in the design of autonomous robots [16]. In this paper we propose a self–programming robotic controller assembled with operative neural blocks that realizes specific tasks. Some blocks behave as truly agents, according to their capacity to perform a useful job without external intervention and satisfying the four conditions of: Autonomy, Social ability, Reactivity and Pro-activeness [17]. Preassembled neural blocks are combined with simulated mechanical elements, to construct a dynamic ambient where robot learning and self-programming progress.

2   The Robot and Its Neural-Mechanical Layout

The general mechanical and neural computer models used in this paper were first discussed in [16]. An updated version is shown in Fig. 6 where multipart mechanical elements coexist with operative neural blocks that act as a controller. The robot is assembled with joints that contain sensors, muscles, rotary linkages and robust coupling. Each joint has a dedicated sigmoidal neuron that activates a corresponding muscle that has both contraction and expansion capabilities. When the driver neuron is at rest (output = 0.5) the muscle and joints remain in a neutral, aligned position. Joins have three sensors that activate when touching a ball, they are coupled to form an arbitrarily long robot bodies with corresponding long chain of driver neurons. An independent system moves the robot toward the wall, applying finite horizontal force that traps the ball against the wall.

Neural blocks specialize in specific tasks. The i-agent block, which has the intrinsic capacity to burn "dark" energy, produces self-motivated signals which in turn activate other blocks behavior. The i-agent will thus operate even if it's associated isolation switches are open, cutting all outside stimulus. The TSR or trainable shift register as neural block that behaves as a synchronous shift register, with a finite set of behaviors, selectable through the inputs <down, stop, up>. The position predictor is a one hidden layer network that receives raw sensors signals as input and produces sparse signaling as output. The comparator is a trained net that processes two sparse signals and produce three error signals used by the i-agent (Fig. 1).

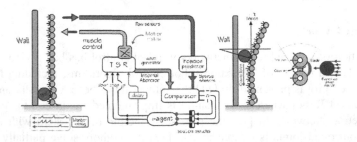

Fig. 1. The neural controller. A multi-joint robot and its associated neural blocks have to learn to fully lift a heavy ball laying in the floor. The mechanical hardware is a long chain of operative joints with independent muscles and neural controllability. The resultant robotic complex must produce a moveable vertical lift force, synchronized with sensors and internal timing.

The master timer block generates ramp-like firing pulses with different repeat periods. The motion matrix contains weights that connects the output of the TSR with the robot muscles, creating massive joints controllability. The neural and mechanical components are connected with clusters of neural signals that carry muscle activation and raw sensory information. When functioning the robot has to solve the "coconut dance problem" in which a heavy slippery ball (coconut) is placed between the robot and a fixed vertical wall. The solution requires for the robot to move its joints in a coordinate way, creating a continuous force component against gravity (lift force), a moving mechanical wave synchronized with sensors and timing signals. Other mechanical requirements, like robot equilibrium and energy efficiency, complicate the overall lifting process. We show i-agent internal self-motivation boosts the learning capacities of the robot and make possible highly efficient self-programming routines. Our results suggest that this agent driven structures can be used in to other machine learning processes, where complex sensing, learning and timing are required.

3 Self-motivated Behavior Initiation

3.1 Structured Neural Chaos: The i-agent

From the fruit fly studies it is deduced that in living brains a few, energy consuming neurons, have the internal capacity to create important changes in behavior. As an original contribution this work proposes an artificial neural network called i-agent, which constantly burns energy resembling the dark energy in the brain and provides the key component of self-motivation in our controllers. A basic i-agent is built with a finite chain of sigmoidal neurons operating in real time (Fig. 2). The neurons inhibit each other with common negative weights (usually -0.1) and share a common self-activating excitatory input ramp K, which begins at zero with all neuron outputs set to 0.1. From there on K continuously increases, heating the system and forcing all participant neurons in a racing toward a 1.0 output. After certain time one of the members crosses a pre fixed threshold (usually 0.7) and the i-agent "fires", raising the output of the winner neuron to 0.9 and lowering all others output to 0.1. Due to internal restrictions and internal noise *only one chaotic winner per firing is allowed*. Inside the robot each winner initiates a robot behavior in a one-to-one basis i.e. winner (i) activates behavior (i).

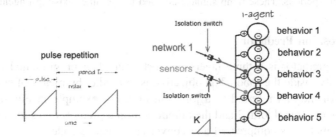

Fig. 2. The i-agent. A finite chain of sigmoidal neurons operating in real time inhibit each other with identical inhibitory weights. Neurons are all equally excited by a repetitive ramp K. In each repetition the i-agent burns "dark energy", fires and declares a unique, unpredictable winner, used to activate one conflict-free behavior. The i-agent will keep on working, pushing behaviors from the inside, even if it is isolated from any other sensor or network.

3.2   Influences from the External World

As defined a free running i-agent keeps the robot active even under secluded conditions, when isolation switches are open. The next step is to allow external networks to build weighted connections with the firing neurons in the i-agent, so that the statistic occurrence of behaviors can be influenced. For instance in Fig. 2 if network 1, connected to internal neuron 3 with a positive weight, activates its output then behavior 3 will have more probability to occur.

3.3   The Master Timer

Timing is important in living creatures since sit make possible to control complex thing, from walking to sleeping [18]. To provide a multiple choice of timing conditions to other blocks, our next functional blocks is a modified i-agent which uses a local oscillator and a binary counting scheme to generate trains of firing ramps, with decreasing $1/n^2$ periods. These signal are selectively used to fire i-agents (Fig. 3).

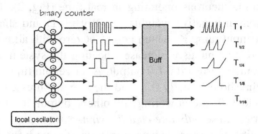

Fig. 3. Master timer. A modified i-agent coupled to a local oscillator accomplish a binary counting that, with the help of buffering neurons, is used to generate trains of firing pulses with sub divided $1/n^2$ periods. These ramp signals are used to fire other existing i-agents.

3.4   The Position Predictor

The position predictor is a three layers network trained or programmed to carry out sensory activity inside the robot. The objective is to predict by means of sparse coding the position of the ball referred to a joint number. For example in Fig. 4 the ball is touching sensors around joint 2 and the output neuron 2 predicts this situation. The ball position information is compressed and converted to sparse code.

3.5   The Wave Generator

Our next block represent, through sparse coding, the internal interest of the robot defined by a dedicated i-agent that behaves as a programmable shift register (Fig. 5). The generator has three independent inputs and a set of short term memory cells, used to store past states. As established the local i-agent output is always a sparse coding vector that looks like 0000100000000000, where the solitary 1 can be shifted around one position per firing, according to the network input vector (up, stop, down) and in synchronism with the firing pulse. The generator thus has three basic behaviors

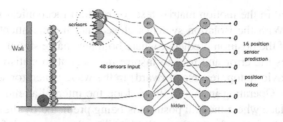

Fig. 4. The position predictor. A three layers network is trained to produce sensory information that indicates the position of the sensed ball in terms of joint numbers. From 48 sensors, 16 sparse coded outputs are derived. Besides compressing the data, sparse signal conveys important correlations with the spatial distribution of sensor in the robot joins.

activated by their respective inputs: shift up, no shift, shift down. The spatial position of the solitary 1, called index, represents the internal attention of the robot i.e. where its muscle commanding force concentrates. In this example the internal attention varies between 0 and 15. The output layer, which directly controls muscles, stays connected to the hidden layer through a weights' matrix (Fig. 5 right). Since the hidden layer is an i-agent and activates one row at a time, each row of weights represents a massive mechanical deformation along the robot body. This matrix will be referred to as the **motion matrix** and in principle it can be adjusted by learning algorithms as to produce mechanical waves that move in synchronism with the shift register.

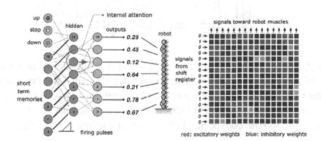

Fig. 5. The wave generator. A dedicated i-agent takes the place of the hidden layer and is trained to work as a programmable shift register, where the winner is referred to as the internal attention. The network has three basic behaviors, activated through inputs. The output layer massively control muscles through a weights motion matrix that connects the hidden and output layers. Learning algorithms can modify the matrix and produce complex mechanical contortions synchronized with other networks through the inputs (behavior selectors) up-stop-down.

4   Self-programming

4.1   Sensory Attraction

Consider the system in Fig. 6 with the isolation switches open and the motion matrix weights set to random values. Thanks to its internal self-motivation, the i-agent keeps on generating random behaviors in the rank (up, stop, down). In response, using information stored in the motion matrix, a set of random mechanical waves will travel the robot body. With the isolation switches closed the internal attention is compared with the output of the position predictor, where both are sparse signals. The comparator network evaluates the error and tries to inspire the i-agent to statistically activate the appropriated behavior (stop, reverse, forward) in the wave generator so that the error is kept near to zero. Operating in this feedback loop the internal attention of the robot is attracted to the place where the ball position is being predicted by the sensors network, so after a while the internal attention will "lock" to the sensory information. In this particular situation an interesting phenomenon occurs: although the system is supposed to be in equilibrium, the self-motivated chaotic nature of the i-agent will keep on going, burning dark energy to explore new equilibrium situation. In other words the lock condition is not deterministic but rather a stochastic event where the i-agent burns dark energy to deviate from time to time, exploring territories. For our robot this represents a good situation for machine learning because now the controller automatically concentrates its muscle control capacity (winner of the wave generator) in the zone were the ball is predicted to be and maintains and self-motivated exploratory activity in the neighborhood.

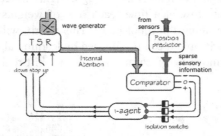

Fig. 6. Sensory Attraction. With the isolation switches closed the internal attention is compared with the output of the position predictor. The comparator evaluates the error and, through the "stop, reverse, forward" signals, tries to encourage the i-agent to keep the error near zero. When this condition is met the internal attention locks to the sensory activity but the i-agent keeps on burning dark energy to initiate unexpected behaviors that explore the vicinities.

5 Self-programming: Searching for the Optimal Lifting Wave Form

With the isolation switches closed the robot will move its internal attention toward the ball laying in the floor. In this conditions if random weights are assigned to the motion matrix, the robot enters a turmoil state, where its internal attention persistently moves around the ball, using dark energy to explore the surrounding and showing almost inexistent lifting capacity.

The problem now is to modify the motion matrix so that an appropriate and steady lifting force appears. For our current example the motion matrix has 256 entries. If we impose the strong restriction that weights can assume only five possible values, say (4, 2, 0, −2, −4) the number of possible weights combination becomes $5^{256} = 8.64 * 10^{178}$, so the problem cannot be solved by brute force search algorithms.

5.1   Step 1: Find a Localized Lifting Solution

To create an appropriated motion matrix all weights are initially set to zero, leaving the robot in a stable upright position that corners the ball between the wall and the floor (Fig. 7). For simplicity weights can assume only one of five possible values (4, 2, 0, −2, −4).

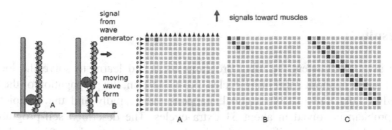

Fig. 7. Self Programming. The robot burns dark energy and does a random weight search in the upper left corner of the motion matrix (A). The localized solution must lift the ball in an efficient way, keep the robot in an upright position and consume as little energy. Once the localized solution is found the robot again uses dark energy to copy the originated weights in the next diagonal matrix position (B). When a new lift height is reached the diagonal copying process is repeated. After the initial success in (A) the overall motion matrix solution is found very rapidly in a few firing cycles (C). A related video can be seen at https://www.youtube.com/watch?v=-cEImJ_tm-o&feature=youtu.be

Since the controller automatically moves the internal attention to the ball position (now lying in the floor) after a while the solitary 1 output of the wave generator will move around the row zero of the motion matrix, so changes in this row will produce big changes in body movement. The internal attention locking to the sensory information represents an unstable equilibrium situation where the i-agents maintains an independent activity, exploring nearby equilibrium points.

With the given initial conditions the lifting problem is solved by the following search algorithm, which dynamically combines different robot parameters and uses dark energy to explore new territories. The found solution will be valid for the upper left corner of the motion matrix.

1. Fill the first four entries (left to right) in the first row with random values.
2. Choose a ramp period (one out of five possible periods).
3. Use dark energy to: Evaluate the lift capacity (how much the ball is lifted from the floor), Evaluate upright position (how much the robot head moves away from the robot base), Evaluate the energy consumption (how many firing cycles are required to reach the current lift).
4. Repeat until maximum lift, upright position and a minimal energy is found.

After about 1300 trial the robot finds the of solution shown in Fig. 7-A with a weight combination composed by the values −4, 0, 4, 0. This arrangement combined with other found parameters, creates a body bending that significantly lift the ball, keeps the robot in upright position and uses about 7 firing cycles to lift the ball.

5.2   Step 2: Propagate the Knowledge

Once an efficient set of weights is found for the upper left corner, the robot uses dark energy to copy the resultant weights' combination along the next empty space in the matrix diagonal. As soon as the ball is lifted to a new height the robot repeats the copying process creating a diagonal pattern of repetitive weights that efficiently lift the ball all the way up (Fig. 7).

6   Results

For the given parameters the robot programs itself and learns to solve the localized lifting solution in about 2500 firing cycles. From there on, the propagation of the lifting knowledge along the matrix diagonal, happens very rapidly and the complete ball lifting problem is solved in about 31 extra cycles. The described self-programming algorithm was tested with different robot parameters such as number of joints, ball size and firing pulse periods, showing a generic, sturdy learning capacity.

7   Conclusions

This paper proposes Brain-Inspired robot controllers based on a neural structure called i-agent that burns dark energy to promote the self-motivated initiation of behaviors. In our method a composite neural-mechanical system is kept in a near to equilibrium situation, where the internal attention of the robot is locked to the local sensory information with the mediation of a self-motivated agent, which uses dark energy to explore the existence of solutions near the equilibrium point. This focalized, proactive attitude is used to boost the self-programming capacities of a virtual multi-joint robot with many moving parts, muscles, sensors and neural components, interacting with elements that obey Newtonian laws. We prove that the localized internal self-motivation generates efficient self-programming routines that in turn create robots satisfying requirements of massive muscle activation, energy efficiency, timing and balancing conditions. This developed near equilibrium method, with self-motivated exploratory attitude, may be useful in other machine learning scenarios.

References

1. Martinez, H., Bengio, Y., Yannakakis, G.: Learning deep physiological models of affect. IEEE Comput. Intell. Mag. **8**(2), 20–33 (2013). https://doi.org/10.1109/MCI.2013.2247823
2. Bengio, Y.: Learning deep architectures for AI. Found. Trends Mach. Learn. **2**(1), 1–127 (2009). https://doi.org/10.1561/2200000006
3. Maye, A., Hsieh, Ch., Sugihara, G., Brembs, B.: Order in spontaneous behavior. PLoS One **10**(1371) (2007). https://doi.org/10.1371/journal.pone.0000443
4. Brembs, B.: Genetic analysis of behavior in drosophila. Cognition and Behavioral Neuroscience. Online Publication Date February 2017. https://doi.org/10.1093/oxfordhb/9780190456757.013.37

5. Raichle, M., Snyder, A.Z.: A default mode of brain function: a brief history of an evolving idea. Neuroimage **37**(4), 1083–1090 (2007). https://doi.org/10.1016/j.neuroimage.2007.02. 041

6. Raichle, M.E.: Two views of brain function. Trends Cogn. Sci. **14**(4), 180–190 (2010). https://doi.org/10.1016/j.tics.2010.01.008

7. Eban-Rothschild, A., Bloch, G.: Circadian rhythms and sleep in honey bees. In: Galizia, C., Eisenhardt, D., Giurfa, M. (eds.) Honeybee Neurobiology and Behavior, pp. 31–45. Springer, Dordrecht (2012). https://doi.org/10.1007/978-94-007-2099-2_3

8. Palyanov, A., Khayrulin, S., Larson, S.D., Dibert, A.: Towards a virtual C. elegans: a framework for simulation and visualization of the neuromuscular system in a 3D physical environment. In Silico Biol. **11**(3–4), 137–147 (2012). https://doi.org/10.3233/isb-2012-0445

9. Huerta, R.: Learning pattern recognition and decision making in the insect brain. In: AIP Conference Proceedings, vol. 1510, pp. 101–191 (2013). https://doi.org/10.1063/1.4776507

10. Yiming, J., Chenguang, Y., Jing, N., Guang, L., Yanan, L., Junpei, Z.: A brief review of neural networks based learning and control and their applications for robots. Hindawi Complex. **2017**, article ID 1895897, 14 p. (2017). https://doi.org/10.1155/2017/1895897

11. Ran, L., Zhang, Y., Zhang, Q., Yang, T.: Convolutional neural network-based robot navigation using uncalibrated spherical images. **17**(6) (2017). https://doi.org/10.3390/ s17061341

12. Ritcher, Ch., Jentzsch, S., Hostettler, R.: Musculoskeletal robots: scalability in neural control. IEEE Robot. Autom. Mag. **23**, 4 (2016). https://doi.org/10.1109/MRA.2016. 2535081

13. Heess, N., Hunt, J., Lillicrap, T., Silver, D.: Memory-based control with recurrent neural networks. CoRR abs/1512.04455 (2015). http://arxiv.org/abs/1512.04455

14. Chang, O.: Evolving cooperative neural agents for controlling vision guided mobile robots. In: Proceedings of 2009 8th IEEE International Conference on Cybernetic Intelligent Systems, 9–10 September 2009, Birmingham University, UK (2009)

15. Shackleford, B.: Neural data structures: programming with neurons. Hewlett-Packard J. **40**(3), 69–78 (1989)

16. Chang, O.: Autonomous robots and behavior initiators. In: Human-Robot Interaction, Theory and Application (2018, in Press). ISBN 978-953-51-5611-6

17. Woolridge, M., Jennings, N.R.: Intelligent agents: theory and practice. Knowl. Eng. Rev. **10**(2) (1994)

18. Rensing, L., Meyer-Grahle, U., Ruoff, P.: Biological timing and the clock metaphor: oscillatory and hourglass mechanisms. Chronobiol. Int. **18**(3), 329–369 (2001)

EEG-Based Subjects Identification Based on Biometrics of Imagined Speech Using EMD

Luis Alfredo Moctezuma[✉] and Marta Molinas

Department of Engineering Cybernetics, Norwegian University of Science and Technology, Trondheim, Norway
luisalfredomoctezuma@gmail.com, marta.molinas@ntnu.no

Abstract. When brain activity ions, the potential for human capacities augmentation is promising. In this paper, EMD is used to decompose EEG signals during Imagined Speech in order to use it as a biometric marker for creating a Biometric Recognition System. For each EEG channel, the most relevant Intrinsic Mode Functions (IMFs) are decided based on the Minkowski distance, and for each IMF 4 features are computed: *Instantaneous and Teager energy distribution* and *Higuchi and Petrosian Fractal Dimension*. To test the proposed method, a dataset with 20 Subjects who imagined 30 repetitions of 5 words in Spanish, is used. Four classifiers are used for this task - *random forest, SVM, naive Bayes*, and *k-NN* - and their performances are compared. The accuracy obtained (up to 0.92 using Linear SVM) after 10-folds cross-validation suggest that the proposed method based on EMD can be valuable for creating EEG-based biometrics of imagined speech for Subject identification.

Keywords: Biometric security · Subject identification
Imagined speech · Electroencephalograms (EEG)
Empirical Mode Decomposition (EMD)

1 Introduction

Electroencephalography (EEG) is a popular non-invasive technique of Brain Computer Interface (BCI), and it refers to the exploration of bioelectrical brain activity registered during different activation functions. EEG does not require any type of surgery, however, compared with invasive techniques the signals obtained are weaker. Another important term is the Electrophysiological source, that refers to the neurological mechanisms adopted by a BCI user to stimulate the brain signals [1].

Due to the easy setup and the little training required, this paper uses the Electrophysiological source *Imagined Speech* [2], that refers to imagined or internal speech without uttering-sounds/articulating-gestures, to create a biometric system for Subject identification.

© Springer Nature Switzerland AG 2018
S. Wang et al. (Eds.): BI 2018, LNAI 11309, pp. 458–467, 2018.
https://doi.org/10.1007/978-3-030-05587-5_43

Due to the non-stationary and non-linear nature of brain signals, signal processing tools like the Wavelet Transform [3–5] and power spectral density (PSD) [6] capable of dealing with these properties, have been reported in the literature. Most recent works have shown wavelets as a powerful tool to analyze brain signals. However, its main disadvantage is the need to fit the best mother function for the signal. This means that mother functions will be different depending on the task/neuro-paradigm/environment adopted.

Recently, the Empirical Mode Decomposition (EMD) has been employed to analyze brain signals corresponding to different tasks. It has shown to be robust in decomposing non-stationary and non-linear time series, with the advantage that it does not need a-priory definition of specific parameters to the signal, in contrast with wavelet transform.

The interest in biometric recognition systems has increased in the last years, since traditional security systems (security guards, smart cards, etc) poses serious challenges of increased vulnerabilities. Current biometric security systems are vulnerable due to a variety of attacks to skip the authentication process [7]. This is because authentication systems cannot discriminate between authorized users and an intruder who fraudulently obtains the access privileges.

To tackle this problem, some researchers have explored the use of brain signals as a measure for a biometric security system. This is possible because any human physiological and/or behavioral characteristic can be used as a biometric feature as long as it satisfies the following requirements: *universality, permanence, collectability, performance, acceptability and circumvention*. A biometric recognition system is able to perform automatic Subject identification based on their physiological and/or behavioral features [7] with the advantage that a single biometric trait can be used for the access into several accounts.

In that context, the main neuro-paradigms in the state-of-the-art are: sensorimotor activity, imagination of activities (Visual Counting and geometric figure Rotation [8]) and mental composition of letters [9], among others [10]. One of the challenges for Subject identification task is the feature extraction stage in order to represent the brain signal captured from different electrodes with a single vector, since it is impractical and computationally costly to use all data generated by the brain.

Some authors report the use of imagined speech, for example [6] used EEG signals from a small population of 6 Subjects while imagining the syllables */ba/* and */ku/*. The collected database consisted of 6 sessions and for each one 20 trials per Subject from 128 channels with a sampling frequency of 1024 Hz. using Electrical Geodesics device. For feature extraction they used the PSD for each EEG signal, then autoregressive (AR) model coefficients were computed for each electrode using the Burg method [11]. The classification stage was performed using the linear kernel of Support Vector Machine (SVM) classifier and using 1-Nearest-Neighbor (k-NN). For these two syllables they obtained 99.76% and 99.41% of accuracy respectively. In the work presented in [5], resting-states were used for Subject identification using *Linear SVM*. The dataset used consisted of 40 Subjects, and 192 instances per Subject. The sampling frequency was 256 Hz with 64 channels. First, for pre-processing a band-pass filter (0.5–40 Hz) and then the Common Average Reference were applied. For feature extraction the Morlet Wavelet was used to extract power spectrum of 7 frequency bands, to finally apply a downsampling to 32 Hz. The accuracies obtained in the best cases were 100%, 96% and 72% respectively for 3 lengths of the signal (300, 60 and 30 s). However, in a real application, the registry of 300, 60 or even 30 s of a signal can be impractical and with high computational cost for real-time. In addition the use of 128 or 64 channels does not support the portability of the device.

As a first step to create a robust method without *a-priory* definition of additional parameters, a method based on EMD to extract features from brain signals of Imagined Speech, is presented here.

1.1 Empirical Mode Decomposition

The EMD method is useful to decompose non-linear and non-stationary signals into a finite number of Intrinsic Mode Functions (IMFs) that satisfies two conditions [12]:

1. The number of extrema and the number of zero crossings must be either equal or differ at most by one.
2. At any point, the mean value of the envelope defined by the local maxima and the envelope defined by the local minima is zero.

The method decomposes a signal into oscillatory components by applying a process called *sifting*. The sifting process for the signal $x(t)$ can be summarized as shown in the Algorithm 1:

Data: Time serie = $x(t)$
Result: IMFs
sifting = True;
while *sifting = True* **do**
    1. Identify all upper extrema in $x(t)$
    2. Interpolate the local maxima to form an upper envelope $u(x)$.
    3. Identify all lower extrema of $x(t)$
    4. Interpolate the local minima to form an lower envelope $l(x)$
    5. Calculate the mean envelope:
       $m(t) = \frac{u(x)+l(x)}{2}$
    6. Extract the mean from the signal:
       $h(t) = x(t) - m(t)$

    if $h(t)$ *satisfies the two IMF conditions* **then**
       $h(t)$ is an IMF;
       sifting = False ;   ▷ Stop sifting
    else
       x(t)= h(t);
       sifting = True ;   ▷ Keep sifting
    end
    if $x(t)$ *is not monotonic* **then**
       Continue;
    else
       Break;
    end
end

Algorithm 1. The sifting process for a signal $x(t)$

1.2 IMFs Selection

The EMD is a powerful tool to decompose a non-stationary signal, however some IMFs that contain limited information may appear in the decomposition because the numerical procedure is susceptible to errors [13]. To select the IMFs that contain the most relevant information about the signal, the methods presented in [14,15] were applied and compared, to finally use the method proposed in [15] that employs the Minkowski Distance (d_{mink}), as follow.

$$d_{mink} = \left(\sum_{i=1}^{n} |x_i - y_i|^2 \right)^{1/2} \tag{1}$$

where x_i and y_i are the i-th respective samples of the observed signal and the extracted IMF.

According to the authors, the redundant IMFs have a shape and frequency content different than those of the original signal, which means that when a IMF is not appropriate, the d_{mink} presents a maximum value.

In this work, a new method for feature extraction based on EMD is proposed. In the next section the method is described in brief. Then, the application of the proposed method for Subject identification is explained.

2 Description of the Method

The main contribution of the proposed method is the feature extraction stage, that consists on applying the Empirical Mode Decomposition (EMD) to obtain 5 Intrinsic Mode Functions (IMF) per channel of the EEG data.

To select the most relevant IMFs, the Minkowski Distance was computed [15]. Once the most relevant IMFs from all instances in the dataset were obtained, it turned out that the number of IMFs was different depending of the size of the signal and the imagined word. However, to obtain meaningful features it is necessary to have the same number of IMFs from all instances. To cope with this, the IMFs selected were limited to the minimum relevant IMFs in all instances, which in this case were only the first 2 IMFs.

Then for each IMF, 4 features were computed: *Instantaneous energy, Teager energy, Higuchi fractal dimension* and *Petrosian fractal dimension*, as it is shown in the Fig. 1. All features per IMF and per channel were concatenated to obtain a feature vector per instance. Once the feature vectors were obtained, they were used to train 4 machine learning-based classifiers (*random forest, naive Bayes, Support Vector Machine (SVM)* and *K-Nearest Neighbors (k-NN)*) in order to compare their performances.

In the following, the step-by-step procedure proposed in this work to identify Subjects by using the EEG of their imagined speech, is described.

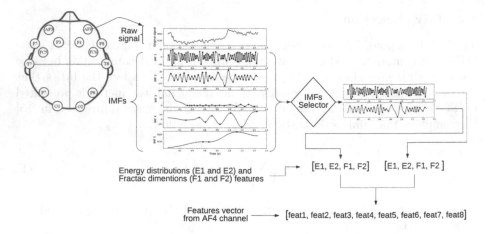

Fig. 1. Flowchart summarizing the feature extraction stage.

2.1   Feature Extraction

When the most relevant IMFs were selected, 4 features were computed for each one in order to reduce the feature vector to obtain a good representation of the signal. The first 2 features used are related with the energy distribution and the others two with Fractal dimensions. Each feature tested in this work is here described.

- INSTANTANEOUS ENERGY: gives the energy distribution in each band [16]:

$$f_j = log_{10}\left(\frac{1}{N_j}\sum_{r=1}^{N_j}(w_j(r))^2\right) \tag{2}$$

- TEAGER ENERGY: This energy operator reflects variations in both amplitude and frequency of the signal and it is a robust parameter as it attenuates auditory noise [16, 17].

$$f_j = log_{10}\left(\frac{1}{N_j}\sum_{r=1}^{N_j-1}\left|(w_j(r))^2 - w_j(r-1)*w_j(r+1)\right|\right) \tag{3}$$

- HIGUCHI FRACTAL DIMENSION: The algorithm approximates the mean length of the curve using segments of k samples and estimates the dimension of a time-varying signal directly in the time domain [18]. Considered a finite set of observations taken at a regular interval: $X(1), X(2), X(3), .., X(N)$. From this series, a new one X_k^m must be constructed,

$$X_k^m : X(m), X(m+k), X(m+2k), .., X\left(m + \left(\frac{N-m}{k}\right)k\right) \tag{4}$$

Where $m = 1, 2, .., k$, m indicate the initial time and k the interval time. Then, the length of the curve associated to each time series X_k^m can be computed as follow:

$$L_m(k) = \frac{1}{k} \left(\sum_{i=1}^{\frac{N-m}{k}} \left(X(m+ik) - X\left(m + (i-1)k\right)\right) \right) \left(\frac{N-1}{\left(\frac{N-m}{k}\right)k} \right) \quad (5)$$

Higuchi takes the mean length of the curve for each k, as the average value of $L_m(k)$, for $m = 1, 2, ..., k$ and $k = 1, 2, ..., k_{max}$, that it is calculated as:

$$L(k) = \frac{1}{k} \sum_{m-1}^{k} (L_m(k)) \quad (6)$$

– PETROSIAN FRACTAL DIMENSION: can be used to provide a fast computation of the fractal dimension of a signal by translating the series into a binary sequence [19].

$$FD_{Petrosian} = \frac{\log_{10} n}{\log_{10} n + \log_{10}\left(\frac{n}{n+0.4N_\triangledown}\right)} \quad (7)$$

Where n is the length of the sequence and $N_\triangledown$ is the number of sign changes in the binary sequence.

2.2 Classifiers and Validation

At this point, the features vector have the same features per each instance with an assigned tag corresponding to the Subject-Id. This allows the use of machine learning methods. In this work, the machine learning methods *random forest, naive Bayes, SVM* and *k-NN* were used. For *SVM*, all experiments were reproduced with the kernels *Linear, RBF (Radial Basis Function)* and *Sigmoid*. In the *random forest* case, the experiments were reproduced with different tree depths (2, 3, 4, 5) using the *Gini* impurity. *k-NN* was tested with different number of neighbors (1, 2, 3, 4, 5, 6, 7, 8, 9).

The accuracy with the 4 classifiers was estimated to evaluate their performances using 10-folds cross-validation.

3 Dataset and Experiments

In this section, the dataset used to test the proposed method in two different experiments for Subject identification is described in brief.

The purpose of the first experiment is to show that the Subject can be identified regardless of the imagined word, to show if a biometric system using different password per Subject can be possible. The second experiment aim is to find whether the accuracy is higher if the password is pre-defined. In others words, using the same imagined word as biometric security measure.

3.1 Dataset

The complete dataset consists of EEG signals from 27 subjects recorded using EMOTIV EPOC device while imagining 33 repetitions of five imagined words in Spanish; *arriba, abajo, izquierda, derecha* and *seleccion*, corresponding to the English words *up, down, left, right* and *select*.

EEG signals with a mean size of $\lceil 2 \rceil$ seconds were recorded from 14 channels which were placed on the head according to the 10–20 international system [20], with a sample frequency of 128 Hz. Each set of imagined words were recorded in a different session, and each repetition of a word was separated by a resting-state and with markers that indicate when exactly the Subject imagines the indicated word. The protocol for EEG signal acquisition is described in details in [4].

3.2 Setup

For the next experiments the first 20 Subjects and the first 30 repetitions per each of the 5 imagined words were used. In summary, the terms used along the paper are the following.

- $S_{\nabla} = 20$: Subjects.
- $W_{\nabla} = 5$: The imagined words in the dataset.
- $R_{\nabla} = 30$: Repetitions per imagined word.
- $C_{\nabla} = 14$: Channels used in all instances.
- $IMFs_{\nabla} = 2$: IMF per channel.
- $F_{\nabla} = 4$: Features per IMF, corresponding to *Teager energy, Instantaneous energy, Higuchi Fractal Dimension* and *Petrosian Fractal Dimension*.

According to the proposed method the feature vector size per Subject is $F_{\nabla} * IMFs_{\nabla} * C_{\nabla}$. Next, the specific setup for the experiments and the results are presented.

3.3 Subject Level Analysis

In this experiment, 4 classifiers were used in order to compare their performances and each classifier has S_{∇} classes, and per class $R_{\nabla} * W_{\nabla}$ instances. The instances for each Subject correspond to all the 5 imagined words, because the aim of the experiment is to show that brain signals corresponding to different words in the group of 5 words can be used to identify the Subject. In Table 1 the accuracies obtained with the proposed method are shown.

The aim of this experiment is to show that the method can be used for Subject identification with high accuracy rates. According to the results in Table 1, the classifier SVM was the best. As it was mentioned before, SVM was tested with different kernels and for this experiment the best one was the *Linear SVM*.

Table 1. Accuracy obtained when all imagined words were grouped for Subject identification

Classifier	Accuracy
random forest	0.64
SVM	0.84
naive Bayes	0.68
k-NN	0.78

3.4 Word Level Analysis

In this experiment, the classifiers were trained using all words separately, in order to explore if the proposed method works best for Subject identification using a specific word. Each classifier has S_∇ classes (corresponding to the Subjects-id), and per class R_∇ instances (repetitions of the imagined word). Table 2 shows the results obtained for Subject identification using EEG-based brain signals for each imagined word separately.

Table 2. Accuracy obtained per imagined word for Subject identification

Classifier	Up	Down	Left	Right	Select
random forest	0.78	0.77	0.73	0.73	0.75
SVM	0.91	0.87	0.88	0.84	0.92
naive Bayes	0.90	0.85	0.88	0.85	0.89
k-NN	0.85	0.80	0.81	0.79	0.88

In this experiment, also the highest accuracy was obtained when using the *SVM* classifier with the *Linear* kernel, obtaining an accuracy of 0.92. On the other hand, the lowest performance was obtained using the classifier *random forest*

4 Discussion and Conclusions

In this paper, a method based on EMD for Subject identification from EEG signals of imagined speech was presented. The proposed method was applied to a dataset of Imagine Speech with encouraging results. The accuracies obtained suggest that the use of imagined speech for Subject identification, specially using the classifier *Linear SVM*, can be effective and worth exploring further.

When the imagined words were grouped together to observe if it is possible to identify a Subject regardless of the imagined word, the highest accuracy obtained was 0.84 using *Linear SVM*. Then, when the second experiment was carried out to observe the accuracies using the imagined words separately, the maximum accuracies reached were also using *Linear SVM*: 0.91, 0.87, 0.88, 0.84 and 0.92 respectively per each imagined word.

In the work presented in [21] the Common Average Reference (CAR) [22] was used to improve the signal-to-noise ratio. Then, the feature extraction was based on *Instantaneous* and *Teager* energy distribution of 4 decomposition levels of Wavelet using the mother function Biorthogonal 2.2, and *random forest* for classification. The accuracies obtained using the imagined word *select* were 0.96 and 0.93 respectively. In this paper, the highest accuracy (Using Linear SVM) obtained for the imagined word *select* was 0.92, which is slightly lower than the above ones. However, with the inherent adaptivity of EMD for feature extraction, there is no need to pre-define any mother function for the particular task or neuro-paradigm. In addition, the EMD inherently improves the signal-to-noise ratio by removing the noise in the first IMFs.

A limitation of the proposed method is the use of a dataset of brain signals from only 20 Subjects. In future, it will be necessary to reproduce the experiments using a larger population in order produce an alternative competitive system to the current biometric security systems used in industry. Further efforts will be made to explore alternative techniques for IMFs selection and for EEG channels selection, since it is well known that specific channels will provide more relevant information than others for the distinct task selected for Subject identification.

Acknowledgments. This work was supported by Enabling Technologies - NTNU, under the project "David versus Goliath: single-channel EEG unravels its power through adaptive signal analysis - FlexEEG".

References

1. Bashashati, A., Fatourechi, M., Ward, R.K., Birch, G.E.: A survey of signal processing algorithms in brain-computer interfaces based on electrical brain signals. J. Neural Eng. **4**(2), R32 (2007)
2. Desain, P., Farquhar, J., Haselager, P., Hesse, C., Schaefer, R.S.: What BCI research needs. In: Proceedings of the ACM CHI 2008 Conference on Human Factors in Computing Systems, Venice, Italy (2008)
3. Moctezuma, L.A., Carrillo, M., Villaseñor Pineda, L., Torres García, A.A.: Hacia la clasificación de actividad e inactividad lingüistica a partir de senales de electroencefalogramas (EEG). Res. Comput. Sci. **140**, 135–149 (2017)
4. Torres-García, A.A., Reyes-García, C.A., Villaseñor-Pineda, L., Ramírez-Cortís, J.M.: Análisis de señales electroencefalográficas para la clasificación de habla imaginada. Revista mexicana de ingeniería biomédica **34**(1), 23–39 (2013)
5. Nishimoto, T., Azuma, Y., Morioka, H., Ishii, S.: Individual identification by resting-state EEG using common dictionary learning. In: Lintas, A., Rovetta, S., Verschure, P.F.M.J., Villa, A.E.P. (eds.) ICANN 2017. LNCS, vol. 10613, pp. 199–207. Springer, Cham (2017). https://doi.org/10.1007/978-3-319-68600-4_24
6. Brigham, K., Vijaya Kumar, B.V.K.: Subject identification from electroencephalogram (EEG) signals during imagined speech. In: 2010 Fourth IEEE International Conference on Biometrics: Theory Applications and Systems (BTAS), pp. 1–8 (2010)

7. Jain, A.K., Ross, A., Uludag, U: Biometric template security: challenges and solutions. In: 2005 13th European Signal Processing Conference, pp. 1–4 (2005)
8. Ashby, C., Bhatia, A., Tenore, F., Vogelstein, J.: Low-cost electroencephalogram (EEG) based authentication. In: 2011 5th International IEEE/EMBS Conference on Neural Engineering (NER), pp. 442–445 (2011)
9. Palaniappan, R.: Electroencephalogram signals from imagined activities: a novel biometric identifier for a small population. In: Corchado, E., Yin, H., Botti, V., Fyfe, C. (eds.) IDEAL 2006. LNCS, vol. 4224, pp. 604–611. Springer, Heidelberg (2006). https://doi.org/10.1007/11875581_73
10. Del Pozo-Banos, M., Alonso, J.B., Ticay-Rivas, J.R., Travieso, C.M.: Electroencephalogram subject identification: a review. Expert. Syst. Appl. **41**(15), 6537–6554 (2014)
11. Steven, M.K.: Modern Spectral Estimation: Theory and Application. Signal Processing Series (1988)
12. Huang, N.E., et al.: The empirical mode decomposition and the Hilbert spectrum for nonlinear and non-stationary time series analysis. In: Proceedings of the Royal Society of London A: Mathematical, Physical and Engineering Sciences, vol. 454, no. 1971, pp. 903–995 (1998)
13. Rilling, G., Flandrin, P., Goncalves, P.: On empirical mode decomposition and its algorithms. In: IEEE-EURASIP Workshop on Nonlinear Signal and Image Processing, vol. 3 NSIP-03, Grado (I), pp. 8–11 (2003)
14. de Souza, D.B., Chanussot, J., Favre, A.-C.: On selecting relevant intrinsic mode functions in empirical mode decomposition: an energy-based approach. In: 2014 IEEE International Conference on Acoustics, Speech and Signal Processing (ICASSP), pp. 325–329 (2014)
15. Boutana, D., Benidir, M., Barkat, B.: On the selection of intrinsic mode function in EMD method: application on heart sound signal. In: 2010 3rd International Symposium on Applied Sciences in Biomedical and Communication Technologies (ISABEL), pp. 1–5 (2010)
16. Didiot, E., Illina, I., Fohr, D., Mella, O.: A wavelet-based parameterization for speechmusic discrimination. Comput. Speech Lang. **24**(2), 341–357 (2010)
17. Jabloun, F., Enis Cetin, A.: The Teager energy based feature parameters for robust speech recognition in car noise. In: 1999 IEEE International Conference on Acoustics, Speech, and Signal Processing, vol. 1, pp. 273–276 (1999)
18. Higuchi, T.: Approach to an irregular time series on the basis of the fractal theory. Phys. D Nonlinear Phenom. **31**, 277–283 (1988)
19. Petrosian, A.: Kolmogorov complexity of finite sequences and recognition of different preictal EEG patterns. In: Proceedings of the Eighth IEEE Symposium on Computer-Based Medical Systems, pp. 212–217 (1995)
20. Jasper, H.: Report of the committee on methods of clinical examination in electroencephalography. Electroencephalogr. Clin. Neurophysiol. **10**, 370–375 (1958)
21. Moctezuma, L.A., Molinas, M., Torres García, A.A., Villaseñor Pineda, L., Carrillo, M.: Towards an API for EEG-based imagined speech classification. In: International Conference on Time Series and Forecasting (2018)
22. Bertrand, O., Perrin, F., Pernier, J.: A theoretical justification of the average reference in topographic evoked potential studies. Electroencephalogr. Clin. Neurophysiol./Evoked Potentials Sect. **62**(6), 462–464 (1985)

Simulating Phishing Email Processing with Instance-Based Learning and Cognitive Chunk Activation

Matthew Shonman[✉], Xiangyang Li[✉], Haoruo Zhang[✉],
and Anton Dahbura[✉]

Johns Hopkins University Information Security Institute, Baltimore 21218, USA
{mshonmal, xyli, zhanghaoruo, antondahbura}@jhu.edu

Abstract. We present preliminary steps applying computational cognitive modeling to research decision-making of cybersecurity users. Building from a recent empirical study, we adapt Instance-Based Learning Theory and ACT-R's description of memory chunk activation in a cognitive model representing the mental process of users processing emails. In this model, a user classifies emails as phishing or legitimate by counting the number of suspicious-seeming cues in each email; these cues are themselves classified by examining similar, past classifications in long-term memory. When the sum of suspicious cues passes a threshold value, that email is classified as phishing. In a simulation, we manipulate three parameters (suspicion threshold; maximum number of cues processed; weight of similarity term) and examine their effects on accuracy, false positive/negative rates, and email processing time.

Keywords: Phishing · Cognitive modeling · Chunk activation

1 Introduction

While reliable estimates vary, hundreds of millions of phishing emails at a minimum are sent every year [4]. Despite the gradual emergence of automated anti-phish defenses, human judgment remains a significant, and typically sole, means for distinguishing legitimate emails from malicious attacks. Many research efforts identify personality traits and informational cues that relate to processing legitimate and suspicious emails, quantifying their impact on user performance through empirical studies [8, 9, 11].

Computational cognitive modeling offers an additional route to study this process. Computational models, including ACT-R and SOAR [2, 7], describe the underlying psychological operations producing human behaviors in physiological movement and problem solving. Compared to "black box" or "product theory" models of phishing and security behavior, which mainly describe correlation between inputs and outputs, these models can offer greater insights into the interactions between a user and a task environment. In addition to predicting potential issues, such as errors in decision making or delays in reaching a task goal, these techniques enable researchers to diagnose plausible causes, based on emerging cognitive conditions, and discern an appropriate remedy.

© Springer Nature Switzerland AG 2018
S. Wang et al. (Eds.): BI 2018, LNAI 11309, pp. 468–478, 2018.
https://doi.org/10.1007/978-3-030-05587-5_44

This work builds from two significant research efforts: the sole notable study using computational cognitive modeling to examine cybersecurity decision-making [6] and a recent empirical study of users making phishing classifications [12]. Our model, based upon Instance-Based Learning Theory (IBLT) and the chunk activation mechanism of ACT-R, portrays users as drawing upon past memory "instances" to determine whether individual cues (such as the email title or presence of poor grammar) are themselves suspicious. Users decide whether a cue is suspicious by matching it with a single previously-encountered cue stored as a memory instance, called a chunk; this "activated" instance is selected from many others according to ACT-R's chunk activation calculation, with the "winner" having the highest value. If a sufficient number of cues in an email are deemed suspicious, the email is classified as phishing.

This simulation study examines the influence of three control parameters on classification accuracy and task completion time:

- *Suspicion threshold.* This term denotes the minimum number of suspicious cues detected before the user marks an email as phishing.
- *Maximum cues processed.* This term denotes the total number of cues per email that a user would likely inspect.
- *Weight of the similarity term in chunk activation calculation.* The ACT-R memory activation formula considers the recency and frequency of an instance's past retrievals and its similarity to the cue currently under consideration.

Our work strives to make several contributions. It is the first study to apply computational cognitive modeling to user security behavior in phishing, widening this important research subject. It presents a comprehensive model of email processing that significantly extends the IBL model integrating cognition chunk activation. Moreover, we are aiming at a systematic effort that also examines data from an empirical study for comparison and validation.

2 Related Work

2.1 Chunk Activation in ACT-R and Instance Based Learning Theory (IBLT)

Anderson [2] proposed the ACT-R cognitive architecture in 1993. In this model, declarative knowledge is stored as discrete "chunks" in long-term memory. ACT-R models a process through which information in memory is retrieved if selected as relevant to a present situation. Relevant information chunks are selected according to an activation value calculation equation, simplified in Kaur et al. [6] as:

$$A_i = B_i + Sim_i + \varepsilon_i. \tag{1}$$

B_i represents a base-level activation, combining the recency and frequency of a chunk's prior retrievals. Sim_i denotes the association or similarity between a chunk and the current situation. ε_i is a random noise term to model imperfection in human cognition. This activation process forms a core component of our own model.

In further detail, for the ith memory chunk (equations drawn from Kaur et al. [6]):

$$B_i = \ln\left(\sum_{t_i \in \{1,\ldots,t-1\}} (t - t_i)^{-d}\right) \qquad (2)$$

$\{1,\ldots,t-1\}$ represents the set of past activation times for the given chunk. $(t - t_i)$ represents the lapse between current time t and a given past activation time t_i. Decay term d has a default value of 0.5. Our study used relative time, omitting duration units.

$$Sim_i = \sum_{l=1}^{k} P_l * M_{li} \qquad (3)$$

P_l is a weight with value -0.01. M_{li} represents the raw similarity score comparing the lth information attribute with the situation represented by the chunk.

$$\varepsilon_i = s * \ln\left(\frac{1 - \eta_i}{\eta_i}\right) \qquad (4)$$

η_i is drawn from a uniform random distribution between 0 and 1 exclusive. Weight s has a default value of 0.25. 90% of ε_i values lie between ± 0.736.

Gonzales et al. [3] developed instance-based learning theory (IBLT) to describe a learning process linked to dynamic decision-making. Experiences are stored in memory as instances with three components: situation (relevant environmental cues), decision (action taken in response to a situation), and utility (post-hoc evaluation of a decision). In order to determine the appropriate action for a current situation, the model considers the utilities of past actions taken in response to similar situations.

2.2 Cognitive Modeling and Computer Security

A limited range of research has thus far applied cognitive modeling to enhance the study of computer security. Veksler et al. [10] discuss several potential uses of cognitive modeling in cybersecurity contexts, such as comparing the effects of training strategies on users and understanding the psychology of attackers, defenders and users to facilitate security improvements and predict human errors. However, this work offers few specifics on implementing its proposals. Veksler and Buchler [9] present three simulations demonstrating that techniques such as model tracing and dynamic parameter adjustment allow computational cognitive models, in the context of social security games, to outperform normative game theory in predicting and responding to cyber attackers. Similarly, Jones et al. [5] describe the use of cognitive agents developed with the Soar architecture to improve training simulations for cyber operators. These agents can consider goals and context in attack and defensive scenarios; they also exhibit generative mechanisms to produce new tactics and learn from experience.

2.3 Computational Cognitive Modeling of Security Decision Making

The sole published work on *computational* cognitive modeling of individual users in computer security is the simulation research of Kaur et al. [6]. Their method draws upon IBLT to describe the behavior of a security analyst determining whether a series of network events constitutes a cyberattack. In this model, situation information is represented as a series of attributes denoting particular details of a network event, including the network location, alert, and operation result. Security analysts classify individual events as threat or non-threat by examining the selected chunk from a past similar experience in memory. A counter for each event sequence increments for each new event judged as a threat. When the counter surpasses a set threshold, the entire sequence is classified as a cyberattack. Each event under consideration is compared to all instances stored in memory. The instance with the highest ACT-R activation score is retrieved from memory, with its utility used to classify the event under consideration.

Our model differs from the above study in several ways:

- In the Kaur et al. simulation, all incidents (event sequences) are attacks (although individual normal events are present). In our model, an email (the equivalent of a full event sequence) may be either phishing or normal.
- In Kaur et al., the analyst continues to score events in a sequence until either the preset number of threat events have been classified, or all events in the sequence have been classified without triggering the suspicion counter. We change this by adding a maximum-cues-considered parameter.
- In Kaur et al., all network events are of identical structure and all decisions draw upon a single shared pool of memory instances. In our model, cues are of various types and decisions for a given type draw only upon memories of that same type.
- Kaur et al. held the suspicion threshold constant. We vary suspicion threshold as one experimental parameter.
- Moreover, we have conducted an empirical study [12] that collects data from real users, providing rich information for further assistance to the modeling effort.

3 A User Experiment of Email Classification

The user task described fully in Zhang et al. [12] provides context for our current work. Study participants were directed to classify 40 randomly-ordered emails as "keep" or "suspicious." 20 emails were legitimate and the remaining 20 were phishing. All phishing emails were link-based attacks.

3.1 Condition-Based User Study Task Sets

Two independent variables were manipulated, each with two levels. Participants were randomly assigned to one of four experimental conditions: (1) Multitasking with Incentive; (2) No-Multitasking with Incentive; (3) Multitasking with No Incentive; and (4) No Multitasking and No Incentive.

Multitasking participants answered 20 sets of questions in an online survey system while completing the email sorting task in Roundcube, a webmail system. Each question set was presented for a maximum of two minutes; participants could manually advance to the next question set after one minute elapsed. Thus, multitasking participants had 40 min at most to complete both tasks. For the no multitasking condition, participants were given 30 min to complete only the email sorting task.

For the incentive conditions, participants could earn additional monetary compensation based on the number of correctly sorted emails. For Condition 1 participants, extra money earned depended on accuracy of both the email sorting and multitasking tasks. For the no incentive conditions, participants received no additional compensation.

3.2 Email Design and Phishing Cues

All 40 emails were created from real emails with personally identifiable information modified. Phishing emails were derived from a semi-random sample of emails in Cornell University's "Phish Bowl" database (it.cornell.edu/phish-bowl). Legitimate emails were derived from emails received by the research team.

We defined a series of cues, contained within the email, implying whether those emails are legitimate or phishing. Crucially, legitimate emails may contain individual suspicious cues, such as misspellings or an absent greeting, while phishing emails may contain enough non-suspicious cues to seem legitimate. However, phishing emails on average contained more suspicious cues than did legitimate emails, providing a path to accurate classification. The original cue definitions are in Zhang et al. [12]; for the present simulation, the "URL Hyperlink" cue was expanded to encompass two other link cues, while a "Subject" cue was added, for a total of 13 cues shown in Table 1.

Table 1. Phishing cue definitions.

Cue type	Cue definition
Branding/Logos	Does the email contain company branding and/or logos?
Overall design	Does the overall email quality appear poor?
Suspicious sender name	Does the subject line appear suspicious?
Subject	Does the subject line direct the receiver to take an action?
Lack of signer details	Does the email provide sender information beyond a name?
Generic greeting	Is the email greeting absent/not addressed to the individual?
URL Hyperlink (possibly multiple cues per email)	Scored according to presence or absence of two attributes: • Does the hyperlink text suggest a webpage different from the true link? • Does the hyperlink website match the email sender?
Spelling/Grammar	Does the text contain any spelling/grammar mistakes?
Time pressure	Does the email request include a deadline?
Threatening language	Does the email threaten a negative consequence if instructions unfollowed?

(continued)

Table 1. (*continued*)

Cue type	Cue definition
Emotional appeal	Does the email elicit a sympathetic or otherwise emotional response?
Too good to be true offer	Does the email present a too-good-to-be-true offer?
Personal information	Does the email request personal information?

3.3 Experiment Results

Out of 205 participants recruited through Amazon Mechanical Turk, 177 progressed through the full study, with 146 classifying all 40 emails in the given time. Participants were randomly assigned into the four experimental condition groups.

For email sorting accuracy, analysis of variance (ANOVA) testing indicated a significant effect of condition on email classification accuracy, using significance level α at 0.05. Overall multitasking significantly worsened subjects' sorting accuracy, but incentive alone made no difference in either multitasking or no-multitasking cases. Significant differences were also present between phishing sorting error rates for conditions 1, 2, and 3. However, there was no significant difference between conditions for legitimate email sorting error rates.

Average email processing time was calculated for each email for every condition. Multitasking and incentive showed opposite effects: multitasking reduced users' processing time, while the incentive increased this value. Spending more time on individual emails did not always guarantee better sorting accuracy. For instance, condition 1 participants spent more time per email compared to those in condition 3, without increased accuracy. Although these participants were more "carefully" sorting emails, switching between tasks seemed to pose a challenge.

4   A Cognitive Model of Phishing Judgment Process

4.1   Model Design

Our study greatly extended the Kaur et al. model to fit the single-task design of the above phishing empirical study. Users classify an email by evaluating the email's individual cues (Table 1) as "threat" or "non-threat." The model maintains a counter variable for every email, which increments by one for each cue judged as threat. An email is classified as phishing when the number of cues so judged passes a threshold level.

The cue current in processing is classified according to the long-term memory chunk with the highest activation score at that moment. Chunks in long-term memory represent past email cues for which the email nature (phishing/non-phishing) is known, and contain the following parameters:

- *Cue type.* One of the 13 different types of cues.
- *Attribute score.* Attributes are coded 0 if the question (Table 1) is answered "No," and 1 otherwise. Hyperlink cues feature two attributes, while all others have one.
- *Utility.* The utility value is 0 if the email associated with this past cue was normal; 1 for phishing.

For this simulation study, long-term memory was populated with chunks derived from all 572 cues drawn from the 40 emails. This produced a memory store containing 40 chunks per cue type (one per source email) except for the hyperlink type; the emails contained 0–13 hyperlinks each, all encoded as distinct chunks. In this way, the 40 emails represent the "real" population distribution of cue chunks associated with legitimate and phishing emails, an assumption that we can re-examine and change in future simulations.

In a departure from the Kaur et al. model, not all cues are processed for each email. As more cues are classified, the likelihood increases that even normal emails will be scored as phishing (since normal emails tend to contain cues that are similar to those contained in phishing emails). In order to balance the likelihood of phishing and normal classifications, the model featured a parameter determining the maximum number of cues which would be classified per email, separate from the suspicion threshold. When this number is reached, the email is immediately scored as normal if the suspicion threshold has not been crossed.

Cues are visited in an order that combines fixed steps and random elements. Expert input and observation through a pilot study suggest that email readers tend to view the following elements in sequence: limited text visuals, sender, subject, greeting, and "story" text. As a result, the model visits the six cues analogous to these elements (the first six cues in Table 1) in a linear order. Because no inherent order emerges for the remaining cues, their order is not fixed. All these cues are stored together in the user's working buffer. For this stage of cue processing, all memory chunks corresponding to these seven cue types are likewise pooled together; the memory chunk being activated determines which cue will be processed next. Once a cue has been processed, chunks of that type are skipped over for future rounds of processing. This sequence resets for each new email classified.

4.2 Simulation Setting

This study sought general insights as to the experimental parameters' influence on the simulation results; thus, we placed limited focus on the impact of specific parameter settings. The maximum number of cues processed per email varied between 7 and 12. The minimum bound ensured that at least one of the remaining cues beyond the first six (fixed-ordered) cues would be classified, while the maximum bound was selected because one email only had 12 cues, without any hyperlinks. The suspicion threshold varied between 2 and 6, always remaining beneath the maximum-cues-processed parameter. Finally, the ACT-R similarity weight P_l took the values -1, -2, and -3. This variation allowed us to examine the similarity term's interaction with the base-level learning and noise terms. Similarity was calculated as the difference between the respective attribute(s) of the cue under consideration and a memory chunk.

The simulation was coded in Python, with chunk management in long-term memory taken directly from the Python ACT-R source code [1]. The simulation was run 100 times for each of the 90 parameter combinations. Output metrics included number of cues processed per email (analogous to total time spent scoring email), classification accuracy, false negative rate (FNR) and false positive rate (FPR). 95% confidence intervals were computed for all simulation results, with ranges of ±0.425 (maximum cues processed), ±0.025 (accuracy), ±0.072 (FNR), and ±0.064 (FPR).

5   Results

Controlling for maximum cue number, accuracy was generally highest for mid-range suspicion threshold values (usually 4 on a 2–6 range). High maximum cue values, though, defied this trend, continuing to increase for high suspicion threshold values. Greater similarity weights were associated with greater accuracy values, but also with greater variation in accuracy for the maximum-cues-considered parameter at high suspicion thresholds.

The mean cues processed metric is equivalent to the average time spent processing an email. This value increased with both greater suspicion thresholds and greater maximum cue levels. Similarity weight had minimal influence on this output (Figs. 1 and 2).

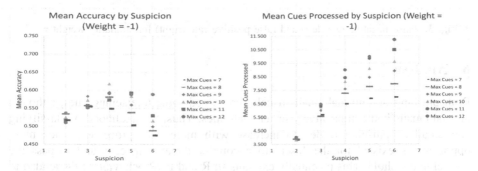

Fig. 1. Mean accuracy (left) and mean cues processed (right) for similarity weight = −1.

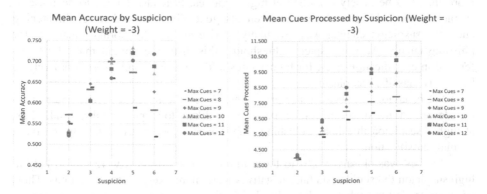

Fig. 2. Mean accuracy (left) and mean cues processed (right) for similarity weight = −3.

FPR tended to decrease as the suspicion threshold was raised. Controlling for suspicion threshold, FPR rose as the maximum cue number increased. Greater similarity weights generally lowered FPR. FNR tended to increase with a greater suspicion threshold. Controlling for suspicion, FNR was generally highest for the lowest maximum cue numbers. Generally, FNR decreased slightly as similarity weight was raised, although some individual points broke with this trend (Fig. 3).

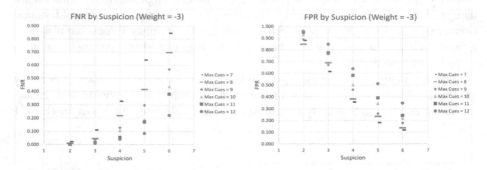

Fig. 3. False negative rate (left) and false positive rate (right) for similarity weight = −3.

6 Analysis

Both phishing and normal emails usually contained some threatening cues, although normal emails had comparatively fewer such cues. Thus, the likelihood of classifying any email as phishing tended to increase with more cues processed, since more opportunities existed for the "user" to encounter threatening cues and surpass the suspicion threshold. This potentially explains FPR and FNR behaviors. FPR tended to increase as the max-cues-processed parameter rose: even if phishing emails were accurately classified at both lower and higher parameter values, normal emails were more likely to be falsely classified at higher values. FPR also tended to decrease as suspicion threshold rose: since normal emails generally contained fewer threatening cues, the suspicion counter was less likely to rise as high for normal emails as for phishing emails. At low suspicion thresholds, this distinction might make little difference in classification rates; for higher thresholds, normal emails were less likely to be falsely classified as phishing.

FNR behavior followed similar principles. When the max-cues-processed parameter decreased, the suspicion counter became less likely to surpass the threshold. Thus, at higher suspicion thresholds, phishing emails were more likely to falsely receive a normal classification.

Accuracy was closely linked to these trends. False positives were more likely at high suspicion thresholds, and false negatives were more likely at low thresholds. Thus, accuracy tended to peak at medium threshold values. Greater similarity weights tended to lower both FPR and FNR, increasing accuracy. Lower weights de-emphasized similarity and increased the recency and frequency effects of past behavior on current decisions; memory instances activated early in a classification round held greater impact on later behavior, increasing the tendency for single instances to be activated for many email cues. This shows the importance of users remaining focused and current, while avoiding internal and external interruptions that might complicate this routine task.

Suspicion threshold and max-cues-processed held expected, positive relationships with the mean number of cues processed per email. Consistent with the user study, spending more time classifying did not correlate with better classification accuracies.

7 Conclusion

This simulation study represents first steps toward a computational cognitive model describing the psychological processes that underlie phishing email classification. Our results imply one initial conclusion: accuracy generally improved when similarity was emphasized over recency and frequency. This suggests that successful security analysts should adopt a strategy that pays more attention to the current state than to details of emails recently encountered. Our manipulations of the maximum cue and suspicion threshold parameters provide additional insights into the decision-making process for this classification problem.

Computational cognitive modeling can offer powerful insights into the mindsets of cybersecurity operators, but few empirical studies have explored this topic. We plan further research to follow this simulation, beginning with fitting our model to population subgroups from the user study. Future work might explore the effect of phishing content changing over time, as phishing senders adapt their techniques to target skeptical recipients. We hope that our work combining simulation and empirical data will continue to enhance the study of human security informatics.

Acknowledgement. This work is supported under the National Science Foundation Award No. 1544493.

References

1. ACT-R Software. http://act-r.psy.cmu.edu/software/
2. Anderson, J.R.: ACT: a simple theory of complex cognition. Am. Psychol. **51**(4), 355–365 (1995)
3. Gonzalez, C., Lerch, J.F., Lebiere, C.: Instance-based learning in dynamic decision making. Cogn. Sci. **27**, 591–635 (2003)
4. Gudkova, D., Vergelis, M., Shcherbakova, T., Demidova, N.: Spam and phishing in 2017. Securelist (2018). https://securelist.com/spam-and-phishing-in-2017/83833. Accessed 8 Oct 2018
5. Jones, R.M., et al.: Modeling and integrating cognitive agents within the emerging cyber domain. In: Interservice/Industry Training, Simulation, and Education Conference (2015)
6. Kaur, A., Dutt, V., Gonzalez, C.: Modelling the security analyst's role: effects of similarity and past experience on cyber attack detection. In: Proceedings of the 22nd Annual Conference on Behavior Representation in Modeling and Simulation (2013)
7. Laird, J.: The Soar Cognitive Architecture. MIT Press, Cambridge (2012)

8. Molinaro, K., Bolton, M.L.: Evaluating the applicability of the double system lens model to the analysis of phishing email judgments. Comput. Secur. **77**, 128–137 (2018). https://doi.org/10.1016/j.cose.2018.03.012

9. Veksler, V.D., Buchler, N.: Know your enemy: applying cognitive modeling in security domain. In: 38th Annual Meeting of the Cognitive Science Society, Philadelphia (2016)

10. Veksler, V.D., et al.: Simulations in cyber-security: a review of cognitive modeling of network attackers, defenders, and users. Front. Psychol. **9** (2018). https://doi.org/10.3389/fpsyg.2018.00691

11. Vishwanath, A., Harrison, B., Ng, Y.J.: Suspicion, Cognition, Automaticity Model (SCAM) of Phishing Susceptibility. Communication Research (in-press)

12. Zhang, H., Singh, S., Li, X., Dahbura, A., Xie, M.: Multitasking and monetary incentive in a realistic phishing study. In: British Human Computer Interaction Conference (2018)

Sparse Sampling and Fully-3D Fast Total Variation Based Imaging Reconstruction for Chemical Shift Imaging in Magnetic Resonance Spectroscopy

Zigen Song[1,2], Melinda Baxter[1], Mingwu Jin[3], Jian-Xiong Wang[4], Ren-Cang Li[1], Talon Johnson[1], and Jianzhong Su[1(✉)]

[1] Department of Mathematics, University of Texas at Arlington, Arlington, USA
su@uta.edu
[2] College of Information Technology,
Shanghai Ocean University, Shanghai, China
[3] Department of Physics, University of Texas at Arlington, Arlington, USA
[4] Advanced Imaging Research Center Radiology Department,
University of Texas Southwestern Medical Center, Dallas, USA

Abstract. We propose a 3-dimensional sparse sampling reconstruction method, aiming for chemical shift imaging in magnetic resonance spectroscopy. The method is a Compressed Sensing (CS) method based on the interior point optimization technique that can substantially reduce the number of sampling points required, and the method has been tested successfully in hyperpolarized ^{13}C experimental data using two different sampling strategies.

Keywords: Imaging reconstruction · Chemical shift imaging
3D Compressed Sensing · Sparse sampling of MRSI data

1 Introduction

Advanced brain imaging in recent years has been greatly influenced by technology advances in magnetic resonance imaging modalities, particularly magnetic resonance spectroscopy that is capable of imaging brain chemical elements and metabolism through their spectrum distributions. Fueled by hyperpolarized contrast agents, parallel imaging, and high speed imaging techniques, magnetic resonance spectroscopy (MRS) is transiting from single-voxel metabolite signal spectrum to multiple-voxel metabolite spectral mapping, i.e. chemical shift imaging (CSI) [1, 2]. These new information will serve key roles for diagnosing brain tumor or other brain diseases in their early stages, as CSI can successfully detect their metabolic inhomogeneity. For instance, the chemical spectrum from a brain tumor is quite different from a spectrum from the actively growing healthy brain tissues, and high-resolution MRSI can provide data and information for diagnosis and prognosis of brain cancer. In [3], MRSI data was able to generate a discriminant function to differentiate between high-grade and low-grade tumors based on the ratios of N-acetyl aspartate/choline and Choline (norm) (Wilks' lambda, $P = 0.001$; 89.5% of the cases were correctly classified). The MRSI

© Springer Nature Switzerland AG 2018
S. Wang et al. (Eds.): BI 2018, LNAI 11309, pp. 479–485, 2018.
https://doi.org/10.1007/978-3-030-05587-5_45

imaging data has become a rich source for brain informatics, but it requires a long acquisition period for patients. The compressed sensing (CS) techniques [4, 5] have been sought to speed up the MR data acquisition, which is particularly valuable for hyperpolarized ^{13}C CSI due to the nonrenewable polarization [2]. Recently, we proposed to use a fully three-dimensional (3D) Compressed Sensing (CS) method based on the interior point optimization technique [5] that can substantially reduce the number of excitations required for imaging hyperpolarized metabolites. In this work, we further present a method, originally developed in the thesis [6], by investigating sparse sampling in the k-space and using the interior point technique via the log-barrier functions and test it successfully on hyperpolarized ^{13}C experimental data. The new method is called the Three Dimensional Image Reconstruction (3DIRECT) method, as in [6], for constrained total-variation (TV) minimization reconstruction to obtain minimal total variation in 3D.

2   3DIRECT

Sparseness of the k-space data is exploited in two phase encoding directions by two different undersampling patterns, i.e. the radial line pattern proposed in this work and the center-weighted random pattern used in [4], as shown in Fig. 1(Left) and (Middle). The radial line pattern has a natural dense sampling at the central region of the k-space. The un-acquired phase encoding readouts are set as zero initial values for the CS optimization. The 3D sparse image reconstruction problem is modeled by

$$\min \text{ TV}(X) \quad \text{subject to } \| A(X) - B \|_2 \leq \varepsilon, \tag{1}$$

where A: $\mathbf{R}^{16\times16\times256} \longmapsto \mathbf{R}^{16\times16\times256}$ is a sparsifying linear transform, B: $\mathbf{R}^{16\times16\times256}$ is the measured observation of sampled pixels of an image in the k-space, and TV: $\mathbf{R}^{16\times16\times256} \longmapsto \mathbf{R}$ is the sum of the magnitudes of the gradient of X in the x-, y-, and z-directions. Extending the 2D l_1-Magic method [5], the 3DIRECT method [6] casts the problem into a Second Order Cone Problem (SCOP). Specifically, we solve the following optimization problem

Fig. 1. Left: Radial line pattern with $L = 3$ for sparse phase encoding matrix; Middle: Center-weighted random pattern with the sampling rate 20%; Right: Proton image of the phantom containing ^{13}C-enriched lactate, alanine, formic acid, and bicarbonate in four individual cylinders.

$$\min_{X,T} \sum_{i,j,k=1}^{n} T_{i,j,k} \text{ subject to}$$

$$\|D_{i,j,k}X\|_2 \le T_{i,j,k} \text{ and } \|A(X) - B\|_2 \le \varepsilon, \tag{2}$$

where $D_{i,j,k} X$ is the numerical differential of X. It is solved by the interior point method via the log-barrier functions that enforce the inequality constraints in (2) [6]. For that purpose, we first define

$$f_{T_{i,j,k}} = \frac{1}{2}\left(\|D_{i,j,k}X\|_2^2 - T_{i,j,k}^2\right), \quad i,j,k = 1,\cdots,n \text{ and}$$

$$f_\varepsilon = \frac{1}{2}\left(\|A(X) - B\|_2^2 - \varepsilon^2\right). \tag{3}$$

We then use the log-barrier functions to implicitly enforce the inequality constraints in (2) to get the objective function as follows

$$F(z) = \langle c_0, z \rangle - \frac{1}{\tau}\left(\sum_{i,j,k} \log\left(-f_{T_{i,j,k}}(z)\right) + \log(-f_\varepsilon(z))\right), \tag{4}$$

where $\tau > 0$ is an accuracy parameter and $c_0 = (0_{n^3}, 1_{n^3})^T$, $z = (x, t)^T$. We use $0_{n^3}, 1_{n^3}$ to denote the column vectors of 0's and 1's of length n^3, respectively. Thus, if we assume a feasible z, the direction Δz along which $F(z)$ is to be approximately minimized is the solution to the following system of linear equations

$$H_z \Delta z = -g_z, \tag{5}$$

where

$$g_z = c_0 + \frac{1}{\tau}\left(\sum_{i,j,k} \frac{1}{-f_{T_{i,j,k}}(z)} \nabla f_{T_{i,j,k}}(z) + \frac{1}{-f_\varepsilon(z)} \nabla f_\varepsilon(z)\right), \tag{6}$$

and

$$H_z = \frac{1}{\tau}\left(\sum_{i,j,k} \frac{1}{f_{T_{i,j,k}}(z)^2} \nabla f_{T_{i,j,k}}(z)\left(\nabla f_{T_{i,j,k}}(z)\right)^T + \sum_{i,j,k} \frac{1}{-f_{T_{i,j,k}}(z)} \nabla^2 f_{T_{i,j,k}}(z)\right.$$
$$\left. + \frac{1}{f_\varepsilon(z)^2} \nabla f_\varepsilon(z)(\nabla f_\varepsilon(z))^T + \frac{1}{-f_\varepsilon(z)} \nabla^2 f_\varepsilon(z)\right). \tag{7}$$

We use the Conjugate Gradient (CG) method to solve (5) [6].

3   Experiments and Evaluation Metrics

To test the method in hyperpolarized ^{13}C CSI, a phantom made of four metabolites: lactate, alanine, formic acid, and bicarbonate, is used for the imaging experiment. All metabolites were labeled with hyperpolarized ^{13}C. Then, the phantom was imaged using MRSI sequence on a 3T GE Discovery MR750w scanner (GE Healthcare, Waukesha, Wisconsin) with a single channel (birdcage) ^{1}H/^{13}C dual-tuned rat size coil [4]. 16x16 spatial phase encoding and spectrum length of 256 points were acquired. Figure 1(Right) shows the proton reference image of the phantom. We test the proposed 3DIRECT with both the radial line under-sampling for the number of lines $L = 5, 3, 2$, representing a sampling rate $R = 27\%$, 16.8%, and 11.3% of the full data, respectively, and the center-weighted random under-sampling at the corresponding sampling rates.

To evaluate the quality of reconstructed images, we used two criteria: (1) the structural similarity (SSIM) index [7]; and (2) the normalized root mean square error (nRMSE). The SSIM index is used to evaluate the similarity on intensity, contrast and structure between the ground-truth image (fully sampled) and the images reconstructed by 3DRECT using sparse samples, while nRMSE is used to measure the overall reconstruction accuracy. The SSIM index is defined as follows [7]:

$$SSIM(X^{Tru}, X^{Rec}) = \frac{(2\mu_{X^{Tru}}\mu_{X^{Rec}} + C_1)(2\sigma_{X^{Tru}X^{Rec}} + C_2)}{(\mu^2_{X^{Tru}} + \mu^2_{X^{Rec}} + C_1)(\sigma^2_{X^{Tru}} + \sigma^2_{X^{Rec}} + C_2)}, \quad (8)$$

where X^{Tru} and X^{Rec} denote the ground-truth image and the reconstructed image, respectively, μ's are the averages of respective image intensities, σ's are the variances and covariances, and $C_1 = (k_1 \ L)^2$, $C_2 = (k_2 \ L)^2$ are two variables to stabilize the division with small denominator. L is the dynamic range of pixel values and $k_1 = 0.01$, and $k_2 = 0.03$. Two identical images will have a maximum SSIM value of 1. The nRMSE is defined as

$$nRMSE = \frac{\sqrt{[\sum_i^N (X_i^{Tru} - X_i^{Rec})^2]/N}}{\text{mean}(X^{Tru})}, \quad (9)$$

where i denotes the ith pixel of the image and mean($\bullet$) is the mean intensity of the image. The smaller the value of nRMSE, the more accurate the reconstructed image. The SSIM was calculated for each of 256 frequency slices and the nRMSE was averaged over all slices.

4   Results

Figure 2 shows the reconstructed CSI images with four different ^{13}C-enriched substrates employing two different under-sampling patterns. The fully acquired data were reconstructed as a reference (Fig. 1A). As can be seen, Fig. 2B ($L = 5$) is visually identical to the reference image. Minor artifacts can be observed with $L = 3$ with a large data reduction. However when $L = 2$, the errors become large and many artifacts appear. Similar results have been observed for the center-weighted random under-sampling pattern, as shown in Figs. 2(E)–(G). The reconstruction performance of the 3DIRECT is shown in Fig. 3 for $L = 5$ and $L = 2$ with the radial line under-sampling pattern using the structural similarity (SSIM) index for 256 frequency components. 3DIRECT is more effective for $L = 5$ than $L = 2$ in bringing the reconstructed CSI components back to the ground truth. The normalized root mean square error (nRMSE), as a function of the sampling rate is shown in Fig. 4, where the red squares are for the radial line pattern and the blue circles are for the center-weighted random pattern. The low nRMSE values for $L \geq 3$ (and sampling rate R $\geq$ 16.8%) represent good reconstruction accuracy. When L is reduced to 2, the nRMSE value is dramatically increased for the radial line pattern. In general, for sampling rate $R \geq$ 16.8% the radial line under-sampling pattern achieves a better reconstruction accuracy than the center-weighted random under-sampling pattern.

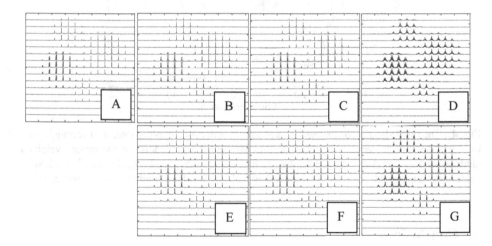

Fig. 2. Reconstructed CSI spectroscopic images with four different ^{13}C-enriched substrates. A: The reference image using full data. B-D: Reconstructed images using the radial line under-sampling pattern with the number of lines $L = 5$, 3, and 2, respectively. E-G: Reconstructed images using the center-weighted random pattern with the sampling rate $R = 27\%$, 16.8%, and 11.3%, corresponding to $L = 5$, 3, and 2, respectively.

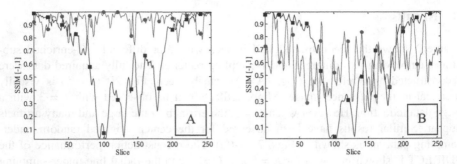

Fig. 3. Comparison of the pre-reconstruction SSIM (black) and post-reconstruction SSIM (blue) with the radial line under-sampling pattern (A) $L = 5$ and (B) $L = 2$, where higher SSIM means that the reconstructed image is closer to the reference image. (Color figure online)

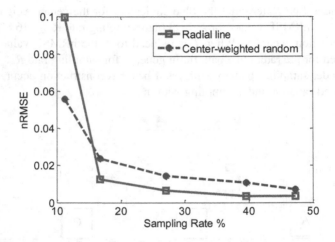

Fig. 4. The nRMSE of reconstructed images as a function of sampling rate. Red rectangles are for the radial line pattern ($L = 2, 3, 5, 8$, and 10) and the blue dots for the center-weighted random pattern (sampling rate $R = 11.3\%, 16.8\%, 27\%, 39.5\%$, and 47.2%). The low nRMSE values for sampling rate $R \geq 16.8\%$ (equivalent to $L \geq 3$) reflect good reconstruction accuracy.

5   Conclusions

Our results show that 3DIRECT is feasible for CSI acceleration of hyperpolarized ^{13}C metabolic imaging. The results show that this 3D CS method can achieve high reconstruction accuracy with the number of radial lines greater than 3 (or equivalently equal to or greater than sampling rate 16.8%). Future work will be focused on comparison with our previous method in [2] in terms of sampling rate, reconstruction accuracy, and reconstruction speed.

Acknowledgment. Zigen Song's research is supported in part by the National Natural Science Foundation of China under Grant No. 11672177.

References

1. Posse, S., Otazo, R., Dager, S.R., Alger, J.: MR spectroscopic imaging: principles and recent advances. J. Magn. Reson. Imaging **37**(6), 1301–1325 (2013)
2. Wang, J.X., Merritt, M.E., Dean Sherry, A., Malloy, C.R.: Accelerated chemical shift imaging of hyperpolarized ^{13}C metabolites. Magn. Reson. Med. **76**, 1033–1038 (2016)
3. Hourani, R., et al.: Proton magnetic resonance spectroscopic imaging to differentiate between nonneoplastic lesions and brain tumors in children. J. Magn. Reson. Imaging **23**(2), 99–107 (2006)
4. Lustig, M., Donoho, D., Pauly, J.M.: Sparse MRI: the application of compressed sensing for rapid MR imaging. Magn. Reson. Med. **58**, 1182–1195 (2007)
5. Candes, E., Romberg, J.: L1-magic: recovery of sparse signals via convex programming (2005). http://www.users.ece.gatech.edu/justin/l1magic/downloads/l1magic.pdf
6. Melinda, M.A.: Three dimensional image reconstruction (3DIRECT) of sparse signal with MRI application. Ph.D. thesis, The University of Texas at Arlington (2016)
7. Wang, Z., Bovik, A.C., Sheikh, H.R., Simoncelli, E.P.: Image quality assessment: from error visibility to structural similarity. IEEE Trans. Image Process. **13**, 600–612 (2004)

An Auto TCD Probe Design and Visualization

Yi Huang[1(✉)], Peng Wen[1(✉)], Bo Song[2(✉)], and Yan Li[2(✉)]

[1] School of Mechanical and Electrical Engineering,
Faculty of Health, Engineering and Sciences, University of Southern
Queensland, Toowoomba, QLD, Australia
u1093597@umail.usq.edu.au, Peng.Wen@usq.edu.au
[2] School of Agricultural, Computational and Environmental Sciences,
Faculty of Health, Engineering and Sciences, University of Southern
Queensland, Toowoomba, QLD, Australia
{Bo.Song, Yan.Li}@usq.edu.au

Abstract. Transcranial Doppler ultrasound (TCD) is a non-invasive ultrasound method used to examine blood circulation within the brain. During TCD, ultrasound waves are transmitted through the tissues including skull. These sound waves reflect off blood cells moving within the blood vessels, allowing the radiologist to interpret their speed and direction. In this paper, an auto TCD probe is developed to control the 2D deflection angles of the probe. The techniques of Magnetic Resonance Angiography (MRA) and Magnetic Resource Imagine (MRI) have been used to build the 3D human head model and generate the structure of cerebral arteries. The K-Nearest Neighbors (KNN) algorithm as a non-parametric method has been used for signal classification and regression of corresponding arteries. Finally, a global search and local search algorithms are used to locate the ultrasound focal zone and obtain a stronger signal efficient and more accurate result.

Keywords: Auto TCD probe · K-nearest neighbor
Signal search and classification

1 Introduction

Transcranial Doppler ultrasound (TCD) is the non-invasive ultrasound technique, which was first described in 1982 [1, 8]. The function of TCD is to monitor cerebral blood flow velocity (CBF-V) and vessel pulsatility [5]. The system of TCD is inexpensive and repeatable for using. Also, it is possible to use for continuous bedside monitoring of CBF-V, which has a positive effect on using in the intensive care [4].

According to the Doppler Effect, ultrasound waves are transmitted through the tissues including skull and the sound waves reflect off blood cells moving within the blood vessels. As a result, the radiologist can interpret the speed and direction of the blood flow. However, during TCD system, it is difficult to pin point and hold the ultrasound probe to the right direction manually, which is experience-dependent and time-consuming. The existing auto TCD probes are two degrees of freedom rotation device, and they do not have fixed axis in the flexible constrains [3, 9]. In this way, the

© Springer Nature Switzerland AG 2018
S. Wang et al. (Eds.): BI 2018, LNAI 11309, pp. 486–495, 2018.
https://doi.org/10.1007/978-3-030-05587-5_46

auto ultrasound probe cannot locate the right position accurately and driving routine is not repeatable.

This paper aims to design and develop a freehand auto TCD probe, which can sweep and search brain blood vessels automatically without human intervention. In this study, efficient algorithms to detect and track blood flow signals are proposed with 3D outputs in visualization. In addition, the proposed algorithms drive each small ultrasound transducers independently for better accuracy.

2 Methodology

2.1 Auto Probe Design

The ultrasound probe is made up of two major components. One is the Doppler ultrasound probe, which used the 2 MHz transmission frequency to emit the ultrasound waves from the transducers. The ultrasound probe used in this study is a one dimension ultrasound transducer and there is only one ultrasound wave emitted for each time. The ultrasound transducer connected with two micro motors (motor X and motor Y) by two poles. The two motors control the deflection angles at x and y axis and z axis is the direction of ultrasound waves. The other part is the probe headset, which keeps the probe to the proper position in the temporal ultrasound window. Therefore, the patient can wear the headset in a comfortable state and the clinicians can do the constant monitoring instead of holding the ultrasound probe to measure the blood flow velocity all the time.

The frequency of ultrasound probe utilized in this study is 2 MHz, which can provide the deeper of the ultrasound waves, over 80 mm, because of a lower degree of attenuation [7]. In this study, only left, transtemporal window is used to perform the signal scanning because the Circle of Willis is generally symmetric in theory. For one side of the cerebral arteries, the range of depth 80 mm can be covered the area from the ultrasound window to the middle of the cerebral artery [6].

In order to explore the influence of sampling depths, the ultrasound sampling depths in the same direction varies starting from 40 to 80 mm with an incremental setting of 5 mm. In addition, the deflection angles of each micro motor is configured as 1 degree while the range is between −70 and +70° and the increment of the angles each time is 1 degree. For the direction of x and y poles, there are both 141 cases and the total cases are $141 \times 141 = 19881$.

Overall, the designed ultrasound probe can meet the requirements of scanning. Firstly, the sampling depth of ultrasound waves can reach over 80 mm by using the 2 MHz ultrasound transducer, which satisfies the distance from the ultrasound window to the middle cerebral artery. Secondly, using two micro motors with two poles connected to the transducer can easily change the deflection angles of the ultrasound waves and the driving routine is repeatable. Thirdly, the scanning range is large enough, which can cover the half area of the Circle of Willis by using one side of the ultrasound probe.

2.2 Global Search and Algorithm

The global search is to use the ultrasound probe to scan the area of the Circle of Willis within the brains and identify the targeted blood vessel sections. According to the MRI and MRA techniques, it is possible to obtain the data of the corresponding position of each cerebral artery, and then using the finite element method (FEM) to acquire the accurate location of each artery, including the locations in the ultrasound window of a skull. The location of the ultrasound window is the position where placed the ultrasound probe.

Firstly, it is necessary to process the FEM data and do coordinates origin translation. The origin (0, 0, 0) of the original FEM data is predefined as the starting pixel of the MRI volume and this point is later translated to the center of the left ultrasound window. To be specific, there are 118 FEM points of left ultrasound window. The Eqs. 1 to 3 are the average evaluations for the location of x, y and z axis, and the central point that obtained is (120.5096, 122.0414, 162.3302).

$$x_0 = \frac{x_1 + x_2 + x_3 + \ldots + x_{118}}{118} \tag{1}$$

$$y_0 = \frac{y_1 + y_2 + y_3 + \ldots + y_{118}}{118} \tag{2}$$

$$z_0 = \frac{z_1 + z_2 + z_3 + \ldots + z_{118}}{118} \tag{3}$$

Secondly, after obtaining the central point of the ultrasound window, the next step is to change the origin of coordinates. While doing the coordinate transformation, the key point is to find the vector of the conversion. The conversion vector is (x_0, y_0, z_0) and all locations of arteries need to be transformed based on the conversion vector. Then, the new location of each artery can be acquired based on the origin of coordinates of the ultrasound window.

Thirdly, set the sampling depth of ultrasound waves and offset the X and Y micro motors, which can control the reflection angles of transmission. Between the ranges of deflection angles, the angle increment of each time is one degree. So, there are 141 deflection angles for each motor and the total cases of ultrasound wave are 141 x 141 (19981).

The outcome of a global search is to locate the ultrasound focal zone. After the global search for the area of the Circle of Willis at a certain depth, the closest point in the space can be found by using k-nearest neighbor search (KNN) algorithm, which is an optimization method to find the nearest point in the scale space. The echo ultrasound signals are generally stronger when the ultrasound wave is closer to the near arteries. Calculating the Euclidean distance (Eq. 4) between the detected ultrasound signals and the near sample points of arteries is an efficient method to determine the strength of signals. There are twelve arteries constructed by a total of 10597 FEM points in this study.

$$d = \sqrt{\sum_{k=1}^{n} (x_{1k} - x_{2k})^2} \tag{4}$$

Applying the KNN algorithm, the k value is set as 10, which means there are 10 neighbor points to the detected signals should be calculated. For the 19881 detected signals, there are 198810 neighbor points calculated in total. The calculation is based on each point of detected signals to their corresponding 10 closest points. According to all values, the next step is to find the minimum distance between test signals and samples from all the scanning signals. The result obtained is 3813. From the 19881 detected signals, the number of 3813 signal has a corresponding 10 closest signals at the sampling depth of ultrasound wave is 50 mm.

2.3   Local Search Approach

The local search is performed after the global search, which helps to improve the accuracy of searching outputs. From the global search, the coordinate point of the 3813th detected signal $(x_1 = 22.5133, \ y_1 = 34.0999, \ z_1 = 28.8157)$. Then, the deflection angle of this detected signal can be calculated in Eqs. 5 and 6. $\theta_y = -43°, \theta_x = -38°$.

$$\theta_y = -(\arcsin(\frac{y_1}{D})) \times 360°/2\pi \tag{5}$$

$$\theta_x = -(\arctan(\frac{x_1}{z_1})) \times 360°/2\pi \tag{6}$$

Once getting the deflection angle of the strongest detected signal, the local search can start. The sampling depth of the ultrasound probe is still at 50 mm and changing the deflection angles of θ_x and θ_y, and the increment of the deflection angle of X and Y motors is 1°. The scanning area is in a circle with the point of (x_1, y_1, z_1) as the center point. Using KNN to search for the nearest 10 neighbor points. According to the obtained signal points to calculate the distance between the points and the Circle of Willis. Using the Eq. 4 to calculate the Euclidean distance of the nearest 10 neighbor points and matching these points to their corresponding arteries.

The purpose of the local search is to acquire the continuous and stable signal spectrum. When doing the global search, the signal image is intermittent, unless continuous signals are detected from certain areas. When acquiring the strong signal from the global search, it is not easy to determine that the nearby search area of signal points can output stable and continuous signal images. Furthermore, when a patient coughs during the process of operation, a false strong signal might be produced and output on the Doppler ultrasound system. The system may misinterpret the false signal as the strongest signal after finishing the global search. Therefore, it cannot search any signals at that certain area during the process of local search and also it cannot display stable and continuous signals on the Doppler ultrasound system.

2.4   Signal Classification and Implementation

The method used for the signal classification is the K-Nearest Neighbor (KNN). In the KNN classification, the output is determined by the "majority vote" of its neighbor, and the most common classification of the nearest neighbor determines the category to which the object is assigned [2]. If k = 1, the object's class is given directly by the nearest node [10]. The first step of the KNN algorithm is to calculate the distance between the detected signal and each training data and then sorting the data according to the increasing relation of distance. The second step is to select K points with the smallest distance and then determining the occurrence frequency of the category of the first K points. The last step is to return the category with the highest frequency in the K points before as the prediction classification of test data.

Figure 1 demonstrates 12 main cerebral arteries with the different color, which has been divided into two categories, the left and right sides. The red circle represents the position of left side ultrasound probe and the left cerebral arteries are at the downside. The red color of the Circle of Willis represents the anterior cerebral artery (ACA), the blue color represents the anterior communicating artery (COA), the yellow color displays the internal carotid artery (ICA), the cyan color shows the MCA, the black color represents the middle cerebral artery (MCA) and the pink color displays superior cerebellar artery (SCBA). The Circle of Willis has been divided into eight regions in Table 1.

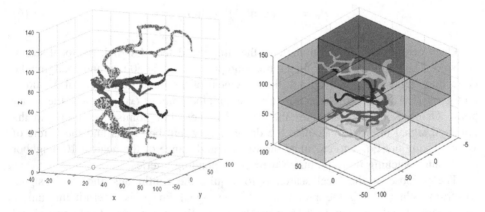

Fig. 1. Circle of Willis and divided into eight regions.

The advantage of dividing the Circle of Willis into eight regions is reducing the amount of calculation and it is also more convenient to classify the signal data. After setting the sampling depth of the ultrasound wave and the deflection angles of X and Y motors, it can be classified as the signal to its corresponding region (Table 2).

The first step is to estimate the location of the detected signal. When the sampling depth of the ultrasound wave is 45 mm and the deflection angles are −10 and −5, the detected signal is in the green region. From Table 1, there are six cerebral arteries in the

Table 1. The arteries are divided into eight regions

Region	The corresponding arteries in the region
Red	RICA, RMCA, LPCA, RPCA, LSCBA, RSCBA
Blue	LACA, RACA, RCOA, RICA, RMCA, RPCA
Yellow	LCOA, LICA, LMCA, LPCA, LSCBA, RSCBA
Green	LACA, RACA, LCOA, LICA, LMCA, LPCA
Black	RACA, RMCA
Light Blue	LACA, RACA, RMCA
Pink	LACA, LMCA, LPCA
White	LACA, LMCA

Table 2. Classify random signals.

Depth (mm)	Deflection angle (X)	Deflection angle (Y)	Region
45	−5	−10	Green
60	15	10	Green
50	5	−45	White
55	−30	−20	Yellow
70	25	45	Non

green region. Compared with the global classification, it is necessary to calculate the distance of the six arteries instead of all twelve arteries with the detected signal, which has a positive effect on reducing the calculations in half. The important step when doing the signal classification is to calculate the ration of closest points from all of 10 points to each artery. In Fig. 2, all 10 closest points are from the same artery, LMCA. As a result, the detected signal can be classified to LMCA.

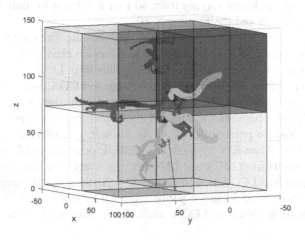

Fig. 2. Classification. Sampling depth at 45 mm and deflection angles are −10 and −5.

Figure 3 shows a different case and the sampling depth of ultrasound wave is 62 mm and the deflection angles are −10 and −8. Firstly, estimating the detected signal is a green region. Then calculating the 10 closest sample points in the green region. The 10 nearby points are divided into three different arteries, LCOA, LICA, and LMCA. It is obvious that there are three points for the light blue color (LMCA), five points for the blue color (LCOA) and only two yellow points (LICA). The percentage of the blue color points is highest, at 50%. Therefore, the detected signal belongs to LCOA.

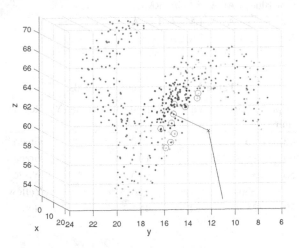

Fig. 3. Classification. Sampling depth at 62 mm and deflection angles are −8 and −10

3 Results

3.1 Analyzing the Data

The Table 3 displays the signals classification based on the global search and the local search at the sampling depths varying from 40 mm to 80 mm for only the left side of ultrasound transmission and the K value is 10.

To evaluate the effect of K value on classification results. The sampling depth of the ultrasound wave is selected as 62 mm and the K values are changed from 3 to 5, 15 and 20 (Fig. 4). When K = 3, there are two sample points from LCOA and only one point is from LICA. Therefore, the detected signal belongs to LCOA. When K = 5, there are both 2 sample points from LMCA and LCOA and only one point is from LICA. However, the distance between the detected signal and the sample points of LCOA is shorter than the sample points of LMCA. As a result, the detected signal should be classified to LCOA. When K = 15, there are 7 sample points from LCOA and there are 3 and 5 sample points from LICA and LMCA respectively. The signal classification of the detected signal is to LCOA as well. When K = 20, there are 10 sample points from LCOA and there are both 5 sample points from LICA and LMCA. The signal classification results from above are LCOA when the K value is different.

Table 3. Classifies the detected signals varying the sampling depth from 40 mm to 80 mm.

Depth (mm)	Classify the signal to Artery
40	LMCA
45	LMCA
50	LMCA
55	LMCA
60	LICA
65	LACA
70	LPCA
75	LACA
80	LSCBA

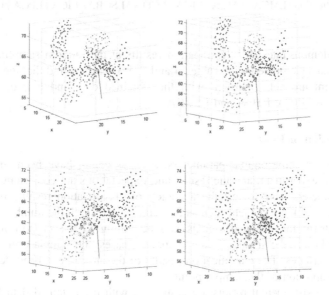

Fig. 4. Sampling depth at 62 mm and deflection angles are −8 and −10. K = 3, 5, 15 and 20.

3.2   Findings

Table 4 shows the characteristic of cerebral vasculature, including the sampling depth of cerebral arteries, which helps to compare the data accuracy

Compared the Table 3 with Table 4, at the sampling depths of ultrasound waves are 40, 45, 50, 55, 65, 70, 75 and 80, the signals classification results are consistent with the data obtained in Table 4. At the sampling depth of ultrasound wave is 60 mm, the classification of the detected signal is belong to the LICA, which is different with the obtained data in Table 4 (the depth of LICA is between 65 and 80 mm). To verify the accuracy of the comparison, a number of random and irregular sampling depths, such as 52, 57 and 63 are selected as shown in Table 5.

Table 4. Characteristics of cerebral vasculature (Naqvi et al. 2013)

Artery	Depth (mm)	Adult MFV(cm/s)
LMCA	30–65	55 ± 12
LACA	60–75	50 ± 11
LPCA	60–70	40 ± 10
LCOA	45–55	21 ± 5
LICA	65–80	41 ± 15
LSCBA	80–12	41 ± 10

Table 5. Classify the detected signals at random sampling depths

Depth (mm)	43	47	58	64	67	69	73	78
Classification	LMCA	LMCA	LICA	LCOA	LSCBA	LICA	LPCA	LPCA

Table 5 demonstrates the classification results at the random sampling depths of detected signals. Compared with Tables 4 and 5, it is easy to find that the results from the experiment are not consistent with the obtained data and biased, such as the classification results of LPCA and LSCBA.

3.3   Discussion of Result

Firstly, there are some regular parameters, such as depth, have been set to test the outputs of the experiment, and the results and expectations are consistent. Also, some specific parameters have to test the accuracy of classification results. For example, different values of k are chosen, such as 3, 5 and 20, to search the number of K nearest sample points to the detected signals and according to the proportion of sample numbers to classify the signals. In some specific cases, the sample points distributed into different arteries. The classification results of the artery have been determined by the higher proportion of the sample points.

When the experimental results are compared with the obtained data from the literature review, the results still produce errors. It is worth mentioning that the original FEM data of the Circle of Willis is from a specific patient. In practice, the cerebral artery locations of different subjects are different, such as the blood vessels vary in thickness, and also other factors, such as the attenuation effect for the sampling depth of ultrasound waves. In data comparison, the error of classification results is affected by external factors. But the results of the experiment itself by using KNN classifier in this paper is accurate.

4   Conclusion

During the TCD, it is difficult to pin point and hold the ultrasound probe to the right direction manually, which is experience-dependent and time-consuming. This study proposed and developed an auto TCD probe, which can search and find the right direction automatically. In the designing, the signal scanning range is a critical factor to accuracy. For the sampling depth of ultrasound waves, 2 MHz ultrasound probe can transmit the ultrasound waves over 80 mm, which is suitable for scanning one side of cerebral arteries. Two micro motors with pole connection with the transducer is a suitable design for controlling deflection angles of ultrasound waves. Combined with the global search and the local search using KNN, the proposed auto TCD probe is able to search, locate and lock-in the corresponding arteries and provide accurate and reliable TCD signals.

In the future work, the internal factors of the cerebral blood flow will be considered and also a time optimal controller will be designed and implemented to shorten the search time.

References

1. Aaslid, R., Markwalder, T.M., Nornes, H.: Noninvasive transcranial Doppler ultra-sound recording of flow velocity in basal cerebral arteries. J. Neurosurg. **57**(6), 769–774 (1982)
2. Hwang, W.J., Wen, K.W.: Fast kNN classification algorithm based on partial distance search. Electron. Lett. **34**(21), 2062–2063 (1998)
3. Loschak, P.M., Degirmenci, A., Tenzer, Y., Tschabrunn, C.M., Anter, E., Howe, R.D.: A four degree of freedom robot for positioning ultrasound imaging catheters. J. Mech. Robot. **8**(5), 051016 (2016)
4. Moppett, I.K., Mahajan, R.P.: Transcranial Doppler ultrasonography in anaesthesia and intensive care. Br. J. Anaesth. **93**(5), 710–724 (2004)
5. Naqvi, J., Yap, K.H., Ahmad, G., Ghosh, J.: Transcranial Doppler ultrasound: a review of the physical principles and major applications in critical care. Int. J. Vasc. Med. (2013)
6. Nicoletto, H.A., Burkman, M.H.: Transcranial Doppler series part II: performing a transcranial Doppler. Am. J. Electroneurodiagnostic Technol. **49**(1), 14–27 (2009)
7. Pfaffenberger, S., et al.: 2 MHz ultra-sound enhances t-PA-mediated thrombolysis: comparison of continuous versus pulsed ultrasound and standing versus travelling acoustic waves. Thromb. Haemost. **90**(03), 583–589 (2003)
8. Purkayastha, S., Sorond, F.: Transcranial Doppler ultrasound: technique and application. Semin. Neurol. **32**(4), 411 (2012)
9. Sherebrin, S., Fenster, A., Rankin, R.N., Spence, D.: Freehand three-dimensional ultrasound: implementation and applications. In: Medical Imaging 1996: Physics of Medical Imaging, 2708, pp. 296–304 (1996)
10. Weinberger, K.Q., Saul, L.K.: Distance metric learning for large margin nearest neighbor classification. J. Mach. Learn. Res. **10**, 207–244 (2009)

Author Index

Printed in the United States
By Bookmasters